Thirty-Three Lessons on *Capital*

Thirty-Three Lessons on *Capital*
Reading Marx Politically

Harry Cleaver

First published 2019 by Pluto Press
345 Archway Road, London N6 5AA

www.plutobooks.com

Copyright © Harry Cleaver 2019

The right of Harry Cleaver to be identified as the author of this work has been
asserted by him in accordance with the Copyright, Designs and Patents Act 1988.

Every effort has been made to trace copyright holders and to obtain their permission
for the use of copyright material in this book. The publisher apologises for any errors
or omissions in this respect and would be grateful if notified of any corrections that
should be incorporated in future reprints or editions.

British Library Cataloguing in Publication Data
A catalogue record for this book is available from the British Library

ISBN   978 0 7453 3998 6   Hardback
ISBN   978 0 7453 3997 9   Paperback
ISBN   978 1 7868 0514 0   PDF eBook
ISBN   978 1 7868 0516 4   Kindle eBook
ISBN   978 1 7868 0515 7   EPUB eBook

This book is printed on paper suitable for recycling and made from fully managed
and sustained forest sources. Logging, pulping and manufacturing processes are
expected to conform to the environmental standards of the country of origin.

Typeset by Stanford DTP Services, Northampton, England
Printed and bound by CPI Group (UK) Ltd, Croydon, CR0 4YY
Simultaneously printed in the United Kingdom and United States of America

Contents

Acknowledgments   vi

Sources and Citations   vii

 1 Introduction   1

 2 *Capital: A Critique of Political Economy*   14

 3 Part Eight: So-called Primitive Accumulation
     Chapters 26–33   16

 4 Part One: Commodities and Money
     Chapters 1–3   98

 5 Part Two: The Transformation of Money into Capital
     Chapters 4–6   168

 6 Part Three: The Production of Absolute Surplus-Value
     Chapters 7–11   186

 7 Part Four: The Production of Relative Surplus-Value
     Chapters 12–15   272

 8 Part Five: The Production of Absolute and Relative
   Surplus-Value
     Chapters 16–18   347

 9 Part Six: Wages
     Chapters 19–22   361

10 Part Seven: The Process of Accumulation of Capital
     Chapters 23–25   406

11 Conclusion   477

Index   486

Acknowledgments

First, and most profoundly, to all of my students who truly engaged with Marx's *Capital* and with the interpretations I offered in lectures, my online "study guide" and informal discussions. Their questions and challenges helped both them and me think more clearly—especially when they turned my attention to things I hadn't thought about before.

Second, I also want to thank friends who read some of the material in this book as it was being crafted and gave me constructive and useful feedback, including ideas and editing, both of which improved the text considerably. These included Brett Caraway, Robert Ovetz and especially my brother William Cleaver.

Sources and Citations

The primary source materials for this book are Volume I of *Capital*, translated by Ben Fowkes and published by Penguin Press and the now completed 50 volumes of *Karl Marx Frederich Engels Collected Works* (*MECW*), published by Progress Publishers, Moscow, Lawrence & Wishart, London and International Publishers in New York. The 33 analyses of the 33 chapters of Volume I that I offer here only engage to a very limited degree with a number of other important theoretical works now available in English: 1) the prefaces written by Marx and Engels to various editions of *Capital*; 2) the "unpublished 6th Chapter," available in the Penguin edition of Volume I as an appendix, titled "Results of the Immediate Process of Production"; 3) the second and third volumes of *Capital*; 4) the intended fourth volume, edited and published by Karl Kautsky (1854–1938) after Marx's death as *Theories of Surplus Value* (1861–63); and 5) various other manuscripts composed in the years before Volume I was prepared for publication, such as the *1844 Manuscripts*, the *Grundrisse* (1857), the *Contribution to the Critique of Political Economy* (1859) and the draft of Volume III included in the *Manuscript of 1864–1865*.

Quoted and cited material from *Capital*, *Volumes I–III* and the *Grundrisse* are all from the Penguin editions of those works, because I assume them to be more readily available to most readers than the volumes of *MECW*. Most other citations of writings by Marx and Engels are to *MECW*. References to the Penguin editions just give their title and page number, e.g., *Capital, Vol. I*, p. xxx, whereas *MECW* references provide volume and page numbers. In some cases, references are given to both editions. Because the translations in these two editions are different, fastidious readers—with the time and inclination—might want to compare the two. They might also check www.marxist.org for other translations from other sources. Some of the difficulties in the various English translations have recently been pointed out by Wolfgang Fritz Haug in his "On the Need for a New English Translation of Marx's *Capital*," *Socialism and Democracy*, vol. 31, no. 1, January 2017, pp. 60–86. Those who can read French might want to study the translation in that language of Volume I of *Capital*, revised by Marx from the German original. Those who can read German can consult *Marx-Engels-Gesamtausgabe* (*MEGA*), the largest published collection of Marx and Engels's writings and one that reproduces them in their original languages. The collection is still expanding under the stewardship of the

Internationale Marx-Engels-Stiftung (*IMES*) in Amsterdam. For more information on *MEGA*, see its entry in Wikipedia.

Many of the songs cited herein are available on YouTube. Lyrics are quoted from the following:

"The 6th Sense (Something You Feel)," by Albert Johnson, Lonnie Rashid Lynn, Chris E. Martin, Kejuan W. Muchita and Bilal S. Oliver © 2000 Juvenile Hell Publ./Universal Music-MGB Songs.

"9 to 5," by Dolly Parton, © 1980 Velvet Apple Music/Warner-Tamerlane Pub.

"The Big Money," by Neil Peart, Alex Lifeson and Geddy Lee © 1985 Core Music Publishing/Anthem Entertainment Group.

"Commercialization," by Jimmy Cliff © 1973 Jimmy Cliff.

"Corrido de Delano," by Lalo Guerrero © 1966 Lalo Guerrero.

"Factory," by Bruce Springsteen © 1978 Bruce Springsteen.

"The Great Eel Robbery," by Men of No Property © 1971 Men of No Property.

"I Don't Like Mondays," by Bob Geldof and Johnnie Fingers © 1979 Music Sales Corp.

"Machines," by Lol Mason, Michael Chetwynd Slamer and Terence Roy Ward © 1979 Atlantic Recording Corporation.

"Maggie's Farm," by Bob Dylan © 1965 Bob Dylan.

"Magnificent Seven," by Mick Jones, Joe Strummer, Topper Headon, Norman Watt-Roy and Micky Gallagher © 1980 Nineden Ltd.

"Money," by Roger Waters © 1973 Pink Floyd Music Publishers Ltd./ Hampshire House Publishing Corp.

"Money Machine," by James Taylor © 1978 Country Road Music Inc.

"Nine to Five," by Ray Davies © 1974/75 Sony/ATV Tunes LLC.

"Piss Factory," by Patti Smith and Richard Sohl © 1974 Druse Music Inc.

"Rain on the Scarecrow," by John Cougar Mellencamp © 1985 John Mellencamp.

"Richard Cory," by Paul Simon © 1965 Paul Simon Music.

"Rush Hour Blues," by Ray Davies © 1974/75 Sony/ATV Tunes LLC.

"Seven Cent Cotton," by Bob Miller and Emma Dermer © 1929 Bob Miller and Emma Dermer.

"Step Right Up," by Tom Waits © 1976 Elektra/Asylum/Nonesuch Records.

"Welcome to the Working Week," by Elvis Costello © 1977 Universal Music Publishing.

1
Introduction

Thirty-three lessons on the 33 chapters of Volume I of Karl Marx's *Capital*. What?! Yet another book on *Capital*? Why read this one, among so many? Well, if you are looking for a scholarly text that interprets *Capital* as a work of economics or philosophy, this one is probably not for you. If you are seeking an interpretation designed to justify some partisan political platform, skip this one. If you need a philological treatise that draws on all editions and translations, look elsewhere. But, if you want to discover how what Marx wrote 150 years ago can help us understand our struggles and figure out what to do next, then this particular appropriation might provide some of what you are looking for.

The basic premise behind this book is the notion that Marx wrote *Capital* to put a political weapon into the hands of those of us opposed to capitalism and struggling to get beyond it. What kind of weapon? Above all, a theoretical one, designed to vivisect capitalism in ways that reveal how it dominates, exploits and alienates us, but also its vulnerabilities. Although committing surgery on living *animals* for research, testing or education is vile, vivisecting capitalism theoretically to figure out how to disrupt it, defeat it and create real alternatives, is all too necessary.[1] Fortunately, Marx has not only given us tools for just such a purpose but has also shown us how to use them. This book aims to sharpen those tools—by demonstrating how even the most abstract concepts in *Capital* designate aspects of the antagonistic social relationships of capitalism in ways that help us resist and escape them. *Capital* was written as a political document; we do well to read it as such and put it to use.

At the time of its publication in 1867, Marx's long-time engagement in the workers' movements of the mid-nineteenth century made the political character of *Capital* quite clear.[2] Yet, unlike earlier works, such as the relatively short and pithy *Communist Manifesto* of 1848, written with Engels for the Communist League at the beginning of the Revolutions of 1848,

---

1. Visit the website of the US National Anti-Vivisection Society (NAVS).
2. Indeed, recognizing its subversive character, the French government sought to impede the publication of *Capital* and eventually put the publisher out of business. "Note des Éditeurs", Karl Marx, *Le Capital: critique de l'économie politique*, Livre Premier, Paris: Éditions Sociales, 1969, p. 8.

Capital is a massive tome, rivaling in length and complexity such classic works as Adam Smith's *Wealth of Nations* (1776) or Hegel's *Phenomenology of the Spirit* (1807). So, it is not surprising that economists have taken *Capital* to be offering an alternative economic analysis of capitalism and philosophers have read it as proposing an alternative philosophical science. But for those being exploited by capitalists at the time and doing their best—often with Marx's support—to organize resistance, *Capital* provided both historical perspective and analytical tools. True then; still true today.

An example of his history-telling can be found in Chapter 10, where he sketches how capitalists, as they gained power, extended the length of the working day, forcing workers to work longer and longer. But he also sketches how workers, supported by social reformers, pushed back—forcing the government to create factory inspectors and then to pass Factory Acts imposing shorter hours. For workers, these were battles over how much of their lives they had to give up to their employers and how much they could retain for their own purposes. But his history is framed by his theory of *absolute surplus-value* (Chapters 7–11), which showed them how central such struggles were, not only to how much of their lives they were giving up, but how success in forcing down the length of the working day opened new possibilities for struggle. By creating more and more free time, successful work reduction made it possible to allocate more of their time and energy to exploring alternatives to capitalist ways of organizing their lives. By the time workers in the United States were fighting for a working day of eight hours, their slogan was "Eight hours of work, eight hours of sleep and eight hours for what we will!"

Similarly, his historical analysis of the increasing displacement of workers by machinery (Chapters 12–15) emphasized how it was a response to their struggles to work less. Against capitalists and their political economists who touted the use of machinery as making it possible to produce more with less work (higher productivity), *Capital* shows how capitalists use machines in a strategy of *relative surplus-value* to undermine workers' self-organization and increase profits by intensifying work! Armed with *Capital*, workers could argue, "Sure, we'll go along with new machines, but only if the increased productivity results in our having to work less! Machines should make our work both shorter and less onerous, not longer and more intense!"

Against employer and political economists' arguments that increases in wages were impossible given the limits of the "Wages Fund" or would reduce the wages of other workers, Chapter 24 of *Capital* provided an analysis that permitted workers to argue how, within the context of rising productivity, not only were increased wages compatible with increased profits but wages could rise at the same time that work was reduced. "Enough with the bosses arrogating the entire fruits of increased productivity to themselves, they must share!"

But that was 150 years ago, give or take. What about today? How relevant are these issues and these analytical categories now? Unfortunately, struggles over the time of labor and the use of machines are still very much with us, not only in factories and offices but throughout society.

For the first half of the twentieth century, workers continued to hammer down the length of the working day, forcing capitalists to rely more and more on machines. Prototypical of the latter were the scientific management methods of Frederick Taylor (1856–1915) applied on the assembly lines of Henry Ford (1863–1947).[3] So iconic were these that some analysts characterize the whole period as one of "Fordism." For a while, in the 1940s and 1950s, work time was stabilized for a great many at about 40 hours a week and deals cut over productivity won higher wages but not less work. But a new cycle of struggle in the 1960s, often by workers wanting more free time to enjoy their higher wages, not only undermined absolute surplus-value through absenteeism and wildcat strikes but also undermined the capitalist use of machines through playing on the job and sabotage. The growth in productivity slowed and then declined, subverting relative surplus-value. The capitalist counterattack was multipronged but ultimately, by the beginning of the 1980s, they succeeded in reducing wages and increasing working hours. The decades-long, on-again, off-again march of workers toward zerowork was reversed and ever since capitalists have been using every ploy possible to increase work time.

Similarly, as computers—in both manufacturing and service industries—have become the most ubiquitous machines of our time, capitalists have deployed them systematically both to raise productivity and to extort more work. Early on, this extortion was obvious as personal computers displaced typewriters and programs were written to count secretarial keystrokes per minute, providing overseers with the means of pressuring typists to work faster, much as control over the speed of Ford's assembly line provided the means to force manufacturing workers to work harder. Today, the widespread use of computers to compile data, "metrics," is aimed at providing employers with new tools to increase workloads. At the same time, the deregulation of finance, the use of computer algorithms to guide speculation and the manipulation of debt have combined to enrich some capitalists while undermining workers' income and wealth (mostly dependent on home ownership), forcing workers into longer hours or second jobs.

---

3. See Frederick Taylor, *The Principles of Scientific Management*, London: Harper & Brothers, 1911; and Henry Ford, *My Life and Work*, Garden City, NY: Doubleday, 1922.

Finally, all these phenomena can be found far beyond the walls of factories and offices. They permeate schools, homes and everyday life in ways Marx never dreamed of, but whose character can still be illuminated by applying his theories. And this is true not only of capitalist methods but of our resistance. Against Fordist methods which had provided a template for the organization of schools, students in the 1960s rebelled, demanding less work and more time for self-defined, even self-organized studies. One result was "grade inflation" or higher grades for less work. Another was the creation of whole new fields, e.g., Black, Mexican-American or Women's Studies. As schools substituted programmed, handheld computers for slide rules or calculators, students who were once asked to solve only one or two problems are today expected to solve dozens. Not less work, but more work. As with metrics in offices and factories, computer tracking of grades has given professors and administrators a tool to fight "grade inflation" and impose speed-up and more schoolwork. As women resisted subservience to housework, capital responded with household appliances, increasingly programmed and operated by built-in software. Although such equipment might be expected to result in less work, studies show that media-promulgated, ever-increased standards of cleanliness and expectations of beautiful homes and gardens have resulted in more housework rather than less.[4] While the Internet and social media have provided workers, students and housewives with the means to organize against all this work, it has also provided capital with the means to track and subvert such organization, while spreading propaganda designed to accentuate well-known methods of dividing and conquering, i.e., the use of race, gender, ethnicity and national identity.

In short, what we have today are new forms of old conflicts. In an age where capitalists have sought to convert all of society into a social factory, resistance and struggle are everywhere and *Capital* still provides us with many tools for understanding the strategies arrayed against us and some insight into how the resistance of those who came before us may still be relevant to our actions today. The obvious question is what are those tools and how do we discover their usefulness?

If, as I argued in *Reading Capital Politically* (*RCP*), "capital" is not a thing but an antagonistic set of social relationships analyzed by Marx in *Capital*, then each and every category he deploys in the development and presen-

---

4. *Homes & Gardens* magazine, published since 1919, is prototypical of a wide range of such efforts, in print, television, Instagram, etc., to set standards for making homes "beautiful"—standards that require ever-increased expenditure of time, energy and money.

tation of his theory denotes some aspect of those relationships.[5] Above I mentioned his concepts of absolute and relative surplus-value. My formulation of the phenomena these two categories denote are the result of my particular—some say idiosyncratic—understanding of what Marx means by "value," a much-disputed concept among both Marxists and their critics.

In *RCP*, I dissected Chapter 1 of Volume I on "The Commodity" and showed how each of the abstract concepts of the substance, measure and form of value can be understood not only as designating aspects of commodities, commodity exchange and money, but also as revealing aspects of the class struggles of capitalism—of the antagonistic conflicts between capitalist efforts to subordinate life to commodity production and our resistance to such subordination. This new book systematically extends that kind of analysis to the other chapters of Volume I of *Capital*.

Both *RCP* and this book are byproducts of some four decades of teaching, first at the L'Université de Sherbrooke in Quebec, then in the graduate program of the New School for Social Research in New York City and then at the University of Texas at Austin. The notes that became *RCP* were drafted in New York and turned into a book in Austin. As years went by and time permitted, to help students work their way through the first volume of *Capital*, I supplemented my undergraduate lectures by creating outlines and writing commentaries on Chapters 2–33, amplifying what I had time to say in the classroom for students to study at their leisure, independently of class times or office hours.

When the World Wide Web became available and *RCP* went out of print, I scanned the book, used OCR to create a digital version, used basic HTML to code it, and uploaded it, along with my existing outlines and commentaries to the course website as a "study guide," illustrated with images, excerpts from literature, songs and textbook-like concepts and questions for review (http://la.utexas.edu/users/hcleaver/357k/357ksg. html). From that point on, I prepared new outlines and commentaries directly in HTML.

Convinced by many folks that I should meld *RCP*'s treatment of Chapter 1 with my notes on all the other chapters and publish the lot in the form of a hard-copy book, I decided to try. I copied and pasted the study guide webpages into MSWord documents and edited them, removing course-specific material, revising the text to reduce the number of words to a count consistent with an editor's notion of a reasonably sized book. In the process, I realized that I also needed to revise the substantive chapters of *RCP* to correspond to the mode of my treatment of the other chapters.

---

5. *Reading Capital Politically* (1979), 2nd edn., Leeds: Antithesis; and Brooklyn, NY: AK Press, 2000.

In the process, I found myself writing an entirely new book, not merely an expansion of *RCP*. Eventually, the contents of this book will be merged with the fully illustrated versions of the commentaries and course materials on the web.

The notes and commentaries on each chapter reflect the multiple objectives that I pursued in teaching Marx's ideas. I came to study Marx, as I believe many do, as the result of dissatisfaction with alternative approaches to struggles in which I was personally engaged and to others I judged significant. I discovered, bit by bit, diverse "Marxist" interpretations of *Capital*—a diversity that reflects the contradictory politics of his interpreters. Trying to sort out those contradictions led me to examine their common source. As Friedrich Nietzsche (1844–1900) said of history, so I have come to say of Marx, the best reason to study the man's writings is because they can enrich our lives, by informing our efforts to free ourselves of the constraints that limit us and by helping us discover freer ways to live, as individuals and as a society.[6]

OBJECTIVES AND ELABORATIONS

My primary objectives in my courses on Marx were twofold: rejecting the roundabout approach of a survey course, I offered students who wanted to study his ideas: 1) the opportunity to read his original writings; and 2) what I judged to be one useful interpretation. Because I had come to believe that the indispensable core of his theory is his labor theory of value, I also decided that the most appropriate place to start was Volume I of *Capital*, his most systematic presentation of that theory, where he deploys it to reveal the nature of capitalism, the struggles to which it inevitably gives rise and the possibilities for transcending it.

But "teaching" *Capital* raised other pedagogical problems. In small graduate classes, everyone could read the same material, sit around a table and discuss it, with individuals' contributions informed by their own preoccupations, e.g., other things they were studying or the subject of their thesis or dissertation. In large undergraduate classes, for the most part lecturing dominated. In both cases, my contributions—in discussions or lectures— reflected my reading of the material being covered. Because I agree that all readings involve interpretation, I never pretended that mine was a true and accurate exposition of "what Marx really meant." On the contrary, I presented my reading/interpretation as one of many possible alternatives.

---

6. See "On the Use and Disadvantages of History for Life" in Friedrich Nietzsche", *Untimely Meditations* (1874), Chicago, IL: University of Chicago Press, 1997, pp. 59–123.

Therefore, I suggested to my students that their studies could most usefully proceed through two stages. First, read and study *Capital* on their own, interpreting his words in terms of their own experience and knowledge of the world. Second, listen to and study my interpretation offered in discussions, in lectures and in answers to their questions, while juxtaposing their interpretation to mine. That process would not only help maintain a critical distance from both Marx and my reading of him but also provide a basis for studying the writings of other Marxists, should they so choose.[7]

A third objective was to demonstrate the contemporary relevance of Marx's theory, despite it being formulated in the mid-nineteenth century and based on observation and analysis of relationships and events of that period. Ever since first reading it, I have taken his Eleventh Thesis on Feuerbach, like Nietzsche's verdict on history, as fundamental. The point of studying the world—including the past and others' writings—is not just to understand it but to use that understanding to change it.[8] I originally approached Marx skeptically. In a graduate course on the history of economic thought, I was taught all the usual reasons for rejecting his theory. Nevertheless, I came to conclude that although much has changed since he wrote, the core of his theory of capitalism still illuminates its essential characteristics and helps us see clearly not only what we are fighting against, but how it impedes our efforts to craft real alternatives.

A fourth objective derived from teaching in North America, given that most of Marx's examples and illustrations are drawn from the history of British and European capitalism. Sadly, given the usual superficiality of high school history courses in the US, for most of my students that history was largely unknown. Therefore, in my commentaries I presented what I hoped were more familiar local examples. So, for example, where Marx analyzed the enclosures and anti-vagrant legislation in England and Scotland, I pointed to the dynamics of enclosure on the Western frontier and the anti-vagrancy laws in the post-Civil War South that forced freed slaves into near-slave labor.

A fifth objective responded to students finding much of *Capital* abstract, dry and dense. Although for those with the necessary background, both his text and footnotes are quite rich in literary and cultural illustrations and allusions, they often proved obscure to my students, whose course

---

7. That suggestion grew out of the work-minimizing efforts of some students to just read my notes instead of studying *Capital*, in the mistaken belief that on tests or in essays all I wanted to find were my own words repeated back to me. I will make the same suggestion to readers of this book. It should be read critically as one person's appropriation of the ideas in *Capital*, not as a substitute.

8. "The philosophers have only *interpreted* the world in various ways; the point is to *change* it." *MECW*, vol. 5, p. 5.

loads rarely left them time to seek out and study the original material. To partially compensate, I included in the web version of these notes colorful illustrations, drawn sometimes from historical or contemporary analyses, sometimes from literature, art, poetry or music dealing with the class struggles of capitalism in the past and in the present. I drew illustrations from nineteenth-century novels portraying the capitalist crimes against which Marx wrote and fought in the Britain of his time and others from US novelists addressing more recent but parallel conflicts closer to home.[9] I also included poems and songs that lament those crimes—against humanity and nature—or celebrate the struggles against them. In the web notes, where possible, I included hyperlinks to performances. However, to reduce those notes to book length, most illustrations have been eliminated or sharply abbreviated.

A sixth objective was to *amplify* the material in Volume I with other writings by Marx that I felt made explicit things that are only implicit in *Capital*. For example, although I discover therein an exploration of the concrete forms of alienation caused by the capitalist subordination of life to work within industry, I also find it useful to draw upon his earlier writings that provide a framework for organizing our understanding of such alienation—a framework that he did not explicitly evoke in *Capital*. Therefore, in these notes you will sometimes find discussions of other writings.

EXTENSIONS

Composed in the 1860s and published in 1867, Volume I of *Capital* is clearly dated.[10] Therefore, I have sought, in a limited way, to examine the relevance of his analysis to aspects of capitalism to which he paid scant attention, but which have since become extremely important. I address its relevance to developments that I have found to be either fundamental to the reshaping of the capitalist world in the years since Marx wrote or most immediately familiar because of our common experiences at home and in schools.

---

9.   Commenting on extensive passages from Jacques Peuchet (1758–1830) on suicide, Marx argued, "It is by no means only to the French 'socialist' writers proper that one must look for the critical presentation of social conditions; but to writers in every sphere of literature, and in particular of novels and memoirs." "Peuchet: On Suicide", *MECW*, *vol. 4*, p. 597. To appreciate Marx's own use of cultural material, see S. S. Prawer, *Karl Marx and World Literature*, 2nd edn., London: Verso, 2011.

10.   Marx did make a few changes in subsequent editions of *Capital*, especially the French translation, and Engels added notes to the German and English versions that reflected some subsequent experience in the nineteenth century.

For example, Marx recognized how from its very beginning capitalism created a labor force, or working class, that included *both* the waged and the unwaged. In Part Eight on primitive accumulation, he points to the enclosures that drove people from their homes, tools and land, leaving them without any source of income and putting pressure on them to seek a wage in the labor market. Some got jobs and a wage, many did not. In Chapter 25, dealing with ongoing accumulation, he analyzed those without a wage as part of a "reserve army." As capitalism rampaged across the face of the earth, through colonialism and then neo-colonialism down to contemporary neoliberal globalization, it has repeatedly enclosed commons and imposed waged labor; but it has simultaneously imposed many kinds of unwaged work. Understanding those impositions, and finding effective forms of resistance, I argue, can be usefully informed by extending Marx's analysis to their study.

One of the most important early forms of unwaged labor within capitalism was slavery. Putting unwaged, enslaved Africans to work—providing raw materials for manufacturing factories manned by waged labor—shaped the entire subsequent history of capitalism. Even today, illegal slavery persists in forms such as human trafficking, and prisons impose de facto slavery by forcing prisoners to work for little or nothing. Moreover, racial discrimination and racist ideologies and behaviors continue to be widespread vehicles of capitalist domination, limiting the efforts of African-Americans and others to improve their lives.

Two other important sectors of the mostly unwaged have been peasants or small farmers in the countryside (often surviving on as yet unenclosed commons and part-time waged labor) and unwaged workers in cities—frequently migrants from rural areas or from other countries—who make up what is often called the "informal" sector of those who manage to get by with little or no access to wages. Indeed, the majority of those involved in the great uprisings of the twentieth century—the Mexican, Russian and Chinese Revolutions—were mostly unwaged peasants. So too with virtually all anti-colonial struggles such as those of the Vietnamese against French, Japanese and American domination. So too with the Zapatista indigenous rebellion in Chiapas, Mexico against racism, cultural genocide and capitalism at the end of the twentieth century, which catalyzed what are now ongoing struggles for democracy in that country and the global rise of both an indigenous renaissance and an anti-capitalist movement. Therefore, I show the ways, and the degree to which, Marx's analysis of the unwaged can be extended to peasants, small farmers and so-called urban "marginals" and deepened by drawing upon the rest of his work.

But those have not been the only important sectors of the unwaged. When Marx was writing, men, women and children were all being driven into factories and other capitalist-organized waged work sites. But the struggles he describes in Chapter 10 to reduce the "working day" of wage labor eventually bore fruit in some parts of the world and resulted in substantial reductions in the time of waged work, e.g., in the US from 75 to 80 hours/week in 1880 down to approximately 40 hours/week in 1940. Over that same period, reformers succeeded in getting laws passed against most child labor and restrictions were placed on waged jobs for women. The resulting "liberation" of children and women—together constituting over half of the population—from waged labor, posed serious problems for a capitalist system that bases most of its control on the imposition of work.

Faced with the loss of the ability to control women and children directly, capitalists had to find other organizational ways of managing them. What it found and propagated were the nuclear family and public schooling, both structured to produce and reproduce the population as endlessly subordinated to the capitalist organization of life around work. In other words, capital invaded and colonized the time liberated from waged labor to make sure that women and children continued to work for it, but without a wage. Women would work as mothers and wives to procreate and reproduce the labor force (both waged and unwaged) and children would be incarcerated and disciplined for future roles as waged or unwaged workers. The relegation of most women to unwaged domestic work together with most waged women being limited to low-waged jobs, reinforced gender as an essential means by which capital has divided people to control them. Like racism and racial discrimination, sexism and gender discrimination predated capitalism but have been systematically reproduced and cultivated for purposes of social control. Therefore, I return again and again to the relevance of Marx's analysis of waged labor for analyzing and understanding unwaged housework and unwaged schoolwork, and the racial and gender divisions that characterize unwaged as well as waged work.

Finally, because Marx was primarily analyzing the characteristics of capitalism (the book, after all, is titled *Capital*) the bulk of the text is concerned with what capitalists have sought to impose: their own modes of organizing social life. He does make clear, however, that from the beginning and continuing throughout the history of the capitalist era, people have resisted having their lives subordinated to those modes and have fought to liberate themselves and to create alternatives. Unfortunately, he devoted relatively few words to describing or analyzing those struggles. There are exceptions, such as Chapter 10 which includes a discussion of the struggles to limit and then reduce the time of waged labor; but for the most part his analyses of capitalist ways of organizing every aspect of life are not accompanied by equally detailed treatments of the struggles against those ways and for alternatives. To overcome this limitation, I have sought to do two things:

first, to bring in some of his writings that *do* address such struggles, and second, to amplify what he did write with the studies of others who *have* investigated and analyzed, in greater detail, the efforts of people to avoid being reduced to the status of mere worker both individually and collectively. So, for example, to complement Marx's discussion in Chapter 27 of enclosure in England, I have brought in some of the work of bottom-up British Marxist historians who have unearthed long-buried stories of resistance to enclosure and of struggles to reverse it.

The degree to which I have pursued these multiple objectives varies from chapter to chapter depending on their content and my familiarity with both the subject and relevant treatment by other authors. But in general, in each case, a brief outline of the content of Marx's analysis is followed by a commentary addressed to an elucidation of some aspects of his theory and to an examination of the degree to which that theory can be usefully extended to domains and times that neither he nor Engels sufficiently explored.

SITUATING MYSELF

These objectives and efforts have been shaped by a half-century of political engagement within universities, first as a student, then as a professor. During those years, I was either directly involved in various struggles, on and off campus, or supporting those of my students. My last extended, direct participation was in the networks of solidarity supporting the Zapatista rebellion in Chiapas, Mexico, the pro-democracy movement it catalyzed in that country and the alter-globalization movement to which it gave birth around the world.

Because of that personal history, I have struggled to avoid—not always successfully—the tendency of academics to situate themselves as *outside* observers and objective analysts of the world and its conflicts. Sometimes it's unavoidable, as when you are writing about historical events in which you did not participate. You can make your sympathies clear, but that's about it. Having been *inside* various struggles, however, has had consequences for my teaching, research and writing. *First*, as a salaried professor, I have always shared—with my mostly unwaged students—my analysis of the situation in which we found ourselves, with all its carefully arranged structures of power, including the hierarchical relationships among professors, students and administrators. Whether in graduate seminar conversations or in lectures to huge classes, I would ask students to consider the constraints on our ability to share knowledge and learn from each other. *Second*, my choice of both course content and research topics has always been determined by my politics, beginning with my early work on the Green Revolution, an outgrowth of a study group trying to understand the non-military aspects of the US government's war against Vietnamese independence. That study, which revealed how capitalists have used money to subordinate scientific research to the political needs of policymakers, led me to gear my own work to helping those they were trying to control. So, I created courses in response to student demands and pursued research to contribute either to particular struggles or to the development of what I judged theory useful to such research. *Third*, believing that authors should not hide behind some pretended objectivity, I have tried to speak and write in ways that make my own political position explicit. Adopting Marxian analytical tools helps to achieve that objective, because they embody a critique of capitalism. But given the diversity of interpretations of Marx mentioned above, I have sometimes critiqued other's writings and analyses to differentiate my own position. *Fourth*, having chosen *what to research* and *which theory to deploy*, I have repeatedly faced the problem of *how to write* in ways that make my own position and politics clear.[11] I addressed this problem in my preface to *Rupturing the Dialectic* (2017) and have tried, in this book, to follow the approach chosen there:

> Frequently in this book I use the first-person plural pronouns "we" and "our"—despite recognizing them as problematic. Sometimes they refer to all living beings, as in "our very existence is threatened by the way capitalist industry poisons land, air and water"; sometimes they refer to all of us who struggle against the way capitalism organizes society, as in "we struggle against the subordination of our lives to capitalist-imposed work." My use of these terms, however, should not be read as a reductionism that ignores the complex heterogeneity of either living beings or of those of us who struggle. As I hope will be clear in what follows, I am not only acutely aware of those complexities but make no pretense of speaking *for* specific groups of which I am clearly not a member. Yet, I use these terms because I want to avoid the academic practice of analyzing conflict from outside and above, as if an objective observer, by being clear that what I have to say here is one expression of my political stance among those opposed to capitalism and striving to create alternatives. I also use these pronouns, where it seems reasonable to do so, to emphasize how capitalist ways of organizing the world impose common problems

---

11.   There is yet another problem, namely that of the capitalist appropriation of Marxian theory. Recognizing that it happens raises the problem of how to minimize the likelihood that what we write will be of use to our enemies. See H. Cleaver, "Karl Marx: Economist or Revolutionary?", in Suzanne W. Helburn and David F. Bramhall (eds.), *Marx, Schumpeter & Keynes*, Armonk, NY: M. E. Sharpe, 1986, pp. 121–146.

on us and how we have often found in the past, and can hopefully find in the future, complementary ways to struggle.[12]

Although minimal in my commentaries on the history laid out in Part Eight, but more frequently in Parts One through Seven, I explicitly situate myself as a worker, as a member of the working class. I recognize that doing so is controversial. Throughout most of the history of Marxism, neither students nor professors have been seen as members of the working class, often defined purely as waged factory workers. At best, with Antonio Gramsci (1891–1937), students and professors might aspire to becoming "organic intellectuals" allied with workers, but still apart. Only recently, for reasons that will appear in my commentaries, have universities been seen as "edu-factories" and professors as one sort of white-collar worker laboring within them and struggling against their constraints.

A final note: neither this book, nor my online "study guide," attempts to confront *everything* written in *Capital*. The book is an amazingly rich compendium of history and analysis, informed and illuminated by a wealth of references. There is no adequate substitute for reading and studying the original.

---

12. Harry Cleaver, *Rupturing the Dialectic: The Struggle against Work, Money and Financialization*, New York: AK Press, 2017, p. 1.

2
Capital: A Critique of Political Economy

Famous, because it provides the most detailed and systematic *critique* of capitalism ever written[1] and because it has inspired generations of rebels in their thinking and actions, *Capital, Volume I*, has nevertheless been cited, condemned or praised far more often than it has been read. Although Marx did warn, in his Preface to the book, that "Beginnings are always difficult" and "The understanding of the first chapter... will therefore present the greatest difficulty,"[2] he also thought that he had organized it in a way that would make it accessible to everyone, including "young people, etc., who are thirsting for knowledge."[3] He was also delighted when it was published serially in France for workers (August 1872–May 1875).[4] But over the years since his time, it has become a commonplace that most of those who start at the beginning—Part One, Chapters 1–3, containing the basics of his labor theory of value—fail to read the rest of the book.

The usual explanation for that failure attributes it to the way in which he presented his theory. Despite his good intentions, instead of some clever hook to draw readers in, he filled those first pages with abstract categories deployed in a dense analysis of commodities (things bought and sold) and money. Although both commodities and money are familiar to everyone, neither the abstract categories of his theory nor his method of presentation

1. There are other books on capitalism just as long and detailed—such as Adam Smith's *Wealth of Nations*—but despite containing a few criticisms of this or that aspect of the system, they have been dedicated to solving its problems and offering policy recommendations for its promulgation, the very opposite of Marx's critique, which is aimed at helping find ways to transcend it.
2. "Preface to the First Edition", *Capital, Volume I*, p. 89; *MECW, vol. 35*, p. 7. Marx offered a similar warning in his Preface to the French edition: "the method of analysis I have employed... makes the reading of the first chapters rather arduous... [But] there is no royal road to science, and only those who do not dread the fatiguing climb of its steep paths have a chance of gaining its luminous summits." *Capital, Vol. I*, p. 104.
3. Marx to Engels, June 22, 1867, *MECW, vol. 42*, p. 384.
4. "Note des Éditeurs", p. 7. To the publisher, Marx wrote "I applaud your idea of publishing the translation of *Capital* as a serial. In this form the book will be more accessible to the working class, a consideration which to me outweighs everything else." "Preface to the French Edition", *Capital, Vol. I*, p. 104.

are well known. While the logic of the presentation is clear enough—gradually adding determinations to move from the more abstract to the more concrete—why it is worthwhile to work through the abstractions and figure out what they all add up to has not been clear to generations of those who have tried but given up. Those who have struggled through the first chapters and then continued through the book, have discovered how vitally important all those abstractions are, a discovery that inevitably leads one back to rereading the opening chapters in the light of all that follows, and then rereading all that follows in the light of a clearer understanding of the basic concepts.

One result of this perception—by those of us who have found reading and studying the whole book worthwhile—has been recurrent admonitions to start reading, not from the beginning, but from some later point in the text. For example, French Communist Party philosopher Louis Althusser (1918–90) advised readers to skip Part One, begin with Part Two, Chapters 4–6, read the whole book through and then return to Part One.[5] Although the order I suggested to my students differed, it was nevertheless very much in the same spirit. For those new to Volume I, I recommended beginning with Marx's analysis of the historical origins of capitalism in Part Eight on Primitive Accumulation (Chapters 26–33) and then taking up his theory in Parts One through Seven. I suggested that order, and organized my lectures and discussion accordingly, because material in Part Eight consists of vivid historical analyses that make the abstractions of Part One easier to understand. While reading everything in the book after Part One, as Althusser recommended, would certainly make it obvious where Marx was going in those first three chapters, reading only Part Eight is enough, I have found, to reveal why he developed a *labor* theory of value and therefore why it is worth the trouble of studying his detailed but abstract presentation of that theory in Part I. Moreover, because the rest of the book, Parts Two through Seven, deploys the categories developed in Part One to analyze all of the different aspects of capitalism addressed, how you understand those categories shapes how you understand those subsequent analyses. The same is true with respect to the second and third volumes of *Capital*. Compiled from his notebooks, by his friends and followers after his death in 1883, the material assembled in those two volumes use the same concepts presented in Volume I to analyze whole new aspects of the class relationships of capitalism. This book follows the same suggested order as my lectures and my online study guide. Because the bulk of my commentaries were written and organized on the basis of that order, comments on a given chapter often assume previous discussions or allude to later ones.

---

5. Louis Althusser, "Avertissement aux Lecteurs du Livre I du Capital", in Karl Marx, *Le Capital: critique de l'économie politique*, p. 13.

3
Part Eight
So-called Primitive Accumulation

These last chapters, 26–33, provide an easy-to-understand historical context for the more theoretical analysis in Chapters 1–25. Those earlier chapters spell out, step by step, Marx's analysis of the antagonistic social relationships of capitalism, beginning with a quite abstract presentation of his labor theory of value and building, gradually to a more concrete analysis of how those relationships are reproduced on an ever-expanding scale. What these final chapters make clear is why Marx formulated a *labor* theory of value as his primary theoretical tool. He shows us how capitalism came into the world as a new form of social domination whose most fundamental method of controlling society was the endless imposition of work. In Marx's analysis, that imposition generated an antagonistic two-class structure: a capitalist class that imposes work and a working class that resists. The chapters in Part Eight are organized in a way that highlights the creation of these two classes:

Chapter 26: The Secret of Primitive Accumulation. This introductory chapter reveals the hidden "secret" of the creation of a new kind of class society, how most people were stripped of their means of living independently, forcing them to work for a new class of overlords.

Chapter 27: The Expropriation of the Agricultural Population from the Land. Sketching the first step in the historical creation of the working class, Chapter 27 analyzes and illustrates how and when people's pre-capitalist ways of life were violently destroyed. Most of the examples are from England and Scotland, for which Marx had the most material. The violence of the expropriation lay both in the use of physical force to overcome resistance to being dispossessed and in the wholescale destruction of traditional ways of living.

Chapter 28: Bloody Legislation Against the Expropriated. In the second step of creating a working class, the expropriated were forced into the labor market to sell their ability and willingness to work to some capitalist. Here again, violence was required because even stripped of the means of independent livelihood a great many people turned to vagabondage or direct appropriation, rather than selling their abilities to capitalists.

Chapter 29: The Genesis of the Capitalist Farmer. Marx's analysis of the emergence of the capitalist class, a new ruling class whose power to impose work was progressively based on having enough money to hire workers and purchase the means of production necessary to put them to work producing commodities, begins with the appearance of agrarian capitalists. Instead of merely collecting rents from tenants, the owners of great landed estates or those hired by such landowners, reorganized agriculture to produce for the market.

Chapter 30: Impact of the Agricultural Revolution on Industry. The Creation of a Home Market for Industrial Capital. Expropriated and dispossessed, people were forced to buy what they needed to live, creating markets for the commodities many of them now produced for their capitalist employers.

Chapter 31: The Genesis of the Industrial Capitalist. Alongside agrarian capitalists came captains of industry, capitalists able to amass sufficient fortunes to hire workers and purchase the means of production necessary for manufacturing and then large-scale industry. Their means included state subsidies, profitable loans to the government and colonial pillage and exploitation.

Chapter 32: The Historical Tendency of Capitalist Accumulation. This chapter provides both a historical summation and a logical conclusion, not only to Part Eight, but to the whole book. It provides sweeping overviews of the rise of capitalism as a new historical phenomenon, of how its methods of imposing work and exploiting people generates resistance and, finally, of how that resistance has the potential to become revolution, overthrowing and transcending it.

Chapter 33: The Modern Theory of Colonialism. In what amounts to an appendix to Chapter 31's brief evocation of colonialism as one of the means through which capitalists amassed enough money to finance investment, Marx analyzes the writings of one economist who not only understood how capitalism requires the creation of a working class but proposed some policies for achieving it.

CHAPTER 26: THE SECRET OF PRIMITIVE ACCUMULATION

Outline of Marx's Analysis

The myth of political economy:
  – frugal elite (who accumulated wealth) vs lazy rascals (who spent it all and were left with nothing but their skins to sell)
Actual history:
  – capitalists replaced guild masters (or feudal lords) and created:
  – a working class, displaced from the soil, stripped of their tools and autonomy
  – capitalists gained control of the means of production via "conquest, enslavement, robbery, murder, in short, force"[1]
  – primitive accumulation, therefore is "the historical process of divorcing the producer from the means of production."[2]
  – workers are freed in a double sense:
      1. neither are they owned as means of production, i.e., as slaves
      2. nor do they own the means of production: they suffer a change in form of servitude
  – capitalist era dates from the sixteenth century.

Commentary

What makes capitalism a new kind of society has been the creation of two new classes: a capitalist one made up of those who seek to organize most people's lives around the work of producing commodities and another, a class of workers, made up of those whose lives are subordinated to that organization. The *secret* of this creation—hidden by pro-capitalist political apologists in the telling of history—is that the emerging class of capitalists *imposed this social order with brutality and violence,* forcibly separating people from their means of livelihood and destroying their ways of life. Those means included: privately owned tools, formal and informal land tenure and commons, such as pastures, fishing waters, forests and often language and culture to which everyone in a community had access. Although this forcible separation created a situation where the reality (and threat) of destitution and starvation would largely replace the lash as a coercive instrument of control, violence has continued to provide capitalists with a supplementary weapon for keeping people subordinated, right down to the

---

1. *Capital, Vol. I,* p. 874.
2. Ibid., p. 875.

present. This is true whether the violence has been wielded by corporate goons, paramilitary thugs or by government police and military.

Marx both *critiques* political economy by showing it to be at once apologetic and false and *gives an overview of the actual processes* through which capitalism emerged as a new kind of social order—an outline of the history he examines more thoroughly in the subsequent chapters.[3]

His analysis temporarily ignores the central subjects of political economy—the interactions of "money and commodities"—to focus on the social conflicts that shaped the new world in which those things came to figure so centrally. The violence that capitalists required to impose their order reveals the depth of resistance. The agents of this new order, the "knights of industry," exploited every opportunity to achieve power, to subordinate the exploited classes of the old order in a new way and to usurp the power of the feudal lords, the "knights of the sword."

The Myths of Political Economy

Myths about the class structure of capitalism have served to justify both its historical origins and ongoing class disparities. The central myth, still promulgated today, is a morality tale that portrays capitalists as obtaining their wealth by frugally saving and investing. It suggests that everyone has always been able to become a capitalist by the same means, and those who do not, have no one to blame but themselves.

In nineteenth-century English literature, this myth was already the object of ridicule far more acerbic than Marx's. For example, in Charles Dickens's (1812–70) 1854 novel *Hard Times*, which narrates the lives and tragedies of several people in a fictional Manchester-style, manufacturing city called Coketown, we find many passages where various persons are repeating this myth. Examples include the self-praising speeches of Mr. Josiah Bounderby—the novel's central capitalist—constantly bragging (falsely it turns out) about how he raised himself out of the mud to his present august position as mill owner and banker.[4] More concise is a pretty exchange between Bounderby's ex-housekeeper Mrs. Sparsit and Bitzer, his light porter, general spy and informer at the bank, in which the repetition of the myth reveals both a disdain for those irrational creatures (workers)

---

3. This opening makes clear why the subtitle of Volume I of *Capital* is "A Critique of Political Economy." His critique does not provide an alternative political economy or economic theory of capitalism, but rather an analysis designed to inform struggles to overthrow it.

4. Dickens's character, Mr. Josiah Bounderby, has found a real-life incarnation in Donald Trump; the parallels between their incessant, narcissistic bragging and their lies about the sources of their wealth are striking.

who put human relationships before personal profit and a self-delusion about the origins of wealth. Both, of course, are merely repeating the self-justifying truisms of Bounderby in an almost ritual, and mutually reinforcing, manner.[5] The effect is both comic and appalling.

A subtler, but even more biting indictment of the myth of the self-made man, is contained in *The Professor* by Charlotte Brontë (1816–55), written in 1846. The protagonist, a young man who becomes a school teacher, only achieves success by fully participating in a dog-eat-dog world fully shaped by the laissez-faire, competitive capitalism of the nineteenth century. The novel portrays the necessary combination of aggressiveness and defensiveness required for survival, as well as the ultimate loneliness and isolation of even the most successful competitors for status and love. It is an amazingly modern treatment of the psychological consequences of what Marx in his *1844 Manuscripts* and social critics in the twentieth century call the *alienation* of individuals in capitalist society. The pressures to which the young professor succumbs and the behaviors that he adopts continue to be depressingly widespread in contemporary academia where academics are pitted against each other in an endless struggle for publication, research funds and promotion.

In American literature and popular culture, this myth has taken many forms, including the novels for young adults of Horatio Alger (1832–99). With the rise of the modern corporation with its many-leveled wage and salary hierarchy, the myth has taken the form of stories of energetic individuals who work hard and scheme their way up that hierarchy, perhaps even to the top. From Horatio Alger's young men to Michael J. Fox in *The Secret of My Success* (1987) or Melanie Griffith in *Working Girl* (1988), the myth has changed little. It has, however, also been repeatedly critiqued, in novels such as Sinclair Lewis's *Babbitt* (1922) or poems such as Edwin Robertson's "Richard Cory" (1897), made famous in Simon and Garfunkel's musical interpretation (1966).[6] I return to these critiques in my commentary on Chapter 7.

Controversy: Was Marx an "Historical Materialist"?

Declining to take on the history of capitalism everywhere, Marx announces that he will take the example of England as the "classic" case. Indeed, throughout *Capital* most of Marx's examples are drawn from British history although from time to time, including in this section on primitive accumulation, he brings in experiences in other countries. However, since

5. Here too are parallels with the sycophants with which Trump surrounds himself.
6. Edwin Arlington Robinson, *Selected Poems*, New York: Penguin Classics, 1997.

Capital was published in 1867, there are many—including his best friend and collaborator Friedrich Engels (1820–95)—who have tried to turn Marx's analysis of the rise of capitalism into a general theory of history, i.e., *historical materialism*. Engels's efforts in this direction built on a few generalizations that he and Marx had made in their early joint works *The German Ideology* (c. 1846) and *The Communist Manifesto* (1848). In the former, they insisted on the material foundations of human life in the genesis of ideology. In the latter, aimed at differentiating their *communist* movement from a variety of *socialist* efforts, they famously wrote: "The history of all hitherto existing society is the history of class struggles." A decade later, in his brief preface to his *Contribution to the Critique of Political Economy* (1859), Marx wrote:

> In the social production of their existence, men inevitably enter into definite relations, which are independent of their will, namely relations of production appropriate to a given stage in the development of their material forces of production. The totality of these relations of production constitutes the economic structure of society, the real foundation, on which arises a legal and political superstructure and to which correspond definite forms of social consciousness. The mode of production of material life conditions the general process of social, political and intellectual life. It is not the consciousness of men that determines their existence, but their social existence that determines their consciousness. At a certain stage of development, the material productive forces of society come into conflict with the existing relations of production or— this merely expresses the same thing in legal terms—with the property relations within the framework of which they have operated hitherto. From forms of development of the productive forces these relations turn into their fetters. Then begins an era of social revolution. The changes in the economic foundation lead sooner or later to the transformation of the whole immense superstructure.[7]

Given the generic character of this passage, characterizing human history in general, it is easy enough to understand why some would see it as a first step toward a general theory of human history. Engels, but not Marx, went on to attempt the elaboration of such a general theory in writings such as *Anti-Dühring* (1878) and in *The Dialectics of Nature* (1883), where he pushed beyond a general theory of history, to sketch a virtual cosmology—a *dialectical materialism* encompassing all of nature as well as human history, a

---

7. *MECW, vol. 29*, p. 263.

cosmology in which historical materialism constituted a subset of a broader vision.

These works became essential references for official Soviet ideology, referred to in shorthand as *histomat* and *diamat*. At their nadir, during Stalin's regime, both were reduced to a virtual catechism to which all Soviet intellectuals were forced to adhere. They were also used to justify—when it suited Soviet interests—demands that members of the Soviet-organized Third International in regions of the Global South support the development of capitalism against so-called "feudal forces." In the wake of Stalin's death in 1953 and of the Soviet crushing of the Hungarian Revolution in 1956, the theory was refurbished as an elaborate structural model by Althusser and his collaborators. The ongoing appeal of one version of historical materialism or another is evident in the continuing publication of the academic journal *Historical Materialism* (1997–), its conferences and its book series.

Unfortunately for those attached to the idea of a general theory of history, Marx wrote his own commentary on this kind of interpretation of his work. One author to whom Marx took exception was Nicolai K. Mikhailovski (1842–1904) who had used Marx's analysis of primitive accumulation to argue the historical necessity for all countries, including Russia, to pass through the stage of capitalism. Yes, the czar should be overthrown, but that overthrow must be followed by accelerating capitalist industrialization of the country. This was a highly political issue in Russia in the 1870s and remained so right through the Russian Revolution when the Bolsheviks seized power and pursued precisely such a policy. Others, such as the populists, recognized no such inevitability, argued and organized for a revolution of workers and peasants that would undercut the beginnings of capitalism in Russia and permit a direct passage from the traditional village *mir* (a communal form of organization) to communism. In the process of rejecting Mikhailovski's interpretation, Marx refused the conversion of his theory into "historical materialism":

> It is absolutely necessary for him to metamorphose my historical sketch of the genesis of capitalism in Western Europe into a historico-philosophical theory of general development, imposed by fate for all peoples, whatever the historical circumstances in which they are placed.[8]

Elsewhere in the same letter, to illustrate his objection to applying his analysis willy-nilly, Marx points out how the expropriation of peasants in ancient Rome led not to wage labor but to slavery.

---

8.   Marx to *Otechestvenniye Zapiski*, November 1877, *MECW, vol. 24*, p. 200.

Four years later, in a letter to Vera Zasulich (1849–1919), one of his translators, he again rejected the generalization of his theory and insisted on the open-ended possibilities of the Russian village *mir* as the possible basis of a new society:

> The historical inevitability of this process [the genesis of capitalist production] is expressly limited to the *countries of Western Europe*. . . Hence, the analysis presented in *Capital* does not adduce reasons either for or against the viability of the rural commune, but the special study which I have made of it, and the material which I drew from original sources, has convinced me that this commune is the fulcrum of the social regeneration in Russia.[9]

He hoped, we now know, vainly, that revolution might give the *mir* a chance to become the point of departure for the growth of an alternative, more attractive culture and civilization.[10]

From these notes and from the treatment in *Capital*, I draw two conclusions: first, this section on primitive accumulation shows the conditions and processes through which capitalism emerged and which it must maintain to reproduce its social order. People must be separated from alternative means of livelihood and driven into the labor market, where they can gain their bread only by working for business.[11] Second, it is a mistake to see this analysis as a linear stages theory that says all peoples must pass through these processes.

Even today, when it can be argued that all countries have long been caught up in the capitalist web and their people fitted into its net of exploitation, there is nothing in Marx that argues each subordinated group must progress through predetermined stages of development before they can fight to be free of capitalism. In a world organized around an extremely complex multinational division of labor, it makes no sense to interpret the

---

9.   Marx to Vera Zasulich, March 8, 1881, *MECW, vol. 24*, pp. 370–371. Also available in the same volume are three drafts of the letter. See pp. 346–369.

10.   These letters have played a role in efforts to show how Marx's later work escaped what seemed to be its early limitations. See Teodor Shanin, *Late Marx and the Russian Road: Marx and the Peripheries of Capitalism*, New York: Monthly Review Press, 1983 and Kevin Anderson, *Marx at the Margins: On Nationalism, Ethnicity and Non-Western Societies*, Chicago, IL: University of Chicago Press, 2016.

11.   In recent years, a debate arose about whether Marx's analysis of primitive accumulation is only applicable to the period of the rise of capitalism or also explains continuing processes of enclosure, dispossession and the imposition of markets in contemporary capitalism. See the articles collected in the second issue of the online journal *The Commoner*, September 2001.

call for a "universal development of productive forces" as a call for universal industrialization. Marx shows us how capitalist development has always involved underdevelopment, both as a process and as a strategy. The development of capitalism is not only based on the underdevelopment and impoverishment of all other modes of life but in the process, it generates a poverty it can never abolish because it provides an ongoing threat that not being directly exploited by capitalism can be worse than being exploited by it.[12] The division of labor, a corresponding income hierarchy and the promise of upward mobility have provided capitalists with carrots to induce acceptance of its rules of the game, but also with the sticks of unemployment and poverty to club people into line when the carrot does not provide sufficient motivation.

Extensions: Capitalism Can Not Eliminate the Alternatives

As he argues here, and again in Chapter 25 on accumulation, capitalist development never means giving everyone a living wage in exchange for work. On the contrary, many, perhaps most (on a world scale) of those whose ways of life are progressively destroyed are doomed to remain unwaged and poor.

This is one reason why so many people have resisted and fought to preserve their independence as communities and their uniqueness as cultures. In the United States, as in other so-called developed capitalist countries, most people have lost that struggle and been swept into the world of factories, offices, ghettos and suburbs. Some have preserved unique cultural attributes by forming rural or urban communities. We have the Amish in the countryside, Native Americans on reservations, and ethnic communities in cities. Others, from time to time, have broken away to form intentional communities that escape, to some degree, subordination to wage labor. But most people have been integrated into the waged/unwaged hierarchies of capitalist society. In the Global South, where factories have been fewer and capitalist development has concentrated its poverty, a higher percentage of people have had better luck in preserving some land, some control over their means of production and more of their traditional culture. They are not outside of capitalism, they too are exploited, as we will see, in a variety of ways, yet they still have some space that supports their ongoing struggle for autonomy. In *Capital*, Marx does not talk much about these situations

---

12.   This point was apparently made so frequently by the English economist Joan Robinson that the statement "The only thing worse than being exploited by capitalism is not being exploited by capitalism" has been repeatedly attributed to her. See her *An Essay on Marxist Economics*, London: Palgrave Macmillan, 2nd rev. edn., 1967.

because his historical examples are mostly drawn from the British Isles, where very little of pre-capitalist social forms and culture survived.[13]

One place where access to land and community cohesion have made possible resistance to total subsumption to capitalism and a certain degree of autonomy is Mexico. In the early 1990s, in the run-up to the passage of the North American Free Trade Agreement (NAFTA), the Mexican government pushed through a constitutional amendment aimed at undercutting one of the few fruits of the Mexican Revolution (1910–20) won by peasants and the indigenous: the collective ownership of land in the form of *ejidos* where the land belonged to communities and not to individuals and could not be bought and sold. While not organized like the Russian *mir*, the *ejidos* nevertheless provided the material foundations for peasant, especially indigenous, communities to survive and preserve elements of their languages, music, dress and self-organization quite different from the institutions of the centralized Mexican state. Thus, they have formed unwanted rigidities to Mexican and American business with an interest in expanding their investments and tapping more people as cheap labor.

While the amendment of the Mexican constitution pleased business, indigenous communities saw it as a death knell foretelling widespread ethnic genocide. As a result, in the southern state of Chiapas the indigenous members of many communities united to form, equip and launch a rebellion against such a destiny. These are the Zapatistas, self-named after one of the heroes of the Mexican Revolution, Emiliano Zapata (1879–1919), a peasant from the state of Morelos who became leader of the Liberation Army of the South.

On January 1, 1994, the same day NAFTA went into effect, fighters of the *Ejército Zapatista de Liberación Nacional* (EZLN, or Zapatista Army

---

13. Fortunately, a bit more has survived in England's first colonies, Wales (1282), Ireland (1603) and Scotland (1707), especially, for those of us who appreciate things Celtic, their traditional language, music and folklore. Capitalists, of course, try to co-opt/instrumentalize all such survivals—just as they do with wholly new artistic and musical creations—by turning them into profitable commodities and spectacles. Thus, folk and even protest music often wind up being sold for a profit. Of course, in the process capitalist commodification often becomes a vehicle for the widespread circulation of anti-capitalist messages and struggle. In the place of wandering troubadours such as Joe Hill (1879–1915) and Woody Guthrie (1912–67), who inspired workers' struggles as they moved from place to place, came LP recordings of Pete Seeger (1919–2014) spreading their songs across the USA, and Bob Dylan (1941–) inspiring the cultural revolution of the 1960s through LPs, tapes and televised performances. Today, with peer-to-peer digital sharing, YouTube and various social media, capitalist commodification has become more difficult and the circulation of anti-capitalist art and music more widespread than ever before. See Brett Caraway, "Survey of File-Sharing Culture", *International Journal of Communication*, no. 6, 2012, pp. 564–584.

of National Liberation) poured out of the jungles and forests and seized six cities in Chiapas. As they did so, they explained their rebellion as a last-ditch defense against their extermination as peoples and demanded official recognition of their rights to preserve and evolve, in their own ways, their traditional forms of social organization. The Mexican government counterattacked with troops but was soon forced into negotiations by widespread protests all over Mexico and around the world. Those protests were sparked by the ability of the Zapatistas, especially their main early spokesperson Subcomandante Marcos, to clearly articulate not only NAFTA's threat to their communities and their demands for autonomy, but also a more general critique of neoliberalism that resonated around the world—so much so as even to inspire foreign musicians, such as the band Rage Against the Machine to celebrate their rebellion in the song "People of the Sun."[14] Outflanked and defeated repeatedly in the subsequent political struggle, the state attacked again in early 1995 and was again forced to back off.

Over the last two decades, the conflict has continued and so far, despite the constitutional amendment permitting communities to be privatized, broken up, sold off and dispersed, the indigenous of the Zapatista movement have been successful in resisting such pressures. Indeed, they have continued to reorganize themselves in more and more explicitly anti-capitalist ways and carried those efforts to the rest of grassroots Mexico seeking ways of building a nationwide, anti-capitalist movement.[15] They continue to resist the final enclosure of the Mexican countryside and the completion of the kinds of processes described by Marx in these chapters.

Because many pre-capitalist forms in Britain were also exploitative, such as the rural world of tenants dominated by a landed aristocracy, Marx had no nostalgia for them. In many areas of the rest of the world, however, those cultures which predated capitalism were either not exploitative,

---

14.   "People of the Sun" got Rage Against the Machine banned by the Mexican government until 1999 when they were finally able to stage a concert in Mexico City. See their video *The Battle of Mexico City* (2001). The Zapatistas and their supporters have made extensive use of social media, beginning with email and webpages, to circulate information about their struggles and to coordinate resistance to government repression. See H. Cleaver, "The Zapatistas and the Electronic Circulation of Struggle" (1995), in John Holloway and Eloina Peláez (eds.), *Zapatista! Reinventing Revolution in Mexico*, Sterling, VA: Pluto Press, 1998, pp. 81–103.

15.   This was the objective of "The Other Campaign" launched in 2005 as an alternative to presidential elections in Mexico. Having won a certain freedom to travel by dint of continuous struggle, a group of Zapatista spokespeople carried their message and questions about democratic alternatives to Mexico's formal electoral system throughout Mexico.

or the people had spheres of autonomy filled with their own traditions, skills and rituals, as in Mexico where strong elements of pre-Columbian, Mesoamerican culture have survived and evolved.[16] Where capitalism has succeeded in destroying such cultures, the world has suffered an absolute loss of cultural diversity and human meaning with little to take their place other than the alienated world of capitalist poverty. Where capitalism has failed to impose its own rules of the game because of peoples' resistance, the conflict continues.

Late in his life, Marx not only studied the peasant *mir* in Russia but also delved into anthropological works on so-called primitive cultures, looking, his notebooks suggest, for further possibilities of avoiding the evils of capitalism through the further development of autonomous cultural practices.[17]

Today, we can look around the world, to some degree in the US and in the other developed capitalist countries, but to a larger degree in the Global South and see the wide variety of distinct ways of life that still offer a diverse array of alternatives to the dominant culture of capitalism. Whether these alternatives are judged satisfying or seen as points of departure, they show something extremely important: capital has never been able to shape the world entirely according to its own rules.

Beyond the survival of pre-capitalist cultural practices, people have also repeatedly created new kinds of social relationships that are incompatible with capitalist rules of the game and in the process, have posed new alternatives to it. In his theoretical chapters, Marx shows capitalism really has no creativity at all but lives by absorbing and harnessing the creativity of those it dominates. The realization of this constant failure of capital to bend all people during all their lives to its demands alerts us to the essential source of potential change: those alternatives created and elaborated through struggle.

With these notes of warning about too simplistic an adoption of Marx's analysis as being universally valid in its details, and even more so as a prescription for a painful but necessary historical passage, we can proceed to examine the elements of this original accumulation which Marx selected for more detailed treatment.

---

16.   See Guillermo Bonfil Batalla, *Mexico Profundo: Reclaiming a Civilization*, Austin: University of Texas Press, 1996.

17.   See Lawrence Krader (ed.), *The Ethnological Notebooks of Karl Marx: Studies of Morgan, Phear, Maine, Lubbock*, Amsterdam: Van Gorcum & Co., 1972 and Anderson, *Marx at the Margins*.

CHAPTER 27: THE EXPROPRIATION OF THE AGRICULTURAL POPULATION FROM THE LAND

Outline of Marx's Analysis

England: serfdom disappeared by last part of fourteenth century
- mostly independent peasants in fifteenth century
- part-time laborers
- right to common land for grazing, timber, etc.
- small peasant properties

Prelude to Revolution: last third of fifteenth century to first third of sixteenth century
- dissolution of bands of feudal retainers
- partly by royal power reducing wealth of aristocracy
- partly by feudal lords
- driving peasants from land for sheep walks (to take advantage of increased price of wool)
- usurping commons
- destruction of houses—futile legislation for 150 years after Henry VII (1489) tried to stem this trend, i.e., to 1630.

Sixteenth century: Reformation
- colossal spoliation of Catholic Church property, ex-feudal proprietor of land
- dissolution of monasteries
- estates given to royal favorites, drove out hereditary sub-tenants
- estates sold at nominal prices

Seventeenth century: "Glorious Revolution" of William of Orange
- theft of state lands, seized and given away or sold at low prices

Eighteenth century: Law becomes tool of land theft
- "Bills for the Enclosure of Commons" by Parliament dominated by "landed and capitalist profit grubbers"

Nineteenth century: "the clearing of the estates"
- clearing of cottages and people
- particularly dramatic in Scotland, e.g., by the Duchess of Sutherland:
- 15,000 people pushed out by British soldiers in appropriation of 794,000 acres of land, pushed to seashore,
- later driven away when seashore was let to London fishmongers.
- conversion of sheep walks to "deer-forests" for sport (led to famine)

Results
1. destruction of yeomanry (independent peasants) by 1750
   - replaced by tenants at will, small farmers on yearly leases, a servile rabble, sheep/deer, and agricultural labor
2. destruction of a whole system of private property and its replacement by another
3. driving of people into the manufacturing towns: creation of the human material to be shaped into an industrial working class, "driven from the land and forbidden to emigrate"

Commentary

This historical analysis of the first step in the creation of the working class centers the forcible expropriation of the means of livelihood of peasants and craftspeople. In England, some six million acres or one quarter of the cultivated acreage was enclosed by direct act of Parliament. Another four to seven million acres are estimated to have been enclosed privately.[18] By these actions, millions of people were rendered homeless and without income. This expropriation of the land was a long process, 300 to 400 years, and only through considerable violence were these changes accomplished. Vast numbers resisted and had to be forcibly dispossessed, a violence that forced them to seek refuge in woodland or cities or even flee abroad.

One area of dispossession, which Marx highlights, is the highlands in Scotland where the Duchess of Sutherland and others drove their clansmen from the land. Such enclosures and the human misery produced were fought by those directly victimized and protested by sympathizers.

The long and tragic history of the enclosures with their terrible costs to humans and to nature left an indelible mark on the various cultures of the "British" Isles. These costs were a central issue in the transformation wrought by the rise of capitalism, the commercialization of agriculture and the industrialization of manufacturing. Not surprisingly, they have also become the inspiration of folk music that remembers and laments. "The Highland Clearances," written by Andy Stewart, blasts Queen Victoria for sanctioning the kind of highland clearances carried out by the Duchess of Sutherland, evokes the burning of the peasant crofts and recalls those who were forced to take ship for the New, and hopefully better, World.[19]

While the new capitalist farmers were on the offensive, they found it no easy task to drive off and pauperize the population. There was violent resistance to physical removal; there were polemics written by economists and others, and from time to time, there was even legislation against the process—though largely ignored and unenforced. As we see in the subsequent chapter, the dispossessed also turned to "vagabondage and brigandry" out of desperation and to avenge themselves for the loss of their land and livelihoods.

This process that Marx analyzes in Britain has been universal throughout the bloody history of the creation of the capitalist world. Marx mentions

---

18. The area enclosed officially is from the estimate by J. D. Chambers and G. E. Mingay, *The Agricultural Revolution, 1750–1880*, London: Batsford, 1966, p. 77. The estimate of privately enclosed land is from Lord Ernle, *English Farming Past and Present*, London: Longmans Green, 1941, p. 163.

19. Silly Wizard, *So Many Partings*, Shanachie Records, 1980.

Germany, Sweden and France in passing, but it has been employed everywhere capitalists invaded, from Asia, through the Middle East and Africa
to the Western Hemisphere. In all those regions, British capitalists, backed
by their government's army and navy, established private property by force
and fiat against the indigenous peoples and their customs, no matter how
varied. So too did the Dutch in the East Indies. In the lands of the Incas and
Aztecs, the violence of the Spanish conquistadors and expropriators is well
known. Both Spaniards and Portuguese established huge colonial empires
in South America, bequeathing the region the title of *Latin* America
following the imposition of their own languages on indigenous peoples.[20]
The Dutch also carved out pieces of South America and Southern Africa.
Throughout the "Age of Imperialism," capitalists, backed by their governments, competed, both economically and militarily, frequently displacing
one another in wars for the control of the peoples, resources, markets and
investment opportunities throughout the world.

Over time, "primitive" accumulation became a recurrent aspect of capitalist development. Despite capitalist efforts to extend their control
throughout the world, that world was just too large and its people too
numerous and too resisting for capitalist investment to expand as rapidly
as its colonial control. As we see in Chapter 25, capitalists have sought to
use un-dispossessed people left on the land as a vast, latent "reserve army"
to be expelled and exploited when needed. Today, these conflicts continue
as capital repeatedly seeks to steal what little land remains in the hands of
small farmers, peasants and indigenous communities. Undeterred by government regulation, private capitalists clear-cut tropical rainforests, which
remain the home of diverse traditional cultures. Governments seize both
private and public lands for corporate investors in airports, golf courses
or mining. As such enclosures continue, so too do the struggles against
enclosure, sometimes in the courts, sometimes in the streets and forests.[21]

Because his subject is the creation of the working class, Marx's focuses
on the dispossession of independent peasants and does not dwell either on
the general nature of the pre-capitalist system, or on details of the ways of
life being wiped out. His general interpretive analysis grasps the transition
in terms of where it is headed but gives little sense of the kind of societies

---

20.   From the beginning of colonialism, colonial powers imposed not only work but
also their own languages on the indigenous populations. For an interesting account of
introduction of this method of domination to the founders of the Spanish empire, see
Ivan Illich, *Shadow Work*, Cape Town: University of Cape Town, 1980.

21.   Within the United States, the current Trump administration's shrinking of
National Monuments and the sale of mining, lumbering and grazing rights on public
lands are prime examples of contemporary government-managed enclosure of the
commons.

that were being destroyed. As a result, he leaves us no feeling for either the world of the peasants who are being driven off their land, or for the world of the landed estates whose "retainers" were being let go to join the unemployed, potentially waged labor force.

Marx's reasons for this absence can be explained partly by ignorance, partly by just not taking the time away from trying to understand the kind of world capitalists were imposing to examine the world(s) it was replacing. Certainly, Marx had no nostalgia for any kind of feudalism, nor was he a pastoralist wanting to turn history back to mythical peasant utopias. What little attention he did pay to peasant struggles before writing *Capital*—mainly those of French peasants—led him to be dismissive of their revolutionary potential.[22] However, as I have mentioned, years after *Capital* was published, debates in Russia over the importance of peasant life as a potential point of departure for a post-capitalist future led him to a much more sympathetic examination of the peasant *mir*.[23]

Whatever Marx's reasons for largely neglecting the study of the world(s) resisting capitalist enclosure, similar ongoing struggles—many of which have survived for hundreds of years—demand that we do the work he only began with his investigation of Russian peasant life and try to understand what such people have been fighting to protect. (See below, the last part of these commentaries on this chapter.)

Literary Illustrations

Traces of this great drama abound in English literature. While several middle- or upper-class poets wrote pastoral verses idealizing a vanishing world they knew only as tourists, lamenting its passing through enclosure, a handful of those who worked the land also chronicled the destruction of their world. One such was John Clare (1793–1864). Born in the village of Helpstone, Northamptonshire, Clare was a landless agricultural laborer who worked various jobs. He was also an acute and sympathetic observer of the countryside around him and a harsh critic of the way nature and the people who worked it were being wiped out by enclosures. His poem "The Mores" begins with an evocation of a beautiful, wide-open natural area of "unbounded freedom," unmolested by fence or plow, where Clare had spent his boyhood. But then comes enclosure that builds fences, "improves" the land, trampling on labor's rights and turning the poor into slaves. Clare's

---

22. See his essays "Class Struggles in France" about the Revolution of 1848, *MECW, vol. 10*, pp. 118–123, and "The Eighteenth Brumaire of Louis Bonaparte", *MECW, vol. 11*, pp. 187–192.

23. See the discussion of this in my analysis of Chapter 26 and the question of whether Marx was an historical materialist.

contempt for this process and the character of those responsible are crystal clear:

Fence now meets fence in owner's little bounds
Of fields and meadow large as garden grounds
In little parcels little minds to please
With men and flocks imprisoned ill at ease.[24]

The drama of this long period lay both in the loss of those various rural ways of life that Marx failed to study and in their replacement by the highly urbanized world of industrial capitalism, with its satanic mills, money values and new kinds of class antagonism. The so-called "industrial novels" of the nineteenth century, however, reflected and nourished political and philosophical debates about the human meaning of these changes. More than "fiction," these novels are invaluable historical canvases on which their authors painted, in rich detail, their changing world. While the central interests in novels are their characters, whose personal dramas and development make up the narrative structure, the books also contain a variety of vivid portrayals of various aspects of English society: some disappearing and some coming to dominate.

One of those novelists who was preoccupied in her writing with the social and human meanings of the transition was Elizabeth Gaskell (1810–65). Her novel *Mary Barton: A Story of Manchester Life* was published in 1848, the same year as Marx and Engels's *Communist Manifesto*. The wife of a Unitarian minister in Manchester, Gaskell was intimately familiar with the working-class world she portrayed and although, unlike Marx, she hoped for a reconciliation of the classes, her novel gives a sympathetic and very human portrayal of the difficult lives and struggles of manufacturing workers. While *Mary Barton* only marginally evokes the transition from an agrarian England to an industrializing one, through the character of Alice Wilson, another of Gaskell's novels, *North and South* (1855) deals with it quite directly.[25] The "South" of the novel is the largely agrarian south of England—from which the main heroine of the story comes—and the "North" is the increasingly industrial north of that country—to which the heroine moves. Discovering a whole new world, she reflects upon all the differences between the two. Here too, Gaskell portrays the class struggles of industrial capitalism, this time through the eyes of the daughter of a disillusioned minister.

---

24.   John Clare, *Selected Poems*, London: Penguin Books, 1990, p. 170.
25.   The book was made into a TV mini-series *North & South*, Brian Percival (dir.), BBC One, 2004.

Writing under the pseudonym of George Eliot, Mary Ann Evans (1819–80) is perhaps best known for *Silas Marner* (1861) and *Middlemarch* (1872). But she also published *Felix Holt: The Radical* in 1866, just before Marx published Volume I of *Capital*. In that novel, Eliot constructs a dramatic tableau of provincial English life with working-class coal miners on one side and the old rural gentry on the other. Her portrayal of the latter conveys just the intense feeling for this disappearing world that is missing in Marx.

While only a reading of the whole novel, with its poetic and striking presentation of individual lives, can do it justice, it includes brilliant snapshots of the world being displaced by capitalism. Her metaphor of the dinosaur evokes the quantitative importance of those estate "retainers" whose dismissal preoccupies Marx and of the imminent extinction of the class which had subordinated so many people, at such great expense, to its own luxurious lifestyle:

> But a man of Sir Maximus's rank is like those antediluvian animals whom the system of things condemned to carry such a huge bulk that they really could not inspect their bodily appurtenance, and had no conception of their own tails: their parasites doubtless had a merry time of it, and after did extremely well when the high-bred saurian himself was ill at ease. Treby Manor, measured from the front saloon to the remotest shed, was as large as a moderate-sized village, and there were certainly more lights burning in it every evening, more wine, spirits, and ale drunk, more waste and more folly, than could be found in some large villages. There was fast revelry in the steward's room, and slow revelry in the Scotch bailiff's room; short whist, costume, and flirtation in the housekeeper's room, and the same at a lower price in the servants' hall; a select Olympian feast in the private apartment of the cook, who was a much grander person than her ladyship, and wore gold and jewelry to a vast amount of suet; a gambling group in the stables, and the coachman, perhaps the most innocent member of the establishment, tippling in majestic solitude by a fire in the harness room. For Sir Maximus, as everyone said, was a gentleman of the right sort, condescended to no mean inquires, greeted his head-servants with a 'good evening, gentlemen', when he met them in the park, and only snarled in a subdued way when he looked over the accounts, willing to endure some personal inconvenience in order to keep up the institutions of the country, to maintain his hereditary establishment, and do his duty in that station of life—the station of a long-tailed saurian—to which it had pleased Providence to call him.[26]

---

26. George Eliot, *Felix Holt, The Radical*, New York: Penguin Classics, 1987, pp. 182–183.

The passing of such grand estates was often gradual and often due to their owners' resistance to changing times, such as the need to modernize the agriculture upon which their rents and incomes were based. Such resistance is part of the tale told in the hugely popular, ITV/PBS Masterpiece Theatre mini-series *Downton Abbey* (2010–15).[27]

Tales of Resistance

Marx's analysis also lacks a detailed examination of the resistance that shaped and forced changes in capital's expropriation and organization of labor. Marx tells us what was done, but he rarely gives a satisfying analysis of the power shifts that made it possible. The Russian anarchist Peter Kropotkin (1842–1921) spells out what needs to be done for the study of all worker struggles, overtly revolutionary or otherwise:

> In the histories hitherto written we do not yet see the people; nor do we see how revolutions began. The stereotyped phrases about the desperate condition of people previous to revolutions fail to explain whence amid this desperation came the hope of something better—whence came the revolutionary spirit. And therefore, after reading these histories, we put them aside, and going back to first sources, try to learn from them what caused the people to rise and what was its true part in revolutions, what advantages it obtained from a revolution, what ideas it launched into circulation, what faults of tactics it committed.[28]

This perspective suggests some areas of Marx's argument that need more research:

1. Dissolution of feudal retainers: the reduction of wealth of the feudal nobility that forced them to let servants go is cited but not analyzed. The dismissal of servants is easy to understand: they could hardly fight to stay, though the above passage from George Eliot suggests why they might want

---

27.   Conflict arises in season four of the series, over whether the estate's income from tenants should be supplemented by producing pigs for the market. Opinions are divided by generations, with Lord Grantham resisting while Tom, Matthew and Mary embrace this very capitalist venture. See Mollie Burton's commentary "Pig Farming and Downton's Bright Future" at www.k-state.edu/english/westmank/downton/pigs.burton.html.
28.   Peter Kropotkin, "Modern Science and Anarchism" (1901), reprinted in Roger Baldwin (ed.), *Kropotkin's Revolutionary Pamphlets*, New York: Vanguard Press, 1927, pp. 186–187. Kropotkin carried out just such research into the role of peasants and the urban poor in the French Revolution and published the results as Peter Kropotkin, *The Great French Revolution* (1909), New York: Black Rose Books, 1989.

to do so. The issue is what did they do when dismissed, how did they live and struggle?

2. Similarly, the issue of the reformation and the overthrow of the hegemony of the Catholic Church needs an examination of the popular forces at play in the English Reformation—forces which not only displaced the Roman church but nearly overthrew the whole regime during the English Revolution of the seventeenth century (see below).

3. More important are the usurpation of the common lands through enclosure. Why this was desired, Marx makes clear. How the power was mobilized to do so, he does not. How did the peasants resist? How was the clearing carried out so that peasant resistance was crushed? British troops were used at times. but how were they turned against their own people? One can speculate but Marx tells us very little about the actual dynamics of this "decomposition" of the peasantry. We get neither analysis of politico-military tactics of repression nor of the tactics of resistance that failed (Kropotkin's "faults of tactics").

4. Laws were passed against enclosure for 150 years, but to no avail—a clear split between legislative and executive action. Why? What were the forces that led the latter to defy the former?

Fortunately, we can gain some insights into these things by studying the writings of historians such as E. P. Thompson (1924–93). In his *Making of the English Working Class* (1963), he revealed new information about agrarian struggles in the period 1790–1830. "How was it possible,... for the labourer to be held at brute subsistence level?" he asks and begins to give an answer that takes into account peasant resistance.[29] (Note that he is discussing labor revolt in the later stages of expropriation, the last gasp of the resisting peasantry and the continuing resistance of the new class of agricultural workers.)

On the side of resistance, he cites various kinds of actions: threats to overseers, sporadic sabotage (burning corn ricks), sullen and discontented spirits, turnip-pilfering, alehouse scrounging, poaching and layabouts. In 1816, after the Napoleonic War years (1793–1815) when the return of troops caused problems in East Anglia, dispossessed field laborers rose up demanding minimum wages and price maxims. There were "food riots, forced levies for money from the gentry, and the destruction of

---

29.   E. P. Thompson, *The Making of the English Working Class*, New York: Vintage, 1966, p. 218.

[labor-displacing] threshing machines."[30] The Laborers' Revolt of 1830 included multi-village strikes, thresher breaking, demand for land, extortion of money, robbery, etc. This movement gained the sympathy of many in the middle class and some concessions.

On the side of the capitalist farmers and gentry, Thompson mentions various means that were used to repress such rebellions: mobilization of servants and retainers, grooms, huntsmen, gamekeepers with pistols, shotguns, etc.; as well as the use of government troops.

Overall, he sketches relatively isolated revolts on which superior military force could be focused. Isolation due to the inability to organize beyond local villages was, in turn, due to the difficulty of communication as well as the unevenness of exploitation. Enclosures were not carried out everywhere at once but piece by piece. Isolated in both space and time, peasant resistance could be destroyed by local goons and government troops.

As we ask these questions of enclosures in the present period, so too must we ask them of those of the fifteenth to nineteenth centuries. We ask them so that we can learn of past strengths and weaknesses in order to do better today. Land is still being seized, people are still being displaced and resistance continues. The peasantry or land question and the capitalist need for labor are still pressing ones. Even when the question is of a shift from unwaged exploitation to waged exploitation (or vice versa) rather than of "primitive" accumulation, the fundamental conflict still plagues us.

Reversing Enclosure?

> Was the earth made to preserve a few covetous proud men
> to live at ease, and for them to bag and barn up the treasures
> of the Earth from others that these may beg or starve in a
> fruitful land; or was it made to preserve all her children?[31]

Gerard Winstanley (1609–76) was a leader of the "Diggers" or "True Levellers" movement against enclosures, a movement that not only resisted but sought to reverse the process by seizing and working unused, enclosed land. One important moment of those struggles took place in 1649, a time of explosive political conflicts in England. The poor harvests of 1648 had led to widespread hunger and unemployment and the urgency of demands for change had led to widespread radical demands, even within Cromwell's army. Marxist historian Christopher Hill (1912–2003), a compatriot of

---

30. Ibid., pp. 225–226.
31. Gerard Winstanley, *The New Law of Righteousness* (1649), www.diggers.org/diggers-ENGLISH-1649/NEW-LAW-OF-RIGHTEOUSNESS-1648-Winstanley.pdf (accessed January 15, 2019).

E. P. Thompson, did the research necessary to provide a detailed description of the struggles and repression of the Diggers in 1649 in his book *The World Turned Upside Down* (1984).[32]

As part of those struggles Winstanley wrote a battle song, "You Noble Diggers All," calling workers to battle to reclaim common lands from the greedy hands of private property.[33] The song blasts not only the landlords and their violence but also the lawyers who manipulated the laws to the landlords' advantage and the priests who wielded their religious doctrine to condemn workers and justify the violence used against them. In a fine example of reappropriating past struggles, Leon Rosselson not only resurrected Winstanley's song, but wrote one of his own, whose title "World Turned Upside Down" was probably taken from Christopher Hill's book.[34] Scotsman Dick Gaughan, who has performed the song, wrote this about it: "The mark of a great song is its ability to speak universals about specific happenings and to be relevant to all times. Sometimes we (Scots and Irish) forget that the first colony of the British Empire was in fact England."[35] For a visual, and visceral, sense of the struggles, see the 1975 film *Winstanley* directed by Kevin Brownlow and Andrew Mollo, noted for the quality of its attention to historical detail.

The Diggers' attempt to reverse the process of enclosure and clearing failed. But that failure was only one moment in a multitude of struggles that shaped the emerging class composition of England. And the Diggers' visions, of the common use of the land, and of the right of people to eat and to determine their own lives are still shared by many and not all "diggers" have failed.

The twentieth century saw a vast resurgence of demands for "land reform," the restoration to people of land previously taken from them. During the Mexican Revolution begun in 1910, Mexican peasants cut barbed wire fences and retook their land in revolts dramatically portrayed in the film *Viva Zapata!* (1952).[36] During the Russian Revolution of 1917, with the slogan "Bread and Land" millions of peasants reappropri-

---

32.   Christopher Hill, *The World Turned Upside Down: Radical Ideas During the English Revolution*, London: Penguin, 1984, pp. 107–124. See too the 1975 film *Winstanley*, Kevin Brownlow and Andrew Mollo (dirs).

33.   Gerrard Sabine and George Holland (eds.), *The Works of Gerrard Winstanley* (1941), New York: Russell & Russell, 1965, p. 663.

34.   Leon Rosselson, *Harry's Gone Fishing*, Wimbley Park: Fuse Records, 1999 (CFCD 007).

35.   Gaughan recorded and released this album in the wake of the political turmoil surrounding the general election of 1979 that brought Margaret Thatcher to power.

36.   This not-to-miss film's screenplay was written by John Steinbeck, directed by Elia Kazan and starred Marlon Brando as Emiliano Zapata.

ated what had once been theirs. In China in 1927, Mao Zedong visited Hunan province and discovered that the revolution had begun without him; poor peasants were expropriating the rich and redistributing the land. In Vietnam, peasants joined the Vietminh against colonialists who had seized their land for rice and rubber production for export, fighting in turn, the French, the Japanese, the French again and finally the Americans. Those were four great revolutionary moments when the reappropriation of land, the reversal of enclosure, was a central issue. We could multiply the examples of such conflicts a thousand-fold, throughout Asia, Africa and the Americas. Today, two current struggles come immediately to mind: those of the Landless Laborers in Brazil (MST) and of the Zapatistas in southern Mexico who have fought to reclaim lands previously stolen and concentrated in the hands of capitalist farmers.

Enclosing Water

Echoing the sad tale of Highlanders pushed to the seashore by the Duchess of Sutherland, who then "let the seashore to the big London fishmongers," an Irish song tells the story of the resistance of fishermen in Northern Ireland to their dispossession by British colonialism.[37] The original expropriation of eel-fishing rights was carried out under the orders of King Charles I in the mid-1600s. The Toome Eel Fishery referred to in the song was formed in the late 1950s and was awarded exclusive fishing rights by a British court in 1963. Lough Neagh is both the largest freshwater lake in the British Isles (153 square miles) and the largest eel fishing area in Northern Ireland, with an annual take of about 600 tons.

On the jacket of their record *This is Free Belfast*, the Men of No Property give the following background: "Northern Ireland's great Lough Neagh is the richest fishing ground of Western Europe. Instead of this natural treasure being the heritage and property of all the people, the fishing rights to its greatest catch: eels, are controlled exclusively by one company, the Dutch-controlled Toome Eel Fisheries (N.I.) Ltd. This company prosecutes the fishermen and can revoke their licences."[38]

The lyrics of "The Great Eel Robbery" include these lines:

> The waters of Lough Neagh we fished
> As our fathers did before,
> But because of the Toome Eel Fishery

---

37. *Capital, Vol. I*, p. 892.
38. Men of No Property, *This is Free Belfast: Irish Rebel Songs of the Six Counties*, New York: Paredon Records, 1971 (P1006).

We cannot fish no more.

. . .

But though we've had a setback
The decision we'll reverse,

. . .

We'll smash that great monopoly
On Lough Neagh's rocky shore,
And Irishmen will gain their right
To fish there ever more.

The song ends with a promise of continuing struggle to win back fishing rights for local fishermen. And indeed, the fishermen formed a Lough Neagh Fisherman's Association and registered as a trade union to fight for their rights. According to one account, the fishermen successfully formed a "Cooperative Society" that was able to buy 20 percent of the shares of Toome Eel Fishery (NI) Ltd. When the majority shareholders counterattacked by refusing to buy eels from the Irish fishing cooperative, the latter bypassed Toome and developed new markets in Europe. With the profits they realized from those markets, they were able to buy out the other 80 percent of the shares of Toome and as forecast in the song, the full rights to eel fishing finally reverted to local Irish fishermen![39]

There is another interesting dimension to this story. The song notes that the Dutch company held a "great monopoly that stretches Europe round." Leaving aside the empirical question of the exact market share of the company, fishing, not just in Europe but around the world, has become increasingly concentrated in the hands of huge multinational corporations using "advanced" technology to maximize their take and profits. One result has been global overfishing and a dramatic depletion of many species of fish. Moreover, because fish eat fish, this has caused a disruption of ocean ecological balance creating a growing crisis, one that cannot be overcome by the substitution of aquaculture or farm fishing for wild catch. The Associated Press reports that this overfishing and depletion includes the European eel.[40] Not only are prices rising rapidly as supply shrinks, but the reduction in the eel population is also creating worries about the impact on other animals who eat them, e.g., cormorants, herons, otters and other European wildlife.

---

39.   Rev. Oliver P. Kennedy, "The Lough Neagh Eel Fishery", *Inland Waterways News*, vol. 27, no. 3, Autumn 2000.
40.   Toby Sterling, "Europe's Eel Population Collapsing", *The Associated Press*, August 15, 2004.

In contrast to this overfishing, the Irish fishermen of Lough Neagh carefully manage their fishing in ways designed to sustain the eel population on which their livelihood depends. This is often the case with local fishing, as with local agriculture. A multinational corporation can deplete what they see as a "resource" and move on; local populations, dependent on the sustainability of their ecosystem, are often more careful in how they interact with it.[41]

Enclosures in the United States

In North America the initial expropriation of the "agricultural population" was the displacement and extermination of Native Americans. Forming a diverse array of cultures based on various mixtures of agriculture, hunting and gathering, these peoples filled the land when the Europeans invaded. Their hunting and gathering spread out over wide regions, and their agricultural methods often involved shifting and moving about. To the Europeans, used to dense populations where virtually every available hectare of arable land was cultivated, or given over to city building, North America looked "empty," or so they pretended. As the Europeans pushed inland, they sought to either subordinate or eliminate those in their way. For the most part, the indigenous population never accepted assimilation. With few exceptions, they were never put to work directly, either as slaves or as wage labor—they simply refused, preferring to fight or to die. In some cases, the European invaders were able to tap the Indians' labor indirectly through the fur trade but mostly they simply pushed them out of the way and killed them when they resisted.

That resistance, of course, was great, long and bloody. It took a 200-year war to secure the majority of the land and to eliminate most of the Indians, confining the few who remained to reservations. This is a history that has been, for the most part, passed over quickly at all levels of school, from elementary to university. Ignorance of Native American culture and stereotypical images of barbaric savages were promulgated to rationalize their destruction and only recently have begun to be replaced by more informed and less racist knowledge and treatments. With respect to Native American resistance, for a long time about the only aspects of that history whose memory was preserved with respect were some of their more effective armed struggles—preserved ironically by the military forces that defeated them, but that still honor the brilliance of their strategies and tactics of war.

---

41. Just how widespread these struggles are can be seen in Mariarosa Dalla Costa and Monica Chilese, *Our Mother Ocean: Enclosure, Commons, and the Global Fishermen's Movement*, Brooklyn, NY: Common Notions, 2014.

Fortunately, the neglect and failure to appreciate the resilience and creativity of Native American resistance has been increasingly countered in recent years, first by student struggles to create space and to gain resources for Native American Studies and second, by histories written from the point of view of the indigenous.[42]

Beyond these accounts of primitive accumulation in Britain and North America—understood as the creation of the classes of capitalist society—we must also recognize that both processes cannot be properly analyzed within national or even continental bounds. Because the indigenous population would not work for a wage, and because indentured European servants often escaped their servitude, the North American working class was constructed, in part, through the enslavement of Africans. That enslavement ripped people from their land and forcibly transported them across the Atlantic to plantations where they were put to work on land stolen from the Cherokee (Tsalaqi), the Creek (Muskogee), the Chickasaw (Chikasha), the Choctaw (Chahta) and the Seminole (Meskwaki). Just as the displaced agricultural population in Britain migrated from rural areas toward cities and even abroad, so too did the African slave trade force a migration that contributed to the formation of a working class throughout much of the Atlantic basin. Thus, primitive accumulation in the New World was closely interlocked with that of Europe and Africa, making it mandatory to study the formation of an *Atlantic* working class rather than a purely North American one.[43]

This history and its study is complicated by the process of separating people from the land being repeatedly renewed. European settlers, who displaced the indigenous population, used the land they seized to ground their own independence from the growing capitalist demands for labor. For the most part, the frontier was not settled by capitalist plantation owners and ranchers employing slave or waged labor, but by family farmers who came west precisely to escape the factories and slums of both Western Europe and the American East Coast. The frontier moved west year after year and generation after generation as part of a struggle for freedom from exploitation—even as the indigenous population lost its freedom, and often its very existence.

---

42.   See Winona LaDuke, *All Our Relations: Native Struggles for Land and Life*, Boston, MA: South End Press, 1999; Ward Churchill, *Struggle for the Land: Native American Resistance to Genocide, Ecocide and Colonization*, San Francisco, CA: City Lights, 2nd edn., 2002; and David Treuer, *The Heartbeat of Wounded Knee: Native America from 1890 to the Present*, New York: Riverhead Books, 2019.

43.   Such has been the objective of Peter Linebaugh and Marcus Rediker in their *Many-headed Hydra: Sailors, Slaves, Commoners, and the Hidden History of the Revolutionary Atlantic*, Boston, MA: Beacon Press, 2000.

This westward movement of pioneers, mountain men and homesteaders provided not only the inspiration for ideals such as Jefferson's agrarian democracy, but also an ongoing problem for capitalists who wanted to integrate the labor of these independent agriculturalists into a wider project of accumulation. As late as the nineteenth century, most US citizens still lived on the land and their labor (like that of the indigenous before them) could only be tapped through the market. They could only be exploited through unequal exchange in which they sold agricultural produce that took a great deal of labor to create and bought manufactured products that took much less. With the development of capitalist banking and finance, they were also exploited through mortgages and bank loans. Over the years, these methods all worked together to generate a slow but inexorable process of dispossession, through which the vast majority of independent farmers lost their farms and were forced into wage labor. This process is still going on, even though only 3 or 4 percent of Americans still live on the land. It accelerates in hard times, when farm prices are low and mortgages and bank loans cannot be repaid, and slows during upturns when expanding demand and government subsidies keep farm output prices up and credit cheap.

As might be expected, this process, like earlier periods, generated considerable resistance. From the Whiskey Rebellion (1791–94) through the Populist Revolt of the nineteenth century to the American Farm Movement of the 1970s (supported by Willie Nelson's Farm Aid concerts), it has been a long and bitter history. Repeatedly, the dreams of independence of many generations of American farmers have been crushed and, like the British yeomen and Native Americans before them, they and their families have been driven from the land.

Typical of the popular music of farmer resistance are two songs, one from the period of the Populist Revolt and the second from that of the American Farm Movement. "The Farmer is the Man" originated among western farmers after the Civil War and became famous during the Populist Revolt of the 1890s. In that song, those responsible for the exploitation and ultimate enclosure of family farmers' lands and tools are the mortgage men and bankers who "get it all."[44] The more recent song about the loss of family farms is "Rain on the Scarecrow" by John Cougar Mellencamp.[45] This song is bleaker, more about loss than about struggle, but fitting, given that most farmers have lost and very few remain. The story is the same: "The crops we

---

44. Pete Seeger, *American Industrial Ballads*, Smithsonian Folkway Records, 1992 (CD SF 40058).
45. John Cougar Mellencamp, *Scarecrow*, PolyGram Records, 1985 (824 865-2 M-1).

grew last summer weren't enough to pay the loans / Couldn't buy the seed to plant this Spring, and the Farmers Bank foreclosed."

Women, Witches and the Enclosure of the Body

Marx's analysis of the enclosures focuses on the theft of peasants' land, one of their basic means of subsistence and sources of power to resist exploitation by others (whether landlords who charge rent or capitalists who profit from paying low wages). The loss of land was often accompanied by the loss of most other means of subsistence including home and tools (such as spinning wheels, axes, saws, looms, cauldrons) which allowed peasants to provide themselves with housing, furniture, clothes and food. Thus, along with the expropriation of the means of production went that of the means of reproduction—of reproducing daily life for oneself and one's family.

Accompanying this expropriation of land and the material means of reproduction came another expropriation even more intimate: that of women's bodies. During this period, a wide variety of women's social practices and rights came under attack including their right to regulate their own fertility and their equality with men in both work and struggle. Their proper roles were redefined as brood mare and housewife. Their rights and possibilities were dramatically reduced as they were more deeply subordinated to men in both homes and waged work places.

The nadir of this repression unfolded in Britain and Western Europe during 1550–1650, the period of the "Great Witch Hunt," which saw tens of thousands of women tortured and executed for once common practices that had been criminalized. Most of the victims of this repression were poor peasant women singled out in a population that was resisting the enclosures. In Britain, this period is bracketed by the 1549 Ketts Rebellion against enclosures and the English Revolution, which sought to turn the whole new order "upside down." During those years, the state, in collaboration with both Catholic and Protestant Churches, accelerated a wave of repression against women that had been growing with the rise of capitalism and popular resistance to it. Midwives (*sage femmes*, or wise women, in French) were accused of being in league with the devil and preventing procreation or committing infanticide. This persecution was the beginning of a process where women were forced to procreate more workers for the labor market and increasingly excluded from all aspects of obstetrics and gynecology which were taken over by men and the state.

Rebellious women who spoke out or who insisted on their rights and their desires were accused of witchcraft and killed, as examples to all others. Such attacks struck directly at the important roles women had played in peasant revolt. Any and all manifestations of sexual desire outside of marriage—adultery, procreation, prostitution, etc.—were criminalized.[46] The sexuality of the young was repressed, of the old ridiculed—indeed, the stereotypical image of the witch as an old, evil and lascivious crone dates from this period. Women in general were accused by demonologists of "insatiable sexuality" capable of dominating men and causing impotence.[47]

The attack on women was orchestrated also to strike at men's sexual freedom and to undermine any solidarity between men and women while redirecting the energy of both into work for capital.[48] Women were to procreate and recreate the working class, while men were to do the work of disciplining women—and eventually both would be driven into the factory. Not surprisingly, along with the aggravation of antagonistic relations between men and women, the period of the witch hunts also saw the demonization and criminalization of all other "unproductive" sexual activity, such as homosexuality and public, collective sexuality, both of which had been common during the Middle Ages.[49]

---

46. Such repressive laws, such as those calling for sexually active but unwed women to be put to death, had already been attacked vehemently at the beginning of the sixteenth century by Ludovico Ariosto in his epic romantic poem *Orlando Furioso* (1516), Part One, Canto IV, New York: Penguin Classics, 1975. In that poem, one of the main characters, a chivalrous knight named Rinaldo, learns of a princess who had been set up for death by a spurned suitor. The suitor achieved his revenge by making it seem as if she had made love with another outside of wedlock—this in Scotland where such behavior was punishable by death. Rinaldo's reaction expresses Ariosto's own feelings about such repressive laws: "This inequality in law much wrong / Has done to women. / With God's help I mean / To show that to have suffered it so long / The greatest of inequities has been. / A curse upon the legislator's head!"

47. Such fear of women's sexuality has continued to haunt gender relationships long after demonologists became mere subjects of horror films. It poisoned medicine and early psychology, where female sexuality was diagnosed in terms of hysteria and can still be found among insecure men and misogynistic defenders of male dominance.

48. Freud's argument in *Civilization and its Discontents* (1930) that civilization is based on the sublimation of libidinal energy into work was taken over by Herbert Marcuse (1898–1979) for the case of capitalism in *Eros and Civilization*, New York: Beacon Press, 1955. One doesn't have to agree with either's theoretical apparatus to see the appropriateness of the analysis in a society which tries to channel all energy into work.

49. The argument of this section is based, in part, on two critical overviews of the studies of English and European witch hunts: Richard A. Horsley, "Who Were the Witches? The Social Roles of the Accused in the European Witch Trials", *Journal of Interdisciplinary History*, vol. IX, no. 4, Spring 1979, pp. 689–715; and Silvia Federici, "The Great Witch Hunt", *The Maine Scholar*, vol. 1, no. 1, Autumn 1988, pp. 31–52. More recently, Federici has given us a much more complete history of both women's struggles in this period and their violent repression in her books: *Caliban and the Witch: Women, the Body and Primitive Accumulation*, New York: Autonomedia, 2004 and *Witches, Witch Hunting and Women*, Oakland, CA and Brooklyn, NY: PM Press, Autonomedia, Common Notions, 2018.

Land, Capital and the Struggle for the Preservation of Cultural Diversity

For much of the world, the kind of enclosure Marx is talking about has meant the destruction of entire ways of life that were deeply rooted in people's relationships to the land, both material and spiritual. In capitalism, land becomes a commodity, something to be bought and sold, a source of profits, and mainly, a vehicle for the control and exploitation of other humans. Unlike indigenous cultures, capitalism has no place for a spiritual relation to the land (or to the other creatures who dwell upon it). Instead of being one with the rest of nature, capitalism sees it all as usable and exploitable "resources."[50] For thousands of years, Native Americans lived in balance on the land, hunting and gathering only what they needed for their limited populations and cultivating a little ground for a few crops. Instead of shaping human culture in harmony with the surrounding ecology, capitalism wantonly destroys and pillages the earth. The commons are drawn and quartered into "little parcels little minds to please." Forests are clear-cut for lumber and left as wasteland. Whole species, such as the buffalo, are hunted to near extinction. Grasslands are stripped through overgrazing and turned into deserts. Mountains are ripped apart by "mountain-top removal" and strip-mining more generally. Rivers are turned into open sewers and lakes into cesspools or sterilized with acid rain. Oceans are polluted, overfished and littered with plastic waste. The only spaces spared this exploitation are those that have been fought for and won against the logic of capitalist economics: a few reservations where Native Americans have refused the temptation of selling their mineral rights, a few National Parks and areas of wilderness, and a variety of so-far commercially value-less lands.

Understanding the human meaning of this destruction requires studying the cultures being destroyed and their ongoing struggles to preserve what is left. Much has been learned by anthropologists and sympathetic outsiders who have observed and tried to understand in the years since Marx studied those few reports available to him.[51] From indigenous communities in southern Mexico to hunter-gatherers in the Amazon and beyond, people whose cultures contain strong pre- or anti-capitalist elements still survive and resist. In a few cases, resistance has mutated into efforts to expand, often through land seizure, to obtain more space for these cultures to grow and evolve. However limited our ability to understand those cultures, we can realize the rich diversity of human being which is at stake and measure the losses humanity has sustained as capitalism has done its best to extermi-

50.   See Vandana Shiva's essay "Resources", in Wolfgang Sachs, *The Development Dictionary: A Guide to Knowledge as Power*, London: Zed Books, 1992, pp. 206–218.

51.   Krader, *The Ethnological Notebooks of Karl Marx*.

nate all but the most superficial differences around the world, to undermine people's ability to live differently through the expropriation of their land, of their tools, of control over their bodies, integrating them poorly equipped into its spiritless world of endless work.

Recent decades have seen the flourishing of resistance both to capitalist ecological destruction and to the cultural genocide it perpetrates. Films dealing with these tragedies include *The Emerald Forest* (1985), *Amazonia: Voices from the Rainforest* (1991), *Medicine Man* (1992), *Ferngully* (1992), *Zapatista* (1999), *The Burning Season* (2008) and *Avatar* (2009). *The Emerald Forest* shows some of the classic methods used in the Amazon by its invaders: pitting tribe against tribe, murder and the slaughter of the forest. But it also shows some of the spiritual richness of the indigenous culture and the close relations between humans and the animal world. *Amazonia* contains numerous interviews with Brazilian Indians and rubber tappers, once enemies, now increasingly allied in the attempt to defend the rainforest and the autonomy of their lives against the inroads of ranchers, miners and government "development" projects such as roads and dams. It also points out that of the 900 tribes in the Amazon at the time of colonial conquest, only 180 remain; the other 720 were wiped out. *Medicine Man* deals with how the destruction of the rainforests also involves the destruction of a rich and diverse source of medicinal "resources." *Ferngully*, an animated feature-length fantasy film, simply celebrates the beauty of the forests. *Zapatista* documents the indigenous uprising in Chiapas while providing background that makes it understandable. *The Burning Season* documents forest clearance for commercial palm oil production in Indonesia and its impact on orangutans and global warming. Although science fiction and located on another, fictional planet, the critical acclaim and worldwide popularity of *Avatar's* portrayal of the conflict between a rapacious capitalist corporation and an indigenous people demonstrates the degree to which people all over have become sympathetic to the struggle against capitalist depredations. There are many more films dealing with these issues.

CHAPTER 28: BLOODY LEGISLATION AGAINST THE EXPROPRIATED

Commentary

The conversion of dispossessed peasants and artisans, into waged and potentially waged workers involved a long and brutal campaign to drive them into the labor market—a campaign whose difficulty was due to resistance, documented in centuries of "bloody legislation" aimed at its suppression.

Outline of Marx's Analysis

People resisted, choosing to become "beggars, robbers and vagabonds" instead of exploited factory workers. Thus, the use of violence to reduce them to a "labor force"

1530: Henry VIII (1491–1547):

- whipping
- slicing off ears
- hanging
- 72,000 thieves put to death

1547: Edward VI (1537–53):

- slavery
- whip and chains
- branded V on chest of vagabonds
- execution
- children taken

1572: Elizabeth (1533–1603):

- branded ear
- execution

James I (1566–1625):

- public whipping
- branded R on left shoulder
- execution

Early period: "direct extra-economic force"
Later period: "silent compulsion of economic relations" or "natural laws"
The state: "the rising bourgeoisie needs the power of the state"

- to lengthen the working day (Chapter 10)
- to set maximum wages (punishment more severe for acceptance than payment)
- outlawing of "combinations, contracts, oaths" from fourteenth century to the nineteenth century, until:
- "laws against combinations of workers collapsed in 1825 in the face of the threatening attitude of the proletariat"
- "only against its will, and under the pressure of the masses, did the English Parliament give up the laws against strikes and trade unions"

In part, resistance was a refusal of the factory and the refusal to be reduced to a machine among machines in that factory. The following statement by one American manager reveals how capitalists saw workers: "I regard my work-people just as I regard my machinery. . . . They must look out for themselves as I do for myself. When my machines get old and useless, I reject them and get new, and these people are part of my machinery."[52] No residue here of the paternalism of feudal times, much less the closeness and mutual support of so-called primitive cultures, only the most violent redefinition of human beings as animate tools, an attitude echoed in more recent times by economists who consider workers "human capital."[53]

Charlie Chaplin's classic film *Modern Times* (1936) presents an eloquent visual representation of workers as part of the machinery, paced by machinery, eaten up by machinery and driven crazy by the factory. Although it concerns the assembly line of Fordism in the twentieth century, its basic vision is every bit as valid for earlier periods.

As early as 1857, Marx observed in his *Grundrisse* notebooks, "They must be forced to work within the conditions posited by capital."[54] They do not go willingly from fields, forests and villages to the "satanic mills" of early capitalist factories and into the dank tenements available to them. Force must be used because they resist. Marx cites begging, vagabondage and robbing as forms taken by the resistance and he describes the bloody legislation passed to repress them. However, he does not analyze these activities in any detail; we get no texture of this resistance, only of punishment by whip and branding iron. When he analyzes the factory in Chapters 13, 14 and 15 on cooperation, the division of labor, machinery and modern industry, he *does* show how the struggle continued inside the factories through machine breaking, strikes and so on.

The continuing brutality of factory work, described by Rebecca Harding Davis in her book *Life in the Iron Mills* (1861), through that portrayed by Bruce Springsteen in his song "Factory" (1978), goes far to explain why so many have resisted being forced to work in them.[55] The day-to-day violence of work and of the struggle over that work have shaped our world both on the job and off. Both Davis and Springsteen portray the conse-

---

52.   Norman Ware, *The Industrial Worker, 1840–1860*, Chicago, IL: Quadrangle Books, 1964, p. 77.

53.   See Gary Becker, *Human Capital: A Theoretical and Empirical Analysis, with Special Reference to Education (1964)*, Chicago, IL: The University of Chicago Press, 3rd edn., 1993.

54.   *Grundrisse*, p. 736.

55.   Rebecca Harding Davis, *Life in the Iron Mills*, New York: The Feminist Press, 1972. Originally written 1861 in the city of Wheeling on the Ohio River. Bruce Springsteen, *Darkness on the Edge of Town*, Columbia Records, 1978 (JC-35318).

quences of factory work for community and family life. She evokes men "laired by day in dens of drunkenness and infamy," while he remembers his daddy coming home "with death in his eyes" and "Somebody's gonna get hurt tonight."

The Street as an Alternative to the Factory

Begging was already a form of refusal in the feudal period, where various persons made use of a certain space created by Catholic attitudes toward alms-giving to live without working. This was a struggle because there was, even then, an attempt to distinguish between "deserving" and "undeserving" beggars and the undeserving included those judged able to work. By the fifteenth and sixteenth centuries, the attempts to control begging advanced with the need for labor in the emerging capitalist factories, and with the growing militancy of the beggars. In 1529, a Great Riot exploded in Lyons, France:

> mobs of destitute people pillaged the homes of the rich, broke into the municipal granary, and occupied the city hall in protest against the soaring price of bread. The *Grande Rebeine* caused profound concern in Lyons, and over the next few years the new system of poor relief was put into effect.[56]

The Lyons system of poor relief had two sides: 1) it granted bread, etc., and 2) it aimed at regulating the poor and forcing them to work. Tickets were allocated (like food stamps) for bread. Children were housed in "hospital asylums," vocational training was provided, they were then placed in domestic service or apprenticed. The city government also provided support for industry, especially the Lyons silk industry, to help provide jobs. Finally, begging was forbidden, a new special police force was set up, the *chasse-coquins*, and if any beggars were caught, they were put to work at hard labor or thrown into jail. This was the kind of treatment so thoroughly portrayed in Victor Hugo's great novel *Les Misérables* (1862).

Despite such state tactics, begging remained widespread. Beggars used many kinds of tricks in their trade. Some feigned illnesses by chewing soap, foaming at the mouth and acting epileptic. There were at one time 19 secret societies in Rome ranging from "gibbering idiots," "illness fakirs" to

---

56.   John A. Garraty, *Unemployment in History*, New York: Harper Colophon, 1978, p. 25. Something similar happened with the widespread urban uprisings of the mid-1960s. They were followed by a massive expansion of the Federal Food Stamp program.

tradesmen who had lost their jobs. In 1627, an Italian monk listed 33 types of false beggars that included "tears at will," "flour for communion wafers," "mad as result of tarantula bite," and so on. Sir Thomas Moore complained of "sturdy and valiante beggars, cloking their idle lyfe under the colors of some disease or sickness."[57]

Clearly, many people preferred the colorful life of the street to the drab drudgery of the factory and the grim grey existence of the factory family. Henry Mayhew (1812–87), a playwright and a founder of the satirical weekly *Punch*, was also an investigative reporter. He interviewed vagrants, both the temporarily jobless and the permanently unwaged, gathered their stories, published them in the *Morning Chronicle* in London and later in his book *London Labour and the London Poor* (1851). The vagrants often juxtaposed the joys of wandering and begging to the drudgery of waged labor.[58]

History has also recorded considerable *sympathy for beggars* among common people—to the point of helping them resist arrest—probably because most workers knew they might become beggars themselves, by choice or because of downturns in the industrial cycle. Garraty notes, "French archives contain evidence showing that the *police were often harassed by crowds* when they attempted to arrest beggars."[59]

Even more colorful, the history of "robbery" and "crime" provides rich material for the beginning of a class analysis of crimes against property.[60] On the one side, *workers* directly appropriate what they have produced but is now owned by capitalists, whether on the job or in the larger society. On the other side, *capitalist* theft is legalized, from their domestic enclosure of land, homes and tools to their foreign conquests. Such analysis reveals how business has succeeded in pitting workers against workers, from communities where desperate workers rob other workers, nativists against immigrants and colonial armies to carry out the dirty work of spreading capitalist theft across the face of the earth.

---

57. Thomas Moore, *Utopia* (1516), Book 2, Part 2, New York: Penguin Classics, 2003.
58. Henry Mayhew, *London Labour and the London Poor*, New York: Penguin Classics, 1985, pp. 383–385.
59. Garraty, *Unemployment in History*, p. 55.
60. Essential contributions to the analysis of the class politics of crime in this period can be found in E. P. Thompson, Douglas Hay, Peter Linebaugh, John G. Rule and Cal Winslow, *Albion's Fatal Tree: Crime and Society in Eighteenth-Century England*, New York: Pantheon, 1975. On Jack Sheppard and the working-class art of excarceration, see Peter Linebaugh, *The London Hanged: Crime and Civil Society in the Eighteenth Century*, London: Allen Lane, 1991, Chapter 1: "'The Common Discourse of the Whole Nation': Jack Sheppard and the Art of Escape."

Controversy: The Nature of the State

Marx doesn't analyze the state in the abstract but rather shows us con-cretely.[61] Here the state appears as government, as legislation (Statute of Laborers, etc.), as the House of Commons, as police and armies. In this period, capital succeeds in turning the state-as-government into a tool, an organ of its class rule. This is done both via laws *for* capital that *are* enforced, and via laws *against* capital that are *not* enforced (such as those against enclosures).[62] Yet the passage of some laws that favor the working class shows that the government is also *a terrain of class conflict*. What ulti-mately matters are neither debate nor votes, but acts. Which and whether laws are passed and enforced is a function of class power.

During this period of "bloody legislation," capital succeeded in using state power for its own ends, against workers and against the old landed aristocracy. Capitalist power is clearly greater than that of workers, yet the balance of power also shifts and causes shifts in government action. Marx attributes the collapse of laws against combinations of workers in 1825 to the "threatening attitude of the proletariat."[63] Similarly, the abandonment of laws against strikes was done only "under the pressure of the masses."[64] Similar shifts in power, resulting in changes in laws concerning the length of the working day, are analyzed in Chapter 10.

Two observations can be made: *first*, government appears as an organ of capitalist class rule only to the degree that it acts in the interests of that class. It is also a terrain, a space where struggle ensues, and working-class power may be reflected in both parliamentary debate and in executive action. Today the growth of working-class power has resulted in many enforced laws which benefit workers to the detriment of capital. This does not mean that government is a neutral third-party, mediating between the classes as sometimes depicted. It does mean that no simple theory of government as capitalist-state will suffice. *Second*, although Marx does mention some of the victories won by the working class as well as some defeats, he does not analyze or describe the struggles that produced these changes. While we can see both the need for struggle and its possible effectiveness, we

---

61.   One result has been a proliferation of Marxist efforts to "fill the gap" in his theory by conjuring up a Marxist theory of the state. Among the many contributions to that effort, see the issues of the journal *Kapitalistate* (1973–83).

62.   The non-enforcement of laws and regulation costly to business became public policy under the Reagan administration that systematically sought to undermine exist-ing labor rights and environmental protection laws by eliminating them where possible and refusing to enforce them elsewhere. This practice has been renewed under Donald Trump.

63.   *Capital, Vol. I*, p. 903.

64.   Ibid.

learn nothing of the methods used and how they succeeded. What concretely constituted the "threatening attitude of the proletariat"? How did the "masses" exert pressure? Of these things we learn little.

Working-Class Struggles

E. P. Thompson's *Making of the English Working Class* reveals something of those struggles which Marx mentions but fails to analyze in detail. Examining the period between the Combination Acts of 1799 and 1800 and their repeal in 1824–25,[65] he shows us how the rising anger and militancy of both reformist intellectuals and workers took a number of forms including clandestine political groupings and secret unionism but never congealed into any centralized movement. He shows how such underground activity developed rapidly in response to the anti-combination laws and acts. Workers drew together and swore secret oaths in multiple conspiracies. When they could not strike openly, they developed covert methods for sabotaging production, methods that would leave little evidence for prosecution.[66]

In such ways were the "threatening attitudes" of the proletariat expressed and the Combination Acts undermined to such a degree that by 1824 a repeal bill was moved through Parliament by men arguing that the Acts had *favored* combination and needed to be abolished to undermine the growth of working-class organizations! Much to these persons' despair, however, repeal was followed immediately by widespread, now legal, strikes and conflict. Efforts to reinstate the Acts in 1825 were immediately attacked by a "storm of protests, petitions, meetings, and deputations from every trade." The reinstatement efforts failed, opening the way for "the great wave of general unionism between 1832 and 1834."[67]

We need this kind of history and analysis to complement Marx's sketch in *Capital*. We need to examine how those before us fought being forced into the labor market and factories, and then how they fought once there—how they fought singly, in small groups, in relationship to political groups and to the emerging unions. We need to examine how their struggles interacted with the plans of capital. What methods worked; which did not. Beyond understanding how capital imposed its system, and maintained it only by fierce repression of widespread militancy, we need to learn lessons for today from the history of those struggles.

---

65. Thompson, *Making of the English Working Class*, pp. 497–521.
66. Ibid., pp. 514–515.
67. Ibid., p. 520.

Vagrancy Laws during Reconstruction

In the United States, the early post-Civil War period provided a very close parallel to this use of vicious legislation to force a population freed from the land into service to capital. Large numbers of newly freed slaves, together with many uprooted and burned out whites, roamed the South wanting only "forty acres and a mule" to begin a new life. The failure of the Reconstruction Act of 1867 to include land reform—the breakup and redistribution of the old plantation land to those who had worked it—condemned the war-freed and uprooted population to search for work where they could find it. Southern land owners, of course, wanted to reinstitute the plantation system via wage labor, under conditions similar to the slavery they had lost. Most of the freed and uprooted, however, refused to return to those conditions. Failing to entice these potential workers into such employment, the capitalists used force in a method strikingly like that used in England.

Harsh laws in most southern states criminalized vagabondage, petty pilfering and other crimes against "property," resulting in a rapid increase in the number of people thrown into prison. In some cases, such as the notorious Parchman Penitentiary, a huge prison plantation in the Mississippi, the government imposed what amounted to slave labor. To help finance the penal system, it also supplied a large quantity of cheap labor to capitalists who were unwilling to pay sufficiently high wages to attract a work force. State governments would lease out prisoners to work in chain gangs at nominal cost to local and national capitalists. C. Vann Woodward (1908–99) in his book *Origins of the New South* (1951) provides us with horrifying descriptions.[68]

The conditions in these state-provisioned labor camps rivaled not only the brutality of the English situation in the sixteenth and seventeenth centuries, but the Soviet gulag and Nazis camps of the twentieth century. It is always worth remembering the slogan over the entrance to the German concentration camp at Auschwitz was the very capitalist slogan *Arbeit Mach Frei*—"Work Makes You Free." In some ways, labor camps and prison labor are the quintessential expression of capitalist society. They are among the few places where the illusions of freedom are discarded, and work is imposed directly and brutally.

With this kind of treatment, death rates were high. But it didn't matter because there were always more vagabonds or petty criminals to be shipped out to the mines or swamps to be worked to death for the sake of capitalist

---

68.   C. Vann Woodward, *Origins of the New South, 1817–1913*, Baton Rouge: Louisiana State University Press, 1951, pp. 213–214.

profits.[69] This was very similar to the period when the slave trade supplied so many slaves that cheap new muscle could be had to replace that driven into the grave. In Chapter 10, Marx discusses the abuses capitalists inflict when the supply of labor is cheap:

> Hence the Negro labour in the southern states of the American Union preserved a moderately patriarchal character as long as production was chiefly directed to the satisfaction of immediate local requirements. But in proportion as the export of cotton became of vital interest to those states, the over-working of the Negro and sometimes the consumption of his life in seven years of labour, became a factor in a calculated and calculating system.[70]

Once the slave trade was abolished and slaves became hard to replace, their treatment improved—to insure reproduction! In the post-Civil War South, the roaming masses provided the same kind of surplus labor supply as the slave hunting-grounds of Africa—with the same kinds of abuses.

Workers did not accept such barbaric treatment passively. Crime grew in response to repression, and in turn swelled the ranks of prison labor. Non-prison labor finding itself undercut by cheap convict labor fought against this involuntary servitude of so many of their number. When convicts were used to break strikes and displace legal laborers, open conflict over this issue became widespread. Woodward quotes one Colonel Colyar who was the Tennessee Democratic leader and general counsel to the Tennessee Coal, Iron and Railroad Company: "we found that we were right in calculating that free laborers would be loath to enter upon strikes when they saw that the company was amply provided with convict labor."[71] By 1891, however, the good Colonel's workers had had enough. When the company offered a contract with no-strike and other objectionable clauses and the workers refused it,

> the company ordered convicts to tear down their houses and build stockades for the convicts who were to replace free labor. The evicted miners then marched in force on the stockades and, without bloodshed, compelled guards, officers and convicts to board a train for Knoxville.

---

69.   For a visual, though tame, taste of this regime, see the film *Cool Hand Luke* (1967) with Paul Newman in a modern chain gang. Just in case you think that vicious corporal punishment has been banned from the capitalist world in this new twenty-first century, take a look at documentation compiled by World Corporal Punishment Research—or do some research on the Abu Ghraib prison run by the US in Iraq.

70.   *Capital, Vol. I*, p. 345.

71.   Woodward, *Origins of the New South*, p. 233.

Governor John P. Buchanan, with three companies of militia promptly returned the convicts to the stockades. A few days later more than a thousand armed miners packed the guards and convicts off to Knoxville a second time, and those of another company along with them, again without bloodshed.

The conflict over convict labor continued until October 31, 1891 when the workers "forcibly freed the convicts of the Tennessee Coal Mine Company, allowed them all to escape, and burned down the stockades. They repeated the same tactics later at two other mining companies, releasing in all some five hundred convicts. The mine operators of the area then employed free labor. . ."[72] In other words, in this instance the workers won and defeated this strategy of capital by using armed force. Unfortunately, even today, almost two decades into the twenty-first century, penal labor is thriving. Many prisons in the US are still being run as gulags with their inmates either put to work by the prison itself or rented out to private capital.[73]

Controversy: The Wage, Its Absence and the Imposition of Work

Although primitive accumulation has often been defined as the creation of a waged proletariat, we have seen how that very process also involved the creation of the unwaged, from vagabonds through slaves to housewives and children.

Regarding slavery, Marxists have debated the status of slaves because they are not waged. Some, such as historian Eugene Genovese (1930–2012), have argued that slavery constituted a different kind of social system articulated with capitalism. Others, myself included, see American slave labor as a peculiar form of labor within capitalism, a form of unwaged labor essential to the functioning of both Southern and Atlantic capitalism. Cotton slavery in the US was the material foundation of the cotton textile mills in Manchester, England. In *Capital*, Marx often described wage labor as "wage-slavery" or as "veiled" or "indirect" slavery marking the similarity

---

72. Ibid., pp. 233–234.
73. For an example of the former, see the documentary *Angola for Life: Rehabilitation and Reform Inside the Louisiana State Penitentiary* (2015) and the article about it by Whitney Benns, "American Slavery, Reinvented", *The Atlantic Monthly*, September 21, 2015. See also Vicky Paláez, "The Prison Industry in the United States, Big Business or a New Form of Slavery", Center for Research on Globalization, March 2008. Compare with the recent imposition of forced labor in China where ethnic minorities are being incarcerated in labor camps and forced to work for American companies. See Dake Kang, Martha Mendoza and Yanan Wang, "In Locked Compound, Minorities in China Make Clothes for US", *Associated Press*, December 18, 2018.

of wage to slave labor. Clearly the distance between the two for him was not great.[74] Elsewhere he wrote:

> I do not mean indirect slavery, the slavery of the proletariat; I mean direct slavery, the slavery of the Blacks in Surinam, in Brazil, in the southern regions of North America. Direct slavery is the pivot of our industrialism today as much as machinery, credit, etc. Without slavery, you have no cotton, without cotton you have no modern industry. It is slavery that has given value to the colonies; it was the colonies that created world trade; it is world trade that is the necessary condition for large-scale industry.[75]

On the other hand, in Chapter 3, he contrasts enclosure-freeing of Englishmen who entered the capitalist labor market with the impoverishment of Roman plebs through debt. The latter led to slavery and former to capitalism. His analysis grasps slavery within its historical context. In the ancient world, it defines a social system. In the capitalist nineteenth century, it is a peculiar form of labor control within a system based more on exchange than on direct coercion. Yet the coercion of the market is not far from that of the whip.

During the late slave period, just before the Civil War, the South was beginning to industrialize, partly in response to resentment over terms of trade between the raw materials of the South and the industrial products of the North. Robert S. Starobin (1939–71), in a book on this industrialization effort, noted how the situation of the slave was being transformed by the needs of industry for greater labor mobility.[76] Rather than being inseparable from the plantation, some slaves were being sent out by their owners to seek work for wages! The industrially employed slaves would then turn over part of their wage to their owner. This meant a dramatic transformation in the day-to-day habits and behavior of the slaves as well as their relationship with their owners. In short, they were acting less like slaves and more like wage labor.

Eric Williams (1911–81) argued that slavery itself originated from the struggles of both "free" waged workers and indentured workers in the colonies. Capital had to seek out new sources of cheap and totally controlled labor to compensate for the concessions made to workers at home

---

74. *Capital, Vol. I,* p. 625.
75. "Marx to Pavel Vasilyevich Annenkov" (December 28, 1846), *MECW, vol. 38,* p. 101.
76. Robert S. Starobin, *Industrial Slavery in the Old South,* Oxford: Oxford University Press, 1971.

and the facility with which the indentured could escape.[77] Slaves, of course, fought for freedom, through overt revolts and by escaping.[78] At least some English workers saw the freedom of slaves as beneficial to them. Marx even wrote to Lincoln congratulating him on the freeing of the slaves and his re-election in 1864 in a letter on behalf of the International Working Men's Association (the First International).[79] During the Civil War, British textile capitalists supported the Southern cause, because they depended upon cheap, slave-produced Southern cotton. Some even argued that Britain should enter the war on the Southern side. Demonstrations by British workers helped block such intervention.

Within the US, many Northern workers also saw, to some degree, that their ability to win higher wages and better working conditions depended upon ending a situation where some workers were literally made slaves—to work at extremely low "wages." In Chapter 10, Marx notes,

In the United States of America, every independent worker's movement was paralyzed as long as slavery disfigured a part of the republic. Labor in a white skin cannot emancipate itself where it is branded in a black skin. However, a new life immediately arose from the death of slavery. The first fruit of the American Civil War was the eight hours agitation which ran from the Atlantic to the Pacific...[80]

As the struggles of the waged and unwaged were linked, so too are many (and eventually all) conflicts between various groups of workers and capital interconnected. If the power of American workers in the North and of British workers was limited by slavery in the early nineteenth century, today we see plenty of evidence of how the power of those same workers is limited by the weakness of workers in the Global South. Multinational corporations and free trade have increased capital's ability to shift jobs from high to low wage areas, undercutting the livelihoods of workers in the

---

77. Eric Williams, *Capitalism and Slavery*, Chapel Hill: University of North Carolina Press, 1944, which is directly indebted to C. L. R. James's book *The Black Jacobins: Toussaint L'Ouverture and the San Domingo Revolution (1938)*, rev. 2nd edn., New York: Vintage Books, 1963 (see Williams's bibliographic notes III.B. at the end of his book).
78. Escaping in the US often made use of the underground railroad; escaping in Latin America and the Caribbean often involved flight into the hinterland and the establishment of "maroon" communities, sometimes with indigenous peoples. See Richard Price, *Maroon Societies: Rebel Slave Communities in the Americas*, 3rd edn., Baltimore, MD: Johns Hopkins University Press, 1996.
79. Karl Marx, "To Abraham Lincoln, President of the United States of America", *MECW, vol. 20*, pp. 19–21.
80. *Capital, Vol. I*, p. 414.

former areas with little or no improvement for workers in the latter ones. The solution to this problem today, as in the nineteenth century, is an acceleration of the international circulation of struggle via the self-conscious collaboration between higher, lower and unwaged workers.[81]

CHAPTER 29: THE GENESIS OF
THE CAPITALIST FARMER

Outline of Marx's Analysis

Genesis of the capitalist farmer: "was a slow process" evolving through many centuries

For England:

1) First form: the bailiff, himself a serf, like Roman *villicus*
2) Second form: emerging in second half of the fourteenth century was the farmer, provided by the landlord with seed, cattle and farm implements, exploits more wage labor
3) Third form: *metayer*, or sharecropper, who advances part of inputs, rest advanced by landowner and they divide the output
4) Fourth form: fifteenth century on, capitalist farmer proper, owns capital, employs wage labor and pays rent

This emerging class gets boost in fifteenth/sixteenth century from:

1) "Usurpation of the common lands" which allows expansion in cattle and manure
2) Fall in value of gold causing a rise in prices (e.g., agricultural output), undermining real wages and rents, raising profits.

So, by the end of the sixteenth century, England had a "class of capitalist farmers"

Commentary

Analyzing the emergence of the capitalist class, Marx begins in the countryside, where he began his discussion of the genesis of the working class. The expropriation of the rural population also involved landed proprietors reorganizing the countryside, directly or through intermediaries. In some cases, landlords took over supervision of waged workers on their enlarged domains. In most, they hired others to reorganize agricultural produc-

---

81.   See slides prepared for a debate on "outsourcing" in 2004 at http://la.utexas.edu/users/hcleaver/outsourcing.ppt.

tion increasing its commercialization, demanding only their share of the surplus-value as rent. The examples Marx gives shows the decreasing control of landlords, per se, and the increasing control of the emerging class of capitalist farmers. Like the capitalist class more generally, in order to emerge as a dominant class, agrarian capitalists had to first gain control over production, independent of the landlords, and second, employ a reorganized labor force to produce a marketable surplus.

As the point of departure of this process in Europe varied enormously, so too did the paths along which the new class emerged. They varied from region to region and country to country. The history in the United States was just as varied, starting from family farming, waged labor and plantation slavery. After slavery was ended by revolt and civil war, small farmers, whether independent or sharecroppers, were slowly squeezed off the land in an ongoing process of enclosure by large-scale capitalist agribusiness, with considerable help from the US government.

The Resistance to Market Forces in American Farming

In the United States, the westward movement of people seeking alternatives to the emerging factories (in Europe and on the East Coast of America) created a class of independent family farmers linked together in many kinds of community. These farmers were akin to the independent yeoman farmers Marx saw being wiped out in England. Obtaining land by displacing Native Americans, their labor could only be harnessed/exploited by the emerging capitalist system through the market (the manipulation of domestic terms of trade and high interest rates). Such exploitation culminated in the Populist Revolt in the late nineteenth century, when millions of American farmers joined together to protest, among other things, the falling ratio of the prices they received for their crops to the prices they paid for their tools, seeds, etc. They also protested the limitation of the money supply to gold—that kept supplies of money limited, prices down and interest rates up—and demanded the monetization of silver.[82]

---

82. On the agrarian Populist Revolt in the United States, see the following works: John Hicks, *The Populist Revolt*, Minneapolis: University of Minneapolis Press, 1931; C. Vann Woodward, *Tom Watson: Agrarian Rebel*, New York: Oxford University Press, 1963; Lawrence Goodwyn, *The Populist Movement: A Short History of the Agrarian Revolt in America*, New York: Oxford University Press, 1978; Robert Klepper, *The Economic Bases for Agrarian Protest Movements in the U.S., 1870–1900*, New York: Arno, 1978; Bruce Palmer, *"Man Over Money": The Southern Populist Critique of American Capitalism*, Chapel Hill: University of Northern Carolina Press, 1980; Donna Barnes, *Farmers in Rebellion: the Rise and Fall of the Southern Farmer's Alliance and People's Party in Texas*, Austin: University of Texas Press, 1984. For an allegorical treatment of the populist battle for the monetarization of silver, see Frank Baum, *The Wonderful Wizard of Oz*,

Throughout much of the following twentieth century, farmers had to struggle against a tendency for the terms of their trade to fall and thus for their situation to worsen.[83] A blues song, "Seven Cent Cotton," composed in 1927 by Sampson Pittman, dealt with just such a problem: low prices for cotton and high prices for just about everything the farmers had to buy. The song begins: "7¢ cotton and 40¢ meat / How in the world / Can a poor man eat? / Flour up high and / Cotton down low / How in the world / Can we raise the dough?"[84]

Other methods of exploitation included debt peonage through which farmers would become indebted to landowners, banks or suppliers and forced to produce commercial crops to pay off their debt. This was the fate of many ex-slaves after the Civil War. For those who escaped imprisonment and de facto slavery (see my commentary on Chapter 28) and were unable to obtain land, they often found themselves "sharecropping" others' land and trapped in perpetual debt.[85] Others have been subordinated via the modern "putting out" or "contract farming" system, whereby small farm owners sign contracts with food chains or food processing corporations and must follow the methods and instructions of their buyers. In both cases, as in the case of slavery, people's skills and labor have been manipulated and exploited by capital without this being done through the wage.

Capitalists have not always found it easy to entice or compel American family farmers to produce for the market, and thus expose themselves to exploitation. The traditional American family farm is a complex combination of animal husbandry, vegetable and grain growing, designed from the first to be largely self-supporting. Animal wastes are returned to the soil as nutrients; the animals feed on grain or their byproducts or on fallow pastures being renewed by nitrogen-fixing crops. Drying, butchering, salting, canning and more recently freezing have provided farm families

---

Chicago, IL: George M. Hill Co., 1900. You can also re-examine the 1939 film version, but its makers changed Dorothy's magical shoes from silver (symbolic of free silver) to ruby (looked better on the screen) and thus obfuscated a main point!

83.   This problem with relative prices deserves two further comments: 1) the ratio has sometimes been quite consciously manipulated by policymakers to exploit farmers, the most notorious case being the Stalinist government in the Soviet Union that wielded the "scissors" against peasants; 2) concern with just such problems on an international scale was raised by Raul Prebisch and others in Latin America who argued that the raw material exporting Third World as a whole was chronically faced with falling terms of trade.

84.   For one rendition of this song, and for the rest of the lyrics, see Pete Seeger, *American Industrial Ballads*, Folkways, 1957 (5251), Smithsonian/Folkways, 1992 (CD SF 40058). Others, but not Pete's, are available on YouTube.

85.   See Edward Royce, *The Origins of Southern Sharecropping*, Philadelphia, PA: Temple University Press, 1993.

with food the year round. In these circumstances, it is possible for small farmers, if they are not caught by the debt traps of suppliers or bankers, to produce for the market only to the degree that they choose, selling just enough to buy things they cannot produce. In research for his PhD dissertation, Ricardo Salvatore discovered how the refusal of New England farmers to produce hides for even a regional leather market forced East Coast shoe producers to import hides from as far away as Argentina and California.[86] Those farmers who refused to subordinate their production to the market were opting for a certain culture and way of life in which they were working for themselves and their own self-defined needs.

In a process that Marx analyzes with respect to industry in Chapter 25, American agriculture has suffered gradual processes of both proletarianization and centralization. Exploited and then foreclosed, most small farmers have been driven off the land and into rural or urban labor markets. Some, in self-defense, have survived by banding together in farmer cooperatives.[87] Parallel has been the rise of larger, more wealthy farmers and ranchers and their takeover by Eastern or European investment companies. American agribusiness emerged from open range wars, where the stronger stole from the weaker, and from some buying up others' land, often at cut-rate prices from foreclosing banks. The big farms and ranches fenced the land and hired ever more laborers, including cowboys to manage herds and cattle drives—armed cowboys who, sometimes, struck for higher wages.[88] In these ways, the experience of England has been essentially repeated in North America, albeit with some variation.

The period of the Populist Revolt was the last important instance of large and small American farmers combining in a common political cause. Subsequently, the state, through the Department of Agriculture, went out of its way to destroy this alliance by supporting the growth of the American Farm Federation that catered to large farmers and by directing its increasing number of agricultural extension agents to push new technology mainly toward more affluent farmers who could afford the necessary investment.[89]

---

86. Ricardo D. Salvatore, "Class Struggle and International Trade: Rio de la Plata's Commerce and the Atlantic Proletariat, 1790–1850", University of Texas at Austin, PhD dissertation, 1987. The problem of controlling a hide-producing proletariat reappeared in the Pampas, where fiercely independent gauchos only killed wild cattle for hides when they needed money.

87. See the discussion of cooperatives in my commentary on Chapter 13.

88. See Ruth Allen, *Chapters in the History of Organized Labor in Texas*, Austin: University of Texas Press, 1941.

89. On how the alliance between small and large farmers was irretrievably broken with help from the Department of Agriculture, see Grant McConnell, *The Decline of Agrarian Democracy*, New York: Atheneum, 1969.

In recent years, the revival of the "farm movement" in response to the latest credit crunches and crises of parity in output and input prices has been supported by those few small farmers who are left, and some large farmers who stand to gain from price supports. This "movement" is on a very small scale in comparison to the Populist Revolt, in large measure because while in 1870 almost 50 percent of Americans still worked the land, today that number has been reduced to 3–4 percent and is still declining.

As its operations and the need for cheap farm labor grew, agribusiness turned to immigrant labor, both legal—through the Bracero Program— and illegal. By the 1960s, however, field workers (mostly Mexican, or Mexican American) began to form unions, fight for union recognition, higher wages and better working conditions in the central valley of California. They fought in part through strikes and in part through a nationwide grape boycott that mobilized millions of shoppers (mainly housewives) in their support. Many of us who were supporting the resistance of peasants in Southeast Asia to US government counterinsurgency war also lent our time and energy to support that struggle in the American countryside.

The struggles of farmworkers have been commemorated in song. An early one, "Deportee (Plane Wreck at Los Gatos)" (1948) by Woody Guthrie, lamented the exploitation of immigrant workers. Another, the "Corrido de Delano" or the "Ballad of Delano" by Lalo Guerrero (1916–2005), celebrated the battles of the United Farm Workers in California. The song begins: "In 1965 or 1966, more or less / Our people rose up / In the fields of Delano / Demanding better wages / For working the land." Among the many other musical expressions of such rural conflicts in that period was "Maggie's Farm" by Bob Dylan. His song, however, was more than an expression of *rural* revolt; it expressed a whole cycle of social struggles of the late 1960s: the revolt against capitalist work in all its forms. "Maggie's Farm" could be any farm, factory, office or schoolroom where people were put to work and mistreated. The miseries that Dylan describes are those of all workers: ideas which can't be realized because work drains away energy, low wages, penalties for the infraction of stupid rules, the blindness of bosses to anything besides their pursuit of profit, their frequent enjoyment of their power over workers, the shadow of the state standing behind them to protect them from workers' revolt, ideology that hides hypocrisy. Yet, the song reveals the struggle for self-realization despite the oppressions of boring work. It begins: "I ain't gonna work on Maggie's farm no more / No, I ain't gonna work on Maggie's farm no more / Well, I wake up in the morning / Hold my hands and pray for rain / I got a head full of ideas that are driving me insane / It's a shame the way she makes me scrub the floor."

Parallels in the Global South

Colonial plantations, on land stolen from indigenous populations, faced resistance and had to resort to many different forms of coerced labor.[90] For the most part, such agriculture produced raw materials for the industries of the colonizing countries, e.g., American, Egyptian or Indian cotton, Caribbean sugar or Vietnamese rice and rubber. See the films *Burn!* (1969) and *The Mission* (1986) for dramatic portrayals of the colonial period in Latin America. The post-colonial period perpetuated the same pattern of dependence on former colonial trade.

Like some American family farmers, many peasant communities have refused to gear their production to the demands of the market. Some, seduced by market income in the past, have withdrawn after nasty experiences of finding their income subject to wild fluctuations in market prices. Periods of downturns in crop prices have shown them that their medium- and long-run income, not to mention their cultural ways of life, are more secure when their production is essentially organized to meet their own needs and only surpluses are offered to the market.

On the other hand, in the post-colonial era, influential commercial producers reacted to such market price instability by demanding considerable state intervention to lessen such fluctuations and stabilize income. In this way new independent governments gained some control over their economies, which had been and continued to be dependent on former colonial trade. Such interventions—such as subsidizing the prices of basic food crops—were long opposed by development economists and foreign governments who wanted to open those markets to their own exports.

That long opposition culminated in the trumpeted free-market, neoliberal ideology of the Reagan administration in the 1980s. On every front, the US government pressured foreign governments to "open their markets" and reduce government "regulation." The *ideology* was that of eighteenth- and nineteenth-century liberalism: "free markets are the best solution to all economic problems."[91] The actual *strategy* was merely a variant of colonial force: hammer down all those defenses that local groups had erected to their subordination by multinational capital. During the 1982 debt crisis in Mexico, for instance, the International Monetary Fund demanded the elimination of subsidies supporting the price of the basic food crop, maize, as one condition (among many) for debt rollover. It was accepted and enforced by the Mexican government. The result was a drop in maize prices

---

90.   See Marx's comments on the attitudes of freed slaves in Jamaica, cited in my commentary on Chapter 10.

91.   Of course, markets have never been free, neither then nor now, but are carefully organized to benefit those capitalists with the most clout in shaping trade policies.

and a flood of maize imports from the US that convinced many peasants to abandon market-geared monoculture and return to more diverse production patterns designed for local needs. This pattern has been replicated worldwide.

Such neoliberal policies have continued to be pursued by Democratic as well as Republican administrations. A decade after Mexico's de facto default, the Clinton administration pushed through the neoliberal NAFTA that went into effect on January 1, 1994, an implementation met by the indigenous Zapatista uprising. Within a year, the peso went belly-up and that same administration demanded further opening of the Mexican economy to foreign investment and trade as conditions for bailing out speculators. In all these cases, the welfare of both farmers and consumers was subordinated to that of multinational corporations, including agribusiness.

The Use of Inflation in Primitive and Mature Accumulation

Marx's analysis of the way inflation (a general rise of prices) enriched capitalist farmers in the sixteenth century is still instructive in our own period. The utilization of inflation by capitalists to transfer value from waged workers (and others on fixed income) to themselves (the owners of the commodities whose prices are rising) became a conscious policy in the 1940s–1960s, a period in which capitalist macroeconomic policy was dominated by the thought of John Maynard Keynes (1883–1946). Keynes had seen how inflation could be used to undermine real wages in the presence of "money illusion." Then development economists such as Sir William Arthur Lewis (1915–91) recommended state-generated inflation as a way to increase savings and investment to spur accumulation in the Global South.[92] In some countries, such as Brazil, this was institutionalized, not only with inflation but with differential indexation whereby wages were indexed at a lower rate than capital values.

In the 1970s rapid inflation was the only way capital could undermine real wages, given that, in the late 1960s, nominal wages had grown more rapidly than productivity and undermined profits. Thus, the acceptance by US capital of the quadrupling of oil prices by the Organization of Petroleum Exporting Countries (OPEC) in 1974 and again in 1978, in

---

92. See W. A. Lewis's classic article on development and the use of inflation against the working class: "Development with Unlimited Supplies of Labor", *Manchester School*, May 1954, pp. 139–191. On Keynes and "money illusion," see his *General Theory*, 1936. For a class analysis of the dynamics of inflation politics in Brazil, see Nathan Dudley, "Worker Struggle and Wage Compression: The Rise and Fall of Indexation in Brazil", University of Texas, MA thesis, May 1988; and Conrad Herold, "Working Class Struggle and the Brazilian Debt Crisis", University of Texas, PhD dissertation, 1994.

the hope and expectation that hundreds of billions of "petrodollars" would be recycled through Western banks and become available for capital to use against workers.[93] Inflation successfully prevented the rapid rise of real wages and an accelerated fall in the share of profits. However, workers' continued success in raising nominal wages generated accelerating inflation that became, for business, more of a problem than a useful strategy. At that point, policies "attacking inflation" became a euphemism for what were really "attacks on wages."

This points to a basic lesson to be learned from the study of this part of *Capital*: in his analysis of the period of primitive accumulation, Marx outlines and analyzes then *new* phenomena, which become *established* patterns of mature accumulation. We can approach primitive accumulation by looking backward and asking how the mechanisms of capitalist domination became established, but we can also examine the ongoing patterns of accumulation to discover how the same mechanisms have been continually re-employed. Land, for example, is still being enclosed and people continue to struggle against enclosure or to reverse it, seeking the re-establishment of ever larger commons as one vehicle for escaping capitalist domination. Certainly, the structure of the section, two chapters on the emergence of the working class, and three on the emergence of the capitalist class, points to a fundamental point which many Marxists have overlooked: socially speaking, accumulation is an accumulation of classes and the accumulating quantities of money, means of production, commodities, factories, etc., are only moments, or elements, in the social accumulation of the antagonistic social struggles which make up the interactions of those classes.

CHAPTER 30: IMPACT OF THE AGRICULTURAL REVOLUTION ON INDUSTRY. THE CREATION OF A HOME MARKET FOR INDUSTRIAL CAPITAL

Commentary

The expropriation of land and the bloody legislation against the expropriated produced not only a proletariat available for work in capitalist industry, but also a market for the goods being produced by that industry. Previously, that market was quite limited because most people produced

---

93.   US negotiators let OPEC know that it would not oppose increases in oil prices. When European governments sought to form a "buyers' cartel" to manipulate demand against OPEC's manipulation of supply, the US refused to go along. See V. H. Oppenheim, "Why Oil Prices Go Up: The Past: We Pushed Them", *Foreign Policy*, no. 25, Winter 1976–1977, pp. 24–57.

Outline of Marx's Analysis

Point of departure: largely self-sufficient peasantry, which worked the land, produced raw materials and processed them into final consumption goods, e.g., raised sheep, worked wool into thread and hence into cloth and clothes

Expropriation of the land had three results:

1. Peasants became workers and landlords either became or hired agrarian capitalists
2. Produced raw materials, along with the land, became the property of the agrarian capitalists
3. The destruction of independent artisanal and handicraft production so that all consumer goods had to be purchased

Destruction of artisanal production:

- begins with expropriation of the land which often involved the destruction of villages and means of artisanal tools such as looms
- is temporarily limited by the rise of cottage industry, subordinated to merchant capital
- this begins the period of manufacturing controlled by merchants, in isolated workshops, with the aim of profits
- is completed with the rise of industrial factories in which production and workers are concentrated in "labor barracks"
- creates the home market which replaces homemade or artisan goods produced to meet local needs

Home market means demand for food, clothes, housing, etc. all from people who had previously provided their own but are now working for wages and buying what they need on the market.

what they needed. It was restricted to the wealthy with money to spend or to local exchange, often under conditions of barter or reciprocity within a community. Marx points out that the rise of a waged working class also meant the rise of a class of consumers who increasingly bought everything they needed in the market.

The Imposition of the Market

As we saw in Chapter 28, throwing peasants off the land does not necessarily mean they will present themselves at the factory gates or constitute an immediate market for capitalists' goods. The inability to produce one's own food or clothing does not mean those who need to eat or to be clothed will have the money necessary to buy what they need or that buying them is the only way to obtain them. They could also be appropriated directly. In legend, Robin Hood and his merry men poached the king's deer. As commons were enclosed, peasants continued to gather wood in forests for huts and fires and poached game on now private land.[94] Along with the laws against vagabondage, aimed at creating a class of waged workers, came other laws aimed at preventing such direct appropriation, i.e., property laws that imposed the market as the only legal way to acquire goods. These laws were every bit as bloody, perhaps more so, than those against vagabondage. In the seventeenth and eighteenth centuries, British courts regularly hanged people for petty "theft." Historian Peter Linebaugh coined the term "thanatocracy" for this rule by death.[95]

While this distinction between direct appropriation and buying with a wage may seem clear cut, historically it was not so neatly defined. During the period of manufacturing, it was commonplace in many trades, for the workers to take part of their income in the form of directly appropriated means of production. For example, silk workers would appropriate scraps of silk cloth, shoemakers would keep excess leather, shipwrights would help themselves to scrap lumber, sailors would take tobacco being transported in their ships, cowboys could take part of their pay in calves or put their own brand on mavericks, and so on. In each case the workers would either consume the material directly, sell it for money or work it up into a product (e.g., leather into shoes) and sell that for money.[96] Eventually, this kind of activity was criminalized; laws were passed attacking these non-wage forms of income and through them the real wage was lowered, making the workers poorer and the employers richer. Moreover, the struggle over such appropriation led to a variety of new methods of production: from hogsheads (large wooden barrels) in shipping (to make "pilfering" more difficult) to Mirabeau's *fabriques réunies* in which workers could be watched over, their labor process more carefully controlled and "waste" limited.

---

94.   See Peter Linebaugh, "Karl Marx, the Theft of Wood, and Working-Class Composition: A Contribution to the Current Debate", *Crime and Social Justice*, no. 6, Fall–Winter 1976, pp. 5–16 on Marx's early interest in such direct appropriation. See also Douglas Hay, "Poaching and the Game Laws on Cannock Chase", in Thompson et al., *Albion's Fatal Tree*.

95.   See Linebaugh, *The London Hanged*, Chapter Two: "'Old Mr Gory' and the Thanatocracy."

96.   Linebaugh analyzes several of these situations, both the direct appropriation that supplemented money wages and its criminalization. Ibid., Chapters 5, 8 and 11. See also Allen, *Chapters in the History of Organized Labor in Texas*.

Valorization and Disvalorization

Another way of looking at the emergence of the "home market" is the commodification of production, that is to say how goods which had been produced for use came to be produced for sale. This is characteristic of the capitalist organization of life; capitalists convert human activities into commodity producing ones. The people capitalists put to work produce not just useful items or services but commodities that can be sold to make a profit (or so the capitalists hope). This whole process of putting people to work producing commodities, sold to realize a profit, which is then reinvested to begin the whole process over again, Marx calls (in Chapter 7) "valorization" or the "self-valorization" of capital.[97]

Capitalist valorization is quite the reverse from the point of view of displaced peasants and artisans. Peasants displaced from the land lose their ability to farm, not only in the direct sense that without land they cannot grow food, but over time the very skills necessary for farming are lost within a generation. Their children, raised away from the land, never acquire the skills of their parents. Artisans, who knew how to spin thread or weave cloth but lost their spinning wheels and looms, soon lose their skills in those handicrafts. Their children never gain them. Thus, the creation of value for the capitalist means the creation of what Ivan Illich has called "disvalue" for the expropriated.[98] This loss of skill, this loss of the ability to produce for oneself to meet one's own needs, involves two related processes, *de*valorization and *dis*valorization. Where certain skills and abilities and knowledges are lost completely, not just by the individual but by society, we can say there has been *de*valorization or the destruction of value. Where the skills and abilities are lost to individuals but taken over and incorporated into capital and the production of commodities, we can say the people have suffered *dis*valorization—the displacement of personal and communal skills into the production of commodities.[99]

These processes, although begun in the earliest period of primitive accumulation, continue to this day. In Chapter 15 of *Capital*, on machinery

---

97. As opposed to the self-valorization of workers. In the Introduction to *Reading Capital Politically*, I point out how this term "self-valorization" was appropriated and redefined by the autonomist Marxist Antonio Negri to designate, not the self-valorization of capital, but the self-activities of workers valorizing their own lives.

98. On the concept of disvalue, see Ivan Illich's essay "Useful Unemployment and its Professional Enemies" in his book *Towards a History of Needs*, Berkeley, CA: Heyday Books, 1977.

99. For further methodological considerations on valorization and disvalorization, see Harry Cleaver, "The Inversion of Class Perspective in Marxian Theory: from Valorization to Self-Valorization", in Werner Bonefeld, Richard Gunn and Kosmas Psychopedis (eds.), *Open Marxism*, vol. 2, *Theory and Practice*, London: Pluto, 1992, pp. 106–144.

and modern industry, Marx analyzes this process in terms of *deskilling*. He shows how the development of machines has involved the mechanical reproduction of skills that workers then no longer exercise. The more this process develops, the fewer aspects of traditional skill are exercised by the workers. The result is a real process of "abstraction" through which work is steadily reduced to simple machine tending.

Today, the processes of devalorization and disvalorization are most evident in the Third World. In barrios and villages, we find people whose abilities to meet their own needs are being undermined by the intrusion of the market. Sometimes, as in the case of the substitution of marketed baby formula for breastfeeding, the results have been dramatic: malnourishment, crippling and even death.[100] In other cases, say the substitution of store-bought clothing for homespun, the results are not so immediately obvious or dramatic but, in the long run, cultural traditions and ways of life are lost, e.g., patterns unique to communities woven into clothing, traditional reverence for the earth. The creation of the home market replaces diverse cultural practices and ways of being by a single way of doing things and similar goods. Capitalists like to point with pride to the array of colors and styles available in your average department store, or the array of foods available in supermarkets. But compared to the pre-existing diversity of styles in clothing and cuisines, their vaunted "choices" pale, mere variations to maximize sales.

Under these circumstances, people have long fought against the subordination of their activities to capitalist accumulation and for the preservation of their cultures, which cannot survive independently of the structure of those activities. Just as peasants struggled against the expropriation of their land, so too did the artisans among them struggle against the destruction or subordination of their tools and crafts. As described in Chapter 15, during the early period of manufacture workers sometimes smashed machines that would subordinate their skills, increase their work and lower their income.[101] Such struggles also constituted a defense of ways of life, of patterns of interactions, within a community and between generations (parent–child, apprenticeships).

Looking primarily at Europe, Marx saw the rigidities of the guilds with their strict rules that limited production, the number of journeymen working under a master, and so on. In those conditions, he saw capitalism bringing a certain freeing up, a liberation of production from artificial

---

100. Such results led to an international boycott of Nestlé for pushing baby formula to the poor in the Global South and to the formation of the International Baby Food Action Network (IBFA).

101. *Capital, Vol. I,* pp. 554–555.

restraint, thus an historically progressive force. But the guilds were mainly city institutions and Marx never closely explored the great variety of cultural practices in the countryside—at least not until late in his life, long after *Capital* was written. Then, he began to read ethnographic studies and was drawn into debates about the Russian *mir*, or peasant commune. As a result, he showed a greater appreciation of such alternative forms of social organization. Unfortunately, none of this shows up in *Capital*; it was never revised to take account of this new appreciation.

The Realities and Costs of Agricultural Development

Marx does address a fundamental difficulty inherent in the rise of an industry based on a labor force separated from the land. If expropriation led to a fall in production of foodstuffs, because of fewer people working the land and agrarian capitalists replacing food production with raw material production for multiplying factories, there would be a serious problem in feeding those forced off. However, he was aware of two factors that tended to offset such a difficulty. First, England had increasing recourse to importing foodstuffs from the continent.[102] Second, the concentration of the land in the hands of an emerging capitalist class was accompanied by an increase in agricultural productivity, an early "green revolution" that involved innovations such as crop rotation, the spreading use of nitrogen-fixing crops, drainage, land reclamation and water meadows.[103] These improved methods were implemented primarily by the greater cooperation and intensity of work by wage laborers under the control of agrarian capitalists. Under these circumstances, the "setting free" of part of the agricultural population was accompanied by a similar "setting free" of part of the product of the soil, now sold in the market to those forced into the cities.[104]

---

102. With England in the lead in the development of manufacturing, many countries on the continent, from Revolutionary France to Czarist Russia exported grain to England in order to buy manufactured goods, including machinery to expand their own industry. This would only pose a problem in times of war, e.g., the Napoleonic Wars (1803–15) when grain imports were cut off.

103. See G. E. Mingay, *Agricultural Revolution: Changes in Agriculture, 1650–1880*, London: A & C Black Publishers, 1977.

104. This history was forgotten by economists who expected, after World War II, to be able to move some 25 percent of the agricultural labor force in Eastern Europe into manufacturing labor with no reduction in output. They were wrong and soon had to revise their plans to include increased investment in agriculture to raise productivity. See Paul Rosenstein-Rodan's classic "Problems of Industrialization of Eastern and South-Eastern Europe", *Economic Journal*, vol. 53, no. 210/211, 1943, pp. 202–211. A later example of the less optimistic efforts to find ways of imposing work is John C. H. Fei and Gustav Ranis, *Development of the Labor Surplus Economy: Theory and Policy*, Chicago, IL: Homewood, 1964.

Increased productivity has often been used as a justification for changes in land tenure by policymakers in Western capitalist countries as well as by those in the Soviet bloc who imposed collectivization. But two points temper this rationale. First, it is easy to find many areas of the world where land was expropriated but then not cultivated at all and so productivity did not rise. In some cases, the land was monopolized purely with the intent of preventing the indigenous population from having recourse to subsistence farming. Examples are common in Central America. When the CIA overthrew the government of Guatemala in 1954, it was partly because its democratically elected president, Jacobo Árbenz Guzmán (1913–71), had appropriated unused lands of the United Fruit Company for distribution to landless peasants.[105] In other areas, expropriated lands have been used productively and then abandoned but not given back to their original owners, e.g., in the Brazilian northeast where, when the price of sugar dropped, sugar cane lands were abandoned. In the Soviet Union and other so-called socialist countries, peasant resentment and resistance to forced labor systematically undermined the productivity of the state or collective farms.

Second, the basic argument that changes in land tenure can raise productivity is, itself, questionable. Questionable not because data on productivity, such as pounds of wool per acre or per hour of labor, do not show a rise, but because of the narrow notion of productivity. Traditional self-sustaining agriculture has almost always involved a complex mix of interrelated activities—well-known in traditional American family farming that long dominated US agriculture. The traditional family farm engaged in both cropping and husbandry. Corn provided food for the table, feed for cattle as well as marketable produce. Cattle provided milk and milk by-products, meat, income through the sale of meat and hides as well as fertilizer for the fields. Rotated nitrogen fixing crops such as alfalfa or clover provided feed for the cattle as well as fertilizer to the soil. Gardens provided a balance of vegetables and fruit for the table, and sometimes for sale in local markets. Pigs absorbed table waste while producing meat for consumption or sale, and so on. The replacement of a large number of such farms by a few commercial agribusiness operations that produce just one crop, such as hybrid corn, or feedlot cattle or pigs, has involved the substitution of a simple monoculture system, whose productivity is narrowly defined and easy to measure, for a complex system whose productivity is not so simply measured, or even conceptualized. That complex system was a way of life

---

105. Richard H. Immerman, *The CIA in Guatemala*, Austin: University of Texas Press, 1982. Also see the now released CIA assassination plans for the overthrow of the Arbenz government and the "cleansing" of his supporters.

that integrated humans and nature as well as nature itself.[106] Destroying such ways of life replaces complex, balanced ecosystems by simplified, unbalanced ones, often with disastrous consequences for the land, for water and for human life.[107] In short, the decline of traditional farming involved tremendous human and ecological costs in terms of the destruction of ways of being that could not be legitimately compared with or compensated for by increased productivity. What has been true in the United States has also been true around the world, from the destruction of Mexican *milpas* and communities to the commercialization of Asian wet-paddy rice culture.

CHAPTER 31: THE GENESIS OF THE INDUSTRIAL CAPITALIST

Outline of Marx's Analysis

Industrial capital grew up more rapidly than agrarian capital
- less through gradual accumulation by workers or artisans
- more through the annexation of labor by merchant or usurer capital
- despite traditional restrictions of guilds, etc.
- began in sea ports and villages beyond such constraints
- accelerated and solidified through the victory of capital over the feudal ruling classes
- financed by wealth accumulated through force

The wealth that financed the rise of industry was not accumulated through frugality
- but rather by force
- above all, in the beginning, by colonialism
- "enslavement and entombment in mines" of the indigenous population of America
- "conquest and plunder of India"
- enslavement of Africans
- monopolization of trade (including the opium trade in China)
- but also, the use of banks, the national debt and taxation
- "Force is the midwife of every old society which is pregnant with a new one"

▶

---

106.   See Wendell Berry, *The Unsettling of America: Culture & Agriculture*, Berkeley, CA: Counterpoint, 1977, 2015.

107.   Examples include the impoverishment of the soil by monocropping, the runoff of excess inorganic fertilizers into waterways causing eutrophication and the overuse of pesticides poisoning workers in the fields, consumers and a variety of non-human animals, most recently honeybees, whose colony collapses are threatening entire industries requiring them for pollination.

Colonialism: Dutch, English, Spanish
- violence and the plunder of wealth
- massacre and the direct theft of land and riches
- enslavement of populations
- monopolization of trade (including the slave trade)
- English East India Company in India: salt, tea, betel, opium
- Dutch East Indies Company in Indonesia: slaves
- trade: exports of local wealth, imports from the home country
- concentrated wealth in the hands of those who invested it in industry
- led to commercial wars between competing colonial powers

Public debt: one of the earliest and longest lasting mechanisms
- private finance capital loaned money to the state in exchange for negotiable bonds
- the state used the money to finance the violence of primitive accumulation: army, navy
- repaid the debt with interest, through the imposition of taxes on the people
- which concentrated more money in the hands of finance capital
- the circulation of state debt and the creation of large-scale banking gives rise to the massive expansion of credit
- in the hands of capitalists
- before the rise of consumer credit

Trade protection: monopolization of trade and the extortion of heavy taxes combine in the use of:
- protective duties
- export premiums
- the destruction of competing industries (e.g., Irish woolens, Indian cottons)
- all of which plundered both the English people and their trading partners and concentrated wealth in the hands of capitalists

These methods financed industrialization

In England:
- the impoverishment of the workers
- the enslavement of their children (who were not free agents in the labor markets)
- cruel working conditions and minimal pay
- the rise of night work: "the beds never get cold"

In the colonies:
- slavery ("the veiled slavery of the wage-labourers in Europe needed the unqualified slavery of the new world as its pedestal")
- scalp hunting and murder

"If money," Marx concludes, "'comes into the world with a congenital blood-stain on one cheek,' capital comes dripping from head to toe, from every pore, with blood and dirt"

Commentary

Industrial capital, the prototypical form of capital, emerged alongside agrarian capitalism. Marx refutes the myth that this emergence was accomplished purely through conscientious frugality and entrepreneurial investment by describing the actual sources of finance for investment that became permanent features of capitalism, well beyond the early period of primitive accumulation.

The Myth of Entrepreneurship

Marx's attack on the myth of entrepreneurial frugality remains important because it still flourishes. It became foundational to the ideology of upward mobility, which claims that anyone who works hard can move up the income hierarchy, even to the very top. Recently, it has been refurbished as part of the right-wing attack on those roles of the state used by workers for their own protection. In the United States, amidst the crisis of Keynesianism in the 1970s, this ideology was elaborated by *neo-conservatives*, and soon became known in the rest of the world by the label *neoliberalism*.[108] Marx accepts the grain of truth that many small guild masters, independent small artisans and even wage-laborers, "transformed themselves. . . into capitalists."[109] But he argues that such personal initiative, savings and investment were not the major mechanisms by which industrial capitalism emerged. Nor we can add, are small businesses today the major source of capitalist expansion.

---

108. The term neo-conservative was adopted in the United States by conservatives who wanted to differentiate themselves not only from "liberals" (which in the US has come to mean vaguely socially progressive) but also from earlier moderate conservatives. Self-proclaimed neo-conservatives emerged on the public scene with the crisis of Keynesianism whose managers—members of what some used to call the Establishment—tended include both "liberals" and "mainstream or moderate conservatives" (as opposed to far-right groups like the John Birch Society and the China Lobby). The neo-conservatives, backed by considerable right-wing money began to build alternative policymaking institutions—such as the Heritage Foundation—and proclaim a "return to first principles," namely a faith in markets and opposition to all government programs benefiting workers. First in Latin American, now pretty much everywhere, the term neoliberal has been used to characterize the policies of those neo-conservatives. The term neoliberal evokes a contemporary version of nineteenth-century liberalism, i.e., the ideology of free trade and faith that markets were the best way to solve most problems—coupled, of course, with the use of the state for the repression of workers' struggles. The worldwide adoption of the term neoliberal accelerated in the wake of the Zapatistas' multinational Encounters against Neoliberalism and for Humanity in 1996 and 1997.

109. *Capital, Vol. I*, p. 914.

Since the 1970s, attacks on the Keynesian social and environmental programs and regulations have been rationalized by the pretense that they undermine entrepreneurship. State paternalism, neoliberals have claimed, whether of welfare state in the West or of socialist governments in the East, creates dependency and tends to snuff out the entrepreneurial spirit vital to the building of free enterprise and society more generally. Targets have included programs that support working-class income and increase workers' ability to resist exploitation, as well as environmental, occupational safety and health regulations that workers have imposed on business to limit damage to both humans and the rest of nature. Neoliberals call for deregulation to cut corporate costs and enhance private profits, the selling off (enclosure) of public lands for purposes of exploitation, the removal of environmental regulations to encourage investment, the reduction or elimination of social safety-net programs, vouchers to finance private schools outside the public-school system, and in countries now freed from Soviet-style regimes, the substitution of private farming for state or collective farms. Hypocrisy is blatant in the steadfast opposition these same capitalist apologists maintain to any reduction in the role of government in the defense and subsidization of corporations and in their repeated support for "supply-side" tax cuts that supposedly increase investment but actually benefit the wealthy at the expense of everyone else. Such policies have rightly given rise to the term "corporate welfare."

Analyzing the rise of industrial capitalism shows us how these arguments are just as ideological and self-serving as those Marx confronted in the nineteenth century. Even during the birth of capitalism, in the supposed golden age of laissez faire, before the rise of "big government" or the welfare state, the role of the state was crucial for the emergence and survival of capitalism. Whether describing the state use of armed violence to capture and maintain colonies for exploitation by "free enterprise" or analyzing the use of national debt and taxation to finance such violence and to transfer income from workers to capital, Marx highlights the ways in which the greatest and most important "entrepreneurial" ability of all was the ability to mobilize, not individual creativity, but state power in the service of capital accumulation. Similarly, he shows how the main beneficiaries of this ability were not small, "entrepreneurial" firms, built with individual initiative, but giant monopolistic trading and industrial enterprises—such as the British and Dutch East India Companies—built and sustained by state charters and armed support.

The myth of entrepreneurship derives its strength partly from the ubiquitous propaganda apparatus of capital, but also from an extremely important truth hidden beneath all its distortions and hypocrisy. Within capitalism, the real sources of creativity and innovation are social individuals working and thinking within a collective process. The myth of entrepreneurship misleads by pointing only to the innovative individual (from Horatio Alger to Steve Jobs), while ignoring both the social fabric enabling such individuals to create and their dependence on capitalist finance, which turns their innovations into new modes of exploitation.

The real source of innovation and wealth, Marx argues, is living labor (including creative thinking). Capitalists, as such, serve as mere managers of a system in which dead labor—in the form of capital, whether means of production or money—dominates living labor. Where those who work and think have the power to force capital to harness rather than repress such creativity, the system accumulates and develops rapidly. Where workers are weak and capital powerful and rigid in its control, the system can accumulate only quantitatively and tends to stagnate. In the West, the right-wing calls for a liberation of entrepreneurship, but their policy prescriptions have been focused primarily on liberating not individuals but multinational corporations from constraints that benefit workers and protect the environment. In the last years of the Cold War, Soviet reformers, such as Mikhail Gorbachev, found themselves caught in a contradiction; they needed looser industrial and political controls (to achieve more flexibility and rapid accumulation) but feared the result would be explosive expressions of discontent they could not manage. Their fears soon proved to be justified, the Berlin Wall fell and their regime with it, soon replaced by a savage mafia-capitalism dedicated to maximum exploitation and repression. The reality of neoliberalism is Trump's authoritarianism and Putin's dictatorship.

Capitalist Development and the Role of the State

Thus, capitalists' attitude toward the state depends entirely on the degree to which it serves their needs. Where, during the early period of primitive accumulation, industrial capitalists did not have the power to use the state to eliminate guild rules inimical to their business interests, they set up operations in sea ports and villages where such restrictions did not obtain. Where and when capitalists were able to usurp state power, they used it to craft a world more to their own convenience. They pillaged the Global South through colonialism. They impoverished and disvalorized their employees through low wages and taxation. In both areas, they imposed a murderously repressive social order based on slavery and the exploitation of children.

The central role of colonialism in the original accumulation of industrial capital consists of a series of mechanisms, some crass and violent, some subtler but still violent, which facilitated amassing the wealth that financed

British industrialization.[110] These mechanisms became quasi-permanent features of capitalism right up to the decolonialization period after World War II. The violence he describes in the initial conquest and plundering was required to overcome the fierce resistance of the people being colonized. The example he cites from the United States—scalping and murdering Native American men, women and children—was far from unique, as people everywhere resisted integration into the invading European capitalist takeover of their lands.

The violence did not disappear with the stabilization of colonial rule because resistance did not disappear. Violence begat violence. In the French colony of Vietnam, for example, military force was required to maintain control against both passive resistance and armed struggle. It took their military defeat at Dien Bien Phu in 1954 to force their withdrawal from Indochina. The history of colonialism is one long drama of invasion, resistance, conquest, exploitation, continued resistance and continued repression. But repression ultimately failed, as one anti-colonial struggle after another succeeded in pushing foreign governments and their repressive apparatus out. Unfortunately, as colonized people were to learn to their chagrin, the end of formal colonialization did not always mean the end to the mechanisms of exploitation.

One such mechanism was trade, trade internal to the colony, trade between the colony and the colonizing country, and trade with the outside world. Marx describes the case of India where the British took over the trade in consumer items such as salt, betel, opium and rice.[111] In the case of rice, he claims that the British created a famine in the process. Indeed, famine became recurrent.[112] Most notorious was the Bengal famine of 1943 in which over 2 million people died. Four years later, the British were finally forced out. Another example of British efforts to monopolize trade within a colony was Nigeria, which came into direct conflict with the market women who had traditionally dominated domestic trade. When the women sought to affirm their traditional rights, the British violently repressed them.[113]

---

110. Socially speaking, real "wealth" in capitalism is not gold or money but social power, the power of capital to command people's lives as labor. Thus, the colonial plundering of gold or other non-human material resources was secondary to the imposition of work on the colonized and the use of the colonized to reinforce the imposition of work within the colonial country.

111. *Capital, Vol. I*, p. 917.

112. See Brian Murton, "VI.4: Famine", in K. F. Kiple and K. C. Ornelas (eds.), *The Cambridge World History of Food*, New York: Cambridge University Press, 2000, pp. 1411–1427.

113. See Judith Van Allen, "Sitting on a Man: Colonialism and the Lost Political Institutions of Igbo Women", *Canadian Journal of African Studies*, vol. VI, no. ii, 1972, pp. 165–181, and the Wikipedia entry on the Abeokuta Women's Revolt.

The rise of British industry at home—the central subject of this chapter—was fueled by the monopolization of colonial foreign trade. Colonialism meant an extension of the markets for industrial output beyond the home market.[114] Colonial powers prevented any other countries' industries from selling in their conquered territories, and destroyed local industry, either directly (by cutting off the thumbs of weavers) or indirectly by underselling at lower prices.[115] In the *Communist Manifesto*, Marx and Engels commented on this aspect of capitalist expansion:

> [The bourgeoisie] has resolved personal worth into exchange-value, and in place of the numberless indefeasible chartered freedoms, has set up that single, unconscionable freedom—Free Trade. . . The cheap prices of its commodities are the heavy artillery with which it batters down all Chinese walls, with which it forces the barbarians' intensely obstinate hatred of foreigners to capitulate.[116]

The reference to "Chinese walls," of course, is not to the Great Wall of China, built to keep out nomadic tribes and to tax commerce on the Silk Road, but to the efforts of the Chinese ruling class to keep out Western capitalist merchants and their cheap and often noxious commodities. The walls were battered down both by cheap commodities and by the gunboats of the Western powers that forced China to accept their trade.[117]

European capitalists not only imposed exports on their colonies, they also demanded *protectionist* measures to limit imports at home to keep prices and profits up. Demands for "free trade" or for "protectionism" depended purely on what was useful to a particular set of capitalists at any point in time.

Arguments for either set of policies could draw on the writings of economists, always ready to provide rationales for capitalist demands. The proponents of "free trade" could draw on classical political economists such as Adam Smith (1723–90) and David Ricardo (1772–1823). The latter was especially useful because he provided a theory of "comparative advantage" that argued that all parties could gain from trade. The proponents of protectionism had not only the arguments of US Secretary of the Treasury Alexander Hamilton (1755–1804) for protecting American industry, but

---

114. The colonies, Marx wrote, "provided a market for the budding manufactures." *Capital, Vol. I*, p. 918.
115. See Michael *Edwards, Growth of the British Cotton Trade 1780–1815*, New York: Augustus M. Kelley Publishers, 1976.
116. *MECW, vol. 6*, pp. 487–488.
117. Classic were the British wars to force China to accept British exports of opium.

the book *The National System of Political Economy* (1841) by Friedrich List (1789–1846) who turned Hamilton's arguments into systematic economic theory.[118] List, who had supported the new German Customs Union to facilitate wider trade, came to modify his embrace of free trade by supporting the argument that "infant-industries" deserve protection until they can get their production costs lowered enough to become competitive in world markets. The imposition of barriers to imports helped create the home markets required by new industry. By limiting supply, protectionist measures raise the prices at which industrialists can sell, boosting their profits and ability to invest. In consumer goods industries, the higher prices undercut the real wages of their customers, who pay this supposedly limited, short-term subsidy for the sake of the development of industry.

In a speech given in January 1848, the year he and Engels published the *Manifesto*, Marx addressed free trade and protectionist policies directly and at length. After reproducing the arguments on all sides, especially mocking capitalist arguments about how one policy or the other would benefit workers, he shows how, on the contrary, workers suffer from both policies. "What is Free Trade," he asks, "under the present conditions of society?" His answer: "Freedom of Capital. . . freedom of Capital to crush the worker." What of protection? "The Protective system is nothing but a means of establishing manufacture upon a large scale, that is to say, of making it dependent upon the market of the world; and from the moment that dependence upon the market of world is established, there is more or less dependence upon Free Trade too."

Given this analysis, he goes on to conclude, "Generally speaking, the Protective system in these days is conservative, while the Free trade system works destructively. It breaks up old nationalities and carries the antagonism of proletariat and bourgeoisie to the uttermost point. In a word, the Free Trade system hastens the Social Revolution. In this revolutionary sense alone, gentlemen, I am in favor of Free Trade."[119]

Today, conflicts over the choice of free trade versus protectionist policies persist. Campaign contributions have bought some industries continuing protection for their markets and their profits, at the expense of those who buy their products. The sugar industry in the US is one durable example. The price of sugar has been, since 1789, artificially raised by tariffs.[120]

---

118.   Friedrich List, *The National System of Political Economy* (1841), New York: Garland Publishing, 1974.

119.   "Speech on the Question of Free Trade", January 9, 1848, *MECW, vol. 6,* pp. 463–465.

120.   While contemplating the cost of the sugar in your drink—and its impact on your health—think too about what it took to produce that sugar and get it to the soft drink factory or dining room table. The history of sugar is one of greed, slavery and

After the Great Depression, multinational corporate interests increasingly demanded free trade. Most economists concurred, arguing that competing protectionist measures had deepened the crisis of the 1930s. The General Agreement on Tariffs and Trade (GATT) of 1947 was formed to reduce obstacles to trade. In the wake of World War II, American companies, less damaged by war than their foreign counterparts, wanted as much freedom to invest and export as possible. Reduced trade barriers and subsidies, such as the Marshall Plan (1948–51), where some 13 billion dollars were loaned to countries in Western Europe, facilitated a huge flow of consumer and capital goods from the US.[121] While policymakers saw the Plan as a way to stabilize Western Europe at the dawn of the Cold War, economists justified it mainly by recourse to Ricardo's arguments for free trade. For economists and for business media, trade is almost universally portrayed in terms of the relationships between nations, rather than between classes. Ricardo laid out his argument about "comparative advantage" and "gains from trade" in terms of trading between England and Portugal. Politicians and TV commentators today talk about improving or worsening trade between countries such as the United States and China. Determining such conflicts and influencing the negotiations between governments, however, are the class forces at work within the individual countries and across borders.

Negotiated in secret collaboration with business interests, NAFTA provides a good example. On the surface, it appeared to be simply an agreement between the governments of the US, Canada and Mexico to form a free trade zone that could compete with the increasingly unified European Union, created in 1993. Both blocs contain huge populations, large internal markets and enormous combined resources. But behind this appearance lay patterns of struggle between capital and labor.

The interest of American and Canadian corporations in including Mexico in a trading bloc derives from the possibilities of pitting Mexican workers against American and Canadian workers who are paid more and have more legal rights. Having already moved thousands of jobs south into Mexico, corporations have used the threat of moving to Mexico, where

---

imperialism. Along with the 1969 film *Burn!*, which dramatizes some early Caribbean sugar history, read Sidney W. Mintz's *Sweetness and Power: The Place of Sugar in Modern History*, New York: Penguin, 1985. One of the more interesting ways to explore the interconnections of capitalism is to trace the "material circuits" of various commodities, from the point of production to the point of consumption (and in some cases to the disposition of by-products and waste). These circuits often prove to be not only paths of capitalist valorization and devalorization, but also paths of the circulation of struggle.

121.   Reduced barriers to capital investment, achieved through the rules of the International Monetary Fund, created in 1945, also facilitated a wave of investment by increasingly multinational "American" corporations.

workers are much less powerful, both on the job (lower wages and benefits) and off (little social security, unenforced environmental protection, political repression), as a threat to obtain concessions (lower wages, more flexible work rules, etc.) from American and Canadian workers.[122] Such outsourcing requires that goods once produced in the US or Canada, but now produced in Mexico can be freely exported back into the US and Canada. Without the ability to do so, such a continental strategy against labor could not work.

Opposition to the treaty clarified the class content of trade. Literally thousands of protestors from all three countries—from unions to environmentalists—collaborated to oppose a corporate-friendly NAFTA. Coalitions of hundreds of groups in each country organized to oppose the treaty. Those coalitions, in turn, linked together to support each other through international discussion and the circulation of information. This was the first time that such grassroots organization occurred on this scale.[123] Although those efforts were defeated, and NAFTA went into effect in 1994, the network of new contacts prepared the ground for the subsequent alter-globalization movement that mobilized against the World Trade Organization (WTO), formed to undercut local democracy by imposing global trading rules. Grassroots groups such as People's Global Action organized massive demonstrations in Geneva, Seattle and elsewhere. Just how much of a threat to capitalist interests such mobilization constitutes can be measured by the increasing violence unleashed by the state in Quebec City, in Prague and in Genoa, including beatings, torture and killings. Measured by the breadth of mobilization and the degree of repression, the intensity of class struggle around trade has become great indeed.

Banks, Debt and Taxes

The last of the mechanisms of amassing investible funds that Marx highlights is the manipulation of public debt and taxes. He describes a process that would grow and develop over time to become one of the most powerful levers of capitalist control in our day. He deals with this issue at both the national and international level, and so should we. The process is a simple one, although obscure to most of us. Capitalists loan money to the state to

---

122.   For a dramatic exploration of the consequences to Flint, Michigan of such displacement, watch Michael Moore's film *Roger and Me* (1989) about the results of General Motors moving auto plants and some 30,000 jobs to Mexico.
123.   For a capitalist view of the dangers of such international grassroots mobilization, see Cathryn Thorup, "The Politics of Free Trade and the Dynamics of Cross-Border Coalitions in U.S. Mexican Relations", *Columbia Journal of World Business*, vol. XXVI, no. 11, Summer 1991, pp. 12–26.

finance expenses over and above state revenues (budgetary deficits). The state uses the money to pay for its expenditures—Marx emphasizes those which support the process of primitive accumulation—and then pays back the borrowed money, at interest, with money acquired through taxation, an act which Marx describes as turning money into capital "as with the stroke of an enchanter's wand."[124] Here he emphasizes taxes on subsistence goods, which impoverishes peasants and artisans and results in their expropriation. Augmented, the money loaned becomes capital—finance or usurer's capital. Although not based on the extraction of surplus labor from industrial workers analyzed in the rest of the book, this amassing does make such extraction possible. This process in turn, because national debt takes the form of negotiable securities, provides one basis for the expansion of banking and financial markets, which also facilitate financial intermediation or the pooling of money that can be used to finance industrial capital.

Marx does *not* discuss, at this point, something he knows to be a complicated issue: the conditions under which amassed money-capital becomes available for industrial investment. Already quite familiar with the problem in the 1850s, he analyzed and wrote many articles about it, years before *Capital* went to press. He criticized, at length, the French *Crédit Mobilier*, an early financial institution that claimed to be channeling capital into industry. Marx showed that it greatly overstated the degree to which this was being done and was in fact guilty of a great deal of speculation with other people's money.[125] He claims the development of financial markets played a key role in amassing the money that financed industrialization, but his focus is more on the amassing than on its channeling to industrial investment.

Today, when the United States and many other countries have highly developed financial markets, this remains an issue of contention. One of the most severe critiques of financial deregulation that began at the end of the 1970s has been how it facilitated the diversion of money out of real capital investment and into the "casino economy" with its various forms of speculation, from real estate through stocks to mergers and takeovers.[126]

---

124. *Capital, Vol. I*, p. 919.
125. A study of Marx's examination of the *Crédit Mobilier* can be found in Joseph Ricciardi, "Essays on the Role of Money and Finance in Economic Development", University of Texas at Austin, PhD dissertation, 1985, some of which was more recently published as "Marx on Financial Intermediation: Lessons from the French *Crédit Mobilier* in the *New York Daily Tribune*", *Science & Society*, vol. 79, no. 4, October 2015, pp. 497–526. Marx's writings on this subject are now easily available in *MECW, vol. 15* and thereabouts.
126. See Anthony Bianco, "The Casino Society: Playing with Fire", *BusinessWeek*, September 16, 1985 and Susan Strange, *Casino Capitalism*, New York: Basil Blackwell, 1986.

The result was very slow growth in the real economy, collapse of the US savings and loan industry and the stock market crash of 1987. Similarly, the freeing of financial markets from state regulation has been contentious in the Global South. Free market economists make the kind of claim Marx is making in this chapter: that the development of such markets would speed investment. But, is Marx's analysis of the *Crédit Mobilier* more to the point? To what degree does such freeing simply result in financial swindling and speculation rather than investment in new factories? The international financial crises associated with the European Exchange Rate Mechanism (ERM) in 1992; the Peso crisis of 1994; the Asia crisis of 1997; the Russian financial crisis of 1998; the repeated failures in the late 1990s to implement the European Monetary Union; the Turkish financial crisis in 2000; and the 2001–02 financial crisis in Argentina and, most recently, the financial crisis of 2007–09 have kept the issue alive.

The repayment of sovereign debt as a risk-free use of the state's power of taxation to multiply the capital of finance capitalists has certainly become a permanent feature of capitalism. The current US federal deficit is a case in point. Excesses of government expenditures over tax revenues have been financed with hundreds of billions of dollars of debt, loans from private capitalists being repaid at market rates of interest with taxpayers' money.

Ever since Marx was writing, international loans to foreign governments have also provided a lucrative way to convert bank money into finance capital. In the early twentieth century, Western bankers sought, with their nations' gunboats and marines, to obtain a slice of the royal Chinese debt.[127] After World War II, the Marshall Plan initiated decades of US government loans to other governments, in return for concessions to US diplomatic objectives and the interests of multinational corporations. More recently, in the 1970s, OPEC petrodollars, deposited in Western banks, were lent to desperate oil-importing countries at flexible rates of interest, to be repaid with export revenues via various forms of taxation. When American monetary policy tightened after 1980, interest rates soared, the world economy was pitched into depression, and those borrowing governments faced a crisis. Unable to raise the sums necessary to repay the sudden spike in repayment obligations, the result was an international debt crisis. Further loans to repay earlier loans were conditional on the imposition of austerity on the workers of the indebted countries.[128]

127.   See Scott Nearing and Joseph Freeman, *Dollar Diplomacy: A Study in American Imperialism*, New York: Monthly Review Press, 1966.
128.   See Cleaver, "Close the IMF, Abolish Debt and End Development: a Class Analysis of the International Debt Crisis", *Capital & Class, vol. 13, issue 3*, no. 39, Winter 1989, pp. 17–50.

Slavery and Child Labor

At the end of the chapter, Marx emphasizes what were clearly to him two of the most obnoxious and reprehensible features of early capitalism: slavery and the exploitation of children. The wage-slavery of the Old World, he argued, had the formal slavery of the New World as its foundation. The taking of slaves in Africa, the trade in slaves that brought them to the Americas and the peculiar institution of plantation slavery were all vital in producing the raw material worked up in British industry: textiles from cotton, rum from sugar and so on.[129] Thus, the capitalism emerging in this period was not just British capitalism but was an Atlantic capitalism of a particularly vicious nature. Not only did it plunder and loot, but it imposed both literal as well as waged slavery.

Though Marx joined others of his day in condemning the exploitation of children in mines and textile mills, decades would pass before effective child labor laws would put an end to the most flagrant abuses of this sort in the US and other industrial centers. That said, the exploitation of children has never ended, not in the US or in other countries around the world. The subjection of children to forced labor for pitiful payment outside any free labor market is still common.[130] This is not about fast food stores hiring teens, or children put to work by television and Hollywood producers, but rather the forced prostitution of children and their exploitation in industrial production (such as carpet making, cocoa production, cobalt mining) around the world under conditions every bit as atrocious as those described by Marx. Most out-and-out slavery, the buying and selling of individuals, has been effectively abolished, with a few exceptions, including the sex trade where children are trafficked along with adults. Groups such as the Anti-Slavery Society and the International Labor Organization periodically publish reports of the depressing extent of such exploitation.[131]

---

129. This infamous pattern is now known as the "Atlantic triangular slave trade." Manufactured goods were traded in Africa for slaves. Slaves were traded to the Western Hemisphere for raw materials. Raw materials were traded to New England, Britain and Europe.

130. If slavery involves legally enforced, unpaid labor, then we should include two other groups of incarcerated workers: children in schools and prisoners in both public and private jails—even if individuals are being neither bought nor sold.

131. Those reports include an ILO textbook (at www.ilo.org/ipec/information resources/wcms_ipec_pub_174/lang--en/index.htm), well worth reading. It has many illustrations and personal testimony from children as well as analysis of the depth of the problem. One such group, the Concerned Center of Child Workers in Nepal, publishes a newsletter (*Voice of Child Workers*) in which you can find ample illustration of the extent of the problem in that country.

These aspects of capitalism have been around since its inception and continue, wherever business has the power to impose them. As Marx points out, if you really want to understand capitalism (or any other social system of class domination) study it where it exists with the fewest constraints.[132]

CHAPTER 32: THE HISTORICAL TENDENCY OF CAPITALIST ACCUMULATION

Outline of Marx's Analysis

Three historical phases:

1. Either: a) slaves, serfs or b) personal private property in means of production

  – based on the labor of its owner
  – peasants' own land, artisans' own tools
  – fragmentation of holdings, excludes large-scale cooperation
  – small-scale industry
  – "first negation: of individual private property"
  – violent and protracted

2. Capitalism: private property in means of production

  – based on expropriation of personal private property
  – cooperation, division of labor in workplace, socialized labor
  – large-scale industry, application of science
  – expropriation of capitalists by capitalists via centralization of capital
  – internationalization of production and markets
  – growth in mass of misery, oppression, slavery, exploitation
  – growth in the revolt of the working class
  – expropriation of the expropriators
  – "second negation: of capitalist private property"
  – quicker, less violent

3. Social property in the means of production

  – founded on changes under capitalism
  – based on the carrying on of production by society
  – cooperation and possession in common of means of production

---

132. *Capital, Vol. I,* p. 916, footnote 4.

Commentary

This chapter sums up both the historical processes of primitive accumulation and the dynamics of capitalist development itself, especially the processes of centralization of capital and class struggle, which Marx argues will bring the overthrow of capitalism.

The Ideology of Private Property

Marx juxtaposes *capitalist private property* to small-scale, *personal private property* in the means of production, e.g., land and tools, which he notes existed to some degree under most earlier social systems. He contemptuously condemns the capitalist ideology of private property, not only because it serves as a justification for violence and exploitation, but also because it ignores how the creation of *capitalist* private property involved the mass destruction of earlier forms of property.

Private property is usually justified by appealing to people's sense that it is only proper for *individuals* to have property/control/possession of the fruits of their own labor. Farmers who work the land should have property rights in that land and whatever their cultivation can produce. Artisans who weave cloth should own their looms and the cloth they have woven and be free to determine what becomes of it. Anyone who works, gets paid a wage, and uses that wage to buy something has a right to the personal ownership of that thing because, in a transformed way, it was obtained through personal effort. Such were the kind of arguments put forward by John Locke (1632–1704) in his *Second Treatise of Civil Government* in 1690.[133]

Marx argues that such reasoning, based on individual effort, is hypocritically used to justify something very different: the *capitalist* ownership and control of goods produced by other people (i.e., the workers in the factories owned and controlled by the capitalists). A concept of justice that makes sense at the level of the individual does not necessarily make sense at the social level, if applied to property relations between factory owners and workers. This distinction is ignored or skimmed over for the sake of justifying capitalist control over their workers' products. But why should capitalists "own" the products of workers? Because the capitalists own the machines and raw materials? But labor is just as vital, perhaps more so, and that is "owned" by the workers. Shouldn't *both* capitalists and workers own the products and share in whatever revenue comes from their sale? In Chapter 6, Marx argues that because they purchase workers' "labor-power"

---

133.   John Locke, *Two Treatises of Government*, Peter Laslett (ed.), Cambridge: Cambridge University Press, 1960, student edn., 1988.

(their ability and willingness to labor) capitalists own everything in the production process, i.e., both means of production and the labor of their workers, and therefore have unique property right to the products. However, one judges this situation, it is quite clearly not covered by an ideology based on the situation of individuals.

As the material in this section of primitive accumulation has made clear, the capitalists used violence to wipe out the personal means of production of most people, monopolizing them in their own hands. In this process, they showed no respect for "private property." How hypocritical then to use moral principles applicable to the individual to justify the results of the violation of those principles.

One other note on this mutation of property rights: while today there are many cases of personally owned, small businesses (mostly short-lived), the vast bulk of capitalist operations are organized through limited liability corporations in which "ownership" is diffused among a great many anonymous shareholders and their "property" is controlled by a handful of managers and, perhaps, a few shareholders who own substantial blocks of stock. Because of this mutation, capitalists sought, successfully, to have property laws rewritten in such a way that "corporations" are treated in much the same way as individuals with respect to property and other rights but not with respect to liability.[134] Rights are concentrated; liability is limited. This is the hypocritical context of the ideology of property rights: the property of giant multinational corporations (who often exercise power greater than many nations) is justified using ethical arguments applicable to a very different reality.

Revolution and Communism

Although he does not use the terms revolution and communism in this chapter, the "expropriation of the expropriators" clearly refers to the revolutionary overthrow of capitalists, while "social property" or the "possession in common of the land and the means of production" also clearly refers to communism as the form of post-capitalist society. In *Capital*, Marx makes only passing allusions to these two phenomena. He sets out an analysis of capitalism, but neither an analysis of possible revolutions nor blueprints for post-capitalist society.

Nevertheless, the book has a great deal about class struggle against capitalism. He shows, for example, how alienated workers come to constitute a

---

134. The most notorious recent example has been the *Citizens United v. Federal Election Commission* case in which a conservative Supreme Court used the free speech clause of the First Amendment to the Constitution to grant corporations the same ability to spend money influencing elections as individuals.

threat to the survival of the system by self-organizing in factories—created by capitalists for the purpose of control and exploitation. He mentions such things as strikes (Chapter 10) and machine breaking (Chapter 15), but nothing about actual processes of revolution. In this chapter, the only comment touching this issue is his assertion that the overthrow of capital will be less violent and less protracted than the capitalist overthrow of the earlier modes of production. This will be true, he suggests, because workers are many and capitalists are few. But from such a comment to an analysis of how such an overthrow might take place is obviously a long jump and has been the subject of Marxist debate and organization ever since.

Both before and after he wrote *Capital*, Marx, along with Friedrich Engels and other friends, engaged directly in political struggles against feudal absolutism and against capitalism. Before and during the 1848 Revolutions in Europe, Marx and Engels both contributed to the emergence of a revolution against the absolutist state in Germany through journalism (publishing newspaper articles, the *Communist Manifesto*, etc.) and then, in Engels's case, through direct participation in armed struggle against the state. Although there is relatively little in their writings on the subject of the methods to be used to overthrow capitalism, I think it is fair to say that while they thought many different forms of struggle were appropriate at different times and places, they were not optimistic about the likelihood of capitalists voluntarily stepping aside to allow workers to take over. After Marx's death in 1883, during the years of the Second International (1889–1914), Engels and many other Marxists had great hopes that increases in workers' right to vote (first men, then women) and the rise of social democratic parties could bring about a peaceful end to capitalism. Not only did that dream die with the onset of World War I, but in the decades since, even when social democrats have gained national power through elections, they have either proved complicit with capitalism or been overthrown. As a result, Marxists have split over this issue. Some continue to embrace an electoral path to the transcendence of capitalism; others have thought it impossible and organize for violent revolution.

Given his analysis of the growth of class struggle, always situating its development within the material conditions of the organization of capital and the self-organization of the workers, Marx also thought that the paths through capitalism to communism were multiple. Twenty-two years after the 1848 Revolutions, another revolution erupted in France and created the Paris Commune. Marx followed that revolution—centered in Paris—closely and his commentaries are among the most interesting of his writings. In the *Civil War in France* (1871), he describes and analyzes the sequence of events by which the French government was overthrown, a new revolutionary government established and then crushed by the old regime.[135] Marx drew no formulae from these events, any more than he had from the 1848 Revolutions. In each case, he sought to judge the adequacy of the measures taken in terms of the actual historical conditions obtaining at the time.

This approach made it impossible for Marx to design revolutionary strategies before the fact, a priori; every revolution would be unique in terms of which particular methods would be appropriate and successful. Clearly, he felt this to be the case in the 1870s when he was consulted about the possibilities of revolution in Russia. As I mentioned in my commentary on Chapter 26, he rejected the idea of applying his work on England, without qualification, to Russia and argued that the existence of a materially different situation, especially the existence of the peasant *mir*, implied that another path to and through revolution to "social regeneration" was at least possible.

Something similar can be said about Marx's approach to communism—a term chosen to differentiate his politics from existing ideas of socialism—a post-capitalist, classless society. In *Capital*, very little is said about this. He only mentions "social property" being established "on the basis of the achievements of the capitalist era: namely cooperation and the possession in common of the land and the means of production produced by labor itself."[136] We can assemble a variety of such limited comments from Marx's writings, from the 1840s to those in the 1880s, but nowhere is there a prescription or formula, a design or a blueprint, for either the structure or the workings of a communist society.

In the mass media, the adjective "Marxist" is often used interchangeably with "communist," as in "a Marxist society" or a "Marxist government." Such terms are also used to refer either to some hypothetical post-capitalist society, or to existing societies that call themselves "socialist" or "communist," such as the Union of Soviet Socialist Republics (USSR). Both uses are erroneous. First, Marx everywhere eschewed "utopianism" which, by definition, involves intentionally designing a better society that does not yet exist.[137] There have been many efforts to found utopian communities but

---

135. *MECW, vol. 22*, pp. 307–359.
136. *Capital, Vol. I,* p. 929.
137. For an example of Marx and Engels's friendly, yet critical, comments on the utopian socialists, see the discussion in the *Communist Manifesto*. Given the relatively underdeveloped struggles of workers of their time, they argue, the utopians were led to substitute their own visions for the analysis of the positive directions of the struggles. "Historical action," the utopians hope, "is to yield to their personal inventive action, historically created conditions of emancipation to fantastic ones, and the gradual, spontaneous class organization of the proletariat to an organization of society specially contrived by these inventors. Future history resolves itself, in their eyes, into the propaganda

none of them were designed by Karl Marx. He clearly believed in trying to imagine and in trying to achieve a better society, but he also felt, as in the case of revolution, that the form and content of such a society would be determined as a collective social project based on historical givens, and not on the implementation of any one, or even a few, persons' ideas. Second, the founders and managers of the USSR appropriated Marx's analysis of capitalism in two ways. They used his critique of capitalism to denounce the sins of their Western adversaries during the Cold War and, ironically, they appropriated his analysis of capitalist accumulation as a guide for accumulation within their own system.[138] The resulting "socialism" amounted to a new form of *state capitalism*, with only the mix of planning and markets differing from that in the West.

A basic methodological principle permeates Marx's work on revolution and communism: to understand the direction in which society seems to be evolving, study the social forces at work forcing changes. For some idea about what a future society might be like, look both at those aspects of the current society which people are struggling to eliminate and at those new kinds of relationships they are struggling to bring into being or to nourish to full growth. This approach to understanding social change (as the basis for contributing to it), makes studying Marx still useful.

Dialectics

Towards the end of his analysis in this chapter, Marx uses two obscure terms: "the first negation" and "the negation of the negation." Both derive from the writings of German philosopher Georg Wilhelm Friedrich Hegel (1770–1831) that Marx studied as a student and critiqued in the 1840s.[139]

---

and the practical carrying out of their social plans.... In proportion as the modern class struggle develops and takes definite shape, this fantastic standing apart from the contest, these fantastic attacks on it, lose all practical value and all theoretical justification." *MECW,* vol. *6,* pp. 515–516.

138. This appropriation is clear in an essay by Yevgeni Preobrazhensky (1886–1937) titled "Primitive Socialist Accumulation" (1926) devoted to accelerating investment in industry via the expropriation of peasant surpluses. See Preobrazhensky, *The New Economics,* Oxford: Clarendon Press, 1967, pp. 77–146. The main thing that differentiated his kind of accumulation from that analyzed in this part of *Capital* was the word "socialist." Stalin instituted that expropriation with a vengeance via forced collectivization. See also Rita di Leo, "I Bolscevichi e «il capitale»," *Contropiano,* maggio-agosto, 2/1969, pp. 273–344, and her *Il modello di stalin: il rapporto tra politica e economia nel socialismo realizzato,* Milano: Feltrinelli, 1977.

139. Notably "Critique of the Hegelian Dialectic and Philosophy as a Whole" (1843), *MECW,* vol. *3,* pp. 326–346, and "The German Ideology" (1846), *MECW,* vol. *5,* pp. 15–539.

In Hegel's philosophical system, everything, both thought and the rest of the cosmos, develops "dialectically." That is to say, he saw everything unfolding in a complex kind of movement, which he analyzed in a series of lectures and books. Leaving aside the rest of the cosmos, Marx felt that Hegel was correct in grasping the form of social development that occurred within capitalism as dialectical. Therefore, from time to time, he found Hegelian concepts accurately denoted various aspects of the social relations of capital.

In this case, the "first negation" was capital's destruction of pre-capitalist social relations. As was typical of such a Hegelian concept, this first negation both destroyed some aspects of the old society (personal property), yet at the same time preserved something of the past (private property), while creating something new (capitalist private property).

The "negation of the negation" Marx imagined, would be the suspension of capital's monopolization of the means of production (capitalist private property), with all that entails, through revolution. Yet, again, Marx thought this second negation would also preserve something of the old system (cooperation and a sophisticated system of social production) while eliminating its more obnoxious characteristics (class domination, exploitation and alienation).

The concept of dialectics is most often presented in terms of the famous triad: thesis, anti-thesis, synthesis, in which a thesis (e.g., capitalism) gives rise to its anti-thesis (e.g., the working class), and this contradiction is resolved (e.g., through revolution) in a way that produces fundamental changes (e.g., the elimination of classes) while retaining progressive features of the old contradiction (e.g., socialized production). This triad, however, is only one brief moment of the Hegelian dialectic, spelled out at great length in his *Science of Logic* (1816) and other books, and also only one of the many moments of his analysis which Marx thought relevant to the analysis of social relations under capitalism.

There are reasons, however, to think long and hard about the differences as well as the similarities between Hegel and Marx. For Hegel, his dialectics was a cosmology, a science of an unending reality. There are plenty of reasons, however, to think that while Marx saw the social relationships of capitalism as dialectical—and therefore containing aspects grasped by Hegel—the antagonism of working-class struggle always posed the threat of a revolution in which synthesis would be impossible and the dialectical character of the class relationship ruptured completely. By implication, there is no a priori reason to think that the social relationships of post-capitalist society would be dialectical in the same sense that they are in capitalism.

CHAPTER 33: THE MODERN THEORY
OF COLONIALISM

Outline of Marx's Analysis

True colonies:

- "virgin soil" colonized by free immigrants, e.g., America, Australia
- as opposed to colonies constructed from old societies, e.g., India, Indonesia
- in true, or free, colonies there is a dramatic contradiction between:
- the capitalists who want to hire workers to valorize their capital
- and people who, because of the availability of land, become independent producers

Edward Gibbon Wakefield (1796–1862), a kidnapper, ex-con and English political economist

- looks at this situation in the true colonies
- sees how labor markets are constantly "understocked"
- and capitalists unable to valorize their capital
- deduces the need to deprive people of the possibility of being independent
- so, his solution is to put an artificial price on the land
- to force immigrants to work for capitalists
- and what they eventually pay for the land can be used to import more workers

Marx applauds the honesty of this analysis because:

- Wakefield is admitting to the need to separate people from the land
- in order for capitalism to develop
- and in the process, he [Wakefield] admits people are better off as free producers
- all this ends "the illusion" of "free contracts" between equals in the labor market

However, when approaches such as Wakefield's were tried by the British in Australia:

- they were undermined as the flow of immigrants simply diverted itself to the US
- but eventually the "squandering" of land on aristocrats and capitalists
- together with the influx of gold seekers
- and the destruction of artisans by cheap British imports
- succeeded in producing a labor surplus

Thus, once more, Marx concludes that the secret of primitive accumulation is:

- "the annihilation of that private property. . . the expropriation of the worker"

Commentary

Three interesting dimensions to Marx's analysis stand out. First, the chapter extends his previous comments on the hypocrisy of capitalist ideology of private property. Wakefield's work illustrates clearly how that ideology is set aside when it becomes an obstacle to capital accumulation.[140] Second, it expands his discussion of colonialism in Chapter 31. Third, his reading of Wakefield provides a political methodology for reading other economists.

Land and Power

By demonstrating an acute awareness of how access to land helps people resist the labor market and wage labor, Wakefield confirms Marx's analysis in Chapter 27 of the capitalist use of expropriation. Unlike England, in Australia and in North America, there was too much land to enclose. Immigrants—both those fleeing capital's depredations in Europe and those transported as criminals—fled to unenclosed land to avoid the clutches of waged labor. This goes far toward illuminating the drama of past and current struggles over land tenure and its reform around the world. Unfortunately, the backdrop to this story of struggle between colonizing capitalists and immigrant workers in Australia and in North America, was the expropriation, slaughter and displacement of the aboriginal population.

As we have seen, the struggle over land did not end with the establishment of capitalism. To begin with, the elimination of smallholding peasants and farmers was often very incomplete. Where the incompleteness was substantial, there has been ongoing conflict between small farmers and capitalists over control of land. On the whole, small farmers have lost; their numbers and the proportion of land under their control has declined more or less continuously. But this history of defeat has included dogged resistance. Even today small farmers continue to fight against their expulsion from the land.

At the same time, a great many of the dispossessed, all around the world, have fought to regain what they, or their ancestors, have lost. In some countries, they have achieved considerable success, either through revolutionary or, sometimes, legal means. One important example is Mexico. In the first decades of the twentieth century, the struggle for land was a central issue during the Mexican revolution. Millions of peasants mobilized in 1910 not only to overthrow the Porfiriato, but to retake lands that had

---

140. For more on Wakefield's work within the evolution of classical political economy, see Michael Perelman's *The Invention of Capitalism: Classical Political Economy and the Secret History of Primitive Accumulation*, Durham, NC: Duke University Press, 2000, pp. 324–339.

been stolen from them since colonial times. In 1934, from the government of Lázaro Cárdenas, they won the redistribution of millions of acres of land to *ejidos*—a fundamental reorganization of land tenure from private to unalienable communal property. For decades following that redistribution, capitalists renewed their efforts to once again monopolize land. Finally, in 1991, Mexican President Salinas railroaded through a change in the constitution undermining the legal protections for *ejidal* lands—as one giveaway in negotiations over NAFTA. Three years later, Mexican *campesinos* rose up once again, this time in the form of the EZLN. That rebellion, launched on January 1, 1994, the same day NAFTA went into effect, constituted what indigenous communities in the southern state of Chiapas saw as a life-or-death effort to defend their land, their communities and their ways of life.

Other major examples of peasant revolt in the twentieth century—always including the fight for land—included, most notably, the revolutions in Russia and in China. Despite the way local, revolutionary Marxists argued for the "leading role" of the industrial proletariat in those countries, they were well aware that the vast majority of the population demanding change were peasants. Slogans including "Land and Bread" were designed to appeal to both peasants and industrial workers. Peasant struggles for land also played a key role in many decolonization movements, e.g., India, Vietnam, as well as in battles for land reforms in the post-colonial period. Such struggles continue today all around the world.

Despite such overwhelming evidence of the ability of peasants to mobilize, many "orthodox" Marxists have attacked small landholders, farmers and peasants as structurally reactionary. They have emphasized Marx and Engels's comments on the failure of peasant revolts in Germany, on the limitations of growth potential in English smallholdings, and on the politics of peasants in France.[141] Doing so justified systematically subordinating peasant needs and desires to what they viewed as more progressive objectives of the factory proletariat.[142] The results in the Soviet Union, in

---

141.   Marx's best-known comments on the peasantry are in his essay "The Eighteenth Brumaire of Louis Bonaparte" (1851), *MECW, vol. 11*, pp. 187–192. Engels's most thorough work on the subject was: "The Peasant War in Germany" (1850) in *MECW, vol. 10*, pp. 397–482.

142.   Lenin wrote endlessly on the subject, largely as part of an ongoing debate in Russia, first with the Populists and then among the Bolsheviks. On the Bolshevik debates, see Moshe Lewin and Irene Nove, *Russian Peasants and Soviet Power*, New York: W. W. Norton, 1968, 1975, Chapter 6: "The Party and the Accursed Problem"; and Stephen F. Cohen, *Bukharin and the Bolshevik Revolution*, New York: Vintage, 1971, Chapter 6: "Bukharinism and the Road to Socialism." For an overview of the orthodox Marxist tradition (Engels, Lenin, Mao) of anti-peasant analysis, see Chapter 1 in Ann Lucas de Rouffignac, *The Contemporary Peasantry in Mexico*, New York: Praeger, 1985.

China and elsewhere has been to turn Marxism into an ideology of rural expropriation via collectivization and state control.

Yet, here, as in his comments cited earlier about the Russian peasant commune, we see Marx's appreciation of the advantages of personal property in the land and its associated means of production. In commenting on Wakefield, he emphasizes how control over land "is the secret. . . of the prosperity of the colonies." He points out how Wakefield admits that this control benefits small farmers: "He depicts the mass of the American people as well-to-do, independent, enterprising and comparatively cultured, whereas 'the English agricultural laborer [with no land] is a miserable wretch, a pauper.'"[143] While it is certain that Marx was no Jeffersonian romantic dreaming that all life should be organized around the small farm, it is nevertheless clear that he understood both the benefits and the power that people derive from being self-sufficient and not dependent on capitalists for a wage. Orthodox Marxist-Leninists in the USSR, who justified forced collectivization as "primitive socialist accumulation," understood this as well. Like Mr. Wakefield, they sought to subordinate peasants' labor-power to the accumulation of capital. Unfortunately for their plans, the allocation of small subsistence plots of land to Russian peasants gave them a vital resource to resist their exploitation on collective and state farms. Both Soviet planners, in their day, and Chinese Communist Party leaders were forced, time and again, to capitulate to the long war of attrition peasants have carried out based, in part, on their little plots of land. The struggles have continued in the post-Soviet era in Russia, in Eastern Europe and in China.

Reading Economics Politically

Marx's treatment of Wakefield provides us a paradigm for reading the writings of economists. Unlike many critics who tend to focus on the ideological aspect of capitalist thought, Marx focuses on the strategic meaning of Wakefield's ideas. He is primarily interested in the strategies and tactics that Wakefield proposes for gaining control over workers. Marx's presentation in *Capital* provides us with an insight into the class content of such approaches and the dangers they represent.[144] Here Marx provides a report on the enemy's strategy that both makes sense of some workers' behavior

---

143. *Capital, Vol. I*, p. 938.
144. Marx spent considerable time and energy analyzing bourgeois economics. The main results can be found in the three volumes of *Theories of Surplus Value*, but his insights and comments are scattered through many other works.

on the battlefields of the class war and provides insights that can guide that of others.[145]

In some sub-fields of economics, such as "development" economics (the contemporary counterpart of Wakefield's work), the strategic content of economic theory is often very clear. For example, in my commentary on Chapter 29, I highlight the work of W. A. Lewis who wrote about how to use money and inflation against workers to the benefit of capitalists. In other sub-fields, this content is often less clear and must be deciphered. For example, in Keynesian macroeconomics, aggregation tends to hide class relations in nebulous categories. "Consumption," for example, denotes not just the expenditure of working-class wages and salaries on consumption goods and services but includes that of all receivers of income. Similarly, "savings" includes not only the unexpended income of "households" but retained profits of corporations. Nevertheless, by studying the evolution of the theory within the historical context of class struggle, we can decode such concepts and discover their class meaning.

For example, we can recognize in the centrality of the "consumption function," and of "demand" more generally, Keynes's response to the changing balance of class power in the 1920s and 1930s. His theoretical concepts expressed his recognition of a situation in which working-class wages could no longer be usefully viewed simply in terms of costs—to be held down as much as possible—but had to be understood as the main source of markets for final output. As such, he pointed out how their increase can induce capitalist investment and accumulation. Keynes's genius lay in seeing how, when they could no longer be repressed, workers' demands for wages, unemployment compensation and social security could be harnessed for capitalist development.

Keynes's own ability to read pre-Keynesian economic theory politically can be seen in his reactions to the return of the pound to the gold standard after World War I. In a remarkable series of articles entitled "The Economic Consequences of Mr. Churchill" (1925), Keynes forced into public scrutiny and debate the strategic class meaning of the return to gold.[146] As he showed, it was no mere technical adjustment, but required a direct attack on working-class wages—an attack which could not be publicly admitted but which would inevitably generate a highly unpopular class war. Although he

---

145.   In the introduction to my book *Reading Capital Politically*, I liken this approach to the portrayal in the movie *Patton* (1970) of General George Patton's reading of German Field Marshall Erwin Rommel's book on tank warfare. Patton read Rommel, not to critique him, but to defeat him.

146.   John Maynard Keynes, "The Economic Consequences of Mr. Churchill", in John Maynard Keynes, *Collected Works*, vol. XIII, Cambridge: Cambridge University Press, 1978, pp. 207–230.

was no Marxist, his political reading of this international monetary policy is very similar, methodologically, to Marx's reading of Wakefield. This kind of reading turns the study of economic theory into an adventure in class espionage. Making clear how economics functions as a tool of capitalist management, facilitates our understanding of the strategies that are being woven against us and thus finding ways to defend ourselves.

4

Part One
Commodities and Money

Now we turn to theory. Parts One through Seven (Chapters 1–25) constitute Marx's presentation of his theory of the antagonistic class relationships
of capitalism. We turn to Part One *after* having studied Part Eight because
it provides an historical framework that makes the abstract material of this
first part easier to understand.

Whereas Part Eight highlighted the historical creation of the two new,
antagonistic classes of capitalism, with vivid descriptions of real moments
in history, Part One offers an analysis of value and money mostly stripped
of historical detail. The organization of his presentation—from the most
fundamental and abstract concepts to more and more concrete ones—
resulted from Marx deciding to take Hegel's *Science of Logic* (1812–16) as
a model for his own presentation. In that work, Hegel-the-philosopher
begins with abstract *being* and works his way towards a theory of the very
concrete cosmos. In Chapter 1, Marx-the-social-revolutionary points to
the commodity, the most elementary form of wealth in capitalism, analyses
it and finds it to be produced by *human labor*, which he calls the "substance
of value." This becomes the point of departure for his presentation. The rest
of Chapter 1 elaborates an analysis not only of the "substance" of value, but
also of its "measure" and its "form," ending with the "money form" of value.

Chapter 1: The Commodity. This chapter can be read forward, from
"abstract labor" to the "money form" as a theory of value. Or, it can be read
backward, from the "money form" to "abstract labor" as the beginnings of a
theory of money. Viewed in this second manner, the next two chapters on
exchange and money elaborate the theory. They do not, however, complete
it—because to do so requires grasping money within the circuits of capital,
exploitation and accumulation which come later in the text.

Chapter 2: The Process of Exchange. Abstracting in Chapter 1 from the
human actors involved in exchange made his presentation subject to his
critique of fetishism. In Chapter 2, he begins to de-fetishize his analysis by
pointing out that commodities do not "bring themselves to market" but are
subject to the will of their owners. This is the first step in situating commodities as moments of human social relationships.

Chapter 3: Money, or the Circulation of Commodities. Marx continues his analysis of money within exchange; how its use facilitates buying and selling, provides a measure of value and standard of price, and so on. He treats the usual aspects of money found in economics textbooks but through his theory of value shows how money embodies the substance and form of the antagonistic class relations of capitalism.

CHAPTER 1: THE COMMODITY

Overview of Chapter

Section 1: The Two Factors of the Commodity: Use-Value and Exchange-Value

  Use-Values
  From Exchange-Value to Value

Section 2: The Dual Character of the Labor Embodied in Commodities

  Useful Labor
  Abstract Labor, or Labor as Source of Value
  Socially Necessary Labor Time

Section 3: The Value Form or Exchange-Value

  a) The Simple, Isolated, or Accidental Form of Value
  b) The Expanded Form of Value
  c) The General Form of Value
  d) The Money Form of Value

Section 4: The Fetishism of the Commodity and its Secret

Preliminary Commentary

Marx's presentation begins with the analysis of commodities—of useful products of human labor that are bought and sold—because:

> The wealth of societies in which the capitalist mode of production prevails appears as "an immense collection of commodities," the individual commodity appears as its elementary form. Our investigation therefore begins with the analysis of a commodity.[1]

---

1. In the preface to the first German edition, in which Marx talks about the method he uses in this chapter, he refers to the commodity form as the cell form: "Moreover, in the analysis of economic forms neither microscopes nor chemical reagents are of

His "wealth of societies" echoes the title of Adam Smith's *The Wealth of Nations* (1776), the foundational text of classical political economy. But when he goes on to specify "in which the capitalist mode of production prevails," we know that he will be analyzing wealth in capitalism, not in any random "nation."

Part Eight on Primitive Accumulation explains why wealth appears as commodities in capitalism—because capitalists have imposed the commodity form on both workers and production. They have stripped people of their land and tools (Chapter 27) and have forced them to sell their willingness and ability to work as a commodity for wages (Chapter 28). These processes created a "home market" (Chapter 30) in which most consumer goods take the form of commodities. In Volume II, Marx restates this point explicitly. "The wage-laborers, the mass of direct producers,. . . must constantly be faced with the necessary means of subsistence in purchasable form, i.e., in the form of commodities. . . When production by means of wage-labour becomes universal, commodity production is bound to be the general form of production."[2] With raw materials, machinery, factories and office buildings being produced by capitalist-controlled wage (or slave) labor, this has also been true for producer goods. Finally, the same is true for everything produced for sale to the state or for export abroad.

Beyond a new organization of production—in which wealth takes the form of commodities—Part Eight also explains how work imposed in this manner results in a class society, made up of capitalists who impose work and workers upon whom work is imposed. Workers, unable to escape the factory or office, continue to resist and sometimes create alternatives. To provide an analysis that can help workers overthrow this system, Chapter 1 explains how commodities are not simply "things produced and sold" but embody characteristics of the antagonistic class relationships of capitalism. The real "wealth" of capitalists is their control over people via imposed work. This fundamental bond must be broken to liberate society from the exploitation characteristic of capitalism and the cruel alienation that results.

Figure 1 portrays the overall structure of his analysis. Section 1 analyzes the commodity into use-value and exchange-value, beneath which lurks "value" whose *substance* is abstract labor. Section 2 examines the *measure* of value—socially necessary labor time. Section 3 explores the complexities

---

assistance. The power of abstraction must replace both. But for bourgeois society, the commodity-form of the product of labor, or the value-form of the commodity, is the economic cell-form. To the superficial observer, the analysis of these forms seems to turn upon minutiae. It does in fact deal with minutiae, but so similarly does microscopic anatomy." *Capital, Vol. I*, p. 90.
2. *Capital, Vol. II*, p. 119.

of the *form* of value. Section 4 calls our attention to the fetishism of the presentation up to this point and prepares us for Chapter 2 that begins de-fetishizing the analysis by situating commodities in the hands of their owners.

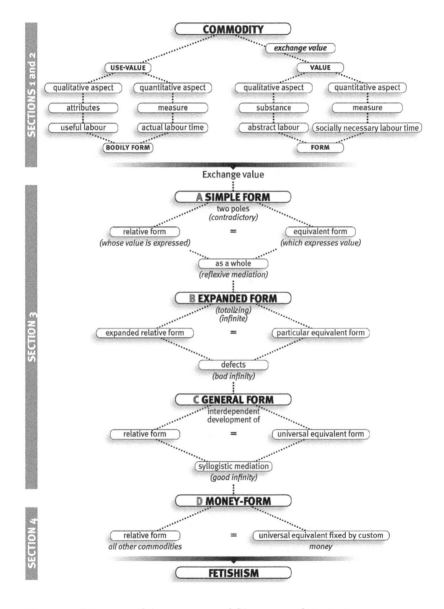

Figure 1   Diagram of the structure of Chapter 1 of *Capital*.

Section 1: The Two Factors of the Commodity: Use-Value and Value

---

Outline of Marx's Analysis

Commodities have two contradictory aspects:

- use-value, or value in use
- exchange-value, or value in exchange
- this contradiction is resolved via exchange

Use-values have qualities and exist as quantities

- various qualities imply various uses
- various qualities imply various measures of quantity
- only realized when used/consumed

Exchange-value appears first as quantity in exchange

- 1 quarter of corn = x cwt of iron
- as use-values corn and iron are different, but
- the equality in exchange implies some common property
- abstracted from their different use-values and
- abstracted from the different useful labors that produced them
- common property = products of undifferentiated labor
- commodities are "crystals of this social substance," abstract labor
- substance of commodity values = abstract labor

Measure of commodity values = labor time socially necessary to produce them

- socially necessary labor time (SNLT) varies with conditions of production

Use-values can exist without value,

- when not produced by labor, e.g., air, unworked soil, wild forests
- when produced by labor but not exchanged, consumed directly

---

Commentary

Marx analyzes the commodity into its two modes of existence. In the first part of Figure 1, we have:

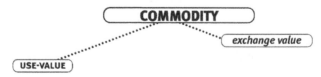

Figure 2   The twofold character of the commodity.

A commodity is a *use-value* because it has a value in use; that is, it "satisfies human wants of some sort or another." It also is an *exchange-value* because it has a value in exchange; that is, it can be exchanged for something else. However, these two different determinations are contradictory. A commodity only becomes a use-value if it used. It only becomes an exchange-value if it is not used but exchanged. Yet, the commodity—sold, bought and consumed—is the unity of these opposites. The strange combination of unity and opposition, in which the opposites only have their meaning vis-à-vis each other and are thus inextricably joined, constitute what Marx means by a *contradiction* or contradictory relation. Just such a contradiction obtains in the antagonistic class relationships of capitalism. Each class stands opposed to the other, but at the same time each exists, as such, only within the relationship. A capitalist class can only exist when those with money can hire people and put them to work; people constitute a working class only in their subordination to capital.[3]

This contradiction, which Marx analyzed in *A Contribution to the Critique of Political Economy*, can only find its solution in the actual exchange process which: "must comprise both the evolution and the solution of these contradictions."[4] He analyzes this solution more fully in Chapter 3, where he describes the realization of the two contradictory aspects in circulation as a *metamorphosis*. Before a commodity is sold and consumed, both use-value and exchange-value have only abstract and potential existences. Selling the commodity results in the metamorphosis of its potential exchange-value into whatever has been obtained in exchange. In Chapter 3, the exchange-value of commodities appears in the form of money. When that money is then exchanged for another commodity, obtained for consumption, exchange-value metamorphoses again into use-value, realized as it is consumed.

The biological metaphor of metamorphosis evokes the *changes in form* through which an insect develops from an egg, through the stages of pupa, larva, chrysalis, to adult; the form and appearance change but the essence remains constant. The Monarch, for example, through all these stages in becoming a butterfly remains *Danaus plexippus*. What remains the same as the commodity goes through its metamorphoses? Marx's answer is

---

3. The contradictory unity of capital and labor is akin to that of masters and slaves analyzed by Hegel in his *Phenomenology of the Spirit* (1807), New York: Oxford University Press, 1977. There, Hegel argues further that masters require that for slaves to be truly slaves, they must acknowledge and accept their servitude. By that criterion neither Spartacus nor Nat Turner were truly slaves. Through their rebellion, they asserted their autonomy and became more than mere workers. The same is true for those who rebel against capitalist control over their lives.

4. *MECW, vol. 29*, p. 285.

"value," whose substance is human labor in the abstract, and whose form is exchange-value. Before turning to how he extracts that answer from his analysis of exchange-value, and what he means by it, let's examine his analysis of use-value in more detail.

Use-Values

At first, Marx suggests that use-values only "provide the material for a special brand of knowledge, namely the commercial knowledge of commodities."[5] Similarly, in *A Contribution to the Critique of Political Economy*, he wrote that use-values "do not express the social relations of production" and that "use-value, as such, lies outside the sphere of investigation of political economy. It belongs in this sphere only when it is itself a determinate form."[6] Despite these comments, throughout his writings we discover that use-value has many "determinate forms," which do express distinct social relations—and are often contested. Even before he published *Capital*, while analyzing how some product can be directly reinvested, Marx notes how this is an example of the importance of "the analysis of *use-value for the determination of economic phenomena*."[7] Here, in Volume I, use-value expresses "value" (see Section 3 below); labor-power has varying use-values (Chapters 6 and 7); the manipulation of use-value is one way of cheating workers/consumers (Chapter 10); machines, besides their use in making things, also serve to control workers (Chapter 15). Many years later, in his "Marginal Notes on Adolph Wagner" (1879), Marx explicitly rejects as "drivel" that use-value has no place in his analysis beyond being one aspect of the commodity. Besides the value of a commodity being represented in the use-value of another, he also points out that "behind use-value is useful labor, one aspect of the twofold character of labor which produces commodities" (see Section 2 below) and "surplus-value itself is derived from a 'specific' use-value of labor-power [see Chapter 7 below]. . . etc., etc." He concludes: "for me use-value plays an important part quite different from its part in economics hitherto."[8] Use-value, therefore, is worth considering at some length.

The use-values of commodities have specific *qualities*, or attributes, produced by specific sorts of concrete useful labor, and specific *quantities*, the result of that labor being exerted over measurable amounts of time.

---

5. *Capital, Vol. I*, p. 126.
6. *MECW, vol. 29*, p. 270.
7. *MECW, vol. 32*, p. 120.
8. "Marginal Notes on Adolph Wagner's *Lehrbuch der politischen oekonomie*", *MECW, vol. 24*, pp. 544–546.

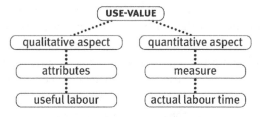

Marx illustrates his argument with a variety of apparently innocuous use-values/commodities—linen, iron, clocks and corn (wheat).[9] I say "apparently" because these played key roles in the period of capitalist development he was analyzing. Linen, a cloth made from flax was, along with wool, then cotton, essential to the development of the textile industry, the core of the British industrialization. Iron, along with coal, was required in the production of machinery for industry and weapons for controlling workers both at home and throughout the expanding British Empire. Clocks (and eventually watches) became tools for measuring work and maximizing exploitation. Wheat bread was the basic means of subsistence for the working class in England. In the same spirit, in *Reading Capital Politically*, I examined food and energy more generally than just bread and coal. While food provides us with nutrition and pleasure, both in consumption and in the opportunities for social bonding, control over its production provides capitalists with profit and control over the rest of us—because they make food a commodity and write laws that force us to buy what we need and want and thus to work for wages. While human energy provides us with life and non-human energy with the means to reduce work and make life more pleasant (heating and lighting our homes, etc.), capitalists exploit our energy as part of our labor-power and, like food, turn non-human energy into commodities they sell for profits or use against us (Chapters 12–15). Here, let's turn from the production of things to that of services, now the dominant commodity-producing sector of the economy.

Although in the nineteenth century the limited commercialization of services meant Marx felt he could largely ignore them, services now make up the majority of commodities and include transportation, finance, entertainment, medical aid, housekeeping, care-giving, communication and schooling. In each case, the use-value to their purchasers depends upon the nature of the service. Their use-value to capital, besides exchange-value, parallels that of food and energy: control over those who need or desire them. Also, in each case, a vast number of differentiated services are offered to workers, corporations and government.

---

9. In British usage, and in this context, "corn" refers to important cereal crops. In England that was wheat; in Ireland and Scotland oats, in Mexico maize, in China rice.

Narrowing our focus to just one kind of service—the loaning of money and the resulting debt of the borrower—we can easily see the differences in use-values for borrowers and lenders. In Marx's time, most lending was by capitalists to each other and to governments because workers had very low, precarious wages and little or no collateral to cover default on debt. As we saw in Chapter 31, the immediate use-value to those who loaned money to governments was the profit they received via interest—profit that could be loaned out again. Over time, financial institutions increasingly loaned to businesses that used their borrowings for either speculation or real investment, i.e., putting people to work. A secondary use-value was the leverage lenders gained over the behavior of borrowers. By the end of the nineteenth century, the Austrian Marxist Rudolf Hilferding (1877–1941) argued that businesses had become so dependent on banks as to give the later considerable power over the former.[10] In the twentieth century, as workers' struggles succeeded in repeatedly raising wages, they gained access to various kinds of credit. As a result, we are able to obtain other services and things such as washing machines (credit cards), automobiles (car loans) or houses (mortgages). Such borrowing allows us to enjoy use-values before we have enough cash-on-hand to pay for them. Yet, the form of such lending—the fine print and fraudulent practices—often traps us in perpetual debt, endless worry and the need to work and work and work to meet our repayment obligations. The result, of course, has been intense conflicts between debtors and creditors.

These stark differences between the use-values of commodities to workers and their use-values to capital have resulted in struggle over the qualities and prices of commodities. "Consumerism" has involved not only the efforts of capitalists to persuade people that they need more and more of this and that through advertising and ideology, but also the self-organization of workers-qua-consumers, who have contested various qualities of commodities, e.g., dangerous automobiles, poisonous effects of the "chemical feast," and even their very existence, e.g., hydrocarbon energy commodities that many want to replace with renewable ones to stave off both immediate harm to people and their environment and long-term effects on global warming and all of its emerging, catastrophic consequences.

From Exchange-Value to Value

Marx begins his analysis of exchange-value much the way Adam Smith did: with simple barter, the exchange of a given quantity of one thing for a

---

10.   See his book *Finance Capital: A Study in the Latest Phase of Capitalist Development* (1910), London: Routledge & Kegan Paul, 1985.

given quantity of another. Whereas Smith evoked hunting and gathering societies that exchanged such things as pelts, hides, fish or tools, Marx chose, as we have seen, commodities important for British capitalism, e.g., 1 quarter of corn = x cwt of iron.[11] Whether we consider Marx's choices or the more contemporary ones I have suggested, we quickly see that the *meanings* of the exchange-value of any given commodity are not the same for workers and capitalists.

We can easily see this in the domain of finance, looking (as above) only at the loaning of money and the resulting debt of the borrower. The higher the rate of interest (and accompanying fees), the more profit capitalist lenders will rake in and the "deeper" the debt of borrowers.[12] For those institutions that make such loans out of monies in their possession, e.g., automobile companies or banks, the objective is the extraction of as much interest as possible, to maximize their profits. So, whether the loans are made to businesses, government or individuals, lenders encourage: 1) the very partial repayment of the principal borrowed, e.g., a minimum repayment that only slowly reduces the principal upon which interest is charged; and 2) refinancing of debt that prolongs the period during which they can extract interest and profit. Beyond such simple financial calculations, keeping people, business or governments in perpetual debt with continuing obligations to repay grants leverage and power over borrowers. Hilferding made this point about bank loans to businesses, millions of workers today live under constant threat of dispossession (of automobiles by the "repo" man, or of homes by sheriffs or bailiffs with notices of eviction). Many governments facing difficulty in repaying their debt out of current revenue choose to cut expenditures—imposing austerity on workers—instead of raising taxes.[13]

In the 1970s, when capitalists responded to worker success in raising wages by raising prices, the resulting accelerating inflation undercut real interest rates. Lenders responded by imposing flexible rate loans. When President Jimmy Carter brought Paul Volcker in to chair the Federal Reserve and attack inflation, i.e., wages, he increased interest rates, drove up loan repayment costs and pitched the world economy into a depression. Coupled

---

11.   In British Imperial weight measures, a quarter of corn = 28 pounds and cwt = hundredweight = four quarters or 112 pounds. In this and other examples of exchange, the equals symbol (=) should be read "is worth" because clearly iron is not the same as corn.
12.   The real cost of borrowing derives not merely from interest and fees but often from a whole host of ancillary conditions, including time and conditions of repayment.
13.   Such was the case in New York City in 1974 when lenders would rollover loans to the city government only when it accepted to impose austerity on city workers and welfare recipients. See Donna Demac and Philip Mattera, "Developing and Underdeveloping New York: The 'Fiscal Crisis' and the Imposition of Austerity", *Zerowork #2*, Fall 1977, pp. 113–139.

with simultaneous financial deregulation, the result was the international debt crisis of the 1980s and 1990s, the imposition of austerity on workers, rising unemployment, falling wages and widespread recourse by workers to debt to maintain their standard of living. All of which prepared the ground for further financial crisis, first the collapse of the savings and loan industry in the late 1980s and then that of 2006–08 in which millions lost jobs and homes, prompting protests and demands for increased regulation, e.g., the Consumer Financial Protection Bureau, and debt-forgiveness, e.g., the widespread demands to cancel student debts and make education free.

Value

To return to barter, the implied *equivalence*, accepted by the exchangers, cannot lie in the use-values of the items exchanged because they are qualitatively different and have quite different use-values. Nor can it lie in the concrete useful labor that produced them because those labors were also quite distinct. In his example of 1 quarter of corn = x cwt of iron, cultivating and harvesting labor is obviously quite different from mining and smelting labor even if both extract something usable from the earth. So, what is the source of equivalence perceived by the exchangers?

For Marx, equivalence must lie in some *common property*. Abstracting from both use-value and the concrete, useful labors that produce use-values, he writes that:

> exchange-values [commodities] can only differ in quantity, and therefore do not contain an atom of use-value. If then we disregard the use-value of commodities, only one property remains, that of being products of labor... Nor [are they] any longer the product of... any particular kind of productive labor... [they] are all together reduced to the same kind of labor, human labor in the abstract... they are merely congealed quantities of homogeneous human labor... crystals of this social substance, which is common to them all, they are values—commodity values.[14]

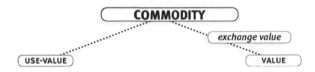

Marx's argument that "only one property remains, that of being products of labor" has been repeatedly challenged with counterarguments that

---

14.   *Capital, Vol. I*, p. 128. Marx doesn't consider the possibility of *non-equivalent reciprocity*, where exchange merely satisfies both participants, with no underlying common property or common measure at all.

strike at the heart of the "labor" theory of value. For example, some have argued that labor is not the only universal factor of production, energy is another. Already in Marx's time, non-human sources of energy were rapidly replacing human muscle-power as capitalists invested in machinery, driven by water, then steam, then electrical power. All commodities, therefore, can also be understood as "products of energy." Why, then, privilege a *labor* theory of value over an *energy* theory of value?

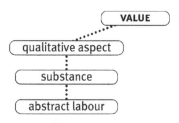

Marx was neither economist nor engineer; he does not offer a *technical theory* based on inputs and outputs, as expressed, for example, in economists' production functions of the sort $Q = f(K, L, E)$ where output, Q, is a function of inputs capital, K, e.g., machinery and raw materials, labor, L, and energy, E. He is not interested in just any "common property." What interests him is the "social substance," because his is a *social theory* in which he centers the key social relationship of capitalism: imposed labor (and the resistance to it). We see this in Part Eight, where imposed labor forms the primary means through which capital subordinates most people's lives to its own organizational forms.[15]

Can this "abstract labor," the substance of value, have any semantic meaning beyond being the fruit of a logical deduction? There are at least two ways in which I think it does.

First, Marx argues that as it develops, the capitalist division of labor tends to simplify skills to the point where workers can be moved easily from task to task. If the forms of labor are increasingly secondary, then it makes sense to speak of labor abstracted from those changing forms. This argument has been accepted by many as sufficient justification for considering "abstract labor" the substance of value.[16]

---

15. In the fourth section of this chapter, Marx's social focus is clear when he laments "the dull and tedious dispute [among economists] over the part played by nature in the formation of exchange-value. Because exchange-value is a definite social manner of expressing the labor bestowed on a thing, it can have not more natural content than has, for example, the rate of exchange." p. 176.

16. See, for example, Paul Sweezy, *The Theory of Capitalist Development: Principles of Marxian Political Economy* (1949), New York: Monthly Review Press, 1968; and Ronald Meek, *Studies in the Labor Theory of Value*, New York: Monthly Review Press, 1956.

Second, in what sense is the varying content—different kinds of useful labor—*secondary*? There are many important passages in *Capital* where the concrete form of useful labor is vitally important to Marx's analysis. For example, in Chapters 12–15 repeated alterations in the technical composition of capital (the shop floor arrangement of workers, tools, machines and raw materials) are shown to have been essential in maintaining or regaining control over workers. But, in capitalism, "control" means, above all, keeping people working at producing commodities. Therefore, there is a second, more profound semantic meaning to his "abstract labor;" the *substance of value* is precisely the social control over people's lives provided by any form of labor, independently of its content or form. Capitalism structures people's lives and society around work, no matter the nature of the work, which changes over time as technology evolves within the dynamics of struggle between the imposition of work and people's resistance to it. In other words, "value" expresses the particular social use-value of labor to capital as its primary means of social control. Marx's labor theory of value is a theory of the value of labor to capital.

Section 2: The Dual Character of the Labor Embodied in Commodities

---

Outline of Marx's Analysis

1) Useful labor

Social division of labor involves heterogeneous use-values and forms of labor

- qualitatively different use-values, e.g., cloth and coats, produced by:
- qualitatively different forms of labor, e.g., weaving and tailoring
- in Indian villages, use-values are *not* commodities
- in capitalism, use-values *are* commodities

Labor as creator of use-values, or useful labor, is:

- a "condition of human existence"
- an eternal natural necessity
- mediates the metabolism between humans and nature
- Petty: labor is the father of material wealth, the earth is its mother

2) Abstract labor, or labor as source of value

- labor abstracted from useful or determinate qualities
- labor as simple expenditure of human labor-power   ▶

- value of a commodity represents human labor pure and simple
- simple average labor produced by simple, i.e., average, labor-power
- complex labor = intensified or multiplied simple labor
- magnitude of value determined by labor time
- if one coat has same value as 20 yards of linen, both embody same amount (duration) of labor
- value varies with productivity, or output per hour of concrete *useful* labor
- increased productivity *increases* material wealth or output per hour
- increased productivity *decreases* value per unit

Commentary

This section provides, as Marx says, a "further elucidation" of the arguments in Section 1 about the twofold nature of the labor contained in commodities. His elucidation, therefore, is divided into two parts: the first elaborates his previous analysis of useful labor, the second deepens his previous analysis of abstract labor, or the substance of value. The former elaboration has been much less controversial than the second.

Useful Labor

Useful labor is heterogeneous. People do all kinds of useful labor, producing all kinds of useful things (and services). With the textile industry the heart of British industrialization, Marx points to the useful labor that weaves linen thread (made from flax) into linen cloth and the quite distinct useful tailoring labor that cuts and sews that cloth into linen coats. He might have added the horticultural labor that grows the flax, the harvest labor that reaps it, the labor that rets it, the labor that scutches it, the labor that heckles the fibers and the spinning labor that spins the long flax fibers into the thread necessary to weave/produce linen cloth. Because humans discovered many kinds of labor early on, there has always been a social division of labor, where some folks undertake some kinds of useful labor and others undertake other kinds. But only in capitalism have the diverse use-values produced by the diverse forms of useful labor generally taken the form of commodities, of things and services that are sold to others. Why this has been so, is explained in his analysis of primitive accumulation.

His emphasis on how human labor "mediates the metabolism between man and nature" foreshadows an analysis he elaborates in Chapter 7 on

"The Labor Process."[17] Here, by asserting that labor is "a condition of human existence" and "an eternal natural necessity," he frames his concept of useful labor as generic and a-historical, applicable throughout human history. The formulation by William Petty (1623–87) that labor is the father of material wealth and earth the mother, Marx proposes true for all time.[18] In so doing, he sets the stage for differentiating "abstract labor" from useful labor as a characteristic of capitalism alone.

Abstract Labor, or Labor as Source of Value

Section 1 arrived at the *concept* of abstract labor by abstracting from the diverse determinate forms of useful labor. Here, Marx defines labor as the "simple expenditure of human labor-power," without regard to the particular skills involved; he suggests two corresponding concepts: 1) "simple labor-power" and 2) "simple average labor" performable by "every ordinary man" (with "ordinary" explicitly understood to evolve over time with society).

The idea of an undeveloped" "simple labor" implies its contrary, that of more developed, or skilled "complex labor." To explain the relationship between the two, Marx offers, "More complex labor counts only as intensified, or rather multiplied simple labor, so that a smaller quantity of complex labor is considered equal to a larger quantity of simple labor." But who is doing the counting; who is considering, or making the judgement about what equals what? Marx doesn't say, but merely argues that "this reduction [of complex to simple] is constantly being made. . . behind the backs of the producers." How?

The lack of precision about the "who" and the "how" has led to various interpretations trying to clarify these statements. The most common interpretation perceives a "reduction" problem solved through market mechanisms of exchange, an optimistic logic akin to that of economists' wishful expectations of tendencies toward equilibrium. This interpretation finds consistency in another statement that Marx makes here, namely, "through its value [a commodity] is posited as equal to the product of simple labor." This reading sees "value" as revealed in exchange, not the varying exchange-values resulting from market fluctuations, but some underlying value which anchors those fluctuations. Once "prices" are accepted as the monetary expression of exchange-value (at the end of this chapter, and then in Volume III), this "reduction" problem re-emerges as the so-called

---

17.   In *Capital*, like most writers in his day, Marx used the term "man" to designate the human species. When not directly quoting Marx, I use non-sexist alternatives such as humanity or humans.

18.   *Capital, Vol. I*, p. 134.

"transformation problem" of whether and in what manner values determine prices.

My alternative interpretation, consistent with my suggestion that Marx's labor theory of value is a theory of the value of labor to capital, is the following. If the *substance of value* (denoted by the concept of abstract labor) is precisely the social control over people's lives that any labor, independently of its content or form, provides capital, then that substance becomes the determinate character of whatever kind of useful labor we care to consider—quite independently of whatever "complexity" or skill is being exercised. As to "who" counts or considers, the answer becomes "capital" or "capitalists" or "capitalist policymakers," who worry, first and foremost, not about the kinds of useful labor being imposed but the overall success of business in putting people to work. Here is the real-world "reduction;" forget complexity and ask rather how many and for how long are those ordinary men and women being employed? When Marx says this happens "behind the backs of the producers," many Marxists think "behind the backs of the capitalists," forgetting that "the producers" are the workers they employ. The reduction of the problem that concerns workers—of whether the existing complex assortment of concrete labors are producing what they need—to that of how successfully work is being imposed overall, not only happens "behind their backs" but usually behind closed doors, among policymakers dedicated to preserving and expanding capital's way of organizing life around imposed labor. "Simple labor" then, is not so much a characterization of some basic ability as it is a concept denoting the simple fact of being put to work—in more or less complex ways. Thus the "value" of a commodity is "equal to" or determined by the amount of work that can be imposed in producing it.

Socially Necessary Labor Time

But how is the "amount" of work measured? Assuming the "intensity" of labor constant, Marx argues that the amount of labor and the corresponding magnitude of value are determined by the *time of labor*, irrespective of complexity or skill.[19] Not the concrete labor time required to produce a given commodity, in a given production setting, but the *average* amount, or *socially necessary labor time* (SNLT) required. Thus, from a capitalist point of view, two commodities produced with the same amount of labor have equal values. They have equal values because their production provides equal opportunities for putting people to work.

---

19. In Chapter 15, Section 3c, he drops the assumption and examines how capital seeks to intensify labor as a means of imposing more work and extracting more value.

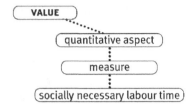

With the amount or quantity of value now seen to be determined by the time of labor, Marx turns to the effects on variations in the effectiveness, or productivity (e.g., output per hour), of useful labor.[20] A *doubling* of productivity, brought about, for instance, through the introduction of machines, or better machines, will cut in half the value of each unit of output, because each unit takes only half the time to produce. Or, the value of each unit of that commodity to capital will be cut in half because producing it provides only half the opportunity for putting people to work.

These results clarify the distinction between the meanings of useful labor and abstract labor—one determines actual production, the other the value of the labor employed to capital as its primary means of social control—and lay the basis for further analysis. In the next section, Marx examines quantitative changes in exchange rates due to changes in productivity. In Chapter 3 on money, he examines how changes in the productivity of labor producing metals used for money are related to changes in prices. In his extensive analysis of technological change in Chapters 12–15, he explores how productivity evolves as an aspect of class struggle over the imposition of work and resistance to it.

Section 3: The Value Form or Exchange-Value

a) The Simple, Isolated, or Accidental Form of Value
b) The Total or Expanded Form of Value
c) The General Form of Value
d) The Money Form of Value

Preliminary Commentary

This frequently neglected section on the form of value, begins with the simplest form—where one good represents the value of another—and ends

---

20.   NB: although in microeconomic models each factor of production has its own productivity (output per unit of input), in Marx's analysis the focus is on labor productivity because labor is the source of value for capital. Henceforth, unless otherwise specified, all references to changes in productivity are to changes in the productivity of useful labor.

with the money form, where some historically and socially determined money represents the value of every commodity. Further determinations of the character and roles of money are analyzed in Chapters 2 and 3, which build on the complexities examined in this section.

Marx shows us how, just as use-value receives an expression and existence in the bodily form of the commodity, so too does value receive an independent expression and existence in the form of money. In the *Grundrisse*, before he had worked out the mode of presentation used in *Capital*, the understanding of money was a central concern of his studies of value and abstract labor. In the early notebooks comprising the "chapter on money" a great many of the determinations of Chapter 1 are discussed, not as abstract qualities of commodities in general, but directly as determinations of money, the ultimate commodity.[21]

Unfortunately, most Marxists have had little to say about the form of value or the complexities hidden within the money form but revealed in this section. For example, both Paul Sweezy and Ronald Meek, two widely read and influential Marxist economists, focused on the substance and measure of value almost totally ignoring its form. Sweezy's "qualitative value problem" concerns only the qualities of abstract labor and socially necessary labor time and ignores form completely.[22] Meek's commentary on Chapter 1 devotes 15 pages to the quantitative reduction problem and only one very short paragraph to the form of value (to which Marx devotes 24 pages).[23] He justified this neglect by quoting Engels, who thought all the detail was just about how the emergence of money overcame the inefficiencies of barter exchange.

This neglect, however, is quite inexcusable. Not only does this section reveal many subtle aspects of exchange and money, but because both are elements of the class relationship, these same aspects can be discovered throughout the social relationships of capitalism.

---

21. *Grundrisse*, Notebooks I and II.
22. Sweezy, *The Theory of Capitalist Development*, pp. 23–40.
23. Meek, *Studies in the Labor Theory of Value*, pp. 173–174. A. Leontiev gives about four pages to the form of value in his *Political Economy: A Beginner's Course* (1935), San Francisco, CA: Proletarian Publishers, n.d., pp. 64–67 and Isaak Illich Rubin (1886–1937), in his *Essays on Marx's Theory of Value* (1928), Detroit, MI: Black & Red, 1972, pp. 115–123, does only a little better. One might be tempted to simply attribute this to an intellectual error, but, as I argued in *Reading Capital Politically* this neglect of the form of value can be seen as only one manifestation of a much broader failure to confront the question of form throughout the class struggle. See *RCP*, 2nd edn., pp. 136–138.

a) The Simple, Isolated, or Accidental Form of Value

Outline of Marx's Analysis

Commodities' character as value is purely social

- that character appears in the social relation of exchange
- commonly recognized value form is the money form
- objective: reveal, through analysis, what lies *within* the money form
- simple form: $xA = yB$, e.g., 20 yards of linen = 1 coat
  - relative form: value of xA is expressed by yB
  - equivalent form: yB
    - expresses the value of xA,
    - is form of existence of the value of xA
    - is material embodiment of the value of xA
- most focus on quantities, x and y, but:
- quantitative equality requires a common quantum, i.e., value
- exchange gives value a form distinct from use-value
- 20 yds linen = 1 coat implies equation of weaving with tailoring
  - what is equal in the two kinds of labor is:
  - their common quality of being human labor in general
- labor *creates* value, but is not value
  - *becomes* value in its coagulated state, in objective form, a materially different thing
  - so, in exchange, the coat (in equivalent form) represents more than it does alone
- in exchange, yB becomes a *mirror* for the value of xA
  - i.e., yB *reflexively mediates A's* relation to its value
- x and y, the quantities of A and B, change with productivity
  - changes in productivity in production of A, changes value per unit
    - which changes amount y of B required to represent the value of A
  - changes in productivity in production of B also changes required y

---

Commentary

Marx devotes more words to presenting his analysis of the simple form of value than to any of the other forms, including that of money. The reason for this he explained to Engels in 1867. "The simplest commodity-form," he wrote, "contains the whole secret of the money form and with it in embryo, of all the bourgeois forms of the product of labor."[24] Through the exchange of some quantity x of commodity A for some quantity y of commodity B, or

$$xA = yB,$$

the value of commodity A finds an independent expression and a concrete manifestation in commodity B. This simple, or elementary, exchange relation is also called *accidental* because it is accidental which commodity expresses the value of another. This relationship, although pictured above in the form of an equation, is not a mathematical, reversible equation. Marx is careful to explain that the equals sign is short for *is worth*. As it is written, $xA = yB$ says that xA *is worth* yB meaning that yB expresses the value of xA. To obtain an expression of the worth of yB, the relationship must be rewritten as $yB = xA$, i.e., yB *is worth* xA, where now xA expresses the value of yB. Most of the analysis of this section consists of analyzing the meanings of this relation.

Marx first deals with the *qualitative* aspects of this relation, ignoring the quantitative constants x and y. He formalizes the unsymmetrical nature of the expression by analyzing the two forms within the simple form: the relative form and the equivalent form.

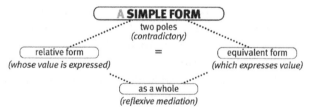

In the exchange $xA = yB$, Marx calls commodity A the *relative value form* because its value is expressed in, and relative to, commodity B. He calls commodity B the *equivalent form* because it serves as the material equivalent for the value of commodity A. In other words, commodity A gets its value expressed, while (the corporeal use-value of) commodity B provides a phenomenal expression of the value of A. Therefore, when the value of commodity B is expressed by xA in $yB = xA$, then B has the relative form and A the equivalent form.

As with the relationship between use-value and exchange-value, we find an opposition and a unity. We have an *opposition* because the relative value form and the equivalent form exist as two opposed, contradictory poles.

---

24.   Mark to Engels, June 22, 1867, *MECW, vol.* 42, p. 384.

We have *unity* in the sense that they are "mutually dependent and insep-arable." *A* only has the relative form if it has an equivalent *B*; *B* is only an equivalent when expressing the value of some other *A*. The two expressions represent the two sides of an actual exchange process. When a commodity is brought to market its owner only finds out what it *is worth* by exchanging it. The commodity acquired is accepted as the equivalent of the value of the commodity given up.[25]

As with use-value and exchange-value, this unity of opposites has the form of the class struggle: two opposed perspectives and forces bound in one contradictory totality. This is obvious in the case where the commodity brought to market is the labor-power of workers. When they sell their labor-power to capital, it has the relative form and the value received (the wage or other income) has the equivalent form. An examination of each of these forms—in this chapter carried out only with respect to the exchange of random commodities—further clarifies this kind of relationship.

The Relative Form of Value

Why is it value that is being expressed by *B* and not something else? Because the only thing commodity *B* has in common with *A* that matters to capital is value, i.e., the value of being products of labor-in-general, of being vehicles for the imposition of work and social control. It is in this sense, within the framework of capitalism, that commodity *A* achieves an independent expression of its value to capital in *B*. In a simple exchange of "use-values" between friends, outside of any capitalist market, no such common value need exist or be postulated.[26] For example, I prepare and serve you a meal (an objectivization of some of my skills); you reward me with a smile and a request for second helping. There is no basis—common value—for equivalence in such a case.[27]

---

25.   Keep in mind that here, as in most of the book, Marx assumes equal exchange, i.e., no cheating, in which one commodity owner would wind up with another commodity of lesser value. Why he makes this assumption becomes clear in his analysis of exploita-tion in Chapter 7.

26.   I put *use-value* in quotes because outside of capitalism, either before its historical rise, or in a future post-capitalist world, there seems no reason to use this generic term, invented to differentiate values-in-use from value-to-capital, to characterize things we make or ways we help each other. As we struggle for that future world, free of capital, we can also abandon the vocabulary developed to analyze this insane society that we want to leave behind.

27.   In non-capitalist systems of reciprocity, it might be natural for the person so gifted to estimate the time and energy that went into preparing said meal in order to recip-rocate, more or less in kind, at some point in the future. But such estimations are more likely to be manifestations of the desire to demonstrate roughly equal appreciation, honor or love than of the desire to calculate equal opportunities to impose work.

But in capitalism, where the value of things to capital is measured by the amount of work that can be imposed in their production, Marx points out that these relations between the two commodities necessarily represent the relations between the labor contained in them. The equation of the two products of labor distinguishes the substance of their value—abstract labor—from the useful labors that produced them as distinct commodities. The exchange equation expresses the reduction of the various kinds of useful labor to abstract labor, the common value to capital of all kinds of labor that produce commodities.

His analysis of the *quantitative aspect* of the relative form of value, having established that the only way magnitude can be expressed relatively is in terms of the same quantum of quality, shows how the quantity of the value of one commodity, A, can be expressed by a quantity of another, B. Inevitably, the expression of value will vary with *changes in the productivity* of either commodity A or commodity B. Earlier, in Section 1, we saw the impact of variations in productivity during the analysis of socially necessary labor time and in Section 2 we saw how this was grounded in changes in useful labor, while abstract labor remained constant. If the intensity of labor is constant, an increase in the productivity of the labor required to produce some good, A, implies a drop in the socially necessary labor time per unit and a reduction in its per unit value. As more use-values embody the same total value, each unit embodies less. In this section, we see the implications for the simple form of value and the quantitative expression, yB, of changes in the value of commodity xA.

If the productivity of the labor producing commodity A rises, so that its per unit value *falls*, and if the productivity in the production of B has not changed, then a *decreased* amount y of the equivalent commodity B will be sufficient to express the value of xA. If the productivity of the useful labor producing B rises, reducing its value per unit, while that producing A remains constant, then there must be an *increase* in the amount y of B expressing the value of xA. If the productivity of both changes, then the quantitative variation can be calculated by taking both effects into account. This illustrates a further reason why the relative value form is called relative. The relative value of commodity A can change (because of a change in the value of commodity B), although its value (in terms of socially necessary labor time) remains the same. Or, its relative value can remain the same, even if the value of A changes.

The Equivalent Form and Reflexivity

When we say that B *expresses* the value of A, we are speaking of a relation of mediation known as *reflection*. In this kind of mediation, one thing (in this case, commodity *A*) is related to an aspect of itself (value) through another thing (in this case, commodity *B*). Familiar examples of this kind of mediation are how we all come to know our image through a mirror, or aspects of ourselves (from image to abilities) through the comments of others.[28] In speaking of how the equivalent performs such a service, Marx says: "In order to act as such a mirror of value, tailoring itself [producing commodity *B*, the coat] must reflect nothing apart from its own abstract quality of being human labor."[29] In a footnote, Marx notes that Hegel called this kind of relation "determinations of reflection" [*Reflexionsbestimmungen*]."[30] In the first German edition of *Capital*, Marx wrote: "Its [coat's] status as an equivalent is [so to speak] only a *reflexion-determination* of linen."[31] Also, "the relative value-form of a commodity is *mediated*; namely through its relationship to another commodity."[32] In other words, commodity *A* can come explicitly into relation to itself as value only through the mediation of another commodity (*B*) expressing a single aspect of commodity *A*. We can represent this relation of reflective mediation as:

xA ◄——— yB

---

28.   For a detailed analysis of this kind of mediation between humans, see the analysis of l'autrui (the other) in Jean-Paul Sartre, *L'être et le néant: Essai d'ontologie phénoménologique* (1943), or *Being and Nothingness: An Essay on Phenomenological Ontology* (1966).

29.   *Capital, Vol. I*, p. 150.

30.   Ibid., p. 149n. This follows Hegel's analysis of reflection in his *Logic*, upon which Marx undoubtedly drew—as Ben Fowkes recognizes in an editorial footnote. Hegel's analysis appears fittingly in the Book of Essence, which is divided into three parts: essence, appearance and actuality. For Hegel, essence is "being coming into mediation with itself through the negativity of itself" (*A* related to its value thru *B*). The metaphor of a mirror which Marx uses to discuss the revelation of essence through reflection is used by Hegel: "The word reflection is originally applied, when a ray of light in a straight-line impinging upon the surface of a mirror is thrown back from it." Or, "reflection or light thrown into itself, constitutes the distinction between essence and immediate being, and is the peculiar characteristic of essence itself" (§112). The existence of essence, however, must be grounded "not in itself but on something else" (§131), not in commodity *A* but on *B*. Marx's analysis is thus very close to Hegel's and the lecture of the latter can inform the analysis of the former. The fact that Hegel is indulging in an exercise in philosophy while Marx is analyzing the commodity form of the class struggle should not obscure this relationship. It should only keep us on our toes to be able to grasp not only the similarities but also the differences between the two. See *Hegel's Logic, Being Part One of the Encyclopaedia of the Philosophical Sciences* (1830), Oxford: Clarendon Press, 1975.

31.   "The Commodity" (Chapter 1 of the first German edition of Volume I of *Capital*), in *Value: Studies by Karl Marx*, translated and edited by Albert Dragstedt, London: New Park Publications, 1976, p. 24.

32.   "The Form of Value", ibid., p. 60.

As with two randomly exchanged commodities, this relationship of reflective mediation is also an aspect of the commodity form of the class relation. Individuals and capital stand as opposed poles just like the relative and equivalent value forms. Just as the relative value form finds its meaning only in the equivalent form, so too do individuals recognize themselves as workers only through their relation to their employers.[33] It is not just a matter of perception. Within capitalism individuals can only exist as workers, and collectively constitute a working class, within that relation. Put in the language above, the mass of workers has their joint condition as working class reflected to them through capital acting as a mirror which mediates this recognition. In this way, the class gains both definition and self-recognition. This is true both in terms of class-in-itself, in which all workers have in common is the exchange of their labor-power for income, and in terms of class-for-itself in which workers discover their unity through struggle. Just as the equivalent form brings out and expresses a unique quality in other commodities, value, so too does capital reflect a unique quality of people, their labor-power, or their ability and willingness to be put to work. Inversely, those with money can only be capitalists when they are able to hire people and put them to work. But the relation is not parallel. People can break out of this reciprocal relationship—rejecting and smashing the mirror—and remain people, complete with all their skills, now freed to build new worlds. Whereas if we deprive capital (or capitalists, the functionaries of capital-as-social-relation) of its ability to impose work on us, it loses its control over us and with it, its ability to organize society, leaving the rest of us free to experiment with new modes of *self*-organization.

The analysis, so far, shows us how all the elements which we have analyzed—use-value, exchange-value, abstract labor, socially necessary labor time, and so on—are combined in their elementary interrelationships in this simple value form. In the expanded, general, and money forms which follow, further determinations are taken into account to achieve a more complete and more complex expression of value.

The Insufficiency of the Simple Form and the Transition to the Expanded Form

While the simple form gives the value of *A* an independent expression in *B*, there is nevertheless a contradiction between this form and the nature of

33. In footnote 22, where Marx evokes *Reflexionsbestimmungen*, he prepares the ground for this insight by commenting "one man is king only because other men stand in the relation of subjects to him. They on the other hand, imagine that they are subjects because he is king."

value. This is the "insufficiency" of the simple form of value. The simple form fails to represent "*A*'s qualitative equality with all other commodities and its quantitative proportionality to them."[34] Why should it? The reason lies in his previous analysis of value. In Section 1, he designated the substance of value as abstract labor. Abstract labor, in turn, denotes the peculiar character of all concrete forms of useful labor as serving capital as its primary mode of organizing its control over society. In Section 2, socially necessary labor time was based on averages across the whole commodity-producing society. Now, if the substance and measure of value reflect this universality of the commodity form, then so too must the phenomenal form of value. The value form must represent these interconnections among *all* commodities. His exposition of his analysis of the value form progresses in this direction.

b) The Total or Expanded Form of Value

If, in the elementary form, *A* finds its expression in one other commodity, *B*, and if, furthermore, the *B* chosen is accidental, then *any* commodity could be so chosen. "The number of such possible expressions," Marx writes, [of the value of *A*] "is limited only by the number of different kinds of commodities distinct from it."[35] This is why the second form of value, the expanded form of commodity *A*'s value, consists of "an indefinitely expandable series of different simple expressions of that value."[36] In this way, the immediate contradiction between the individual representation of *A*'s value and the multiplicity of commodities (universality of value) is resolved. This new form, a more complete expression of value, can be represented in the following manner.

$$xA = yB$$
$$xA = wC$$
$$xA = zD \text{ etc.}$$

or

$$xA = \begin{cases} yB \\ wC \\ zD \text{ etc.} \end{cases}$$

The relation of reflection, by which the relative value of *A* is given independent expression through a particular equivalent, is now multiplied. "Every other commodity now becomes a mirror of linen's value."[37] This is why

---

34. *Capital, Vol. I*, p. 154.
35. Ibid.
36. Ibid.
37. Ibid., p. 155.

Marx calls the relative form "expanded." The equivalent form remains *particular* in the sense that, although there is an endless list of equivalents, each is a particular expression of *A*'s relative value. In this way, the various kinds of useful labor that produced all these commodities are expressed as equal through the interrelation of the products.

Each of these many expressions of the value of *A* has the characteristics of the simple value form: the polarity between relative and equivalent forms, the unity of opposites, reflectiveness, and so on. In this way, the more complete form preserves the previous form containing all the latter's relations to the class struggle. What analysis of this expanded form reveals, however, is much more than a mere list of possibilities.

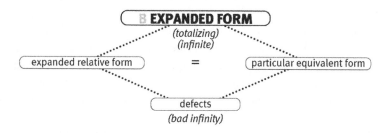

The importance of this new form lies in its comprehensiveness. Because all commodities are involved, accidentality disappears. The form provides a representation of the *totality* of generalized commodity production under capitalism. By including the production of all commodities, not just of things and services but also of labor-power, the representation expresses much of capital's social totality.[38]

Because the number of expressions of value is limited only by the number of commodities, for which there is no theoretical limit, the form also expresses capital's tendency to expand *infinitely*. It seeks to constantly expand its way of organizing society, forever bringing more and more people, activities, and materials, under its control by forcing them to become elements of the production of commodities. This tendency toward infinite extension is not provoked "from the outside." Capitalist social relationships generate, through their mutual antagonism, their own self-expansion, only one part of which is the expansion of the commodity world. Those antagonistic social relationships—especially the struggles of workers—force capitalists to seek out and invest in new sources of all the elements that make it up. Whether we are speaking of its expansion internationally, as different parts of the world are brought into the orbit of its imposition of

---

38.   Much, but not all. Left out are all those relations not involving exchange, e.g., the activities of the unwaged.

social control through work, or of its expansion into all sectors of production, or of its expansion into all aspects of the reproduction of labor-power, in each case the new "areas" of control are not mere additions. They grow out of dynamics internal to the class struggle and constitute moments of reorganization as capital tries to retain or expand overall control.

In Marx's time, that tendency was manifested not only in the commodification of everyday life, but also in colonialism, as capitalists in countries such as Britain, France and The Netherlands built empires, annexing ever greater numbers of people, their lands, "resources" and activities throughout the world. This tendency of capitalism toward infinity, moreover, does not merely involve *adding* something new to existing social orders, it has always been one of *subsuming* them, of transforming them into moments of existing relationships. Controlling the cheap and often slave labor employed in raw material production in colonies facilitated control of workers in British factories. These dynamics continue in the form of vertical integration in industry, outsourcing and immigration to pit foreign cheap labor against more expensive local labor. In this way capitalism is also totalizing; in the language of contemporary literary criticism, it seeks to impose its own narrative on the world.[39]

Today, we can recognize this tendency in both neoliberal globalization and in the ever-multiplying number of commodities imposed upon us. We can also recognize it in the privatization of space exploration and colonization. In the United States, NASA has been turning over ever more of its programs to private corporations such as SpaceX and United Launch Alliance. Corporations already own and operate satellites and are preparing to build and operate space shuttles and orbital hotels for wealthy tourists. As many science fiction writers have long foreseen, unchecked capitalism will expand throughout the solar system and, if possible, bring its nightmarish form of society to the stars. The expanded form expresses this tendency toward infinite expansion. In more optimistic sci-fi, such as *Star Trek*, we figure out how to get rid of capitalism and expand into the universe largely free of its constraints.[40]

Unfortunately for capital, however, the realization of its efforts to find ever more opportunities to impose work requires the mobilization of workers' (our) imagination and creativity. As Marx discusses in later chapters, living

---

39. Many theorists of "new social movements" have accused Marx of seeking to impose a totalizing narrative of class on a world full of other complexities, e.g., racial, ethnic and gender discrimination and resistance. The accusation fails to recognize that it was not *his* narrative but that of capital he was analyzing and critiquing.

40. I say "largely" because the galaxy is still plagued by Ferengi capitalists. Alternatively, as in the two versions of the film *The Day the Earth Stood Still* (1951), (2008), a wiser galactic civilization stops a humanity still enthralled to capitalism in its tracks.

labor—our activity—is the only source of innovation and change within capitalism. Inevitably, despite capital's efforts to constrain and harness that power for its own purposes, we, both individually and collectively, discover our own kind of infinity—that of the potentially infinite possibilities for living realizable only through freedom from the constraints of capitalism. In the very movement whereby capital multiplies a world of proliferating commodities, we discover vast potential beyond capital itself, which tries to restrict our possibilities to those in its own interest.[41]

Defects of the Expanded Form

Although this form gives us a more complete representation of value, by making the interrelationship among all commodities explicit, Marx points out why even this form is inadequate. He lists its defects. First from the point of view of the relative value form, the series of equations representing the relative expression of value is interminable, a pieced-together mosaic of independent expressions, and there is no common representation of value which would express its universality. And then, from the point of view of the equivalent form, because we have particular equivalents, we have a series of unrelated, fragmentary equivalent forms, the labor embodied in each equivalent thus appears only as particular not general, or abstract labor. Abstract labor, therefore, is only manifested through the totality of its particular forms, but that totality is an ever-incomplete series lacking internal unity.

In short, an adequate expression of value must represent the interaction of all the (potentially infinite) commodities capital succeeds in forcing us to produce, but in a way that expresses their common character. In the expanded form the common substance of abstract labor remains unexpressed because we have no unique or common expression for the value of each commodity. This critique by Marx of the expanded form is similar to Hegel's critique of the *bad infinity*—also an unlinked, interminable series.[42]

c) The General Form of Value

The answer to the defect of the expanded form is implicit in that form. While the expanded form appears as a natural extension of the simple form, because the equivalent chosen in the simple form is arbitrary, the *general form* emerges from a reversal in perspective. When *A* is exchanged against *B*, *C*, *D*, those commodities express the value of *A*. But it is also true

---

41. *Grundrisse*, Notebook IV, pp. 408–409.
42. See Hegel's *Logic*, §94–§95, pp. 137–141.

that *B, C, D*, and so on are being exchanged for *A*. Consequently, *A*, viewed as equivalent, expresses the value of *B, C, D*. This gives a *common expression* for the value of all commodities, namely *xA*. We now have a potentially infinite list, but one that is no longer fragmentary because all commodities are linked through a common or general expression of value in *A*.

$$\left.\begin{array}{l} y\text{B} \\ w\text{C} \\ z\text{D etc.} \end{array}\right\} = x\text{A}$$

For each commodity, the expression of its value takes place in its exchange with another commodity, *yB* = *xA*, but when the equivalent is the same for all, the form taken as a whole is unified. A unique aspect of all commodities, value now has a unique representative. By being equated to this single representative, the value of any commodity is not only distinguished from its bodily use-value, but its representation also expresses what it has in common with all other commodities.

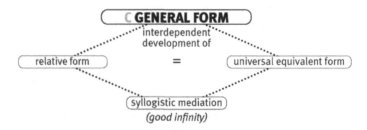

This form is general, or universal, in all its parts. The relative form of any given commodity is universal "because it is the relative value-form of all other commodities at the same time."[43] The equivalent form is universal because the equivalent has become the unique form of appearance of value for all commodities. Because of this, the labor producing it "acquires as a result a general social form, the form of equality with all other kinds of labor. . . the general form of appearance of undifferentiated human labor" or abstract labor.[44] That abstraction from concrete specificity within capitalism makes the universal equivalent the embodiment and symbol of the core class relationship: the imposition of work as the fundamental vehicle for the organization of society.

Within this general form, the internal contradictions characteristic of the earlier forms still obtain. The irreversible and contradictory polarity

---

43. *Value: Studies by Karl Marx*, p. 29.
44. *Capital, Vol. I*, p. 159.

and reflectiveness of the simple form, the totalizing and infinite aspects of the expanded form, all remain characteristics of the general form. But now something new appears. Because the universal equivalent has acquired the character of direct exchangeability with every other commodity, all other commodities have lost that quality. They are longer exchanged for each other but must first be exchanged for the universal equivalent.

This observation highlights a fundamental aspect of the general form—namely, as the equivalent form becomes the universal equivalent for the value of all other commodities, it also becomes *the universal mediator* between them all. Earlier, we saw how individual commodities related to their own value through the mediation of an equivalent (through reflection). We now see how reflexive mediation, as a characteristic of the general form, is part of another kind of mediation played by the universal equivalent: "All commodities by mirroring themselves in one and the same commodity as quantities of value, reflect themselves reciprocally as quantities of value."[45] Reciprocal reflection, but mediated through the universal equivalent.[46] That equivalent has become a mediator for the expression of value of each commodity *and* for the relation of all commodities to each other as values.

This second form of mediation between two distinct commodities is *syllogistic mediation*. In a syllogism, two distinct entities are related via a third.[47] The universal equivalent, xA, mediates the relationship between yB and wC.

$$\left.\begin{array}{l} yB \\ wC \\ zD \text{ etc.} \end{array}\right\} = xA$$

or

$$yB - xA - wC$$

Expressing the value of each individual commodity, the universal mediator binds them together. It explicitly incorporates each individual commodity into the universal value relation. By having a common expression of value, the otherwise disparate exchanges become parts of an interconnected commodity world. The series grows, potentially infinitely. But that infinity

---

45. *Value: Studies by Karl Marx*, p. 30.
46. This reciprocity between any two commodities is, in some ways, like that of Hegel's Civil Society. But the mediation of the reciprocal relation through a universal equivalent is different from Hegel's concept of reciprocity. Marx's introduction of the syllogistic mediation, which Hegel introduces in the Book of the Notion, makes it quite distinct.
47. A classic example of a syllogism in logic textbooks is: Caesar is a man; all men are mortal; therefore, Caesar is mortal. What interested both Hegel and Marx is not the logic of the deduction, but how Caesar's existence as a man mediates his relation to mortality.

is no longer a tiresome mosaic of separate elements. Like Hegel's "good infinity," the capitalist commodity world is now expressed as an integrated and united whole in which the repeated appearance of new commodities no longer means only the creation of new finites, but the continuation of a tendentially infinite process.

Syllogistic mediation plays a fundamental role, not only in how capital organizes the world of commodities but in how it organizes its control over workers. Just as the universal equivalent mediates between all commodities, capital tries to mediate all relations in the social factory, between workers producing commodities, between producers and consumers, between parents and children, between teachers and students, between spouses, between ethnicities, races, age groups and genders, between locals and immigrants, and so on.

But what does it mean to say that capital intervenes as a mediating force everywhere? We have already seen how capital imposes money as universal, mediating equivalent (more on this in the next section). We have also seen how it uses the state, e.g., troops for enclosure, property laws and police to impose the commodity form, maximum or minimum wage laws, and so on. Seeing how some of us are organized to mediate capital's relations with others is often less obvious. In *RCP*, I illustrated this kind of mediation with several examples: in the relations between the waged, in those between waged men and unwaged women, between teachers and students and between domestic and immigrant workers. In each case, capital sets up a hierarchy, of higher waged over lower waged, waged men over unwaged women, waged teachers over unwaged students, and domestic workers over immigrants. Through these hierarchies it seeks to pit us against one another and use some of us to manage others—both by imposing work on those ranked lower and by absorbing the ire of those imposed upon. To reinforce these mediations, capital also makes use of racial, gender, ethnic, religious or national differences among workers. So, in a place like Texas, local Anglo workers tend to be higher paid and hold managerial positions vis-à-vis lower paid African- or Mexican-American workers.

Understanding this kind of mediation in the class struggle not only helps illuminate its complexity, but also suggests how we can take the initiative to rupture and destroy it, forcing a recomposition of class relations. This happens when we *refuse the mediation and bypass it*. In industry, in wildcat strikes rank-and-file workers organize autonomously and bypass both foremen and trade union officials to confront employers directly. In education, when university students occupy an administration building, demanding an end to school complicity with war, or a termination of cuts to programs important to them, they are bypassing the mediation of professors and directly confronting the administrators of capital's edu-factories.

When students in K-12 schools walk out—as they did during the "Sí, se puede!" immigrant rights marches in the spring of 2006 and in March 2018 during the National School Walkout, in the wake of the shootings at Marjory Stoneman Douglas High School—they are bypassing both teachers and administrators. Today, "Dreamers," threatened by Trump's efforts to end Deferred Action for Childhood Arrivals (DACA), and by resurgent racism and nativism, school children, threatened by repeated mass shootings, and black youth, threatened by police murders of unarmed civilians, are also on the march. In echoes of the Civil Rights Movement, they are all bypassing local mediations and demanding security from deportation, from the profit-hungry arms industry and from racist police through changes in laws both local and national. In the great "Women's Marches" of 2017–19, millions of women have acted collectively, bypassing all of capital's mediations.[48]

These mediations can also be *broken* as well as bypassed. That happens when they result in such harsh conflict as to no longer function as intended. University students generally carry their struggles directly to the administration or beyond. But in K-12 schools, student refusal of discipline rarely bypasses teachers to strike directly at administrators—as in the walkouts in 2006 and 2018. Instead, anger flares against teachers, sometimes to such a degree that the latter cannot retain control. This has spurred the proliferation of teacher unions, changing the relationship between administrators and teachers. Acting in federations, mobilizing at the level of the state, they make demands for collective instead of individual bargaining over salaries and conditions of work. The work of having to impose discipline in an increasingly rebellious classroom is the equivalent of speed-up on an assembly line—it increases the intensity of the workday and the requirements for reproducing labor-power. In these circumstances, militant teacher unions are creating a whole new alignment of power in education. Faced with teacher refusal to try to impose discipline in dangerous situations, school administrations and city governments are being forced to pay higher wages, to bring in security guards, metal detectors and police, so on.

At the same time, such developments raise serious problems for working-class strategy. How can this growing power of students and teachers be organized so that it is directed more against capital than against each other? The autonomous power of students has forced the creation of a new level of autonomous organization and power among teachers—a recomposition of class relations. But as long as the dynamic and direction

---

48. Many men, refusing their assigned role of mediators, have also marched alongside those women, just as some teachers have marched with their students and all kinds of whites have joined Black Lives Matter marches.

of these developments are not understood, there is the danger of ultimate collapse and defeat.

In universities we have seen such dangers. In the 1960s, the struggles of students forced a recomposition of the teaching staff that included a new generation of radicals and new fields of study initially aimed at supporting further protest, e.g., Black Studies, Mexican-American Studies, Women's Studies, Peace Studies. The changes undermined the ability of higher education to discipline, plan and organize the supply of labor. But the insurgent spirit that created those new programs has been constantly undermined by both the usual neutralizing institutional measures, e.g., competition for funding and promotion,[49] and by outside attacks by conservative forces, e.g., the National Association of Scholars or, more recently, Turning Point USA. In the same period, student pressures undermined grade tracking, generating grade inflation. But as a result, experiments are underway to find other modes of judging the ability and willingness of students to work. All these developments have led to the current attempt by capital to reimpose work discipline in the schools through fiscal crisis, and a nationwide restructuring of education. Such a restructuring necessarily involves attempts to find new kinds of mediation to replace those which student and teacher/professors' struggles have rendered less reliable. Being clear about mediation can help in discovering vulnerabilities and modes of subversion. Recognizing the dynamics of mediation can facilitate their refusal and defeat, as when students join teacher strikes, seen lately in West Virginia, Oklahoma, Arizona, Kentucky, Colorado and Los Angeles.[50]

Ultimately, we must destroy the divisions and intra-class antagonisms which capital imposes. But while students and professors may struggle against administrator plans, or men and women, whites and blacks, locals and immigrants seek ways to destroy the mediations, solutions are never so simple as "unite and fight." As I argued in the section on abstract labor, the divisions are real and hierarchical; they are power divisions, and collaboration requires a power struggle not only of different segments of the working class against capital but also, at times, between those segments. Our problem of political organization is how to develop our intra-class struggles, not as a circular firing squad, but in ways that strengthen all of us.

---

49. Thus, the continuing relevance of Marcuse's analysis of "repressive tolerance" in Herbert Marcuse, Barrington Moore and Robert Paul Wolff, *A Critique of Pure Tolerance*, Boston, MA: Beacon Press, 1965, 1969.

50. Jeffery R. Webber, "Return of the Strike: A Forum on the Teachers' Rebellion in the United States", *Historical Materialism*, vol. 26, issue 4, 2018, pp. 1–46.

d) The Money Form of Value

The transition from the general form to the money form is much simpler than the previous transitions. The money form differs from the general form only in so far as the universal equivalent has become fixed by social custom into some one commodity. Once this happens, the universal equivalent functions as money and we have the money form.

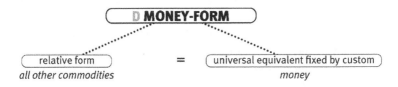

The *money form* is the total relationship,

$$\left.\begin{array}{l} y\text{B} \\ w\text{C} \\ z\text{D etc.} \end{array}\right\} = x \text{ gold}$$

and must be differentiated from *money* which, in this case, is gold. This money form contains all the determinations of the prior forms. It has the contradictory unity and reflective relations between the relative form and the equivalent form brought out in the simple form. It has the totality and infinitude brought out in the expanded form and welded together in the general form. And it has the mediated character of the general form. Like capital, then, the money form is contradictory, reflexive, totalizing, infinite and mediated.

Marx's whole analysis in this first chapter has been leading to the money form. We can now reverse the process and reassess each step as elements of a theory of money. *Money* is partly defined as a universal equivalent, not simply one element of this totality but expressing this totality. Money is one commodity among many, *and* the unique general expression of their value to capital as vehicles for the imposition of work. Money, by expressing all commodities as values, expresses the domain of capital—the social relations which turn use-values into commodities. As a moment in the money form, money is a moment of the whole of capitalism. If capital is most basically the social relations of the commodity form (of which the commodity world is a part), then money is the quintessential expression of the commodity form itself. In capitalist society, to have a coin in the hand is to have a golden drop of that society itself. Look deeply into that coin, as you might with a crystal ball, and behind its golden luster, which has stopped many an eye, you discover the blood and sweat of the class struggle.

When we look back at the roles of the equivalent form in the various relations we have examined, we now know we were looking at the roles of money. For example, money stands as equivalent in contradictory unity with labor-power. It does the same with all other commodities and, by so doing, shows them (through reflection) their character as values, and thus as parts of capital. The tendency for capital to expand infinitely is partly the tendency to turn social relations into money relations, that is, to convert all use-values into values by utilizing their production as a means of social control and by setting them equal to money. Money becomes the magic wand by which capital incorporates both old and new elements of the world into itself.

To set an object equal to money is to give it a *price*. Thus, the *price form* is a sub-form of the money form, in which any

$$yB = x \, gold$$

But the price form never stands alone. It is part of the money form. Setting any commodity equal to some quantity of money, by giving it a price, instantly ties it into the whole world of capital.[51] How? By setting a price, it is affirmed that this use-value, having been produced by useful labor of some sort, is only one special product of that universal tool of capital's control: work. Setting an object equal to money sets it equal to all other commodities and equates the labor which produced it to all other labor, affirms its common usefulness to capital as means of social control. (We ignore, as Marx does, cases where prices are set on things that are not the products of labor, e.g., unworked land.) It makes no difference whether the quantity of embodied labor is socially necessary or not—as we have seen earlier, this is often not the case. The *qualitative* equality of work has been affirmed and the quantity set socially. Money shows to the commodity its value for capital, i.e., the usefulness of the labor that produced it as a vehicle for controlling society.

Money not only equates all commodities as products of labor but also stands as the *universal mediator* between all these different elements of capital. In the exchange of labor-power for money, money mediates its

---

51. Already in his analysis of the production and circulation of commodities, Marx saw how setting a price on a product incorporated it into capital, even when it was produced by unwaged labor. See *Capital, Vol. II*, Chapter 4, pp. 109–111. Today, from the perspective of the social factory, in which so-called non-capitalist modes of production are understood as ways of organizing unwaged labor, this is even more true.

owner's relation to capital, not only to direct employers but to other workers and to all commodities. The money wage, M, is one way in which capital, K, mediates its relation to our labor-power, LP: $K - M - LP$. There are many others, as we saw in the preceding section, but the money wage is the most common and most revealing. As such it also establishes the importance of the *unwaged* relation to capital.

As we have seen, unwaged relations may be mediated in a variety of ways, e.g., men mediating the relation of their unwaged wives or professors mediating that of students to capital. All workers, waged and unwaged, must obtain the means of subsistence, but not always directly through wages. School children work for capital to the extent that they produce their labor-power for future roles as workers (waged and unwaged), but most receive no direct money payment. As unwaged housewives are supported by the resources (money) obtained by a waged husband, so children are supported by one or more waged parent. The relation with capital is mediated directly for whoever is paid a money wage, but that person mediates for unwaged family members. In these circumstances, the ways those at home work for capital is hidden by the absence of direct money payment.[52]

This brings out an important consideration about money that is often overlooked—namely, that for money to play the role of mediator or universal equivalent, there must be many relations where it does *not* mediate directly. The place in *Capital* where Marx makes this clearest is in his analysis—in Chapter 25—of the waged and unwaged. For capital to be able to use the money wage to mediate its relation to waged workers, it must maintain a *reserve army of unwaged workers* as a check on the power of the former. But to say that there must always be such an army is to say that money is the universal mediator in a peculiar way. Ultimately, everyone must get commodities to survive, but not necessarily through their personal command of a wage. Money, however, remains the universal mediator because it even defines its absence. The unwaged are defined with deference to the waged—defined by their *lack* of control over some money. Unwaged spouses and children may not receive money directly from capital, but they either receive some through the waged member of the household or receive what money buys—what they lack is control over the money supporting them, buying their food, etc. This is exactly why the struggle of the unwaged has often been for wages, not because they want to expand capital's dominion—they

---

52. See the more detailed analysis in my commentaries on the chapters on the wage (especially Chapters 19 and 21).

already suffer that—but to gain greater powers of self-determination. This was the objective of the Wages for Housework Campaign.[53]

The maintenance of non-monied, or unwaged, relations are important to capital in many ways. The image of the milling crowd at the factory gates begging for jobs or protesting their absence is one traditional but limited vision. To it we must add unwaged students, women and street-dwellers in the developed world. But, as we saw in the analysis of primitive accumulation, the case of the Global South is even more dramatic. Through colonialism, capital created and maintained vast, partially self-supporting global reserves of unwaged labor-power—a worldwide reserve army. Despite the defeat of most formal colonial empires, poverty continues to be the tool by which vast millions are kept alive but (capitalists hope) available when needed. These reserves are drawn upon either for immigration into areas where their cheap labor can be used to hold down the wage demands of more powerful workers (e.g., Mexican and Caribbean labor in the US; Mediterranean, East European and African workers in Western Europe) or for employment in their own areas when runaway shops seek out their cheap, and often politically repressed, labor locally. Of course, time and again things have not worked out so well and the struggles of the unwaged have often made them unprofitable for capital's factories.

That money is a mediator—interposed between capital and the working class—means two things. First, for workers, attacks on capital can both use and refuse this mediation, exactly as women and students have used and bypassed men and professors, respectively. In strikes, workers refuse the wage mediation and attack capital directly with refusal of work, sabotage, factory seizure, and so on. So too, direct appropriation involves the refusal of capital's prices of other commodities, e.g., changing labels in a supermarket, using free slugs instead of purchased tokens in the subway, or the total elimination of price through shoplifting, sneaking into movie theatres, employee theft, or collective Black Christmases where commodities are seized.[54] It involves the self-reduction or bypassing of utility or housing

---

53. On the logic of the "wages for housework" analysis of the work of women in the home and their demands for payment for their work, see the seminal essay by Mariarosa Dalla Costa, "Women and the Subversion of the Community" (1971), in Barbagallo (ed.), *Women and the Subversion of the Community: A Mariarosa Dalla Costa Reader*, Brooklyn, NY: PM Press, 2019. For some history of that campaign, see Louise Toupin, *Le salaire au travail ménager: Chronique d'une lutte féminist international*, Montreal: les éditions du remoue-ménage, 2014; and Silvia Federici (ed.), *Wages for Housework: The New York Committee 1972–1977, History, Theory, Documents*, Brooklyn, NY: Autonomedia, 2017.

54. "Black Christmases" refers to the direct appropriation of goods during electrical blackouts, such as the one that occurred in New York City in 2003. The same kind of

prices, e.g., collective refusal to pay, illegally taping electrical lines or gas pipes, squatting abandoned buildings.[55] This refusal of price is a refusal of capital's rules of the game. Refusing to accept the role of money amounts to the refusal to accept everything we have seen going into the determination of money—the whole set of value relations. This is a working-class perspective with a vengeance.

The only question one might ask is whether it makes any difference that today gold has been largely demonetized and replaced by paper and bank accounts. Marx shows in Chapter 3 that it does not; I return to this question in my commentary on that chapter.

Howsoever capital manipulates money, whether through corporations, national governments, or international agreement, it should now be clear that the actual object of the manipulations is the value relation between workers and capital. We have seen the complex way money expresses this class relation and the complex roles it plays at the heart of that relation. Many roles and institutions of money are not analyzed in Chapter 1, but the analysis of the universal equivalent in the money form and the price form has given us some fundamental and basic insights into the role of money as medium of circulation and as mediator between the classes. It permits us to see, if not the details, at least the basic character of money in every period of class struggle.

Section 4: The Fetishism of the Commodity and its Secret

Outline of Marx's Analysis

Commodities seem simple but are very strange, enigmatic things
 – not as sensuous use-values, not as products of useful labor
 – but as values, as products of abstract labor
 – such that the relationships between their producers "take on the
   form of a social relation between the products of labor"
Thus *fetishism*,
 – where social relations among producers assume "the fantastic form of
   a relation between things"

▶

---

appropriation occurred during the urban uprisings of the mid-1960s, from Watts in California to Newark, New Jersey, and in moments of crisis, in the absence of outside aid, e.g., New Orleans in the wake of Hurricane Katrina in 2005.

55.   For examples of the collective self-reduction of prices, see Bruno Ramirez, "The Working-Class Struggle Against the Crisis: Self-Reduction of Prices in Italy", *Zerowork* #1, 1975, pp. 143–150, or the mass refusal to pay jacked up water prices in Detroit in 2014 or Baltimore in 2016.

– akin to religion where "the products of the human brain appear as
autonomous figures"

– attaches itself to products of labor

– social relations among producers exist only through the mediation of
exchange

Its *secret*,

– producers see only the relationship between objects that are
exchanged

– but equating different products in exchange, equates different kinds
of labor

– thus, fetishism hides value, or, the value hidden within the
commodity form

– commodities become social hieroglyphs that must be deciphered

Value,

– deciphering becomes possible through the *quantitative* equality
revealed in the exchange of commodities

– at first random, but eventually "firmly established" through repeated
exchanges

– amidst fluctuations, socially necessary labor time "asserts itself"

– determination of the magnitude of value by labor time is therefore "a
secret" hidden under random fluctuations

– analysis of prices led to determination of the magnitude of value

– analysis of their common expression in money led to the establishment of their character as values

– but the money form *conceals* the social character of an individual's
labor

Social character of private labor,

– hidden in capitalism

– in plain view in *Robinson Crusoe*, in feudal society, in associations of
free men

– in all these cases, social relations are *not* disguised as social relations
between things

Classical political economy,

– analyzed value and its magnitude, but:

– never clearly differentiated between "labor as it appears in the value
of a product" and "labor as it appears in the product's use-value"

– never asked why labor is expressed in value, why labor time is
expressed in the magnitude of value

– never saw that purely quantitative distinctions presuppose their qualitative unity, "reduction to abstract human labor"

– never succeeded "in discovering the form of value which in fact turns
value into exchange-value"

Commentary

This fourth section has a strange relationship with the three sections that precede it. Whereas those three exposit a theory of the value of labor to capital and explore many of its aspects, the arguments in this section critique what has just been laid out for failing to *explicitly* situate commodities as moments of a set of social relationships. Although throughout this section Marx refers only to the social relationships of commodity producing society, he also makes clear that the only fully developed one is capitalism.[56]

There are two main points to this section. The first identifies *fetishism*, or how omnipresent commodity exchange hides the social relationships that have generated that phenomenon. The second, partly through lengthy footnotes, illustrates this fetishism by pointing to how poorly economists have seen through it, remaining stuck at the analysis of the relationships among things. By failing to perceive how the interactions among things have been determined by the social relationships that produced them and they have never been able to understand "value" in terms of those social relationships.

Fetishism

In my experience of teaching, I have found that for most students, their only notion of fetishism has been limited to that of a sexual fetish, i.e., some body part or thing upon which people have a sexual fixation—thus missing the idea of something hidden behind the fetish. Because of this limitation, I have often used the example of Chinese foot fetishism as an illustration of the kind of thing Marx discusses with respect to commodities. In that particularly obnoxious case, the subordination and domination of Chinese women achieved through the painful breaking and binding of their feet—often inflicted by their mothers—was camouflaged by making those crippled feet into supposedly desirable, sexually stimulating objects. Indeed, specialized shoes were sometimes constructed, covered with sexually evocative imagery, diverting attention from the real social relationship of domination to that of sexual excitation.[57] Marx's own choice—religion—to illustrate fetishism posed several problems for my students.

---

56.   Among other places where he states this clearly is in footnote 34, where he writes: "The value-form of the product of labor is the most abstract, but also the most universal form of the bourgeois mode of production; by that fact it stamps the bourgeois mode of production as a particular kind of social production of a historical and transitory nature." *Capital, Vol. I*, p. 174.

57.   See Michel Beurdeley and Kristopher Schipper, *Chinese Erotic Art*, Rutland, VT: C. E. Tuttle Co., 1969 and the attack on foot-binding by Qiu Jin (1875–1907) in Amy Dooling, *Women's Literary Feminism in Twentieth-Century China*, New York: Palgrave Macmillan, 2005.

In "the misty realm" of religion, Marx argues, "the products of the human brain appear as autonomous figures endowed with a life of their own, which enter into relations both with each other and with the human race."[58] Where is the fetishism? In the way the preoccupation of religious people with their gods (or, for Deists, their God) blinds them to how their imagined deities are indeed "the products of the human brain." This analysis amounts to what is sometimes called a "projection" theory of religion. Marx was neither the first to embrace such a theory—he was preceded by both conservative thinkers such as Thomas Hobbes (1588–1679) and David Hume (1711–76) and radical ones such as Ludwig Feuerbach (1804–72)—nor the last, as we find similar concepts in the work of Nietzsche and in modern psychology where interest in "projection" has shifted from a preoccupation with religion to one with interpersonal relationships, e.g., individuals who project their own traits onto the behavior of others, whether those traits be desirable or not.[59]

My students' problems with Marx's theory of religion included 1) perceiving it as a harsh attack on religion in general, and 2) perceiving it as an attack on their own beliefs. Where gods and goddesses have been incarnations of natural forces or personifications of particular human traits, e.g., Aphrodite or Venus as goddess of beauty, many students found the idea of projection easy enough to grasp, and even accept. But those who believed in a singular, unique God, e.g., those in the Judeo-Christian-Islamic tradition, found it much harder to see their God as a projection and personification of human ideas of power, of goodness and of the patriarchal social relations of the societies that birthed those religions.

Perceiving Marx's theory as an attack on religion in general usually derived not only from the cited passage in *Capital*, but from his well-known reference to religion as "the opiate of the people" in his *Contribution to the Critique of Hegel's Philosophy of Right* (1843). Marx's phrase has usually been interpreted as condemning religion for promising an illusory "pie up in the sky, after you die" and distracting workers from struggle against their exploiters in the here and now. Today, during an opioid-addiction epidemic, where the primary starting point of addiction has been the use of painkillers, it should be easier to read Marx's characterization of religion in the spirit of his time. In those days, the primary use of opiates was, as it is today, painkilling. There were, to be sure, "opium eaters," both in Britain and in China, where the British East India Company fought two wars to open

---

58. *Capital, Vol. I,* p. 165.
59. A standout example today is Donald Trump, who repeatedly castigates others for behaviors of which he has been frequently guilty, e.g., lying and purveying what he calls "fake news."

the country to its opium. But far more common was the use of morphine (extracted from opium) and of laudanum (opium prepared in an alcoholic solution) as painkillers. Within both that historical context, and within the current epidemic, to call religion an "opiate of the people" appears less of a condemnation and more as simple commentary on how the pains of day-to-day existence are, to some degree, alleviated by religious faith.

With *commodity* fetishism, Marx argues, relationships between producers "take on the form of a social relation between the products of labor." In other words, people see only that mass of commodities, evoked at the beginning of the chapter, being produced by a diverse array of producers, and not the social relationships they embody. This is an everyday experience, as we are bombarded by advertisements touting this or that commodity. As a result, most people only relate to other producers through the market, through buying (or ignoring) the products of their labor. Economists too, Marx observes, have been primarily preoccupied with the analysis of market relations where commodities are bought and sold—to the detriment, he argues, of their ability to understand the social dynamics of capitalism.

The Limited Understanding of Economists

With their attention focused on commodity exchange, Marx argues, economists were inexorably drawn to the analysis of the *quantitative* relationships among commodities, as manifested in their money prices. "It was solely the analysis of the prices of commodities," he writes, "which led to the determination of the magnitude of value, and solely the common expression of all commodities in money which led to the establishment of their character as values."[60] While the classical political economists' theory of value was based on labor, that theory was soon replaced with "neoclassical economics" whose core was "price theory," or what is now called "microeconomics," where market-determined, money price is the only concept of value.[61] Even after the advent of Keynesian "macroeconomics," however, market prices have remained the only recognized universal measure of value. Fetishism obtains throughout because of the way the money form "conceals the social character of private labor" and the social relations among producers, "instead of revealing them plainly."

---

60. Ibid., p. 168.

61. In Part I of *Rupturing the Dialectic*, there is a brief analysis of the replacement of the labor theory of value with theories of price determination based first on a homogenous concept of utility, somewhat akin to a labor theory, and then on heterogeneous personal preferences. A much more detailed account is given in Cheeyakpuvanda Carriappa's "The Unruly Masses in the Development of Economic Thought", PhD dissertation, University of Texas at Austin, August 2003.

Marx's assessment of the limited understanding of classical political economists was based on extensive critical study of their writings, beginning in
the 1840s, that revealed, he felt, both what they had understood and what
they failed to comprehend. By 1863, four years before publishing *Capital*,
he had filled some 23 notebooks, over a thousand pages, with extensive
commentary on the writings of political economists such as Adam Smith
and David Ricardo. Originally intended as Volume IV of *Capital*, some
of that critical material was included in his *Contribution to the Critique of
Political Economy* but most was eventually compiled and published after
his death in the three volumes of *Theories of Surplus Value*. What you find
in this section of Chapter 1 is therefore a very abbreviated set of critical
comments based on that research.

In those comments, Marx highlights what he considers the fundamental
limitation of even the best analyses of the classical political economists:

> As regards value in general, classical political economy in fact nowhere
> distinguishes explicitly and with a clear awareness between labor as it
> appears in the value of a product, and the same labor as it appears in the
> product's use-value. . . It does not occur to the economists that a purely
> quantitative distinction between the kinds of labor presupposes their
> qualitative unity or equality, and therefore their reduction to abstract
> human labor.[62]

In Section 2, Marx considered this distinction "the pivot on which a clear
comprehension of Political Economy turns." He considered his discovery
of this distinction and his working out of its implications, not only for the
critique of classical political economy but for his own theory, essential. He
once wrote to Engels that one of the "best points in my book" was "*the
twofold character of labor, according to whether it is expressed in use-value or
exchange-value.*"[63]

He also claims that "one of the chief failings of classical political
economy" was its inability to discover "the form of value which in fact turns
value into exchange-value." Not only did Smith and Ricardo treat the form
of value as "something of indifference" but by treating capitalism as "the
eternal natural form of social production" they overlooked "the specificity of the value-form, and consequently of the commodity-form together
with its further developments, the money form, the capital form, etc."[64]
This blindness to historical specificity has plagued economics ever since.

---

62. *Capital, Vol. I*, footnote 33, p. 173.
63. Marx to Engels, August 24, 1867, *MECW, vol. 42*, p. 407.
64. These points are made in *Capital, Vol. I*, footnote 34, p. 174.

Whether looking back at history or at the current conjuncture, economists tend to deploy the same a-historical theory in their analysis.

In a final point, let us note Marx's critique of economists' efforts to include "nature" in the determination of exchange-value. He writes, "The degree to which some economists are misled by fetishism. . . is shown, among other things by the dull and tedious dispute over the part played by nature in the formation of exchange-value."[65] Because, he argues, "exchange-value is a definite social manner of expressing the labor bestowed on a thing, it can have no. . . natural content." As he pointed out in Section 2, labor mediates humans' relationship to nature, but his theory of value is a social theory of that mediation, not, as the economists would have it, a theory that sees labor as one input into production and "nature" (in whatever form) another input. In formulations such as the production function $Q = f(K, L, N)$, economists only achieve the homogeneity of both inputs (K, L, N) and output Q, necessary to the utilization of such equations, by measuring everything in terms of exchange-value (money), thus deriving their equations based on an assumption that not only capital and labor, but also "nature" can be measured in such a fashion.

CHAPTER 2: THE PROCESS OF EXCHANGE

Outline of Marx's Analysis

Analysis of fetishism means we must move from the study of commodities to that of their owners'
  – possession
  – embodied will
  – consenting alienation
  – private property and contract
Contradiction: commodities must be:
  – values before use-values
  – use-values before values
  – resolution = exchange
Money
  – "crystallizes" out of exchange
History of exchange
  – reciprocity instead of exchange
  – exchange of excess
  – production for exchange
  – emergence of money

---

65. *Capital, Vol. I*, p. 176.

Commentary

Here Marx responds to his critique of the fetishism of his own presentation in Sections 1–3 of Chapter 1 because it only dealt with the relationships between commodities independently of the social relations of which they are a part.

From Things to Social Processes

Against his previous descriptions of commodities "doing this" and "doing that" (e.g., expressing value here, reflecting an essence there), he notes that "commodities cannot themselves go to market. . . we must, therefore have recourse to their guardians."[66] In so doing, we pass from the abstract world of Chapter 1, to the more realistic world of actual exchange—to the market where the owners of commodities meet, trade and realize the form of value.

Marx starts with an analysis of the relation between commodities and their owners, then passes to a summary of the logic of money as a requirement of generalized exchange, and finally to a sketch of the historical emergence of exchange and money. His analysis of the relations between commodities and their owners, and among owners, is very close to Hegel's in his *Philosophy of Right* (1820).[67]

1. Owners have possession of commodities.
2. Owners are in relation to each other as having their "will" in the objects.
3. Alienation of commodities only occurs in consenting acts.
4. Juridical expressions of this are private property and contracts of exchange.

The primary and most fundamental example of this in capitalism is the exchange of labor-power for the means of subsistence. In that case, we have already seen in Part Eight the meaning of the above four conditions. The worker must have possession of his labor-power (not be a slave or a serf). The capitalist must have possession of the means of production (having taken them from the workers). Given this pattern of possession, the two

---

66. *Capital, Vol. I*, p. 178.

67. For Hegel's analysis, on which Marx draws, see G. W. F. Hegel, *Outlines of the Philosophy of Right*, translated by T. M. Knox, revised by Stephen Houlgate, Oxford: Oxford University Press, 2008, First Part: "Abstract Right", Section 1: "Property" and Section 2: "Contract." You might also want to read the Third Part: section 2 on "Civil Society"; Subsection A on the "System of Needs", which contains his analysis of needs, work, capital and class divisions.

parties are "free" to act. This "freedom" appears as an act of free "will" as well as an act between two freely consenting property owners. That Marx goes beyond Hegel on this was already apparent in Part Eight in his ironic attack on the meaning of such "freedom." This will recur in Chapter 6 on the "Sale and Purchase of labor-power." Finally, the exchange of labor-power for the means of subsistence takes the form of a legal contract, verbal or written. The union contract formed through collective bargaining being a recent formal example.

The introduction of the owner adds concreteness to the analysis of the exchange process, partly because the owner, unlike the commodity, is not interested in just any exchange but in some specific exchange. "[The commodity] is always ready to exchange not only soul, but body, with each and every other commodity... the owner makes up for this lack [of specificity] in the commodity of a sense of the concrete, physical body of the other commodity by his own five and more senses."[68] In other words, the owner goes into the market with a will, with the objective of acquiring some other particular commodity—directly, in the case of barter, indirectly in the case of markets where money is used.

At this point Marx points out a contradiction—an analysis carried over from his earlier work *A Contribution to the Critique of Political Economy* and from his analysis in Chapter 1 of the two sides of the commodity: use-value and exchange-value. First, sellers' only interest in their own commodities are their exchange-values, "for himself its only direct use-value is as a bearer of exchange-value... all commodities are non-use-values for their owners... consequently [and this is the first point] commodities must be realized as values [which is to say exchanged] before they can be realized as use-values [consumed]." Second, to be exchanged someone must see them as potential use-values: "they must stand the test as use-values before they can be realized as values."[69] There is the contradiction. Before they can be use-values they must be exchange-values but before they can be exchange-values they must be use-values. To be complete as commodities they must be both.

Money in Exchange

In this contradiction Marx sees the origin of the need for money in exchange. In so far as each owner of commodities looks at other commodities "as the particular equivalent of his own commodities [and]. . . his own commodity is the universal equivalent for all others. . . there is

68. *Capital, Vol. I*, p. 179.
69. All quotations from *Capital, Vol. I*, p. 179.

in fact no commodity acting as universal equivalent." This problem was already discussed in Chapter 1 somewhat more abstractly (the problem of the expanded form) and the solution perceived: the money form. But this, he notes, cannot be solved in the abstract, at the formal level of Chapter 1:

> Only the action of society can turn a particular commodity into the universal equivalent. . . through the agency of the social process it becomes the specific social function of the commodity which has been set apart to be the universal equivalent. It thus becomes—money. Money necessarily crystalizes out of the process of exchange.[70]

In other words, the rise of the universal equivalent, i.e., money, is a concrete social phenomenon, not an abstract one; it emerges within the historical development of exchange. It comes with the "broadening and deepening of the phenomenon of exchange." The "need to give an external expression to this opposition [between use-value and exchange-value] for the purposes of commercial intercourse produces the drive towards an independent form of value." So, money within exchange is the historical outgrowth of the exchanging of commodities by their owners. Here again Marx fights the fetishism which would deal with these matters purely in terms of the relations between things.

The rest of this chapter is devoted to a sketch of the process by which money as universal equivalent emerged from widening exchange. Howsoever accurate Marx's treatment, the major methodological point is that we must locate this phenomenon in the real world of exchange, understand what is being designated by the term universal equivalent (money) and not be bemused by commodity fetishism into an equally mistaken money fetishism. As he terminates the chapter: "The riddle of the money fetish is therefore the riddle of the commodity fetish, now become visible and dazzling to our eyes."[71]

Then and Now

1. There is no reciprocal isolation or foreignness in the "primitive" community—whether of patriarchal family, Indian commune or Inca state.
2. Exchange begins at the boundaries of communities, of things not produced for exchange.
3. Commodities come to be produced for exchange.

---

70. Ibid., p. 180.
71. Ibid., p. 187.

4. Repetition makes normal, fixes values at definite magnitudes.
5. Articles come to only momentary equivalence with universal equivalent.
6. The universal equivalent crystallizes out as the money form— attached to most important articles of exchange from outside, or to local mobile wealth, i.e., cattle.
7. Natural selection leads to the money commodity being chosen among those that can be divisible at will and uniform in quality, i.e., precious metals.
8. Value of money is determined by socially necessary labor time of its production.

All of this is a synopsis of his analysis in *A Contribution to the Critique of Political Economy* and in the *Grundrisse*'s chapter on money, both of which can be consulted for a more detailed account.

This sketch of the historical origins of money has led some to interpret this chapter, as well as Chapters 1 and 3, as being about money in all kinds of society where money and exchange have existed, not just about money and exchange in capitalism. Of such interpretations I say: the primary analysis in each chapter in Part One is about the determinations of exchange within *a fully developed system of exchange*. The *only* fully developed system of exchange is capitalism, for reasons that are presented in Part Eight and elsewhere (Volume II, Part One). Certainly, he does give examples, such as those above, which draw on pre-capitalist societies, while making the point that money as universal equivalent is not an abstraction but designates a real social phenomenon within the history of exchange.[72] And at times he points to the historical roots of various aspects of capital. Here it is money; in Volume III it is merchant capital, rent, etc. But I would recall his injunction in the introduction to *A Contribution to the Critique of Political Economy* that while bourgeois economy can provide a key to the past, one should not equate the past with the present.[73]

Commodification of Life

One aspect of Marx's analysis of the centrality of exchange in capitalism which has struck a sympathetic chord in many, even those who would never

---

72. Along with Marx's own review of the history of the development of money and exchange, you might also want to look at Pierre Vilar, *A History of Gold and Money, 1450–1920*, New York: Verso, 1991 (originally published in Spain in 1960).
73. Originally written for the *Contribution*, the Introduction was set aside and replaced with a shorter Preface. It now appears in *MECW, vol. 28*, pp. 37–45.

call themselves Marxists, is how, in the pursuit of profit and social control, capitalism tends to convert both things and relationships into commodities. This tendency toward the "commodification of life" has been recognized and deplored by a great many novelists, poets, social commentators and songwriters. From Balzac's caustic condemnations of an infinitely invasive commercial logic to popular music, the tendency has long been denounced, made fun of and rejected in prose and song lyrics.

In reggae musician Jimmy Cliff's song "Commercialization" (1973), this aspect of capitalist Babylon is attacked vigorously. He decries the commercialization—"the notion of [capitalist] civilization"—of women, people in general, food, drugs, war and time.[74]

More lighthearted, Tom Waits's song "Step Right Up" (1976) makes carnivalesque fun of advertising and the pretense that any and all problems can be solved by the purchase of some commodity, from the drudgery of housework to fears about personal appearance and relationships.[75] Interlaced with sound bites of advertising hype and sexual innuendo is the real message of the song: all the junk is being sold for profit at the expense of the buyer ("How do we do it? Volume, volume turn up the volume," "We'll give you the business," "The large print giveth and the small print taketh away"). In this case the very length of the song (five minutes and 40 seconds) is both a reproduction and a critique of the endlessness of the advertising noise that constantly bombards us.

In 1979 the British rock group The Clash also took up this theme more directly, attacking the idea that one can buy a "personality" through the purchase of commodities. Instead of being a "happy shopper" constructing his life through his purchases, the singer in "Lost in the Supermarket" wanders confused amidst the mountains of commodities.[76] He has done as the ads say, clipped his coupons, listened to the "hit" music and drunk his bottle of social brew; but lo and behold, the alienation doesn't go away no matter how much he participates in "exchange."

Finally, the Reagan years (1981–89) of "greed is good" justifying tax breaks for the rich, the Bush II years (2001–09) of war, economic crisis and more tax breaks for the rich, and Trump's most recent (2017) additional tax breaks for the one percent have only reinforced such critical views of

---

74. On the commodification of war, see Doug Kellner, *The Persian Gulf TV War*, Boulder, CO: Westview Press, 1992 on how the Pentagon and the news networks packaged and sold the Gulf War to the American people, against one of the most rapidly mobilized and nationwide anti-war movements in US history. For further background, see his earlier book, *Television and the Crisis of Democracy*, Boulder, CO: Westview Press, 1990.
75. *Small Change*, Asylum Records, 1995.
76. *London Calling*, CBS, 1979.

the commercialization of life and the narrow concept of self-interest that pervades the ideology that has accompanied it. Such critique has found its way into the repertoires of even the most popular, non-radical rock and country singers. One example is Shania Twain in "Ka-ching!" (2003) who mocks/laments the capitalist seduction that "more is better," the compulsion to buy, the dangers of credit and the notion that having more money and the stuff it buys brings happiness.[77]

CHAPTER 3: MONEY, OR THE CIRCULATION OF COMMODITIES

Overview of Chapter
Section 1: The Measures of Value Section 2: The Means of Circulation Section 3: Money

Preliminary Commentary

First and foremost, in capitalism money is power. Money gives capital the power to impose work on us and, when successful, bestows the power (through profits and investment) to do it again on an expanded scale. At the same time, from the point of view of the rest of us, money—if only we can get our hands on enough of it—gives us the power to resist or refuse work, to struggle against the exploitation and alienation that comes with it and some resources to craft alternatives.

Not surprisingly then, money is a frequent subject of popular music. Money—especially corporate wealth—is desired for the power it gives and feared for the threat that it carries. Pink Floyd in their 1973 song "Money," written in a period when capitalists were resisting wage increases, mock the ideological contradictions of such a situation. "Money so they say / is the root of all evil today / but if you ask for a rise / it's no surprise / that they are giving none away."[78] "They," of course, are the capitalists and their apologists who preach the evils of money to the working class while using it for their own purposes of domination. Rush, in a song written during the Reagan years when capital was wielding its money like a bludgeon against the working class, are blunter about the power of money. Taking the title "The Big Money," from John Dos Passos's 1936 novel of the same name,

---

77. *UP!*, Mercury Records, 2002.
78. *The Dark Side of the Moon*, Harvest Records, 1973.

they sing, "Big money goes around the world... pushing people around... got a mean streak... got no soul."[79]

In another song, written only three years later, still during the unapologetic reign of Reagan/Bush and their rich capitalist friends, Randy Newman makes the same point in his own low-key, ironic manner in the song "It's Money that Matters."[80] How is it, he wonders, as so many of us have, that the best and the brightest often just scrape by while the wheelers and dealers, the slime balls and the crooks are living high off the hog in their "great big houses" with their "great big swimming pools." The answer, of course, is money. Of course, most of us understand that "it's money that matters" and not just in the USA but throughout the whole capitalist world. The difficult questions concern why money matters and how it can be a weapon, both for and against capitalism.

Coming from the streets, a lot of hip-hop music is preoccupied with money, so often out of reach, far from those streets. But what's the point of getting it? In 2000, Common suggested in "The 6th Sense" that the "revolution is here" and money can buy change.

> I'd be lying if I said I didn't want millions
> More than money saved, I wanna save children
> Dealing with alcoholism and Afrocentricity
>
> ...
>
> I'm Morpheus in this hip-hop Matrix, exposing fake shit[81]

Marx's analysis broadens our understanding about how and why money is power beyond Chapter 1, where we only got as far as the *money form* of value, where that universal equivalent is a socially accepted commodity. In

$$\left.\begin{array}{l} y\text{B} \\ w\text{C} \\ z\text{D etc.} \end{array}\right\} = x\text{ gold}$$

we saw that each mediated relation, e.g., $yB - x\,gold - wC$, has the form of what Marx calls "simple commodity exchange," or $C - M - C$, in the case of the labor market, $LP - M - C(MS)$. The aggregation of all such exchanges constitutes "circulation" as a whole.

---

79. *Power Windows*, Anthem Entertainment, 1985.
80. *Land of Dreams*, Reprise Records, 1988.
81. *Like Water for Chocolate*, MCA Records, 2000.

Structure of the Chapter

Marx's analysis begins with money within nation-states—because of the way national governments have come to create and regulate money—then moves on to examine money at the international level. Both analyses add concreteness to the much more abstract analysis of Chapter 1 where there was no such reference to nation-states and their role in exchange. He discusses five aspects of money:

1. Money as measure of value
2. Money as standard of price
3. Money as means of circulation
4. Money as hoard or store of value
5. Money as means of payment (credit)

Section 1: The Measure of Values

Outline of Marx's Analysis

a. money as measure of value
  – ideal vs real

b. money as standard of price
  – fixed weight of metal
  – weight names
  – money names

Commentary

Marx begins by distinguishing between money serving as the *measure of values* and as a *standard of price*. In both cases, when he writes of an ideal or imaginary expression of value or price, he is referring to the situation *before* commodities are sold. In terms of $C - M - C$, we are only at the first C, neither $C - M$ (sale) nor $M - C$ (purchase) has been completed. We can picture this phase of the analysis as:

C – potential M – potential C

C is produced and real, but M is only a desired goal, as is the subsequent $M - C$.

Now we saw in the money form how *qualitatively* money expresses the value of commodities and how *quantitatively* its magnitude measures that value.[82] We also saw in the price form, $yB = xgold$, how a single commodity money (e.g., gold), expresses price. Money is a *standard of price* in so far as "it is a fixed weight of metal," i.e., a measure of the quantity x of gold. Governments set this standard. They set both the *weight unit* or quantum with which to measure the amount of gold, e.g., an ounce, and they give *money names* to those units, e.g., 1 oz. of gold is $35.00, or 1/35 oz. of gold = $1.00.[83]

For example, suppose: *1 ton of iron = 1 oz. of gold* because the amount of socially necessary labor time that can be imposed producing one ton of iron is the same as the amount that can be imposed producing 1 oz. of gold. The ounce of gold serves as an equivalent of the value of the ton of iron to capital.[84] The 1 oz. of gold simultaneously serves as standard of price. The 1 oz. is the *weight-name* for the price of iron. The *money-name* is $35.00. In the days of commodity money, these money-names were attached to gold *coins* minted at a given, standard weight. To summarize:

Commodity: iron
Quantity: 1 ton
Measure of value: = 1 oz. of gold
Standard of Price: = 1 oz. of gold or 35 dollars

Various examples include:

Country	Weight of gold	Money name	Coins
United States	1 oz. of gold	35 dollars	7 five-dollar coins
United Kingdom	1 oz. of gold	12 pounds sterling	12 one-pound coins
France	20 grams of gold	100 francs	10 ten-franc coins

Simple wear and tear gradually separate money names of coins from their value. When worn down and no longer containing their original weight of

---

82. Because so many things and relationships become commodities in capitalism, money comes to be seen as the measure of everything, even things which might otherwise be thought of with no reference to money. In his song "Money Machine,"' on his album *In The Pocket*, James Taylor sings "you can measure your manhood by it."
83. I give $35 here because for many years the exchange-value of gold was fixed by the US government at $35/oz. That was the price it would pay for gold and that was the amount of gold it would give up (to foreigners) in exchange for their dollars. Since gold was demonetized in 1971 after the onset of the international monetary crisis, the price of gold has been set by supply and demand in the gold market and its price has varied enormously. In September 2017, 1 oz. of gold was selling for about $1,900.
84. This is an imaginary example, not based on any empirical evidence.

metal, then as standards of price coins misrepresent value. Precious metal coins were also intentionally debased by governments by adulterating precious with base metals, in efforts to surreptitiously increase their supply of money. Marx mentions "the continuous debasement of the currency by kings and princes."[85]

More interesting, from a worker's point of view, was debasement through the filing or clipping of metal from precious metal coins. Anyone who could get their hands on a coin could shave off a bit here and there—a challenge not only to the power of the state but to the class relations embodied in money.[86] With such debasement, a gold coin that was worth $10 upon coinage, after clipping might be worth only $9.95 or $9.90 because it contains less gold. Yet it would continue to be exchanged as if it were worth $10—until, of course, a general perception of the debasement led to its rejection as a standard. This posed a danger to exchange and to the power of the state. As a result, such "clipping" was made illegal and the mint responsible for coinage was invariably preoccupied with ferreting out and prosecuting those responsible for such attacks on the value of money.

This is one reason why the distinction between money as measure of value and as standard of price is important. Values can change and leave prices unaffected, or prices can change with value unaffected. Suppose, for example, price increases due to a sudden surge in demand, i.e., suddenly everyone wants to buy some commodity x. The price of x will rise as a reaction to the sudden increase in demand but its value—the socially necessary labor time required to produce it—has not changed. Inversely, there may be an inability to sell said commodity at a price which equals its

---

85. *Capital, Vol. I*, p. 194. In Section 1 of Chapter 10, Marx refers in footnote 2, to "the little shilling men," who he had previously identified in his *Contribution to the Critique of Political Economy* as those who advocated repayment of debt in debased shillings as a solution to currency problems. See, *MECW, vol. 29*, p. 319. In Marx's time, British monetary units included the pound sterling, which was divided into 20 shillings, each of which was divided into 12 pence (pennies), each of which was divided into four farthings. The farthing was demonetized in 1961 and after the conversion to a decimal system in 1971, the pound was divided into 100 pence and the shilling coin was replaced by a new five-pence piece. The shilling was demonetized in 1991. He returns to the issue of debasement in Section 3, subsection c) Coin.

86. The class politics of the debasement of money receive an illuminating treatment in George Caffentzis's book *Clipped Coins, Abused Words and Civil Government: John Locke's Philosophy of Money*, Brooklyn, NY: Autonomedia, 1989. Even today, when our coins contain very little precious metal (usually copper at most) we still find little reeded edges around the circumference of many coins (dimes, quarters, half-dollars and some dollar coins in the US), originally placed to help reveal if a coin had been clipped or filed and so lost some of its precious metal and value. They exist today purely for historical continuity.

value, and it is either sold at a price under its value or not sold at all. In such cases the full value of the commodity is not realized. It is either devalued or if the price goes to zero, it has no value at all. This is called the *realization problem*. For a commodity to have value it must achieve exchange-value. If the price is above or below the value, then there is unequal exchange. If this persists, there will be a change in the production of the commodity. If it can't be sold, it will no longer be produced, and its production will no longer provide an opportunity for putting people to work. If the price rises, to increase production more workers may be hired.

However, Marx usually abstracts from such discrepancies and assumes that prices equal values. This simplifies his analysis and exposition. However, he is quite explicit about some commodities having a price but no value, e.g., conscience, honor, unworked land.[87] Moreover, he recognizes that with constantly fluctuating markets, prices rarely equal value. He recognizes that supply and demand change far more rapidly than changes in the socially necessary labor time required to produce commodities.[88] He can abstract from such situations because his primary purpose here is a social/class understanding of the role of money in capitalism rather than explaining price variations.

Because economists are preoccupied with prices, many have dismissed Marx's theory in Chapters 1–3 because it does not provide tools for analyzing market-driven fluctuations in relative prices. Even if we knew the relative amounts of socially necessary labor time to produce various commodities, they argue, that would not explain the frequent divergence in relative prices from relative values. True, but it is not the purpose of Marx's theory. Neoclassical microeconomic theory (or "price theory"), with its focus on the determination of supply and demand, was designed for the analysis of just such market forces. However, unlike neoclassical theory, Marx's theory provides an analysis of money prices as a moment of the antagonistic class relations of capitalism. Neoclassical economic theory doesn't even recognize the existence of classes. Moreover, when we examine Marx's analyses of historical price fluctuations, we find that he uses a mixture of his labor theory and supply and demand analysis to understand price changes.[89]

---

87. *Capital, Vol. I*, p. 197.
88. This becomes important to his critique of Thomas Robert Malthus (1766–1834) on the causes of changes in wage levels. See my commentary on Chapter 25.
89. Marx's analysis of supply and demand, however, is *not* the same as that of contemporary microeconomics. He, like almost every economist of his time, was working before anyone (with the exception of a little-known French economist named Antoine Cournot, 1801–77) had developed an analysis of supply and demand in terms of mathematical functions relating price and quantity changes. You will not find in Marx's

Section 2: The Means of Circulation

Outline of Marx's Analysis

a. metamorphosis of commodities

$C - M - C, (P - U - I)$

b. the circuit of money

qualitative: $M - C - M$

quantitative: $M = PQ/V$

c. coin and symbols of value

– role of the state

– paper money

Commentary

Money serves as a medium of circulation of commodities, as M in $C - M$ – C. Marx characterizes this combination of sale, $C - M$, and purchase, M – C, as a "social metabolism"—one in which money facilitates commodities passing from hand to hand. Analyzing this process, and elaborating on the metaphor of metabolism, Marx suggests changes in the form of value are akin to the metamorphoses undergone by insects in their development.[90]

a) Metamorphoses

In a sale, when a commodity C is exchanged for money M, the owner of C realizes its exchange-value. The exchange-value of C now exists in the form of the money M. This original owner of C, Marx says, has accomplished the *first metamorphosis* or change of form.

When this money (the exchange-value of C) is then used as means of purchase $(M - C)$, the second change of form occurs—the *second metamor-phosis*—as the value of the original commodity is transformed by exchange into a particular use-value to be consumed. Thus, exchange resolves the original contradiction between the use-value and the exchange-value of the commodity, discussed at length in Chapter 1, by actual exchange-value and actual use-value replacing potential exchange-value and potential use-value.

---

analysis, therefore, distinctions such as those between the quantity demanded at a price and "demand" conceived in terms of a downward sloping curve. That said, you will find as competent an analysis of market fluctuations as was available in the mid-nineteenth century.

90.   On his use of this biological analogy, see my commentary on Section 1 of Chapter 1.

Two obvious things can occur to rupture this sequence and cause such circulation to break down. First, if produced goods cannot be sold at acceptable prices, they may not even be brought to market and may be destroyed.[91] A second rupture can occur if C is successfully sold, but then the M obtained is held without being spent, such that no $M - C$ takes place. The choice to hold onto cash rather than spend it, often becomes more common during times of uncertainty and declining confidence in the future.[92] "The division of exchange into purchase and sale," he writes, ". . . contains the general possibility of commercial crisis, essentially because the contradiction of commodity and money is the abstract and general form of all contradictions inherent in the bourgeois mode of labor."[93]

Commercial crises arise when such ruptures proliferate on a large scale. Understanding them requires their origins and consequences be analyzed in terms of the underlying antagonistic polarity of capitalist class relations.[94] As Marx writes in *A Contribution to the Critique of Political Economy*: "The 'antagonistic' nature of bourgeois production is, moreover expressed in the antithesis of buyer and seller."[95] That antagonistic nature, of course, lies in the relationship between capitalists and workers, a relationship which includes the exchange of labor-power for a wage and the subsequent exchange of the wage for consumer goods, topics he takes up in Chapter 6.

Because the series of such exchanges is unlimited, potentially infinite, and because it is interlocked, that infinity is of the "good" variety—self-related and mediated by the universal mediator.[96] This is an essential point. Capital organizes all market exchanges into one huge circuit of circuits in which

91. Examples of such aborted commodity production include the destruction of cows and pigs on farms during the Great Depression when their market price fell below the cost of keeping them alive and the burning of coffee beans in Brazil to restrict supply and keep prices high.

92. John Maynard Keynes, deploying an analytical framework quite different from Marx's, also demonstrated how such a shift toward increased savings could cause a crisis for the economy. Contradicting the assumption that greater savings would result in greater investment and growth, he pointed out that decreased spending could undermine investment and slow growth.

93. Ibid., p. 332.

94. Among classical political economists, there was a heated debate about whether such large-scale ruptures were possible. Some, such as Ricardo, argued that while individual commodities might fail to find buyers, in the aggregate "supply creates demand" (Say's Law) and widespread rupture was impossible. Others, most notably Malthus, looked at the increasingly common commercial crises of the time and replied "Nonsense!" to Ricardo (and Say) whose theory proved repeatedly unable to account for those crises.

95. *MECW, vol. 29*, p. 331.

96. On the "good infinity," see the analysis of the general form of value in my commentary on Section 3 of Chapter 1.

NB: $C - M - C$ represents but one moment in the general circulation of commodities and is linked to others. To picture circulation as simply the sum of the circuits, albeit tempting, would be misleading because each part of the circuit $C - M - C$ is also a part of two other circuits. The *sale*, $C - M$, is also simultaneously a *purchase* from the point of view of the owner of money M who spends it on C. From the perspective of the owner and seller of C, M is the transformed value of C. But for the owner of M, its nature is not derived from C but, perhaps, from some previous commodity C which was sold. When the owner of the original C then spends the equivalent M to buy a new commodity, i.e., the second C in $C - M - C$, that purchase is simultaneously a sale from the point of view of its seller. Therefore, $C - M - C$ implies at the very least, three actors, each participating in a different circuit of commodity exchange.

exchange-value and use-value are defined within the whole. The role of money as mediator is even clearer now than when we studied the money form.

In the relation $C - M - C$, we also have a clear syllogistic form of mediation, which Marx identifies as an example of the Hegelian syllogism $P - U - I$, or Particularity – Universality – Individuality.[97] The seller only cares about a *particular aspect* of C, its potential exchange-value. Once sold, the value of the commodity takes the form of money, which is the *universal* equivalent. When spent, the money is exchanged for some *individual* commodity, which is consumed for its use-value. Money therefore mediates the two extremes of production and consumption. The most important such mediation, of course, is capital's imposition of the money wage between the working class and consumer goods, i.e., $LP - M - C(MS)$.

b) The Circulation of Money: Quality

In its role as universal mediator in the circulation of commodities, money also circulates. It passes from hand to hand, leaving one hand to purchase, received by another as payment. Its parallel circulation, Marx represents as $M - C - M$. In *A Contribution to the Critique of Political Economy*, the two forms are set out immediately together:

$C - M - C$
$M - C - M$

---

97.   *MECW, vol. 29*, p. 331.

In *Capital*, the second is talked about but not specified in this way until Chapter 4 on the general formula for capital. The reason is clear enough. $M - C - M$ makes no sense in and of itself. As Marx says, when we look at $M - C - M$, "one will immediately recognize the predominant form of bourgeois production."[98] But in capitalism $M - C - M$ must be $M - C - M'$, with $M' > M$, the expenditure of money to make more money.[99] Marx doesn't want to talk specifically about this expanding aspect of capital just yet, and therefore restricts himself to dealing with the circulation of money as a moment of the circulation of commodities. Unlike commodities that have been produced to be sold and ultimately drop out of circulation into consumption, money, Marx writes, "haunts the sphere of circulation," repeatedly passing from buyers to sellers. This raises the question of "how much money this sphere constantly absorbs."[100]

b) The Circulation of Money: Quantity

Highlighting his question, Marx immediately passes over to an analysis of the *quantitative aspect* of money as medium of circulation—the amount required to circulate a given quantity and value of commodities. The backdrop to his analysis was considerable debate—dating back to the mercantilists—about the relation between the amount of money, M, and the prices, P, of goods, Q, in circulation. For example, John Locke argued that the prices of goods would be proportional to the quantity of money that circulated them.[101] The more money, the higher the prices of a given quantity of goods in circulation.[102] Symbolically:

$$M = PQ, \ or \ P = M/Q$$

Where, with Q given, $P = f(M)$ and $dP/dM > 0$. Before long, Richard Cantillon (1680–1734), who investigated the concrete processes involved in an expansion of the money supply, pointed out that the *velocity* of money,

---

98. Ibid., p. 357.
99. In $M - C - M'$, money appears as the initiator of the process and its object, which helps make it a fetish, hiding the centrality of the production process, the control over labor-power and the production of commodities, including labor-power.
100.   *Capital, Vol. I*, p. 213.
101.   This theory was also propounded by Charles-Louis de Montesquieu (1689–1755) and David Hume (1711–76), both of whom Marx cites in this section. Hume is critiqued more thoroughly in *A Contribution to the Critique of Political Economy*.
102.   See Locke's "Some Considerations of the Consequences of the Lowering of Interest and the Raising the Value of Money" (1691), in *Locke on Money*, vol. 1, Clarendon Edition of the Works of John Locke, Oxford: Clarendon Press, 1991.

or how frequently each unit of money was being employed in a given period, had to be taken into account, because the more frequently a unit of money is used in exchange, the less is needed for any given period. If you could use money twice as frequently, you would only need half as much to circulate the same value of goods.[103] The result came to be known as the "quantity theory" of classical political economy, usually written these days as:

$$MV = PQ, \text{ or } MV = \Sigma p_i q_i, \text{ or } M = PQ/V, \text{ or } P = MV/Q^{104}$$

By assuming that Q and V are given in the short run, the usual interpretation became a variation on Locke's earlier, simpler idea that the prices of commodities will be determined by the amount of money thrown into the economy. For example, applied to the European inflation in the sixteenth century, in the wake of huge inflows of gold and silver from the Spanish and Portuguese colonies of the New World, the theory implied that the resulting increase in the amount of precious metals, M, in circulation drove up prices, P, i.e., $\uparrow M \Rightarrow \uparrow PQ/V$, or $\uparrow P \Leftarrow \uparrow MV/Q$. This Marx calls a "false conclusion" and an "illusion." He offers a quite different analysis.

Whereas the analysis above is all in terms of market prices, with no reference to any other value, Marx, as we have seen in the price form, $yB = xgold$, saw price as a monetary expression of value understood as socially necessary labor time (SNLT), i.e., some amount x of *gold* expresses the value of some amount y of B. For him, in a world of a commodity money such as gold, prices must be understood in terms of the value both of the commodity being exchanged (B) and of the money commodity (*gold*). So, if $y = 1$ and yB = a unit of B, then $xgold$ = the price of a unit of B. For multiple, n, units of B, their total value = $n(xgold)$. Where Locke or Cantillon would be happy with PQ, or $\Sigma p_i q_i$, as expressions of the market value of the goods in circulation, Marx begins instead with $\Sigma v_i q_i$, or Q_v, their total value measured in terms of SNLT.

The amount x of *gold* required to circulate a given value of commodities, Q_v, he argues, is determined by the value of *gold* and the average

---

103. See Cantillon's "Essai sur la nature du commerce en général" (1755), *Essay on the Nature of Trade in General*, Indianapolis, IN: Liberty Fund, 2015. Cantillon also recognized that under some conditions increases in the quantity of money could stimulate investment, increasing Q and thus modifying the effects of changes in the amount of money in circulation. In this section, footnote 27, Marx cites Guillaume-François Le Trosne (1728–80) and in footnote 29, William Petty on velocity, rather than Cantillon.
104. For those unfamiliar with the notation, p_i = price of individual good i, q_i = quantity of individual good i, $p_i q_i$ = the market value of good i and $\Sigma p_i q_i$ = sum of the market values of all goods.

velocity, V, of its use, i.e., $xgold = f(Q_{ev}V)$.[105] "We know," he writes, "that the values of commodities remaining constant, their prices vary with the value of gold (the material of money), rising in proportion as it falls, and falling in proportion as it rises."[106] Instead of prices being determined solely by the *amount* of money in circulation, i.e., $P = f(M)$, they are determined by both the amount and by the value of gold. Therefore, he explains the inflation of the sixteenth century by how the looting of the Inca and Aztec civilizations and of the subsequent use of slave labor in the mines of the Western Hemisphere not only produced new flows of gold into Europe, but also dramatically reduced the costs of producing gold and lowered its value. With a lower value for gold, it took more of it to represent the unchanged values, Q_{ev}, of the commodities being bought and sold in Europe. Hence, increases in prices denominated in gold of a lower value.[107]

On events closer to his own time, Marx's deploys his theory to reject the idea that crises are brought on by a lack of money. "Popular opinion," he writes, "is naturally inclined to attribute [stagnation] to a quantitative deficiency in the circulating medium."[108] Whereas, he argues, the real deficiency usually lies in a contraction of markets or a crisis in production, or, more rarely, a change in the value of money.[109]

c) Coin. The Symbol of Value

Metal money circulating is called coin. National governments mint coins at legally determined weights of precious metal, as we saw in Section 1. But we also saw how debasement can separate the money names of coins from their value, yet they still circulate, symbols of their original value. Therefore, coins of baser metal (tokens) and even paper, e.g., bank notes, can serve as symbols of the appropriate amounts of gold. But because any symbol can represent a given value, different amounts of paper money, i.e., pieces of paper upon which money-names are printed, can represent the same

---

105.   In this Marx agreed with the mercantilist John Law (1671–1729). See Law's *Money and Trade Considered* (1705), Charleston, SC: BiblioLife, 2009. In modern economic parlance, this is called an "endogenous" theory of money, as opposed to an "exogenous" one where it is supposed the state can control the supply of money in circulation. As the behavior of the Bank of England was based on the latter theory, Marx was often amused when its efforts to control the money supply failed and it was forced to respond to the demands of circulation to stave off deeper crises.

106.   *Capital, Vol. I*, p. 213.

107.   Ibid., p. 214.

108.   Ibid., p. 217.

109.   Ibid., pp. 217–219.

amount of value. In these circumstances, where value and price differ, the quantity theory requires reinterpretation. Instead of:

(1) $M = xgold = Q_v/V$ with Q_v = value of commodities in circulation and V = velocity,

we can rewrite the formula as:

(2) $M_p = paper\ money = Q_v/V$

As long as the nominal (face) value of M_p represents the amount of gold coin required to circulate Q_v at velocity V, Marx argues, the two expressions are equivalent. But the nominal value of inconvertible paper money issued by the state need not match the value of gold required. If, for example, the state decides to finance expenditures with huge increases in paper money, the amount of M_p will rise quickly. With prices, P, expressed in paper money-names, they too will rise as a result. For example, if M_p is quickly doubled then on the average P will double if the value of Q_v and V remain constant (assuming no feedback on production Q_v or V from the injection of money). Because the value represented by the doubled quantity of paper money will not have changed, the value represented by an aliquot portion of paper money (e.g. one dollar) will be halved. Paper money will have been *devalued* in the sense that each unit now buys only half the value of commodities. In other words, usual interpretation of the quantity theory holds in the case of paper money. The value represented by paper money is seen to be a function of its own quantity as well as the values it represents. The same is true with respect to credit money, whether tracked and measured on paper or digitally.[110] The failure of the classical political economists to clearly distinguish between value and prices hindered them from seeing this.

---

110. For some Marxists, the demonetization of gold and its replacement with purely fiat money has caused a crisis for Marx's analysis. For others, the basic lesson remains: money represents value, whether it is a commodity like gold with its own value, or purely a symbol. Domestically, gold was demonetized in the US in 1933, during the Great Depression, when the government stopped offering gold in exchange for notes and private holdings of gold were nationalized. Internationally, the role of gold as an international money—a declining complement to the dollar in the decades following World War II—collapsed in August 1971 when President Richard Nixon announced that the US would no longer exchange gold for dollars. See George Caffentzis, "Marxism after the Death of Gold", in Marcel van der Linden and Karl Heinz Roth, eds, *Beyond Marx: Theorizing the Global Labour Relations of the Twenty-First Century*, Chicago, IL: Haymarket Books, 2014, pp. 395–415.

Section 3: Money

Outline of Marx's Analysis

a. Hoarding
   - money as store of value
   - monetary reserves

b. Means of payment
   - credit
   - credit and class struggle
   - credit and crisis

c. World money
   - extension of analysis to world level
   - universal means of payment
   - means of purchase
   - embodiment of wealth

Commentary

a) Hoarding

When money drops out of circulation and its owners just hold onto it, not using it for anything except as a store of value, Marx calls it "hoard." The term is more familiar today from the reality TV series *Hoarders* about people who, suffering from "compulsive hoarding disorder," fill their houses with all kinds of junk. The only kind of hoard that interests Marx is money. With commodity money, such as gold or silver, hoard is simply money squirreled away, under a mattress or in a bank vault, or transformed into various "aesthetic forms" such as jewelry, which can always be melted down and converted to coin if needed.[111] Today, even though precious metals have been demonetized, some money is still regularly held as hoard. Both individuals and businesses often hold money for short periods in safes or banks for expected expenditures. Such hoard is accumulated "in preparation for the days when the sums which are owing fall due."[112] Money is

---

111.   Marx cites the burying of silver in India. The expression "stashing one's cash under the mattress" derived from actual hoarding, regardless of where the stash was hidden. Today the expression commonly refers to savings of any sort, although it seems to be favored by gold sellers evoking traditional practices. Safes continue to be sold to those with enough hoarded money to protect, whether individuals or businesses.

112.   *Capital, Vol. I,* p. 240.

also hoarded as a precaution against unexpected need.[113] Hoarded money, moreover, may be local or foreign; today multinational corporations, governments and some supranational institutions, such as the International Monetary Fund (IMF), hold "foreign exchange reserves" that can be drawn upon at need.[114]

Such hoard must be differentiated from savings that take the form of interest-bearing assets, because the sellers of those assets put the money they receive back into circulation, e.g., banks loan out money deposited in savings accounts or spent on certificates of deposit, corporations sell stocks and bonds to acquire funds for investment, governments sell bonds to cover excess spending over revenue.

Money, Marx argues, is still money even when held out of circulation. But in what sense? Holding the M acquired from the exchange $C - M$ out of circulation, breaks the flow $C - M - C$ and the first metamorphosis is not followed by the second. Yet this solidification or "petrification" of money as hoard, whatever its form, plays a necessary role in the functioning of money as means of circulation.

First, qualitatively, only by dropping out of circulation and then returning as means of purchase, i.e., as universal equivalent in $M - C$, do various forms of money prove themselves as such. Thus, the paradox that any would-be universal equivalent only becomes money as non-means of circulation. "The withdrawal of commodities from circulation in the form of gold," Marx writes, "is thus the only means of keeping them (gold and silver) continually in circulation (as money)."[115] Hoard is not separate from circulation, but integral to it, i.e., flowing in and out over shorter or longer periods. In the post-World War II period, the increasing quantity of foreign dollar reserves signaled the ascendency of the dollar as the primary international money.

Second, quantitatively, the amount of money in circulation is determined by the flow of money into and out of hoard. As value, price, quantity and velocity change, the M required by Q_c/V changes. When the need for money lessens, more of it is added to hoard; when the need grows, hoard provides a reserve that can be drawn upon. Hoard, therefore, serves as a reserve which provides the system with flexibility. This is perhaps most obvious in recent

---

113. These two reasons—"transactions demand" and "precautionary demand"—for holding money were recognized by Keynes along with a third motive, speculation, also recognized by Marx because widespread in his day.

114. The IMF is an organization that pools foreign exchange reserves from member governments and makes them available, under agreed upon conditions, to cover such things as temporary trade deficits.

115. *MECW, vol. 29*, pp. 361–362.

years in the case of central and international banks where foreign exchange reserves grow when exports (that bring in money) exceed imports (that require the expenditure of money) and are drained in periods when imports exceed exports and are paid for out of hoarded reserves. One dramatic such case unfolded in the wake of the quadrupling of oil export prices by OPEC in 1973–74 and again in 1978. The sudden increase in prices to those countries dependent upon oil imports required the disgorging of foreign exchange reserves to cover the increased costs. Given the limits to those national reserves, the IMF created an emergency "Oil Facility," allowing members to draw more reserves than standard rules permitted.

Therefore, hoarders who behave as misers are caught in a contradiction. In their greed, they pile up money in hoard, and store value. But by removing it from circulation, they are also removing it from any opportunity to expand via investment. No matter how much money the miser stores away, there is always a contrast between the endless possibility of acquiring more and the limited achievement. The miser is thus driven to pile up money endlessly. This kind of hoarder Marx labels "a martyr to exchange-value." Unlike the capitalist who understands that the way to accumulate ever increasing quantities of money is to continuously throw it back into circulation, the miser appears as the "holy ascetic seated at the top of a metal column."[116] Another way of saying this, in the language of Section 4 of Chapter 1, is that misers are the victims of their own money fetishism. Unlike the capitalist who understands that the purpose of money is investment and putting people to work, the miser thinks that the object of making money is the money itself. Perhaps Marx had in mind the title character of George Eliot's novel *Silas Marner: The Weaver of Raveloe* (1861). A miser, Marner is devastated when his hoard of gold is stolen. Only later, through caring for the orphaned child Eppie, does he discover that there is much more to life than money.

This narrow and limited fetishism was found among the early mercantile "bullionists" who believed that the objective of foreign trade and government policy should be to enrich a country through the gathering of precious metals, or "treasure" as they often called it. They wanted to restrict imports (and thus gold or silver outflow) while encouraging exports (and thus gold or silver inflow). This view was attacked both by more sophisticated mercantilists, such as Thomas Mun (1571–1641) and Richard Cantillon, and by classical economists, such as Adam Smith, who demonstrated how the export of gold and silver (spending money abroad) could result in even more gold and silver being brought into the country (from subsequent exports).

---

116. Ibid., p. 367.

b) Means of Payment

This is the form money takes when used to pay for something *after* the act of purchase and the acquisition of the item or service purchased. Instead of $M - C$, purchase, we have buying on credit where the good C is obtained *before* the payment of money M takes place. In this case, M is credit money, generally an IOU of imaginary money which is later paid. For example, when you use a credit card, you sign a paper as you acquire the commodity, but you have not yet paid. You pay later, with one or more checks drawn on your bank's checking account.[117] Such credit inevitably has a price, usually in the form of interest, and if not repaid on time, fees and possible seizure by the creditor of the purchased item.

The polarity and separation of actions $M - C$ and $C - M$ in credit, like the polarity of simple sale and purchase opens the possibility of the disruption of the circulation process—credit crises. In Marx's time, when most credit was extended to businesses, credit crises often resulted from commercial crises when production outpaced the growth of markets and first merchants and then industrialists found themselves unable to sell and thus unable to meet their debt obligations. In recent times, when many middle- and high-income workers have succeeded in obtaining access to credit, crises have resulted from predatory and fraudulent lending practices, e.g., sub-prime loans, that have fueled unsustainable housing booms. Credit crises have also resulted from governments finding it increasingly difficult or impossible to meet their sovereign debt obligations. Such was the 1974–75 "fiscal" crisis in New York City, which resulted when the banks refused to rollover the city government's loans, or the international debt crisis of the 1980s and 1990s, which resulted from the US Federal Reserve dramatically increasing interest rates, making loans taken out at floating rates in the wake of the oil crises of the 1970s impossible to repay, and plunging the world into depression, or the current debt crisis facing Puerto Rico accentuated by Hurricane Maria that decimated the island's economy.

Although his main interest is crises in the relations between banks and business borrowers, explored at length in Volume III of *Capital* and in his journalism, Marx also points out how the struggle between debtors and creditors has long been an important aspect of class struggle:

The class struggle in the ancient world, for instance, took the form mainly of a contest between debtors and creditors, and ended in Rome

---

117. Marx did not know the credit card, but his theory grasps it easily. Already in this chapter, footnote 54, he marvels at how small a role is played by the actual exchange of cash money (rather than credit) in the accounts of a London merchant bank. *Capital, Vol. I*, p. 238.

with the ruin of the plebeian debtors, who were replaced by slaves. In the Middle Ages, the contest ended with the ruin of the feudal debtors, who lost their political power, together with its economic base. Here, indeed, the money form. . . was only the reflection of an antagonism which lay deeper, at the level of the economic conditions of existence.[118]

Today, the economic conditions of existence are the exploitative and alienating social relations of capitalism. Many workers, through success in forcing up real wages, have gained access to credit. Yet, lenders to workers, from payday loan sharks through credit card and automobile companies to banks, often use obscure, poorly understood fine print (which "taketh away") or out and out fraudulent practices to exploit borrowers. The contest between workers and fraudulent lenders, who sold billions of dollars' worth of sub-prime loans during the recent housing boom that led to the credit crisis of 2007–08, ended with millions of workers losing their jobs and their homes, while the crooked lenders were bailed out at taxpayer expense. Similarly, governments and their lenders do their best to foist the costs of fiscal crises onto workers via the imposition of austerity, regardless of whether the crisis was due to workers' struggles winning higher wages and better services or was due to corrupt practices on the part of government officials and their cronies. This has been true for local governments such as those of New York City or more recently those of Detroit or Puerto Rico, or national governments such as those of Mexico, Argentina and Brazil in the 1980s, or Greece and Spain in the last few years.[119]

Marx notes that once you have a developed system of credit and money as means of payment, then this must be taken into account in the analysis of the amount of money needed to circulate goods. This can be done partly by netting out the payments which cancel each other and by adding on the payments left over to those commodities circulating due to direct payment.[120] The repeated invention of new forms of credit money has made it increasingly difficult for economists to measure the "quantity of

---

118. Ibid., p. 233.

119. On the class politics of the fiscal crisis of New York, which turned out to be the prototype for fiscal crises everywhere, including the US, see Donna Demac and Philp Mattera, "Developing and Underdeveloping New York: The 'Fiscal Crisis' and the Imposition of Austerity", *Zerowork* #2, 1977, pp. 113–139; and Eric Lichten, *Class, Power & Austerity: The New York City Fiscal Crisis*, South Hadley, MA: Bergin & Garvey, 1986. On the class politics of the international debt crisis, see my article "Close the IMF, Abolish Debt and End Development: A Class Analysis of the International Debt Crisis", *Capital & Class*, #39, Winter 1989 and issue #10 of *Midnight Notes* on the "New Enclosures."

120. *Capital, Vol. I*, p. 237.

money." They now have a whole range of measures, which differ primarily by the degree of "liquidity," i.e., the ease with which various kinds of money can be converted into acceptable means of immediate payment.

c) World Money

At the level of the international economy, Marx notes mainly that money loses "the local functions it has acquired, as the standard of prices, coin and small change, and as a symbol of value." Instead it serves mainly in its original form as bullion, as the commodity gold or silver. In this form it serves primarily as:

- universal means of payment to cover debts
- universal means of purchase to circulate goods in international trade
- absolute social materialization of wealth when wealth is to be transferred between countries but not in the form of particular commodities, e.g., "money loans for carrying on wars" or "forced contributions" in the wake of wars.[121]

As commodities are traded internationally, he argues, they "develop their value universally" and the monies for which they are exchanged confront them, just as they do domestically, as their "independent value form." Although Marx does not specify exactly how "universal value," is established, presumably this occurs in the same manner that he has been analyzing for isolated countries and their economies, i.e., through adjustments in production toward socially necessary labor time, with *socially* redefined in terms of the economies of trading partners.

Because international payments fluctuate with world trade and capital flows, just as they fluctuate within countries, he notes the need for international reserves. In his time, when gold and silver were the main international monies, reserves were held as gold or silver bullion.[122] Today, with both gold

---

121. Payments in gold were one part of the "contributions" imposed on Germany after World War I by the Treaty of Versailles. That ill-advised postwar looting of Germany plunged the country into depression, was lambasted by Keynes and contributed to the rise of Nazism. See John Maynard Keynes, *The Economic Consequences of the Peace (1919)*, New York: Harcourt, Brace and Howe, 1920.

122. Engels provides a long footnote (#59, p. 241) on how changes in sources, methods of production and demand were favoring the displacement of silver by gold as money, accelerating the instability of bimetallism, already remarked upon by Marx. For a long time, the displacement was slowed at an international level by the preferences of those in some countries, especially Asia, for silver as opposed to gold. In the United States, despite the demands of farmers and the oratory of William Jennings Byran (1860–1925) during the late nineteenth-century Populist Revolt, silver was marginalized to small coins and silver certificates years before gold itself was demonetized in 1933.

and silver demonetized, such reserves are held primarily as stocks of foreign currencies.

Even from these brief remarks, we can see how Marx extends his analysis of domestic money to the world market. We can do the same with other aspects of his analysis. For example, take the separation of price and value. We can find such a separation of money name from value when paper currency (with a purely symbolic value) increasingly dominated the fixed exchange rate system of Bretton Woods after World War II. The exchange-value of the dollar had been fixed at 1 oz. gold = 35 dollars. But, during the post-World War II period, the gold supply grew more slowly than the rapidly expanding trade that accompanied the recovery of Western Europe and Japan. So, holdings of dollars grew. Eventually, a growing unwillingness of other countries to hold more dollars and of problems at home, the dollar was devalued in 1971.[123] The value of the 1 oz. of gold hadn't necessarily changed but that amount of gold was given a new money name. At the same time, the prices of all other commodities—whose values could also be assumed to remain the same in the short run—denominated in dollars rose. The devaluation of the dollar had no effect on the value of an ounce of gold (or a ton of iron), but the price of that ounce of gold as expressed in its money name rose quickly from $35 to over $500 in the early 1980s. In the longer run, to understand the peak price of gold in 2017 of over $1,900, one would have to examine the technologies involved in gold mining and production to judge whether there was a significant change in the SNLT required to produce 1 oz. of gold.

We must always keep in mind the social relations which money embodies and represents, the class relations of power that are reflected and represented in the exchange form, the money form, etc. International money flows are international rearrangements in those structures of power, as are international commodity flows! It is always tempting to give in to the money fetish, to forget the social realities of money within the class context and be blinded by money and complicated money mechanisms. It is not always easy to avoid fetishism and translate the complexities of money into class terms. But, in our own defense, we must.

One set of examples were the crises around the structure of debt and credit that exploded in oil importing countries in the wake of the two oil crises in the 1970s and in the wake of the fierce tightening of the supply of money in the US in 1979–81 which drove up interest rates and plunged the world into depression. That so-called Third World Debt crisis, however,

---

123.   The dollar was repeatedly devalued between 1971 and 1973 after which it floated against the other currencies and against gold, with the result that gold was effectively demonetized and its role as an international money collapsed.

was not merely the by-product of OPEC price increases and US monetary policies but was also the rotten fruit of class struggles that produced them.

Behind the OPEC price increases lay not merely greedy sheiks, but worker struggles for more income and better standards of living in the oil-producing countries. Behind the tight money policies, inaugurated by President Jimmy Carter, and implemented by Federal Reserve chairman Paul Volcker, lay the urgent need by capitalists to attack a level of working-class power within the United States that was driving an accelerating inflation, undercutting exports, real interest rates and business investment generally. Behind the buildup of massive debt in Mexico, Argentina and Brazil lay the need for resources to cope with social and labor unrest (both through military and police repression and through development, i.e., investment, more jobs and higher wages). Thus, behind the international negotiations between "creditor" and "debtor" nations lay the class politics within each, and within the world as a whole.[124]

Not surprisingly, given the role of money as a weapon of repression and exploitation in the Global South, it is common to find expressions of resentment against money, especially the dollar—the money most frequently used to finance repression—throughout popular music. Such resentment throbs in Peter Tosh's song "The Day the Dollar Die."[125] One of the best-known reggae musicians, Tosh crafted an anticipatory song which celebrates the future death of the dollar (that he obviously thinks inevitable), and of money more generally.

124. See Cleaver, "Close the IMF, Abolish Debt and End Development."
125. *Mystic Man*, Rolling Stones Records, 1979.

5
Part Two
The Transformation
of Money into Capital

After seeing in Part Eight how capitalists took over the world, imposing endless work as their most basic means of social control and in Part One how Marx reformulated the classical economists' labor theory of value as a theory of the value of labor to capital, here, in Part Two, we see how the realization of value makes possible not merely social control in the present but even wider control in the future.

Chapter 4: The General Formula for Capital. Long before the rise of capitalism as a social system, merchants and usurers spent money to make more money, an undertaking that many have equated to capitalism. That objective still obtains within capitalism but discovering how it is achieved poses a puzzle. Merchants buy cheap and sell dear. Usurers exact interest from borrowers. But how do agrarian or industrial capitalists wind up with more than they invested?

Chapter 5: Contradictions in the General Formula. The contradictions confronted in this chapter arise from excluding unequal exchange (cheating) as an explanation for how capitalists achieve a surplus over their investment. If commodities exchange at their value (including in exchange with money), the source of increased value must lie elsewhere.

Chapter 6: The Sale and Purchase of Labour Power. Having concluded that the source of expanded value lies outside exchange, Marx zeros in on the one commodity whose use-value includes the ability to generate more value than it costs. That commodity is labor-power, or the ability and willingness to work for some capitalist. Marx begins by examining the labor market where it is sold and purchased, reserving for the next chapter a closer analysis of the work that employers extract from that labor-power.

CHAPTER 4: THE GENERAL FORMULA FOR CAPITAL

Outline of Marx's Analysis

First form of capital was money
  – merchant's capital
  – usurer's capital
In $M - C - M'$ as opposed to $C - M - C$,
  – commodities are only a means to an end
  – money is alpha and omega
  – only a quantitative expansion
  – valorization

Commentary

Money, Marx says, is the first form of appearance of capital, understood in the limited sense as money being used to make money. Historically, it first appears in the form of merchants' capital (buying goods to sell at a higher price), usurers' capital (loaning money at interest) and monetary wealth. For example, merchant capitalists launch their enterprises with money, M, which they use to buy commodities, C, hoping to sell them for more money, M', where $M' > M$, or $M' = M + \Delta M$, to achieve $M - C - M'$. He points out that $M - C - M$ "would be absurd and empty if the intention were, by using this roundabout route, to exchange two equal sums of money."[1] The problem therefore is to analyze this form to discover its logic.

He highlights a series of formal differences. Below, I follow his analysis, step by step, but whereas Marx concretizes his abstract discussion of $C - M - C$ with the example of farmers selling corn to obtain money to buy cloth, which they need to live, I want to examine the case of workers selling their labor-power, LP, in exchange for a money wage, M, which they then spend on the means of subsistence, $C(MS)$, i.e., $LP - M - C(MS)$. As this is the subject of Chapter 6, I don't go into great detail here, but I choose this case because it is by far the most important form of $C - M - C$ in capitalism.

Phase Inversion

The order of the phases in $M - C - M$ is inverted in comparison with the order of the phases in the circuit of the commodity. We have $M - C$, $C - M$, instead of $C - M$, $M - C$. When we take $LP - M - C(MS)$ as an example of

---

1. *Capital, Vol. I*, p. 248.

$C - M - C$, we know that while workers begin by selling their labor-power $LP - M$, to get money, capitalists begin by investing part of their money to purchase labor-power $M - C(LP)$. The second phase for workers involves the expenditure of the wage, M, on the means of subsistence $M - C(MS)$, while for capitalists the sale of $C(MS)$, or other commodities, constitutes $C - M'$, the second part of their circuit $M - C - M'$.

Different Mediations

In $C - M - C$, or $LP - M - C(MS)$, money mediates, whereas in $M - C - M$, commodities mediate. In the case of $LP - M - C(MS)$, the money mediator is usually the money wage or salary, although it might be some other form of income paid in exchange for labor-power. For workers, money is only a means to an end, it is not an end in itself. Generally speaking, when workers hold on to money, the objective is merely the redistribution of income, from good times to bad, or from working years to retirement.[2] Even those such as Eli Chinoy's autoworkers, who saved as much of their wage as possible to set up some small business, were mostly buying freedom from the assembly line rather than becoming insipient capitalists.[3] For many capitalists, buying commodities, whether LP or the means of production, MP, is merely a means to the objective of making more money. Socially, of course, whether they recognize it or not, investment in labor-power serves to keep people under control by putting them to work.

Spending Money versus Advancing It

In $C - M - C$, or $LP - M - C(MS)$, money is irreversibly *spent*, but in $M - C - M$, it is only *advanced*. While workers spend their money in $M - C(MS)$ to get what they really want (the means of life), capitalists expect to get their money back (augmented, of course).

Different Displacements

Money is displaced twice in $M - C - M$, but the commodity is displaced twice in $C - M - C$, or $LP - M - C(MS)$. For the capitalist, money flows out and back; for the worker, one commodity, LP, is traded away for another, $C(MS)$, which is consumed.

---

2. As noted in my commentary on Chapter 3, the depositing of workers' extra income in savings accounts, while delaying their personal $M - C(MS)$, does not rupture the flow of money because banks loan those savings to borrowers who then spend it.

3. See Eli Chinoy, *Automobile Workers and the American Dream*, Garden City, NY: Doubleday, 1955; 2nd edn., Urbana: University of Illinois Press, 1992. As his study demonstrated, even when such workers did have entrepreneurial dreams, most of their small businesses failed and they were forced back into the labor market.

Loss versus Reflux

In the case of $C - M - C$, or $LP - M - C(MS)$, money spent is money lost, as it passes from one set of hands to another. Whereas in $M - C - M$, money flows back to the original owner as revenue, in a reflux completed as soon as C is sold. This reflux is "conditioned by the very manner in which it is expended," i.e., as an investment.[4]

Different Objectives

In $C - M - C$, or $LP - M - C(MS)$, *use-value* is the final goal; in $M - C - M$, *exchange-value* is the determining purpose. As I argued in my commentary on Chapter 1, workers are mainly interested in the use-values of commodities, $C(MS)$, and only concerned with their exchange-values when they must pay for them. In the case of capital, money is the beginning and the end, the alpha and the omega, the means and the goal. In the case of merchant capital, which buys goods to resell at a higher price, the mediating C is any old commodity for which there is a market. When we turn to industrial capital—the quintessential form of capital for Marx—investigating what happens to this C will take us (in Chapter 7) into the dark heart of production.[5]

Quality versus Quantity

In $C - M - C$, or $LP - M - C(MS)$, the two extremes are qualitatively *different* use-values. In $M - C - M$, the two extremes are qualitatively *identical*; therefore $M - C - M$ cannot draw its meaning from any qualitative change, but only from a quantitative one. Therefore "the complete form of this process is $M - C - M'$," and the increment of M' over M, or ΔM = surplus-value. As translator Ben Fowkes notes, this is the first time this key term appears in the book.[6]

Goals: Limited versus Infinite

Final goal of $C - M - C$, or $LP - M - C(MS)$, is the consumption of use-values whose realization lies outside of circulation in the realization of people's lives. Final goal of $M - C - M'$ is the circulation of capital—"an end in itself"—potentially limitless. (Remember the infinity of the expanded, general and money forms of value.)

---

4. *Capital, Vol. I*, p. 250.
5. Ibid. This characterization, of course, ignores the social role of profit, ΔM, which is to expand the imposition of work. The fetishism of this chapter is overcome in Chapter 7 where Marx brings work back to the fore and analyzes it directly.
6. *Capital, Vol. I*, pp. 251, 252.

As the "conscious bearer of this movement" Marx says, the capitalist has this "boundless drive for enrichment, this passionate chase after value."[7] Thus, the objective content of $M - C - M'$ is the "valorization of value" as increase in magnitude. The subjective content of the capitalist is just this objective movement, so the capitalist acts as "capital personified and endowed with consciousness and a will."[8]

This is pretty much the way Marx treats capitalists throughout the book. He is not interested in them as individuals but as personifications or functionaries of capital. In this volume, which sets out the logic of the class relations of capital, he rarely mentions any behavior on their part that might violate that logic, e.g., an individual capitalist's predilection for consumption over investment. Unlike many anti-capitalists, he does not constantly inveigh against "fat cats," and rarely points his finger at capitalist wealth and ostentatious consumption.[9] His interest is elsewhere: their behavior as they act as capitalists per se: as the agents of investment and the endless imposition of work. We saw this in Part Eight when he drew our attention to the Duchess of Sutherland. In her case, he was not concerned with her wealth but with her role in betraying her clansmen by expropriating and enclosing their lands.[10]

However, despite his lack of interest in the capitalist qua individual, Marx does comment here on the conscious mindset of many capitalists: avarice, a passion for money-making. This kind of individual has often been portrayed and mocked in literature. Such was the greedy and egotistical Mr. Bounderby caricaturized in Dickens's *Hard Times*, evoked in my commentary on Chapter 26. Some capitalists, however, rise above mere greed to positions of policymaking and political responsibility. Those who can see through the money fetish understand that investment organizes society by shaping the lives of most people around jobs and work. Capitalists who come to understand this sometimes acquire a sense of "noblesse oblige," i.e., a sense of responsibility for the general social welfare. Thus, when David Rockefeller said "profits are the measure of our [business's] contribution to society," we can interpret him as meaning: profits are invested, investment creates jobs, jobs make it possible for people to live, thus business "contributes" to society with their profits. No matter that, from a worker's point of view, he has conveniently presented a process of exploitation as a kind of benevolence; he has

---

7.   Ibid., p. 254.
8.   Ibid.
9.   Unlike, say, Thorstein Veblen (1857–1929), who penned an acerbic critique of "conspicuous consumption" in his *Theory of the Leisure Class*, New York: Macmillan, 1899.
10.   See also his article "The Duchess of Sutherland and Slavery", *The New York Daily Tribune*, no. 3687, February 8, 1853, *MECW, vol. 11*, pp. 486–494.

grasped his profit-making activity, $M - C - M'$, in social terms and understood that what is really at stake is the organization of society through work. In their own peculiar, class-biased way, such capitalists achieve something of what Marx's theory provides: an understanding of the social meaning of such frequently fetishized categories as money and profit.

We can now see how the *metamorphosis of capital* is interwoven with the metamorphosis of the commodity. Money and commodities appear only as "different modes of existence" of capital, or "capital is money, capital is commodities."[11] Because Marx sees value as the substance and subject of this movement and its magnitude increasing via changes in form, he writes that "valorization is therefore self-valorization."[12] Here Marx falls back into a Hegelian language in which value, if we fail to remember what it is, appears as a reified (thing-in-itself) relationship that acts independently. But that value which expands itself, we know to be the real social content of the capitalist–worker relationship: work, its imposition and struggle against it. So, it is this work that finds money as its independent expression, and it is this struggle over the imposition of work which is constantly expanding. The capital/labor relation finds the motive of its own expansion within itself—within the antagonism and resultant class struggle.

Because $M - C - M'$ is the form peculiar to merchants' capital, industrial capital and, in the abridged form $M - M'$, to interest-bearing capital, Marx concludes that $M - C - M'$ is the general formula for capital *in the sphere of circulation*. This formula, or representation, is *not* adequate to express capital once we have examined its substance in the sphere of production. Then we must have $M - C \ldots P \ldots C' - M'$, in which we discover in $C \ldots P \ldots C'$ the origin of the prime in M'.

CHAPTER 5: CONTRADICTIONS IN THE GENERAL FORMULA

Outline of Marx's Analysis

Problem: explain source of expanded value in the formula $M - C - M'$

Expanded value:

– assuming equal exchange, it *cannot* originate in exchange
– taken in the aggregate *cannot* originate in cheating
– therefore, the expanded value must originate *outside* exchange

---

11. This simple way of putting the relationship holds a profound truth: not only are money and commodities moments of capital, but all the elements of the relationships Marx investigates in this book are moments of capital.

12. *Capital, Vol. I*, p. 255.

Commentary

Having arrived at the general formula for capital $M - C - M'$ through the analysis of circulation, Marx now addresses the source of the increased or surplus-value in M' (where $M' > M$). He argues that the increased value cannot, in the aggregate, originate within the circulation process. Therefore, we must turn elsewhere (to the sphere of production) for an answer. This chapter provides a transition between the analysis of circulation and that of production—the sphere of labor. If we keep in mind, from our studies of primitive accumulation and Chapters 1–3, the understanding that value is work-for-capital as social control, then it is obvious that surplus-value or surplus work can only originate in the sphere of production. However, let us follow Marx's reasoning.

He begins by noting that $M - C - M'$ contradicts all the laws of exchange, value, money, etc., already developed. How? Presumably because $C - M'$ is unequal exchange. What gives?

First, he looks at the inverted order of succession, $M - C$ and then $C - M'$ rather than $C - M, M - C$, and asks if this can be the source? After tracing the process $M - C$ and $C - M'$ from the point of view of both buyer and seller at each step, he concludes that the order is irrelevant, the actual acts are still those of simple commodity circulation. Therefore, the question must be re-posed, "We must rather look to see whether this simple circulation, by its nature, might permit the valorization of the values [increase in magnitude of value] entering into it and consequently the formation of surplus-value."[13]

To answer this question, he begins with simple exchange, $C - C$, wherein money appears only as money of account—to name price—but does not enter into exchange. In this case Marx argues that in terms of *use-value* it can be said that each side gains because it gains more use-value than it might otherwise have been able to produce. This is basically Ricardo's argument about comparative advantage. But, assuming equal exchange of *values*, there is no reason to think that any gain in value has been made.

Next, he places money in the middle, as means of circulation, $C - M - C$. While this makes sale and purchase distinct acts, it does not change the assumption that equivalents are exchanged, as we have already seen in Chapters 1–3. Changes in form do not imply "a change in the quantity of value."[14]

At this point Marx reverses his line of reasoning, to work backwards from the conclusion to point out logical inconsistencies. He writes, "It

---

13. *Capital, Vol. I*, p. 259.
14. Ibid., p. 260.

is true, that commodities may be sold at prices which diverge from their values."[15] If so, we have two possibilities:

1. Suppose the seller sells commodities above their value, i.e., 110 instead of 100. If all sellers do this, then when the sellers become buyers, they lose the 10 gained. In the aggregate *prices* rise 10 percent but there is no net gain in *value*.
2. Suppose the buyer buys below value. If all do this then this buyer has already lost (in $C - M$, $M - C$) before buying and there is no net gain.

If there is *unequal exchange*, someone sells above value and gets away with it, then that merely *redistributes* value that already exists. If there is a *class* that consistently buys without selling and is cheated therein, they must be getting their money from taxes, expropriation, etc., so the selling class is just getting back some of its own, previously stolen money. Moreover, while cheating can produce a redistribution, it does not raise the total quantity of value in circulation: "The sum of the values in circulation can clearly not be augmented by any change in their distribution."[16]

In illustrating this argument, he uses an example from the colonialism of antiquity: the towns of Asia Minor paid money tribute to Rome and then cheated them when selling to the Romans. They "swindled back from their conquerors a portion of the tribute in the course of trade. Yet for all that, the provincials remained the ones who had been cheated. Their goods were still paid for with their own money."[17] In other words, there was a one-way transfer of real wealth to the Romans. The same might be said concerning the relationship between the working class and capital. No matter how much the working class may cheat capital, either in the exchange $LP - M$ (in which the working class can cheat by failing to work) or in $M - C(MS)$ via shoplifting, changing price tags, or what have you, as long as capital achieves some degree of surplus-value and reinvestment, it is the working class which is, in the end, being cheated—in that part of its life realized as surplus-value (surplus work) and out of that part of its life spent in the reproduction of labor-power.

Therefore, Marx concludes, whether we are speaking of merchants' capital $M - C - M'$ or even of usurers' capital, $M - M'$, the increase in value cannot arise in circulation, at least not in the aggregate (there *can* be redis-

---

15. Ibid., p. 261.
16. Ibid., p. 265.
17. Ibid.

tribution), and "something must take place in the background which is not visible in the circulation itself."[18]

Yet he does not immediately end the chapter. He goes on to spell out the paradoxical situation that even with equal exchange, exchange of equivalents, the capitalist must "at the end of the process withdraw more value from circulation than he threw into it at the beginning." Applying his biological metaphor of metamorphosis to the holder of money striving to turn into a capitalist, he notes that a "money-owner" is "only a capitalist in larval form... His emergence as a butterfly must, and must not, take place in the sphere of circulation."[19]

CHAPTER 6: THE SALE AND PURCHASE OF LABOUR POWER

Outline of Marx's Analysis

Expanded value, $M - C - M'$
 – must originate in C
 – cannot occur in exchange-value of C
 – must occur in use-value of C, in labor-power (LP)

Definition of labor-power
 – aggregate of capabilities to produce use-values

The labor market
 – buying and selling labor-power
 – workers own their labor-power (LP)
 – workers have no means of production (MP)

The value of labor-power
 – socially necessary labor time to produce means of subsistence (MS)
 – MS is historically determined

The use-value of LP
 – source of expanded value
 – ability to work

Commentary

Marx begins the transition from the sphere of circulation to the sphere of production by deducing that the origin of surplus-value lies within the

---

18.   Ibid., p. 268.
19.   Ibid., p. 269.

realization of the use-value of labor-power. In the process, he examines briefly both its exchange-value and its use-value. By focusing on the specific use-value of labor-power as source of surplus-value, he highlights its central value to capital. In later chapters, he returns again and again to the quantitative determination of surplus-value, but he begins here, and continues in Chapter 7, focused on the *qualitative* aspect of the use-value of labor-power. At this point, his concern with the exchange-value of labor-power is only to show that capitalists can extract surplus-value even in the presence of equal exchange. Let us follow Marx from circulation to production.

He reasons as follows:

1. The increase in the value associated with the formula of capital $M - C - M'$ cannot take place within the $M - C$ because the value of C is merely the transformed value of M.

2. Nor can the increase originate in the second act of sale $C - M$, for this too is only a change in form.

3. The increase "must therefore take place in the commodity which is bought in the first act of circulation," in the C acquired through $M - C$.

4. But, it cannot occur within the exchange-value of C if we assume equal exchange.

5. Therefore, "the change can originate only in the actual use-value of the commodity."

6. Therefore, the question: is there a commodity whose use-value "possesses the peculiar property of being a source of value?" Whose consumption involves the creation of value?

7. The answer: yes, the commodity labor-power, or the capacity and willingness to work.

Definition of Labor-Power

"The aggregate of those mental and physical capabilities existing in the physical form, the living personality, of a human being, capabilities which he sets in motion whenever he produces a use-value of any kind."[20]

Although this definition is gendered and a-historical, i.e., abstracted from the specific conditions of capitalism, the whole context—the analysis of capitalism, in a book titled *Capital*—makes it quite clear he is analyzing a set of social relationships within that framework. Although this definition lacks any specificity about "mental and physical capabilities," the one I have

20. Ibid., p. 270.

emphasized, without which all the others are moot, is the *willingness* of people to work for capitalists. Whether obtained by coercions of the types analyzed in the section on primitive accumulation or by more sophisticated modes of education and propaganda that normalize waged and salaried labor, willingness—begrudged or enthusiastic—is a trait capital must engender to get people to actually work once they have been hired in the labor market.

The Labor Market

Marx begins his analysis of the labor market with the *demand* for labor-power, the M that its holder wishes to convert into capital by purchasing workers' labor-power (one part of C) and putting them to work generating surplus-value, to complete $M - C - M'$. How the would-be capitalist comes by enough money to hire workers (and to be able to purchase the necessary means of production) is skipped over in this chapter, although we have seen his historical analysis of this in Part Eight, in Chapter 29 on the rise of agrarian capitalists and in Chapter 31 on the rise of industrial capitalists.

He then specifies two conditions that must be fulfilled for there to be a *supply* of labor-power available for purchase:

1. Workers must be free proprietors of their own labor-power and be able to sell it as a commodity—but only for a limited time. This differentiates workers who sell their labor-power from both slaves and from peons, who are effectively enslaved by endless debt.[21]

2. The workers cannot produce commodities independently of capital, because capital has expropriated the means of production. That expropriation has included the means of producing one's own subsistence, so that all goods and services necessary for survival must be purchased as commodities.

These are exactly the conditions for the creation of a working class, whose historical origins Marx traces in Chapters 27, 28 and 30 in Part Eight. He explains not detailing this history (he does mention it) by saying,

---

21. The examples of peonage given by Marx are in Mexico and Romania. As noted in my commentary on Chapter 29, after the Civil War in the United States, a great many ex-slaves found themselves trapped in sharecropping and exactly the kind of debt peonage Marx describes in this chapter, despite the clause in the Thirteenth Amendment barring involuntary servitude as well as out-and-out slavery.

"We confine ourselves to the fact theoretically, as [the capitalist] does practically."[22]

He then goes on to discuss first the value, and then the use-value of labor-power within capitalism.

The Value of Labor-Power

The value of labor-power, he writes, "is determined. . . by the labor-time [socially] necessary for the *production* and consequently, also the *reproduction* of this specific article [my emphasis]."[23] But what does it mean to "produce" labor-power and how, if at all, is its "reproduction" different from its production? Assuming an already constituted capitalism, the *production* of labor-power evokes at least two elements, both of which he mentions. First, is the procreation of children: "The production of labor-power must include the means necessary for the worker's replacements, i.e., his children."[24] Second is the training of children willing and able to work for capital. For most working-class children of Marx's time, training was on-the-job, sometimes as apprentices or in penal labor in workhouses.[25] In more recent times, mass public education has provided the disciplining and psychological conditioning required for most, although juvenile detention facilities still incarcerate the recalcitrant and "rehabilitation" is usually defined by a return to work. The broader category of the *reproduction* of labor-power also includes day-to-day reproduction, from feeding and clothing to whatever patching up—both physical and psychological—is required for the "maintenance" of workers' ability and willingness to return to work. Moreover, given technological change and the ever-increasing precariousness of jobs, procreation has become an industry and training and retraining have become common not only among the young but among adult workers. Such changes illustrate why Marx notes that what is required for the production and reproduction of labor-power has "a historical and moral element." Requirements have changed over time with the evolution of class relationships. The *reproduction* of labor-power clearly includes the *production* of labor-power as a subset of all those activities involved.[26]

---

22. *Capital, Vol. I*, p. 273.
23. Ibid., p. 274.
24. Ibid., p. 275.
25. See John Locke, "On the Poor Law and Working Schools" (1697), in H. R. Fox Bourne, *The Life of John Locke*, vol. II (1876), London: Henry S. King & Co., 1876, pp. 377–391. There were a few exceptions, such as the schools that the textile manufacturer and reformer Robert Owens (1771–1858) created for his own workers' children under ten years of age, to discipline and train them for future work.
26. This use of terms is consistent with the way Marx uses the term reproduction in Chapters 23–25 where he analyzes the reproduction of the class relationship as a

While all the work involved in the reproduction of labor-power has an impact on its value, Marx *defines* that value as "the value of the means of subsistence necessary for the maintenance of [the] owner of labor-power."[27] In other words, in the little circuit, $LP - M - C(MS)$, the value of labor-power, LP, and hence the amount of money, M, that capital must pay workers is determined by the value of the use-values, $C(MS)$, required for their production and reproduction.[28]

Left out of this definition is all the essential work involved in reproducing labor-power *not* involved in the production of consumer goods, e.g., housework and schoolwork. The work of the waged agricultural laborer who produces food necessary for the reproduction of labor-power is included in this definition, but the work of the unwaged housewife who prepares the food and sets it on the table for consumption and then washes the cooking pots and serving dishes is *not* included. The work of salaried writers, editors, proofreaders, typesetters and bookbinders who create textbooks is included, but the unwaged work of the student who spends hours studying those textbooks is *not* included. Were the housewife hired as cook or waitress in a restaurant, or the student a salaried employee being trained on the job for a new position, their labor would be included.

Both Marx and the classical political economists, such as Adam Smith, were well aware of the existence and necessity of such work. But they saw it as outside of what they felt was capital's new way of organizing work, i.e., profitable commodity production. Smith, for example, juxtaposed putting people to work producing commodities to paying people to provide personal services. The latter, he argued, had to be paid out of some external source of revenue, e.g., land rents for the owners of large estates, such as

---

whole under the rubrics of "simple reproduction" and "expanded reproduction" or "accumulation."

27.   *Capital, Vol. I*, p. 274.

28.   While "pay" is often interpreted narrowly in terms of the direct payment of wages and salaries, the value that capital must consecrate to the reproduction of labor-power should be grasped to include all value diverted from otherwise investible revenue to support the process. In Marx's time there were few employers like Robert Owens who created schools for working-class children. After the Civil War and into the early twentieth century, capitalists became deeply involved in creating private schools, and lobbying for the creation of public-school systems, especially in the largely agrarian southern states, to create a whole new generation of workers—from low-paid manual workers to salaried professionals—better prepared for work in modern industry. In the case of public schools, capitalists sought, from the beginning, to shift the burden of payment onto working-class taxpayers, undermining the value of their wages and salaries. Some capitalists have also profited directly from 1) the building of public schools and their purchase of textbooks and other equipment, 2) the building of for-profit operations, e.g., charter schools, technical training schools and youth detention centers.

the one portrayed in the TV series *Downton Abbey*, or wages or salaries for less well-off individuals. Workers hired by capitalists, however, generate the revenues necessary for their rehiring by producing commodities sold at prices that cover the costs of production plus a profit. Such workers, Smith called "productive," whereas personal servants he dubbed "unproductive." Marx retained this nomenclature with the addition of awarding the title "productive" only to those commodity-producing workers whose products embodied surplus-value.[29]

Not only are housework and schoolwork ignored in this definition, but so too is their impact on the value workers must receive for the purchase of consumer goods and services. For example, the more unwaged domestic food production, via gardening or subsistence farming, the *fewer* food commodities workers need to purchase and therefore the *lower* the value of labor-power and the lower the wage, M, required to buy $C(MS)$. Or, the *more* schoolwork that can be imposed on children, or adults in retraining, the *fewer* waged teachers are required and *lower* the amount of revenue diverted to schools and training programs. Inversely, the *less* housework performed by unwaged housewives—due to escape or rebellion—the *greater* the wage must be to purchase services that were once performed at much lower cost.[30] Similarly, the *less* schoolwork children are willing to do on their own, the *greater* the expense of forcing them to work, via more teacher oversight, police in schools and court enforcement of laws against truancy.

Unlike Marx, we can trace such connections by extending the little circuit $LP - M - C(MS)$ to a full-fledged *circuit of the reproduction of labor-power*, i.e.,

$$LP - M - C(MS) \ldots P_c \ldots LP^*$$

where consumption is organized by capital as the work (P_c) of reproducing labor-power LP^*. The impact of changes in the amount of such work will

---

29. Marx's critique of the limits to Smith's analysis can be found in Volume I of the three volumes of Theories of Surplus Value, *MECW, vol. 31*, pp. 7–31. This analysis by Marx of the distinction between the "productive" labor of waged workers employed by capitalists and the "unproductive" character of other kinds of labor produced a long and strange legacy. Not only have debates raged among Marxist theorists about what labor is and is not "productive," but they have resulted in such bizarre phenomena as the refusal of the Soviet state to include "services" in its Material Product System accounting because "service" labor was judged to be unproductive.

30. Obviously, unwaged housewives have to be supported out of their husband's wage or salary, but such support generally costs far less than that required to hire someone to perform the same work.

depend on the nature of the work. In the case of procreation and the rearing of children, LP^* would have to be greater to meet the needs of an expanding population. In the cases mentioned above, of housework and schoolwork that substitutes for purchased commodities or waged labor, the value of LP^* would be lower.[31]

Differential training requirements for different jobs explain, in part, the wage and salary hierarchy. The greater the complexity of skills required, the greater the expenditure required to produce labor-power. While some expenditure on training occurs directly on the shop floor or in offices by employers or other workers, much more derives from wages and salaries that make it possible for parents to pay for their children's schooling. Data showing that families tend to rear children to similar skill levels tend to confirm this, e.g., university-educated parents tend to have jobs with salaries high enough to send their children to universities.

Toward the end of this discussion there is a curious passage in which Marx writes about a "minimum limit" of the value of labor-power. "The limit is formed by the value of the physically indispensable means of subsistence." Yet he then goes on to say that "if the price of labor-power falls to this minimum, it falls below its value" because the labor-power functions at *less than normal quality*. Less than normal quality work, i.e., lower levels of productivity, we can suppose, would be the consequence of underpaid workers being either malnourished and sick, or disgruntled, angry and resisting work more than usual. So, there would seem to be no such thing as a "minimum limit" after all. Instead, what we have, as integral to the wage and salary hierarchy, are parallel hierarchies in healthiness, illness and willingness to work, where those who are paid more can afford better medical care, those who are paid less cannot and those who are paid the least are frequently malnourished, sick and angry.[32]

What the issue of "minimum limit" evokes is our (workers') judgement of the adequacy of the use-values we receive, in terms of health, both physical and psychological. Can we buy enough commodities—food, clothing,

---

31. I first worked out this circuit while researching some issues in public health. See the Appendix to "Malaria, the Politics of Public Health and the International Crisis", *Review of Radical Political Economics*, vol. 9, issue 1, April 1977, pp. 96–100.

32. Dynamically, the degree of resentment and anger fluctuates with changes in income. Losing a good job with access to decent medical care or gaining some increase in income and health but still at much lower levels than others, can both be sources of discontent. In his time, Marx noted that job loss and wage reductions associated with economic crises often spurred worker uprisings. The latter case was noted by economists and political scientists studying "development" in the Global South. They saw how positive changes, e.g., higher income or access to education, often provoked the demand for even faster improvement and discontent when it was not forthcoming.

housing, toys and services—and enough of the right sort, to be healthy, able and willing to work? Do we have enough time and energy, to "consume" them, i.e., put them to use in our efforts to live lives worth living. So, we try to figure out which commodities we need, what their prices are, and what our wages or salaries can buy. For the most part, we do these things in the order of Marx's little circuit $LP - M - C(MS)$, i.e., we look for and try to find a job that will earn us a wage or salary, $LP - M$, and then spend our money on what we need $M - C(MS)$. But longer term, we often reason in the opposite order: first deciding how we want to live, figuring out what commodities are necessary for that kind of life and then we either look for a job that will bring in enough money so that we can afford to live that way, or if we cannot find one, we take a less remunerative job and then fight for higher wages or for a better-paying position.

Whatever kind of job we obtain, there is no guarantee that what our wage or salary can purchase today will be the same tomorrow. If we are lucky, increases in the productivity of the production of consumer goods will reduce their per unit values and prices so our money income will purchase more goods and services.[33] If we are unlucky, their per unit values and prices will rise so that we can only obtain *fewer* goods and services. Such might be the result of anything that requires more socially necessary labor in the production of either existing goods or new ones required for reproduction. Such changes are easier to see in changes in supply and demand beyond the control of workers. Capital may transfer value to itself by artificially restricting the supply of some goods, e.g., oil or coffee, or stimulate demand (through advertising) to drive up prices, undercut real wages and the value of labor-power. Or, as we saw in Chapter 3, it has often intentionally triggered a general inflation of prices by expanding the supply of fiat money, to transfer value from those on fixed wages to the owners of commodities whose values haven't changed but whose prices have. In each case our income buys fewer or lower quality consumer goods. Another way in which the value of labor-power can be lowered is through the kind of cheating Marx describes in his footnote on the adulteration of bread. When workers spend their wages, they expect to get a commodity of a usual, recognized quality. If the quality is reduced by adulteration— incorporating ingredients of lesser value because requiring less labor—and

---

33. As you will find in Chapter 15, when the value of consumer goods fall, capital has sometimes sought to arrogate to itself all of the gains of increasing productivity. There is, however, no guarantee of success in such endeavor, so the distribution of the fruits of productivity gains has always been decided by the balance of power between workers and capital.

the baking company sells their bread at a price above its now lower value, buyers are cheated and receive less use-value than otherwise.[34]

The Use-Value of Labor-Power

The use-value of labor-power, Marx writes, "consists in the subsequent exercise of that power [of the aggregate mental and physical capabilities. . . of a human being]." The exercise that preoccupies him here produces commodities, which capitalists sell with the aim of making a profit. He is not concerned, for the moment, with the exercise of those capabilities in the production of labor-power itself, e.g., housework and schoolwork, although they are exercised daily in its reproduction. Nor does he examine how those capabilities are sometimes exercised completely outside the circuits of capital, for autonomous purposes of workers, e.g., discovering alternatives to capitalist ways of doing things.

Now, the use-value of labor-power that most vitally concerns capitalists is its "peculiar property of being a source of value, whose actual consumption is therefore an objectification of labor, hence creation of value." As we will see in the next chapter, by "objectification of labor" he means the way workers' abilities, directed by the will of their employers, become embodied in their products, the objects and services they produce.[35] In other words, if labor-power is the capacity to work, then the use-value of labor-power includes not only its exercise, the work of creating commodities embodying surplus-value, but also the use-value of that surplus-value, which can then be used to impose more work. Not just any exercise of human capabilities, but imposed labor, and—through re-investable surplus-value—ever more labor to boot.

The "ever more labor to boot" is essential. "The process of the consumption of labor-power" must be not only "the production process of commodities" but also the genesis of "surplus-value"—required for investment and the expansion of the system. Work is value only when it produces surplus-value, when it contributes to the expansion of value. Work which does not, may serve the function of social control when it occurs, but if it does not result in sufficient surplus-value, then the imposition of that kind of work will cease.[36] I discuss this further in the next chapter.

---

34.   You will find a longer discussion of this phenomenon in Chapter 10 where Marx returns to adulteration.

35.   The kinds of products that he cites are almost always physical objects. As will become clear later, he also recognizes that some commodities are not "objects" in the usual sense, but services that exist only in the kinds of work being done.

36.   In the microeconomic analysis of the firm, such termination as the result of insufficient surplus-value/profit, is called the "shut-down point." Indeed, most commodities

We now pass, as Marx says, fully into "the hidden abode of production where... the secret of profit-making must at last be laid bare." To do so, we must leave the fetishistic realms:

of FREEDOM—free contracts
of EQUALITY—equal exchange
of PROPERTY—each sells his own
and of BENTHAM—each owner looks only to his own advantage.[37]

And enter the capitalist realm of COERCION—where, as we will see, the capitalist rules as a despot, and workers slave as cogs in the machine—at least in as much as the capitalist can make them do so!

---

have a "life cycle;" they are produced, find a profitable market for a while, but eventually demand dwindles, profits decline, and their production is terminated. The intentional shortening of that life cycle—in favor of more profitable substitutes—is called "planned obsolescence."

37.   Jeremy Bentham (1748–1832), a social reformer who influenced Robert Owens, also embraced the idea that humans are always motivated by egotistical self-interest, even when they help others.

6

Part Three
The Production of
Absolute Surplus-Value

Like Dante following Virgil, after making our way through the dark wood of exchange, we follow Marx to descend into the capitalist hell of imposed work, where he unveils the contradictory character of work and its abuse under capitalism.[1]

Chapter 7: The Labor Process and the Valorization Process. Work: people using tools to transform nature. This chapter analyzes first work-as-God-like-creation and then work-under-capitalism, organized to exploit in ways that inflict four different kinds of alienation and thus resistance. Hours worked beyond those required to meet workers' needs constitute an absolute surplus, which is appropriated by their employers.

Chapter 8: Constant and Variable Capital. To put people to work, capitalists invest. The money they spend buying the means of production, Marx calls constant capital because their value was fixed by the labor that created them. The money used to hire workers, he calls variable capital because that investment holds at least the possibility of generating more value than it costs.

Chapter 9: The Rate of Surplus-Value. So, when capitalists are successful and workers' toil exceeds that required to produce what they need, surplus-value results. The ratio of that surplus-value to the labor that workers find necessary, he calls the rate of surplus-value. He deploys this analysis to critique some of the rationalizations of exploitation provided by economists.

Chapter 10: The Working Day. In one of the longest chapters in the book, Marx analyzes the class struggle over just how long capitalists are able

---

1. For an extended riff on this parallel, see William Clare Roberts, *Marx's Inferno: The Political Theory of Capital*, Princeton, NJ: Princeton University Press, 2017.

to compel people to work. Although earlier ruling classes also forced people to work, he argues that only capitalists have sought to impose work endlessly. He sketches the history of their trying to maximize work time and of workers' struggles to limit the portion of their lives given up to their overlords.

Chapter 11: The Rate and Mass of Surplus-Value. This chapter concludes Part Three on absolute surplus-value by illustrating some interrelationships among the factors that determine both its absolute amount and its relative amount vis-à-vis variable capital.

CHAPTER 7: THE LABOR PROCESS AND THE VALORIZATION PROCESS

Overview of Chapter

Section 1: The Labor Process
Section 2: The Valorization Process

Preliminary Commentary

This chapter opens Part Three of Volume I of *Capital*, which deals with the sphere of commodity *production*. This chapter resolves the problem raised in Part Two: the source of surplus-value in the circuit of capital $M - C - M'$. It also further develops the distinction between useful labor and abstract labor, between use-value and value. Moreover, it delves into some of the most central and important issues raised by Marx's whole theory: the meaning of work, what is central and determining in capitalism, the relation between human kind and nature, the social relations of work and domination. So far in *Capital*, Marx has been using the term labor or work without critical definition. This chapter provides that definition.

Section 1: The Labor Process

Commentary

This section provides a generic discussion of work as one kind of human activity—the characteristics of "production in general," independent "of the particular form it assumes under given social conditions." He begins by juxtaposing humanity with the rest of nature. Humans, he says, *confront* the rest of nature as one of its own forces and proceed to shape and transform

Outline of Marx's Analysis

Labor as useful labor—production of use-values
   (independent of social form)
Work—humans and nature are both participants
Humans (active) act on nature (passive), which changes both, nature
   in humanity.
Humans are unique in nature as having self-conscious wills, work as
   one kind of human self-realization

Labor process:

   1. Work—one kind of human activity
   2. Raw materials—worked up and worked upon
   3. Tools—instruments of work

Under capitalism:

   – workers work under control of capital, not autonomously
   – tools, raw materials and product are the property of the capitalist,
   all used for domination.

it to meet their own needs. He sees this confrontation and transformation as a peculiarly human quality and contrasts this with the activities of other animals, e.g., spiders or bees. The difference, he argues, is that other animals act instinctually without thought or intent, whereas humans act with fore-thought and purpose, with a self-conscious will. "But what distinguishes the worst architect from the best of bees," he writes, "is that the architect builds the cell in his mind before he constructs it in wax."[2]

We have here two issues of considerable import: the relationship between humans and the rest of nature and the question of what distin-guishes humans from other species—how we understand "human nature." With respect to the first, the relationship *appears* to be one of opposition, of antagonistic contradictions: humans *confront* nature, humans conquer nature. But there can be no real opposition because nature appears here without any independent will, and thus as a collection of *things* upon which humans act. That collection includes other animals. "The animal," Marx says in the *Economic and Philosophical Manuscripts of 1844*, "is immediately one with its life activity. It does not distinguish itself from it. It is its life activity. Man [on the other hand] makes his life activity itself the object of his will and of his [self-]consciousness. He has conscious life activity."[3] This

---

2.   *Capital, Vol. I*, p. 284.
3.   *MECW, vol. 3*, p. 276. I have inserted [self-] for reasons explained below.

contrast follows Hegel in his *Philosophy of Right* chapters on "property" where "free spirit"—an attribute of human beings—is distinguished from and counterpoised to "the external pure and simple, a thing, something not free, not personal, without rights."[4] In his *Encyclopedia*, Hegel also writes, "the animal on the other hand, because it does not think is also incapable of possessing a will."[5] The French philosopher, Jean-Paul Sartre (1905–80) later made a similar distinction between *being in-itself* and *being for-itself* (human being) in which only the latter has the power of self-transformation, of change, and the former is frozen into sameness, unless acted upon by some outside force.[6] This distinction also exists in Marx's discussion of *class in-itself* and *class for-itself*, where workers are merely part of a class in-itself when they act only as factors of production for capital, whereas, when they act in their own interests against capital, they form part of a class for-itself.

Marx held this vision of humanity as active being, juxtaposed to the rest of nature as passive existence, in one form or another, from a very early period. Yet, nature is also essential. In the *Manuscripts*, he writes, "The worker can create nothing without nature, without the sensuous external world. It is the material on which his labor is realized, in which it is active, from which and by means of which it produces."[7] He also presses beyond the theme of humans confronting nature, even though they are part of it, one of its forces. In both the *Manuscripts* and in *Capital* we find evidence of the way in which Marx saw humans transforming nature and giving it meaning only as a moment of humanity's own existence—a reversal of "humans in nature" to "nature in humanity." In the *Manuscripts* we find Marx defining the being of the human species as residing in its self-conscious treatment of itself "as a universal and therefore a free being."[8] This free being can appropriate all of nature and subordinate it because nature is unfree. "The universality of man appears in practice precisely in the universality which makes all nature his inorganic body—both inasmuch as nature is 1) his direct means of life, and 2) the material, the object, and the instrument of his life activity."[9] Thus, instead of the oft-repeated aim of some Eastern

---

4. *Outlines of the Philosophy of Right*, §42, p. 58. In his "addition" to §42, drawn from Hegel's own notes, Eduard Gans (1797–1839) elaborates: "the soul of an animal has for its object not its soul, itself, but something external."

5. *Hegel's Philosophy of Mind, Being Part Three of the Encyclopedia of the Philosophical Sciences*, translated by William Wallace, Oxford: Oxford University Press, 1971, §468, p. 228.

6. Jean-Paul Sartre elaborates this distinction in *L'être et le néant / Being and Nothingness*.

7. *MECW, vol. 3*, p. 273.

8. Ibid., p. 275.

9. Ibid., p. 276.

religions that humans should seek oneness with nature, here we have humans forging nature's oneness with humankind.

In *Capital*, as we progress through the three volumes of the book, we find an increasing appropriation of nature by humans within capitalism. In this chapter, we find humans extracting use-values from nature as raw materials and turning them into tools and commodities. We also find the domestication of animals and their conversion into both tools and sources of raw materials. In the chapters on machinery and modern industry, we find humans appropriating the forces of nature (wind, water, steam, etc.) to drive machinery. In Volume II, written in the age of sail, we find harnessing the wind essential to trade and empire. In Volume III on ground rent we find the problem that arises when the land has been so worked up that it becomes impossible to distinguish the productivity of the incorporated labor from the "natural" productivity of the soil—thus a conflict between capitalist farmer and landlord.

I offer two comments about Marx and Hegel's sharp distinction between humans and other animals. First, it is obviously very anthropocentric. They assert—on the basis of what little they know about other species—that while those species may be conscious in some sense, they do not think, they are not self-conscious, they do not have a will.[10] Research since their time throws each of these assertions into sharp question. Gorillas have developed vocabularies of hundreds of word-symbols and compose sentences with them. Whales and porpoises who have brains as complicated and as large as human brains, sing and accord each other names. Animals as diverse as chimpanzees and crows have been shown to recognize and solve puzzles. Then there is the question of the making and using of tools (see below). All this suggests that thinking, self-consciousness and will are present in other species—though perhaps neither the form nor the content of their consciousness resembles that of humanity. If this is true then some other differentiating characteristic, or characteristics, will have to be found to indicate what is specifically human about humans. Perhaps only the greater or lesser amounts of, and particular combinations of, characteristics that we share with many other species differentiates humanity.

Second, the above issue is not determining for what follows. Even if other species are conscious and have wills, humans can still be so characterized and analyzed. This chapter deals with the *human* labor process, with a particular kind of interaction with the world. The central issue is the

---

10.   Hegel defines "will" as a kind of thinking: "when intelligence is aware that it is determinative of the content, which is its mode no less than it is a mode of being." Marx's architect, who "builds the cell in his mind" is clearly thinking and planning in preparation for "building the cell" concretely. See Hegel's *Philosophy of Mind*, p. 227.

character of that interaction. That other animals might engage in labor is secondary to its analysis within the human context.[11]

What is important to remember, I think, is that labor, or work, as Marx defines it, is only one kind of possible, purposeful, meaningful activity for humans. In working humans reach out, take possession of some aspect of nature and transform it, usually with tools. Humans obviously have other kinds of relationship with nature. Swimming in the sea, hiking a forest trail or climbing a mountain are all intensive interactions with nature but they involve no intentional transformation of the environment.[12] The same is true with meditation, or contemplation—sitting on a hill and feeling the wind and watching a sunset—or engaging in conversation, and so on. These all involve active, purposeful activities that people find meaningful, yet they involve no intentional transformation of the non-human environment. The labor process, as Marx defines and analyzes it, is a very particular process.

So, what is this labor process? It has, Marx says, three elements: the workers, their tools, and the material on which they work. Here the human worker is the active element, the objects to be transformed and the tools for that transformation are passive—interaction between willful humans and will-less nature. Humans, Marx argues, make nature part of themselves: "nature becomes one of the organs of his activity, which he annexes to his own bodily organs."[13] Vis-à-vis other species, he writes, "The use and construction of instruments of labor although present in germ among certain species of animals, is characteristic of the specifically human labor process, and Franklin therefore defines man as 'a tool-making animal'."[14] So Marx would define humans, in part, as *homo faber*—"man who makes"— even though he recognizes that we are not alone with this trait. In the *Manuscripts*, Marx also based this distinction on the character of the will behind the use of tools. An animal, he says, only produces what it needs,

---

11.   To the degree that domesticated animals do have a will, their subordination to humans makes them slaves; to the degree they are forced to work for capital, a case can be made for seeing them as part of the working class. See Jason Hribal, "Animals are Part of the Working Class: A Challenge to Labor History", *Labor History*, vol. 44, no. 4, 2003, 435–453, and his *Fear of the Animal Planet. The Hidden History of Animal Resistance*, Petrolia/Oakland, CA: Counter Punch/AK Press, 2010.

12.   In all these, transformation is neither the intent nor primary characteristic of the activity. Obviously, swimmers may leave suntan lotion in the sea, a transformation of its chemical make-up that damages coral reefs, too many hikers (or mountain bikers) may cause erosion and mountain climbers can pound so many pitons into cracks that they widen them, or leave their waste and discarded junk on the mountain to such a degree as to have an impact on the local ecology. But these, as in many other activities are unintended (un-willed) side effects and not the objectives of the activity.

13.   *Capital, Vol. I*, p. 285.

14.   Ibid., p. 286.

"It produces one-sidedly, whilst man produces universally. It produces only under the dominion of immediate physical need, whilst man produces even when he is free from physical need and only truly produces in freedom therefrom."[15]

Given the concept of humans acting upon passive nature with their will, labor appears as a kind of activity in which humans by transforming nature (raw material through the use of tools) impress their ideas (and thus themselves) upon it.[16] In *Capital* Marx describes this process as follows:

> In the labor process, therefore, man's activity, via the instruments of labor, effects an alteration in the object of labor which was intended from the outset... the product is a use-value... Labor has become bound up in its object: labor has been objectified, the object has been worked on. What on the side of the worker appeared in the form of unrest [*Unruhe*] now appears, on the side of the product, in the form of being [*Sein*], as a fixed immobile characteristic.[17]

In other words, in the kind of human activity Marx calls labor or work, humans translate their ideas into objects, create those objects and by so doing externalize themselves in those objects. But these objects, even though created by humans, are again but things, fixed and immobile. The robot is one advanced example of humans putting themselves into things—creating a machine that performs many of their own actions.[18] Androids, such as the robots of Isaac Asimov's stories and novels (1939 on) and Lieutenant Commander Data in TV's *Star Trek: The Next Generation* (1987–94), would be machines more fully in their own image. Hence also the fear of creating a self-acting, thinking robot that could have a will— potentially hostile—of its own, e.g., from *Collossus: The Forbin Project* (1970) to *Blade Runner* (1982, 2017) and *Terminator* (1984, 2015). Thus too, Isaac Asimov's *Three Rules of Robotics* so that they never become a threat—rules which are currently being ignored by developers of robots for military use, despite calls for their banning.[19]

---

15. *MECW, vol. 3*, pp. 276–277. For more on the diversity of animals who use tools, see the Wikipedia entry on "Tool using animals." There you will find some evidence that contradicts Marx, namely that some animals make tools for play, not out of need.
16. This is Hegel's second form of taking possession of a thing: by forming it; see §54–56 in the *Philosophy of Right*.
17. *Capital, Vol. I*, p. 287.
18. In Chapter 15, he describes how machines developed as engineers figured out how to mechanically replicate human actions. He also points out how the ancient Greeks dreamed of robots, long before they could be built. See my commentary on that chapter.
19. See Toby Walsh, *It's Alive!: Artificial Intelligence from the Logic Piano to Killer Robots*, Melbourne: La Trobe University Press and Black Inc, 2017. See also The 2017

As nature transformed by humans, use-values appear to be an element of humankind's "inorganic body;" they embody the will of humans and are thus extensions of their creators. Here we have moved behind that fetishism of commodities that Marx discussed in Section 4 of Chapter 1: "The mysterious character of the commodity-form consists therefore simply in the fact that the commodity reflects the social characteristics of men's own labor as objective characteristics of the products of labor themselves, as the socio-natural properties of these things."[20] Commodities are not things-in-themselves, they are things-for-us that we have created. Furthermore, they have been created within certain social conditions and bear their stamp. But we will come to this anon.

To emphasize and sharpen his distinction between the active element, workers working, and the passive element, means of production, Marx uses a vivid gothic metaphor: that of necromancy. "Living labor must seize upon these things, awaken them from the dead, change them from merely possible into real and effective use-values. Bathed in the fire of labor, appropriated as part of its organism, and infused with vital energy..."[21] We can almost see Dr. Frankenstein hovering over his stitched-together chunks of dead flesh infusing the whole with energy, bringing it to life. Here the view of the human/nature relationship as one of active/passive becomes one of living/dead. This is a powerful metaphor and one to which Marx returns with many variations. As we will see, he finds this process malevolent *only* when it falls under the control of capital—only when Dr. Frankenstein works under the command of a capitalist does his creation become a monster. At this stage of his analysis, on the contrary, it is a positive, life-giving process. Humans give life to unfree, passive things by incorporating them into the human world. Human life, at least from the view of humans (Marx) is the only true life. Obviously, animals like sheep, cows and pigs are alive in the biological sense, but they become alive for humankind only in so far as they become the object of its labor. Hegel is explicit about this and Marx undoubtedly agrees: "What I do to the organic does not remain external to it but is assimilated by it. Examples are the tilling of the soil, the cultivation of plants, the taming and feeding of animals..."[22]

It should be obvious at this point why Marx used the example of religion in his discussion of fetishism in Chapter 1. Whereas, for him, humans imbue other things with life through their labor, he sees the

---

Open Letter, signed by 116 founders of robotics and artificial intelligence companies from 26 countries.

20. *Capital, Vol. I*, pp. 164–165.
21. Ibid., p. 289.
22. *Philosophy of Right*, §56.

Judeo-Christian-Islamic tradition of a "God" creating humankind as a projection of this quality that humans themselves possess. The same would be true with respect to other "creation myths," such as the Mayan myth that the Oldest Gods created the Mayan people from corn, and therefore call themselves "the people of the corn."[23] One can imagine Marx commenting: "What's really going on here is that the Mayan people recreate themselves, day by day, year after year, through their *milpas* [plots of corn] that they have cultivated and from which they live. They have merely projected this fundamental aspect of their own lives, their own creativity, in an idealized form."

Now, if it is true that other species are endowed with consciousness and will, then truly humans have been involved not only in interspecies slavery but also mass murder. The view that humans alone have a will and impart life to other things is not limited to Marx but has been a central feature and justification for much of our way of life. To believe, or to discover otherwise has the most profound ramifications. Ecologists and vegans push this kind of thinking and demand that we find ways of living that do not kill off other species, either because they view the species as complementary to each other in an ecological balance or for simpler moral reasons: you don't murder other sentient and probably sapient beings. With scattered exceptions, down through the centuries, this has not been the dominant human view of things. Through various social forms, from ancient societies to the present, we have been a self-serving species, subordinating other species to the needs of our own.

Thus, Marx speaks in the *Manuscripts* of humans as "species-beings." "In creating a world of objects by his practical activity, in his work upon inorganic nature, man proves himself a conscious species-being, i.e., as a being that treats the species as its own essential being, or that treats itself as a species-being."[24] In other words, humans act together as a species as they create things out of the rest of nature, as they transform the world in which they live for themselves. As they treat their own species as their own essential being; they act for themselves rather than for something else, or for someone else.

Abstracted from any historical context, labor appears, in this account, as simply a form of "spontaneous, free activity," one that transforms nature. "The object of labor is, therefore, the objectification of man's species-life: for he duplicates himself... he sees himself in a world that he has created."[25] It is free activity, free expression of life precisely because humans act

---

23. See *Popol Vuh: The Mayan Book of the Dawn of Life*, translated by Dennis Tedlock, rev. edn., New York: Touchstone, 1996.
24. *MECW, vol. 3*, p. 276.
25. Ibid., p. 277.

according to their will: being a conscious being means that humans' own lives are objects for them. "Only because of that is... activity free activity."[26] Abstracted as it is from any concrete set of social relationships, this generic concept of labor has serious shortcomings. Most obviously, within class societies—those characterized by some class dominating other classes— the human activity of labor is not free, but subject to crippling constraints. In the case that preoccupies Marx in this book, capitalists impose their own will on the labor of workers in production—whether of producer or consumer goods and services—but they have also reached beyond the factory and sought to shape individual consumption to reproduce them as workers and *not* as free human beings.

Labor as a General Category

Elsewhere, in an essay titled "Work is *Still* the Central Issue!," I have critiqued Marx's analysis of labor or work as a generic concept.[27] I do, however, find it appropriate *within capitalism*. The following is a slightly revised excerpt.

Marx took the concept of work or labor from both the philosophy and the political economy of his times. His use of a general concept that covers all kinds of specific productive activities makes sense in capitalism for a couple of reasons—regardless of whether it is appropriate to any other period, past or future. First, as Marx argued:

> when it is economically conceived in this simplicity [labor as such], 'labor' is as modern a category as are the relations which create this simple abstraction... Indifference toward any specific kind of labor, presupposes a very developed totality of real kinds of labor, of which no single one is any longer predominant.

It is precisely in capitalism that no single form of labor predominates. What is produced and how it is produced changes again and again but capitalists are happy to deploy any and all kinds of labor to maintain social order. Second, the real indifference toward any specific kind of labor is not that of the workers, we often have very distinct preferences, but that of capital. In commodity-producing, profit-generating, reinvesting capitalism, the kinds of work that produce commodities are entirely secondary—as long as their sale realizes a profit, which can be used to put people to work all over again

---

26. Ibid., p. 276.
27. This included a critique of Engels's differentiation between work and labor. The essay can be found in Ana C. Dinerstein and Michael Neary (eds.), *The Labour Debate: An Investigation into the Theory and Reality of Capitalist Work*, Farnham: Ashgate, 2002, pp. 135–148.

on an expanded scale. Under such circumstances it is reasonable to refer to these diverse activities under one rubric: work (or labor) that refers not to the specificity of the activity but to its central role in maintaining order. As I argued in my commentary on Chapter 1, it is this social dimension of work that is designated by what Marx calls the "substance of value" or "abstract labor," measured by socially necessary labor time and with the form of exchange.

The Labor Process in Reproduction

Given capital's shaping of working-class *consumption* to make sure that it results in the *production* of labor-power, and thus is *productive* for capital, we must ask ourselves to what degree Marx's analysis of the labor process is also applicable to the work of producing and reproducing labor-power. His analysis was developed primarily with respect to the factory. In that context, his analysis of the labor process as consisting of the three elements labor, tools and raw materials seems straightforward. But do these elements also obtain in the activities that produce labor-power? If they do, then it would make sense to treat that production as also involving "labor processes" and to analyze them much as Marx does in the factory.

Given the common capitalist ideologies of love, family and education, one's most immediate reaction is a virulent "No!" We are *not* passive objects, open to manipulation by some external subject. Our relationships of friendship, of marriage, of parent and child are surely more profound and meaningful than simple relations of labor! Are we not active, willing human beings, interacting with each other in hopefully creative, mutually fulfilling ways? Even when we fail, are we not still involved in human relationships far more complex than mere work?

Unfortunately, when we consider the character of labor-power as the ability and willingness to work *for* capital, according to *its* bidding and *its* designs, and for *its* profit, we see that the applicability of Marx's categories of analysis are *all too appropriate*. The production of labor-power is the production of people who are willing and able to set aside their own humanity/will to become the instruments/tools of their employers' wills, objects to be used, abused and exploited. Therefore, those involved in producing labor-power are also tools of capital, every bit as much as the labor-power they shape. The capitalist orchestration of reproduction treats people as things, suppresses or subverts their will, their subjectivity, shaping them and subverting *self*-activity into activity-*for-capital*. In short, to the degree that capital can manage it, the various activities that are involved in the reproduction of human beings dehumanize both producers and the produced.

Some examples follow. 1) We would like to view procreation, gestation, birthing and child rearing as activities of loving mothers, but to the degree that women are used as brood mares of a labor force, they are turned into tools of capital. Whether their affections are co-opted by capital, or they are pressured (sometimes verbally, sometimes physically) to do the work of cooking for, and serving meals to, of cleaning up after, of nursing when ill, they also serve as tools for reproducing the labor-power of their children and spouse. 2) Children, regardless of the love and care of their parents and their own curiosity about the world, find themselves doomed to years of tedious and mind-deadening labor in schools designed to mold them, as objects, into productive workers.[28] 3) Teachers who might like to help children learn but who find themselves forced to impose fixed curricula and standardized tests in classrooms of too many children for any individual attention, and therefore filled with resentful students who must be disciplined, find themselves doing the hard, and sometimes dangerous, work of hammering lives into labor-power.

In all these cases, the work of producing labor-power, has secondary effects. The work of reproduction, as with work in production, leaves poisonous residues with which individuals and families must cope. In "Factory" (1978), Bruce Springsteen sings of how, at the end of the working day "Men walk through these gates with death in their eyes / And you just better believe, boy, somebody's gonna get hurt tonight." Some of those men may well cope by taking out their frustrations violently. Others may internalize and repress the same emotions tonight, but explode later, develop ulcers or take drugs. So too must wives subjected to the stresses of housework and children subjected to those of schoolwork find ways of coping with the psychological by-products of their work producing labor-power. Whatever ways they choose also constitute elements of that work.[29]

Therefore, yes, just as Marx explores the concrete forms of the labor process in the sphere of production, in the factory, so must we explore the concrete forms of the labor process in the sphere of reproduction, in the home, the school and community. As we study the chapters where he carries out such exploration in the factory, such as his analyses of cooperation (Chapter 13), the division of labor (Chapter 14) and technological change (Chapter 15), so too should we examine the parallels between factories, homes and schools as well as the differences and the peculiarities

---

28. I ignore here all those children who are put to work directly producing commodities, whether in the fields, at looms or in a brothel, where they are treated as objects and shaped directly by their exploiters.

29. Shiloh Whitney offers a perceptive analysis of such labor in "Byproductive Labor: A Feminist Theory of Affective Labor, Beyond the Productive-Reproductive Distinction", *Philosophy and Social Criticism*, vol. 44, issue 6, July 2018, pp. 637–660.

of the various labor processes involved in the production and reproduction of labor-power. Who does what work? Which tools are deployed and how? In what ways are people treated as mere raw materials, or as tools for the shaping of others?

At the same time, as we examine and critique how capital has organized both production and reproduction, we must also recognize and analyze both resistance and the creation of alternatives. In all the examples cited above, the women, children, students and teachers caught in such situations often resent and sometimes rebel—both individually and eventually, collectively, in women's and students' movements and teachers' efforts to form unions in self-defense.[30] Resistance, as we will see, has undermined and forced transformations in capital's methods, so that we can only understand those methods within the historical class dynamics through which they have evolved. In so far as resistance has invented autonomous alternatives, even when those fail or are absorbed, they foreshadow the transcendence of capitalism. *Capital* provides an analysis of what we do *not* want; and therefore, helps in judging the degree to which proposed alternatives are truly different. Judging the desirability of alternatives requires whole new sets of alternative values as the basis for constructing new worlds.

Section 2: The Valorization Process

Outline of Marx's Analysis

Labor within capitalism:
- as abstract labor
- production of surplus-value/surplus labor time
- distinct through its extension in time

Historical:
- formal subsumption of labor to capital
- real subsumption of labor to capital

Capitalist concern is with labor time, not production as such; with exchange-value/value rather than with use-value

Value of product = $c + v + s$ = (value of means of production) + (value of labor-power) + (surplus-value)

New labor time = $v + s$, problem of capital is to make sure labor time exceeds v

Measured by *SNLT*, focus is on *how long* workers are forced to work

Capitalist production of commodities = unity of labor process + valorization process (realization of surplus-value)

---

30. Or, as we saw recently in West Virginia, rebel in wildcat strikes against both school administrators and lax union leadership.

Commentary

Turning from production in general, or the labor process in general, to production and the labor process within capitalism, involves turning (in the language of Chapter 1) from the analysis of useful labor to that of abstract labor, the substance of value, and the capitalist focus on extracting surplus labor, or surplus-value. Noting that what businesses purchase in the market are the means of production and labor-power, Marx makes an historical observation: namely that as capitalists appear on the historical scene and take over control of production, they take control of *existing* labor processes:

> The general character of the labor process is evidently not changed by the fact that the worker works for the capitalist instead of for himself; moreover, the particular methods and operations employed. . . are not immediately altered. . . The transformation of the mode of production itself which results from the subordination of labor to capital can only occur later on, and we shall therefore deal with it in a later chapter.[31]

This distinction, which Marx later develops (in Chapters 14 and 15 and in "Results of the Immediate Process of Production"), is between the "*formal* subsumption of labor to capital" and the "*real* subsumption of labor to capital." In the former, the labor process is unmodified, and conflict primarily concerns how much labor capital is able to impose; in the later, capitalists transform the labor process and conflict also turns on the organization of production and its implications for productivity. This distinction is emphasized in *Capital* by the division between Part Three, on Absolute Surplus-Value where the focus is on "how long" workers work, and Part Four, on Relative Surplus-Value where the focus is on transformations of the labor process, increases in productivity and resulting increases in surplus-value.

If the labor process is at first untransformed then what *does* change when capital takes over? Marx's answer at the end of Section 1 of this chapter is twofold. First, "the worker works under the control of the capitalist to whom his labor [power] belongs." Second, the "product is the property of the capitalist."[32] People lose their status as independent peasants and artisans and are subordinated to and controlled by their employers, who by owning the labor-power-set-in-motion, and eventually the tools and the raw materials, also own the product.[33] Section 2 considers the labor process from the point

---

31. *Capital, Vol. I,* p. 291.
32. Ibid., pp. 291–292.
33. During the rise of capitalism, ownership and thus control over both production and the product shifted progressively in favor of capitalists. In the early putting-out system, artisans still controlled their tools but increasingly bought raw materials from

of view of the goals and intentions of capitalists—the realization of an increase in value over investment, M, or a surplus-value, $M' - M > 0$.

Here we discover that for labor to have the quality of value, capitalists must succeed in extracting a surplus, over and beyond the labor necessary to produce the means of subsistence required to reproduce the labor-power of their workers. Success in extracting surplus labor means the generation of surplus-value, the *sin qua non* for capitalism's expanded reproduction. Therefore, to truly understand value, we must re-study it from the capitalist optic of surplus-value. From the point of view of the labor process, we examined actual labor and the means of production. From the point of view of surplus-value, what counts is the distinction between necessary labor and surplus labor. Although the labor embodied in the means of production and the labor required to produce the means of subsistence are both necessary (the former has already been performed in the past), Marx reserves the term *necessary labor* to whatever SNLT is necessary to produce the consumer goods required to reproduce the working class.

This distinction between necessary labor and surplus labor—the heart of Marx's concept of exploitation—has been attacked by his detractors, especially by economists who would limit the concept of exploitation to situations in which the marginal value of the product of labor exceeds the wage.[34] If, as Marx assumes, today's surplus labor is invested in improving production, they argue, and if those improvements raise the productivity of consumer good production and the standard of living, then it hardly makes sense to speak of "surplus" labor! Shouldn't we rather speak of labor necessary today and labor necessary for the future? There are at least four answers to this attack.

---

merchant capitalists and then sold them their product. As they succeeded in herding workers into factories, capitalists came to own, and thus control via their ownership, all of the elements of production. With the rise of the joint-stock company—in which ownership became widely distributed among stockholders—managers increasingly replaced owners as the primary agents of control. In Volume III of *Capital*, Marx recognizes this, calling managers "functionaries of capital" rather than "capitalists." "Functionaries" because the primary function of their job as managers continued to be the capitalist mandate for continued control over society at large: the imposition of work and surplus work to expand that control.

34. In microeconomics, with perfect competition each factor of production receives a value equal to that of its marginal product. Economists recognize that this may not occur under circumstances of "imperfect" competition, e.g., of monopsony in labor markets. Within "growth theory," economists are happy to talk about surplus; they just don't recognize it as resulting from exploitation, preferring to treat it as savings out of current income, often ignoring the source, the difference between savings by workers out of wages and those by capitalists out of profits.

First, there is no guarantee that the investment of surplus labor will raise the productivity of consumer good production or improve standards of living. Investment make take place in the production of 1) only the means of production required for producing more producer goods,[35] 2) goods that make no positive contribution to the standard of living, e.g., the products of the military-industrial-prison complex, 3) luxury goods beyond the purchasing power of virtually all workers, e.g., multi-million-dollar condos, mansions, yachts or private jet planes, or 4) instruments of speculation through which workers are defrauded of their savings and become victims of financial crises.

Second, there is also no guarantee that even investment that does raise the productivity of consumer good production (lowering their per unit value) will result in higher real wages and increased standards of living. Capitalists may succeed in capturing the fruits of such increased productivity by lowering wages and increasing surplus-value (profits). Indeed, much of Marx's analysis in Chapters 12–15 assumes such success.

Third, there are no guarantees that investment in consumer good production will be carried out in ways that avoid negative externalities, either of the goods produced, e.g., dangerous products that harm their purchasers, or of production processes that are destructive of consumers' environment. Capitalists regularly produce products with poisons that undermine their consumers' health. Mountain top removal for coal mining and fracking for natural gas both produce energy products purchased by workers but poison the environment. Such negative externalities may offset any apparent gains from greater access to consumer goods.

Fourth, the most general objection, however, concerns how in capitalism the extraction of surplus labor serves to expand the imposition of labor-as-social-control, *tout court*. Economists who worship markets pretend that ultimately capitalists produce what worker-qua-consumers demand. Supply is determined by demand. That pretense is undermined by the obvious fact that much of demand derives not from workers but from capitalists and governments that they control and as a result a great deal of what is produced, and the labor required, is *not* determined by workers' demands. It also ignores the ways and degrees to which what we do demand is shaped by capitalist investment in advertising, the cultivation of consumerism and pro-capitalist ideologies.

Were, of course, all surplus labor performed to meet workers' future self-defined needs alone, then the economists would be correct, today's

---

35. Prime example: the years of rapid Soviet industrialization where most surplus-value was plowed into building up industrial capacity rather than improving standards of living.

surplus labor would be necessary to meet tomorrow's needs. But that will only take place in a post-capitalist world of what Marx called "associated producers" or communism—the antithesis of capitalism, a world where one works to live, rather than living to work.

Capitalists want the new labor expended in the labor process to be of sufficient quantity to cover the costs of labor-power *and* generate an investable surplus. As he elaborates in the next chapter, under those circumstances the value of the product embodies the value of the means of production (*constant* capital—*constant* because this value does not change) and new value incorporated in the product. This new value derives from employing purchased labor-power (*variable* capital—*variable* because the amount of work performed can vary) sufficiently to pay workers the value of their labor-power plus a surplus-value. Symbolically,

$$investment = c \ (in \ MP) + v \ (in \ LP)$$
$$LP \ in \dots P \dots produces \ v + s$$
$$the \ value \ of \ the \ product = c + v + s$$

where c = value (the SNLT) embodied in the means of production and $v + s$ = newly produced value (the SNLT expended in this labor process), of which v = the SNLT required to produce the workers' necessary means of subsistence, and s = surplus labor or surplus-value. "Therefore, the value of labor-power, and the value which that labor-power valorizes in the labor process are two entirely different magnitudes."[36] Assuming the intensity and productivity of labor constant (as he has done up to this point), then the amount of labor is measured by time or duration of the labor process. This issue: the hours of labor ($v + s$) is the central subject of Chapters 7–10 and is determined by class struggle.

There is an important interaction here between qualitative and quantitative factors, central to the understanding of capitalist production. If the workers work only so long as is necessary to reproduce themselves (this may happen directly in agriculture if they are paid part of the crop, indirectly in manufacturing) then the employer obtains no surplus-value and fails as a capitalist. To be successful, employers must extract surplus-value to finance future investment.[37]

This is vital to his whole discussion—that the major *qualitative* determination of what is peculiar to capitalist control of the labor process is

---

36.   Ibid., p. 300.

37.   Future investment may be used to expand the scale of production, putting more workers to work using existing technology, or to increase the productivity of current workers by purchasing new technology. The latter is the focus of Chapters 12–15.

the *amount* of work imposed! What we have here is a concretization of the tendency that we discovered in the expanded form of value analyzed in Chapter 1, i.e., capital's tendency to continuously expand. Here, at the social core, is expansion of the amount of work it imposes, via reinvestment of surplus-value, and thus the expansion of its hold on human life, either bringing an increased number of people under its control or tightening its grip on current workers.

The purpose of labor when workers control the process is the transformation of nature to supply whatever they judge necessary to satisfy and fulfill their lives, individually and socially. The purpose of labor under capital is more labor than the workers would perform for themselves—surplus labor—in order to expand its control over society. For the moment Marx does not question or analyze the reasons for this unending quest by capital for surplus labor. We can see the imposition of labor as the imposition of a certain kind of social control, but why does this expand? Why the quest for more and more control over more people, over more of their energy and the hours/days/weeks/months and years of their lives? This is not answered here. Marx simply notes that this is the case and goes on to analyze the implications of this for human beings managed through labor.

Alienation

Besides imposing *more* work, control by capital transforms the *meaning* of work. Because capitalists control tools, the raw materials and direct the labor process, workers work for their employers and not for themselves. It is the capitalist who brings living labor, *LP*, and dead labor, *MP*, together. It is the capitalist that orders the worker to infuse life into the dead. But this God-like necromancy has turned malevolent. The dead flesh endowed with life becomes "an animated monster" who, turning against its creator, slowly strangles the worker.

How? If the product is a machine, capitalists will use it to exploit workers. If the product is a consumer good or service, then workers will only have legal access to it to the degree that they accept the despotism of capitalists over their lives by prostituting themselves in the labor market. Workers' labor is no longer simply one form of life activity in which they interact with nature; it becomes the means through which they are controlled and dominated. Where in the case of the free human, work would appear as one "free manifestation of life, hence as an enjoyment of life,"[38] under capitalism this interaction becomes "an alienation of life." Whereas for the free human this kind of activity would be one way of affirming "the specific nature of

---

38.   *MECW, vol. 3,* p. 228.

my individuality," an exteriorization of myself in things, under capital this work process in which my own being and talents are embodied in a product is one in which the product is alien to me, owned by the capitalist and used against me: "it is a forced activity and one imposed on me" only through "an external [capitalist] fortuitous need, not through an inner, essential one."[39]

This theme of the *alienation* of work and of the products of work was elaborated by Marx in the 1840s and remains in his analysis even through *Capital.* It was particularly present and developed in the *Economic and Philosophical Manuscripts of 1844* and in his "Comments on James Mill" (1844).[40] The *alienation* of work means that with capitalists in control of the labor process, work is no longer the autonomous means of self-expression and fulfillment to workers but is rather an alien force imposed on them, dominating them. The alienation of the product of labor means that the product, rather than being a fulfilling objectification of the worker's personality becomes a weapon for controlling the worker.

Work as a form of life is alienated above all because it is forced from the outside, imposed by capital:

> His labor is therefore not voluntary, but coerced; it is forced labor. It is therefore not the satisfaction of a need; it is merely a means to satisfy needs external to it. Its alien character emerges clearly in the fact that as soon as no physical or other compulsion exists, labor is shunned like the plague. . . it [labor] is not his own, but someone else's, that it does not belong to him, that in it he belongs, not to himself, but to another. . . it is the loss of his self.[41]

The Resentment of Work

There are two elements here: first, the labor is forced, second, the worker feels it as such and shuns it. The first of these is the main point; whether the second is true is secondary. In some jobs, some workers may feel that work is pleasant or enjoyable even though the work is being done for capital. While much of capitalist schooling and ideology seek to instill a work ethic, even for unpleasant jobs, it is also true that some of us are able to get paid for doing work that interests us, that we would choose to do even if we had an independent source of income that freed us from the labor market and capital's dominion.[42] But whether we enjoy our work, or resent

---

39.   Ibid.
40.   Ibid., pp. 270–282.
41.   *MECW, vol. 3,* p. 274.
42.   In the case of academics, this can be seen in how even after retirement from salaried labor, many ex-professors continue their research, writing and speaking.

it, is secondary to the reality of its imposition. It may be that, as Marx says: "The worker therefore only feels himself outside his work, and in his work feels outside himself. He feels at home when he is not working. . ." But then we may also have lucked out, obtained an interesting job, or decided, consciously or not, to "make the best of a bad situation" and learned to enjoy working. The issue of psychological alienation is important—because so many experience it—but is entirely secondary to Marx's analysis.

However secondary it may be, dislike for work pervades capitalist society. We are surrounded with cultural manifestations of people's resentment of work: from bumper stickers "Work Sucks, But I Need the Bucks" or "I'm in No Hurry, I'm On My Way to Work," through desk and office signs announcing "Work May Not Hurt You, But Why Take The Chance" or "I Love My Job, It's The Work I Hate" or "Work is a Four-letter Word," to such widely appreciated cultural icons as the Garfield cartoon strip in which the main character detests Monday and "lives for the weekend." People identify with this attitude despite the way Garfield never goes to work, no matter what day it is! It is the attitude that matters, the almost universal loathing of the obligated return to the working week. At the end of that week, the most common prayer in America, regardless of one's religious faith, is "Thank God, It's Friday" or TGIF which, among other things, was adopted by the TGI Friday restaurant chain because of its widespread appeal.

During the countercultural revolution of the 1960s, the term alienation came to be used quite broadly to refer to all feelings of estrangement. Marx's *Economic and Philosophic Manuscripts of 1844* coupled with *Capital* provides theoretical weapons to understand not only alienation in work but the experience of alienation throughout life—once we recognize how capitalism has succeeded in converting so much of life to imposed work. Two songs from the 1960s express such feelings of general alienation, "The Sound of Silence" by Simon and Garfunkel and "Eleanor Rigby" by The Beatles.[43]

In the first of these songs, the singer wanders the streets alone amidst thousands of equally isolated individuals talking and talking but never connecting—precisely the experience of the alienation of worker from worker, of person from person when all are merely workers-for-capital instead of being involved with each other as a result of their own self-activity.

43. Released, respectively, on *Sounds of Silence*, 1966 and *Revolver*, 1966. Two Marxist treatments of alienation that seek to expand upon Marx's ideas are Ivan Mézáros, *Marx's Theory of Alienation* (1970), 5th edn., London: Merlin Press, 2006 and Bertell Ollman, *Alienation: Marx's Conception of Man in Capitalist Society*, Cambridge: Cambridge University Press, 1971. There is today an enormous literature on alienation as a result of a virtual explosion of activity on the part of sociologists and psychologists in the wake of the cultural revolution of the 1960s and in response to widespread job dissatisfaction.

The second portrays two isolated individuals, ignored and abandoned by others. Those songs gave voice to individual experiences and feelings of alienation within mass urbanized society and resonated in the emotions of millions. They are not intellectual essays on alienation, like Marx's texts; they are, instead, poetic evocations of daily pain. Their favorable reception over the years (measured by recording sales and views on YouTube) has demonstrated just how widespread that pain has been. In the years since, anti-work songs have proliferated—several are discussed in my commentary on Chapter 10, Section 5.

Aliens and Monsters

Irrespective of the feelings of workers, however, work *is* imposed and the product of the labor process is used to control the producers, so work becomes:

> something alien, as a power independent of the producer.... Under these economic conditions this realization of Labor appears as loss of realization for the workers; objectification as loss of the object and bondage to it; appropriation as estrangement, as alienation. . . the greater this product, the less is he himself. . . the life which he has conferred on the object confronts him as something hostile and alien.[44]

As property of the capitalist, as either means of production or means of subsistence, the product of labor becomes the means of forcing people to work, it becomes capital. The alien in this horror movie is capital. The worker has imbued dead, objectified means of production with life, created something new, but then this product, raised from the dead, turns monster and dominates its creator.

This is a complete reversal of the labor process described in the first part of Chapter 7. There humans are god-like, mobilizing passive or dead things, and endowing them with life. Here capital, by using dead things, *MP and MS*, as moments of itself, mobilizes and dominates living labor. It subordinates work as one kind of life activity to itself, the worker "is lost to himself" and has the misfortune to be "a living capital." Here the worker appears as a zombie, the living dead, human life suspended and used by death. Instead of working to live, we have living to work—the ideal of the capitalist work ethic. Humans become, as Marx says, "nothing more than workers."[45] Or again in the *Grundrisse*: "the positing of an individual's

44. *MECW, vol. 3*, p. 272.
45. Ibid., p. 283.

entire time as labor time, and his degradation therefore to mere worker, subsumption under labor."[46] Instead of work providing one form of fulfilling being for humans, all forms of human being are subordinated to work. Thus, under capital, alienation takes four forms:

1. The *alienation of workers from their labor*: living labor becomes an alien means for controlling them rather than fulfilling them.

2. The *alienation of workers from their product*: the products they create become alien to them. Owned by the capitalists, they are separated from them and then used for dominating and controlling them.

3. The *alienation of workers from each other*: the stripping away of their self-realization within their species means the "estrangement of man from man... What applies to a man's relation to his work, to the product of his work, and to himself, also holds of a man's relation to the other man. . ."[47] Thus capital ruptures the interactions between people and forces them to exist and to act according to its directions. First, the domination of their lives by work means that they have, effectively, very little time and energy available for relationships with each other. They are alienated from each other in the simplest sense: being separated. Second, the capitalist imposition of competition and hierarchy pits them against one another, estranges them from one another precisely in so far as their lives are defined only in terms of their relation to capital and not in terms of unmediated relationships between each other—thus the loneliness and separateness of life in capitalist society portrayed in the songs above.

4. The *alienation of workers from their "species-being"*: therefore work, which was one means of human interaction, one way of fulfilling human species-being as a collectivity, becomes merely a means to insure individual existence. "In tearing away from [humans] the object of [their] production [the product] estranged labor tears away from [them their] species-life, [their] real objectivity as a member of the species."[48]

Absent are the positive phenomena associated with the interaction of humans with each other in their work and in the sharing of their products such as Marx imagined existing in some society free of capitalist domination:

> In your enjoyment or use of my product I would have the direct enjoyment both of being conscious of having satisfied a human need

---

46. *Grundrisse*, p. 708.
47. *MECW, vol. 3*, p. 277.
48. Ibid.

by my work, that is, of having objectified man's essential nature, and of having thus created an object corresponding to the need of another man's essential nature. I would have been for you the mediator between you and the species. . . in the individual expression of my life I would have directly created your expression of your life, and therefore in my individual activity I would have directly confirmed and realized my true nature, my human nature, my communal nature. Our products would be so many mirrors in which we saw reflected our essential nature.[49]

Thus, capital undermines not only our individual self-realization through the transformation of nature, but also our mutual interactions as we carry on these activities communally.

In *Capital*, all of this discussion is left out. Marx does not insert this long analysis of the *Manuscripts* into *Capital* which he wrote years later. This has led some interpreters to see a sharp rupture between the "young" Marx of the 1840s and the "mature" Marx of the 1860s. Yet, there are clearly important elements of this analysis which persist, indeed are amplified, in *Capital*.[50]

Here, in Chapter 7, value, through the labor process, becomes an "animated monster."[51] Later, in Chapter 10, we find this monster is pictured by Marx as a *vampire*! "Capital is dead labor, which, vampire-like, lives only by sucking living labor, and lives the more, the more labor it sucks."[52] The evocation, of course, is not of the vampire who kills quickly at one feeding, but who returns again and again to slowly sap the life force of its victim. The dead labor is precisely the products produced by workers, products that have become alien objects, part of capital, and are used to dominate workers. The expression "sucking living labor" clearly means forcing humans to work, and the more they are forced to work the more products are produced, the more surplus-value, the more capital thrives. He also speaks of capital's "werewolf-like hunger for surplus labor," again the alien monster seeking ever to impose more work.[53] And then in Chapter 11 we find, in somewhat less picturesque language,

---

49. *MECW, vol. 3*, p. 228. Note the evocation of reflexive mediation analyzed in Chapter 1.
50. This was the position of Louis Althusser and his co-authors in their book *Lire le Capital* (1965), Tomes I–IV, Paris: Maspero (Petite collection), 1973, in which they argued the existence of an "epistemological break" between the "young" Marx of the *Manuscripts* and the "mature" Marx of *Capital*.
51. *Capital, Vol. I*, p. 302.
52. Ibid., p. 342.
53. Ibid., p. 353.

It is no longer the worker who employs the means of production, but the means of production which employ the worker. Instead of being consumed by him as material elements of his productive activity, they consume him as the ferment necessary to their own life-process, and the life-process consists solely in its own motion as self-valorizing value.[54]

Further, in the chapters on machinery and modern industry there is a whole discussion about how under capital the worker comes to serve the machine, rather than vice versa. Clearly, the core of the analysis of alienation is very much alive in *Capital* in so far as it concerns the way capital distorts humans' self-activity and relationships with each other. Rather than creating things as extensions of self, individual and collective, humans become the tools of capital and their creations turned against them. What is missing, it seems, is the way Marx in the early writings spoke of the feelings of workers. There he discoursed freely about workers "enjoying" activity, or finding it "hateful," of "feeling at home" or of "feeling outside," etc. Absent in *Capital* is any extended discussion of working-class consciousness and its relationship to their situation. Marx is concerned here with the dynamics of capitalist domination and with working-class struggle against it, but he no longer spends time exploring the relationship between what is going on and what workers think or feel about it. He examines their subjectivity in their actions rather than in their minds.

Alienation in Reproduction

As suggested earlier, the ever more extensive intervention of capital into the management of people's lives off-the-shop-floor, out-of-office, in homes and families, in schools and spaces of recreation, demands not only the recognition of its efforts to reduce our lives to the work of creating and recreating our labor-power, but also an analysis of the kinds of alienation that must inevitably be associated with such intervention.

Let us examine, one after another, the degree to which Marx's four aspects of alienation are present within the sphere of reproduction and whatever differences there may be with their presence within production.

The first form of alienation for waged workers is from their labor. With their labor processes defined for them by their employers, their work activities are clearly not free expressions of their own will and creativity. In the sphere of reproduction, on the contrary, people appear to be on their own, self-directing. In Section 1, I mentioned, as examples of the unwaged work of reproduction, "procreation, gestation, child rearing, teaching, training,

---

54. Ibid., p. 425.

disciplining or retraining." Each of these may include a variety of different, concrete labor processes but the key issue vis-à-vis alienation are the ways and the degree to which capital dictates such processes and strips those performing them of their autonomous control and ability to exercise their own will/creativity.

Clearly, the sub-spheres of reproduction where there is the least *direct* control by capital pose the greatest challenge to the relevance of Marx's analysis of alienation in production. So, let's examine what some have argued is the freest such sub-sphere: the home. Some consider the home and family as entirely free of capitalist relations, indeed as refuges from the exploitation and alienation suffered in waged and salaried jobs. No obvious employer stands over those doing housework, telling them what to do and how to do it. At the end of the waged working day, do not many flee the office or factory and seek the sanctuary of home, free of the boss's oversight and demands? Surely, exhausted workers jam evening rush-hour traffic, hurrying home, seeking relief, relaxation, friendly faces, dinner and sleep in the private haven of their apartments and houses. To what degree does the home provide an actual refuge? I did argue, after all, in my commentary on the general form of value, that capital has arranged various forms of mediation within the home and family. Has such intervention been conscious policy?

Well, throughout the twentieth century (and even before, though not in so comprehensive a fashion) capital has indeed quite consciously intervened in the home, to shape, adjust and dictate what does and does not go on in that supposed sanctuary. The institutions of such intervention have been both private and public. Following, but soon exceeding efforts by other capitalists, the well-known robber baron John Rockefeller set up the General Education Board (GEB) in 1902 with the goal of transforming low-productivity, mainly agrarian southern workers into a more productive and more profitable-to-employ labor force. The GEB worked to engineer changes in both schooling and the family; it hired lobbyists to push for a generalization of public schooling and, working through the US Department of Agriculture, helped launch home economics by setting up a network of girls' canning clubs to teach modern methods of food preparation and preservation. The purpose was to change the character of the family by transforming the tasks that were performed within it. In the words of Dr. Seaman A. Knapp, a prime mover for the GEB in this domain,

The home eventually controls the viewpoint of man; and you may do all that you are a mind to do in the schools, but unless you reach in and get hold of that home and change its conditions you are nullifying the uplift of the school. We are reaching for the home.[55]

Similar programs were implemented to shape the huge numbers of largely peasant immigrants flowing into the United States in the late 1800s and early 1900s. Here too, agents, both private and public, worked to change the habits of people who came to the US from rural areas to those demanded by industry. Again, such programs were aimed at both the habits of waged labor, from working by the sun to working by the clock, and at those of unwaged work in the home.[56]

Worker success in achieving less work and higher wages widened the demand for consumer goods and services, inducing business to increase and diversify their production. But business shaped both products and their advertising to cultivate modes of consumption and behavior judged compatible with capitalist ideas about the nature of a proper work force and proper modes of its reproduction. When labor laws to protect, and sometimes to exclude, women from production were enacted, so that more women were spending more time in the home, consumer goods designed for the home were peddled with screeds preaching their proper use, and thus the proper modes of labor in the home. Similarly, and I return to this in my comments on piecework in Chapter 21, along with the production of soaps, washing machines, dishwashers, vacuum cleaners, carpet cleaners, etc. came ever increasing standards of "cleanliness" such that not only did the machines regulate the work of cleaning, but the standards dictated more such work as well.

In schools, the early work of the GEB soon became regular courses on home economics where children, mainly girls, were trained in the various skills of "homemaking"—cooking, sewing and so on—under the common assumption that most girls would become married women and need those skills for the work of reproducing labor-power. Instead of mothers passing along their often ethnically distinct skills to their daughters, all were being taught the same skills by virtually identical institutions.

At the same time, governments, acting primarily as agents of business, wrote laws to regulate family relations of property, marriage, child protection, taxation and so on (forms of $M - K - W$, analyzed in my commentary on Section 3 of Chapter 1). So, although the ideology of capitalism has held

---

55. Cited in Grace E. Frysinger, "Home Demonstration Work, 1922", USDA, Department Circular 314, June 1924. For a more detailed account of the various objectives and programs of the GEB, see Chapter 3 of my dissertation "The Origins of the Green Revolution", Stanford University, 1975 and the references contained therein.

56. See Herbert Gutman, *Work, Culture and Society*, New York: Vintage Books, 1977.

the family and home up as the quintessential "private sphere," in fact the state has been busy implementing regulations and specifying what could, and what could not, go on there, both among adults and between adults and children. Because those laws and regulations are only as effective as their enforcement, the police and judiciary also played increasingly important roles in structuring family life. Laws may forbid a man to beat his wife if she didn't do her work properly (according to his assessment) or to rape her if she wasn't compliant with his sexual desires, but if the police do not arrest him, nor the courts convict him, laws against marital violence are meaningless.

In all these ways, and many more, capital has shaped family life and the behavior of people within the home. What seems private and protected from the pressures of the work-a-day world, upon closer examination turns out to be highly determined by capital, sometimes to an amazingly detailed degree, through a wide variety of mechanisms. Reared within such institutions and accustomed to their structures, people often internalize the behaviors they have experienced while remaining blind to the forces that have shaped them—a blindness which helps perpetuate the myth of the home-as-sanctuary.

All this is not to say that such intervention cannot be resisted, or that people have not sought to build family relationships based on non-capitalist criteria. But a clear understanding of how capitalists have tried to shape family and home would seem to improve our chances of successfully creating alternatives. As in industry, being clear about what we do not want can help us as we strive to create alternatives.

Turning to *the second form of alienation*—the alienation of workers from their product—how relevant is this to the sphere of reproduction? The product of the work of reproduction is labor-power, a willingness and ability to work that can be sold to some capitalist employer. In this case, the alienation of the product is inherent in the product itself. One trains children (as a parent or teacher) or trains/disciplines oneself, to work long and hard to acquire marketable abilities and the willingness to exercise those abilities under the direction of some employer. Moreover, as with other products, once in the hands of the capitalist, the product is then employed against those who sold it, by structuring their work both to control them immediately on the job and to exploit them by extracting surplus-value.

But what of those whose labor-power does not wind up being sold to capitalists? What of houseworkers, mostly housewives, who never enter the labor market? What of the unemployed who strive fruitlessly to prostitute themselves on the labor market, or who, disgusted, turn their back on it? In the case of children who are trained in housework and who go on to work only in the home, we have already seen how, to some degree, they will be doing the work of producing labor-power for capital. To the degree that they are reproducing their own labor-power, or that of others (spouses or children), they are working for capital. In as much as their product is for capital and will be used by it for its own purposes, then that product—the commodity labor-power—is every bit as alienated from them as the commodities produced by factory or office workers.

In the case of the so-called unemployed, searching for jobs is clearly work for capital: it makes the labor market function and, as Marx discusses in Chapter 25, helps keep down others' wages. Since the 1940s in the United States some have been paid for this work, in the form of unemployment compensation.[57] To obtain such compensation, workers must generally provide proof of job search interviews with prospective employers. Such workers are not working for wages per se, but whether they receive compensation or not, they are undertaking a labor vital to the functioning of the system as a whole. Moreover, the "products" of their labor, namely the opportunities they provide capitalists to reorganize their labor force through firing and hiring and the downward pressure on current employee wages are surely not things which belong to them; they are services provided to capitalists.

With respect to *the third form of alienation*—of worker from worker—we must ask if this too can be found within the home, within the family unit or in any other sphere of reproduction. The answer given by youth and feminist revolt in the 1960s and 1970s was a resounding, and very public, YES! "The crisis of the family" has haunted capitalist policymakers ever since.

The youth revolt of the 1960s was a revolt against virtually every aspect of modern capitalist society but three dimensions were particularly evident: a revolt against parental authority, a revolt against school, especially against the imposition of curricula determined from above, and a revolt against societal injustice of many forms, from the absence of civil rights to imperialist war. All these revolts took place mainly within the sphere of reproduction: within the family, the school and the community rather than the waged job place. They were all engendered by revulsion against a life (and possible death) structured and organized by capital in the alienated ways mentioned above.

Within the home the rebellion of children against parental authority was reinforced by, and sometimes spun off from, women's revolt against the patriarchal authority of their husbands and fathers. The feminist movement

---

57. In France, workers were strong enough to get laws enacted forcing their current employers to subsidize their search for jobs or retraining if laid off. Such laws are now under attack by Macron's new policies designed to make firing easier and cheaper for employers—one source of the anger that spawned protests by "les gilets jaunes."

was formed by women escaping the isolation of the home to the public sphere of collective action and struggle.

The division of labor within the nuclear family, which in the twentieth century became a norm, wherein husbands worked at waged jobs and women worked at unwaged housework, involved, as I pointed out in my commentary on the general form of value, a hierarchical power relationship in which the men who commanded the wage were also in a position to command their wives, and thus mediate those women's relationship with capital. That command was the most immediate manifestation and concrete form of the capitalist shaping of the family and home and of women's lives. Individually, and then collectively, women revolted against that command, ruptured the mediation and broke out of the hierarchy, the home and the family to seek better working conditions and better pay, whether those conditions were within or outside the home and whether the pay was a formal wage or a better share of family income.

Women also revolted against the perpetuation of patriarchal power within various social movements that challenged this or that aspect of capitalist society. Whether in the anti-war or black power or student rights movements young men, no doubt following the pattern of their fathers, often sought to lead and get their fellow female rebels to follow that lead—to make the coffee and clean up the mess after meetings. But young women increasingly would have none of it; they spoke up and spoke out and soon formed their own autonomous organizations, vital steps in the emergence of militant wings of the feminist movement.

In all these cases we find young men and women, and then older men and women following their lead, revolting against what they saw as intolerable conditions of alienation in the home, in the school and in the community. As students, they were sick of being pitted against each other in a highly competitive educational system in which only a few were promoted to higher education and many were discarded or dropped out along the way. They sought cooperation and collective action as a substitute for competition and a dog-eat-dog scrabble for grades and scholarships. In universities, they wanted some control of their curricula and fought for new fields and programs that better met their needs. They also fought against the imposition of too much work, so they would have time to learn on their own, both in libraries and in the streets. Professors and administrators came under pressure, grading became easier, "grade inflation" was born, and whole new programs of study were created on the basis of militant student desires, e.g., Black Studies, radical economics, insurgent sociology, women's studies and Chicano studies.

Blurring the distinction between private and public life, they experimented—often openly and to the horror of the ideologs of the nuclear family—with new family structures: open marriages, communal living arrangements, homosexual partnerships, and so on. The "crisis of the family" was created by such innovating rebels. Capitalist responses have been varied. Some have adapted and accepted new family structures, as long as they too serve to produce and reproduce labor-power. Others have counter-attacked in efforts to restore the patriarchal nuclear family, most obviously in efforts to ban contraception and abortion—essential to women's control over their own bodies—and in repressive "conversion therapy" programs and the refusal to recognize LGBTQ rights.

Finally, with respect to *the fourth form of alienation*—that of workers from their species-being—because this involves the substitution of the capital-ist will for that of workers, both individually and collectively, then to the degree that capital has succeeded in shaping the sphere of reproduction such that we do what it wants/needs, the way it wants and specifies, we are stripped of our humanity every bit as much as we are in the factory or office.

When parents become truant officers enforcing capitalist hours on learning, or drill sergeants ferociously imposing the arduous work of com-petitive sports on their children, then neither parents nor children are living autonomously but are both playing predesignated roles in the cap-italist machine. When parents expect and husbands demand that young women become brood mares to perpetuate the family (i.e., the labor force) and either set aside their own dreams and autonomous plans or take them up only as a second job alongside their "primary" one within the home, then both the women and those imposing these standards are, once again, playing predesignated roles within capitalist accumulation and have effec-tively given up the free exercise of their own wills.

That some people have consciously embraced the capitalist values and roles of such institutions doesn't obviate their loss of autonomy, and thus of their humanity. Given Marx's theory of human species-being as the exercise of the will, we must conclude that a human or a group of humans, can, after all, choose to be less than human by giving up its exercise. And this is true whether we are dealing with the sphere of production or that of reproduc-tion. It is also true whether we are dealing with workers or capitalists.

Resistance

Whether in the spheres of production—factories, fields or offices—or in those of reproduction—family or school—all of these forms of alienation have been resisted or subverted. On the job, workers have autonomously modified labor processes to make them easier and safer or they have sabotaged them to shut down production and escape. In families, house-wives have resisted outside efforts to shape their efforts and increase their workloads, sometimes choosing to escape completely. In schools, students have demanded changes in curricula and refused work in both classrooms and at home, sometimes dropping out entirely. On the job, workers have directly appropriated their products or sabotaged them. In families, adults have helped each other and their children resist pressures to become nothing more than mere workers. In schools, by pursuing their own intellectual and political goals, students have diverted time and energy from the production of labor-power. On the job, workers have overcome capital's imposed divisive divisions (of race, gender and ethnicity) to collaborate, from informal shop-floor organizing to formal organizations such as unions as vehicles for collective bargaining. In families, women have demanded, and many husbands and children have agreed, to share housework, subverting the patriarchal hierarchy of the nuclear family. More generally, a generation of women have overtly challenged that hierarchy and forced men to recognize its existence and agree to find or invent alternative, more rewarding relationships. Similarly, in rejecting absolute parental authority, children have demanded and often achieved more equitable relationships within the home and vis-à-vis outside activities such as schoolwork. In schools, students have resisted being pitted against each other. Rejecting competition and embracing collaboration, they have organized for collective action both within schools and in the larger community. In all these actions, on the job and off, by asserting their own wills, individually and collectively, people have affirmed, to one degree or another, what Marx calls their species-being.

The Alienated Capitalist

Although Marx was unconcerned with capitalists as individuals, many social commentators, novelists, poets, songwriters and filmmakers have been. A recurring theme in their treatment of the fate of individuals who become capitalists or "functionaries of capital" has been that "success" in the rat race does not breed happiness—"success," of course, being defined in terms of moving up the capitalist wage and salary hierarchy, of moving into positions where you are more of a manager of others and less of a worker being managed. The payoff for such movement is income and power, wealth and status. The image of the successful capitalist has largely been substituted in contemporary society for older images of the royalty and nobility. Against such ideology, which portrays the successful businessperson as the hero of capitalist society, has been pitted the more critical view that while "success" is materially rewarding, its achievement is also spiritually and socially exhausting. The cost of competing has been the isolation of the workaholic—which is not all that different from the isolation of the worker chained to the assembly line, or the housewife trapped in the home. In each case, life is reduced to work with all its alienations, especially the isolation from ful-filling relationships with others. Sometimes this theme has been developed as critical commentary, sometimes as a warning to those tempted by the obvious payoffs of "success" but blind to the costs. One such treatment in the 1960s was Simon and Garfunkel's song "Richard Cory," an adaptation of a poem by Edwin Arlington Robinson (1869–1935), in which, much to the dismay of one of his workers who envied him, the successful businessman goes home one night and puts a "bullet through his head."[58]

CHAPTER 8: CONSTANT AND VARIABLE CAPITAL

Outline of Marx's Analysis

Constant capital = *c*
  – value *invested* in the means of production, *MP*
  – value *embodied* in *MP*
Variable capital = *v*
  – value *invested* in the hiring of labor-power, *LP*
  – hired labor-power *LP*
Labor
  – preserves old value, by virtue of its character as useful labor
  – creates new value, by virtue of its character as abstract labor
Workers
  – create new value; more work, more value
  – if more than the value of their labor-power (*v*), they create surplus-value (*s*)
MP
  – transfer their value to the product as they are used up
  – quickly for raw materials
  – over time for tools and machinery (depreciation)
  – "their value undergoes a metempsychosis. It deserts the consumed body to occupy the newly created one."
Secondary points:
  1) Marx treats the repairs of machines, i.e., the value imparted to them during repairs, the same as their original creation. The repair labor is added to the original labor to determine their value. Depreciation is that "which no doctor can cure."
  2) with the value embodied in the product = *c* + *v* + *s*,
      – rise or fall of the *SNLT* required for producing *MP* or *LP* ⇒ rise or fall in value of *c* + *v*
      – *s* will diminish or increase

---

58. For some analysis of the original version of "Richard Cory," see the comments on the poem by Robinson at www.english.illinois.edu/maps/poets/m_r/robinson/robinson.htm.

Commentary

Although aimed at clarifying and elaborating the content of the previous chapter, Marx's use of language in this chapter is misleading. Writing of labor "preserving," "transferring" or "creating" value makes value sound like some metaphysical essence, some ethereal substance which can be conjured into being, conserved or transferred from one object to another. This is particularly true when he writes of value undergoing a "metempsychosis," a term which usually refers to the transmigration of souls from one body to another. These verbs, preserve, create, transfer, are all transitive verbs that seem to have an object: value. Because value is not an object, but a sociopolitical aspect of labor, these words obscure the phenomena they are intended to evoke. We can, however, bring those phenomena into the light.

"Creating" value is nothing more than the simple act of working within the context of capitalist institutions. Workers "create" value every time their labor performs the roles capital assigns to it, i.e., creating commodities that are sold and on which a surplus-value is realized, and, in the process, serving to keep people's lives centered on work, now and in the future. "Preserving" or "transferring" value refers simply to how useful labor, if it is performed competently, guarantees that the SNLT previously embodied in raw materials and machinery becomes part of the total SNLT required for the creation of the final product. Incompetent labor (or intentional sabotage), which results in wasted raw materials, broken machinery or flawed products, not only fails to add new value but nullifies the previous labor that went into producing the means of production.

In this chapter, as in Chapter 7, Marx further develops the fundamental dichotomy he set out in Chapter 1 between useful labor and abstract labor. Here it is the useful labor—the actual concrete processes of labor that produce a use-value—which preserves, through its competence, the labor already invested in prior stages of production. It is the additional characteristic of that useful labor as abstract labor, that makes it count as additional value.

With respect to his comments on the repair of machinery, his point is a simple one: the labor it takes to create a machine and the labor it takes to keep it running are all necessary for its continued functioning and counts as value. However, his analysis of the labor that repairs machinery can be extended to the labor that repairs labor-power. Later on, in Chapter 23 of *Capital*, Marx offers some analysis of this issue, but we can at least notice it here.

Repairing and Producing Labor-Power

In Chapter 6, the labor required to reproduce the ability and willingness to work was defined as that embodied in the means of subsistence. The labor of repairing labor-power, analogous to that which repairs machinery, raises new issues. Operating coffee machines at work to obtain the caffeine necessary to stay alert on-the-job is labor that obviously repairs and maintains labor-power. But brewing off-the-job morning coffee to wake up, get up, get to work and begin work, also renews labor-power. Then there's the work of caring for those on sick leave, of patching up the psychological wounds incurred on the job. In short, much of housework contributes to the daily, weekly and annual repair of labor-power. This labor neither creates commodities purchased with the wage, nor does it create commodities that the capitalist purchases and then provides to the worker. Such labor, because it does not produce a capitalist marketed good, is not counted in the value of labor-power. It certainly influences that value, as I pointed out in my commentary on Chapter 6, but unlike the labor that repairs machinery, it is not counted in the value of labor-power.

Yet, the amount of work involved in repairing labor-power is probably much greater than that involved in repairing machinery. When you count all the work done by individuals taking care of themselves and all the work done by other family members and friends, you have a tremendous amount. Unaccounted for in Marx's value theory, it also remains uncounted in cap-italist measures of labor performed or of (market) value produced, e.g., national product accounting that only tallies up the market values of sold commodities. Only when such work is done by professional cooks, house-keepers, cleaning establishments, prostitutes, psychotherapists, and so on, are the hours of work measured and the purchased service counted as part of the value of labor-power.

Against this almost universal refusal to recognize the importance and quantity of housework, some Marxist feminists have pointed out its essential role in the reproduction of capital and created an international "wages for housework" campaign of women demanding regular payment for their work of procreating, rearing and *repairing* labor-power. In some places, government pro-natalist policies have indirectly recognized the validity of these arguments by awarding money to women for having children. In some recent divorce and separation legal cases, women and some hired economists have argued persuasively that such work has economic value. A few economists have argued that housework should have a value imputed to it and should be included in measures of Gross National Product.

CHAPTER 9: THE RATE OF SURPLUS-VALUE

Overview of Chapter

Section 1: The Degree of Exploitation of Labor-Power
Section 2: The Representation of Components of Value by Parts of
      the Product
Section 3: Senior's "Last Hour"
Section 4: Surplus Product

Preliminary Commentary

Partly, this chapter sets out some basic definitions that Marx utilizes in the rest of the text. Partly, he is explaining some of the implications of the last two chapters where he introduced surplus-value, constant capital and variable capital. One implication is how his analysis provides the basis for repudiating an argument by Oxford Professor Nassau W. Senior (1790–1864) against any reduction in the length of the working day.

Section 1: The Degree of Exploitation of Labor-Power

Outline of Marx's Analysis

Surplus-value (s)
   = excess of value of product over value of inputs
Value of capital advanced, C
   = value of inputs = constant capital (c) + variable capital (v) = $c + v$
Total value of product:
   = $C' = (c + v) + s$
Constant capital (c)
   – refers to: the concrete fixed capital (machinery, factories, etc.) +
     raw materials used in production, but also
   – refers to: the value of investment in these inputs
   – fixed capital gives up only a part of its value (c_1) in each period
   – raw materials (c_2) are completely used up
   – so, $c = c_1 + c_2$
New value = $v + s$
   v = variable capital = value of investment in labor-power, LP ▶

---

v = value of LP

    = value required to reproduce LP

    = $SNLT$ for production of $C(MS)$ = necessary labor time = necessary labor

s = extra labor time over necessary labor = surplus labor time = surplus labor

Rates of extraction of s:

s/v = rate of surplus-value = rate of exploitation = surplus labor/ necessary labor

$s/(c+v)$ = rate of profit

Commentary

A redefinition: whereas up to this point, Marx has mostly used the term *necessary labor* purely within the context of the socially necessary labor time required to produce all commodities, in this section, with apology (see footnote 5), he narrows his usage of the term to denote the socially necessary labor time required to produce the $C(MS)$ required to reproduce labor-power. Henceforth, *necessary labor* refers to the labor necessary for the reproduction of this key commodity; necessary, he points out, not only from the point of view of workers' survival, but also for capital, "because the continued existence of the worker is the basis of that world."[59]

The most interesting thing in this section concerns the difference between two measures of the rate of extracting a surplus from the workers. The *rate of surplus-value*, s/v, compares surplus labor time, s, with necessary labor time, v. With $v + s$ = total labor time, ratio s/v measures the proportion of the workers' day given up to the capitalist versus the amount spent on self-reproduction, i.e., reproducing the value of labor-power. This is very much a worker's view, because the focus is on workers' time and how much of it is appropriated by their employers with no compensation. Because theft is involved, Marx also calls the rate of surplus-value the *rate of exploitation*. Clearly, the higher the ratio s/v, the higher percentage of the workers' day is being appropriated by the capitalist and the smaller the proportion workers are laboring to meet their own needs.

---

59. *Capital, Vol. I*, p. 325. While this is true in the aggregate, at the level of the class relationship, obviously capital could care less about the survival of individuals per se. Thus, its forever profligate expenditure of workers' lives in production, in wars, in police and paramilitary violence, in its use of the death penalty, and at the bottom of the unwaged/wage hierarchy, in poverty, malnourishment and death by disease and starvation.

The *rate of profit*, $s/(c + v)$, on the other hand, compares surplus labor time, s, with the capitalist's total investment, $c + v$. This measure, which, as Marx points out, dramatically underestimates the degree of exploitation, preoccupies capitalists, because it measures how much they earn in relation to how much they invest. Expressing the rate of profit in value terms reveals the exploitation hidden behind the similar, more familiar calculations of monetary rates of profit, net revenue/costs, calculated by business to measure their success.[60]

The rate of surplus-value is never calculated by capitalists for three reasons. First, it's impractical. Despite the way in which all capitalists carefully measure work time and labor productivity (the labor time required for each unit of output), to extract the most surplus labor possible (see Chapters 12–15), such work time data is never available in forms that would make it possible to distinguish between v and s.[61] Second, even if it were, both v and s are measured by SNLT, whose measurement would require that ALL producers keep and make available such data. Third, it would be too revealing. Capitalists are not inclined to make such calculations, because the results would draw attention to the distinction between the time workers work for their bosses versus the time they work for themselves. This of course is precisely one objective of Marx's value theory: to reveal what is going on from the workers' point of view, the reality hidden by capitalists' usual monetary calculations. In footnote 3, he points this out, "the rate of profit is no mystery when one knows the laws of surplus-value. But if one works in the reverse direction, one comprehends neither the one nor the other."[62]

Section 2: The Representation of Components of Value by Parts of the Product

> **Outline of Marx's Analysis**
>
> *Stage 1:* c, v and s
>   – can be represented by proportional parts of the product
>   – because each part embodies a given amount of labor time. ▶

---

60.   *Estimates* of potential rates of profit are also used to compare alternative investment possibilities, a habit that grounds Keynes's marginal efficiency of capital curve, central to his theory of the impact of central bank decisions about money supply and the likely impact of changes in interest rates on investment.

61.   In monetary calculations of the rate of profit such distinction is not necessary because $c + v$ = costs of production.

62.   *Capital, Vol. I*, p. 324.

With prices = values, assume:
- 1 shilling (s) = 0.5-hour *SNLT*
- a total product (*C'*) of 20 lb of cotton yarn is worth 30s
- components of that value are:
   - *c* = cost of constant capital = 24s, of which
      - 20 lb of raw cotton cost 20s
      - depreciation of the spindles used to produce the 20 lb of yarn = 4s
   - *v* = cost of variable capital = 3s (or 6 hrs of new labor)
   - *s* = surplus-value or profit = 3s (or 6 hrs of new labor)
   These values of 24s, 3s and 3s can be represented by 16 lb, 2 lb and 2 lb of yarn respectively.

Stage 2: *C'* embodies 60 hrs *SNLT*:
- 48 to produce *c*,
- 6 to produce *v*,
- 6 to produce *s*

Stage 3: temporal progression in production

Commentary

The purpose of this rather tedious section is to clarify the set of relationships used in the next section to debunk Nassau Senior's argument that a shortening of the working day by one hour would wipe out all surplus-value. Marx's presentation progresses through three stages. First, he shows how the value of the various components of the final product can be represented by proportional parts of that product. Second, he then presents the amount of labor time involved in producing both components and final product. Finally, he traces the temporal sequence of that labor.

Stage 1 corresponds to the title of this section, "The Representation of Components of Value by Parts of the Product." To illustrate how such representation can be done, he conjures up a hypothetical example, namely the production of 20 pounds of cotton yarn, requiring 20 lb of cotton, spindles for spinning[63] and 12 hours of spinning labor. His example assumes both that the cotton yarn is a commodity being produced by workers for some capitalist who wants to turn his money into capital by extracting a surplus-value or profit, and that monetary prices are equal to, and can

---

63.   At various points, he says that constant capital also includes "auxiliary materials," including steam engines, coal, oil, etc. So, his numerical example is a simplification of all the values used up in the operations of a spinning mill.

therefore represent, values. This last assumption justifies his analysis of the value of the product and its inputs in terms of shillings rather than SNLT.[64]

Assuming the value of the 20 lb of cotton yarn when sold to be 30 shillings (30s) and the cost of production consisting of the value of the cotton from which it is spun, 20s, the depreciation (value lost through wear and tear) of the spindles, 4s, and the wages of the spinners, 3s, that investment of 27s (20s + 4s + 3s), returns a surplus-value of 3s (30s − 27s). Given the values of these components, the amounts of yarn that represent or embody those values are the following. The value of the constant capital (20s + 4s) is embodied in and can be represented by 16 lb of yarn (13⅓ lb for value of the cotton, 2⅔ lb for depreciated value of the spindles). The remaining 4 lb of yarn embodies both the value of labor-power (3s) and the surplus-value (3s), so the value of labor-power is embodied in 2 lb of yarn and the surplus-value in 2 lb. In other words, we have the following correspondences:

$$C' = c + v + s$$
$$30s = 24s + 3s + 3s$$
$$20\ lb = 16\ lb + 2\ lb + 2\ lb$$

Stage 2 begins when he switches from calculating corresponding values and weights of product to calculating the amounts of *SNLT* embodied in the various components and final product. This has, of course, been implicit in the assumption that prices (in shillings) are equal to values, but diving behind shillings into labor time leads to new revelations.

The take-off point for this dive is the observation that the 12 hours of *SNLT* that produced the cotton yarn results in a new value of 6s (3s + 3s), or one hour of *SNLT* results in .5s of value. Therefore, assuming the correspondence between labor time and shillings has remained the same from the previous period, in which the cotton and spindle were produced, and the current period, when the cotton yarn is produced, the amount of *SNLT* required to generate a value of 30s is 60 hours. But only 12 of these hours are new, those expended to produce the cotton yarn. The other 48 hours of labor were expended in the previous period to produce the cotton and the depreciated part of the spindles.

Stage 3 of his exposition imagines, as the production of the yarn proceeds, an association of additional hours of labor and value, with factors of production. Producing 1⅔ lb of yarn per hour (20lb/12hrs), in 8 hrs the spinner can produce 13⅓ lb of yarn, which embodies the value of the cotton. As his laboring continues, the spinner produces more yarn, embodying the value

---

64.   See footnote in the commentary on Chapter 3, Section 1.

of the depreciated spindles, the value of labor-power and surplus-value. Then, using the same example, Marx notes how the same components of value: c, v and s can be represented in terms of proportional parts of the total *SNLT* employed in production, i.e., 12 hrs. In this case the values of c = 24s, v = 3s and s = 3s, are the result of 9 hrs 38 min, 1 hr 12 min and 1 hr 12 min of labor, respectively. But while this accounting process correlates the amounts produced with the labor time expended on and by various factors of production, both old and new, it is a mistake—one committed by capitalist sycophants such as Senior and debunked in the next section—to associate particular hours of labor with particular elements of value, especially to think that only the last hour of labor produces surplus-value and therefore cannot be cut without wiping it out.

Section 3: Senior's "Last Hour"

Outline of Marx's Analysis

Nassau Senior:
  - reducing the working day by one hour would wipe out all manu-
    facturing profits, s
  - the component parts of the total value of the final product can be
    represented by parts of the time worked
  - i.e., $c + v$ = 10.5 hrs, s = 1 hr
  - reduce work time by one hour ⇒ 0 s

Marx's critique:
  - in each hour of the working day constant capital is being used up
  - reduce work time by one hour
    ⇒ reduction of c
    ⇒ less reduction of s

Commentary

This section builds on the previous one to elaborate Marx's critique of Nassau Senior, who supported the opposition of British manufacturers to the Factory Acts by arguing that proposed reductions in work time would wipe out profits (or surplus-value) and destroy British industry. Here, he shows how Senior used the argument that the components of value can be "represented" either by parts of the product, or by parts of the time used to produce the product to oppose work time reductions.

Marx's critique is simple enough. He shows the fallacy of Senior's reasoning by recalling that each hour of production processes elements of constant capital (raw cotton spun with spindles into yarn) and by demonstrating how that simple fact undermines Senior's argument. He concludes his argument in showing how the rate of surplus-value will only drop from 100 percent to 82.6 percent. Some may find this argument troubling, however, not because it is wrong, in Marx's terms, but because it is not framed in terms of profit (or net profit) as Senior would have it. It is, however, easy to frame the conclusion in terms of absolute levels of profit, the rate of profit or the rate of exploitation.

Restating Senior's initial example in Marx's terms, an 11.5-hour day gives the following results:

> $C' = 115,000$ (total value of product),
> $c = 95,000$ (constant capital, including depreciation), and
> $v = 10,000$ (wages).
> So, investment costs $= c + v = 105,000$
> Assuming, as Senior does, that $s/v = 1$, or 100 percent (10,000/10,000)
> Net profit or $s = 10,000$ $(C' - \{c + v\})$ or $(115,000 - 105,000)$
> Therefore, the rate of profit: $s/(c + v) = 10,000/105,000 = 9.5\ percent$

The results of *a one hour drop in the working day* (from 11.5 to 10.5 hours) can be calculated:

> $C' = 105,000$ (assuming production falls proportionately, prices constant)
> $(\{115,000/11.5\}10.5 = 105,000)$
> $c = 86,739.1$ (assuming costs fall proportionately)
> $(\{95,000/11.5\}10.5 = 86,739.1)$
> $v = 10,000$ (assuming the wage bill remains the same)
> So, investment costs $= c + v = 96,739.1$
> Continuing to assume, as Senior does, that $s/v = 1$, or 100 percent, then
> Net profit $s = 8,260.9$ (105,000 − 96,739.1)
> Therefore, the rate of profit: $s/(c + v) = 8.5\ percent$ [8,260.9/(96,739.1)],
>   and
> $s/v = 82.6\ percent$ (as in Marx's calculations)

So, we see in Senior's example that if the working day is reduced one hour, the result would be a drop in absolute profits from 10,000 to 8,260.9 or a drop in the rate of profit from 9.5 percent to 8.5 percent, both of which confirm the argument Marx is making that Senior drastically overstates the potential negative impact of the 10 hours law on profits. We can also note, that in the more likely case that the wage *rate* rather than the wage *bill* remained the same, the reduction of one hour would drop the wage bill (v) from 10,000 to 9,130.4, c would still be at 86,739.1 and profits, $C' - (c + v)$, would therefore only fall to 9,130.5+ with a resultant negligible change in s/v and $s/(c + v)$!

The history of Senior's hour, and of all other episodes like it—such as the one Marx cites in 1848—bespeak much more than false logic. The desperate arguments put forward by capitalists and their apologists to resist any reduction of work time reflect more than fear of losing profits. Their arguments, foretelling doom and societal collapse, reflect a deeper intuition that all reductions in work time threaten the social fabric of capitalism as a civilization built on the subordination of life to work. This can be seen in the argument by Andrew Ure (1778–1857), which Marx cites in a footnote, that a life not structured by work would be both idle and immoral.[65] Marx's long footnote 11 provides antidotes to Ure in quotations from the Inspectors of Factories reports revealing the immorality of capitalism, in the horrible working conditions in textile manufacturing.[66] Down the path of less and less work lies another kind of world, one in which capitalists as a class are completely superfluous.

Section 4: Surplus Product

Outline of Marx's Analysis

Surplus product = the portion of the product that represents surplus-value

Rate of surplus product = surplus product/necessary product

---

65. Andrew Ure, *The Philosophy of Manufactures: Or an Exposition of the Scientific, Moral, and Commercial Economy of the Factory System of Great Britain*, London: Charles Knight, 1835, especially Book the Third on "The Moral Economy of the Factory System" (available online as a pdf). The architects of classical political economy were hardly the first to have this preoccupation. The writings of their predecessors, the mercantilists, were rife with such worries. See, for example, Thomas Mun, "Englands Treasure by Forraign Trade. Or The Ballance of our Forraign Trade is the Rule of our Treasure" (1664) in Thomas Mun, *The Complete Works: Economics and Trade*, Newton Page, 2013, where he praised the Dutch for their hard work and lamented the degree to which the English followed their pleasures, "besotting" themselves "with pipe and pot, in a beastly manner, sucking smoak, and drinking healths" (available online as a pdf). Nor were the classical political economists the last. We are still plagued with sanctimonious teachings of "work ethics" and moral condemnations of time wasted in leisure, despite the widespread structuring and commodification of leisure by capital itself.

66. Marx draws upon these same sources at greater length in Chapter 10.

Commentary

In this last, short section, Marx simply finishes his parallels between the distribution of value and the distribution of product. He emphasizes the ratio of surplus product to necessary product (i.e., the part that goes to working-class consumption) for the same reason he emphasizes the ratio s/v: they both highlight distribution between the classes.

In the final footnote of this section (#13), Marx quotes T. Hopkins who writes: "To an individual with a capital of £20,000, whose profits were £2,000 per annum, it would be a matter quite indifferent whether his capital would employ a hundred or thousand men [. . .]."

Such indifference characterizes only what I call narrow-minded, fetishistic capitalists who cannot see beyond their bottom line—those who think that the point of business is merely profit-making and self-enrichment. Such capitalists rarely rise to the level of policymaking because they cannot see that it often *does* matter whether a hundred or a thousand people are employed. Organizing society around the endless and universal imposition of work, capitalists collectively *must* worry about whether they provide enough employment to absorb the existing labor force and whether investment will create enough new jobs to absorb new entrants to that labor force. If they do not, and unemployment grows too large, their ability to control society is threatened.

In the nineteenth century, worker uprisings tended to occur during periods of crisis and soaring unemployment, e.g., the crisis of 1847 was followed by the revolutions of 1848. This continued into the twentieth century, right up through the Great Depression that saw nationwide mobilizations of those unable to find jobs. In the post-World War II era, concern continued as policymakers sought to provide "full employment" to reintegrate returning soldiers and a new, baby-boom generation of workers. It also preoccupied post-colonial regimes as local elites, replacing foreign ones, faced the familiar problem of providing jobs to control populations increasingly being driven from the land into cities. Development economists have worried about the issue of "appropriate technology," i.e., the degree to which a given technology introduced into the Global South by either local or multinational corporate investment would contribute to putting rural–urban migrants to work. In all these cases, the most threating rebels have been the unwaged, angry at their loss of waged income or unable to find waged or salaried employment.[67] Such preoccupations led the International

---

67. Or, in the case of the educated, unable to find jobs appropriate to their level of schooling. American counterinsurgency experts saw discontented intellectuals, unable to find suitable jobs, as prime candidates for leading rebellions. One solution was to

Labor Organization to warn of the need for the creation of a billion jobs by the end of the twentieth century to absorb the growth in the world's labor force, or risk widespread unrest. More recently wars in the Middle East and Africa and genocide in Myanmar, are creating historically high levels of refugee migration, leading to more problems for capitalist policymakers of finding enough jobs to insure integration into the labor force.

CHAPTER 10: THE WORKING DAY

Overview of Chapter

Section 1: "The Limits of the Working Day"
Section 2: The Voracious Appetite for Surplus Labor
Section 3: Sectors of Industry with No Legal Limits
Section 4: Day and Night Work
Section 5: Struggle Over Extension of Work Day
Section 6: Struggle for the Limitation of Working Hours
Section 7: The Impact of English Legislation on Other Countries

---

Preliminary Commentary

The choice of a "working *day*" rather than a working week, month or year was natural in a period where workers were working at least six days a week and day-labor was common.[68] Today, in the US and many other countries we more frequently speak of the working *week*, because decades of workers' struggles culminated in the creation of the five-day work week (and thus the weekend—a previously unknown concept). This victory was followed by demands for shorter working *years* (more vacation time or paid holidays) and shorter working *lives* (earlier retirement). By the 1970s, after two decades of generally rising wages, the then standard working week of five days came under attack by rank-and-file unionists who demanded negotiations for a four-day week or for the reduction of the 40-hour week to the 36 hours. More recently, since the early 1980s, by imposing serious wage

---

employ them as teachers, which, of course, merely multiplied the problems as their students progressed and found themselves in similar situations. See Martin Carnoy, *Education as Cultural Imperialism*, New York: Longman, 1974.

68.   Obviously, day-labor still exists where low-waged, unemployed workers gather on street corners hoping to be picked up by some contractor and put to work for a day's wage.

cuts, the capitalist class has regained the initiative and has succeeded in imposing longer working days and later retirement, although the weekend is still largely intact.[69]

Missing in *Capital*, but now mandatory, is extending Marx's analysis beyond the sphere of waged and salaried work to a "working day" that includes not only the work of producing commodities on whose sale a surplus-value is realized, but also the work of reproducing life as labor-power. This extension is required not only because capital has come to exercise its despotism beyond the factory—in the home, family, school and community—but because our struggles have also developed in these areas. The terrain of conflict over the "working day" has expanded accordingly.

Section 1: "The Limits of the Working Day"

Outline of Marx's Analysis

1. The working day can be represented either by $v + s$ or by
   A------B------C, where
      A------B represents those hours that generate the value of labor-power, v, and
      B------C represents those hours that generate surplus-value, s
      B------C is "variable," longer or shorter, depending on the balance of class power
2. But there are limits:
   There is a *minimum limit* to:
      A---B for workers to reproduce their labor-power
      B---C must at least result in the average rate of profit (or capitalists will withdraw from this form of investment)
   There is a *maximum limit* of A----B--C, which is a function of:
     – the "physical limits" set by workers' needs for sleep, food, etc. and
     – a "moral/social" limit set by workers' needs for intellectual and social requirements
     – both of these are elastic though within 24 hours ▶

---

69. Largely intact for the waged, but often not for the salaried whose work time is not measured by the clock, who often work at home via computer, and who are all too often subject to employer contact and demands via cell phone. Less intact too, for all those whose work carries over into their "off-work" hours by preoccupation with their work, or even drawing from their home lives to enrich their work, e.g., sitcom writers.

3. In *LP – M* and *M – LP* we have two different perspectives on the exchange:
   Capitalists: demand as much use of labor-power, *LP*, as they can extract in exchange for wages, *M*
   Workers: demand enough time to both reproduce *LP* and live, i.e., a normal working day
4. Thus, capitalist rights as purchaser vs workers' rights as sellers:
   "Between equal rights force decides. Hence it is that in the history of capitalist production, the determination of what is a working day, presents itself as the result of a struggle, a struggle between collective capital, i.e., the class of capitalists and collective labor, i.e., the working class."

Commentary

Marx's analysis in this section, which sets the tone for the rest of the chapter, portrays two subjects in contention: the capitalist and working classes. Capital demands one thing, workers demand another. Capitalists demand their rights as purchasers of labor-power and workers demand their rights as sellers. In the Hegelian language of Chapter 2, two wills or sets of wills confront each other, not just in the labor market, but throughout the sphere of production and, in extension, in the sphere of reproduction. The length of the working day emerges through struggle between opposing forces. True of work time, true of most of the key variables in Marx's analysis, they denote moments of class conflict and are determined by struggle.

As with the circuit of capital, Marx constructs a visual representation of the working day:

A------B------C

For a 12-hour working day, the first segment *A------B* (six dashes for six hours of labor) represents necessary labor, i.e., that part of the working day during which workers produce the value necessary for the reproduction of their labor-power, *v*. The second segment, *B------C* (six dashes for six hours), represents surplus hours and surplus-value, *s*, that capital extracts over and above the time required to produce the value they must render to workers in exchange for their labor-power. While Marx, like the classical political economists, assumes the first segment is fixed at subsistence, the number of surplus hours can vary. How many extra hours capitalists can impose and the amount of surplus-value they can extract will depend on how much power they have vis-à-vis workers. Varied too will be the resulting rates of surplus-value, s/v, and profit, $s/(c+v)$.

The working day, $v + s$, Marx insists, has a *minimum limit* because in general capitalists demand at least the average rate of profit, $s/(c+v) = \pi$, to continue a given investment. If π falls below the average for very long, the capitalist will close shop.[70] As with the rate of exploitation, what determines the average rate of profit is the balance of class forces. This minimum, as Marx defines it here, is purely in terms of waged hours in production. With the unwaged hours of capitalist-organized *re*production included in the working day, the minimum amount of working time (waged and unwaged) is still defined in terms of what is required for the reproduction of labor-power and the generation of an average rate of profit under existing circumstances.

In the case of the *maximum limit* to the length of the working day, we can see a shift in the balance of class power over time. Early on, capital pushed to maximize commodity-producing working hours and tried to minimize the times of reproduction, e.g., meal times and sleep. The ferocity of that push provoked Marx to characterize capital in Gothic terms: "Vampire-like, [capital] lives only by sucking living labor, and lives the more, the more labor it sucks"[71] (see Sections 3–5 below for detail on various aspects of those efforts). In response, workers resisted, and demanded enough free time to reproduce their labor-power without having their lives shortened by overwork.[72] Within this history, what Marx calls the "moral" limits to the length of the working day have varied according to workers' ability to gain time for "intellectual and social activity." When and as they have been able, workers have hammered down the length of the working day (Section 6), reducing the maximum limit. The reduction of the working day creates more and more time for the fulfillment of workers' own, self-defined needs. Yet, as I have previously noted, capital has invaded and colonized those ostensibly free hours in ways designed to reduce them to the mere

---

70.   This argument predates and foreshadows the neoclassical microeconomic concept of a firm's "shut-down point," the point at which revenues no longer cover the variable costs of production and continuing to operate only generates losses.

71.   *Capital, Vol. I*, p. 342.

72.   Marx here couches workers' arguments in terms of having enough time and energy to reach the average working-class life expectancy of some 30 years. In Section 3 below, we see why when he highlights the case of a young woman worker killed prematurely by overwork. Thanks to workers' struggles, the average worker's life expectancy in the US has expanded from those 30 years to 75–80 years today. Despite this, death by overwork—via fatigue-induced accidents on the job or stress-provoked heart disease, etc.—continues in modern capitalism to such an extent that the Japanese have a specialized term for it: *karōshi* (過労死).

reproduction of labor-power, e.g., by controlling children's time through educational institutions and that of adults through laws, cultural norms and diversions. Every hour has become another time of struggle.

Section 2: The Voracious Appetite for Surplus Labor

Outline of Marx's Analysis

1. "Capital did not invent surplus labor"
   – surplus labor has been extracted in many class societies
2. Where use-value predominates
   – surplus labor is limited by the set of wants
3. Where exchange-value (capitalist market) dominates
   – a boundless thirst, whose aim is not use-value and therefore not limited by wants
   – this comes with capitalist world market and production for export
   – e.g., in the US slavery transformed from paternalism to the using up of slaves' lives to maximize exchange-value and profit
4. Corvée labor
   – in the Danubian Principalities, *Règlement Organique* (1831)
   – a positive expression of thirst for surplus labor, positive because explicitly defined
   – surplus labor is obvious, i.e., so many days of work on a seignorial estate
5. Factory Acts in Britain (1850)
   – negative expression of thirst, negative because the Acts set limits to surplus labor
   – limits set through the state, forced by working-class struggle and exhaustion of *LP*
   – capital responds with "nibbling and cribbling" at the working day
6. Full-timers, half-timers: people defined as personified labor time

Commentary

Capitalism as Endless Work

Points 1–3 in the outline above add historical concreteness to an aspect of Marx's analysis we first encountered in Chapter 1's discussion of the expanded form of value: capital's tendency to infinity or limitless expansion. The existence of *surplus* labor, he argues, neither makes capitalism unique nor defines it. Ruling classes have imposed surplus labor in many different kinds of societies. Marx names several. It is the *boundlessness* of surplus labor in capitalism that makes it unique. In other class societies, e.g., ancient slavery or feudalism, surplus labor was subordinated to useful labor, to the production of use-values for the ruling classes, e.g., a pyramid for a pharaoh, a palace for a Roman emperor, a Forbidden City for a Chinese one, a castle for a feudal lord. In capitalism, it is the other way around, the imposition of useful labor is subordinated to surplus labor, i.e., the extraction of surplus-value. This is fundamental to his critique of capitalism. Significantly, Marx discusses it here without regard to the value form. Form in capitalism is important, but not as fundamental as the content. Capital seeks endless amounts of surplus labor, but only secondarily through the commodity form, where surplus labor appears in the form of surplus-value, and ultimately surplus money and profit. Marx even uses American slavery to illustrate capital's boundless thirst for surplus labor even though slaves do not receive wages—the most common form of domination in capitalism.[73]

Because capitalism is not defined by the existence of surplus labor, the end of capitalism cannot be defined by the end of surplus labor. What must be ended to bring about a post-capitalist society, is the endlessness of surplus labor and the subordination of useful labor to surplus labor. We must reverse the relationship and subordinate surplus labor to our own multidimensional needs as we define them in post-capitalist society. Thus, post-capitalist society is not a no-growth society but one whose growth is subordinated to meeting needs and not the other way around.

This can also be put in terms of the relation between work time and leisure time, or between production-time and reproduction-time. In capitalism, we see an effort to subordinate reproduction to production, to organize non-factory life so that it only prepares one to enter or re-enter factories, fields or offices. This includes the subordination of culture to capitalist-organized work and education as discipline and training for work. Thus, the reversal and overthrow of capital must include the reduction of work to one life choice among many, the subordination of production to cultural flowering, the recasting of education for lives-worth-living not just for job training. Only through these reversals can work become one fruitful element of life, among others, no longer antagonistic because no longer a means of domination.

In points 4 and 5, Marx juxtaposes Danubian corvée to the Factory Acts because although both involved set rules in the former case the extraction

---

73. Marx often marks the parallel between out-and-out slavery and waged labor by referring to the latter as wage-slaves.

of surplus labor is obvious, while in the second, it is hidden.[74] In both cases, the dominant class—of boyars or of capitalists—imposes surplus work. Eventually, the abolition of serfdom in 1864 undermined corvée labor. In the case of the Factory Acts, the working class successfully forced a reduction of work. Such steps in the right direction depend on workers' power to impose them.

Nibbling and Cribbling

Within the context of the waged working day, capitalists must use overseers, foremen and other forms of oversight to keep workers working as steadily and as long as possible.[75] Later, in Chapter 15 he will discuss how the subordination of workers to machines can achieve the same end, but here it is human oversight, from harassment to threats of firing that gets workers to start work, keep working, and return to work after breaks. Ex-railway worker Mark Anthony Priest (present professor of painting at the University of Louisville), in an appropriately titled work, has portrayed one such overseer yelling at a rail repairman "Get Back to Work!" Charlie Chaplin, in *Modern Times*, provides a comic critique of similar harassment along a factory's assembly line.

But unsatisfied with making sure workers labor steadily during their contracted work time, capital also "nibbles and cribbles" at the working day, stealing a few extra minutes from workers here and a few more minutes there.[76] This nineteenth-century pattern persists, notably in salaried work, where tasks are often assigned requiring extra minutes or hours, either inside or outside the office. In schools, many are the salaried, secondary school teachers who must take papers or tests home to grade at night or on weekends; many are the professors who put in uncounted hours in their research. True too for unwaged students, many of whom have experienced classes running over time and most of whom have been assigned homework to do outside school hours.

Unfortunately, Marx's comments are very one-sided. He fails to examine the similar ways in which workers nibble at the time they are forced to give

---

74.   Danubian corvée refers to days of corvée labor performed by serfs for the benefit of the land-owning boyars in the Principalities of Moldavia and Wallachia along the lower Danube River. United in 1859, they formed the core of the Kingdom of Romania.
75.   Today the hulking overseer has often been replaced by electronic surveillance, which watches, measures and signals managers of any slacking.
76.   The verb to *cribble*, which originally meant to pass through a sieve, was already obsolete in the nineteenth century, but was preserved and given special meaning in the vocabulary of workers, as reported by the Factory Inspectors in 1856. *Capital, Vol. I*, p. 352.

to capital, stealing back moments of their lives when they can, biting off big chunks when possible. The struggle over the working day goes on in this piecemeal fashion just as it does at the macro-level of collective battles over legislation setting working hours or vacations. Playing on the job, absenteeism, slowdown, sabotage—"the conscientious withdrawal of efficiency" (Veblen)—are all ways in which workers seek to reduce the amount of their lives they give up to business.[77] Capitalists, of course, denounce employee "time theft" while ignoring how it just involves taking back the time they are stealing from workers.[78]

Several illustrative examples of this kind of "nibbling" were given in a 1971 article on the auto industry: "Counter-Planning on the Shop Floor" by Bill Watson.[79] One recounts the use of sabotage to shut down the line to gain free time. Another describes the organization of "rod-blowing contests" for amusement and time-liberating sabotage. Such conflict goes on throughout the social factory, not just in commodity-producing work. When students arrive late or skip class completely, or text-message during lectures, or blow off studying, this happens on a small scale.[80] When they insist on taking courses such as philosophy, or Marxism, or labor history as vehicles for their own education and needs instead of more "practical" courses that are job-oriented, they are nibbling at the time capital is trying to convert into reproduction-time on a much larger scale. This kind of perpetual conflict characterizes life within capitalist society. When women resist having any, or more, children, they are often fighting for more time for their own life—including, perhaps, life with their husband (or existing children)—and undermining the reproduction of labor-power for capital. Such working-class action is sometimes overt and aggressive, sometimes covert and passive in its resistance, but it is rarely absent. Oversight thus

---

77. Veblen used this expression—taken from the literature of the Industrial Workers of the World—as an appropriate definition of sabotage as used by both workers and business. Thorstein Veblen, *On the Nature and Uses of Sabotage* (1919), New York: Oriole Chapbooks, n.d.

78. Any number of businesses specialize in helping other capitalists fight against workers' "nibbling and cribbling." See, for example, the website of Epay Systems and download its e-book *How to Prevent Workforce Time Theft*.

79. *Radical America*, vol. 5, no. 3, May–June 1971, pp. 77–85. Now available from Zabalaza Books, Johannesburg, South Africa and online at libcom.org.

80. Read J. D. Salinger's classic novel *Catcher in the Rye* (1951), New York: Little, Brown and Co., 1991, or the first-person narrative *Artie Cuts Out* by Arthur Bauman as told to Paul Wallis, New York: Jaguar Press, 1953. And the graduate student protest essay "Wages for Students" (1975), now available in a trilingual edition *Wages for Students*, Brooklyn, NY: Common Notions, 2016. And watch the now classic film *Ferris Bueller's Day Off*, John Hughes (dir.), 1986.

involves not only capitalist efforts to impose extra work but is often a defense against workers' efforts to work less.

Section 3: Sectors of Industry with No Legal Limits

Outline of Marx's Analysis

1. The lace trade: children used up by being worked 15 hours and more
2. Potteries: short life span, chest diseases (pneumonia, asthma, bronchitis, etc.), function of long hours, poor conditions
3. Lucifer matches: tetanus (lockjaw), long hours in rooms with phosphorus
4. Paper hangings: no stoppage for meals
5. Baking: adulteration and overwork related, sleeping on kneading boards
   - workers organized and won the abolition of night labor in some areas, were defeated elsewhere
6. Agricultural workers: long hours, formation of trades union and protests
7. Railway men: accidents from overwork, failure of labor-power
8. Dressmaking (milliners): Mary Anne Walkley, 20, death from overwork
9. Blacksmithing: die at rate of 31 per thousand/year, 11 above mean

---

Commentary

In this section Marx reveals the consequences of long working days. He will do this again in Chapter 15 on relative surplus-value and speed-up. There he will focus on the results of working too fast. Here the ill consequences of working too hard come from working too long. In these examples, we see not only the lengths to which capital will go in extorting absolute surplus-value when the working class is too weak to resist, but also how, in their fetishistic pursuit of monetary profit, some capitalists lose sight of their social role of putting people to work and in their fanaticism result in putting people to death, undermining the very society they are trying to control and structure. Here fetishism is not simply failing to perceive social relations behind things but is a mentality and way of behaving which undermines the reproductive capacity of the system itself.

Although he examines those sectors of industry where the working class is too weak to achieve reductions in hours, Marx does mention from time to time (e.g. bakers in Ireland and agricultural workers in Scotland) instances where workers are or have been struggling to change the situation. What we have little of here, as all too often in *Capital*, is analysis of how some workers were successful and why others were not.[81] Here we have mostly the results.

This section spells out a long series of horror stories about overwork, horrible working conditions and the consequences for both workers and consumers. Marx draws these stories from newspapers, independent studies and government reports. From newspapers, he plucks anecdotes on a few dramatic cases, e.g., the death of Mary Anne Walkley in 1863 or a railway accident in 1866.[82] From government reports, such as those to the Children's Employment Commissioners of Parliament, or of the Royal Commissioner of Inquiry, he extracts a great deal more detail. In a few cases, studies, such as those of George Read on the baking industry, or by Dr. Richardson on overwork, provide him with the results of extensive independent research. Today, similar, and in many cases equally horrifying, information can be amassed from both public and private sources.

One source that Marx did not use were the vivid literary treatments of such appalling conditions portrayed in nineteenth-century "industrial novels." But those stories mattered. They played a considerable role in mobilizing broader support for workers' demands for shorter hours and better working conditions. For example, in *North and South*, Elizabeth Gaskell vividly describes an example of the kind of working situation Marx was writing about.[83] Bessy, a working-class girl whose health has been destroyed by working long hours in the textile mills, describes the circumstances under which she contracted what we now call byssinosis, by breathing in the "fluff," tiny particles of cotton spun off into the air during production.[84]

---

81.   In the case of those Irish journeyman bakers in Cork, whose organizational efforts were defeated, Marx points to their bosses, the "master bakers," "exercising their power of turning the men out of employment," i.e., firing them. Why this method worked in Cork, but not in Wexford, Kilkenny, Clonmel or Waterford, he does not explain. *Capital, Vol. I*, p. 362.
82.   It is not only in Japan that overwork sometimes produces death or only on the assembly line that workers collapse. See a professor's account, "Why I Collapsed on the Job," by Katerina Bodovski in *The Chronicle of Higher Education*, February 15, 2018.
83.   Her novel *Mary Barton* (1848), which also portrays the life of factory workers, is evoked in my commentary on Chapter 27.
84.   Her story thus also illustrates the phenomena the factory inspector described in footnote 11 of Chapter 9. For a striking portrayal of the fluff that filled the air in the cotton mills of that time, watch the BBC television production of *North & South* (2004). For a similar portrayal in cotton mills of more recent times, watch *Norma Rae* (1979). The story of the struggle to get byssinosis recognized by industry and government in the

A half-century later, in his 1905 novel *The Jungle*, about the life and struggles of Lithuanian immigrants in and around the Chicago stockyards, Upton Sinclair (1878–1968) provided equally shocking descriptions of the conditions under which workers were compelled to labor. After losing a better job on the killing floor due to an accident, the main character, Jurgis, is forced to work under conditions like Bessy's, only worse. Where Bessy was forced to breathe in "fluff," Jurgis found himself in a job where he had to breathe in clouds of toxic dust from ground fertilizer.

Sinclair describes the effects of the fertilizer on Jurgis, but he doesn't follow the stuff downstream. We know today that kind of poisoning continues as such materials are applied to the fields by agricultural laborers who, like Jurgis, are exposed to it for hours at a time. Moreover, as the twentieth century has progressed this situation deteriorated as even more toxic pesticides and herbicides have become common in modern corporate farming. The exposure and poisoning of both consumers and farm workers by lethal pesticides such as parathion have been well documented.[85] Farm worker organizations, such as the United Farm Workers in California or the Texas Farm Workers Union have struggled against such practices for years.[86] When they succeed, often with the support of environmentalists and consumers, the corporations producing the chemicals often ship them off to other agribusiness operations in countries where workers are less well organized. Moreover, we now know that along with workers and consumers the entire environment has become increasingly poisoned by the growing quantities of chemicals used in agriculture.

From these observations we can derive a methodology for studying the extent of such problems and struggles around them: follow the material circuits of production, consumption and resistance. In the case of Sinclair's beef industry-derived fertilizer we would want to follow the toxic trail both

---

United States is told in Charles Levenstein and Gregory F. DeLaurier, with Mary Lee Dunn, *The Cotton Dust Papers: Science, Politics, and Power in the "Discovery" of Byssinosis in the U.S.*, Amityville, NY: Baywood Pub. Co., 2002. Better known than the byssinosis of textile workers, or the pulmonary problems of potters that Marx cites in this section, is the pervasive pneumoconiosis, or "black lung" disease, of generations of coal miners, caused by breathing coal dust. These problems have become worse over time as the increasing use of machinery has sped up the processing of the raw materials and the production of toxic dusts.

85. Parathion was developed by I. G. Farben—the German corporation whose Zyklon B poison gas was used in the Holocaust—and deployed as a chemical warfare agent by the British South African Police during the Rhodesian Bush War. See Wikipedia on parathion and its use in Africa in Glenn Cross, *Dirty War: Rhodesia and Chemical Biological Warfare, 1975–1980*, Solihull, UK: Helion & Co., 2017.

86. Besides contacting farm worker organizations for details, listen to Tish Hinojosa's song "Something in the Rain" (1992).

upstream (back through the production and transport of phosphates and creation of beef waste) and downstream (transport, use in fields, effects on workers, consumers and environment) and conflicts at each point. We could examine the hours worked, the conditions of work, the human and environmental costs incurred and how workers have coped. In the process we discover the real costs of production, including all those hidden by capitalists so they won't have to pay for them, or labeled "negative externalities" by economists. This is not ancient history. In recent years, we have seen repeated exposés of the horrors capital is willing to impose, as long as they can get away with it.[87] At the same time, along these material circuits of capitalist valorization and devalorization, we also find paths of the circulation of struggle. As Jurgis moved from slaughterhouse to countryside and back to the city, carrying his experience with him, so have millions of others carried their experiences from one place to another, across boundaries of space, time and moments of capital's circuits, drawing strength from old struggles to inform new ones. Even without workers moving, changes wrought by struggles can ripple along the circuits circulating disruption and revolt, as in the case mentioned above of farm workers' struggles giving rise to consumer boycotts, or revolts in one area inspiring those in others, upstream, or down. Ripples can become waves and waves can become revolutionary tsunamis.[88]

Where workers have the power, they have set strict limits to the time spent in dangerous jobs. For example, there have been jobs in steel mills where the temperature is so high a worker will only work for ten minutes before being replaced. In the nuclear industry, workers also refuse to work for more than a few minutes when exposed to high radiation levels, another kind of heat. These are jobs where longer exposure will kill quickly. On the other hand, there are far more jobs like Bessy's, Jurgis's and those of farm workers, which are ultimately more dangerous because the threat is less obvious and longer term. The killing occurs through poisoning (pesticides) or diseases (white or black lung) that shorten workers' lives but in ways that are not so transparently associated with a particular job. Because so many products of such production contain toxic chemicals (tobacco, food, etc.) the poisoning continues downstream, to consumers. In all such cases business fights tooth and nail to deny any responsibility, even hires researchers and lawyers to dispute connections between working conditions

---

87. For example, watch the films *A Civic Action* (1999), based on the true story of a court case around the pollution of groundwater by a local tannery in Woburn, Massachusetts, and *Erin Brockovich* (2000), based on another true story about Pacific Gas and Electric allowing toxic chemicals to seep into local water supplies in California and the lawyers who were able to expose the crime and gain compensation for the victims.

88. See my "Circuits of Struggle?", *The Political Economy of Communication*, vol. 4, no. 2, pp. 3–34.

and the destruction of workers' health.[89] In this, as in so much of what Marx analyzes about nineteenth-century capitalism, we are forced to say *"plus ça change, plus c'est la même chose"* (the more things change, the more they remain the same).

Book after book has been written on questions of job safety. Struggles to improve working conditions—including the reduction of work time—continue. The Occupational Safety and Health Administration (OSHA) was created as an outcome of these conflicts—but not until 1970! This issue is highly pertinent today. As a result of attacks by recent administrations on safety regulations, wages and employment, many American workers have been forced to accept not only substantial increases in the length of the working week—the first in decades—but also more dangerous working conditions. This situation has worsened with the election of Donald Trump with his appointment of industry shills to many departments, such as ex-governor of Texas, Rick Perry, as head of the Department of Energy, a man who had previously argued for eliminating it, or Scott Pruitt, as head of the Environmental Protection Agency (EPA), a man who had sued the EPA several times and has been systematically gutting the protections for which so many people fought.

Adulteration, Then and Now

The subject of adulteration appears in this section as a by-product of the focus on the long working hours of unregulated business. The effort to extract as much work as possible has always been complemented by capitalist efforts to minimize costs—of both labor and the means of production—to increase profit. Business has always fought both laws and their enforcement that would protect workers on the job and workers as consumers, because regulations increase costs and reduce profits. If the baking industry had been appropriately regulated such that workers had time to go home to sleep, there would have been no "perspiration, discharge of abscesses, etc." on the breadboards. Had adulteration been banned and the law properly enforced, there would have been no chalk in the bread of nineteenth-century London consumers. If chemicals toxic to humans were banned from agriculture, we wouldn't still be eating poisons, and "organics" would be standard rather than something available only to those with higher incomes. The increased costs in all such cases would be borne by the capitalists rather than the workers and consumers.[90]

---

89. Besides efforts to escape responsibility for byssinosis and black lung disease, two other dramatic cases were the efforts of industry to deny the roles of asbestos and tobacco in causing mesothelioma and lung cancer, respectively.

90. Of course, all capitalists try to pass along to consumers, through higher prices, any

In Marx's time, in Britain the factory inspectors turned in reports, which amounted to exposés.[91] At the turn of the century in America such writing by early investigative journalists was called "muckraking." Sinclair's *The Jungle* is such a muckraking work and alongside its vivid descriptions of horrid working conditions, it also details the adulterations common in the meatpacking industry, e.g., in the production of sausage. His vivid descriptions spurred President Theodore Roosevelt (who read the book) to push through the Pure Food and Drug Act and the Meat Inspection Act in 1906. Not long ago, however, despite the meat inspection laws that resulted from Sinclair's novel, *60 Minutes* reported that in American chicken-packing plants as much as 35 percent of the meat is infected with salmonella bacteria. Even more nauseating detail has been provided by Eric Schlosser in his book *Fast Food Nation: The Dark Side of the All-American Meal* (2001).[92] Read it and you'll never again eat a fast-food hamburger. Recent moves by the US Department of Agriculture to allow meat-processing plants to police themselves will only make matters worse.

With pro-business forces in power in both the executive branch and Congress, the only institutions standing between us and a return to nineteenth-century conditions of working and consuming are non-profit labor, consumer and environmental groups who must appeal to the rest of us for financial support and pressure to stem current moves to roll back or remove the laws and regulations that protect us.

Section 4: Day and Night Work

Outline of Marx's Analysis

1. Day and night relay shifts
   - designed to avoid losses due to under-utilization of capacity
2. Mixed night work (men and women)
   - deterioration of "character"   ▶

---

increase in costs imposed by government regulation. The degree to which they can do so, however, depends on the sensitivity of demand to changes in price.

91. Although earlier struggles and public outrage forced the creation of factory inspectors and the public release of their reports, such were by no means common in other capitalist countries. Marx's famous "Workers' Inquiry" of 1880—a set of 100 questions to be put to workers to uncover their working conditions—was composed to put pressure on the French government to create its own system of inspection. See the third issue (online) of *Viewpoint Magazine* devoted to the Inquiry and its modern uses.

92. Eric Schlosser, *Fast Food Nation: The Dark Side of the All-American Meal*, Boston, MA: Houghton Mifflin, 2001. His book inspired Richard Linklater to make the film *Fast Food Nation* (2006). He did so in a way that reflected Upton Sinclair's main concern: the mistreatment of immigrant workers.

3. Night work especially bad for health
   – no sunlight
4. Often sequential shifts
   – incredibly long work days glossed over
5. Children/adult hierarchy

Commentary

Much of what is described in this section still holds true. In some industries, children *may* no longer be used, hours *may* have been shortened, wages raised, etc., but the imposition of night work to maximize capacity utilization and hold down costs remains common. Even where there is no extra cost associated with daily shutdowns of operations, capital continues to seek maximum labor and surplus labor.[93]

Night work has also plagued housework and schoolwork. In the home, childrearing, a notoriously 24-hours-a-day undertaking, has long been imposed on women, but in traditional extended families the work was often shared. In the nuclear family, individual women have borne the vast bulk of the burden alone. Even as women have succeeded in escaping isolation in the home and gaining access to jobs and autonomous income, they have found themselves doing double duty—*la doble jornada*—with no end to their working day. Although Marx provides no detailed account of housework, feminists have been providing the same kind of detailed descriptions of long working hours and difficult working conditions in the home that Marx marshalled for his critique of factory work.[94] As schooling has replaced factory work for children, there too night work has been imposed, as the school working-day has been extended into evening and nighttime in the form of homework (under the spur of piece-rate grades or of the direct disciplinary power of parents doing the unwaged work of making their kids study).

Not surprisingly, resistance has emerged in these unwaged domains, in favor of self-determined activity. Women have insisted that husbands and

---

93. On the profitability of increasing "turnover," the frequency of production within a given period, see Part Two of Volume II of *Capital*.

94. See, for example, Sarah Berk (ed.), Women and Household Labor, Beverly Hills, CA: Sage, 1980; Susan Strasser, *Never Done: A History of American Housework*, Pantheon, 1982 (New York: Holt, 2000). On the applicability of Marx's Workers' Inquiry to unwaged domestic labor, see Alisa Del Re's article "Workers' Inquiry and Reproductive Labor" in the third issue of *Viewpoint Magazine*.

children share the work; students collaborate, or cheat and plagiarize to shorten nighttime homework, or out-and-out refuse.

Section 5: Struggle Over Extension of Work Day

Outline of Marx's Analysis

1. The struggle has two subjects:
   - *capital*, which increases work time as much as it can
   - the *working class* which seeks "time for education, for intellectual development, for the fulfillment of social functions, for social intercourse, for the free play of the vital forces of his body and his mind..."
2. Capital will use up workers' lives quickly
   - if new recruits are available
   - if not, it may have them imported, e.g., from agricultural areas or poor houses by "flesh agents"
   - true for slave labor, true for wage labor
3. This excessive using up of human life
   - not a question of subjective viciousness but
   - one of competition between capitalists that keeps pressure on all
4. The normal working day
   - the result of centuries of struggle between capitalists and workers
   - fourteenth to eighteenth centuries, to force the "free" worker to make a voluntary agreement
   - "to sell his birthright for a mess of pottage"
   - capitalists used the state to extend working hours
5. Up to the epoch of large-scale industry, workers
   - resisted giving up their whole week
   - were attacked as "naturally inclined to ease and indolence"
6. This included:
   - attacks on idleness among children, and
   - praise of Germany where children were "educated from their cradle at least to 'something of employment'"

Commentary

As capitalism spread like a plague through the world, its functionaries gained enough power over the state to enforce an ever greater imposition of work. In that period, the capitalists clearly had the initiative and people were fighting a defensive battle against the loss of their lifetime.

Yet capitalist gains were not won easily. Marx points out how this new form of domination took "centuries" to impose. Even through most of the eighteenth century, workers still preserved some time free from capitalist control.

This period reveals the kind of world capitalists shaped as they gained the power to arrange things according to their own ideas of social order. They created a world in which life was entirely subordinated to work and the mere existence of any time for other activities was derided as a threat to morality and (more accurately) as undermining the submissiveness of the working class.

Marx's comment about workers who could live on four day's wages not wanting to work another two days for the capitalists is reminiscent of his wonderful reference in the *Grundrisse* to a similar situation in the West Indies:

> The *Times* of November 1857 contains an utterly delightful cry of outrage on the part of a West-Indian plantation owner. This advocate analyses with great moral indignation—as a plea for the re-introduction of Negro slavery—how the Quashees (the free blacks of Jamaica) content themselves with producing only what is strictly necessary for their own consumption, and, alongside this "use-value" regard loafing (indulgence and idleness) as the real luxury good; how they do not care a damn for the sugar and the fixed capital invested in the plantations but rather observe the planter's impending bankruptcy with an ironic grin of malicious pleasure.[95]

The capitalist anger and racist hate inspired by this situation can be seen in comments by one of the would-be slavers best-known apologists: Thomas Carlyle (1795–1881). Writing much earlier, Carlyle penned an "Occasional Discourse on the Negro Question" for the December 1849 issue of *Fraser's Magazine*.[96] Inspired by the renewed attention to the circumstances mentioned in *The Times*, Carlyle revised and reissued his essay as a pamphlet in 1853. There we find Carlyle raving against the high price of labor in the presence of sun and rich soil that makes people largely autonomous of the labor market:

> Far over the sea, we have a few black persons rendered extremely "free" indeed. Sitting yonder, with their beautiful muzzles up to the ears in

---

95. *Grundrisse*, Notebook III, pp. 325–326; *MECW, vol. 28*, p. 251.
96. Thomas Carlyle, "Occasional Discourse on the Negro Question", *Fraser's Magazine for Town and Country*, vol. xl, no. ccxl, December 1849, pp. 670–679.

pumpkins, imbibing sweet pulps and juices; the grinder and incisor teeth ready for ever new work, and the pumpkins cheap as grass in those rich climates: while the sugar-crops rot round them uncut, because labour cannot be hired, so cheap are the pumpkins. . . The West Indies, it appears, are short of labour; as indeed is very conceivable in those cir-cumstances. Where a black man, by working about half-an-hour a-day (such is the calculation), can supply himself, by aid of sun and soil, with as much pumpkin as will suffice, he is likely to be a little stiff to raise into hard work![97]

While there is much else in Carlyle's pamphlet worth reading because of what it reveals about capitalist racism, ideology and strategy, the point here is simply the relevance to Marx's discussion of wages. What the situation in Jamaica revealed, once again, is how "natural" circumstances—untamed by the imposition of the social relationships of capitalist-imposed work—may undermine capitalism. Therefore, the need to reimpose those relationships. Like Wakefield in Chapter 33, Carlyle discusses various strategies for doing so, from the reimposition of slavery to a dramatically increased importation of free labor to make land and "pumpkins" so scarce that free labor would be forced into the labor market, the effective imposition of near-slavery.

This phenomenon of workers making enough wages to want to work less, to have the time to enjoy the possibilities created by their wages, has been recurrent in capitalism, growing more common as standards of living have risen. Indeed, success in the wage struggle inevitably leads to inten-sified struggle over time because, from a worker's point of view the real object of wages is to live and life requires time. More and more money (and the wealth it buys) is useless if there is no time to put it to use. Even economists eventually came to recognize how income and leisure are "complementary goods."

Escaping Work

When work is imposed, and the workplace an alienated hell, then escaping from it (with enough means to survive) means a flight to liberty and freedom. As Marx wrote in the *Economic and Philosophic Manuscripts of 1844*, when work is imposed workers often feel "outside" themselves at work and only feel "at home" when they are not working. Thus, escape from work is not only a victory won, but a freeing of the body and, at

---

97. Carlyle, *Occasional Discourse on the Nigger Question* (1853). John Stuart Mill countered Carlyle with an essay on "The Negro Question." The two essays have been published together, e.g., *The Nigger Question and the Negro Question*, Whitefish, MT: Kessinger Publishing Reprints, 2010.

least potentially, a rebirth of the spirit, a rediscovery of life-for-itself after life-as-work-for-capital.

Of course, such escape and such joy of liberty can only be obtained by most workers for brief periods. Processes of primitive accumulation have removed the means of production from most people and thereby the possibility of sustained independence. Freedom can last only as long as available resources (saved or directly appropriated) permit. As those resources are used up, and in the absence of nineteenth-century "Poor Laws" or twentieth-century "welfare," workers are driven back to work for the capitalists who alone can provide the wages and salaries necessary for survival.

Nevertheless, the joy of such escapes into freedom from work and into freedom to be and to do independently of the whims of any employer can be sweet indeed—no matter how short or how long. The fleeting opportunities of the weekend or the joys of vacation may not last long, but they can give a taste of freedom and the possibilities of self-valorization. The exhilaration of telling a boss to "Take this job and shove it!" derives partly from casting off alienation, partly from the sweet taste of free activity it makes possible.

Among American writers who have written in protest against the conditions of human life under capitalism, the themes of escape from the universal life sentence of hard labor and of the joy it can bring has been recurrent. In Jack London's short story "The Apostate" (1906) the main character—a boy named Johnny who had spent all his life in factories—finally walks away from a life that had stunted and twisted him. What will become of him we don't know, but in the escape from work there is bliss.[98]

In Sinclair's *The Jungle*, a very similar event occurs in the life of the main character Jurgis Rudkus, who flees the hell of working-class Chicago and briefly escapes from work and all its miseries. This event occurs late in the novel, after he and his family have been exploited and beaten down on the job and off, after all their hopes and dreams have been destroyed, after his wife has died in an unheated garret and his baby son drowned in an unrepaired street. After all this, Jurgis—like London's Johnny—jumps a train and flees the city and the horrors of his life. But in Sinclair's novel, unlike London's short story, we find out what happens next. Jurgis soon finds himself in the countryside, a countryside not so unlike what he had known in Lithuania as a peasant child before immigrating to America.

Avoiding any pastoral romanticism, Sinclair has Jurgis soon learn that the American countryside is also a factory, only organized differently, in

---

98. This story can be found online at http://storyoftheweek.loa.org/2011/09/apostate.html, or in Donald Pizer (ed.), *Jack London: Novels & Stories*, New York: Library of America, 1982, pp. 797–816.

farms rather than in plants. He learns the ways of tramps but also of the migrant agricultural labor force—with plenty of work and good wages for a few months in the fall and no work and no wages throughout the long months of winter. Thus, the escape into freedom proves only temporary and as the story unfolds, Sinclair makes it very clear that such flights by individuals can only be temporary and fleeting. The momentary joys of the individual in these stories figure as evocations of the possibilities open to humankind through the transcendence of capitalism.

No other modern film exalts such escape with as much humor as *Ferris Bueller's Day Off* (1986). In this case the escapees are students, not waged workers, but the portrayal of their temporary escape from school incarceration and testing quickly became a beloved celebration of grabbing free time when you can. As Ferris says in the opening sequence, "Life moves pretty fast, if you don't stop and look around once and awhile you could miss it." Stopping and looking around takes time, time away from work, whether in factory, office or school.

The Struggle over Free Time

Although the working class was ultimately able to block the capitalist expansion of the working day, as Marx shows in the next section, and was eventually able to pass over to the offensive and successfully reduce its length, capitalists are forever trying to increase the amount of work they get out of workers, not only on-the-job (as this section discusses—and as recent calls to delay the age of retirement illustrate—but also during unwaged hours.

Sometimes, the effort to convert free time into a part of the working day is obvious, many times it is not. In many jobs, employers expect workers to use their free time for company business. Salaried corporate employees, for example, are often expected to take work home at night if necessary, as well as putting in long formal hours. One example I discovered at a Motorola factory in Austin, Texas, was an effort to convince techies to spend their time driving to and from work listening to recorded articles on the latest developments in their area of expertise.[99] Similarly, students are expected to use their free time for homework. And those with aspirations

---

99. For several years I took advantage of tours offered at the local Motorola "campus" to show my students what a modern, high-tech factory was like. We discovered the corporation's strategy to steal commuting time while visiting the corporate library, where articles were read out aloud and recorded on cassette tapes. Given the distances and congestion of Austin's roads—due to the influx of high-tech firms—commuting itself was already uncompensated work for Motorola. Listening to tapes while navigating to and from home amounted to an intensification of that work.

for higher education must also sacrifice free time to all kinds of "extra-curricular" activities to beef up their future applications. As I noted in my commentary on Section 2, secondary school teachers are regularly forced, by the size of their classes and other obligations of their work, to take home tests or papers to be graded. University professors, whose promotions and "merit" salary increases depend upon publishing, inevitably convert many hours that might be "free" into work. All too often, hard-pressed, underpaid teachers, adjunct professors and students find themselves forced to seek extra, waged night work just to survive. Perhaps the most extreme example of such capitalist efforts to convert leisure to work has been the hope (so far disappointed) that through hypnopedia, or sleep-learning, everyone could be subjected to recordings at night and go on working while asleep! Such have been modern versions of the capitalist fantasies Marx relates in the seventeenth through the nineteenth centuries.

While Marxist cultural critics have elaborated extensive critiques of the capitalist colonialization of free time through the structuring of consumption, the most instructive of what has been written on this theme has been composed by women. For the distinction between work time and free time has always been nebulous for housewives. Unlike factory workers where work time and free time are ostensibly separated by the gates of the plant or the doors of the office, women working in the home and community have no clear-cut division between housework and time for self. As any number of feminist writers have pointed out, much of what has been justified as fulfilling "love and nurturing" has often been work—either for men or for capital or for both—with little or no *self*-fulfillment involved.[100] Shopping, house cleaning, childcare and even sexual activity can and often has been reduced to the work of reproducing labor-power. The increasingly common observation that husbands retire but housewives never do, reflects this muddled boundary between work and freedom. We must also recognize the society of the spectacle, as the Situationists have done, to see how workers' time is structured and diverted to merely restore the vitality necessary to work rather than infusing energy for struggle. Observations such as these lead us to see how the boundary between work and non-work has been obscured and often erased, as capital has structured "non-work" time to reproduce work time.

However, unlike those who see only domination and no effective struggle in such spheres, who see, for example, only the instrumentalization of the wage struggle—wage-driven consumer demand contributing to the

---

100. See, for example, Giovanna Franca Dalla Costa, *The Work of Love: Unpaid Housework, Poverty and Sexual Violence at the Dawn of the 21st Century*, Brooklyn, NY: Autonomedia, 2008.

expansion of capital—we must also see the ways struggle often ruptures accumulation and causes crisis. One critical theorist, Herbert Marcuse, understood how the autonomous appropriation of consumption had revolutionary potential in the youth revolts of the 1960s. But, having written off the industrial working class as sold out, he failed to see how the rupture of the Keynesian productivity deal in the factories could also undermine capital and lead to the refusal of what he, following Freud, called the sublimation of libidinal energies into work.[101]

We can recast the critical theorists' critique of consumerism by seeing not only how consumption is shaped by capital to reinforce a life based on work but how this is resisted. Critical theorists have often argued that consumption has replaced work as the key category of advanced capitalism.[102] What they have failed to demonstrate is any reversal in the subordination of consumption to work. On the contrary, it is rather easy to show not only how most spheres of consumption are structured as spheres of the reproduction of labor-power and how the desire to consume requires the ability to buy and that ability depends on work! So, the most avid consumers end up having to do the most work in order to get the money they need to buy the stuff they want to consume. Consumerism leads directly to workaholism.[103]

But there are manifold struggles against this subordination of free time to life-as-work. We must recognize how students have resisted being conditioned into dutiful workers. We must learn from feminist literature how women have fought against their subordination to men (and to capital). We must examine how the passivity inculcated by the spectacle has been repeatedly ruptured and people have taken the initiative in the shaping of their own and their communities' lives. We must see how people have either refused or taken and subverted the consumerist commodities through which capital has sought to structure our lives. We must listen to hear how music has escaped the limits of commercialism and fired resistance and revolt. We must watch to see how, even in Hollywood, films have reproduced and circulated people's struggles against their integration as passive pawns in others' games. All this involves extending Marx's analysis of the

---

101. Herbert Marcuse, *Eros and Civilization: A Philosophical Inquiry into Freud*, Boston, MA: Beacon Press, 1955.

102. See, for example, Claus Offe, "Work: The Key Sociological Category?", in Claus Offe, *Disorganized Capitalism*, Cambridge, MA: The MIT Press, 1985, pp. 129–150.

103. A wonderful film that illustrates this dynamic is Lulu the Tool (1971), originally *La classe operaia va in paradiso* [The Working Class Goes to Heaven], in which a machine tool operative piles up lots of consumer goods by working harder than everyone else and getting paid more but ruins his marriage, until an accident at work makes him realize there's more to life than stuff.

fierce working-class resistance to the expansion of the working day to the class struggle over whether free time will really be free.

The Work Week and Popular Music

In his pre-radio, pre-moving picture, pre-TV era, Marx illustrated the capitalist imposition of work and workers' struggles for a lesser working day with literary allusions and quotations. But rising wages and new technology facilitated the spread of popular culture from bars, coffee houses, vaudeville and cabarets to juke boxes, vinyl records, cassette tapes, compact discs, TV, film and YouTube. As a result, we can now complement his illustrations with a rich array of contemporary audio-visual ones.

Despite American workers achieving a five-day working week by the early 1940s, with weekends free (at least in principle), a great deal of popular culture has reflected ongoing attacks on the continued domination of life by work. The almost universal critical attitude toward work is manifest in the resentment of, and attacks on, Monday—the day most people must return to work—and celebrations of Friday—the day people escape from work. These attitudes have been articulated, elaborated on and circulated in almost every form of popular music. Rock and roll, country and western, punk, rap and hip-hop songwriters and bands have all contributed to the construction of a corpus of musical denunciation of the working week and of the rhythm of the working days which constitute it. Among the more memorable contributions are the following, in chronological order.

The British rock band The Kinks created a concept album entitled *Soap Opera* (1975). Most of the songs on side A of that album critique moments of the working day and its consequences: before, during and after official work hours. In "Rush Hour Blues," 7 a.m. begins the day, well before the official job itself at 9 o'clock. As this and the other songs make clear, the real working day is much longer than the official one and includes getting ready for the job and getting there. Compare The Kinks' cup of tea with Parton's "cup of ambition" through The Clash's "cold water in the face" (below). The story is the same: there is no spontaneous enthusiasm that brings one springing from bed in joyous anticipation of going to work. On the contrary, dreams, yawns and reluctance require shock and drug treatment to be overcome. In the Kinks song, the reluctance becomes resistance to being hurried to the unpleasantness of both commuting and work itself. "Rush Hour Blues" laments all the details of the daily annoyances of commuting, "waiting for the train," "rushing up the stairs and in the elevator," being "caught in the crush," being "pushed" and "shoved," "fightin' with my briefcase and my umbrella." And the worst of it is "some people do it every day of their lives!"

The second Kinks' song "Nine to Five" has something of the same tenor as that of The Clash. Work-life "is so incredibly dull," "the hours tick away / the seconds, the minutes, the hours, the days / each day, each week / seems like any other." And the result, "he's starting to lose his mind"—or take it back, depending on your perspective.

Two years later, Elvis Costello launched a general attack in "Welcome to the Working Week" (1977): "I know it won't thrill you / I hope it don't kill you." The points are well taken because not only do most people dislike working but work does kill thousands of people each year, either through on-the-job accidents or through its by-products such as stress and insanity.

Many songs attack Monday, the first and most despised day of the working week. "I Don't Like Mondays" (1979) was co-written by Bob Geldof of the Boomtown Rats in response to the actions of a student in California who, one Monday morning, decided not only that she did not want to go to school but that no one else should go either. To implement her decision, this schoolgirl, who lived across the street from the school, took a 22-caliber rifle and started shooting. The song reflects on the general amazement that followed this event as no one could understand how this hitherto quite ordinary 16-year-old—who was always "good as gold"—could do such a thing. In the Rats interpretation, "the silicon chip inside her head got switched to overload"—in other words her programmed behavior of going to school every Monday became more than her humanity could tolerate. "Why?," everyone asked, "what were the reasons?" Well, the Rats respond, "They can see no reason / Cause there are no reasons / What reasons do you need to be shown?" In other words, what needs explaining is not why she flipped out, but why it didn't happen long before. How was it possible for a healthy human being to be programmed into weekly self-destruction without revolting? That is what needs to be explained, not why she didn't want to go to school. All of this, of course, is based on the understanding that school, like the factory, is a place of incarceration, that schoolwork really is work, and is imposed on people just like other kinds of work; and therefore, that revolt against unwaged schoolwork, like the revolt against waged work is a perfectly sane response. The song is reminiscent of the analyses of schizophrenia and psychosis by R. D. Laing (1927–89) and David Cooper (1931–86) who have argued that people sometimes find themselves in situations to which sane responses appear to be insane.[104] Commonplace in the wake of more recent school shootings, analysis has

---

104.   See R. D. Laing, *The Divided Self: An Existential Study in Sanity and Madness*, Harmondsworth: Penguin, 1960; R. D. Laing and D. G. Cooper, *Reason and Violence*, London: Tavistock Publications, 1964; and D. G. Cooper (ed.), *Psychiatry and Anti-Psychiatry* (1967), New York: Ballantine Books, 1971.

focused on either the character of the shooter or the issue of gun control. The fundamentally repressive nature of schooling is rarely discussed.

Dolly Parton's "9 to 5" (1980), the theme song of the movie of the same name, describes not only the morning rituals of drugging one's self awake and dragging one's self to the job, but also exploitation on the job where "they just use your mind and they never give you credit" and "you're just a step on the boss man's ladder." Without ever speaking of "capitalist society" as such Parton says the same thing in American vernacular: "It's a rich man's game, no matter what they call it / And you spend your life puttin' money in his wallet."

"Magnificent Seven" (1980) by The Clash, probably the second best known British punk band (after the Sex Pistols), like the Kinks' "Nine to Five" and Parton's "9 to 5," rails against the working day—from dragging one's self from bed at 7 a.m. through work, till quitting time and beyond, to a life poisoned by work. The title of the song is, of course, ironic. Seven in the morning is NOT magnificent but rather damned because it is the time you must start getting ready for work: "Move y'self to go again / cold water in the face / brings you back to this awful place." On the job, "clocks go slow in a place of work / minutes drag and the hours jerk" till lunch when you can "wave bu-bub-bub bye to the boss" and get away from the grind. The Clash are very clear about the qualitative nature of time in this song, when they sing about lunchtime stolen from work: "It's our profit, it's his [the boss's] loss" versus work that is the boss's profit and our loss. Work is money for the boss, loss of life for us. Time away from work is life for us, loss of profit for capital. Work in the afternoon, the after-lunch, the after-freedom (such as it is, "watching cops kickin' gypsies on the pavement!") is no better: "So get back to work and sweat some more... It's no good for man to work in cages." But what follows, at the end of the day, once you "get out the door" and escape? The worker "hits the town, he drinks his wages." Workers never make enough money to change their basic condition: "did you notice, you ain't gettin'?" At the end of the song there is an evocation of various people who have struggled against some aspects of capitalism, Marx and Engels, Martin Luther King and Mahatma Gandhi. The reference to Marx and Engels is humorous and refers to Marx being poor and having to borrow money from Engels. The reference to King and Gandhi is much more bitter, "they was murdered by the other team."

The Bangles also complain in "Manic Monday" (1986) about the unpleasantness of getting up and going to work in contrast to the pleasures of Sunday, making love and dreaming. Despite the unpleasantness of a "run day" when she must hurry, hurry, get dressed, catch a train and make it to work on time, the singer gets up and goes to work for the classic reason within capitalism: in order to eat! In this case the pressures on her are even greater because her lover is unemployed and they both depend on her job for survival—the traditional situation of the family with only one wage earner.

Section 6: Struggle for the Limitation of Working Hours

Outline of Marx's Analysis

Capital: last third of eighteenth century:
  – avalanche of violent and unmeasured extensions of working day

Working class: began to resist: "As soon as the working class. . . had recovered its senses. . . it began to offer resistance"
  1802–33 five labor laws are passed in response to working-class struggle
    – but there is no enforcement
    – children and young people are worked all night, all day or both
  1833: The Factory Act of 1833 is passed, will last till 1844
    – applied to cotton, wool, flax and silk factories
    – regulated hours of children and young people
    – set working day at 15 hrs (5:30 a.m.–8:30 p.m.)
    – set maximum hours at 12 (during this 15-hr period)
    – set minimum meal times of 1 1/2 hrs
    – no children under 9 yrs (mostly)
    – set maximum hours of children 9–13 yrs at 8 hrs (except in silk industry with 10 hrs)
    – banned night work for ages 9–18
    – no regulation of adult workers over 18 yrs, could be worked 15 hrs

Capital: the capitalist response was to find new ways to lengthen hours
  – mainly the development of the relay system
  – ages 9–13 worked in two shifts (5:30 a.m.–1:30 p.m.; 1:30 p.m.–8:30 p.m.)
  – made it hard to judge compliance with law
  – sought to lower age of childhood from 13 to 12
  – this was defeated by working class:
  – "'the pressure from without' became more threatening"
  – sought to repeal Corn Laws to lower wages

▶

Working class: workers began to demand the Ten Hours Bill, achieved:
  1844: Factory Act of 7 June 1844
    – protected women workers over 18
    – by limiting hours to 12 and banning night work
    – reduced hours for children under 13 to max. 6 1/2 hrs
    – except silk which got 10 hours for 10–13-yr-olds
    – attacked the relay system (a main object of the law)
    – all labor must end at same time
    – labor-time regulated with public clocks
    – hrs to be posted
    – still no regulation of hours of adult male workers
    – results: generalization of the working day to 12 hrs
  1847: Factory Act of 8 June 1847 (10 Hours Act)
    – reduced hours for young persons (13–18) and all women to 11
      hours
    – hours to be reduced to ten on 1 May 1848
    – still no regulation of hours of adult male workers
  1848: Revolutions of 1848 swept Europe
Capital: the capitalist response to these laws included:
  – use of crisis of 1846–47 to repeal the Corn Laws, proclaim free
    trade
  – reduce wages (about 25 percent)
  – attempt to get workers to demand repeal of Act of 1847 (failed)
  – attack on factory inspectors (failed)
  – counterattack against working class in the wake of uprisings of
    1848
  – dismissals of young people and women (regulated hours)
  – restored night work for adult males
  – shifted meal times to before and after work (failed, courts ordered
    otherwise)
  – reorganized "relay system"
  – divided up hours into "shreds of time"
  – kept workers in factory longer than work hours
  – "hours of enforced idleness" (paid 10 hr wages for control over
    12–15 hrs)
  – Home Secretary George Gray told factory inspectors to lay off
  – local courts acquitted mill-owners of violations of Act
  – 1850: Court of the Exchequer ruled Act of 1844 was meaningless

▶

Working class: against these counterattacks, the workers struggled harder:

> "So, far, the workers had offered a resistance which was passive, though inflexible and unceasing. They now protested in Lancashire and Yorkshire in threatening meetings. . . class antagonisms had reached an unheard-of degree of tension"

1850: The Factory Act of 5 August 1850
- – ended the relay system
- – set work day at 6 a.m. to 6 p.m. (except for children: attack on adults)
- – set 1.5 hrs for mealtime, same time for all
- – but allowed increase in hours of young and women from 10 to 10.5 hrs, M-F, reduced to 7.5 on Saturday—silk again the exception, children 10–13 could still be worked 10.5 in some branches, silk twisting and silk winding

1853: a law was passed limiting time children could be kept at work to 6 a.m. to 6 p.m.
- – forced by adult males who didn't want children used against them
- – cumulative result was to achieve 12-hr day for all, including adult males
- – result: "physical and moral regeneration of the factory workers"
- – "capital's power of resistance gradually weakened, while at the same time the working class's power of attack grew"

1860: dye works and bleach works brought under Factory Act of 1850

1861: lace and stocking factories brought under Factory Act of 1850

1863: earthenware products, matches, percussion caps, cartridges, carpets, baking, etc.

Commentary

Methodology

Throughout his historical sketch, although from time to time discussing specific groups of businessmen and workers, for the most part Marx discusses the class struggle in terms of two personifications of the classes: capital and the working class. He thus carries on his discourse at two levels of abstraction: specific industries, general classes. He even, from time to time, cites specific individuals who took particular actions—a third level of analysis. Clearly, a complete history of this period would require an interweaving of all three levels: class, industry, individual. The point here is to see the circumstances in which he feels free to talk about "capital" in a general way. He does this when and where the actions of specific groups represent or express the interests of classes as a whole. When a specific group of capitalists introduced the relay system to outflank the law, Marx saw them acting as representatives of their class, others followed their lead, they were the most innovative at that point of the class struggle, thus they represented not just themselves but "capital."

There is a fundamental shift from the last section to this section. In the last section (and indeed in the opening sentences of this one, too) Marx was emphasizing the way in which capital was on the offensive, pushing out the limits of the working day, imposing longer hours, etc. He points to the last third of the eighteenth century as a period in which the capitalists, at the height of their power, pushed working hours beyond all bounds. In those circumstances the working class played a defensive role, it merely resisted, even if this resistance was "inflexible and unceasing." But in this section, we see a shift in initiative. Workers' resistance grows to the point where they can block further extension of the working day, and then they pass over to the attack; they take the initiative in the class struggle. From the Factory Act of 1833 on, the regulation of the working day means not only setting a maximum number of hours, but a repeated reduction in that maximum. Capital is forced into defensive maneuvers to defend the long hours they were able to impose earlier and then to resist the reduction of those hours. Despite their best efforts, workers won first less work for children, then less for women and finally less for adult men.

This turning point meant that in the following decades workers were on the offensive the majority of the time. The achievement of ten hours limit on the working day was followed by agitation for the eight-hour day, and by 1940 not only did most workers in the United States achieve the eight-hour day, they also achieved the five-day week with the liberation of the weekend from capitalist time. In the United States, the working week was chopped down by working-class struggle from an average of 75–80 hours in 1880 to 40 hours in 1940.[105] For 30 years after that the struggles shifted from the working week to the working year and life cycle as workers fought for more paid annual holidays and early retirement. Although in recent years capital has regained the initiative, the historical trend throughout most of the twentieth century was repeated reductions in the portion of our lives given

---

105. On the history of struggle over work time in America, see David R. Roediger and Philip S. Foner, *Our Own Time: A History of American Labor and the Working Day*, New York: Verso, 1989.

up to capital.[106] As in early periods, capital resisted every such reduction. It seems to have understood intuitively that a reduction of hours not only threatens its immediate profits but also constitutes a long-run threat to the very survival of the system. As the portion of lifetime devoted directly to work drops, it becomes ever more untenable to demand that the rest of life be subordinated to that diminishing percentage, or to accord prestige and power to those who impose work on others.

We can also discover this distinction between resistance and offense, so clear in Sections 5 and 6 of Chapter 10, in the sphere of reproduction. Two obvious examples in the United States are those of women and students.

After World War II women were pushed out of waged jobs in wartime industries to make room in the labor force for returning soldiers. Then throughout the 1950s, the nuclear family—repeatedly celebrated in new TV shows such as *Father Knows Best* (1954–60)—provided only a narrow terrain for individual women to resist patriarchal oppression. Resistance in isolation did find some reflection on TV in Lucille Ball's coping with marriage in *I Love Lucy* (1951–57) and then on her own in *The Lucy Show* (1962–68) and in a few strong women in Hollywood movies, e.g., Katharine Hepburn. But the mobilizations of the suffragette movement were long past and while many women fought alongside men in union struggles and played essential roles in the Civil Rights Movement, they often had to confront gender discrimination, even within liberal or radical political groups, and found few opportunities for collective action by women. That obviously changed with the rise of Second Wave feminism, in which large numbers of women once again found each other, their voices and the energy to mobilize collectively against the many constraints on their lives.

With respect to school, prior to the mid-1960s most students were fighting defensive battles—often fragmented and individual—where rebels were frequently dismissed as juvenile delinquents. Rather than celebrated as Ferris Buellers, they were dismissed as rebels without a cause.[107] The mid- and late 1960s saw a definitive shift in initiative. Instead of merely resisting the functioning of the school as factory, students took the initiative and attacked its subordination to corporate interests and war; they also demanded more time for their own projects, their own courses of study. So successful were these attacks that a wide variety of spaces were opened for study critical of capitalism and unsubordinated to its needs. By forcing the

---

106. On capital's recent success in extending working hours, see Juliet Schor's book *The Overworked American: The Unexpected Decline of Leisure*, New York: Basic Books, 1991.
107. An allusion to the 1955 film *Rebel Without a Cause*, starring James Dean, that focuses on the troubled personalities of the "rebels."

creation of courses and fields such as women's studies, radical economics, insurgent sociology, Black studies, Chicano studies, and so on, students were beating back their working day and expanding the time available to them for their own purposes. This reduction in the time during which students accepted being disciplined into dutiful workers is analogous to the reductions of factory work time Marx describes in this section.

What is missing in this section, as in other parts of *Capital*, are detailed analyses of just how workers were able to achieve these changes to their benefit. Just as we need to know how they failed to block the extension of work in the previous period, so too do we need to know how they were able to pass over from an ineffective defense to an effective one and then take the initiative. Marx mentions a few things: that workers used Parliament, the Factory Inspectors, the courts and "threatening meetings" to fight for less work. But, to truly understand, we obviously need much more detail and analysis. The same is true about the struggle against the work of reproducing labor-power, e.g., in the school, the home or the community. In the last decades of the twentieth century and the first two of the twenty-first, all of these struggles have continued. Marx's accounts in these sections provide only a starting point and methodology for learning from past struggles to inform the present.

Section 7: The Impact of English Legislation on Other Countries

---

Outline of Marx's Analysis

First point: factory legislation was gradually extended to all of industry

Second Point: isolated workers are helpless; organization is necessary to limit and then reduce the working day

France: "limps slowly behind England," but legislation after 1848 is comprehensive

United States: struggle for less work was impossible as long as slavery survived

– first fruit of Civil War was 8 hours agitation

– 1866 General Congress of Labour in Baltimore calls for 8 hrs

– The International Working Men's Association Congress in September 1866 calls for 8 hrs universally

Conclusion: workers as a class must compel the passing of laws to limit working hours

---

Commentary

The main emphasis in this short section points to the obvious conclusion from the foregoing historical sketch: namely, that to bring about changes beneficial to themselves workers must "put their heads together," organize and fight collectively.[108] They must overcome the divisions which separate and pit them against each other (e.g., wage, ethnic, gender, racial divisions); the strength of some depend on the strength of others. The struggles of "free" workers in the North depended on the defeat of Southern slavery. "Labor in a white skin," he writes, "cannot emancipate itself where it is branded in a black skin."[109] Marx's participation in the International Working Men's Association (the First International) demonstrated how strongly he felt that workers had to organize and circulate the experience of their struggle from country to country and not let themselves be isolated—a guarantee of defeat. He salutes English factory workers "as the champions, not only of the English working class, but of the modern working class in general."[110] The success of English workers in obtaining a whole series of Factory Acts from early in the nineteenth century demonstrated to workers on the continent what could be achieved, and was won by French workers through the Revolution of 1848. Everywhere the following statement by Marx has held true: "The establishment of a normal working day is therefore the product of a protracted and more or less concealed civil war between the capitalist class and the working class."[111] The war is still going on.

Despite the best efforts of the First and then Second International (1889–1914) to unite workers across national boundaries, World War I demonstrated the cost of failure, as workers in some countries were pitted against those of others and over 15 million died. That cost has been demonstrated repeatedly in World War II, in the war in Korea, in the wars throughout Southeast Asia and those of the Middle East, all playing roles in the proliferation of multinational investment and trade that have made up the "globalization" of capital in recent decades.

Just as the struggles of slaves were key to those of their waged counterparts, today the struggle of workers in the Global South, e.g., Mexico, are key to those of workers in the Global North, e.g., the United States. Multinational corporations pit the former against the latter, either by shifting production from where workers are stronger or by importing workers willing to work at lower wages and under worse working conditions. Politicians, bought

---

108.   *Capital, Vol. I,* p. 416.
109.   Ibid., p. 414.
110.   Ibid., p. 413.
111.   Ibid., pp. 412–413.

and paid for by those corporations, reinforce conflicts between workers in different countries the same way they do within countries, by fomenting racism, nativism and ethnic cultural and linguistic discrimination. It continues to be true that only the international circulation of struggle can undermine capital's global hierarchy and strengthen all workers.[112]

Besides the failures of the Internationals,[113] one social democratic attempt—very much in the spirit of the struggles to limit working hours discussed in this chapter—that has, unfortunately, also proved ineffectual, was the creation of the International Labor Organization (ILO) in 1919 to fight for international labor standards. Although the ILO has been able to gather information revealing details of capital's global hierarchy and to formulate rules that would undermine it, it has never been granted any power of enforcement. More effective, although still quite piecemeal, has been the organized collaboration of workers in different countries. Some examples include the widespread international support for the movement against apartheid in South Africa in the 1980s, mobilizations in over 40 countries in support of the indigenous Zapatista rebellion in Chiapas, Mexico in 1994 and again in 1995, the support by stevedores all over the world for the dockers in Liverpool (1995–98) and continuing solidarity around the world with Palestinians suffering Israeli occupation of the West Bank and Gaza. Such specific struggles gave rise to the emergence of a networked, alter-globalization movement against neoliberalism. Ever since the Intercontinental Encounter in Chiapas in 1996, tens of thousands of grassroots and labor organizers have mobilized, from Chiapas to Geneva, from Seattle to Davos, from Prague to Genoa, to attack capitalist institutions and policies.

Just as the success of workers in limiting waged working hours in Britain strengthened similar struggles elsewhere, so too have successes of some women and children in winning less subordination of their lives to the reproduction of labor-power given strength to those in other countries. Examples have included women gaining legal rights to contraception, divorce and jobs; children gaining freedom from corporal punishment and influence over curriculum in schools. Victories in Britain, of course, have not always been the source of inspiration. Today struggles persist, surging

---

112. See the set of slides I prepared for a debate with a business school professor over "outsourcing"—a phenomenon which by 2004 was spreading fear among business school students: http://la.utexas.edu/users/hcleaver/Outsourcing.ppt.

113. Those failures include not only the First and Second Internationals but also the Soviet-sponsored Third and Trotskyist Fourth Internationals. In each case, their spokespersons supported international collaboration among workers, their members sometimes acted accordingly, but success was piecemeal, small-scale and unable to ward off wars.

and ebbing in many different countries, while modern means of communication, both mass and social media have facilitated the circulation of knowledge, inspiration, support and emulation. The international circulation of student struggles in the late 1960s was obvious; so too were the anti-apartheid movement, the Occupy movement, the Arab Spring and the recent "Women's Marches" in 2017–19. Such circulation, in the spheres of both production and reproduction, give hope that Marx's dream of an "international" of workers capable of overthrowing capitalism might, one day, be within reach.

CHAPTER 11: THE RATE AND MASS OF SURPLUS-VALUE

Outline of Marx's Analysis

Assumptions
    Value of average labor-power (v) constant
    Variable capital = $V = v\#$, where $\# =$ number of workers
    Rate of surplus-value $= s/v$

First law:
    Mass of surplus-value $= S = (s/v)V = (s/v)v\#$

Implications of first law:
    Capitalists can only *increase* ($\uparrow$) S by:
      $- \uparrow$ the number, $\#$, of workers, or
      $- \uparrow$ the length the working day, $(v + s)\uparrow$, increasing s (and s/v)
    Capitalists can potentially offset a *reduction* in the mass of surplus-value, S caused by a decline in one factor, $\#$ or s (and s/v), by increasing the other factor,
      e.g., a reduction in employment ($\#\downarrow$) can be offset by an extension of the working day, $(v + s)\uparrow$, and thus $(s/v)\uparrow$.
      e.g., a reduction in working hours $(v + s)\downarrow$, which cuts s and s/v, can be offset by an increase in the number of workers.
    Therefore, S is, to some degree, independent of the supply of workers

Second law:
    But the absolute limit of the average working day, $(v + s) < 24$ hrs, sets an absolute limit to the degree to which the decline in the number of workers can be offset by a rise in s/v through an extension of the working day

                                                   ▶

Third law:

The mass of surplus-value varies directly with the investment in variable capital, i.e., $\Delta S/\Delta V > 0$

- This is not affected by differences or changes in c/v
    - either between different branches of industry
    - or in the same branch
- But this law seems to contradict immediate experience

Observations on the definitions of classes:

Independents: own/control their means of production
    e.g., family farmers and artisans

Capitalists who-also-work: hybrid, e.g., "small masters"
    e.g., small business owner-operators

Capitalists qua capitalists: "capital personified"
    - fully devoted to the "control of the labor of others"
    - comes with an increase in the number of workers controlled
    - for this to happen, some minimum amount of capital must be available to the would-be capitalist

Main points:

1. Capital develops within production until it acquires command over labor
2. This command is coercive:
    - forces people to work more than necessary for their needs
    - more coercive than all earlier systems of directly compulsory labor because unbounded
3. At first this coercion is exercised with no change in technology (formal subsumption)
4. But the relation between workers and their means of production is soon inverted and the *MP*:
    - become the means for the absorption of *LP*
    - come to consume the workers instead of visa versa (real subsumption)

Commentary

This chapter concludes Part Three on absolute surplus-value by illustrating some interrelationships among the variables that determine both its absolute amount and its relative amount vis-à-vis variable capital. Keep in mind that within this analysis the *intensity* and *productivity* of labor are held constant. Marx takes changes in those factors into account when he turns to relative surplus-value in Part Four.

Here, he organizes his presentation around three "laws," or regularities among the relevant variables. Those laws are discussed in terms of both labor time and money. For example, a *rate of surplus-value*, s/v, of 100 percent, generated during a 12-hour working day, can be represented by (6 hrs)/(6 hrs). Or, assuming 1) value = price, 2) price is measured in terms of shillings (s) and 3) that the mining, smelting, minting etc. of the silver in 3s is assumed to require a social average of 6 hours, then the same rate of surplus-value can be expressed in money terms (3s)/(3s), where 3s in the hands of workers buys the means of subsistence produced by 6 hours of labor and 3s in the hands of capitalists buys the means of production produced by 6 hours of labor.[114]

The First Law

Keeping in mind that surplus-value is determined by the amount of surplus labor, Marx's first law states that the mass of surplus-value depends upon the rate of exploitation and the number of workers being exploited. Assuming v per worker is constant and V = the total variable capital invested in hiring # number of workers = v#, then the:

$$\text{mass of surplus-value} = S = (s/v)V = (s/v)v\#$$

An implication of the first law is that the only way capitalists can increase the *mass* of surplus-value, S, at their disposal is by a) increasing the number of workers, #, which would increase both total v and s, because more workers would be generating more surplus-value; and/or b) increasing the length of the working day ($v + s$), which, with v constant, would increase s and s/v. In money terms, increasing # would increase the wage bill, $v\#$, or V (total variable capital), but also profit (surplus-value).[115] With # and the wage bill constant, increasing the length of the working day would increase both the rate of surplus-value and the amount of profit.

If workers succeed in holding the length of the working day constant at $v + s$ and increasing in the value of labor-power, ↑v, the resulting increase in V would *undercut* both the rate and mass of surplus-value. Value would be redistributed from s to v. In other words, the better paid workers would be producing less surplus-value in the same work time. For this reason,

---

114.   Beginning with the Great Recoinage of 1816 in England, 1 shilling was the name given to 5.655 grams of 0.925 fine silver.

115.   Profit here designates the money form of surplus-value, measured in shillings in this chapter. As will be seen below, the rate of surplus-value and the rate of profit are quite different measures, whether expressed in terms of value or money.

Marx assumes v is constant in this chapter and changes in V are due solely to changes in the number of workers.

Let's look at an example, in which a decline in the number of workers is offset by an increase in the length of the working day (which produces an increase in s/v by increasing s). Let's assume:

- a capitalist puts 100 workers to work for 9 hours, such that
  - the total *new* value $(v + s)$ = 900 hours of SNLT
- if the value of one shilling = 2 hours of SNLT, then the total *new* value $(v + s)$ = 450s
- if 6 hours are required to produce the value of the labor-power of each worker (v),
  - the value of variable capital, V, required to set those 100 workers to work is 600 hours
- if, in monetary terms, the value of the labor-power per worker (and thus the wage) = 3s, then
  - the total wage bill required to set those 100 workers to work is 300s

Thus, total mass of surplus-value, S, realized by the capitalist will be $[(v + s) - V]$ or $900 - 600 = 300$ hours, or $450s - 300s = 150s$. In this case, the rate of surplus-value, s/v = 300/600, or 150s/300s, or ½, or .5, or 50 percent.

Now, if for some reason—say, by introducing a new arrangement of production—capitalists lay off some workers, so ↓#, they can try to compensate by getting their remaining workers to work longer so as to raise the rate of surplus-value and keep getting the same mass of surplus-value. For example, if the number of workers falls from 100 to 50, v remains fixed, and V declines from 300 to 150, then, with the same rate of exploitation, s/v, the total mass of surplus-value S would fall to 75, which would obviously displease the capitalist who had reorganized production.[116]

However, if the capitalist had the power to increase the length of the working day from 9 to 12 hours (while holding the value of labor-power, v, constant, such that V = 150) that would raise s from 300 hours to 600 hours and s/v from 300/600 (or .5) to 600/150 (or 4, a 200 percent increase) and an S of 150s would be preserved. Before, 100 workers were producing 300 surplus hours (100 x 3 hours); now 50 workers are producing 300 surplus hours (50 x 6 hours).

---

116. As explained in Part 4, labor-displacing machinery is often introduced not only to get rid of workers (especially militants), but also to increase productivity and by so doing increase the rate of surplus-value. In this example, the only way to increase s is by lengthening the working day.

In other words, the law also implies that if workers somehow manage to reduce the rate of exploitation, e.g., by forcing up v (or wages), then the only other way for the capitalists to maintain their total mass of surplus-value would be by putting more workers to work. (Remember intensity and productivity are assumed fixed.)

The Second Law

The point of the second law is that this process of compensation has its limits and those limits are set by the absolute length of the average working day. Biologically speaking, that absolute limit must be something less than 24 hours because no one can work continuously without rest and sleep without dying in short order. At the height of capitalist power, the level of such an absolute limit was explored as capital pushed the daily number of hours people were forced to work out to 14, 15 even 18 hours. Marx recognized that such extreme limits, although sustainable for some years, had the long-run effect of shortening the life span of workers. This, of course, didn't matter to the capitalist if new recruits were available, from new generations or from immigration or through foreign conquest. Fortunately, as we saw in Chapter 10, the absolute limit came to be set not biologically but socially, by the power of workers to force down the length of the working day. Therefore, the "absolute limit" he evokes here is a very real historical phenomenon which constrains the capitalists' ability to cope with a drop in the number of people they are able to put to work.

In the example given above, with a 9-hour working day, we have seen that the negative effect on the mass of surplus-value, S, of a halving of the labor force (e.g., a drop from 100 to 50 workers) could be fully offset by a doubling of the rate of exploitation, s/v, from 50 to 100 percent so that S stayed at 150 shillings (or 300 hours). However, given some limit to the possible extension of the working day (say 18 hours), at some point the negative effect on S of a drop in the number of workers *cannot* be fully offset in this manner because there is a limit to how much surplus-value can be extracted from each remaining worker. We can calculate that limit in this case by working backward using $S = V(s/v) = (v\#)(s/v)$ to find # given v and the initial S.

Assume the capitalist is forced to lay off workers but wants to keep the mass of surplus-value, S, at 300 hours or 150 shillings. Assuming too that the value of labor-power remains the same (no reduction in the wage or the SNLT required to reproduce the labor-power of the employed workers), then 3s or 6 hours of each worker's working day must continue to be devoted to covering that cost. If the working day is extended from 9 hours to the maximum feasible 18 hours, then for each worker, the capitalist employer will get the now expanded number of surplus hours ($3 + 9 = 12$), or 6 shillings. Under these circumstances the rate of exploitation will have quadrupled from $s/v = 3$ hrs/6 hrs, or 50 percent, to $s/v = 12$ hrs/6 hrs, or 200 percent. Or, from $s/v = 1.5s/3s$ to $6s/3s$. So, the question is how many workers would be required to produce a S of 300 hours or 150 shillings?

If, within this 18-hour working day, each worker is generating 12 hours (or 6 shillings) for their employer, then the answer is obviously $300/12 = 25$ workers. If the number of workers fell below 25, it would be impossible for those remaining to produce 150 shillings worth of surplus-value even working the maximum of 18 hours. A similar calculation will show that there would still be such a limit even if workers could be forced to work 24 hours a day—even if the capitalists had the power to work people until they dropped and died.

For Marx, as he suggests briefly, this limit is important primarily because while capital always seeks to produce the maximum mass of surplus-value, there are also strong tendencies for it to also reduce the number of workers as much as possible in any production process to facilitate control over the remaining workers. He discusses this tendency at length in Part Four on relative surplus-value. It appears as a part of his analysis of the technological changes capitalists introduce to raise the mass and rate of surplus-value by raising productivity and increasing the intensity of labor.

The Third Law

The third law holds that with v and s/v constant, the mass of value and surplus-value produced is exclusively dependent on the mass of labor set in motion. This law is clearly derived directly from the first law. Where $\Delta =$ change, we can also state the third law as: S varies *directly* with the number of workers employed, $\Delta S/\Delta V > 0$ or even, $\Delta S/\Delta\# > 0$.

Marx emphasizes how this holds true regardless of the amount of investment in constant capital. He juxtaposes the cotton spinner who works with a lot of machinery with a baker who requires very little. After showing how surplus-value is uniquely dependent upon the living labor set in motion by the capitalist, Marx turns to the issue of constant capital. He does this because immediate experience suggests that most capitalists earn about the same average rate of profit despite employing very different technologies. Yet this seems to contradict the assertion that s and S depend uniquely on v.

Remembering that the rate of profit $= s/(c + v)$, where c equals the total investment in constant capital, it would certainly seem that differing levels of c would produce differing rates of profit given the same v and s, even if s varies only with v and not with c. Given that c does indeed vary enormously from industry to industry, and even from firm to firm, this would seem to contradict the notion of an average or general rate of profit. Marx does not resolve this apparent contradiction in Volume I of *Capital* but returns to it in Part One of Volume III. There, he argues that the notion of an average or general rate of profit remains valid because of the tendency for capital to reallocate itself across profit rate differentials—from low to high, which raises the low and lowers the high—and by so doing tends to equalize profit rates.

Definitions of Classes and Individual Psychology

Up to this point in *Capital*, Marx's theoretical analysis has differentiated between two interlinked but antagonistic classes: the capitalist class made up of those who impose work on others and the working class upon which work is imposed and which frequently resists. There are many people, however, who do not fit neatly into these categories.

For example, those who have escaped enclosure and reduction to dependence on finding jobs to survive, e.g., subsistence peasants, family farmers or artisans. Such people work-to-live, using whatever tools are appropriate to their craft and circumstances. Then there are capitalists who also work, those whom Marx calls "small masters," a rather archaic term that harkens back to the feudal guilds where, say, goldsmiths would both work at their craft and employ a small number of apprentices. Today, we can find counterparts in the owner-operators of small businesses (including some family farms) with few employees, who impose work on both themselves and their employees. They work, generate value and pay wages, both to themselves and to their employees.

Capitalists qua capitalists, or what Marx calls "capitalists properly speaking," do not work at all, but merely own the means of production and live off the surplus-value produced by those they employ. Of course, for surplus-value to be successfully extorted, *someone* must coordinate and manage employees and as owner-operators ascend to become capitalists properly speaking, they usually hire others to make sure that happens, e.g., overseers, supervisors and managers. For small masters to become such capitalists they must have enough money to put enough people to work to generate a surplus-value greater than that required for their own consumption, large enough to hire managers and finance investment and growth.

With the rise of the joint-stock company, Marx saw that the control over the imposition of work, investment decisions and so on increasingly lay in the hands of managers, not among widely dispersed owners. So, he began to speak less of "capitalists" and more of "functionaries of capital," i.e., that hierarchical array of managers responsible for the execution of the capitalist rules of the game, such as being competitive and earning at least the average rate of profit if not more. (This aspect of capitalism is emphasized and studied by Marx in Part Seven on "accumulation.")

This discussion of intermediate cases, between the extreme class prototypes (the worker who only works and the capitalist who only imposes work on others) is useful not only because it shows Marx's awareness of the complexity of real life, but also because it speaks to the issue of class in the age of the "middle class." While small business owner-operators are generally considered middle class, far more numerous are those middle strata of the wage/salary hierarchy involved in both imposing work and having work imposed upon them. Examination of most people's work lives reveals that virtually everyone in contemporary capitalism lives this dichotomy. Moreover, given how capitalists have structured contemporary social institutions to convert life into labor-power, e.g., the nuclear family and the public-school system, virtually everyone lives this dichotomy internally, psychologically, as well as externally in their work situation. The inculcation of self-discipline, which is a prime prerequisite both for being a housewife and for getting middle and higher waged and salaried jobs, is a primary objective of schooling.

To the degree that such inculcation is successful, each person lives a continual tension between *their capitalist side* that keeps reminding them of their obligation to work and *their working-class side* which repeatedly rebels against the subordination of their life to work. Housewives find themselves torn between a sense of obligation to their spouses and children and the need for at least some autonomous self-realization. Among students, such tension takes the form of internal conflict between the sense of obligation to go to class or to complete assigned homework and desires to play or to follow one's own intellectual curiosity down unassigned, perhaps uncharted, paths. Among waged workers such tension takes the form of conflict between the sensed need to always be on time and always be focused on their work and the desire to steal free time through absenteeism or playing on the job.

Resolution of the tension through the suppression of desire leads to the pathologies of workaholism, one-dimensionality and social isolation.[117] Resolution of the tension through the complete rejection of imposed work while perhaps leading to a happier and psychologically healthier life in the short run, may also lead to problems of survival. Most people experiencing the unending pressures of capital to work and the insurgence of their own needs and desires, struggle to work out a compromise whereby they

---

117. There's a moving scene in the last episode of the second season of the TV series *The Marvelous Mrs. Maisel* where the actor playing Lenny Bruce (1925–66) riffs on the loneliness of committing his whole life energy to his work as a stand-up comedian.

can live with the tension. They learn how to resist the internalized "ought" enough to preserve space for some personal fulfillment, while giving in to it enough to survive. Capital offers an uncomfortable trade-off: the more you are willing to subordinate your life to work, the more (they claim) you will be rewarded with income and status. At least that is the promise. In reality, there are all kinds of limitations (such as sexual or racial discrimination as well as the wage hierarchy itself) which limit rewards no matter how much you internalize the capitalist work ethic, no matter how hard you work.

What all this shows is that the issue of class in capitalism, whether at the collective level or at the level of the individual, concerns the struggle over competing ways of life: the capitalist way in which life is subordinated to work and alternative ways in which life is self-constructed and work is subordinated to that self-construction.

Main Points

In four points Marx sketches what he considers vital aspects of the emergence of capitalism.

First, capital develops within production (or takes it over) until it acquires direct command over labor. Thus, the merchant capitalist becomes an industrial capitalist as first the putting-out system and then the factory provide mechanisms to control and exploit others' labor. Capital is power over others, power to command their lives and limit them to incarnations of labor-power.

Second, this command is coercive. Capital *forces* people to be workers, to be part of the working class; it *forces* them to work *more* than they otherwise would, e.g., *longer* than they would. This was the point of the discussion in Chapter 10 of the capitalist success at forcing out the length of the working day, at introducing night work and so on. Here he repeats what he emphasized in Section 2 of Chapter 10, that capitalism is more fanatical in the imposition of work than all earlier systems of directly compulsory labor. Unlike such earlier systems, where labor was imposed to achieve some finite purpose, the capitalist imposition of work knows no limits; it is unbounded; there is an endless "thirst" for surplus labor and its monetary equivalent. Where the imposition of work is the substance of the social order, the backbone of civilization, then the eternal maintenance of that order requires that such imposition be endless.

Third, command over labor, over life as labor, is prior to any question of technology. The capitalists at first take command, impose work, using the technologies available, whatever they are. The imposition of work is the main thing; how it is imposed is secondary. This priority is obvious in the putting-out system and in early factories where traditional methods of production dominate.

However, fourth, the method of production, as embodied in the means of production themselves, soon becomes the vehicle for capitalist command. The means of production are no longer tools in the hands of workers, but become tools of the capitalist for the control of workers. Instead of being the means workers use to produce useful things, the means of production become, under the control of the capitalists, the means of exploiting the labor-power of others, the means for putting people to work. Instead of the workers consuming their tools in the accomplishment of their own ends, the workers are consumed by the means of production in the accomplishment of the capitalists' ends, which may involve either the fetishistic chase after money or a more sophisticated understanding of the need for jobs to maintain order. Quite independently of the consciousness of the capitalist, investment always involves the imposition of work. Note: there are many times and places where capitalists understand quite explicitly their role in maintaining social order. One common example is in periods of high unemployment when policymakers worry about the lack of jobs leaving too many people too free—people whose free time threatens to be used in ways inimical to capitalist plans. Another example occurs during strikes by schoolteachers in which those same policymakers worry about the dangers of having vast numbers of young people loose in the streets instead of safely incarcerated in school buildings.

This discussion, which ends Part Three on absolute surplus-value, sets up the reader for the next section on relative surplus-value by focusing attention on the issue of technology and the means of production. Relative surplus-value, Marx will show, is that surplus-value obtained through the manipulation of technology for the purpose of imposing more work or of obtaining a greater proportion of the work already being performed.

7

Part Four
The Production of Relative Surplus-Value

Whereas the capitalist strategy of *absolute* surplus-value involves forcing workers to work longer, their strategy of *relative* surplus-value is considerably subtler. More hours of work exhaust workers and, as we saw in Chapter 10, provoke resistance, ultimately effective in forcing a reduction. Faced with defeat on the terrain of working time, capitalists have responded by replacing obstreperous workers with non-human energy sources and machines—all proclaimed to have the virtue of reducing the labor required to produce commodities, but which are wielded as weapons to impose more work.

Chapter 12: The Concept of Relative Surplus-Value. The extraction of relative surplus-value occurs via the introduction of productivity raising technological change that reduces the value of labor-power and the costs of labor to capital. The primary technological changes in Marx's day (and often today as well) involves replacing workers with machinery that raises the productivity of labor, but also often displaces some workers who lose their jobs entirely. Increases in productivity that have the potential to reduce work for everyone become, in capitalism, the means for extracting more work.

Chapter 13: Cooperation. Although relative surplus-value involves technological change, what changes is not only the relation between workers and machines but also the organization of cooperation within a complex division of labor. Marx emphasizes how humans, as social beings, have always cooperated, although the modes of cooperation have changed with the social order. Cooperation, therefore, precedes capitalism, plays a part in the struggle against it and will continue once capitalism has been overcome.

Chapter 14: Manufacturing and the Division of Labor. This chapter examines how industrialization changes the division of labor, the relationship between workers and their tools, how capitalists impose their despotic will within factories but are also subject to the anarchy of markets. Beyond Marx's study of industry, I show how his analysis can also be extended into domains of unwaged labor such as the home and the school, in part because of capitalist efforts to organize those domains to be complementary to industry.

Chapter 15: Machinery and Modern Industry. In one of the longest chapters in the book, Marx analyzes both the development of machinery and how it has been used by capitalists against workers, not only to increase their exploitation via relative surplus-value but as a means to break their self-organized resistance to its control over their lives. To describe the dire consequences, both in the sphere of production and in the larger sphere of reproduction, he draws mostly on detailed government reports, written by official inspectors appalled at their findings, year after year. He ends with an analysis of how the development of capitalism has disrupted natural ecological cycles in ways that threaten both humans and the rest of nature.

CHAPTER 12: THE CONCEPT OF RELATIVE SURPLUS-VALUE

Outline of Marx's Analysis

Alternatives to lengthening labor-time
With $v + s$ fixed, reducing v increases s and s/v
How can v be reduced?
   a. by pushing down the wage?
   b. by pushing down the value of the means of subsistence
Increases in productivity $\Rightarrow$ relative surplus-value
Increasing productivity = increased output per unit of useful labor
   input
Capitalists achieve this by "revolutionizing" the "technical and social
   conditions of the [labor] process"
Relative surplus-value can be achieved either through:
   – an increase in productivity in producing MS
   – an increase in productivity in producing the MP used in the
      production of MS
Competition
   – circulates productivity-raising technological change:
   – an individual capitalist (or corporation) who lowers costs and
      increases profits

▶

- gains a temporary advantage and a greater share of surplus-value vis-à-vis competing capitalists
- the increased productivity, will cut costs, allowing innovating capitalist to sell at lower prices
- assuming increased productivity results in increased production, supply will expand and push down prices
- which threatens other capitalists' profits and market share
- they are therefore under pressure to adopt the same or similar productivity-raising innovations to lower their own costs
- if they do this, their costs will fall, competition increases and the original innovator loses advantage
- as this process unfolds, overall v falls and s/v rises for the capitalists as a class, so relative surplus-value has been realized collectively

Productivity and the working day

Marx is careful to note that although rising productivity makes it *possible* for the amount of work by all workers to be reduced, this "is by no means what is aimed at in capitalist production"

Instead, the only reduction in work is experienced by those workers displaced by machinery and unable to find other work (and thus earn their bread)

Commentary

Even if the "boundaries of the working day" cannot be extended, because of the success of workers' struggles in setting legal limits on working hours—so that $v + s$ is fixed—capitalists can still increase surplus-value *by reducing necessary labor*, v, and thus raising both the amount and the *relative* share of surplus-value.

The reduction in v might be achieved by pushing down wages, but if wages, and the level of v, are at subsistence, as Marx usually assumes, then success at reducing the wage would mean a collapse in the ability of the workers to reproduce themselves and a breakdown in the system. Marx notes that this does happen—especially during crises when layoffs and increased unemployment force those still employed to accept lower wages—but must be assumed away in the analysis of self-sustaining accumulation.[1]

---

1.   Another reason to ignore this possibility: crises and falling wages have been followed by booms and rising wages, keeping average wages over time at subsistence (or rising) levels.

The alternative way to reduce the value of labor-power, v, is by pushing down the value of the means of subsistence, *without* reducing the *real* wage and the ability of the workers to reproduce themselves. This can only be done by *increasing the productivity* of useful labor in the production of the means of subsistence.

This theory of *relative* surplus-value follows that of *absolute* surplus-value. Although he does not spell it out until Chapter 15, the distinction between absolute and relative surplus-value is historical as well as analytical. The capitalist takeover of production is at first merely formal; they take control of production methods as they find them. Only later do capitalists begin to invest heavily in the technological changes at the heart of relative surplus-value. They build factories; they use water, then steam, then electricity to power machinery; they introduce more efficient machines. The pressures which drive this investment are twofold:

1) Workers' success in limiting and then reducing the length of the working day (already discussed in Chapter 10)—which, *ceteris paribus*, reduces s and s/v.

2) Workers' struggles at the point of production which force capitalists to reorganize to regain control. The dynamics of these conflicts are dealt with in more detail in Chapter 15.

Two other pressures that Marx does NOT explore in *Capital* but are implied by his analysis:

3) Increases in wages, or the value of labor-power, imposed by worker struggles. Assuming the length of the working day is fixed or being reduced, these would increase v at the expense of s. We already know from Chapter 6 that the value of labor-power *can* rise and Marx's analysis of workers' historical struggles to limit and then reduce the length of the working day in Chapter 10 can be replicated in an analysis of workers' historical struggles to force up wages. That he did not do so has been lamented and the reasons debated.[2]

4) Successful struggles around the unwaged labor of reproduction, e.g., housework and schoolwork, create pressures a) on family wage-earners,

---

2. His failure, in this context, to analyze the implications of wage struggles appears odd given that he opposed those who argued there was no use fighting for higher wages because capitalists could and always would use crisis and unemployment to roll back any increase workers might achieve in their wages. Among those who have lamented his failure, at some length, are Antonio Negri, *Marx Beyond Marx: Lessons on the Grundrisse*, Brooklyn, NY: Autonomedia, 1991; and Michael Lebovitz, *Beyond Capital: Marx's Political Economy of the Working Class*, 2nd edn., New York: Palgrave Macmillan, 2003.

spurring them to fight for higher wages and salaries, and b) on the state to subsidize workers' income with transfers of value through programs such as family allocations, welfare, unemployment insurance, the GI Bills, Pell Grants, etc.

Relative Surplus-Value as a Strategy

Marx writes of relative surplus-value as an *object*, a certain kind of surplus labor time extracted by capitalists. However, this kind of surplus-value is extracted through the *process* of raising productivity by reorganizing production via new technologies. Such reorganization of work has not only increased productivity but has also constituted an ever more prevalent *strategy* for dealing with workers. As a strategy, relative surplus-value is considerably more subtle than absolute surplus-value.

The *absolute* surplus-value strategy, as we have seen, involves forcing workers to work longer, extra labor time which rebounds to the profit of the capitalist, not to that of workers whose wages (or value of labor-power) Marx assumed constant.[3] In *relative* surplus-value, in the absence of an increase in demand, some workers suffer from the introduction of machinery by losing their jobs, increasing unemployment (driving workers from the active into the reserve army of labor, discussed in Chapter 25). But for those who remain, the costs are not immediately obvious, except where the reorganization of the factory is carried out in a way that undermines workers' self-organization. On the contrary, the increased productivity which lowers costs can not only raise profits but can even be used by the capitalist to meet workers' demands for higher wages. Marx doesn't discuss this possibility here, but it is implicit in the analysis.

Assume a simple (exaggerated) case in which productivity doubles. In Marx's examples, the capitalists always get the full benefit. Suppose that at first, in a fixed working day, a total new value ($v + s$) of 100, embodied in, let's say, 100 bushels of wheat, is evenly divided in real terms and in value terms between the classes such that $v = 50$ (workers are paid 50 bushels), $s = 50$ (capitalists retain 50 bushels) and $s/v = 50/50$, or 100 percent. Now suppose that in the next period, the introduction of tractors doubles productivity such that total output rises to 200. With total working time remaining the same, the per unit value of output would be halved. With real wages fixed, the working class would still receive 50 bushels of wheat

---

3. Even if wages rise with the imposition of extra work time, e.g., "overtime" paid at time-and-a-half, the extra pay can be assumed to merely cover the extra costs of reproducing the increased energy expended by workers. So, even if v increases as $v + s$ increases due to longer work time, s also increases. See Marx's analysis in Chapter 20 and my commentary.

even as v fell to 25, because that amount of value is now embodied in 50 bushels of wheat. Under Marx's assumptions, the capitalists would reap the whole fruit of this doubled productivity by arrogating three-fourths of the value to themselves, by retaining 150 bushels worth 75, so that s rises from 50 to 75 and s/v rises to 75/25, or 300 percent.

However, it is also *possible* for capitalists—under pressure from workers' wage struggles—to concede increases in real wages and still earn larger profits. Suppose workers demanded a real wage increase of, say 50 percent. With a doubling of productivity, the capitalists could grant such an increase, in which v would rise from 25 to 37.5, and surplus-value would still rise from 50 to 62.5! Not only would their absolute amount of profit increase, but so too would the rate of exploitation, s/v, rising from 50/50 (100 percent) to 62.5/37.5 (167 percent). Herein lies the subtlety: relative surplus-value makes it possible for the capitalists to grant an improvement in living conditions to workers, while at the same time retaining and augmenting their own power (measured in terms of value, and thus workers commanded). This possibility provides the capitalists with a new tool for dealing with the working class: not only can new technology be used against them, but those who retain their jobs can be persuaded to cooperate with such change by being paid higher wages.[4]

Rising Productivity and Less Work

While Marx's analysis of relative surplus-value reveals the technical possibility for workers as well as capitalists to gain from increases in productivity, the potential gains are not limited to higher real wages. In the example given above, of a doubling of productivity, there are many possible outcomes. A shift in value distribution from 50/50 to 25/75, occurs only if we assume capitalists reap all the gains, and that the working day ($v + s$) remained fixed. But for workers a doubling of productivity has the potential to mean *less work*:

1. At one extreme, with the same working hours, doubled output can be shared between the classes according to some deal or another.

---

4. A dramatic example of this took place in American coal mining in the 1950s. As a result of the 1950 National Bituminous Coal and Wage Agreement between the United Mine Workers and mine owners, new mining technology was introduced—such as improved hauling equipment for thin seam coal, the spread of the continuous mining machine, new drilling and ripping equipment—allowing wages to rise, but at a cost of over 50 percent of coal miner jobs. See William Cleaver, "Wildcats in the Appalachian Coal Fields", *Zerowork* #1, 1975, pp. 114–127.

2. At the other extreme, the same output, produced by only half as much work, can be shared.

3. In between: some positive increase of output (but less than doubling) together with less work, e.g., a 50 percent increase in output with 25 percent less work.

Indeed, there are an infinite number of possible choices. Such are the *technical* possibilities. The *political* possibilities of realizing what is technically possible, however, have always been determined by the dynamics of class struggle.

This same logic obviously also applies to the unwaged work of reproduction. Theoretically, if rarely in practice, the introduction of labor-saving devices in homes and schools can reduce the amount of work required to achieve required ends. Unfortunately, as already indicated in my commentary on Chapter 7, the "required ends" have, all too often, been expanded such that the potential reduction has not been realized.[5]

In Marx's time, one of rapid British industrialization, capitalists fought to prevent workers taking the fruits of productivity growth in the form of less work, losing that battle only through the acts of Parliament analyzed in Chapter 10. Similar gains were made in the United States by workers who fought for the eight-hour work day and eventually the five-day work week, finally succeeding around 1940. During the subsequent Keynesian era of collective bargaining and union contracts, capitalists would insist that workers take the benefits from rising productivity uniquely in the form of increased wages and other money benefits, e.g., pensions or health care, but avoided all discussion of any further reduction in weekly hours of work below the hard-won 40 hrs/wk. Marx's comment that "the shortening of the working day, therefore, is by no means what is aimed at in capitalist production" continued to be the case.

Nevertheless, beginning in the late 1960s, after three decades of rising real wages, workers began, once again, to demand less work. What, after all, is the point of having higher wages if you have no time to enjoy the life they make possible? In the United States and Western Europe, rank-and-file workers began to pressure union bureaucrats to negotiate a four-day or 36-hour week. Even the Great Recession of 1974–75 failed to dampen the desire for less work as well as higher wages. It took the Carter–Volcker–Reagan engineered depression in 1980–82 that brought high unemployment, a wave of union-busting and deregulation that undercut workers' safety, to wipe these demands from the agenda of American workers. Despite the global spread of that depression, in Europe capitalists were less successful.

---

5. See too my commentary on Chapter 21 on piece-wages.

Demands for less work persisted, and in some cases, such as France and Germany, workers did win a reduction in working hours.

A parallel demand for less housework surged among housewives and for less schoolwork among students as elements of Second Wave feminism and the student movements in the 1960s. In both cases, women and children demanded less work and more time for self-realization, both individual and collective.

Today in 2019, stagnant real wages, increased job precarity, rising debt, continuing attacks on social programs and omnipresent uncertainty undercut our ability to fight for less work even as continuing productivity-raising technological change makes more and more free time technically possible. Capitalists continue to use both absolute and relative surplus-value strategies to impose more work.

Competition

In his account of the circulation and diffusion of technological change, Marx highlights the pressure of competition among capitalists. Once one capitalist introduces new, productivity-raising, cost-cutting methods that make it possible to sell at prices below those of competitors, these last are under pressure to follow suit. This understanding was by no means unique to Marx but was shared by capitalists as well as many political economists and social observers of the period of the industrial revolution.

One literary articulation of this view from the nineteenth century can be found in Charlotte Brontë's 1849 novel *Shirley*, whose story unfolds during the period of Luddite rebellion (circa 1810–12) when workers organized themselves to break machines whose introduction was depriving them of employment and income.[6] In one scene, a group of angry workers confront the capitalist textile mill owner Mr. Moore and demand that he stop, or at least slow, the introduction of new labor-displacing machinery. Their protest comes in the midst of a depression caused by the Napoleonic Wars that cut off British exports to the Continent and caused much unemployment among millworkers. Moore responds that he cannot slow down the introduction of new technology without being swept away by other capitalists who would refuse to do the same. Moore admonishes the workers

6. The period of machine-breaking was much longer than the period of the Luddites. Instances of machine-breaking began in the eighteenth century and continued into the 1930s. See Marx's discussion in Chapter 15; Charles Poulsen, *The English Rebels*, London: Journeyman, 1984, Chapter XIII, "The Reign of King Ludd", pp. 140–146; David Noble, *Progress Without People: In Defense of Luddism*, New York: Charles Kerr, 1993; and Peter Linebaugh, *Ned Ludd & Queen Mab: Machine-Breaking, Romanticism, and the Several Commons of 1811–12*, Brooklyn, NY: PM Press, 2012.

to take up their problems with Parliament but to leave him alone. Even though Moore eventually becomes somewhat more sympathetic to the plight of the workers, at no time does he become an advocate for either government regulation of technological change or for government intervention to help the poor cope with it. On the contrary, Moore will use the government, its troops and judiciary to pursue, prosecute and punish (through transportation to Australia) those workers who attacked his mill and his new machines, exactly the punishment which was meted out by his real-life counterparts.

Within the argument of Moore, we discover the class basis of competition. Moore is confronted by his workers. So too, we can suppose, are all his competitors among the Yorkshire clothiers (as well as others outside the region). Those best able to command their workers will win the competitive battle; those less able will lose. In the novel, as in the history it portrays, there are other capitalists who are beaten down by their workers; that is to say, their mills are burned, and their machinery destroyed. Moore plays tough, introduces cost-reducing machinery and succeeds in defending his mill against a Luddite attack. When the trade blockades are later lifted, he is able to sell his accumulated stocks at a competitive price and expand production using the new technology. Those capitalists who failed to introduce the new machinery due to the resistance of their workers, or whose mills were damaged or destroyed, would obviously be at a competitive disadvantage, if they could function as capitalists at all. In short, competition among capitalists must be seen not merely as a dog-eat-dog game played without reference to the working class, but rather as a sort of social Darwinism through which the power of capital over the working class is maximized. Where workers are strong enough to impede accumulation, their bosses go under and the workers are thrown out of work, into unemployment and find themselves at the mercy of other, stronger, capitalists.

This class analysis of capitalist competition allows us to avoid the widespread practice of interpreting it as a process that goes on independently of the self-activity of workers who are therefore seen as only suffering the consequences of a process beyond their ken. When Marx writes that we can only understand how the "immanent laws of capitalist production manifest themselves in the external movement of individual capitals" and "assert themselves as the coercive laws of competition" by grasping "the inner nature of capital," we must recognize that "inner nature" to be class struggle and interpret competition accordingly.[7] Competition is characteristic of class conflict where the management of capitalist domination is allocated to diverse capitalists whose relative skill in managing (controlling) their

---

7. *Capital, Vol. I*, p. 433.

workers will determine their success. The competitive struggle, therefore, although it appears in the consciousness of many capitalists (and of many Marxists) to be something that goes on only among capitalists, is determined by the dynamics of competition between capital and labor.

CHAPTER 13: COOPERATION

Outline of Marx's Analysis

Capitalist production
- large number of workers
- extensive scale
- large quantities of products
- economies of scale, increasing returns to scale, fall in value per unit of output

Cooperation
- "many workers working together side by side in accordance with a plan"
- either in the same process, same kind of work
- or in different but connected processes
- a "social force," a "new productive power, which is intrinsically a collective one"
- workers strip "off the fetters of [their] individuality, and develop the capabilities of [their] species"

Sources of productive power of cooperation (social labor):
1. heightens mechanical force of labor
2. extends sphere of action over a greater space, or, contracts field of production
3. sets large masses of labor to work at critical moments (e.g., harvests)
4. excites rivalry between individuals
5. creates continuity and many-sidedness
6. simultaneous operations
7. economizes the means of production by use in common
8. lends to individual worker the character of average social labor

Cooperation implies authority:
- to "secure the harmonious cooperation"
- a "special function arising from the nature of the social labor process"
- a "function of the exploitation of a social labor process," i.e., valorization ▶

Cooperation and class struggle:
- increased resistance to the domination of capital
- increased repression of this resistance

Cooperation under capitalist authority:
- "a *plan* drawn up by the capitalist"
- "the powerful will of a being outside them"
- "in form it is purely despotic"
- requires "officers (managers) and NCOs (foremen, overseers)"

Workers are brought together by capital
- they are "incorporated into capital"
- their productive power is a "free gift" to capital, costs it nothing
- their productive power *appears* as "inherent in capital"
- as their numbers increase, so too does their resistance

Earlier forms/results of cooperation:
- Egyptian pyramids and such, under domination of ruling class
- early hunting peoples
- Indian communities with common ownership of *MP*, individuals rooted in tribe or community

Cooperation = "the fundamental form of the capitalist mode of production"

Commentary

Marx's analysis of cooperation in this chapter serves two purposes. First, he lays out the results of his studies of the *social nature* of the capitalist organization of work. Second, he lays the groundwork for continuing his analysis of the technological changes involved in capital's relative surplus-value strategy. In Chapter 7, he defined work in very abstract and theoretical terms, first the labor process and then valorization. In Chapter 12, he launched his analysis of the capitalist strategy of reorganizing the labor process to increase (relative) surplus-value. Here, in Chapter 13, he provides an approach to understanding the qualitative changes involved in such reorganization. Reorganization is, first of all, reorganization of cooperation.

To begin, he emphasizes that work under capitalism is collective. *Cooperation* concerns large numbers of workers brought together by capitalists and put to work. He recognizes that workers have cooperated collectively throughout history; cooperation is not new under capitalism. But capital reorganizes cooperation. This emphasis on cooperation follows from Marx's analysis of labor (and the resistance to labor) as the core of the *social* relations of capitalism. Although capitalists appear to be responsible for cooperation, and thus to "deserve credit" for this social development, Marx insists on the long-standing existence of cooperation. From that perspective, however responsible the capitalists may be for the particular form it takes, it remains a force outside, an autonomous force of the species, which capital must constantly strive to domesticate to its own ends. Part of this force appears to be purely technical: the way in which cooperation results in increases in productivity (output per worker) so that the output of a large number of assembled workers is greater than the sum of the output of the same number of isolated workers. However, even this "technical" aspect of cooperation turns out to be immanently political and related to the dynamics of intra- as well as inter-class relationships.

As we have seen in the analysis of primitive accumulation, capitalists forged a new system of cooperation on the ruins of earlier ones. In the beginning, this was often indirect as many workers came to be controlled (through a putting-out system) by a single merchant capital. But over time, conflicts with workers led capitalists to gather workers together in one place, incarcerate them in factories where they could be observed and controlled. However, this gathering had contradictory effects.

In these new circumstances, some kinds of struggle became much more difficult. For example, artisans who had appropriated the scraps of their raw materials (wood, silk, leather, etc.)—and cut the raw materials so as to maximize the amount of scraps—found themselves increasingly under the eye of the capitalists, or their overseers, who were diligent to eliminate such practices and thus to reduce both their own costs in raw materials and the income of the artisans.[8] On the other hand, bringing workers together in the same place also made communication among them easier—about their conditions of work, their wages, their living conditions, the tactics of their boss and so on. Thus, this gathering together also facilitated collective struggle—a kind of cooperation quite antagonistic to their bosses.

Scale, Authority and "Rivalry"

The growth in the scale of production meant that more and more workers were being subsumed under the command of capitalist managers, a change which initially appears to be only a quantitative one. Sometimes this just meant more workers doing the same thing. But many times, especially in manufacturing, it increasingly meant a qualitative change as more and more people worked on a set of related tasks, which required coordination, the *organization of cooperation*:

---

8. These struggles are vividly portrayed in Peter Linebaugh's *The London Hanged*.

All directly social or communal labor on a large scale requires, to a greater or lesser degree, a directing authority, in order to secure the harmonious cooperation of the activities of individuals, . . . A single violin player is his own conductor: an orchestra requires a separate one.[9]

This issue of the coordination of cooperation, inherent in "the nature of the social labor process," Marx only explores within capitalism. There, he argues, this authority—"the work of directing, superintending and adjusting"—is that of capital. At this point, he passes into a second aspect of the issue: the specificity of the social relations of cooperation under capitalism: class antagonism. As the scale of capitalist undertakings grew, he argued, so did the conflicts and the complexity of the issue of organization. "As the number of the co-operating workers increases, so too does their resistance to the domination of capital. . ."[10] Resistance dictates the need for a whole officer corps of supervisors and overseers to make sure that the growing army of workers actually do as much work as their employers desire, that the "collective power of masses" is maximized. Thus, his analysis of cooperation is two-sided and parallels his earlier analysis of work in Chapter 7: first a discussion of the labor process independently of capital, second, a discussion of the specificity of the process under capitalism, i.e., within valorization:

The control exercised by the capitalist is not only a special function arising from the nature of the social labor process and peculiar to that process, but it is at the same time a function of the exploitation of a social labor process, and is consequently conditioned by the unavoidable antagonism between the exploiter and the raw material of his exploitation.[11]

Marx's analysis, while providing an approach to grasping technological issues in terms of antagonistic class relationships, has sometimes been seized upon as a technologically deterministic justification of hierarchical authority, not only under capitalism but under all large-scale, complex systems of social cooperation, including socialism. Some of the terms and metaphors which he used, especially "directing authority" and "orchestra director" clearly lend themselves to this interpretation. This line of deterministic interpretation was given a powerful boost by an essay penned by Frederick Engels in 1873.[12] That piece, written against anarchist slogans

---

9.   *Capital, Vol. I*, pp. 448–489.
10.   Ibid., p. 449.
11.   Ibid.
12.   F. Engels, "On Authority", in *MECW, vol. 23*, pp. 422–425.

of abolishing authority, argued that "authority" was inherent in technology. In the case of the cotton spinning mill, he wrote, "the authority of steam. . . cares nothing for individual autonomy" and the "forces of nature" subject humans "to a veritable despotism independent of all social organization. Wanting to abolish authority in large-scale industry is tantamount to wanting to abolish industry itself, to destroy the power loom in order to return to the spinning wheel." "If," he argued, "the autonomists confined themselves to saying that the social organization of the future would restrict authority solely to the limits within which the conditions of production render it inevitable, we could understand each other. . ."

The one-sidedness of Engels's argument is striking. It totally ignores the issue of the genesis of the "conditions of production"—how the capitalist organization of production technology has been structured within the context of class antagonism in order to maximize capitalist control over the working class. He is refusing to enter into the analysis demanded by the anarchist attack on authority, namely, an investigation into how the conditions of production can be changed to eliminate a top-down authority and to replace it with democratic decision-making. He fails to question why it is that in industry, as he knows it, "the first condition of the job is a dominant will that settles all subordinate questions." Why is production organized so that this is "the first condition"? At this point in our reading of *Capital* the contrast between Engels's argument and Marx's is not so obvious. Later, when we get to Chapter 15, it will be much clearer. Once we read Marx's analysis of how "it would be possible to write a whole history of the inventions made since 1830 for the sole purpose of providing capital with weapons against working class revolt" we see the one-sidedness and inadequacy of Engels's argument.[13]

Nevertheless, this kind of argument was taken up and elaborated by the Bolsheviks, especially by Vladimir Illyich Ulyanov (Lenin) (1870–1924) who used it to justify the overthrow of worker-created factory committees and soviets and to impose top-down, party-state-managerial despotism. Although he professed to believe that ultimately "every cook could govern," i.e., coordination could occur within cooperation by the workers themselves, he called for, and imposed, measures of hierarchical control that tended to destroy all bottom-up initiatives.[14]

13. *Capital, Vol. I*, p. 563.
14. Lenin's writings which deal with issues of authority and competition include: "The Immediate Tasks of the Soviet Government" (April 1918), in V. I. Lenin, *Collected Works*, vol. 27, pp. 235–277, which was written in the spring following the October Revolution; and "A Great Beginning. Heroism of the Workers in the Rear. 'Communist Subbotniks'" (June 1919), *Collected Works*, vol. 29, pp. 409–434.

In Lenin's view "rivalry" or competition among workers was to be encouraged in the socialist USSR in order to generate the most work possible. His emphasis on competition among workers emulated that encouraged within overtly capitalist countries, albeit justified by an alternative logic. Elsewhere competition was promulgated throughout society as the natural condition of humankind. In the USSR, Lenin promulgated it as a necessary condition for victory in the class struggle against capitalism and for socialism. In December 1917, right after the revolution of October, he argued:

> Far from extinguishing competition, socialism, on the contrary, for the first time creates the opportunity for employing it on a really *wide* and on a really *mass* scale. . . our task is to organize competition. All "communes"—factories, villages, consumers' societies, and committees of supplies—must *compete* with each other as practical organizers of accounting and control of labor and distribution of products.[15]

Here Lenin is calling for new forms of competition among production units—new, but not all that different from competition among capitalist firms. This competition, Lenin demanded, should be organized in such a way as to weed out those who would not work hard enough:

> workers who shirk their work. . . will be put in prison. . . [elsewhere] they will be put to cleaning latrines. . . [elsewhere] they will be provided with "yellow tickets". . . so that everyone shall keep an eye on them, as harmful persons. . . [elsewhere] one out of every ten idlers will be shot on the spot.[16]

And so on. These comments called for the imposition of a new work discipline by whatever means necessary. Those who must be forced to work, as he makes clear, are not only leftover reactionary capitalists and intellectuals out to sabotage the revolution, but also those workers who had revolted, at least in part, to "lighten the burden of labor." But his rhetorical method identifies "slovenliness, carelessness, untidiness, unpunctuality, nervous haste, the inclination to substitute discussion for action, talk for work," etc. with "the educated" and calls on workers, especially the party faithful, to root out such idlers and to identify and correct any such tendencies among members of their own class.[17] In this manner, right at the beginning of

---

15. "How to Organize Competition", in *Collected Works*, Moscow: Progress Publishers, vol. 26, pp. 404–415.
16. Ibid.
17. Ibid.

Bolshevik rule, Lenin made it clear that Bolshevik-style socialism means more, not less, work. Is this Marx? Or rather, are such views lineal descendants of Marx's ideas? Can the despotism of Soviet state capitalism be traced to Marx's own views on technological necessity? I don't think so, but Marx's comments on authority are not his only remarks that have lent themselves to such interpretation and usage.

A second aspect of Marx's analysis of cooperation, which was also used to justify post-capitalist competition, was his notion that one source of the heightened productivity of cooperation derived from the stimulus it gave to "animal spirits:"

> Apart from the new power that arises from the fusion of many forces into a single force, mere social contact begets in most industries a rivalry and a stimulation of the "animal spirits", which heightens the efficiency of each individual worker.[18]

There are two things to say about this. First, capital has generally promulgated rivalry not only to stimulate "animal spirits" to get more work but also to divert workers' energies from resistance to exploitation and alienation into competition with each other. Thus, capitalists promulgate the ideology of dog-eat-dog competition as a natural condition and encourage a pervasive competition among individuals, within families, within schools, among workers, among men vis-à-vis women, among women vis-à-vis men, and so on. Second, we know that people who come together to act in concert (e.g., in work) can provide each other with support and positive feedback that can make both each individual and the collective more productive. Indeed, there is plenty of experimental evidence that collaboration is *more* productive than competition.[19]

There is nothing in Marx's analysis that implies that coordination cannot take place *within* cooperation through the self-management of "associated producers." His observation that any social labor process involving large numbers of people requires coordination seems uncontestable as far as it goes. But it doesn't go very far. As he recognizes, the form of that coordination has varied enormously in the social situations he mentions—slave plantation economies, ancient Egypt, primitive hunting, capitalism. The same is true for his very few words in this chapter on "rivalry" or competition among workers. Both his earlier work in the *1844 Manuscripts* attacking the ways in which capital pits worker against worker and his later

18. *Capital, Vol. I,* p. 443.
19. Alfie Kohn, *No Contest: The Case Against Competition,* Boston, MA: Houghton Mifflin; 2nd rev. edn., 1992.

discussion in *Capital*, Chapters 20 and 21 on how capitalists manipulate wages to encourage competition and hierarchy, suggest that in general he understood "rivalry" to be only one form of "animal spirits" and that various kinds of non-competitive but mutually stimulating interactions would characterize un-alienated, post-capitalist work relations.

Since Marx was writing, we have over 130 more years of experience with a wide diversity of forms of cooperation, most of which have been elaborated within capitalism, but some of which have been developed explicitly against it.

As workers succeeded in reducing work, e.g., the eight-hour working day and five-day working week, and gaining time away from waged work, capital has responded by colonizing that "free" time, the process I discussed in my commentary on Chapter 10. The institutions of that colonization have recreated many of the characteristics of the capitalist factory, including competition. For individuals, the first experiences of being subjected to competition—instead of collaboration—are usually those of the family and the school. Reared by parents who have themselves internalized competitive attitudes, children often find it encouraged at home. In schools, students are prodded from a very early age to compete against each other for grades and honors. In the short run, it is a means of control; in the long run, they are being conditioned to compete in the waged workplace. Such competition in the class room is complemented and reinforced by competition in sports, whether between individuals or teams. In the case of teams, the enflaming of "animal spirits" is central to the realization of the powers of "cooperation"—to the point of encouraging animosity, scorn and hatred against other teams. At the level of the school system, interscholastic competition is institutionally encouraged not only in sports, but also in music, in debate and in science fairs. Along the dark path to popularity and social status, competition is also fostered between boys and girls, and among boys vis-à-vis girls and among girls vis-à-vis boys. In many places, it is also fostered between castes, ethnicities and races. From secondary school through the university, "school spirit" is roused with marshal band music and pep rallies pitting students against students, often with violent language and mob antagonism.[20] Beyond the shop floor, the family and the school, capitalists have fostered competition throughout society, from professional sports through music, film, fashion, beauty and cooking contests to soap operas, electoral politics and the judicial system. Even where it organizes collaboration—from collective school projects through corporate ones to sports teams—it carefully structures it within a wider framework

---

20. Extreme consequences of such conditioning have included riots by hooligans at sports events.

of competition. Always, the overall framework is competition rather than collaboration because collaboration can be turned against it.

Competition also characterizes capitalist organization at the inter-firm level, and even the international level. At both levels, the capitalists with the best control over their workers tend to win. At the inter-firm level, control can involve either the stick of low wages or the carrot of rewarded creativity. At the international level, as many Marxists have pointed out, conflicts between national blocs of capitalists were characteristic of the age of imperialism.[21] Even today, in the age of globalization in which multinational corporations and supranational institutions manage the world's economy, we hear policies favored because, it is argued, they increase the "international competitiveness" of this or that country. Recent anti-refugee and anti-immigrant campaigns throughout the world have fomented rabid nativism to rouse locals against foreigners. This has been apparent from right-wing nationalist groups in Europe to Donald Trump's slogans "Make America Great Again," "America First" and "Build the Wall!"

All of this, of course, undergirds the most fatal competition of all— wars, either civil wars or wars between nation-states, in which workers kill workers. The psychological preparation for war mobilization, the framing of mindsets wherein some workers will willingly kill other workers, requires years of reinforced conditioning at every age, right up to that of military drafts or enlistment. The alienation cultivated in the workplace that pits workers against each other must be accentuated to the point of inspiring hate in some and demonization of others. We saw just such demonization in racist portrayals of the Japanese ("Japs") during World War II, of the Chinese ("Chinks") during the Korean War, of the Vietnamese ("Gooks") during the war in Indochina, of Arabs ("Rag-heads") in the two Gulf Wars and in the contemporary propaganda by Islamist terrorists associated with groups such as Al Qaeda and ISSIL.

Against such forms of capitalist cooperation through competition, workers have formed their own systems of cooperation: in industry, shop floor solidarity and unions; in schools, small group collaboration in cheating and large-scale protest movements; in the community, grassroots organizations of women, gays or other self-organized movements; at the international level, peace movements against war or grassroots organizing against international competition, e.g., continent-wide resistance to so-called Free Trade Agreements. Sometimes such self-organization may

---

21.   Classic Marxist analyses of these phenomena are Nicholai Bukharin, *Imperialism and the World Economy* (1917) and V. I. Lenin, "Imperialism, the Highest State of Capitalism" (1917), *Selected Works*, Volume 1, Moscow: Progress Publishers, 1963, pp. 667–766.

involve the *détournement* or direct subversion of the institutions of capitalist cooperation; at other times it may involve the creation of collaborative counter-movements created especially for the purposes of struggle. In periods of intense class struggle, the workers have often displayed collective imagination through the creation of new approaches to the organization of cooperation, e.g., the Paris Commune in 1871, the soviets in 1905 and 1917, the workers councils in Germany in 1918–19, in Hungary in 1956, in the counter-cultural movements of the 1960s, in resistance to austerity during the international debt crisis of the 1980s–2000s, in the new uses of electronic and social media by indigenous movements for autonomy and during the Arab Spring, by the Occupy movement and most recently by the Black Lives Matter movement and resistance to Trump's attacks on civil rights, environmental protections and the social safety net.

The "Cooperative" Movement

Marx's insistence on the autonomy (vis-à-vis capital) of cooperation as a quality of human social labor was closely related to his understanding that the overthrow of capitalism by workers would not lead to social dissolution and chaos (of which capitalist ideology frequently warns) but to the liberation of cooperation from capitalist command. Thus, those few times when Marx spoke of labor in post-capitalist society he often referred to "associated labor"—which would certainly involve new kinds of social cooperation. Eschewing utopianism, he refused to speculate on, much less design, such future forms of cooperation and focused instead on the study of how cooperation was evolving within capitalism as one aspect of the developing struggle between labor and capital.

Another who was fascinated with the phenomenon of cooperation, and who also saw that it predated capitalism and would certainly post-date it, was the Russian anarchist Peter Kropotkin. A geologist-geographer who developed political concepts in part out of his scientific research, Kropotkin became convinced that the history of other animals as well as that of humans was shaped by natural instincts to social cooperation. Against the vulgar Darwinist notion—so suitable to capitalist ideology—that evolution was the outcome of an endless war of all against all, Kropotkin pitted his studies of natural and human history which showed the endless variety and continuity of cooperation—what he called "mutual aid." From his scientific field experience in Siberia to his historico-political studies of Western society, Kropotkin drew myriad examples of both animal and human cooperation and argued that cooperation was the dominant reality of social life within species. Beings might hunt and kill other species and within species there are sometimes struggles to establish a "pecking order," but, for the most part, their relationships among kindred were cooperative. Kropotkin spent considerable time ferreting out the underground history of bottom-up cooperation in villages and cities, among farmers and artisans, in manufacturing and industry. Like Marx, he refused to design a post-capitalist world and instead studied the trends in the present that pointed to the future.[22]

But, if Marx and Kropotkin refused to design the future, others were much less restrained. Those whom Marx called the "utopian" socialists, such as Robert Owen (1771–1858) in Britain or Charles Fourier (1772–1837) in France designed both plans and experiments based on their own ideas of how cooperation could be reorganized for the benefit of workers.

Owen was a businessman who developed ideas of improving productivity and the lives of workers by reorganizing both industry and private life in relatively small-scale cooperative villages. He began his experiments in his own yarn mills and neighboring village of New Lanark, Scotland. He introduced modern machinery but also improved the living conditions of workers by keeping wages up during depressions, by upgrading housing and sanitary arrangements, building schools, and organizing the supply of workers' commodity needs at cost. Owen believed that through education and the transformation of the whole community, inside and outside the factories, society could be improved and reorganized around democratic cooperation. Because education had to precede democracy, however, Owen felt free to intervene directly in workers' lives, not only improving their material conditions but also monitoring their behavior, to the point of installing colored behavior indicators near each workers' position in the factory to signal the quality of their character from day to day. Eventually, he worked his ideas into a systematic approach to the reorganization of society around cooperative communities, and became involved in a variety of experiments, the best known of which were the New Harmony Village in Indiana (1824–27) and Orbiston in Lanarkshire (1825–27). These and several other such experiments were organized around communal ownership of property and cooperative labor. None lasted very long and despite his own experiments at New Lanark proving profitable, Owen failed to persuade either business or government to finance the spread of his approach.

However, Owen's innovations at his New Lanark mills did become widely known and provided inspiration for a variety of reformers. Some

---

22. For the results of Kropotkin's studies on cooperation among animals and throughout human history, see his book *Mutual Aid: A Factor of Evolution* (1902), London: Freedom Press, 1987. Subsequent historical research has added to and complemented his work. See, for example, Maxine Berg's *The Age of Manufactures 1700–1820*, New York: Oxford University Press, 1986, which presents the results of recent research into the diversity of pre-industrial forms of manufacturing revealing a wide variety of forms of cooperation—many of which proved extremely resistant to capitalist takeover.

carried on his ideas about cooperation, ultimately leading to a worldwide cooperative movement. Indeed, Owen is probably best known today as the father of that movement. Others, inspired by him, included those very wedded to preserving the class distinctions of Old England within the new conditions of industrialization. One such was Benjamin Disraeli (1804–81) who before becoming British prime minister wrote a series of romantic Tory novels lamenting the decline of the old values. These were the three "Young England" novels: *Coningsby, or the New Generation* (1844), *Sybil, or the Two Nations* (1845) and *Tancred, or the New Crusade* (1847). In *Sybil*, for example, Disraeli denounced the capitalist "spirit of rapacious covetousness." Since the Reform Act of 1832, which admitted the industrial middle class to the electorate, he argued,

> the altar of Mammon has blazed with triple worship. To acquire, to accumulate, to plunder each other by virtue of philosophic phrases, to propose an Utopia to consist only of WEALTH and TOIL, this has been the breathless business of enfranchised England for the last twelve years, until we are startled from our voracious strife by the wail of intolerable serfage.[23]

He then followed up graphic descriptions of some of the worst working-class slums with a glowing portrayal of the establishment of one Mr. Trafford, a very Owenite businessman:

> On the banks of his native Mowe he had built a factory which was now one of the marvels of the district. . . holding more than two thousand work-people. . . the whole building was kept at a steady temperature, and little susceptible to atmospheric influence. The physical advantages of thus carrying on the whole work in one chamber are great: in the improved health of the people, the security against dangerous accidents for women and youth, and the reduced fatigue. . . When the workpeople of Mr Trafford left his factory they were not forgotten. Deeply had he pondered on the influence of the employer on the health and content of his workpeople. He knew well that the domestic virtues are dependent on the existence of a home, and one of this first efforts had been to build a village where every family might be well lodged. . . . In every street there was a well: behind the factory were the public baths; the schools were under the direction of the perpetual curate of the church. . .
>
>   And what was the influence of such an employer and such a system of employment on the morals and manners of the employed? Great; infinitely beneficial. . . . Proximity to the employer brings cleanliness and

---

23. *Sybil, or the Two Nations* (1845), New York: Penguin Classic, 1985, p. 56.

order, because it brings observation and encouragement. In the settle-
ment of Trafford crime was positively unknown: and offences were very
slight. . . . The men were well clad; the women had a blooming cheek;
drunkenness was unknown; while the moral condition of the softer sex
was proportionately elevated.[24]

Charles Fourier, about a year younger than Owen, also got his start in
business and went on to design new social institutions around cooperation in labor and society. Like Owen, Fourier's ideal new social units were
small-scale villages based on cooperative principles but linked in a regional
(and ultimately even global) network. Also like Owen, Fourier's plans
extended beyond the workshop to the larger society where he advocated
cooperation in education and even love. His utopia included not only collective work but also collective emotional and sexual linkages designed to
liberate people from the frustrations he felt were inherent in the traditional
family. Basing himself on a theory of desire quite different from Owen
and most other utopian thinkers, Fourier's plans for reorganization sought
to reshape society to meet and balance a well-defined list of intellectual,
psychological, emotional and physical needs. Whereas Owen thought
people could be re-educated to fit into a more rational social order, Fourier
sought to fit the social order to eternal human desires. Unable to achieve
the implementation of his ideas during his lifetime, Fourier's energies were
focused on their theoretical design, the imaginative working through of
how social relationships might be reorganized in a non-competitive, cooperative fashion to achieve individual happiness within social harmony
(which, in his view, necessarily included a considerable dose of rivalry and
competitiveness). It was left to his followers to actually set up working
models of his ideal communities (or "phalanxes"); at least 40 were launched,
especially in America, during the 1840s, but like the Owenite experiments
none lasted very long.[25]

While Marx rejected such approaches to transcending capitalism
as evidence of the immaturity of the proletariat in the early nineteenth
century, he nevertheless considered these inventive social reformers "revolutionary" in "many respects" and applauded the way they identified the
class antagonisms of capitalism and provided "the most valuable materials

---

24. Ibid., pp. 225–226.
25. For chapter length introductions to the ideas and efforts of Robert Owen and
Charles Fourier and their followers, see Keith Taylor, *The Political Ideas of the Utopian
Socialists*, London: Frank Cass, 1982. For a sample of Owen's own work, see Robert
Owen, *A New View of Society and Other Writings*, London: Penguin, 1991. For a taste of
Fourier's writings, see Mark Poster (ed.), *Harmonian Man. Selected Writings of Charles
Fourier*, New York: Doubleday, 1971.

for the enlightenment of the working class."[26] He saw producer cooperatives as inspiring forerunners of the future:

> We speak of the cooperative movement, especially of the cooperative factories raised by the unassisted efforts of a few bold "hands". The value of these great social experiments cannot be over-rated. By deed, instead of by argument, they have shown that production on a large scale, and in accord with the best of modern science, may be carried on without the existence of a class of masters employing a class of hands.[27]

While many cooperatives have organized collective production, e.g., peasant or farmer cooperatives where individual family farmers collaborate to share equipment and jointly market their output, others have reorganized the sphere of reproduction, e.g., consumer, housing, financial or caregiving cooperatives.[28] The utopians left in their wake a tradition of scattered, isolated and usually short-lived "intentional communities." The organization of cooperatives, in contrast, became a whole social movement, which has spread the ideology and practice of "cooperation" across the face of the Earth. From their origins in Britain and France to the US and many other countries, "cooperatives" have been held out as an alternative path to the dog-eat-dog competition of capitalism.[29] The history of the class struggle is, in part, a history of the struggle over the creation and utilization of new forms of cooperation.

CHAPTER 14: MANUFACTURING AND THE DIVISION OF LABOR

Overview of Chapter

Section 1: The Dual Origin of Manufacture
Section 2: The Specialized Worker and His Tools
Section 3: The Two Fundamental Forms of Manufacture
Section 4: The Division of Labor in Manufacture and Society
Section 5: The Capitalist Character of Manufacture

---

26. "The Manifesto of the Communist Party", *MECW, vol. 6*, p. 516.
27. Karl Marx, "Inaugural Address of the Working Men's International Association", November 1864, in *MECW, vol. 20*, p. 11.
28. See the various examples in ILO, "Promising Practices: How Cooperatives Work for Working Women in Africa" (available online) and the work of the ILO's Cooperative Facility for Africa more generally.
29. See John Curl, *For All the People: Uncovering the Hidden History of Cooperation, Cooperative Movements and Communalism in America*, Oakland, CA: PM Press, 2012.

Preliminary Commentary

Outline of Marx's Analysis

"Manu"-facturing
- workers using their hands and tools to make things
- manufacturing period = mid-sixteenth to last third of the eighteenth century
- "a particular sort of cooperation" based on the division of labor among large numbers of specialized workers
- "division of labor in manufacturing is merely a particular method of creating relative surplus-value"
- "dependent on the strength, skill, quickness and sureness with which the individual worker manipulates his tools"

In this chapter Marx deepens his discussion of cooperation begun in Chapter 13. He examines the organization of cooperation within the context of manufacture, the first reorganization of production beyond the simple annexation of handicraft workers through the putting-out system. In the putting-out system the organization of production remains unaltered, handicraft people continue working as before using their own tools in their old ways. But in manufacturing, the capitalists increasingly impose a new division of labor in which the workers become increasingly specialized, performing only one part of a larger production process involving many workers and many steps. Yet, throughout the manufacturing period, the handicraft worker, however specialized, is still the moving force of production, or what Marx calls "the regulating principle of social production." The word manufacturing derives from two Latin roots: *manus* for hand and *factura* for making. Thus, manufacturing is "making by hand" and it is the workers' control over the use of their hands which regulates the rhythm and quality of the work. Manufacturing work thus corresponds very closely to Marx's analysis of labor in Chapter 7 in which a worker uses tools to transform raw materials. He later juxtaposes this to "machino-facture" in which the rhythm of work is determined largely by the machine and workers are both used by the tools and demoted from their central role, i.e., stripped of their traditional power of controlling the labor process.

Section 1: The Dual Origin of Manufacture

Outline of Marx's Analysis

- from the assembling of large numbers of different or the same kinds of skilled workers
- both cases: an increasing division of labor, increasingly narrow specialization
- decomposes complex handicraft skills into partial operations

---

Commentary

The capitalist bringing together of large numbers of workers leads from a simple assembling of those with handicraft skills to an ever-more complex division of labor. Whether different kinds of craftspeople with complementary skills are assembled, or a large number of those with the same skills, the end result, he argues, has been the same: namely an ever-increasing specialization of work and tools. This division and specialization derives partly from the reorganization of workers to produce a larger number of products at a more rapid pace, i.e., to increase productivity (and thus relative surplus-value). However, the reorganization also serves to undermine workers' control of the production process.

This increasing specialization results in that process of deskilling or "*disvalorization*" of workers that I discussed in my commentaries on primitive accumulation. Whether we are talking about multiskilled peasant farmers reduced to farm labor, midwives reduced to nurses, or craftspeople reduced to narrowly specialized factory workers, in all cases there is a loss of skill and of meaning from the point of view of the individuals and an appropriation and transformation of skill by capital. The transformation includes an unavoidable process of "*devalorization*" as many skills and meanings, both personal and collective, are lost for good. Some of the negative effects of these losses are discussed below.

Section 2: The Specialized Worker and His Tools

Outline of Marx's Analysis

- "collective worker" made up of highly specialized individual workers
- one-sided work means less time in execution and fewer time gaps

▶

> – as the workers become more specialized, so too do their tools
> – tools of specialized worker = differentiated, simplified and adapted to specialized tasks, e.g., 500 varieties of hammer
> – both worker and tool become perfected for narrow task, impoverished for others

Commentary

Marx's analysis of how the varied skills of the handicraft worker become distributed piecemeal across a much larger body of workers leads him to see that larger body as itself constituting a collective worker and each worker an "organ" of the larger body. "The collective worker, formed out of the combination of a number of individual specialized workers, is the item of machinery specifically characteristic of the manufacturing period."[30] Because each of the specialized workers is more effective at their individualized tasks, this collective worker is more productive than an equal number of unspecialized workers who did everything. "The one-sidedness and even the deficiencies of the specialized individual worker become perfections when he is part of the collective worker."[31] This metaphorical way of speaking about a large-scale, social set of complex relationships has certain limitations, but it is nevertheless a very powerful one. It evokes not only the reality of productive cooperation, as these workers learn to work together as one, but also the potential for class struggle wherein these same workers learn to struggle as one, whether in unions or in wildcat strikes, against the capitalists for whom they work.

Part of the source of higher levels of productivity derives simply from specialization—of the workers and of tools, retrained and redesigned for narrowly defined purposes, and hence more effective. But another part, an aspect to which Marx returns in other chapters of the book, is how specialization results in the elimination of the time gaps inherent in the work of handicraft workers as they move from one task to another, changing tools, the organization of material upon which they are working, and so on. While such gaps provide potential moments of rest for handicraft workers, they are time wasted from the point of view of manufacturers. In the next chapter, Marx will analyze how the introduction of machinery further helps bosses extract every possible second of life and joule of energy from their workers.

---

30. *Capital, Vol. I*, p. 468.
31. Ibid., p. 469.

Section 3: The Two Fundamental Forms of Manufacture

Outline of Marx's Analysis

Heterogeneous: parts made separately, then assembled, e.g., watch-making

Organic: production through a series of sequential processes, e.g., needle-making

The "collective worker"
  – "formed from the combination of the many specialized workers"
  – each worker a specialized organ of the whole

Mutual interdependence
  – a given proportionality to achieve continuity of all workers
  – appropriate number of workers for each operation
  – extension of scale by multiplying groups
  – different skills = different training = different values of labor-power
  – hierarchy of labor-powers, hierarchy of wages

Simplification of tasks = devaluation of labor-power, as v decreases, s increases

---

Commentary

Although the concept of the "collective worker" emphasizes unity by its use of a singular figure to represent a complex group, Marx also recognizes the internal divisions and separations which compose this unitary figure. Not only does he show how the collective worker is composed of different kinds of workers populating a complex division of labor, but he recognizes that the division of labor is never a simple horizontal set of differences but rather a vertical hierarchy:

> Since the various functions performed by the collective worker can be simple or complex, high or low, the individual labor-powers, his organs, require different degrees of training, and must therefore possess very different values. Manufacture therefore develops a hierarchy of labor-powers, to which there corresponds a scale of wages.[32]

In other words, the reproduction of workers who require complex training necessitates higher wages. This is an application of the analysis in Chapter

---

32.   Ibid., p. 469.

6 of the value of labor-power. When we consider dramatically different skill levels, such as that of manual workers performing simple tasks and engineers who design machinery or chemists who work out new chemical processes, it seems reasonable that on the assumption that such workers tend to produce offspring of the same character, engineers and chemists would require higher wages to rear children capable of achieving the same level of education and training. Within a generation on the other hand, it is not quite so obvious why engineers should require higher income than manual workers to reproduce themselves as such. We can imagine that they need more resources for continuing education, communication with their peers, books, tools of their trade and so on, but this is speculative. Marx certainly doesn't present any such evidence. Therefore, as in Chapter 6 we can take his suggestion here as only a step toward a theory of the wage hierarchy in manufacturing.

One thing is certain, no matter how trivial the actual differences between production tasks, or however tenuous the connections to the costs of reproducing labor-power, capitalists always impose a wage hierarchy as a means of dividing and controlling the collective worker. As the recent movement by women for equal wages on the basis of "comparable worth" has repeatedly demonstrated, many wage differentials have no relationship either to the complexity of the job or to the value of labor-power. When he turns to the subject of wages in Chapters 19–22, Marx further develops his analysis of the relationship between the wages and hierarchy.

What consideration of the hierarchy of labor-powers and wages brings out is that the division of labor involves not merely differences in tasks, it also involves differentials in power. It is not just that some are highly skilled and some less skilled or unskilled. The highly skilled receive more wages than the less skilled just as the less skilled receive more than the unskilled. In as much as wages represent not only power to command the means of life but also power to struggle, the hierarchy of wages involves a hierarchy of power among workers and in their respective and joint relations with capital.

Recognition of these relations by a number of Marxists in the post-World War II period led both to empirical studies of historical changes in the makeup of the collective worker and to the development of a new set of Marxist concepts to understand them. Whereas Marx spoke of the division of labor, these Marxists came to speak of the complex set of power relationships woven out of, and constructed against, the division of labor in terms of a particular "class composition."[33] Historical studies of the changing

---

33. See Steve Wright, *Storming Heaven: Class Composition and Struggle in Italian Autonomist Marxism*, 2nd edn., London: Pluto Press, 2017.

division of labor in the twentieth century led to an interpretation of how the rise of Taylorism and then Fordism led to a particular figure of the collective worker they called "the mass worker."[34] *Taylorism* denotes the meticulous analysis of the labor process and subsequent use of that analysis to impose the most detailed and efficient specialization possible on the collective worker. Taylor quite consciously carried out the redesign of the production process and of the pattern of cooperation to achieve precisely that concentrated power of command in the hands of capital at the expense of the worker that Marx describes so well in this chapter. Taylor's work was dedicated to the final destruction of the power of handicraft and skilled workers to exert any control at all over the work process and, indirectly, to undercut the power of craft unions formed by such skilled workers, e.g., in the US, the American Federation of Labor (AFL) (1886–1955). *Fordism* is a term given to the manner in which Henry Ford reorganized the Taylorist division of labor around assembly line production of standardized products. In the process, he completed what Taylor had begun through the subordination of all moments of work to a single interconnected machine, what the French call "La Chaine," a nice term that evokes the chains of slavery. The mass worker, who emerged within this restructured labor process, was a new kind of collective worker, one totally alienated from work and capable of self-organization at the level of industry. In the US, industrial unions, such as the United Auto Workers (1935–), and federations of industrial unions, such as the Congress of Industrial Organizations (1935–55) and then the AFL-CIO (1955–) were products of the self-activity of the mass worker.

Section 4: The Division of Labor in Manufacture and Society

Outline of Marx's Analysis

Division of labor in manufacture
  – unmediated by exchange
  – planned, organized by the despotism of capitalists
  – depends for its development on growth of the *social* division of labor

Social division of labor in society
  – mediated by exchange of commodities (anarchy), e.g., cattle-breeding, tanning, shoemaking

---

34.   See Sergio Bologna, "The Theory and History of the Mass Worker in Italy" (1987), published in English in two parts in *Common Sense*, no. 11, Winter 1991, pp. 16–29, and no. 12, Summer 1992, pp. 52–78.

- division of labor in general (agriculture vs industry, etc.)
- division of labor in particular (particular industries)
- division of labor in detail (within the workshop)
- foundation of every division of labor = the separation of town from country

Division of labor at each level has an impact on the division of labor on other levels
- ultimately, the division of labor "seizes upon, not only the economic, but every other sphere of society"

Earlier forms of society: e.g., ancient Indian communities
- fixed, authoritative plan of division of labor and village
- blending of agriculture and handicrafts
- mostly "self-sufficing" communities, production for use
- each individual craftsman conducts in his workshop all the operations of his handicraft in the traditional way
- medieval guilds
- separated, isolated and perfected handicrafts
- master, limited number of journeymen
- worker and tools closely united

Commentary

In this section, Marx widens his analysis of the division of labor from factory shop floors to manufacturing as a whole. Workers are gathered in factories to make it easier to control them. Along with such means of control as overseers, time clocks and wage hierarchies, capitalists also carefully organize the division of labor with the same objective. Instead of leaving it to their workers to discover the most effective way of organizing their work, capitalists impose what Marx calls, accurately but pejoratively, *despotic* plans, top-down assignments of the layout of work and machines, of workers to tasks and so on. To some degree such plans are determined by the technologies involved, e.g., sequential tasks requiring different machines are usually organized spatially to minimize time lost in moving material from work station to work station. But, at the same time, managers also try to organize the spatial distribution of work to minimize the costs of oversight, required to make sure employees keep at their work.[35] Worker

---

35. The classic mode of such spatial reorganization is the panopticon, whether implemented in factories, schools or prisons. See Jeremy Bentham, *Panopticon: Or, The Inspection House* (1791), and critiques such as Gertrude Himmelfarb, "The Haunted House of

challenges to all such plans, even if offered with suggestions of how to improve productivity, are often rejected purely to maintain "managerial pre-rogative" or the absolute authority of managers to control everything that goes on.[36]

Such despotic plans Marx juxtaposes to how the division of labor on a wider scale is largely mediated by unplanned markets, "anarchic" because subject to uncoordinated actions by buyers and sellers. In speaking of the anarchy of markets, Marx's choice of the term anarchy to characterize markets where competition reigns (as opposed to monopolies or markets organized as oligopolies) is, perhaps, not merely a vernacular use of the word, but a by-product of his long-standing debate with anarchists. Despite his disagreements, he was certainly aware that many, perhaps most, anar-chists wanted, like himself, the regulation of production and distribution to be taken out of the hands of capitalists and placed in those of workers. For some, of course, their anti-statism has taken the form of belief in unregu-lated free markets, ideas peddled today under the rubric of libertarianism.[37]

In organizing his sketch of the division of labor in industry as a whole, Marx reintroduces moments of the Hegelian syllogism that he used in Chapter 1 to analyze the general form of value. He does this by juxtaposing divisions of labor "in general" (that is, the Hegelian category of universal), e.g., agriculture versus manufacturing, "in particular" (that is, the Hegelian category of the particular), e.g., separate manufacturing industries, to "in detail" (that is, the Hegelian category of the individual or singular), e.g., within the factory. Although he doesn't do much with these designations, their use suggests the need to grasp each division of labor as mediating the relations among the others, as in the syllogism. For example, he writes, the "anarchy in the social division of labor and despotism in the manufacturing division of labor mutually condition each other."[38]

Jeremy Bentham", in Richard Herr and Harold Parker, *Ideas in History*, Durham, NC: Duke University Press, 1965 and Michel Foucault, *Discipline and Punish: The Birth of the Prison*, New York: Random House, 1975. Nowadays, direct visual surveillance has been supplemented by electronic means of monitoring workers in production and in daily life via the collection of personal data via social media. See Shoshana Zuboff, *In the Age of the Smart Machine: The Future of Work and Power*, New York: Basic Books, 1988.

36. This was a major failing of twentieth-century American management. In the auto industry, for example, how the refusal of workers' ideas impeded the improvement of productivity was revealed when Japanese firms—whose managers had discovered how to take advantage of such suggestions, without losing control—invaded the North American market and were able to outcompete local producers.

37. As with Marxism, anarchism is not monolithic; there are many different anarchist ideas about how to get beyond capitalism. That the ideas of some anarchists overlap, or draw upon Marxism, is obvious among those who call themselves anarcho-communists.

38. *Capital, Vol. I*, p. 477.

One of the ways despotism in factories has conditioned the social division of labor—and in the process expanded the scope of capitalist planning and undercut market mediations—has been workers' struggles against that despotism that have led to 1) the creation of industry-wide and even international unions and 2) ever greater regulation by the state, both national and supranational. Time and again, competitive markets have been replaced by broader capitalist planning. The organization of industrial unions has led to industry-wide labor contracts, negotiated between unions and industrial management, often within frameworks specified by the government. The multinationalization of corporate investment, once limited to a few government-chartered companies in the colonial period, has become widespread, allowing managers to plan the division of labor—and hence their modes of labor control—across borders, oceans and cultures. Keynesian economic policies, with their intentional manipulations of both fiscal and monetary policy, have amounted to capitalist planning on a national scale. Such planning has been extended to the international level, through such supranational institutions as the International Monetary Fund and the World Trade Organization, which help regulate investment opportunities for multinational corporations.[39]

The sketches of pre-capitalist divisions of labor, of Asian communities and feudal guilds, that Marx draws at the end of the section, are clearly intended to differentiate the way capital organizes production as opposed to the way others have done so. However accurate his descriptions—based here on colonialist accounts—he emphasizes the rigidity of traditional divisions of labor as opposed to the greater fluidity characteristic of capitalism.[40]

Despite the title of this section evoking the *division of labor in society*, Marx restricts his analysis to industry and fails to address divisions beyond the capitalist realms of waged labor. Although at one point he hints that

---

39. A perceptive analysis of how workers struggles have driven this historical expansion of capitalist planning can be found in Raniero Panzieri, "Surplus Value and Planning: Notes on the Reading of *Capital*", in *The Labour Process and Class Strategies*, CSE Pamphlet, no. 1, London: Stage 1, 1976, pp. 4–25 (also at http://libcom.org/library/surplus-value-planning-raniero-panzieri), originally "Sull'uso capitalistico delle macchine nel neocapitalismo", *Quaderni Rossi*, no. 1, 1961, pp. 53–72.

40. Marx's writings on Indian and Javanese society grew out of his efforts to understand the evolution of colonialism within the British and Dutch empires and within global capitalism more generally. Characteristically, he looked for an understanding of the relationship between the nation-states (colonizing and colonized) in the class dynamics within each and the linkages between social antagonisms in England and those in the colonies through trade, investment and war. For a collection of his writings, see S. Aveneri (ed.), *Karl Marx on Colonialism and Modernization*, New York: Doubleday, 1969. Virtually all his writings on India are now available in the volumes of the *Collected Works*.

the division of labor "seizes upon, not only the economic, but every other sphere of society," he does not develop this.[41] Unfortunately, many efforts to update Marx's analysis, including research on the mass worker, have also failed to analyze the evolution of the division of labor outside the factory, despite recognizing how, by intervening throughout society, capital was turning it into one big *social factory*.[42]

Marx's failure to extend the analysis of the division of labor beyond the factory can be understood from two perspectives, one personal, one historical. At the personal level, Marx was a man of the nineteenth century, patriarchal middle class—university-educated, a journalist and writer by trade—and according to his biographers he was never substantially involved in either housework within his own home or in his children's education, two key terrains of the labor of reproduction. At the historical level, he was writing in a period in which virtually everyone in the working class, men, women and children, were being forced into waged labor. As we saw in Chapter 10, he recognized and tracked workers' efforts to reduce the length of the working day, but real success came only after his death. While that real success liberated hours from waged labor, it also led to capitalist efforts to colonize the time set free, imposing new divisions of labor that have long demanded recognition and analysis. The analysis of the division of labor of reproduction, including that within housework and schoolwork, are clearly required for any complete understanding of the class composition in any given period. It also forces us to recognize that Marx's collective worker includes not only the waged but the unwaged as well.[43]

Examination of the division of labor in reproduction has revealed that the tendency toward specialization being imposed in the factory has been much less present in housework and schoolwork. Chapter 30, on the rise of the "home market," focused on how expropriated workers were forced to buy items they once had produced for themselves. While those commodities were being produced by the increasingly specialized types of labor Marx describes, the flip side of this process was a certain deskilling of household workers (mainly women, but also children), e.g., buying vegetables or baked bread or clothes reduced the necessity and incentive

---

41. *Capital, Vol. I*, p. 474.
42. See Mario Tronti, "La fabbrica e la società", *Quaderni Rossi*, no. 2, giugno 1962, pp. 1–31, and his "Social Capital", *Telos*, #17, Fall 1973, pp. 98–121, originally "Il Piano del capitale", in *Quaderni Rossi*, no. 3, 1963, pp. 44–73; Sergio Bologna, "Il rapporto societa-fabbrica come categoria storica", *Primo Maggio*, no. 2, Ottobre 1973, pp. 1–8; Modern Times Collective (Cleveland) "The Social Factory", *The Activist*, #36, vol. 15, Nos. 1, 2, Spring 1975, pp. 38–41.
43. See Alisa Del Re, "Workers' Inquiry and Reproductive Labor", *Viewpoint Magazine*, no. 3, September 25, 2013.

to learn to garden or bake or sew, or pass those skills along to the next generation. Along the same path, however, other skills had to be acquired, e.g., figuring out how best to spend the wage, to evaluate the consumer goods available in the market, and added to already existing skills, such as cooking, cleaning, healing (both physical and psychological) and a wide array of affective skills managing relationships within the home. Clearly, household labor has never been subjected to the kind of narrow specialized task-work characteristic of Taylorism and Fordism. All those tasks we regroup under the rubric housework have always and continue to require a complex set of skills.

The same has largely been true for that other obvious terrain of the labor of reproduction: education. In the epochs of handicraft labor and manufacturing, the education of working-class children often consisted of little more than apprenticeships to learn required skills or workhouses to instill discipline. As the division of labor came to demand narrow specialization, apprenticeships were replaced by a few minutes of on-the-job training. But as workers won child labor laws, excluding them from mines and mills and factories, and demanded education for their offspring, schools were built to incarcerate and discipline them for future jobs. Repeatedly modeled on factories, schools have imposed new divisions of labor—that varied with the age of the students and the level of the school—designed to prepare students for different kinds of jobs. While all students have been forced to assimilate a common set of skills, e.g., reading, writing and arithmetic, eventually they have been tracked into courses such as industrial arts, designed to prepare students for waged jobs, or college preparatory classes, designed to prepare students for mostly unwaged university studies and eventual salaried jobs. Within colleges and universities, there are all the divisions of labor associated with academic fields and subfields, as well as those associated with administration and all the staff jobs required in such institutions. The majority of these jobs, however specialized with respect to the overall division of labor, still require a complex set of skills, irreducible to the mindless, automaton labor that became characteristic of the factory in the age of Fordism and the mass worker. In recent years, as the advance of computerization and robotics have eliminated many specialized jobs typical of the mass worker, more and more jobs require a complex set of cognitive, intellectual or affective skills and schools have been trying to adapt to prepare students accordingly.

Just as Marx drew upon both literature and factory inspectors' reports to study the division of labor within the waged workplace, extending such analysis to the unwaged work of reproduction requires researching whatever evidence is available about how the divisions of such labor have been organized, resisted and reorganized over time. For such evidence we too can turn to literature and specialized studies to understand the family and schools within the dynamics of the larger class composition in any period. In the home, we can examine the labor of childrearing, cleaning, cooking, and so on, and ask how it has been shared within the family and community? Who undertook which tasks? How much of the work has been done by unwaged women, how much by unwaged children, how much by waged or salaried men and women, how much by hired help and how have these proportions changed over time and in response to what? Doing so helps us understand such phenomena as the rise of autonomous women's movements, organized for the most part by unwaged housewives. In schools, we can ask the same kind of questions in order to understand student disaffection, drug addiction, delinquency, rebellion and the rise of student movements.

Elizabeth Gaskell's novel of working-class life, *Mary Barton*, written the same year that Marx and Engels published their *Communist Manifesto*, opened a window for many middle-class readers on to the inferno of Manchester's rapid industrialization and the division of labor in families and in working-class communities. Although in her story most housework is undertaken by women—the men leaving the preparation of tea and food to the women in the opening chapter, Job Leah's ignorance about how to care for an infant during his return trip from London, John Barton leaving the care of his dead wife's body to his daughter, and so on—there are also working-class men able and willing to assume roles of nurturing and caring. Under both normal circumstances (the opening walk in the countryside) and emergencies (the starvation of William Davenport and his family), they have the knowledge necessary and willingness to nurture, shop for food and medicine, cook, administer to the sick and comfort the bereaved. Overall, her story of the lives of some working-class millworkers and their families portrays much less of a strict gender division of labor than we might have expected.

Today, there is a much richer array of materials upon which we can draw to extend Marx's analysis of the division of labor into the home, the community and the school. Not surprisingly, just as among novelists of the nineteenth century mostly women authors such as Gaskell, Jane Austin or the Brontë sisters explored these issues, since his time it has been primarily women, whether novelists, activists or academic scholars, who have pushed Marxist research in this direction. Moreover, it has mainly been within the context of upsurges in women's or student struggles that such work has been undertaken.

Section 5: The Capitalist Character of Manufacture

Outline of Marx's Analysis

– productive power of collective worker "appears as the productive power of capital"

– "knowledge, judgment and will. . . is lost to specialized workers, is concentrated in the capital which confronts them"

– counterpart to this is the impoverishment, mutilating and crippling of the specialized worker

– capitalism is the first system "to provide the materials and the impetus for industrial pathology"

– Greeks understood the division of labor only in terms of use-value

– main obstacle: resistance of handicraft workers who are still "the regulating principle of social production," skills of handicraft workers in manufacturing gives them power to be insubordinate

– results: failure to seize all disposable labor time, manufactures must follow movement of workers

– solution: introduction of machinery which will "abolish the role of the handicraftsman as the regulating principle of social production."

Commentary

The division of labor in manufacturing constructs a more highly productive collective worker out of the activities of its constituent specialized individuals in part by making each of them more effective in the narrow task assigned. While capitalists want to claim credit, they usually avoid recognizing the price paid by workers for that enhanced effectiveness. Endless labor at one narrow task cripples their other real or potential abilities. "Constant labor of one uniform kind disturbs the intensity and flow of a man's vital forces, which find recreation and delight in the change of activity itself."[44]

Manufacture. . . seizes labor-power by its roots. It converts the worker into a crippled monstrosity by furthering his particular skill as in a forcing-house, through the suppression of a whole world of productive drives and inclinations, just as in the states of La Plata they butcher a whole beast for the sake of his hide or his tallow. . . the individual

---

44. *Capital, Vol. I*, p. 460.

himself is divided up, and transformed into the automatic motor of a detail operation. . .[45]

Although he recognizes that any division of labor in any kind of society will involve some restriction on the potential development of the individual, Marx argues that in capitalism this is carried to a barbaric extreme. "Since manufacture. . . attacks the individual at the very roots of his life, it is the first system to provide the materials and the impetus for industrial pathology."[46]

Marx was far from the first to take up this theme. In Chapter 14 he points out that Adam Smith before him had commented on this kind of negative impact on the individual worker and that Smith learned of it from his own teacher Adam Ferguson.[47] Where Marx goes beyond Ferguson and Smith is in providing a *class analysis* of the dynamics of these relations, especially in analyzing their role in the class struggle (see below).

In his analysis of the collective activities of a glass factory Marx ends with the production of the glass bottle.[48] In "The Apostate" (1906), Jack London describes Johnny as one of those one-sided, specialized and crippled workers of whom Marx speaks:

It was simple work, the tying of glass stoppers into small bottles. At his waist he carried a bundle of twine. He held the bottles between his knees so that he might work with both hands. Thus, in a sitting position and bending over his own knees, his narrow shoulders grew humped and his chest was contracted for ten hours each day. This was not good for the lungs, but he tied three hundred dozen bottles a day. . . he had attained machine-like perfection. All waste movements were eliminated. Every motion of his thin arms, every movement of a muscle in the thin fingers was swift and accurate. He worked at high tension, and the result was that he grew nervous. At night his muscles twitched in his sleep, and in the daytime, he could not relax and rest. He remained keyed up and his muscles continued to twitch. Also, he grew sallow and his lint-cough grew worse. The pneumonia laid hold of the feeble lungs within the contracted chest and he lost his job in the glass-works.[49]

---

45. Ibid., p. 481. La Plata refers to the area in Argentina where wild cattle were killed by gauchos who sold the hides for cash. The hides constituted an important element of Argentine exports in the eighteenth and nineteenth centuries, providing leather to the US and Europe for shoes, boots and machinery drive belts.
46. Ibid., p. 484.
47. Ibid., p. 483.
48. Ibid., pp. 466–467.
49. London, *Revolution. Stories and Essays*, p. 807.

Whether the worker portrayed in this short story was drawn from life is not known. He might well have been because London worked in many of the industries described in his stories. But even if he was not, the portrayal gives vivid concreteness to an all too common phenomenon in the nineteenth and even the twenty-first century.

This problem of the crippling caused by highly specialized work has grown with capitalism and has continued to be the object of both working-class struggle and academic study. In the post-World War II period, for example, farm workers fought against the "short-handled hoe," a tool imposed on them by capitalists who wanted their overseers to be able to immediately identify a worker who stopped working (by standing up straight). It didn't matter to the agribusiness corporations in California and elsewhere that the result of eight hours or more of stoop labor was physically crippling to the workers. Nor is this a problem only for blue-collar workers; think of carpel tunnel syndrome, common among those whose work demands ceaseless typing, hunched over keyboards. Even in the domain of mental labor—foreseen by Ferguson in 1767—over-specialization has led to an inability of workers (including the graduates of professional schools) to understand enough of the background and framework of a problem to generate creative solutions.

Since Marx's time, the development of capitalist industry has brought with it an ever-greater mass of disease, poisonings, cripplings and other injuries for industrial pathologists to study. When we broaden our attention to the social factory, we can begin to recognize how all kinds of pathologies from drug use and suicides to environmental degradation have been just as integral to capitalist development as the factory-based problems that preoccupied Marx. Inevitably, workers have fought such conditions of work and life, both through the fight for safety and health regulation within the official workplace and through the battles for a wide variety of health, consumer and environmental programs in the society at large.

Already in his 1857 *Grundrisse* manuscripts, Marx, following Fourier, had foreseen the necessary condition for overcoming this problem: not the abandonment of the division of labor, as some romantic pastoralists have suggested, but such a drastic reduction in work time that people's work could be enriched by a diversity of life experiences. Where Marx went beyond Fourier was in identifying the forces at work in the class struggles that were pushing society in this direction. His early synthesis in the *Grundrisse* laid out the analysis most clearly: how working-class struggle forced capital to substitute machinery for labor, raising the productivity of labor and creating the *technical possibility* of less work, and the *political potential* to replace labor-time as a measure of value with disposable time for all.[50] Some of that analysis reappears in Chapter 10 of *Capital* in the discussion of working-class struggle for less work. Some more can be found in Chapter 25 where he analyses the genesis of the reserve army of the unemployed. Still more can be found in the *Grundrisse* and in Volume III of *Capital* where Marx analyses how this constant substitution of constant for variable capital reducing the need for labor, increases the difficulty in putting people to work. These analyses lead to his discussion of the "realm of freedom" where work is reduced to a single component of a multifaceted social life and value of labor to capital is replaced by increased disposable time for everyone.

The Class Struggle

Much of Marx's analysis focuses on the benefits to capital of the division of labor in manufacture irrespective of the costs to workers. But there is another side to Marx's analysis, the side that recognizes the power that workers do have even within this division. Precisely because manufacturing is still based on handicraft skills, workers' command over those skills gives them power over the labor process—power to produce and power to refuse to produce:

> Since handicraft skill is the foundation of manufacture, and since the mechanism of manufacture as a whole possesses no objective framework which would be independent of the workers themselves, capital is constantly compelled to wrestle with the insubordination of the workers.[51]

He goes on to quote Andrew Ure that "the more skillful the workman, the more self-willed and intractable he is apt to become."[52] Skilled workpeople can be self-willed and intractable because they control the rhythm and pace of certain phases of the production process. They wield tools and know the most efficient way to use them; they also know less efficient ways. In conflict with capitalists—say, over the conditions of labor or the length of the working day—it is therefore possible for such workers to slow down or sabotage the production process without the capitalists or their overseers being able to understand when or how this is done. Early in the chapter, Marx noted how the craftsman creates "gaps in his working day" as he shifts from one operation to another.[53] The capitalist refinement of the

---

50.   The passage in the *Grundrisse* is the famous "Fragment on Machines", pp. 699–712.
51.   Ibid., pp. 489–490.
52.   Ibid., p. 490.
53.   Ibid., p. 460.

division of labor tends to eliminate such shifts, and thus the gaps, but never completely. At the end of the chapter, he concludes that the proof of the still remaining power of handicraft workers in the manufacturing division of labor lay in the failure of capital to "seize control of the whole disposable labor-time of the manufacturing workers."[54] It was only through the introduction of machinery that Frederick Taylor and Henry Ford would be able to strip the last shreds of power from the hands of production line workers. Unfortunately for the capitalists, the response of the workers to being blocked in one source of power would be to develop others!

When we expand our attention from the factory to the sphere of reproduction with its own evolving division of labor, we can also find endless examples of people using their command over work processes to resist the imposition of labor. Whether we examine the struggles of unwaged housewives or students, we discover a myriad of methods, subtle or blatant to refuse work. The housewife, fed up with being condemned to life as a brood mare, withdraws "affective labor," evokes the proverbial evening headache to avoid sex, and uses her knowledge of her own body to resist conception and procreation. Waged spouses, called upon by their significant unwaged others to share housework, feign incompetence in the hope, conscious or unconscious, that their partners will give up and do the work themselves. Students, bored or annoyed with imposed school work, feign dullness—or wit—to distract teachers, sit in the back of the classroom and text their friends or browse the Internet, opening gaps for play or contemplation in the school day.[55]

Chapter 15: Machinery and Modern Industry

Overview of Chapter

Section 1: The Development of Machinery
Section 2: The Value Transferred by the Machinery to the Product
Section 3: The Most Immediate Effects of Machine Production on the Worker
Section 4: The Factory
Section 5: The Struggle between Worker and Machine
Section 6: The Compensation Theory, with Regard to the Workers Displaced by Machinery ▶

---

54. Ibid.
55. See Douglas Foley's amusing ethnographic account of "playing around in the classroom" in Chapter 4 of his *Learning Capitalist Culture: Deep in the Heart of Texas*, Philadelphia: University of Pennsylvania Press, 1990, 2010.

Section 7:   Repulsion and Attraction of Workers through the Devel-
             opment of Machine Production, Crises in the Cotton
             Industry
Section 8:   The Revolutionary Impact of Large-scale Industry on
             Manufacture, Handicrafts and on the Division of Labor
Section 9:   The Health and Education Clauses of the Factory
             Acts. The General Extension of Factory Legislation in
             England
Section 10: Large-scale Industry and Agriculture

Preliminary Commentary

Because we are still very much in the age of modern industry and so much of our lives involve one kind of machinery or another, this very long chapter treats phenomena of continuing importance. The machines Marx analyzes here are primarily those in the factories of his day; yet his understanding of "automatic systems of machines" applies as much today, in the age of robotization and "smart machines," as it did in the mid-nineteenth century. Perhaps the biggest difference between then and now has been the proliferation of machines beyond the factory, into the organization of our daily lives. Remember intercity railroads were just being built when he was writing. Horse-drawn vehicles had yet to be replaced by automobiles and trucks. Sailing ships had only recently begun to be replaced by steam-driven ships. Faraday's method of generating electricity only became commercial in 1870, three years after Volume I of *Capital* was published. Most of the machinery commonly found in today's homes and schools had yet to be invented. Indeed, although we speak easily of washing or drying "machines," we are less inclined to place the televisions we watch or the computers, tablets and smart phones we work and play with in the same category. Nevertheless, just as capitalists learned how machines could be used to regulate the rhythm of work on the factory floor, so too have they learned how to use these other machines to regulate the rhythm of our lives.

Section 1: The Development of Machinery

Outline of Marx's Analysis

Mill: machines have not lightened toil
Marx: machines are the means for producing relative surplus-value

Rise of machinery = conversion of tools into machines
Machines are:
  – complex tools driven by natural force
  – motor mechanism + transmitting mechanism + tool
  – tools have become implements of a mechanism
  – mechanisms:
    – perform with their tools the same operations as workers
      formerly did with similar tools
    – soon become elements in a complex system of machinery
Complex systems of machinery:
  – simple cooperation of similar machines
    – "a connected series of graduated processes carried out by a
      chain of mutually complementary machines of various kinds"
    – "the cooperation by division of labor which is peculiar to
      manufacture, but now it appears as a combination of machines
      with specific functions"
  – fixed proportions established by their capacities, numbers, speed
  – "collective working machine" = "articulated system"
  – "constitutes itself a vast automaton"
    – automatic system of machinery when the machines "elaborate
      the raw material, without workers' help, and need only supple-
      mentary assistance from workers"
    – "a mechanical monster"
  – development in one sector led to development in connected spheres
    – large-scale industry required to produce machines, i.e.,
      machines built by machines
  – replacement of the worker-subject by an "objective organization"
  – organization of machinery technically requires cooperation of
    labor

Commentary

An opening quote by John Stuart Mill (1806–73) sets the tone of much of this chapter. Machines, he wrote, have not "lightened the day's toil of any human being."[56] Marx's analysis shows why: machinery is not introduced by capitalists to lighten toil but to increase work and relative surplus-value. In this way, he introduces a fundamental paradox of the capitalist age, that

---

56. *Capital, Vol. I*, p. 492.

the ever-increasing number of machines that reduce the human effort required to produce a given product results in more work rather than less.

He begins by pointing out how machines accomplish the same tasks as those previously carried out by workers. They substitute both non-human for human energy and mechanical contrivances for the various gestures and operations previously carried out by workers with their tools. He traces the development of machines from relatively simple substitutes for particular operations to complex systems of machinery. The story is always the same: human-built machines accomplish that same transformation of non-human nature that he identified in Chapter 7 as the character of human work. Thus, particular machines replace particular workers and systems of machines replace large numbers of cooperating workers. In the place of the cooperation of humans, we have the cooperation of machines.[57] As this replacement progresses, some humans are rendered redundant and expelled from production and others are reduced to being mere tenders of machines.

While Marx's analysis is clearly focused on the factories of nineteenth-century British industry, bringing his analysis up to date requires its application to the world outside the factory that has also been transformed by the proliferation of machines. Increasingly throughout the twentieth century, machines were developed not merely as mechanisms of production but also as elements of consumption. To some degree, Marx anticipates this when he notes:

> But as well as this, the revolution in the modes of production of industry and agriculture made necessary a revolution in the general conditions of the social process of production, i.e., in the means of communication and transport... Hence quite apart from the immense transformation which took place in shipbuilding, the means of communication and transport gradually adapted themselves to the mode of production of large-scale industry by means of a system of river steamers, railways, ocean steamers and telegraphs.[58]

These "adaptations" to the rise of machine systems in factories carried those systems into the extra-factory world of everyday life. Moreover, ocean steamers and railways are not only adjuncts to production but, as Marx notes in Part One of Volume II of *Capital*, they are systems of production themselves, providing the service of transporting raw materials, labor and final

---

57. Although speaking of the cooperation of machines draws a parallel with cooperation among humans, machines have no will—to either cooperate or compete—therefore, the expression merely evokes how machines are organized to form complex systems.

58. *Capital, Vol. I*, pp. 505–506.

goods. To the degree that they serve to transport workers to and from jobs, whether close by (think commuter rail) or distant (the travel of immigrant workers), they play a role in the reproduction of labor-power. Moreover, to varying degrees, they also produce a personal consumption good: the service of transportation for travelers of all sorts, including tourists. In these various roles, these modes of transport become terrains and vehicles of struggle and self-valorization. To his examples, we can add the twentieth-century proliferation of automobiles, trucks, airplanes, telephone, radio and television and computer networks. Just as Marx studied the implications of this transformation for our understanding of the dynamics of exploitation and class struggle in the factory, so can we study the implications for this wider proliferation for our struggles and our desires.

Marx's analysis provides a methodological point of departure for querying the nature and meaning of machine technology wherever we find it, whether in factories, on roads or rails, in the air, at sea, or in homes and schools. Let's look briefly at these last two domains.

The introduction of machines into homes, beginning in the nineteenth and accelerating in the twentieth century, was largely driven by the resistance of housewives to the drudgery of the housework imposed upon them by a capitalism that had turned the patriarchal gender hierarchy it inherited to its own advantage. Housewives, with help from children, did the vast majority of the unwaged work of reproducing labor-power. Besides direct resistance—withholding time and energy from household tasks—housewives also fought to divert family income to market demand for labor-saving devices. On the supply side, their efforts were complemented by the advertising campaigns of consumer goods industries.[59] One example, among many, was the introduction of machines for the washing and drying of fabrics. Like the industrial machines that Marx discusses, washers and driers substitute mechanisms for human hands, attention and energy. Handwashing in a tub with a rub board, passing the washed materials through a clothes wringer (if available) and then drying clothes and linens on lines requires long, hard physical labor, whether in a commercial establishment or in the home.[60] Along with the washing itself, a stove

---

59. For an illustrated introduction to housework and the new machines introduced in the US in the nineteenth and twentieth centuries, see Harvey Green, *The Light of the Home: An Intimate View of the lives of Women in Victorian America*, New York: Pantheon Books, 1983, especially Chapter 3, "Cleanliness and Godliness: The Tyranny of Housework."

60. While in India in 1976, I observed women washing their clothes in irrigation ditches. No tub, no rub boards, no mechanical wringers, only their hands, to scrub, beat on rocks and wring. Such methods are common among peasants throughout the Global South.

had to be used to heat water for the tub, first for washing, then for rinsing. Early washing machines—washtubs on stands with a flywheel-driven set of beaters—reduced that labor somewhat; later versions reduced it more (with hot water piped from a heater and automatic shifts through washing and spinning cycles). Drying machines eliminated the work of carrying wet cloth to clothes lines, pinning them up and taking them down.[61]

Sometimes used in capitalist enterprise, laundromats or commercial linen cleaning businesses servicing hotels, hospitals, and so on, washers and dryers have also become a common fixture in most middle-income households. Technically the role is the same, but socially and politically it is quite different. In the business enterprise, the machine substitutes for waged labor and allows managers to process more fabric (clothes, linen, etc.) while reducing reliance on workers. In the home, the washing machine allows the unwaged houseworker (mostly housewives) to accomplish the same tasks of cleaning but in much less time and with much less effort. Whereas, as we will see in Section 5 below, the threat of unemployment often led waged workers to resist and attack machines, unwaged housewives have more commonly fought for them, because of the hoped-for reduction in their workloads. Except for upper middle-class homes, where it might result in fewer domestic servants, the purchase of such machines doesn't result in the displacement of workers typical of industry.[62] Such expenditure, diverting the wage in a direction that benefits unwaged housewives much more than waged husbands, has both reflected and contributed to a shift in burdens of work and power. As such, the proliferation of such labor-savings devices in the twentieth century was certainly, at least in part, a reflection of the growing power of women to escape servitude and improve their lives vis-à-vis men.

Unfortunately, another parallel between the capitalist use of the machine in the factory and the housewife's use of such machines in the home concerns the actual impact on work time. Just as in industry, where capitalists have sought to manipulate the use of machines to increase work, so too have the dynamics of capitalist intervention in the home tended to increase the very work whose reduction has been made possible by such machines. How? First, through both commercial advertising and through advice columns in newspapers and women's magazines, the peddlers of both washing machines and their associated products, e.g., soaps, detergents,

---

61. The electric iron complemented these machines by reducing the labor, not of ironing per se, but of repeatedly maintaining the stove which heated a typical assortment of pre-electric flatirons.

62. The ready availability of such labor-saving devices may also reduce marriage and birth rates of those who feel less need of a spouse or child as domestic workers.

starch and fabric softeners, have jacked up expectations and standards of acceptable levels of "cleanliness" in order to generate much more frequent washing than ever before. Advertisements, condemning "ring around the collar" that might offend employers or draw visiting mother-in-law condemnation, spur housewives to more frequent and more thorough cleaning. Despite these "labor-saving" devices, there is some evidence that in many families the total amount of housework has not been reduced by the introduction of such machines—and thus, to the degree that is so, their potential for liberation from work has not been realized.[63]

Turning briefly to schools, another domain of the work of producing labor-power, we find similar patterns of potential labor-saving offset by increased demands. In many courses requiring mathematical calculations, pen-and-paper figuring was first replaced by calculators and then by computers, dramatically reducing the time and energy required for any one calculation. Instead of reducing work, however, teachers and professors have generally multiplied their demands for such calculations. Whereas one linear regression, laboriously calculated by hand, once sufficed to demonstrate competence, now large numbers are required in repetitive homework. In courses requiring research papers, a few references dug out of card catalogs and the stacks of libraries sufficed to demonstrate effort, knowledge and method; today, the Internet and the digitization of library materials not only makes possible but raises expectations of much more thoroughly researched essays. In every case where papers must be turned in, the advent and availability of first typewriters and then word processing programs with spell-checking sub-routines has led to the refusal of hand-written copy and the demand for neat, typed or printed copy. Thus, as in industry and the home, the time and energy savings made possible by the availability of machines to students have been offset by greater demands on work to be performed.

That said, in schools as in factories, the use of machines to impose more work has been met by resistance. Old methods of refusal have adapted: students who may once have explained the absence of a paper by "my dog ate it" have learned to claim, "my hard disk crashed!" While the Internet provides access to a vast knowledge-commons, it also opens doors to online alternatives to unrewarding homework, e.g., access to others' papers that can be altered and handed in, or to others' hired labor at pay-per-page rates. The introduction of machines alters the composition of class relationships, but it does not overcome the alienations involved.

---

63.   See Ruth Schwartz Cowan, *More Work for Mother: The Ironies of Household Technology from the Open Hearth to the Microwave*, 2nd edn., New York: Basic Books, 1985.

Section 2: The Value Transferred by the Machinery to the Product

---

Outline of Marx's Analysis

Natural forces cost capital nothing, but their exploitation through machinery requires investment

Machinery:
- – enters useful labor wholly, the whole machine is engaged
- – enters valorization bit by bit, adds what it loses by depreciation
- – so, the more labor required to produce the machine and the quicker it is used up, the greater the contribution of the labor that built the machine to the value of the final product
- – as the mass of machinery per worker grows, so does c/v, the ratio of the value embodied in machinery (+ raw materials + intermediate goods) to the value of labor-power

Condition for introduction of machinery: lower cost relative to labor

Therefore: in general,
- – the lower the wage, the less incentive for the introduction of machines
- – low wages = "squandering of human labor-power for despicable purposes"

Commentary

There are two basic messages in this section. The first is the same as that of Chapter 8 on constant and variable capital. The second concerns the conditions determining capitalist decisions whether to invest in machines. Also evoked in his analysis of machinery are the roles of science and technology in their creation.

As stated in Chapter 8, machinery contributes to the value of the final product only the value created in the manufacture of the machine itself. The SNLT that goes into the creation of a machine fixes its potential contribution to the value of the products produced with it. The contribution *per unit* of product, therefore, depends on the amount produced. The greater the total product, the less contribution per unit. So, the longer a machine lasts and the more it produces, *ceteris paribus*, the smaller the role of the original labor that produced the machine plays in the creation of each final product.

The second message concerns the impact of the relative costs of labor and machines on the decisions about how much of either to buy and deploy in production. Put succinctly, the more expensive labor-power becomes, relative to the cost of machinery, the greater the incentive to introduce machinery, especially machinery that substitutes for or displaces workers. Inversely, the lower the wage, the less incentive for investment in machines. Therefore, the tendency of capitalists to hold down wages tends to undermine the incentive to invest in productivity-raising machines and the greater the success of workers at raising wages, the greater the likelihood that capitalists will decide to substitute machinery for workers.

In modern neoclassical microeconomics, the analysis of these relationships is formulated in terms of mathematical production and cost functions, but lead to the same conclusions. Assuming that capitalists desire to maximize their profits, they will utilize each input (labor or machines) up to the point at which the value of its marginal product equals its price. So, if the price of labor rises, then capitalists can increase their profits by introducing machinery that shifts the production function and raises the marginal product of labor. With the cost of labor-power, like the length of the working day, determined by workers struggles, both theoretical formulations show how successful struggles by workers can spur investment in machinery and capitalist development. Inversely, capitalist success at holding down wages, while allowing greater profits in the short run, undermines development in the long run by discouraging investment in new technologies.[64]

There are two essential ingredients in the creation of machines and in their functioning, which deserve more comment than Marx gives them in this section: "natural forces" and "science." For Marx, "natural forces" include both non-human forces like water, steam, etc. and human forces like "the productive forces resulting from cooperation." Although he doesn't define "science," it is certainly one of the elements of human cooperation. Science has developed as a collective way of thinking about and interacting with the world through the interconnected activities of vast numbers of people. Instead of writing, as he does in footnote 23 that "'Alien' science is incorporated by capital just as 'alien' labor is," Marx would have been more accurate if he wrote of science "as one aspect of 'alien' labor." For what is science if not the collective development and elaboration of just that thinking "will" which Marx defined in Chapter 7 as making the worst of architects better than the best of bees?

As with science, so too with "technology," traditionally defined as the "application of science to industry." In footnote 4 of the previous section, Marx noted that "a critical history of technology would show how little any of the inventions of the eighteenth century are the work of a single

---

64. NB: this argument is quite distinct from the Keynesian macroeconomic argument that high wages increase the demand for final goods, spurring investment, while low wages that limit consumption demand undermines investment and growth.

individual."[65] With this he was insisting on the collective character of technological change. As with science, working out its application usually involves many individuals and groups across space and time. The contributions of individuals are often critical, but they are always building on the work of others before them and alongside them. They "invent" in response to perceived real problems, generally having considerable experience and related materials close at hand.

Unfortunately, the voluminous history of scientific and technological development written since Marx's time remains unknown to most people. Instead, popular ideas are often derived from 1) science fiction literature and films dominated by images of isolated "mad scientists" and 2) history textbooks that highlight the contributions of individuals without contextualizing them.

In the literature of science fiction, classic examples include Jules Verne's *Twenty Thousand Leagues Under the Sea* (1870) and H. G. Wells's *The Time Machine* (1895). In both cases, isolated individuals (Captain Nemo and The Time Traveler) invent and create in isolation. This same portrayal persisted in films based on these books. The hugely popular film *Back to the Future* (1985) and its sequels have continued this misrepresentation of scientific research, creation and invention, in the person of Dr. Emmett Brown. So too has the more recent film *Iron Man* (2008) and its sequels, in which the lead character develops his superhero technology in isolation, first in a cave, then in an industrial laboratory.

In the 1950s as the centrality of science and technology to industrial development (via productivity increases and relative surplus-value) became preoccupations of policymakers, the negative public perception of scientists came to be perceived as a problem. In an era when Sputnik and aggregate production functions dictated increased investment in human capital and the expansion of science curriculum in public schools, efforts were made to change both popular images and the habits of scientists who wrote only for each other in technical and mathematical jargon indecipherable by the public. One result has been the emergence of scientists able to write for the public at large, e.g., Carl Sagan (1934–96) who produced the 1980 television documentary series *Cosmos: A Personal Voyage* and wrote the hard-science fiction book *Contact* (1985), later turned into a film (1997) staring Jodi Foster as a SETI (search for extraterrestrial intelligence) scientist.[66] In that film, and in more recent ones, such as *Hidden Figures* (2016)

65.   *Capital, Vol. I*, p. 493.
66.   *Cosmos: A Personal Voyage*, Carl Sagan (dir.), KCET TV, Carl Sagan Productions/ BBC, 1980; Carl Sagan, *Contact*, New York: Simon & Schuster, 1985; *Contact*, Robert Zemeckis (dir.), Warner Bros., 1997.

based on the non-fiction book by Margo Shetterly about NASA mathematicians, creative scientists have been more realistically portrayed as members of a community of collaborating (and sometimes competing) researchers.[67]

In the case of school textbooks, it is common at the elementary and secondary level to teach children about "great inventors" and their inventions in ways which totally abstract from the socio-historical contexts within which they worked. School books make names such as Edison, Einstein or Hawking familiar, without providing the history of developments in their fields upon which they drew. Institutions such as the Royal Swedish Academy of Sciences that awards the Nobel Prize in Physics, Chemistry and Economics to individuals reinforce this tendency. The purpose is undoubtedly ideological, reinforcing bourgeois individualism and encouraging competition (that pits scientists against each other), and pedagogical: you, the individual child, can hope to achieve great things. But the method obfuscates any real understanding of how invention and technological change arise out of collective endeavors. It transforms the "inventors" into magicians and their creativity into a totally magical art. Well-meaning teachers who pressure every student to be an "inventor" through obligatory and competitive "invention fairs" complete the alienation from collective creativity by asking children to "invent" in isolation from the normal social contexts and processes in which real invention takes place. Under these circumstances, most of the children have nothing substantial to suggest and wind up feeling silly and inadequate in comparison with the inventors and inventions they are given as role models.[68] The result is the opposite of that intended: an alienation from imagination of those who cannot understand that their lack of ideas derives from a social rather than an individual failing.

At the university level, students majoring in science and technology are introduced to a more realistic understanding of how their field develops, directly in laboratories and indirectly, through literature—often authored by many individuals—that reveals research conclusions to be the result of team efforts. The more familiar students become with the field and the

67. *Hidden Figures*, Theodore Melfi (dir.), Fox 2000 Pictures, 2016. Margo Shetterly, *Hidden Figures: The American Dream and the Untold Story of the Black Women Mathematicians Who Helped Win the Space Race*, New York: William Morrow, 2016.
68. It is not just children who may be disillusioned. There is a recent (2017) TV commercial for General Electric in which a young girl is portrayed as an inventor who begins by creating gadgets to solve problems of housework and schoolwork and who winds up reprogramming robots to increase productivity in the production of jet engines. Although a welcome portrayal of the potential of girls and women in science and technology, at least one father I know reacted by exclaiming, "What's wrong with my kids?! Why aren't they inventing things like that?!"

literature, the clearer it becomes that they must learn to work within a globe-girdling network, some of which is private, some of which is public. For those who become professional researchers, they also learn something about the various political factors determining the size and direction of flows of funding. Unfortunately, their understanding is too often limited by partisan politics and fails to either recognize or confront the class dynamics at work.

What is missing from Marx's mentions of science and technology, not only here but elsewhere in *Capital*, is any analysis of the division of labor and the dynamics of investment in science and technology on a par with his analysis of these things in industrial production. The increasing role of relative surplus-value strategies by capitalists for dealing with workers has, of course, driven a parallel and necessary preoccupation with investment in research and development, not only on the part of corporations but on the part of government as the result of corporate lobbying to tap tax revenue to fund research to subsidize their own efforts. Thus, in the US such institutions as the National Science Foundation (NSF), the National Institute of Health (NIH) and the Department of Defense (DoD) channel billions of tax dollars into research whose direct beneficiaries are corporations, subsidizing either their efforts to develop new production technologies useful for dealing with workers or to develop new products that can be sold for a profit. In short, STEM (Science, Technology, Engineering and Mathematics) are not just academic disciplines but domains of production where Marx's methodology can be, indeed must be, applied.

Section 3: The Most Immediate Effects of Machine Production on the Worker

---

Outline of Marx's Analysis

(a) Machinery draws in women and children
  – by reducing the need for muscle power, machinery makes it possible to employ less muscular women and children to "break" the resistance of male workers
  – so, the whole family enters the factory
  – this reduces time for housework, time for play
  – less time to cook, to care for infants, to sew; thus, the need to buy substitute commodities
  – less time for children to learn these domestic skills
  – male labor devalorized, family wage spread across earnings of all family members ▶

- $M - LP$ less free, as parents forced by low wages to sell children's labor-power $\approx$ slavery
- devastating impact on children's health
- "thrown into a situation physically and morally polluted"
- high infant death rates
- insufficient nourishment, dosing with opiates
- intentional starving and poisoning
- "intellectual degeneration," unenforced or subverted laws mandating schooling
- some "schools" were not really schools at all
- overcrowded, too few teachers, too few materials
- close, noisome atmosphere

(b) Machinery prolongs the working day
- machinery as "perpetual motion," limited only by worker endurance and resistance
- use of women and children lessens resistance of class as a whole
- increased working day means more rapid turnover of machinery, more surplus-value
- increasing the length of working day reduces marginal costs fixed in machinery
- this is of increasing importance as c/v rises
- monopoly introduction of machinery by individual capital lowers costs and gives increased surplus-value
- contradiction: increase in c displaces v and potential for v
- displacement of v by c offsets rise in s/v and creates pressure for capitalists to compensate for loss in relative surplus-value by increasing working day and absolute surplus-value
- displacement of v produces "a surplus working population"
- by "revolutionizing" "the mode of labor as well as the social organism" machinery breaks the resistance of workers

Paradox: most powerful instrument for reducing work increases it instead—so much for the dreams of Aristotle, Antipater and Stolberg

(c) Machinery intensifies labor
- limitation of length of working day leads to increased use of machinery
- to increase the intensity of labor and thus surplus-value
- intensification via "heightened tension of labor-power"

▶

- intensification via "a closer filling up of the pores of the working day"
- labor-time now "acquires a measure of its intensity, or degree of density"
- intensification achieved via piece wages
- shortening of labor time makes increased intensity possible— "subjective condition"
- intensification achieved via speed-up of machines
- intensification achieved via having one worker tend more machines, e.g., cotton looms
- intensification undermines workers' health, e.g., exhaustion, lung disease
- intensification leads to further struggle for shortening of working day, e.g., eight-hours movement

Commentary

The Great Paradox

The "most immediate effects of machinery on the worker" which Marx describes here are all negative: the introduction of machinery is used by capital to impose work on women and children, to prolong the working day and to intensify labor. The great paradox which Marx sees in the capitalist use of machinery appears fully elaborated here: the machine reduces the need for muscle power—which should lighten labor—but draws in and exhausts women and children; the machine makes it possible to produce more in a shorter period—which should lighten labor—but it is used instead to prolong it; the machine which allows one to accomplish the work of many faster than ever—which should lighten labor—is used to make the one work at an exhaustingly rapid pace. Thus, at the end of section (b) he writes:

> Hence too the economic paradox that the most powerful instrument for reducing labor-time suffers a dialectical inversion and becomes the most unfailing means for turning the whole lifetime of the worker and his family into labor-time at capital's disposal for its own valorization.[69]

In quoting from Aristotle's *Politics* and the poetry of Antipater and Stolberg, Marx is showing how this capitalist use of the machine amounts

---

69. *Capital, Vol. I*, p. 532.

to a betrayal of the dreams and hopes of humanity. From time immemorial, humans have sought to use their intelligence and imagination not only to improve their world but to reduce their drudgery and free themselves for new and more diverse pursuits. In some ways, as Marx and Engels argued in the *Communist Manifesto*, capitalism liberates the possibilities for such developments by destroying many traditional barriers to innovation and change. But even in its historically unprecedented flexibility, capitalism imposes new barriers—especially the endlessness of work.

The Historical Relation Between Absolute and Relative Surplus-Value

Although, as this chapter makes clear, absolute and relative surplus-value often coexist as capitalist strategies, Marx nevertheless suggests a fundamental historical linkage between the two approaches. During the period of the "formal" subordination of labor to capital, before there is any capitalist modification of the labor process, absolute surplus-value dominates, i.e., the main way capitalists seek to extract more surplus labor is through making workers work longer. But eventually workers' resistance to absolute surplus-value forces capital to shift its emphasis to relative surplus-value:

> As soon as the gradual upsurge of working-class revolt had compelled Parliament compulsorily to shorten the hours of labor, and to begin by imposing a normal working day on factories properly so called, i.e., from the moment that it was made impossible once and for all to increase the production of surplus-value by prolonging the working day, capital threw itself with all its might, and in full awareness of the situation, into the production of relative surplus-value, by speeding up the development of the machine system.[70]

> Capital's tendency, as soon as a prolongation of the hours of labor is once and for all forbidden, is to compensate for this by systematically raising the intensity of labor and converting every improvement in machinery into a more perfect means for soaking up labor-power.[71]

It is not an exaggeration, therefore, to argue that throughout the last 150 years, as the working class has been on the offensive attacking absolute surplus-value by reducing the amount of official waged work time, capital has come increasingly to depend upon relative surplus-value strategies for its survival and expansion. Indeed, with the development of the Keynesian state in the period following the Great Depression of the 1930s, capital

---

70. Ibid., pp. 533–534.
71. Ibid., p. 542.

sought the institutionalization of relative surplus-value through a variety of productivity deals, formal and informal, that linked rising wages and profits to rising productivity. By creating an institutional framework within which workers' struggles for less work and more pay could be paid for by increased investment and rising productivity, relative surplus-value became systematized as a key component of capitalist strategy and growth. This formalization can be seen partly in collective bargaining and industrial union contracts and partly in the tax and investment policies of the state that has quite consciously fostered technological change with the object of achieving steady growth in productivity. While such policies have consistently favored investment in new and better capital equipment in private industry, they have also expanded investment in science and technology outside the factory both through research and development programs and through human capital investment in education. The contemporary preoccupation with "high-tech" industrialization is only the latest phase in a long history of relative surplus-value strategies.

Machinery and Life Outside the Factory

Although, as we have seen, Marx spends little time in *Capital* analyzing life outside the factory, his discussion of the ways in which the development of machinery allows the capitalist to draw women and children into production leads him to a recognition of the interrelatedness of waged and unwaged work. Factory inspector reports and other sources indicate how time and energy spent by women and children on the waged job dramatically reduces the time and energy available for both the work of reproduction and life more generally. He cites evidence of high infant mortality rates resulting from the neglect or mistreatment of the young by women whose time is eaten up by the factory.[72] He notes how women working long hours cannot keep up with their traditional domestic tasks and young girls forced to work for wages never even learn the skills necessary. As a result, domestic work (e.g., sewing and mending) does not get done and working-class families either go without or are forced to purchase commodities to replace what they might have produced themselves at home

---

72. At this point in the text, Marx's focus is on women and children. But it should be obvious that the long hours and exhausting expenditure of energy required of men also played hob with the relations among fathers, mothers and children. The brutality and violence of the factory has often been brought home. Listen, for example, to the song "Factory" by Bruce Springsteen and note the lines "Dad comes through the gates with death in his eyes, somebody's gonna get hurt tonight." Both blue- and white-collar workers may bring home either physical or psychological brutality transferring their frustration, anger or depression to their spouses and children.

(e.g., new clothes), thus reducing their real disposable income. Evidence from nineteenth-century periods of crisis and high female unemployment when family health improved because of increased time at home resembles contemporary experience in the Global South. There a fall in agricultural export prices sometimes leads to improved peasant health as family effort is redirected from export to subsistence crop production.

More generally, Marx's analysis draws our attention to the close connection between the waged work of production and the unwaged work of reproduction. In the early twentieth century, as restrictions on women's and children's wage labor led to the emergence of the modern nuclear family and the public-school system, early scattered efforts to give waged working-class children some education—that Marx critiques in this chapter—became a much more generalized effort to re-incarcerate, control and discipline all children. Over the last 40 years, as women have re-entered the waged labor market in large and growing numbers, both families and social policymakers have, once again, been concerned with the impact on family life and reproduction. The substitution of collective day-care for parental care, the phenomenon of latch-key children, rising divorce rates and child abuse have all become widely discussed and hotly debated issues. Positions have ranged from feminist and gay efforts to create (and demand the social acceptance of) a wider range of what are considered "healthy" family structures, to conservative attempts to reimpose the rapidly disappearing nuclear family by making alternatives illegal or socially unacceptable. In short, the development of these debates has forced recognition of the very interrelatedness that Marx emphasized back in the 1860s.

As mentioned in the commentary on Section 1 above, machines, and the subordination of life to them, has become omnipresent in the social factory. Besides the domain of housework and schoolwork, already discussed, machines have also been used to organize the time of recreation such that it becomes the re-creation of labor-power. Probably one of the most widely commented examples of this is television, which has generally been portrayed as a device whose entertainment reduces the worker to a passive witness to an ever-changing spectacle. This interpretation has been an application of the analysis of the Frankfort School whose theorists elaborated a critique of traditional "culture" as dividing the population into an active minority—those who perform—and a passive majority—those who witness.

A more recent example of this kind of subordination, only slightly less passive, are computer games demanding only hand–eye motor responses, yet proving, for some, most addictive. The song, "Machines" by City Boy reproduces and comments on such addiction in the case of arcade games. "It's a world of its own / You don't see a thing as the crowd gathers round /

They call out your name but you don't hear a sound / Give me a quarter, a kroner, a yen / We all wind up wasted so try it again." A visit to the arcade centers of any shopping mall will provide opportunities to witness the kind of manic, obsessive behavior critiqued in the song. As computer games moved from arcades into the home on personal computers and video game consoles, more interactive software and increased complexity have widened the possibilities of self-activity. Mere eye–hand coordination games still exist, e.g., virtually all "first person shooter" games. But also available are a wide variety of both stand-alone and online games that require strategic thinking, often in collaboration with other players. Played alone, eye–hand coordination games have an attraction similar to some sports, without the risk of humiliation in failure. They also provide the opportunity for a kind of cathartic release of tension, and perhaps aggression in a harmless manner. On the other hand, players are jumping hoops designed by an unknown programmer rather than crafting their own world, so the games recreate life as experienced by those who believe themselves helpless to change it.

More interesting are the myriad role-playing games that test one's cleverness, wit and imagination. How the appeal of these games differs fundamentally from arcade games has been evident in the spread of do-it-yourself programs with which those without programming skills can nonetheless craft their own worlds to play in. In some cases, the crafting involves marginal changes in the game world; in other cases, as with *Civilization* or *Minecraft*, entire worlds can be dreamed up and created from scratch. At that point, the machines begin to be more like tools in the hands of workers—the kind of thing Marx talks about when discussing handicrafts—rather than machines into which the players merely fit like cogs in a predesigned system. These new forms of "recreation" are created by a huge and growing industry and deserve analysis using the theoretical tools of *Capital* for thinking about the roles the industry and the games play, or can play, in the organization of our lives. An excellent example of such analysis can be found in the book *Games of Empire* (2009) by Nick Dyer-Witheford and Greig de Peuter.[73] The two authors take on not only the impact of these machine-games but analyze the industries of which they are an integral part, revealing their costs to workers, consumers and the environment, as well as their potential as terrains of resistance.

Machinery and Child Labor

Most striking in Marx's survey of the impact of machinery on the family are his descriptions of the virtual slave trade in children whose subjection

---

73. Nick Dyer-Witheford and Greig de Peuter, *Games of Empire: Global Capitalism and Video Games*, Minneapolis: University of Minnesota Press, 2009.

to factory work wipes out today's play and tomorrow's prospects. Both capitalists who want children's labor-power and parents who need the children's wages participate in this trade. Once adult workers succeeded in imposing legal restrictions on the use of young children, both capitalists and some parents would seek to slip underage children past the factory inspectors, each for their own reasons: of exploitation and of survival. In Mary Barton, Elizabeth Gaskell gives voice to one such parent, a mother whose husband has died of starvation and fever and who desperately needs the income of one of her children:

> I'm sure, John Barton, if yo are taking messages to the parliament folk, yo'll not object to telling 'em what a sore trial it is, this law of theirs, keeping children fra' factory work, . . . I han gotten no money to send him t' school, as I would like; and there he is, rampaging about th' streets a' day. . . and th' inspector won't let him in to work in the factory, because he's not right age. . .[74]

Unfortunately, as I have pointed out elsewhere, neither such needs nor such practices have disappeared since Marx was writing. From agribusiness fields through carpet factories to brothels, children are still being sold into virtual or out-and-out slavery by poor parents and are still put to work, often under the vilest of conditions, by capitalists greedy to suck every drop of profit from their veins.

Intensity of Labor

By addressing changes in the intensity of labor, Marx adds a whole new dimension to his analysis, not only of surplus-value but of value itself. Throughout the book, right up to this chapter, he has always held the intensity of work constant. In the discussion of absolute surplus-value, both intensity and productivity were held constant. Then in Chapters 12–14 on relative surplus-value he analyzed the impact of changes in productivity while holding the length of the working day and intensity constant. But in subsection (c) of Section 3 he discusses the implications of changes in intensity. These changes are introduced at this point because they are intimately related to the use of machinery in modern industry. As he shows through many examples, capitalists introduce machinery not only to raise productivity (output per input of labor) but also to increase work. Machines set the rhythm of work, so by speeding them up the capitalists can force

---

74.   Elizabeth Gaskell, *Mary Barton* (1848), London: Penguin Classics, 1988, Chapter 8, p. 129.

the workers who work with them to work faster, and thus harder (and sometimes longer). With machines running continuously, workers find it difficult to create "pores" of free time in the working day.

Under these circumstances, Marx notes "a change took place in the nature of relative surplus-value."[75] Not only are the capitalists getting more surplus-value from increased productivity, but they are also getting more work, more value and surplus-value, in a given work time. This raises an interesting theoretical question. Why does Marx treat increasing intensity as a form of *relative* surplus-value rather than *absolute* surplus-value? After all, working *faster* would seem to be analogous to working *longer* because in both cases capital is extracting more work (rather than just getting a larger share as has been the point of relative surplus-value). How does working faster produce more surplus-value?

Suppose in the aggregate speed-up results in workers working twice as hard and producing twice as much output in a given time. Assuming as Marx does that the value of labor-power hovers around that amount of SNLT required to produce the means of subsistence, then it will be possible to reproduce labor-power with only half the work time as before. The value of labor-power will remain the same, the real consumption of the workers will remain the same, but the capitalists will now arrogate to themselves more of the output and labor time, both in physical and value terms. To illustrate:

At time t_1 assume total output = 100 units (u), V = 50u, S = 50u, V = 4hrs, S = 4hrs (in an 8-hr day), so S/V = 1
At time t_2 let output double = 200 units, but if V = 50u, then S = 150u.
Assuming working twice as fast is the equivalent of working twice as long (16 hrs instead of 8 hrs), and V remains = 4hrs, then S = 12hrs = 16 − 4, so S/V = 12/4 = 3.

So, doubling the intensity of labor has reduced the *relative* value of labor-power while increasing the *relative* amount of surplus-value, a result analogous to what happens when productivity is raised and intensity is constant. This would seem to be why Marx treats the strategy of increasing intensity as a component of the strategy of relative surplus-value instead of absolute surplus-value in which workers work longer.

Marx describes rising intensity as a "heightened tension of labor-power" because workers work more intently, more focused, both physically and consciously on their tasks. In the case of Jack London's Johnny, cited previously, such tension was mainly corporeal as his total focus on his stopper-tying

---

75. *Capital, Vol. I*, p. 534.

reduced his thinking toward zero. In other jobs that necessarily involve calculation, judgment and even the engagement of individuals' personalities, the strain can be more intellectual and emotional than muscular. Today, we are more likely to speak of this in terms of "stress"—the increased nervous tension and emotional drain that comes with high-pressure, intense labor in both factory and office. As in the case of Johnny, or say agricultural workers forced to use short-handled hoes, it is obvious how physical speed-up can lead to physical breakdown. It has also become increasingly clear how psychological stress can lead to psychological breakdown. Moreover, recent research has made the connections between both kinds of stress more apparent. Physical stress can lead to psychological collapse. In Chaplin's *Modern Times*, speeded-up assembly-line work leads Charlie to a nervous breakdown and hospitalization. We also know that psychological stress can lead to physical breakdown, e.g., heart disease and heart attacks.

As capital has penetrated and manipulated the world outside the official workplace, subjecting all of life to the ever-faster rhythm of machine-paced existence—from increased pressure in school for both grades and rapid progress towards program completion, through the commuter freeway to the rapid-fire sensory barrage of television and other forms of "entertainment," including social media—the physical and psychological stresses of the factory have become commonplace throughout the social factory. This phenomenon, whether acknowledged as an element of the capitalist organization of society or not, has been increasingly recognized as constituting pathological conditions by both medical and social critics. From epidemiologists who have come to recognize the connections between stress and disease to psychologists, psychotherapists, psychoanalysts and new age healers of various sorts whose professions have expanded rapidly in response to the demands of overworked, overstressed workers, housewives and students, this recognition has spread in these last decades.

Working-Class Response

Marx highlights two kinds of working-class response to the pressures and injuries caused by the ever-increasing subordination of life to machinery: one is objective: the exhaustion and using up of people's lives; the other is subjective: revolt. "There cannot be the slightest doubt," he writes at the end of the section, "that this process [increasingly intensity] must soon lead once again to a critical point at which a further reduction in the hours of labor will be inevitable."[76] And in footnote 95, he adds: "Agitation for a working day of 8 hours has now (1867) begun in Lancashire among the

76. *Capital, Vol. I,* p. 542.

factory workers."[77] In other words, faced with a speed-up they cannot stop, workers fight for fewer hours.

But this is not the only kind of resistance workers have posed to such speed-up. Far more common has been the day-to-day sabotage of speed-up and periodical revolts that have taken the form of official and wildcat strikes to stop or reverse the process. Remember the excerpt from "Counter-planning on the Shop-floor" by Bill Watson that described how workers organized rod-blowing contests and water fights in auto plants to fight the endless pressure of the assembly line.[78] In *Modern Times*, when Charlie flips out in response to repeated speed-up he does not just walk away, he disrupts the line, squirting oil in the faces of other workers and sabotages the machinery. Today it is not uncommon to read about stressed-out individuals returning to their places of "employment" and shooting bosses and even fellow workers—whether the job place be a post office, a factory, an office or a school.[79]

Resistance can be individual or collective and the latter is usually more effective. The isolated individual worker who tries to sabotage speed-up has a real problem in a collective work situation and may be caught and fired, or, frustrated with lesser efforts, flip out and take ultimately self-destructive action, such as shooting the boss, or drugs, or self. Collective action on the other hand is often highly effective. In the case of sabotage, it is harder for bosses to identify those responsible as workers shield and protect each other. In the case of more formal protest, strikes and wildcat strikes, workers can and have been successful at rolling back speed-ups and at imposing work rules which make such intensification harder to implement. As in the case Marx cites—the struggle for the eight-hour day—such struggles can be successful not only in a particular plant or industry but at the level of national legislation, reducing the need for isolated, less powerful resistance.

If each introduction of new machinery offers the capitalists new opportunities for class decomposition and speed-up, it also sets off another round of struggle against work intensity. An interesting question is what the long-term upshot of this conflict has been. In the period Marx is describing in this chapter the capitalists were clearly on the offensive, accelerating the introduction of machinery and the pace of work. From Marx's description of the excesses to which this led in the mid-nineteenth century, it seems

---

77. Ibid.
78. See commentary on Section 2 of Chapter 10.
79. Noticeably absent in debates over recent school shootings by students or ex-students has been serious discussion of all those aspects of school that drive students to violence. At least in the wake of the Columbine shootings in 1999 there was some discussion of bullying—an inevitable consequence of the pattern of intense competition imposed on schoolchildren.

likely that the intensity of labor reached the maximum intensity possible. Subsequently, worker struggles have periodically reduced the intensity of work, which is probably why capitalists have so frequently sought to increase it. In the long run, therefore, we can imagine, though there is little statistical evidence to substantiate the speculation, that since the height of capitalist power—perhaps around or after the time that the length of the working day was maximized—the general tendency has been for a reduction in intensity, with periodical success by capitalists in raising it.

Section 4: The Factory

Outline of Marx's Analysis

The capitalist factory combines cooperating workers and machines
- collective worker = dominant subject
- automaton = subject, workers = conscious organs
- deskilling means skill distinctions and hierarchy disappear
  - replaced by differences "of age and sex"
  - replaced by distribution of workers among specialized machines
  - some "are actually employed on the machines"
  - some "merely attend them (almost exclusively children)"
  - very small group of "engineers, mechanics, joiners, etc."
    - in part scientifically educated, in part handicraft
  - workers adapt to the machines, are easily replaceable
  - specialty of handling a tool becomes specialty of serving the same machine
  - reduces costs of producing labor-power
  - makes worker helplessly dependent

Machines = power of capital
- embody science and natural forces
  - all of which have been stripped from most workers
  - intellectual faculties separated from manual labor
- factory requires "barrack-like discipline"
  - which requires military-like organization of command
  - of overseers (NCOs) over manual laborers (grunts)
  - discipline imposed through "autocratic code," "book of penalties"
- damage to workers
  - restricts physical activity

▶

> – restricts intellectual activity
> – physical damage from high temperatures, dust, noise, speeded-up machines
> – robbery of necessary space, light, air and protection from dangerous machinery

Commentary

This short section summarizes what has been said before, emphasizing how within the factory the workers are, simultaneously, subordinated to the automatic machine system, deskilled, reduced to organs of the machines and stripped of their freedom. "Factory work... does away with the many-sided play of the muscles, and confiscates every atom of freedom, both in bodily and in intellectual activity."[80]

Marx makes clear, however, that this deskilling and impoverishment of the work process does not result in homogeneity among workers. Capital does not abandon its methods of dividing the workers to conquer them; it merely substitutes new divisions for the old, divisions of young and old, of men and women, of one kind of machine tender versus another. As he has mentioned elsewhere, these divisions have been complemented by those of ethnicity, race, nationality, tribal affiliation and virtually every other potentially divisive difference capital can identify. Marx's distinctions between those employed on machines, those who merely tend them (e.g., feed materials to them) and the more technically trained class of engineers, mechanics and joiners, etc., constitutes a rough beginning to an analysis of the *class composition* of the factory. In any actual factory such an analysis could be considerably refined to bring out relevant distinctions of power, of class allegiance, of income, of the degree to which various kinds of workers are assigned responsibility over others, and so on.[81]

At the end of the section, Marx asks "Was Fourier wrong when he called factories 'mitigated jails'?" This likening of factories to jails is apt from several points of view. Both are sites of incarceration. Both are usually surrounded by walls, fences and guard posts that keep workers in and others out. To a considerable degree jails in capitalism have been workhouses. The Texas penal system, for example, is one great labor camp, a southern gulag in which all inmates are condemned to work. In the most profound sense,

---

80. *Capital, Vol. I,* p. 548.
81. The Italians who developed the concept of class composition carried out just such detailed investigations, e.g., Romano Alquati, *Sulla FIAT e Altri Scritti,* Milano: Feltrinelli Editore, 1975.

factories are the jails of the working class given the way in which capital condemns one and all to life sentences at hard labor. Indeed, as Michel Foucault has pointed out, incarceration is one paradigm of social control in capitalism. Everywhere you look capitalism has incarcerated social life within closed walls (jails, factories, asylums, hospitals, schools, stadiums, concert halls, shopping malls, swimming pools, the single-family dwellings) at the expense of free life (in the commons, the streets, village square, the open forest, the free-flowing rivers, communal housing, and so on). Much of his analysis of how factories are organized can be extended to those other sites of incarceration.

Section 5: The Struggle between Worker and Machine

Outline of Marx's Analysis

Worker struggles against machines
- eighteenth century: struggles against ribbon looms, wool-shearing machines, sawmill
- nineteenth century: struggles against power-looms by hand-loom weavers
- Luddite movement, early 1800s
- Sheffield file grinders in 1865
- machines become "competitor of the worker himself"
- "section of the working class thus rendered superfluous," e.g., unemployed
- in England, gradual extinction of hand-loom weavers
  - as prices dropped, "many weavers died of starvation"
- in India, "bones of the cotton-weavers are bleaching the plains"
- machines are "a power inimical" to the worker
  - weapon to suppress strikes

Commentary

Workers struggle against machines because machines have been used by capitalists against the workers from the very beginning of their introduction. Marx has shown us one subtle way this has been true, in the strategy of relative surplus-value, wherein the increases in productivity made possible with machines—that have the potential to reduce work—are used to extract more work. But in this section, he highlights the direct conflicts that result from understanding how introductions of machines are aimed at undermining workers. "Hence the character of independence from and estrangement towards the worker, which the capitalist mode of production gives to the conditions of labor and the product of labor, develops into a complete and total antagonism with the advent of machinery."[82] Machinery "is the most powerful weapon for suppressing strikes, those periodic revolts of the working class against the autocracy of capital. . . It would be possible to write a whole history of the inventions made since 1830 for the sole purpose of providing capital with weapons against working-class revolt."[83]

There are several important implications of these passages. First, to the degree that capitalists introduce machinery against workers, we can understand the history of the development of technology as a capitalist response to the struggles of workers. This is different from the usual Marxist view that sees technological development as either an autonomous process (technological determinism) or as the outcome of competition between capitalists. Better, as I argued in my commentary on Chapter 12, to see capitalist competition as an organization of the class struggle in which the success of some capitalists in dealing with their workers, e.g., introducing new machinery that raises productivity and cuts costs, forces others to make similar attacks on workers' power and displaces those who fail to do so successfully.

Second, although in commenting on the Luddite movement Marx notes "it took both time and experience before the workers learnt to distinguish between machinery and its employment by capital, and therefore to transfer their attacks from the material instruments of production to the form of society which utilizes those instruments," he does show precisely how machinery was indeed an "antagonistic" "power inimical" to the workers.[84] His own examples demonstrate how it is really not possible to separate machinery from its use by capital. Machinery is always developed within a concrete context, e.g., to break strikes based on a certain configuration of working-class power, and therefore always embodies a certain class content in its material form. There is no such thing as politically neutral technology. While it may not always be in the workers' best interests to "break" machines, as the Luddites did, the revolutionary transformation of society must certainly involve the transformation of machinery and the relationships between workers and their machinery so that both embody new and changed social relationships. Failure to recognize this can lead to quite reactionary policies, e.g., those of Lenin who favored the introduction of Taylorism in the Soviet Union.[85]

---

82.   Ibid., p. 558. This is one of those points clearly echoing his analysis of alienation in the *1844 Manuscripts*.

83.   Ibid., p. 563.

84.   *Capital, Vol. I*, pp. 554–555.

85.   See Lenin, "The Immediate Tasks of Soviet Government" (1918). As in all things Lenin, there is debate over his relationship to Taylorism. See James Scoville, "The

Third, technological innovation, although used by capital against workers, derives not from capital but from the working class. *Workers* create and innovate. Capital seeks to turn this aspect of the workers' power against them. This is the secret behind Ure's observation that "capital enlists science into her service."[86] "Science," like technology (its application to industry), is but an aspect of the collective knowledge and know-how of labor. "Enlisting" science, means tapping that knowledge and ability in ways which benefit capital at the expense of workers. This is accomplished, in part, through the imposition of a strict division between manual workers and "mental" labor in which the latter are privileged over the former and come to identify and cooperate with the capitalist enterprise instead of their fellow workers. As the numbers of the "mental" workers grow, the same method is then used against them: the imposition of a division of labor that divides to conquer.

Section 6: The Compensation Theory, with Regard to the Workers Displaced by Machinery

---

Outline of Marx's Analysis

Compensation theory:
- more machinery, fewer workers
- fewer workers = lower V
- lower $V \Rightarrow$ capital set free to hire other workers

Critique:
- reduced v, but increased c
- indirect increases in employment
  - may be productive and increase s
  - may be unproductive

Commentary

In this section, Marx makes two critiques of the theory—common among economists in his day—that the displacement of workers by machinery

---

Taylorization of Vladimir Ilich Lenin", *Industrial Relations*, vol. 40, no. 4, October 2001, pp. 620–626; Victor Devinatz, "Lenin as Scientific Manager Under Monopoly Capitalism, State Capitalism, and Socialism: A Response to Scoville", *Industrial Relations*, vol. 42, no. 3, July 2003, pp. 513–520; and Daniel Wren and Arthur Bedeian, "The Taylorization of Lenin: Rhetoric or Reality?", *International Journal of Social Economics*, vol. 31, issue 3, 2004, pp. 287–299.
86. *Capital, Vol. I*, p. 564.

simultaneously liberates the capital once used to employ them to employ the same number of workers elsewhere, thus "compensating" for the initial reduction in employment. First, he shows it is not true, despite how the introduction of machinery can increase employment overall. Second, he shows that much of the employment that does result indirectly from the introduction of machinery is unproductive, in the sense that it does not result in more surplus-value.

His demonstration that the liberation of capital occasioned by displacement of workers does not employ the same number of workers elsewhere is twofold. With respect to the money once used to employ now displaced workers, he points out that part of the money/capital that employed the displaced workers is used to buy a) the machinery that displaces them, plus b) the increased raw materials and intermediary products required for the increased production made possible by the machinery. In other words, much of the money previously invested in variable capital, is invested in constant capital—new machinery and everything that goes with it—and therefore is not available to employ other workers. With respect to the argument that the means of subsistence (*MS*) no longer required by the displaced workers becomes capital to employ other workers, he points out that the reduced demand for those *MS* causes their prices to fall and, if persistent, a drop in employment in those industries producing *MS*. "Our friends the apologists, with their well-tried law of supply and demand," he argues, "prove the opposite, namely that machinery throws workers onto the streets, not only in that branch of production into which it has been introduced, but also in branches into which it has not been introduced."[87]

Marx goes on to recognize and illustrate how the introduction of machinery in one branch of production may *increase* employment in other branches, e.g., the branches that produce machinery and raw materials. Beyond such immediate effects, he also notes indirect ones such as how the machine-based expansion of production increases demand for transportation, canals, docks, tunnels, bridges and the workers required to build them.

More surprising is his second critique: how "the extraordinary increase in the productivity of large-scale industry... permits a larger and larger part of the working class to be employed unproductively."[88] We first examined Marx's notion of "unproductive" labor in Chapter 6. Here he specifies many whose labors fit this category: "men-servants, women-servants, lackeys, etc.," those "too old or too young to work," "'unproductive' women, young persons and children," "members of the government, priests, lawyers,

---

87. *Capital, Vol. I*, p. 567.
88. Ibid., p. 574.

soldiers, etc.," rentiers and usurers, "paupers, vagabonds and criminals."[89] Unusual is his inclusion of capitalists spending surplus-value—like the landed gentry who spent their rents—on servants, to complement their expenditures on luxuries. Unusual because throughout most of *Capital*, he ignores capitalist consumption and only analyzes the deployment of surplus-value in investment.

Section 7: Repulsion and Attraction of Workers through the Development of Machine Production, Crises in the Cotton Industry

---

Outline of Marx's Analysis

Machinery
- displaces some workers
- by increasing overall production creates jobs for others
- enhances flexibility, rapid increases or decreases in production
- accentuates booms and busts
  - internationally
  - cotton famine $\Rightarrow$ crisis, new sources

Commentary

Drawing on data from the Factory Inspectors' reports, the first part of this section continues the analysis of the previous one, describing how machinery displaces some workers, but by accelerating overall growth in production tends to increase the total number of workers, even as the share of investment in their wages (v) declines relative to that in constant capital (c).

The bulk of the section, however, consists of demonstrating how machinery not only increases productivity but also the flexibility of capitalist production, i.e., its ability to expand or contract rapidly in response to changes in demand or the costs of raw materials. This flexibility, when combined with the capitalist tendency to gear the expansion or contraction of production to the maximization of profits, contributes to an increased instability manifested in industrial booms and busts. That instability, he shows, grows with the spread of capitalism through the colonial incorporation of new markets (often based on the destruction of local production) and the creation of new sources of raw materials. India, Australia and the United States all become both providers of raw materials to the British textile

---

89. Ibid.

industry and outlets for its wares and for workers displaced by machinery (or sentenced to transportation due to struggle). In words that echo clarion phrases from the *Communist Manifesto*, he writes of the "cheapness of the articles produced by large-scale industry" providing "weapons for the conquest of foreign markets." The displacement of workers by machinery also "spurs on rapid increases in emigration" and the conversion of colonies into "settlements for growing the raw material of the mother country." The result, he notes, continuing his discussion from Chapter 14, a "new international division of labor."[90]

This expanded division of labor shapes both booms and busts. Although in his detailed listing of sequential periods of prosperity and crisis, 1815–65, his immediate focus remains, as usual, on England, he repeatedly highlights their international dimensions. Moreover, he chooses for his major illustration, how the cotton famine in Britain caused by the American Civil War not only provoked a crisis in the British textile industry but forced producers to turn to poorer quality (shorter, dirtier fiber) Indian cotton with all the negative consequences for both the industry (higher costs) and its workers (worsened working conditions). Analysis of those consequences for workers allows him to cite more of the kind of horror stories we saw in Chapter 10 in those industries subject to no legal limits. In these cases, the source of worsened working conditions were the experiments by capitalists cutting costs in ways that harmed workers' health and cut their wages, e.g., increased use of flour-substitutes for sizing.

Marx also touches on the sphere of reproduction, but only briefly, when he points out how capitalists who own their workers' housing take advantage of dire circumstances to raise rents and deduct them from wages. All reductions in wages during an industrial crisis, regardless of source, worsens the conditions of reproduction for those with no savings and no access to credit beyond the pawning of their few meager belongings. True then, true today.

Section 8: The Revolutionary Impact of Large-scale Industry on Manufacture, Handicrafts and on the Division of Labor

---

Outline of Marx's Analysis

a) Machinery undermines handicraft forms of cooperation
b) Factory system changes other manufacturing
   – new applications of science
   – changes in makeup of collective worker ▶

---

90.   Ibid., p. 579.

c) Illustrations of modern manufacturing
 – industry overworks and poisons
 – industry corrupts
d) Domestic industry – outsourced
e) Changes hastened by Factory Acts

Commentary

This section analyzes the disintegrating impact of machinery on the handicraft and manufacturing forms of cooperation and production, both through direct introduction of machinery and indirect effects on related production where machines have not yet or only partially been introduced.

In the case of handicrafts, machines may simply wipe out previous forms of cooperation. Introduced piecemeal, however, they may temporarily reorganize handicraft modes of production without immediately eliminating them. Marx's examples include needle-making machines and power looms, both of which were, at first, used by individual handicraft workers in their cottages or workshops, but eventually failed due to competition from large factories. Later, in subsection e, he analyzes these dynamics in the case of the sewing machine in the apparel industry, a machine operated by individuals who could be organized either in isolation or in gathered numbers.

As the machine-based factory system expands, it changes the organization of cooperation and the makeup of the collective worker. Even before women and children are herded into factories, introduction of machinery powered by engines makes possible their large-scale employment by outsourcing subsidiary phases of production to domestic industry, i.e., small-scale operations in workers' homes. Marx provides numerous illustrations of how the increasing demand for elements still made by handicraft or manufacturing methods results in a vast expansion of poorly paid labor working under atrocious conditions. Once again drawing on government reports, Marx uses the lace-making and straw-plaiting carried on in homes ("mistresses houses") and small workshops ("schools")—effectively annexed by larger factories and unregulated by the Factory Acts—to illustrate the horrors spawned by the demands of expanding industry. Thus, the contradictory effects of the Factory Acts. Industries covered are forced to overcome obstacles through technical innovation and more machines. Industries *not* covered multiply, employing workers under miserable conditions. This organization adds to the overall flexibility of capitalist production making it easier to expand or contract production, but at the expense of workers, who are sometimes overworked and sometimes allowed to starve.

Although Marx's analysis portrays these various changes as transitional steps toward the universal organization of production in the "factory-system," the flexibility of these different, but interconnected modes of cooperation, have proved too valuable to capital to give up. They persist today, sometimes much as the mid-nineteenth-century reports described them, sometimes in modern versions. One modern example will suffice. In the 1970s, Italian industry, faced with growing militancy among workers concentrated in large factories, began to decentralize production, to literally move machines out of plants and into individual workers' homes or small workshops—recreating precisely the kind of geographic dispersion that Marx describes in this section—and then supplying them with materials and picking up products using trucks or vans. Placing machines in workers' homes both reduced the costs of managing large groups of workers and gave those now-divided workers marginal control over their tools. So widespread did this tactic of breaking up concentrations of workers become that it provoked extended discussion among worker and political militants about the nature of the changes and possible worker responses. The journal *Quaderni del Territorio* published a series of issues and organized a national meeting in the spring of 1978 on *la fabbrica diffusa* (diffused factory).[91] At that meeting, discussion turned around the degree to which this diffusion should be understood simply as a new twist in capitalist strategy of dividing workers to control them, or, as a desperate response to the growing self-organization of the mass worker and an adaptation to the refusal by young workers of factory discipline. This reorganization of cooperation became famous when the Benetton Group, the Italian clothing manufacturer, began outsourcing its production to such modern domestic producers. As with those "domestic industries" Marx describes as being subject to the whims of market fluctuations, so too have their contemporary counterparts been subject to just-in-time production demands, determined by central management in response to fluctuations in sales across outlets.

A final note. In his comments on the "irregular habits of the workers," Marx attributes them partly to a "crudely spontaneous reaction against the tedium of monotonous drudgery" and partly to the fluctuations in demand. As in his discussion of "nibbling and cribbling" in Chapter 10, he fails to analyze such workers' "irregular" behavior as a form of struggle involving choosing when and how hard to work as a function of one's own needs rather than those of capital, which we have seen to demand continuous hard work. Such patterns persist in both production and reproduction. In

---

91. The English counterpart term is "the hollow corporation" where production is outsourced, and central administrative activities consist mainly of coordination, brand advertising and planning.

the latter case think of the common practice of students in putting off studying, in preference for other activities, and then "cramming" at the last minute for exams, papers, etc.

Section 9: The Health and Education Clauses of the Factory Acts. The General Extension of Factory Legislation in England

Outline of Marx's Analysis

Health clauses
  - few protections
  - vehemently opposed by capitalists
Education clauses
  - limited application
  - combining of education and labor makes better workers
  - Owen as exemplar
Modern industry
  - frequent changes in technology
  - requires adaptable workforce
Foreshadows post-capitalism
  - desirable combination of education and labor
  - "totally developed individual"
Evolution of Factory Acts
  - halting, shaped by workers' struggles and capitalist resistance
  - resistance evident in transcripts of hearings
  - as regulations become general, so does struggle

Commentary

This very long section contains a wealth of evidence of both the successes and the failures of the Factory Acts to protect British workers. The overall story of improving, but still insufficient, laws and of failure to enforce continues right down to the present. Seek out contemporary reports on many of the industries described here, e.g., coal mining, and you will still find similar conditions of regulations inadequate to protect miners and outrageous, intentionally lax enforcement. Although workers have long fought both, the inadequacy of enforcement became obvious in the Reagan administration with its emphasis on deregulation (to cut business costs) and on defunding enforcement of regulations not yet removed. The Trump administration is following the same game plan.

With respect to those few clauses in the Factory Acts that concern working conditions, Marx's examples show how limited they were and how little protection they provided. The exceptions for small businesses have a very contemporary ring to them. Think of current small business objections that being forced to provide the levels of benefits, e.g., medical insurance, paid vacations, etc., required of large industry. Providing them, they scream, would put them out of business, or, as Marx puts it, "drive them to the wall." Despite his argument that the dynamics of competition and the generalization of regulation was progressively wiping out small-scale handicrafts, then manufacturing and replacing them with large-scale industry, both have survived, not only in the making of things but in the provision of an ever-greater variety of services. As a result, much that is treated in this section only requires updating.

Perhaps the most interesting elements of his analysis in this section are those concerning education. The enforcement of Factory Act requirements for education, Marx argues, was not only salutary for the children and useful for capitalists in producing better workers but also provided evidence for better ways of rearing children in post-capitalist society. Drawing on Senior's denunciation of the "monotonous, unproductive and long school day" of the children of the upper classes and on Owen's experiments, Marx argues that combining productive labor with "instruction and gymnastics" is "the only method of producing fully developed human beings."[92] The "disposable working population," he argues, "must be replaced by the individual man who is absolutely available for the different kinds of labour required of him... the totally developed individual, for whom the different social functions are different modes of activity he takes up in turn."[93] Such will be possible, of course, only with "the inevitable conquest of political power by the working class."[94]

Will that happen? He concludes the section with this optimistic assessment:

By maturing the material conditions and the social combination of the process of production, [the general extension of factory legislation] matures the contradictions and antagonisms of the capitalist form of that process, and thereby ripens both the elements for forming a new society and the forces tending towards the overthrow of the old one.[95]

---

92. *Capital, Vol. I,* pp. 613–614.
93. Ibid., p. 618.
94. Ibid., p. 619.
95. *Capital, Vol. I,* p. 635.

Section 10: Large-scale Industry and Agriculture

> ### Outline of Marx's Analysis
>
> Traditional agriculture
>   - irrational and slothful
>   - primitive familial union
> Capitalist agriculture
>   - an industry
>   - conscious application of science
>   - less direct harm
>   - greater displacement of labor
> Resistance of workers
>   - less because dispersed
>   - peasantry decimated, become waged
> Negative consequences
>   - urbanization associated with rise of industry
>   - disturbs metabolic interaction between humans and the earth
>   - undermines the fertility of the soil
>   - robs workers, robs soil
> Post-capitalism
>   - systematic restoration of metabolism

Commentary

Promising to provide more analysis later, in this brief section Marx merely notes some of the consequences of the conversion of traditional agriculture into a capitalist industry. Parallels with other industries include the increased use of machinery and science, the displacement and exploitation of workers. The main difference, upon which he dwells, and which has made these passages of great interest in our ecologically conscious age, is how the capitalist exploitation of the earth tends to destroy it, i.e., undermine its fertility. This argument, based primarily on a book by Liebig, has long been debated among agriculturalists, economists and, more recently, ecologists. On the one hand, capitalist apologists point to the conversion of uncultivatable land to agricultural use and the increased use of fertilizers that increases the fertility of the soil. On the other hand, there are plenty of examples of destruction, e.g., ill-managed irrigation combined with inorganic fertilizers leading to salinization and desertification. Or, the substitution of monoculture for complex systems of plants (agronomy and horticulture) and animals (husbandry and aquaculture).

Given contemporary recognition of the considerable wisdom incarnated in many traditional farming methods, Marx's comments about "the previous highly irrational and slothfully traditional way of working" bespeaks ignorance and reflects his anti-pastoral attitudes that interpret the rise of large-scale industry, whatever its shortcomings within capitalism, as progress.[96] Today we know, thanks in part to the efforts of ecologists, not only how those supposedly "irrational" methods survived for thousands of years, but how much we have to learn from them for overcoming the very faults of capitalists' "rational" methods that Marx himself criticizes.

His very comments about how, by concentrating people and production in cities, capitalism "disturbs the metabolic interaction between man and the earth," by preventing "the return to the soil of its constituent elements consumed by man in the form of food and clothing" have been pounced upon by Marxists to highlight the relevance of his writings to ecological critiques of how capitalist agribusiness poisons the earth.[97] Although he doesn't do so here, he might have drawn on passages from Engels's *The Condition of the Working Class in England* (1845) that also pointed to such poisonings, both within cities and in the countryside.[98] However brief his comments, he doesn't hesitate to draw an important conclusion for one thing workers must do, once they have overthrown capitalism, namely organize the "systematic restoration [of the disrupted metabolism] as a regulative law of social production."[99] Kropotkin, whose critiques of capitalist agriculture paralleled Marx's, went even further in his books *The Conquest of Bread* (1892) and *Fields, Factories and Workshops* (1898).[100] Drawing on both new agricultural science and the experience of producers surrounding large cities, he pointed to methods that might contribute to attaining the very goal Marx visualized.

---

96. Ibid., p. 637.

97. See Kohei Saito, *Karl Marx's Ecosocialism. Capitalism, Nature and the Unfinished Critique of Political Economy*, New York: Monthly Review Press, 2017; and John Bellamy Foster and Paul Burkett, *Marx and the Earth. An Anti-critique*, London: Haymarket Books, 2017.

98. Frederick Engels, "The Condition of the Working Class in England", *MECW, vol. 4*, pp. 295–583.

99. *Capital, Vol. I*, p. 638.

100. *The Conquest of Bread* (1892), London: Penguin Classics, 2015 and *Fields, Factories and Workshops* (1898), London: Freedom Press, 1985.

8

Part Five
The Production of Absolute
and Relative Surplus-Value

In Chapters 7–11 on absolute surplus-value and in Chapters 12–15 on relative surplus-value Marx analyzes these strategies of exploitation in terms of value, not in terms of money, an embodiment of value, nor in terms of profit, a monetary form of surplus-value. These three short Chapters 16–18 provide a bridge to Part Six on wages, the money form of the value of labor-power. They both remind the reader of ideas already discussed and begin to analyze some of the consequences of the value of labor-power taking the form of money.

Chapter 16: Absolute and Relative Surplus-Value. Mostly a reminder of the distinction and interrelationships between the two forms of surplus-value with some observations on the concept and historical evolution of productivity. The chapter ends with a critique of the failure of classical political economists and those who followed them to discover the antagonistic social relationships underlying such monetary phenomena as profits and wages.

Chapter 17: Changes of Magnitude in the Price of Labour-Power and in Surplus-Value. The title of this chapter announces the transition from value analysis to money by indicating that the value of labor-power will be discussed in terms of its price. Thus, while reviewing his previous analysis of how absolute and relative surplus-value vary according to changes in productivity, intensity and price of labor-power, he examines the relation between those changes and the price (or wages) of labor. Marx highlights the centrality of rising productivity, not only for the struggle between workers and capitalists over how its fruits are shared but for a post-capitalist future in which rising productivity could be channeled into ever less shared work and ever more shared wealth.

Chapter 18: Different Formulae for the Rate of Surplus-Value. Marx juxtaposes his theory to that of the classical political economists. He argues that their formulations hide the existence of exploitation and create the illusion that workers and capital receive income equal to their contribution to production. He also upholds the reasonableness of characterizing exploitation in terms of the extraction of unpaid labor, i.e., labor performed without compensation.

CHAPTER 16: ABSOLUTE AND RELATIVE SURPLUS-VALUE

Outline of Marx's Analysis

- in capitalism, social labor produces surplus-value
- early on: *formal* subsumption of labor produces *absolute surplus-value* by extending the working day
- later: *real* subsumption of labor produces *relative surplus-value* by reducing necessary labor
- but the means for reducing necessary labor also can increase absolute surplus-value
  - by making the working day longer
- amount of potential surplus labor
  - determined by natural conditions of labor
    - need to master nature leads to development of social division of labor
  - determined by requirements of life
    - where needs are few, a great deal of surplus labor can be imposed
- Ricardo: saw labor productivity as source of profit
- Mill: affirms source of profits in productivity of labor against mercantilist focus on exchange

---

Commentary

In this, the first of the three chapters that take us from analyses in terms of value, to those of the monetary form of the value of labor-power, Marx reminds us of the distinction between absolute and relative surplus-value, of how they are produced and of the relationship between the two. *Absolute surplus-value* emerges early when capitalists only command or subsume the labor of others formally, that is to say, without taking over and transforming tools and how they are used. Under those circumstances, their only available strategy for increasing the extraction of surplus-value involves getting people to work longer. Because workers control their tools and the rhythm of their work, capitalists have little leverage to extract more surplus-value via the intensification of labor. *Relative surplus-value* emerges as capitalists do obtain that leverage, by gaining control over tools and organizing them in factories that facilitate oversight and control. Protected by new property laws, they reshape both tools and their use to raise productivity and increase surplus-value, both by reducing the labor time necessary to produce each unit and by increasing the intensity of labor.

Given the increasing centrality of productivity, he also reminds us of how the conditions and meaning of *productive labor* depends upon the context. At the level of the individual, a productive worker is simply one who produces some product directly, using mind, hands and tools to transform raw materials. That was the generic concept he set out in the first section of Chapter 7. But as human society developed most labor became social, such that individuals came to collaborate in production of ever more things and in so doing formed a collective worker with a division of labor, which he analyzed in some detail in Chapter 14. With the rise of various kinds of class society, including capitalism, antagonistic relationships develop as some are able to impose surplus work on others and appropriate the resulting surplus product. Within capitalism that surplus product takes the form of surplus-value, so that from the point of view of the appropriating capitalists the only productive workers, i.e., the only workers whose labor makes it possible to impose more work, are those who produce surplus-value, i.e., surplus labor whose products can be used to impose more work in the future. As a result, there is a clear distinction between the vernacular, everyday sense of being productive, i.e., being able to produce something, and the only kind of productivity that matters to capitalists. This is consistent with the emphasis we saw in Chapter 1 between use-value and exchange-value/value. Use-values and the ease with which we can obtain them preoccupy those of us who work; the exchange-value of the surplus production preoccupies those who put us to work.

In illustrating the capitalist case, Marx draws a parallel between those industries that produce *things* and those that produce *services*:

> a schoolmaster is a productive worker when, in addition to belaboring the heads of his pupils, he works himself into the ground to enrich the owner of the school. That the latter has laid out his capital in a teaching factory, instead of a sausage factory, makes no difference to the relation.

Given that such "productivity" involves exploitation, he adds that, "To be a productive worker is therefore not a piece of luck, but a misfortune."[1]

---

1. Both this and the quoted passage are from *Capital, Vol. I*, p. 644.

Marx then goes on to remind us of the connections that he demonstrated in Chapter 15 between absolute and relative surplus-value. Namely, how the methods used to produce relative surplus-value, i.e., introducing new machines and new technology, also made possible the prolongation of the working day and the intensification of work, both of which added surplus-value by extracting more work from those subject to the new methods. What he does *not* remind us of here, is how the shift to relative surplus-value strategies was the result of the success of workers' struggles to shorten the working day and by so doing undermine absolute surplus-value.[2] *Nor* does he reiterate his previous analysis of how new machines are designed and new technologies are chosen with the objective of undermining those struggles through the reorganization of the labor process.[3]

These reminders are followed by a brief analysis of the impact of natural conditions on the availability of surplus labor, both potential and actual. Where nature has provided plenty to meet limited needs and wants, as has sometimes been the case in the tropics, little work has been required and this resulted in a lot of spare, disposable time.[4] Marx's remarks here have received substantial support from later studies by anthropologists of what Marshall Sahlins called "original affluent societies."[5] Late in his life, partly as a result of his studies of the Russian peasant commune and its potential for providing the basis of a post-capitalist social regeneration, Marx devoted considerable time to the study of pre-capitalist societies.[6] The importance of his recognition of diverse possible paths to revolution and the transcendence of capitalism has been highlighted by Raya Dunayevskaya.[7] The contemporary renaissance in indigenous resistance to capitalism has led to new critiques of the orthodox Marxist dismissal of such struggles and to new appreciation of the insights being offered by those participating in that resistance into alternatives to capitalist ways of organizing the world. The widespread positive response to, and support for, the Zapatista rebellion in Mexico marked a new level of global awareness among those fighting capitalism; that awareness and support has continued

---

2. Ibid., Chapter 15, Section 2, subsections (b) and (c).

3. Ibid., Chapter 15, Sections 4 and 5.

4. Recall Marx's celebration, cited in my commentary on Section 5 of Chapter 10, of the Quashees of Jamaica thumbing their noses at the capitalist planters.

5. Marshall Sahlins, *Stone Age Economics*, Livingston, NJ: Aldine Transaction, 1974, Chapter 1, "The Original Affluent Society."

6. Lawrence Krader (ed.), *The Ethnographic Notebooks of Karl Marx*, 2nd edn., Assen: Van Gorcum & Co., 1974.

7. Raya Dunayevskaya, "Marx's 'New Humanism' and the Dialectics of Women's Liberation in Primitive and Modern Societies", *Praxis International*, vol. 3, no. 4, 1984, pp. 369–381.

for a wide variety of struggles in many parts of the world. Two examples illustrate the spreading support for the indigenous defense of the sacredness of land against capitalist exploitation. First has been the resistance of First Peoples in Canada to tar sands development, and second has been the resistance of Native Americans in the US to the construction of the Keystone and Dakota Access Pipelines.

In the long run, Marx suggests that the rise in labor productivity has taken place via the organization of social, collective labor and technological development in response to the need to overcome obstacles presented by nature. A certain Eurocentrism *appears* implicit in his suggestion that this has been truer in temperate climates than in tropical ones:

> The mother country of capitalism is not the tropical region, with its luxuriant vegetation, but the temperate zone. It is not the absolute fertility of the soil but its degree of differentiation, the variety of its natural products, which forms the natural basis for the social division of labor, and which, by changes in the natural surroundings, spurs man on to the multiplication of his needs, his capacities and the instruments and modes of this labour.[8]

His illustrations, however, which include waterworks in Egypt, India and Persia as well as Italy and Holland, show that his suggestion here was not Eurocentric. Others, however, have been prone to insist on the climate differences (as they have sometimes done with "racial" differences) between temperate and tropical zones, in trying to explain why early capitalist development seemed to have been concentrated in Europe. Such views have been countered over the years not only by the rediscovery of the independent development of capitalism in places such as India, but also by the recognition of the tremendous natural "differentiation" that obtains in the tropics. Such understanding came first as colonialists discovered competitors to suppress and more and more "resources" to exploit. More recently, modern ecological research has revealed the incredible diversity of life in the tropics. To these discoveries we should also add that of long-ignored indigenous knowledge and innovation in the utilization of plant and animal life for artistic, medicinal and nutritional purposes. The onslaught of biopiracy by the pharmaceutical industry out to patent, monopolize and exploit that

---

8. *Capital, Vol. I,* p. 649. The "tropical region," it is worth remembering, formally lies between the Tropic of Cancer (roughly 23°27' North Latitude) and the Tropic of Capricorn (roughly 23°27' South Latitude). The precise latitude varies from year to year because these tropics, both north and south, are defined by the most northerly or southerly circle of latitude at which the sun appears directly overhead.

knowledge provides perverse testimony to its importance. So, while we may accept Marx's intuition that challenges provoke innovation, we must also recognize that the diversity of innovations throughout the world—both social and technological—has been much greater that he recognized.

Marx ends this chapter with a brief, sarcastic attack on Ricardo—and by implication all the classical political economists of his time—and John Stuart Mill, their successor, for the superficiality of their understanding of monetary phenomena. They did seek to explain such monetary categories as profit, interest and rent, but their efforts to understand their origin stalled at the simple concept of labor. Their failure, he argues, lay in their inability to recognize and analyze the origin of surplus-value—a failure he attributes to their instinct that "it was very dangerous to penetrate too deeply into the burning question of the origins of surplus-value."[9] The question was "burning," of course, because with the development of workers' self-organization, came increasingly intense challenges to the injustice of capitalist profit. While recognizing that "the productive power of labor is the originating cause of profit," Ricardo et al. failed to identify the essence of surplus-value in surplus labor and the exploitative nature of capitalism. Despite this theoretical lacuna, their emphasis on labor as the source of value did lead workers to the inevitable conclusion that if the source of value was labor, then all value should belong to them and none to the capitalists. Equally inevitable was the response of economists who set aside the labor theory of value and replaced it, first with utility theory in the late nineteenth century and then with preference theory early in the twentieth. With this brief evocation of the money form of surplus-value, Marx takes us one step closer to his exposition of the money form of the value of labor-power.

CHAPTER 17: CHANGES OF MAGNITUDE IN THE PRICE OF LABOUR-POWER AND IN SURPLUS-VALUE

Outline of Marx's Analysis

Relative magnitudes of surplus-value, S, and price of labor-power, LP, are a function of:
- length of the working day
- intensity of labor
- the productivity of labor

▶

9. Ibid., pp. 651–652.

1. When only the *productivity of labor varies*:
   - total value remains the same
   - value of LP and S vary inversely
   - although their variation is inverse, the proportionate changes may differ
   - variation in magnitude of S always a consequence of change in value of LP
   - amount of reduction in price of LP depends on *struggle* over fruits of the increase in productivity
   - increasing productivity can result in both workers and capitalists getting more
   - so, both constant and falling prices of LP *can* be accompanied by rise in real standard of living

2. When only *intensity of labor varies*:
   - greater intensity means more output, but also more value, no change in value per unit
   - increased intensity of labor means workers get tired faster, increasing cost of maintaining the same quality of LP
   - so, rise in price of labor-power may not fully compensate for deterioration

3. When only the *length of the working day varies*:
   - if shortened and value of LP remains the same, S is reduced
     - shortening may follow or precede an increase in productivity
   - if lengthened and value of LP remains the same, S is increased, both absolutely and relatively
   - but both price of LP and S can increase, the proportion depends on *struggle*
   - lengthening depletes workers' LP, so value of labor-power rises; wage increases may compensate but as in the case of increased intensity, not completely

4. With *simultaneous variations*:
   - Two important cases:
     (a) decline in productivity, increase in working day
       - increase in working day can compensate for negative impact on S of a decline in productivity
       - 1799–1815 fall in real wages (standard of living)
       - West and Ricardo were wrong that declining productivity lowered S
         - S rose because of increased hours of work and increased intensity of labor   ▶

(b) shortening of working day but increasing intensity and productivity
- the more a working day is intensified, and productivity increased, the greater the shortening possible
- capitalism limits shortening because of its need for S
- capitalism squanders LP and MP on socially superfluous functions
- as necessary labor declines, *potential* free time expands
- end of capitalism will make possible:
- end of leisure for some at the expense of work by others
- universality of labor, but more leisure for all

Commentary

The title of this chapter announces a transition from value analysis to money by making clear that the value of labor-power will be discussed in terms of its price. Price, as we saw in Chapter 1, is the money expression of the value of a commodity, in this case of the value of labor-power. In this chapter, Marx reiterates his analysis of past chapters in terms of changes in both the *value* and the *price* of labor-power and notes how changes in *price* may differ from changes in value. In passing from analysis in terms of value to one in terms of money, Marx must, and does, take into account changes in the real value of money wages, e.g., caused by a change in the price of consumer goods. Therefore, the price of labor-power may not equal its value.

Throughout this analysis, the price of labor-power can be assumed to be wages, in as much as money wages were predominant over other expressions of the value of labor-power in the period in which Marx was writing. (As opposed to wages in kind, salaries, commissions or government payments to the unemployed or the poor.)

While the reiteration of previously explained material has often caused this chapter to be passed over as pure pedantry, there are two reasons for its close study. First, thinking of the value of labor-power in terms of its price, its monetary equivalent, lays the groundwork for Chapters 19–22 on wages. Second, among familiar words and phrases there are also politically important points well worth repetition.

The first of these is his highlighting of how, in the dynamic of capitalist development, despite the existence of some zero-sum relationships where one class can benefit only at the expense of the other, there are situations in which the material situation of both can be improved. The most important of these is when a rise in the productivity of labor results, to use modern terms, in an increase in the size of the pie being produced. When the pie/output grows, it is at least possible for both workers and capitalists to get more of what they want: means of consumption and life for workers, means of production to impose more work for capitalists. Marx writes that it is "possible that owing to an increase in the productivity of labor both the worker and the capitalist may simultaneously be able to appropriate a greater quantity of means of subsistence [or of means of production] without any change in the price of labor-power or in surplus-value."[10] The same mutual benefit is possible with increases in the length and intensity of the working day; where more is produced, more could potentially be shared. In this second case, because longer and/or more intense working hours use up workers' energy faster, any increase in real consumption requires an excess over the necessary compensation for the accelerated wearing out of workers. But it is at least possible for the increase to be large enough.

The importance of these observations is they show how his theory is perfectly compatible with historically observed increases in standards of living among some workers, even as others are thrown into poverty and pauperism. It is also compatible with, and indeed predates, the recognition by neoclassical economists (from at least Alfred and Mary Marshall on) that increases in wages can go hand in hand with increased profits.[11] This was the reality on the basis of which John Maynard Keynes built his theory of how capitalist development could be socially progressive, i.e., one in which growing profits and investment were stimulated by growing wages and benefits.[12] In the process, he overthrew the traditional business view that any increase in wages would undermine profits and therefore had to be resisted by all means possible, including violence when necessary.

Under these circumstances, Marx also points out how the degree to which the fruits of higher productivity and more work are shared depends in large part upon the balance of class forces, i.e., on the struggle between workers seeking to share in increases in the social wealth resulting from increased productivity and the efforts by capitalists to arrogate all increases to themselves. "The new value of labor-power," Marx writes, "depends on the relative weight thrown into the scale by the pressure of capital on the one side, and the resistance of the workers on the other."[13] In the wake of

---

10.   Ibid., p. 659. No change in nominal or money wages, but an increase in real wages because the money buys more due to lower prices of consumption goods.

11.   Neoclassical microeconomics allows wage increases to be compatible with increases in profit as long as the marginal productivity of labor rises.

12.   In Keynesian macroeconomics, rising wages increase consumer demand, which, *ceteris paribus*, induces investment and greater output.

13.   *Capital, Vol. I*, p. 659.

the Russian Revolution and of World War I, Keynes pointed out that the British working class would no longer accept reductions in real wages and was well enough organized to insist on rising real wages. The alternative to provoking a general strike by trying to lower wages, he suggested, was raising productivity (either by shutting down low-productivity operations or by investing in new technology) that could make higher wages possible with no loss to capitalists.

Although Keynes's observations and proposals were made in Britain, similar recognition in the United States underlay the acceptance and legalization by the Roosevelt administration of industrial unions and collective bargaining. Those changes forced capitalists in major industries, such as motor vehicles and mining, to recognize unions, bargain with them collectively and cut "productivity deals" in which workers were allowed to share in the fruits of rising productivity in exchange for cooperation in the introduction of new technology that made that rise possible. Although such deals were written into union–industry contracts, how the agreements worked out in practice continued to depend on struggle and the balance of class power on the shop floor and in the pits.

Marx draws our attention to two cases. The first was during the period of the Napoleonic Wars, 1799–1815. He cites 1799 presumably because it was in November of that year that Napoléon Bonaparte (1769–1821) seized power, ten years after the French revolution. Actual war between the British and French governments began in 1803 as Bonaparte's armies began to conquer much of Europe. He was finally defeated at Waterloo in 1815 after his disastrous withdrawal from Moscow and despite Britain's defeat in the War of 1812 with the United States. During those years of warfare, the ability of Britain to import grain from the European continent was curtailed, both by the French government's closing of its territory to British trade and by the British naval blockade of French ports.[14] As a result, the British economy was forced to rely on less productive local agriculture, especially of corn (the English term for wheat and other grains requiring grinding). The resulting increase in the price of bread for workers helped drive them to accept the longer, harder hours that Marx cites. The increased price of grain and bread not only reduced real wages, but increased ground

---

14. For vivid fictional accounts—often based on real historical documents—of the British blockade from France's northern ports along the Channel to Gibraltar and ports along the Mediterranean coast, see the Napoleonic War novels of C. S. Forester and those of Patrick O'Brian, and the films based upon them. Forester's novels provided the basis for a 1951 film *Captain Horatio Hornblower* starring Gregory Peck and an ITV and A&E TV series *Hornblower* (1998–2003) starring Ioan Gruffudd. O'Brian's Aubrey–Maturin novels provided the material for *Master and Commander: The Far Side of the World* (2003) starring Russell Crowe and Paul Bettany.

rents, profiting landlords. This situation was prolonged after the war by so-called Corn Laws, enacted in 1815, putting tariffs on imported grain. The continued high price of grain and bread intensified class conflicts and led to the famous debate between Malthus, who defended the tariffs as vital to national security, and Ricardo, who critiqued them as harmful to industrial development because they diverted income from profits that could be invested to rents that went largely to luxury consumption by landlords. Capitalists mounted a sustained movement, enlisting workers, to end the Corn Laws, increase wheat imports, and lower the price of bread, an effort that finally succeeded in 1846. Of course, they didn't mention to the workers their plans to lower wages once the price of bread dropped!

The second of the two cases, involving a shortening of the working day but increased intensity and productivity, became dominant in the period of the real subsumption of labor to capital once workers organized themselves effectively enough to force down their hours of work. This forced capitalists to resort to relative surplus-value strategies: in other words, the history analyzed in detail in Chapters 12–15.

What is interesting in Marx's treatment here, is how he draws from that analysis implications for the possibilities beckoning from a future beyond capitalism. In such a future world, he argues, those dreams of Aristotle that he evoked in Chapter 15 could finally be realized. Freed of the capitalist mandate to order society through imposed work, rising productivity could be converted into more and more free time. His brief discussion here echoes Engels's lectures at Elberfeld two decades earlier, where he blasted all the wasteful forms of work that capitalism requires, e.g., police and juridical protection of private property, finance, a military-industrial complex, and so on, imagining all those wasting their time in such activities changing occupations and sharing a declining burden of actually useful labor.[15] No more separate leisure class, freed from work by the labor of others, but an equal sharing by all in less and less work and more and more leisure. Such a future, Marx argues, would allow "the free intellectual and social activity of the individual."[16] Here Marx is also echoing his own words from the *Grundrisse* notebooks a decade before. There he wrote, "The saving of labor time [is] equal to an increase of free time, i.e., time for the full development of the individual, which in turn reacts back upon the productive power of labor as itself the greatest productive power."[17]

A final note: in the midst of pointing out the potentialities created by raising productivity, Marx recognizes how the development of individuals,

---

15. See his two speeches, delivered in February 1845 in *MECW, vol. 4*, pp. 243–264.
16. *Capital, Vol. I*, p. 667.
17. *Grundrisse*, p. 711.

both intellectual and social, changes their aspirations and therefore their needs and desires. As a result, the amount and diversity of labor required to provide the means for satisfying those needs and desires grows. Therefore, "what is now surplus labor would then count as necessary labor, namely the labour which is necessary for the formation of a social fund for reserve and accumulation."[18] In a post-capitalist world, clearly "accumulation" would no longer involve the expanded reproduction of antagonistic class relationships, but rather the growth in all those elements necessary to satisfy changing aspirations. Here we have an answer to an objection long posed by mainstream economists to Marx's theory of surplus labor/value and exploitation within capitalism. "Would not," they have argued, "people in a post-capitalist society still need to do more work than is required to meet their immediate needs in order to create the wherewithal to meet future needs?" Yes, but in such a society, as Marx says here, such extra work would not be "surplus-*value*" because it would not be dedicated to the expanded imposition of social control via more and more work.[19]

CHAPTER 18: DIFFERENT FORMULAE FOR THE RATE OF SURPLUS-VALUE

Outline of Marx's Analysis

Marx's formulae:
- s/v = surplus-value/(value of LP) = (surplus labor)/(necessary labor)

Classical political economy formulae:
- (surplus labor)/(working day) = surplus-value/(value of product) = (surplus product)/(total product)
- working day, value of product, total product = $s+v$ in Marx's terms (leaves out MP or c)

Political economy formulae:
- understates rate of surplus-value
- conceals exchange of wage for LP

▶

---

18.   *Capital, Vol. I,* p. 667.

19.   Mainstream economists, apologists as they are for capitalism, argue that what is produced in capitalism is always a function of people's needs and desires, as manifested in how they spend their money. While making that argument, they completely ignore not only all of the ways in which capitalists manipulate need and desire to create more opportunities for imposing work, but also all of those myriad kinds of work that both Engels and Marx deplored as superfluous to a society freed of capitalist domination.

> – creates the illusion of sharing according to contribution vs actual
>   antagonism
> v = paid labor, s = unpaid labor (popular expressions for (surplus
>   labor)/(necessary labor)
> capital = command over unpaid labor

Commentary

In this chapter Marx, pauses a moment before the section on wages to juxtapose his own formulations to those of classical political economy and to critique the latter in ways that foreshadow the critiques he will make in the next three chapters.

By always comparing surplus-value (or product) to the total value (or product), classical political economists portrayed the relationship between workers and capitalists in ways that 1) hid the existence of exploitation and 2) created an illusion that labor was getting its fair share. The existence of exploitation was hidden by making it appear that each factor of production, i.e., labor and capital, is rewarded according to its contribution to production. So, surplus-value, s, appears to equal capital's contribution and $s/(s + v)$, its share, while by implication, variable capital, v, appears to equal labor's contribution and $v/(v+s)$, its share. Within a few decades after *Capital* was published, neoclassical economists, having substituted utility for labor value, would use the same trick but with fancier mathematics.

Mathematical concepts such as production functions, e.g., $Q = f(K, L)$, permitted the use of calculus to derive marginal products for K (dQ/dK) and L (dQ/dL) and with a few more assumptions, conclude that wages equal market value of dQ/dL, and profits equal the market value of dQ/dK. In the development of this theory of production, the labor theory of value of the classical political economists was set aside, so the only "value" left was money price determined by markets. Yet the conclusion was essentially the same, both the old formulae and the new ones hid exploitation by reducing the antagonistic social relations of production to engineering-like technical relations among things.[20]

---

20. It would not be until the 1960s, when economists at Cambridge University in England, building on the work of Piero Sraffa (1898–1983), attacked these formulations and forced neoclassical economists to admit that they were built on logical flaws, e.g., they pretend to *derive* the price of capital but to do so they must assume the price of capital in order to aggregate heterogeneous capital to come up with "K." See G. C. Harcourt, *Some Cambridge Controversies in the Theory of Capital*, Cambridge: Cambridge University Press, 1972.

For Marx, by formulating the value of labor as one part of the working day, the classical political economic formulation understated what was for him the essential issue: how much of workers' time toiling produced the means of consumption they needed (or their value/money equivalent) and how much of their work time produced the means of production (or their value/money equivalent) capital needed. Clearly, both formulations of the rate of surplus-value, the classical one, $s/(v+s)$, and his own, s/v, are possible measures of capital's share of the total new value created. He preferred s/v because it provided a more direct representation of the division of workers' days. When he notes how $s/(v+s)$ is a "mode of presentation which arises, by the way, out of the capitalist mode of production itself"[21] and promises to return to the point later on, odds have it that he was thinking about the parallel between $s/(v+s)$ and $s/(c+v)$, the rate of profit. He did return to juxtapose the rate of profit to the rate of exploitation in material included in Volume III of *Capital* where he presents the rate of profit as expressing capital's preoccupation with the rate of return on its investment ($c+v$) and the rate of exploitation as expressing the degree to which workers are being exploited, i.e., forced to produce products and value for someone else.[22]

Commenting on the "popular expression" that juxtaposes unpaid to paid labor, instead of surplus to necessary labor, Marx affirms the reasonableness of that way of talking about exploitation in money terms. By pretending to buy labor, rather than labor-power, capitalists argue that all labor is paid for. But as workers grasp intuitively and Marx's analysis in Chapter 6 demonstrated, although fluctuations in supply and demand can push wages above, or drive them below, the value of labor-power, on average workers are only paid wages equivalent to the amount of work that produces the value of their labor-power and capitalists arrogate to themselves the fruits of all excess labor beyond that—with no compensation to those performing it. He concludes, "Capital, therefore, is not only command over labour, as Adam Smith thought. It is essentially the command over unpaid labor. All surplus-value. . . is in substance the materialization of unpaid labor time."[23] But what is the importance of this command over unpaid labor time? We have seen how Marx's focus is on one, and only one, use of surplus-value, or unpaid labor time: investment, i.e., employing it to impose more work in the future!

---

21. *Capital, Vol. I*, p. 670.
22. *Capital, Vol. III*, Part One, Chapter 3: "The Relationship between Rate of Profit and Rate of Surplus-Value."
23. *Capital, Vol. I*, p. 672.

9

Part Six
Wages

In these four chapters, 19–22, Marx analyzes the implications of the value of labor-power taking the form of money wages. These chapters are the only chapters in Volume I of *Capital* in which he examines the monetary form of the variables he has developed for his analysis. Throughout the rest of the book he couches his analysis in terms of value. Later, in Volume III, he takes up the various money forms of surplus-value, i.e., profit, interest and rent. Examining the socio-political implications of various money forms, he focuses on how capital uses wages to hide and enhance exploitation. My comments consider how wages are also a source of power for workers, how they resist the use of the wage form against them and how the wage also hides capital's ability to annex unwaged labor.

Chapter 19: The Transformation of the Value of Labour-Power into Wages. This chapter opens Part Six by focusing on one form that the value of labor-power can take: money wages. It is not the only form, but as the most widespread form in the nineteenth century, it was the object of Marx's analysis. Drawing a parallel between wage labor and slavery and juxtaposing both to corvée labor, he shows how this form hides exploitation. To this I add some notes on how money wages also hide the subordination of unwaged labor to capital.

Chapter 20: Time-Wages. Marx shows how the structure of this first form of money wages, one of several, both hides exploitation and makes it amenable to manipulation to increase the rate of exploitation. I point out the difference between nominal and real wages and how workers, as well as capital, try to manipulate time-wages to their advantage.

Chapter 21: Piece-Wages. Capitalists also use piece-wages to hide exploitation and try to manipulate them to increase it. Marx details the insidious advantages of piece-wages to capital—how they lead to harder work and lower costs of supervision. To complement his analysis of waged work, I apply elements of his analysis to unwaged labor, in schools, in the home and in the countryside.

Chapter 22: National Differences in Wages. With capitalism spreading across the world, Marx confronts the problem of evaluating the resulting international hierarchy of wages. He notes many of the factors that must be taken into account, offers two case studies and ends with a critique of the protectionist arguments of the economist Henry Carey. I then show the relevance of Marx's analysis to contemporary issues surrounding trade and so-called "free trade" agreements.

CHAPTER 19: THE TRANSFORMATION OF THE VALUE OF LABOUR-POWER INTO WAGES

Outline of Marx's Analysis

The value of "labor" cannot be measured by labor. Being "the substance, and the immanent measure of value," labor "has no value itself."

The physiocrats and the classical economists:
  – saw that behind the market price of "labor" lay its costs of production,
  – but conceived of its production in terms of the production of the worker

But what is produced and what the worker sells is not "labor" but *labor-power.*

The worker sells labor-power in exchange for a wage, but
  – the wage form hides the distinction between necessary labor and surplus labor

In corvée labor distinction between labor for self and labor for the lord is clear.

But in slave and wage labor the "form of appearance" hides the "essence"
  – in slave labor all labor seems to be for the owner, hides labor for self
  – in wage labor all labor seems to be for the worker, hides surplus labor for capitalist

The wage is thus one form of appearance of the essential value of labor-power that lies behind it,
  – but the discovery of this essence required clear "scientific" thought

Commentary

The money wage is one form of appearance of the value of labor-power—the most pervasive form in the nineteenth century and still common today. But it is only one form; there are others. For instance, with payment-in-kind, seasonal workers in agriculture are sometimes paid with a share of the harvest, a common practice in the Global South. Or, shoemakers, silk workers and shipyard workers in the eighteenth century were paid in part through tolerance of the appropriation of scraps of the materials they were given to work.[1] Salaries and commissions are other forms of money payment for the value of labor-power. The analysis presented in these chapters provide a general methodology for analyzing all forms of the value of labor-power, and therefore has implications that go far beyond money wages. Here, Marx examines the implications of this one form for both capitalists and workers. In all cases, the analysis of the value of labor-power presented in Chapter 6 underlies the analysis of the wage form in these four chapters and amounts to a prelude to this chapter.

Marx's argument that "Labor is the substance, and the immanent measure of value, but it has no value itself," makes sense because if labor is the measure, or *numéraire*, of value, then we can't speak of the value of that numéraire in the same sense we do of what it measures.[2] Economists, who say that the value of something is its money price, are aware that they cannot speak of the value of money, except in terms of its usefulness as numéraire or in terms of its functional roles, e.g., as a means of circulation. However, we have seen in Part One how Marx's theory of the value of labor to capital explains the value of money to capital, and hence to those against whom it is used.

The distinction that Marx employs between appearance and essence is a very Hegelian one and has been much critiqued in recent years. The primary thrust of that critique has been against the notion that there is one discoverable essence lying behind the appearance of things. This critique has been a by-product of the post-structuralist emphasis on how any object, event, relationship, etc., can be viewed from many points of view and be subject to many different interpretations without any one of them being able to lay claim to the one-and-only "essential truth" about what is being interpreted. In the language of appearance and essence, there are as many essences as there are interpreters. What is seen as essential by one, is perhaps not essential to another. The relevance of this critique to Marx's use of the distinction is only, it seems to me, to remind us that the essence

---

1.   See Peter Linebaugh, *The London Hanged*.
2.   *Capital, Vol. I*, p. 677.

he emphasizes is that it is labor-power, the ability and willingness to work, that is being bought and sold, not work itself. As the development of his argument proceeds, we soon learn that another essential aspect of the relationship is the way this reality is hidden, the way exploitation is made to disappear by the apparent nature of the wage.

How Form Hides Reality

Marx's analysis of how the wage hides the exploitation of labor is reminiscent of his discussion of fetishism in Chapter 1. There he discussed how the commodity and its relationship to money *appeared* to be merely a relationship between things, but upon analysis, both turned out to be moments of the social relationships among people. Here the wage *appears* to be payment for work performed and is often called the price or value of labor. But just as we have seen how price more generally embodies a complex set of class relationships, so too the wage embodies the class relationship of exploitation: the invisible distinction between necessary and surplus labor.

The wage, he argues, makes exploitation invisible by making it seem as if the worker is paid for the labor performed. With most common forms of the wage, e.g., time and piece-wages analyzed in the next two chapters, the more workers work, the more they are paid. There seems to be a one-to-one correspondence between work performed and wages paid. Slavery illustrates the opposite extreme. All of the work of slaves appears to be done for their owners. But some of the work performed by slaves must produce their own means of subsistence (or in capitalism the value thereof) or the slave would soon die. So here too, the real relationship, that slaves work both for themselves and for their masters is hidden from view by the form of the relationship. Marx juxtaposes both these situations to corvée labor. In corvée labor, serfs are forced to spend part of the week working directly for their lord, perhaps in the lord's fields, perhaps building the lord's roads and buildings, and so on. In that case, the distinction between the time the serfs work for themselves (necessary labor) and the time they work for the lord (surplus labor) is clear—just the opposite of the situation under both slavery and capitalism.

In this chapter, serfs and slaves are Marx's only mentions of the unwaged. Serfs toiled in a different kind of class society. Slaves too, in the ancient world, but within capitalism they were workers without wages.[3] In Part Eight, he notes how those expropriated from the land found themselves

---

3.   In the US prior to the Civil War, as Robert Starobin has pointed out, there were exceptions, where slaves worked for wages and returned most of those wages to their owners. See his book *Industrial Slavery in the Old South*, Oxford: Oxford University Press, 1970.

dispossessed and without wages or any other form of income. In Chapter 25, we find his most extensive analysis of the unwaged in capitalism: the reserve army of those surviving without wages. But as I have emphasized in earlier commentaries, since Marx wrote *Capital*, feminist Marxists have pointed out how the unwaged work of procreation and childrearing (mostly by women) and that of schoolwork (mostly by children of both sexes) produce the next generation of labor-power. The mostly unwaged work of repairing the labor-power of both waged and unwaged also reproduces existing labor-power. The absence of direct payment to housewives and most students hides the reality that much of this work benefits capitalists by creating and recreating the labor-power necessary for its very existence. The point is that such work does not *appear* to be done for capital, but that appearance hides the reality of vast amounts of unwaged work.

The way in which the absence of a wage hides such work is now widely recognized. Measures of gross domestic product (GDP), for example, systematically ignore unwaged work and the value of what houseworkers or students produce because there is no wage and no marketed products (other than labor-power). Economists and others who work on countries in which subsistence agricultural production is widespread are well aware that conventional measures of GDP understate the magnitude of aggregate output, and of the amount of work that produced it.[4] Lawyers have also hired economists to present in court—in support of demands for the payment of alimony or palimony—estimates of the value of housework performed by spouses/partners being divorced. In both cases, because there are no market prices, economists impute monetary values to the work performed and products produced.

The Power of the Wage

Although money in the form of the wage gives capital the power to impose labor, that same money, in the hands of those who receive it, grants a different kind of power. While payment in kind, say part of a harvest, has a use-value limited by the nature of the payment, wages paid in the form of money, the universal equivalent, can be spent by workers on whatever they can find and afford in the marketplace. In Marx's time, wages were so low that everyone referred to them as "subsistence" wages because, on average, they provided the minimum amount of money required to feed, clothe and house waged workers and their families. Under such circumstances, it is understandable that not much attention was paid to how workers might spend money for anything beyond survival. But even then, in periods of rapid

4. See Derek Blades and François Lequiller, *Understanding National Accounts*, Paris: OECD, 2006; and Martha Nussbaum, *Creating Capabilities: The Human Development Approach*, Cambridge, MA: Belknap Press of Harvard University, 2013.

economic expansion, as capitalists invested and hired more workers, labor markets tightened, and wages rose above subsistence, workers sometimes found themselves with extra money to spend. Over time as workers became better organized, were able to reduce working hours, force up the value of labor-power and increase their wages, possibilities expanded.

To some degree, workers have used their increased purchasing power simply to improve their lives, e.g., buying better food, clothing or housing, time away from work, or to reduce worries, e.g., more access to medicine and health care, some savings for hard times, or to explore alternative, less stressful ways of being, individually or collectively in play or innovation.

To some degree, however, workers have also used their extra income for purposes of struggle. Time bought away from work has been used to organize, just as it has been used to recuperate and enjoy life. The wider the organizational efforts, the higher the costs of getting people together to discuss tactics and strategies. The use of telephones, the Internet and cell phones, for communication among those organizing, costs money as well as time. So too does travel, by car, bus, train or airplane, to organizational gatherings. Members of unions have pooled some of their extra wage in the form of dues, making it possible to rent spaces to gather, to free some for regular organizing, to create strike funds to replace wages during strikes. Workers anticipating, or already participating in armed revolt have bought guns and ammunition; some have even managed to buy uniforms and other equipment. In all these ways, wages have financed resistance to capitalist domination.

These powers of the wage help explain why those without a wage often seek one. As we saw in Part Eight, many of the expropriated and dispossessed enter the labor market seeking a wage for survival. Even those not threatened with starvation or homelessness, such as the unwaged spouses of waged or salaried partners, may seek a wage to have independent control over their own money. Why? In many one-income marriages, the spouse who earns the wage or salary wields more power than the one who does not. More power exists in two senses. First, the wage (or salary) is in the hands of the person who receives it and that conveys the power to either withhold or share it with a spouse or children.[5] In some arrangements, such income is deposited in a joint bank account accessible to either spouse. In others, the income-earning spouse doles out income to their unwaged partner in the same manner they may give children "allowances." Second, despite the existence of alimony, palimony and co-property laws, command of the wage or salary gives greater power to walk away from a marriage or a

---

5. One form of abuse, both of spouses and of children, has been the withholding of money, depriving the household's unwaged of needed use-values.

cohabitation arrangement, especially a long-lasting one, particularly when the unwaged spouse has little prospect of obtaining a wage or salary high enough to avoid poverty. In every case, asymmetrical income creates hierarchical distributions of power in family relationships, between spouses and between parents and children.

Inevitably, this asymmetrical distribution of power produces antagonism and struggle by those in less powerful positions. Individually, women have battled with husbands, using weapons of the weak when necessary, overt rebellion when possible.[6] Collectively, they have fought for legal rights equal to men, for access to contraception and abortion, for access to schools, for welfare payments or family allocations that vary with the number of children, to have the value of housework recognized and compensated. The Wages for Housework Campaign demanded payment from the state, financed by taxes on business.

Children, whether at home or as students, have resisted the imposition of work through means as varied as playing sick, or using schoolwork to avoid "chores," skipping school, playing around in the classroom and cheating, but they have also fought to be compensated for such work, with some marginal success. In 1911, schoolchildren in dozens of English cities revolted, demanding payment for cleaning blackboards (and an end to corporal punishment).[7] At the university level, scholarships and fellowships, teaching and research assistantships provide some compensation for a few. Some are following the examples of other low-paid workers and forming unions to bargain collectively for higher wages.[8] Others, following the lead of the Wages for Housework Movement, have called for Wages for Schoolwork for all students and an end to the waged/unwaged division in schools that gives those with wages power over those without.[9] Recently, students have launched a national movement for the elimination of student debt acquired to pay the costs of their schoolwork.[10]

---

6. Feminists, such as Simone de Beauvoir in her classic book *Le Deuxième Sexe*, Tomes I et II, Paris: Gallimard, 1949, described such methods of resistance by women. On this kind of resistance by peasants, see James Scott's *Weapons of the Weak: Everyday Forms of Peasant Resistance*, New Haven, CT: Yale University Press, 1985 and *Domination and the Arts of Resistance: Hidden Transcripts*, New Haven, CT: Yale University Press, 1990. Marx, drawing on contemporary accounts, saw both persistent covert sabotage and sometimes open revolt among slaves.

7. See Dave Marston, *Children's Strikes in 1911*, History Workshop, 1973. Online at libcom.org.

8. These efforts are frequently recounted in *The Chronicle of Higher Education* and *Inside Higher Ed* (online).

9. See *Wages for Students*, Brooklyn, NY: Common Notions, 2016.

10. See Strike Debt, *The Debt Resisters' Operations Manual*, Brooklyn, NY: PM Press, 2014.

CHAPTER 20: TIME-WAGES

Outline of Marx's Analysis

Time wages = usually payment per hour or per day
  Nominal wages = money exchange-value of labor-power
  Real wages = the value of the means of subsistence purchased by
  wages
    – can be above or below value of labor-power
Average "price" of labor = average daily value of labor-power divided
  by the average number of hours worked,
    e.g., (daily wage of 3 shillings)/12 hours = hourly price or wage,
    = 3s/12hrs = 36d/12hrs (at 12d per s) = 3d/hr = hourly wage of 3
    pence
If the daily wage is fixed, e.g., 3s, and the capitalists impose *longer*
  hours, the effective hourly wage drops:
With a daily wage of 3s and 1s = 12d,
    – 10 hrs of work implies hourly wage of 3s/10hr = 36d/10/hr =
    3.6d/hr
    – 12 hrs of work, the hourly wage falls to 3s/12hr = 36d/12/hr =
    3d/hr
    – 15 hrs of work, the hourly wage falls to 3s/15hr = 36d/15/hr =
    2.4d/hr
      As we saw in Chapter 10, if the working day is lengthened, with
      no change in the value of labor-power, then the capitalists make
      more surplus-value or profit
If the hourly wage is fixed, then a change in the number of working
  hours will change the workers' income
If daily value of labor-power = 3s, normal working day = 12 hours,
  under these conditions, the hourly wage = 3d, but...
  Suppose the capitalist *reduces* working hours (say during a
  downturn in the business cycle):
    – from 12 to 8, w/wages still 3d/hr, daily wage falls to 2s
    – from 12 to 6, w/wages still 3d/hr, daily wage falls to 1s 6d
  In both cases, the workers are now earning *less* than the wage they
  require for survival
Implication: unless capitalists are constrained by law, e.g., Factory
  Acts, they may manipulate hours and wages for their own benefit,
  to the detriment of the workers

▶

"Hence," Marx writes, "the perfectly rational revolt of the London building workers in 1860 against the attempt of the capitalists to impose on them this sort of wage by the hour." And hence too, the fight for the Factory Acts to put a limit on such manipulations

Overtime = imposition of hours more than the "normal," whatever that happens to be

1. Overtime should be paid at a higher rate, because the deterioration of labor-power accelerates during extra, exhausting hours, and therefore, the value of labor-power (the cost of repairing and reproducing that labor-power) rises. Sometimes the capitalists recognize this and pay a bit more, although Marx suggests that the bit more they pay is not proportional to the cost of repairing the extra wear and tear on the worker

2. If, using methods such as those described above, the capitalist succeeds in lowering wages at current hours, then workers will need, be willing to accept, or even fight for, longer hours

3. The same effect is sometimes achieved by increasing the intensity of work. Higher intensity means more labor being supplied, an increased supply of labor will tend to lower wages, lower wages will lead to more overtime

4. These dynamics are circulated through competition wherein the success of one capitalist in this area will lead other capitalists to seek the same success, because the success of the first allows the undercutting of the others through the reduction in the prices of their wares

Commentary

Value and Price

As we have seen throughout the book, Marx's analysis is developed and presented for the most part in terms of value. Where he has used monetary examples, he uses the simplifying assumption that prices are equal to values. He assumes away cheating in exchange, i.e., cases where unequal values are exchanged. Under that assumption, wages, the price of labor-power, always equal the value of labor-power. Workers are still cheated, however, even when they receive the full value of their labor-power through the extraction of surplus-value. In this analysis of wages, however, his analysis reveals how capitalists' manipulation of the wage to extract more work does sometimes result in workers being cheated out of the full value of their labor-power.

What is negotiated between workers and capitalists are money wages. Consideration of the value of labor-power enters those negotiations only to the degree that workers demand wages that enable them to buy everything they think they need to be able to continue to work. Workers have come to understand the relationship between what they are earning, money-wise, and what they require (or demand) to live. Fairly early on, they learned to distinguish between *nominal* and *real* wages and to recognize that their interests lay in maintaining or increasing the latter. More recently, the demand of low-income workers for a "living wage" roughly approximates a monetary estimate of the level of wages required for minimal levels of reproducing labor-power.[11] In this chapter, Marx shows how capitalist manipulations, in search of higher profits, can result in wages falling *below* the value of labor-power, so that workers are cheated in exchange as well as through the extraction of surplus-value.

Two General Methodological Points

First, Marx is analyzing the peculiarities of one form of a form. Wages are one form of the value of labor-power; time wages are one form of that form. The peculiarities that interest him at this point concern the various ways in which this form of wages can be, and often is, manipulated by capital in its efforts to impose more work. The same will be true in his next chapter on piece-wages. The same would be true if he had analyzed other forms, or if *we* extend his analysis to those other forms. We might note, for example, how salaries—which are paid at a fixed rate, usually so-and-so-much per year (and thus per month)—leave open the amount of actual labor time required. Jobs that pay salaries generally designate the tasks to be performed and those tasks often require far more than the standard number of hours per week, e.g., 40 hours in the US after World War II. Thus, the commonplace that salaried workers wind up spending many extra hours in their offices and go home with briefcases full of work to be done in their supposed free time and, these days, are often on-call via cell phones.

Other forms of working-class income that also support the reproduction of labor-power, e.g., unemployment compensation, welfare payments, grades, public health services, are rarely recognized as such. For example, unemployment compensation is generally presented to the public as a kind of welfare for the temporarily unemployed. However, by forcing those who want to receive compensation to actively seek out employers and then provide evidence of having done so, it is structured to require the work of looking for work, of making the labor market function. In this case, both the amount (low) of the compensation and the rules (how many interviews

---

11. There is a useful Wikipedia entry on living wages that sketches both the history of the idea and the demand.

are required) can be, and are, manipulated to impose more work. In each case, the objective of the analysis should be to identify the ways in which those particular forms of income have been, or are being, manipulated to impose more work reproducing labor-power.

Second, Marx's emphasis here, as in so much of the book, is on the way *capital* tries to manipulate this form of the wage to its own advantage. To the degree that he discusses workers' struggle, it is primarily about their defensive reactions to such manipulations, such as the "revolt of the London building workers of 1860." But surely we can go further than this and look at how workers' wage struggles may be not merely resistance but quite aggressive demands for things they want. We saw this distinction in Marx's treatment in Chapter 10 over the battles over the working day. He sketched how workers *resisted* the lengthening of the working day, but then passed over to the attack, *took the initiative*, and fought for a reduction in the working day. Conflicts over wages, like the battles for *reducing* the working day have often been initiated by workers demanding higher wages and the increased and more varied consumption they can purchase. One obvious, recent example has been the fight by service workers for $15 dollars an hour minimum wage.

Moreover, it should be clear from his analysis that workers have fought to raise wages not only to get more money and better consumption, but to be able to work less! Success at forcing up the hourly wage, especially when workers have been successful in fixing a normal working week, e.g., 40 hours in the post-World War II period, means less compulsion to work. As wages rise, not only is there less compulsion but the rising wage makes more and more activities possible during non-work hours and therefore leads to demands for a *reduction* in working hours. Thus the more or less steady rise in wages after 1945 for many workers—codified in productivity deals—led inevitably to demands in the United States and Europe for reduced working weeks, either 35–36 hours spread out over five days, or the existing 40 hours packed into four days (an effective reduction of working time if you consider—as you must—that the time of preparing for work, going to work, returning from work, etc., is really time working for the boss and not free for your own use).

Where there have been institutional obstacles—such as the reactionary recalcitrance of union bureaucrats to the formal posing of such demands—workers have often simply refused work and appropriated extra free time. Such refusal has included absenteeism, playing on the job, wildcat strikes, sabotage and so on. In the Appalachian coal fields of the 1960s and 1970s, for example, success in raising wages (in part through Keynesian productivity deals that resulted in massive reductions in the number of jobs) led many young miners to seek more free time through wildcat strikes.[12] They would go to work with their hunting rifle or fishing pole in the trunk of their car in anticipation of a wildcat strike that would give most of them the day, or days, off. The possible provocations of such a strike in coal mines were multiple given the dangerous, poisonous character of the work. It was the success in raising wages that made these other struggles possible.

Time-Wages Hide Exploitation

Along with the way time-wages provide one set of tools for capital to exploit workers, and increase that exploitation, so too does their structure play the convenient role of *hiding* that exploitation. In the case of hourly wages, the more hours workers work, the more they are paid—at least in principle. The fewer hours they work, for sure the less they will be paid. To keep track of exactly how long many workers work, capitalists developed "time clocks." There is a traditional one in Chaplin's *Modern Times*, the kind that requires each worker to pick up their personal card from one rack, stick it in the clock mechanism where the time is recorded, and then place the card in another rack. (The use of two racks makes it easier to see if anyone is late or has "clocked-out" early.) Such clocks are still used in some places. One example is the blocky, green Acroprint 125 Mechanical Time Clock manufactured by the Acroprint Time Recorder Company.

Because workers learn to cover for each other, by punching their friend's card in if the friend is a little late, or by punching their friend out if they leave early, capitalists have updated their time clocks. The Acroprint Time Recorder Company—among several such companies—also produces time clocks that use "biometrics," i.e., modern fingerprint recognition equipment, to make sure one worker can't help another and that the corporation extracts the maximum feasible work time from each worker. Similar technologies include things like personalized card swipe units, portable/PDA technology (for geographically dispersed workers) and computer login recordings. For example, in computer tech call centers the workers' logins are automatically recorded the moment they start work—not when they leave home for work, or when they arrive at the company, or even when they walk in the door, but when they put on their headphones and login. Associated with such modern computerized time clocks are software programs to reduce the labor costs of tracking work times and calculating wages due. Take a look, for example, at the reports generated by TimeClock Plus software.[13]

---

12.   See William Cleaver, "Wildcats in the Appalachian Coal Fields."

13.   www.timeclockplus.com/pages/software/v7/professional.aspx.

Where workers are paid per hour, and their work time carefully monitored, it appears that if they work more and are paid more, especially at higher rates, they are not exploited. But this apparent correlation between labor time and pay obscures the existence of surplus labor time. Not surprisingly, when Marx writes about overtime wages, he emphasizes how even when workers are paid extra for working longer, the extra pay may be only a small portion of the value their labor adds to what they are producing and to the profits the capitalists realize upon the sale of those products.

As noted in my previous discussion of "nibbling and cribbling," neither the concept nor the reality of "overtime" are recognized or compensated in the case of salaried workers, or in the case of unwaged labor in the home or for school. Few measure the time of salaried work, or unwaged housework or schoolwork, other than those who find themselves working extra hours! Recent work on "cognitive" labor has highlighted how frequently mental labor on-the-job continues off-the-job, as workers, waged, salaried or unwaged, divert otherwise free time into thinking about their work tasks.[14] Unrecognized as "overtime," few demand compensation.

Overtime and Competition

Marx's discussion of "overtime"—time workers work beyond the current normal working day—was shaped by the widespread use of such extra work in a period in which capitalists were still fighting the Factory Acts discussed in Chapter 10 and sought various ways to subvert any limits on the time over which they could exploit workers. Marx's comments in Section 2 of that chapter on capitalists' "nibbling and cribbling" at the working day—stealing a few minutes here, a few minutes there—gives a sense of the intensity of the struggle in those days. But those struggles, those day-to-day, hour-to-hour struggles between managers and workers never disappeared, not with the Factory Acts nor with more recent labor legislation. Not only has such legislation often not been enforced, but it has often had only partial coverage, leaving many workers unprotected. Marx gives several examples of industries, e.g., paper-staining and bleaching works, in which capitalist manipulation resulted in workers being forced to work overtime; others are easy to find today.

As Juliet Schor documented in her 1993 book *The Overworked American*, the assault on workers in the United States by the Carter and Reagan administrations in the late 1970s and early 1980s resulted in dramatic reductions in hourly wages and other benefits and forced more and more workers to work overtime trying to maintain their real income

---

14. See Yann Moulier-Boutang, *Cognitive Capitalism*, Malden, MA: Polity Press, 2011; and Michael Peters and Ergin Bulut (eds.), *Cognitive Capitalism, Education and Digital Labor*, New York: Peter Lang, 2011.

and standards of living.[15] This was not a change in this industry or that industry, but a change in the overall condition of workers at the national level. By mid-century, capital had learned from John Maynard Keynes and his followers how government macroeconomic policies could be brought to bear against the class as a whole and methods previously used by individual capitalists could be generalized.

Three other worker responses to lowered wages, associated with attempts to maintain the *family* wage, were the entrance of more spouses into the labor market seeking a second wage, the search for second jobs for the same purpose and the taking on of more family debt. In the first two cases, the amount of work being extracted from the working class increased as people worked more hours, whether in old jobs, new jobs or extra jobs. Official statistics on "overtime" naturally fail to take such phenomena into account. In the third case, increased debt inevitably requires increased work to pay it off.

In the case of the baking industry, cited in this chapter, Marx uses a screed from one set of bakers against another set to illustrate how desperate foreign workers and young workers—who "are obliged to accept almost any wages they can obtain"—were being forced to work extra-long hours giving some baking enterprises a competitive advantage over others.[16] In post-World War II Europe and in the United States, the same kind of thing was engineered through the pitting of poor workers from the Mediterranean area or deeper in Africa against better off workers in Northern Europe and poor workers from Mexico, Central America and the Caribbean against better off workers in the USA. More recently, in Europe poor workers from the collapsed communist East have been pitted against the higher waged, shorter working time, better organized workers in Western Europe. In both areas, "globalization" has involved modern multinational corporations closing down operations in the higher-waged West and moving to the lower-waged, longer working time, less organized South and Southeast Asia. Their excuse, as in Marx's time, has been "competition." In a 2004 *New York Times* article we find the following testimony by the representative of one of those multinational corporations. "It's about lowering labor costs," said Peter Gottal, a spokesperson for Siemens, which is based in Munich. "Where we are in a global competition, 35 hours are no longer feasible. We just need more hours."

The article contains many more examples. It also makes clear that hovering behind the current assault on working hours, is a follow-up assault on vacation time. Just as European workers have been more successful than American workers in reducing the length of the working week,

---

15. Juliet Schor, *The Overworked American*, New York: Basic Books, 1993.
16. *Capital, Vol. I*, p. 690.

so too have they been more successful in gaining annual days of vacation. Whereas the average annual vacation in the US is only 12 days, it has been forced up to 18 days in Japan, 25 days in France and 30 in Germany. What we can see here is the contingent relationship between "overtime" and "the normal working day." Obviously, if the "normal working day" (or week, or year) can be redefined legally in a way that lengthens it, then some of what had hitherto been "overtime" and paid a bit more, would become "normal" time and paid at regular rates. Even now, in the twenty-first century, the relevance of Marx's analysis of work time in the mid-nineteenth century is strikingly, and appallingly, relevant.

What this use of desperate immigrant labor and corporate displacement to weaker pools of labor demonstrate is the real class logic behind "competition." The term is used rhetorically, and ideologically, to evoke competition between corporations or between nations, but what we see here is that the capitalist organization of "competition" is really the pitting of workers against workers with the objective of undermining the power of the stronger through the employment of the weaker. The corollary to this strategy is the fanning of racial and ethnic prejudices and the vicious politics that support them. In Germany fomenting the fear of Polish and Turkish workers, or Syrian refugees, feeds Nazis hate groups who, crying "Defense of the Fatherland!," attack those workers and burn their apartment buildings. Similar hate groups in France, egged on not only by Jean Le Pen's minority National Front party, but by official state policies encouraging such competition mount similar campaigns. American politicians have long played the racial card against Black and Chicano workers and against immigrant workers as well. Most recently, and most obviously, Donald Trump's endlessly repeated promises to build a literal wall across the southern US border have clearly been aimed at fomenting racist antagonism against both immigrant workers and refugees. In all these cases, the politics of fear and hate works to divert workers' energy from defending against policies aimed at depriving them of rights won in the past and making it easier for capitalists to drive down wages, impose overtime and redefine "normal work time" upward. After being defeated as a capitalist strategy for almost 40 years in the West, absolute surplus-value has returned with a vengeance.

CHAPTER 21: PIECE-WAGES

Outline of Marx's Analysis

Piece-wage = payment according to the number of pieces produced
Piece-rate = payment per piece
▶

Piece-wage = a form of a form, just like time-wages

Piece-wages *seem* as if workers are paid according to their labor

Piece-wages and time-wages often exist side-by-side:
- in the same industry
- in the same factory

Marx's example as point of departure:
- in 12 hours of SNLT a worker produces 24 pieces
- with total value of 6s (1 shilling = 12 pence) or 72d (pence), value per piece = 3d
- if the piece-rate = 1.5d/piece, in 12 hours worker is paid 1.5d x 24 pieces = 36d or 3s = value of *LP*
- but with the value of 24 pieces = 6s
- the capitalist takes the other 3s as surplus-value = six of the 12 hours

The particularities of piece-wages
1) Setting of piece rates is a source of struggle between workers and capitalists
   - what is the socially necessary labor time (SNLT) per piece?
   - answered by experience.
   - but with new technology or new products there is a struggle
   - whatever the SNLT, that is the standard each worker must meet, or be dismissed
   - standard is set in terms of time, e.g., one waistcoat = 1 hour
   - standard also sets the average intensity of labor required, e.g., to produce a waistcoat within 1 hour
2) With piecework the need for direct "superintendence" is reduced or even eliminated; workers are forced to work fast and well to meet the going standard of production under the threat of losing their job
3) Piece-wages tend to produce hierarchies of wages
   a) The "sweating system" wherein a parasitic middleman "sublets" or "subcontracts" workers and takes a cut of their wages
   b) An employer signs a contract with only one worker who then subcontracts other workers
   c) Individual abilities vary, therefore output and wages vary from individual to individual
4) Piece-wages result in workers being willing, or even desirous, of longer working hours
   - to make more money
   - lowered piece rates make them want to work longer to maintain their total wages

►

5) Technological change increasing the productivity of a given time and intensity of labor will:
   – either, lead to a rise in wages if the piece-rates remain the same
   – or, lead capitalists to try to reduce piece-rates to capture all the fruits of rising productivity

To illustrate this dynamic, Marx assumes productivity doubles. As a result:
   – @ 1.5d/piece our worker's wages would double (assuming the sales price remained the same at 3d/piece)
   – the total product value would double, and both worker and the capitalist would now get 6s each instead of only 3s
   – therefore, the capitalists try to lower the piece rate from 1.5d to .75d to capture all the increased value
   – if successful, of the new total value of 12s the workers would get only 3s while the capitalist walks off with 9s
   – therefore, there is a struggle over who benefits and how much
   – the capitalists accuse the workers who try to share in the increased productivity of "intimidation" and of trying to "establish a duty on mechanical improvements" (p. 700, fn 20)

Commentary

Piecework, to the experienced worker, whether in factory, mine or field, always carries the flavor of exploitation. Capitalists love piecework and piece-wages, because where workers are paid by the piece—whether by the ton of coal cut, or by each part produced in a machine shop, or by the number of vines pruned—to earn a living wage, they must work hard and fast to produce enough pieces, even without someone looking over their shoulder. Most costs of supervision essentially pass from the capitalist to the workers as they internalize the discipline of piecework and impose work on themselves, and all too often, compete with one another.

In Jack London's "The Apostate" (1906), Johnny's supervisor is quite happy with his work:

The superintendent was very proud of him and brought visitors to look at him. In ten hours three hundred dozen bottles passed through his hands. This meant that he had attained machine-like perfection. All waste movements were eliminated. Every motion of his thin arms, every movement of a muscle in the thin fingers, was swift and accurate. He worked at high tension, and the result was that he grew nervous. At night his muscles twitched in his sleep, and in the daytime, he could not relax and rest. He remained keyed up and his muscles continued to twitch.[17]

Even Malthus, who Marx often mocks for his treatment of the poor, recognized that piecework leads to "too much [work] for any human being."[18]

Piece-Wages Hide Exploitation

Marx's comments about how piece-wages make it seem as if workers are paid for their labor, not their labor-power, parallel those in the last chapter on time wages. New and naive workers do not always recognize the subtlety he insists upon. At first piece-wages encourage workers' "sense of liberty, independence and self-control."[19] To them piecework may seem to provide an opportunity for great achievement: the more you work, the more you get paid. They may not see how the *form* of payment leads them to work hard and long, even to demand overtime. They don't realize at first how the piece-rates are set so that even with their greatest efforts they will be exploited by earning little in relation to the value of what they produce. They don't yet see that if they outperform past standards, their higher productivity will be used to lower the piece-rates, undercutting the wages of everyone with the same job. What may be true in the short run (more work equals more wages) is undermined in the long run (more work equals same wages, same value of labor-power).

More immediately obvious to both capitalists and workers, differential skill and sometimes competition pits workers against workers in a wage hierarchy. Those who work the fastest and most effectively produce more pieces and earn more money. Competition among workers diverts workers' frustration and resentment from their bosses to each other, undermining solidarity and collective resistance.

Resistance

However, in reaction to the unpleasantness of piecework exploitation, workers often band together in self-defense. Where they can, they often fight for hourly wages instead of piece-wages to improve their situation.[20] Where that doesn't seem feasible, their primary objective becomes avoiding

---

17.   London, *Revolution. Stories and Essays*, p. 807. This twitching, resulting from endless repetition of the same motions, is portrayed in *Modern Times* to comedic effect as Charlie continues to jerk his hands in the same manner as when wielding his two wrenches on the assembly line.

18.   *Capital, Vol. I*, pp. 698–699.

19.   Ibid., p. 697.

20.   Marx does note one exceptional case in which the reverse is true. Ibid., p. 697.

being drawn into the cruel spiral of more work–lower rates–more work–lower rates, etc. Collaborating to make sure the higher productivity of some is not used to lower piece-rates for all provides one way to limit exploitation. Everyone works at about the same speed and no-one significantly outperforms the others. They know that if this happens the fastest worker's time will be used to set the pace for everyone else, and that the rates will be lowered so even the fastest worker will make little more than before.

Another of London's tales, "South of the Slot" (1909), about a conservative sociologist who got a factory job in order to study "labor," illustrates the conflict that sometimes emerges between cooperating workers and individuals who either don't understand the dangers, or refuse to go along with the collective strategy. In London's story the violence of piece-rates is resisted by a cooperation willing to use worker-against-worker violence to sabotage the system.[21] This situation was undoubtedly one London knew well, because he had worked in just such a cannery himself.

Over 60 years later, this same theme provided the substance of Patti Smith's 1974 autobiographical blast that shook the world of rock and roll. In "Piss Factory," she recounts being set right by another worker when, at age 16, she worked so fast in a factory "inspecting pipe" that she was "screwin' up the quota." When she resisted slowing down, she was warned.

> I get my nerve up. I take a swig of Romilar
> And walk up to hot shit Dot Hook and I say
> "Hey, hey sister, it doesn't matter whether I do labor fast or slow,
> There's always more labor after."
> She's real Catholic, see. She fingers her cross and she says
> "There's one reason. There's one reason. You do it my way or I push your
> face in.
> We knee you in the john if you don't get off your mustang Sally."[22]

The understanding of the danger to workers of piecework became so obvious, and so exposed, that by 1949 workers in the United States were able to pressure Congress into adding an amendment to the 1938 Fair Labor Standards Act governing wages and hours that specified that piece-workers receive wages *at least* as high as the created "minimum wage." Unfortunately, a great many workers were not covered by that legislation and many are still not covered.

---

21. "South of the Slot", in Pizer (ed.), *Jack London: Novels & Stories*, pp. 817–833.
22. On *New Wave*, 1977.

To thoroughly understand the kind of dynamic Marx describes, read the book *A Worker in a Worker's State* by Miklós Haraszti (1945–).[23] It's a short book and well worth the effort. Haraszti worked in the Red Star Tractor Factory in Communist Hungary where piecework was omnipresent, and his book describes in great detail the dynamics of the struggles between the workers and their managers. Indeed, the book reads like an extended amplification of Marx's chapter on piece-wages.

Piece-wages, Then and Now

Marx sees piece-wages as "the form of wage most appropriate to the capitalist mode of production" because they not only provoke speed-up but also "serve as a lever for the lengthening of the working day and the lowering of wages."[24] There are other methods for forcing workers to work faster, such as tying the workers' speed to that of machines, the kind of thing he covered in Chapter 15. But in the absence of such technological methods, imposing piece-wages and keeping piece-rates low puts pressure on workers to work faster and to want to work longer.

For example, in the vineyards of California many workers are paid piece-wages, while others are paid hourly wages (an example of piece and hourly wages existing side-by-side). A study by a professor of the University of California confirmed the perpetuation of the tendency observed by the factory inspectors in Britain and suggested by Marx's theory: pruners in the vineyards paid by the piece, work faster than those paid by the hour. The former took, on average, about 19 hours to prune an acre of vineyard; the latter about 26 hours. The pieceworkers earned a little more—\$6.84 vs \$6.20 per hour—but not much, about 10 percent.

Growers in California, however, have noticed a drawback to piece-wages (that they and their economists call "incentive pay programs"), namely that workers paid piece-wages may just walk off the job when they meet their income goals. In such cases, gains in work due to increased intensity may be offset by a reduction in total labor time and increased costs of hiring replacement workers, a source of considerable cost and annoyance to employers.

Responding to this annoyance with typical concern for the capitalist's worries about such an "income effect," another researcher from the University of California interviewed field workers and concluded that wages were so low that few workers (3 percent) could afford to leave early. A few more (11 percent) left early because of it being too hot in the fields or just disgust

---

23.   Miklós Haraszti, *A Worker in a Worker's State*, New York: Penguin, 1977.
24.   *Capital, Vol. I*, pp. 697–698.

with how hard the work was in comparison to the low wages. Recognizing the tendency of employers to hold rates low to keep wage costs down and profits up, this same researcher studied the implications for profits of higher piece-rates and the higher output per hour induced by those higher rates. He concluded, and sought to convince employers, that, properly managed, higher piece-rates could produce sufficiently higher productivity to give both higher profits and increases in wages sufficient to keep employees working at the faster rates—essentially an argument compatible with the logic of relative surplus-value.[25]

A modern application of the practice of pitting better-performing pieceworkers against others is the practice of using some to set "benchmarks"—identified "best practices"—against which others are judged. A strategy that can and has been used in all sorts of workplaces, from factories to schools to governments, it encourages innovation by some to increase work from all.[26]

Piece-wages and Quality Control

Although piece-wages reduce the need for direct supervision, capitalists cannot leave workers entirely on their own. With standards set for the number of pieces produced (and hence the time and intensity of work), capitalists must make sure that the workers don't cheat, don't create the illusion of having met that standard by working fast but producing shoddy products. Hence the need for "quality control." In any piecework situation, there must be inspectors who examine the quality of the pieces produced to make sure that the quality as well as the quantity is up to snuff. Where large numbers of pieces are produced, only random samples can be checked for quality. If the number is small, all can be checked. For the kind of field workers whose work behavior was examined in the studies of California agriculture mentioned above, the number of vines pruned, or boxes of fruit picked, etc. was certainly large, so the examination of quality was likely only a sampling. Under such circumstances, capitalists try to organize work so it

---

25. See Gregorio Billikopf, "Designing an Effective Piece Rate", University of California at Berkeley College of Natural Resources website. In another study by the same author, he made clear that high "piece rates don't guarantee productivity"—thus the need for careful measurement and management (http://nature.berkeley.edu/ucce50/ag-labor/7research/7calag02.htm).

26. See Isabelle Bruno, "Governing Social Creativity Through Benchmarking. From Xerox Management to 'Innovative Europe'", in Michal Kozlowski, Agnieszka Kurant and Jan Sowa (eds.), *Joy Forever: The Political Economy of Social Creativity*, London: MayFlyBooks/Ephemera, 2014, pp. 143–155.

is obvious which worker produced which piece, a step necessary to identify those responsible for not meeting quality standards.

Shortly after coming to Texas in 1976 I was asked to help Los Obreros Unidos—a union of packing workers employed by Del Monte—in their contract negotiations. I traveled to the factory town of Crystal City where those workers lived and worked and was able to inspect the organization of their work. Among the tasks that I observed was the forking (literally) of cooked spinach into cans by individual workers (mostly women) lined up on each side of a conveyor belt. The belt carried the spinach to the various stations and a can dispenser hung above each station. The cans were marked so that the quality control person sitting at the end of the production line could immediately identify—and chastise—any worker responsible for overfilling, or underfilling, a given can.

Another example, this time from mining: for most of the history of capitalism coal miners were paid by the amount they dug from the earth. They would dig coal and deliver it to be measured, either by the cart or by weight. At delivery, the coal would be inspected to make sure that the miners had not carelessly (or carefully) included rock in with the coal. This was also the point at which the kind of "fraud" Marx alludes to might occur, namely that the scales measuring the amount of coal might be rigged to register less than the actual tonnage, thus resulting in lower wages for the miner and higher profits for the boss. In his novel *King Coal*, Upton Sinclair evoked such fraud and the dangers of challenging it, despite the existence of state laws giving workers that right:

> In the dining room... someone broached the subject of check-weighmen to him, and the whole table heard his scornful laugh. "Let any man ask for a check-weighman!"
> "You mean they would fire him?" asked Hal.
> "Maybe!" was the answer. "Maybe they make him fire himself."
> "How do you mean?"
> "They make his life one damn misery til he go."
> So it was with check-weighman—as with scrip, and with company stores, and with all the provisions of the law to protect the miner against accidents. You might demand your legal rights, but if you did, it was a matter of the boss's temper. He might make your life one damn misery till you went of your own accord. Or you might get a string of curses and an order, "Down the canyon!"—and likely as not the toe of a boot in your trouser-seat, or the muzzle of a revolver under your nose.[27]

---

27. Upton Sinclair, *King Coal*, New York: Macmillan, 1930, Book One, §16, pp. 50–51.

If we switch our attention from the kinds of manual labor that concerned Marx to more contemporary forms of white-collar labor, we often find the same kind of dynamics. For example, there are any number of salespersons who work "on commission," where their income depends on the number of items they sell or the number of tasks they complete. For example, in automobile and truck retail sales, a base salary—often too low to provide a living wage—must be supplemented by working long and hard talking as many people as possible into buying a vehicle. Other examples can be found in proliferating precarious jobs such driving for Uber, providing digital services on a freelance basis through companies such as Upwork Global, Inc., etc. Such is the "gig" economy, the hell of the "precariat."

Another white-collar job, which is structured by the dynamics of piecework, is that of university professors. While most formally receive pay in the form of a salary, in truth the size of that salary is largely determined by piecework. Although universities pretend to value the importance of teaching, large research universities—that dominate higher education and set the standards by which other universities are judged—overwhelmingly base professors' pay not on teaching but on research and publishing. Among scientists working at universities, the income of many is dependent upon pulling in grants to fund their research. To get those grants, they must compete with others. The primary mode of competition is the publication of articles detailing new discoveries. The old saw "publish or perish" has never ceased to be appropriate.[28]

Also characteristic of the working conditions of academic labor, the choice and management of research projects are left up to the individuals involved. Professors are supposed to understand their fields well enough to choose appropriate projects and skilled enough to craft both research and articles reporting on that research without direct supervision. The more research they perform, the more articles they publish, the more likely their promotion and the more likely they are to receive what are now commonly known as "merit" pay increases. They are, in short, paid according to the number of "pieces" they produce. Moreover, like other pieceworkers they are not entirely on their own. They too are subject to quality control when they submit grant proposals or articles to journals. Quality control takes the form of "peer review," wherein other professors evaluate their proposals or articles and decide whether they should receive grants in the one case or publication in the other. This situation, again like other piecework situations, is highly conducive to intense competition. With research funds and

---

28. With the rapidly spreading practice of substituting adjuncts, paid by the course, for tenure track or tenured professors, piecework has taken on a new form in higher education.

space in prestigious journals limited, professors compete for both—as well, of course, for tenure and promotion. For almost four decades—the last 20 years of the twentieth century and the first 18 of the twenty-first—conservative politicians have used tax reductions on the rich to produce rising fiscal deficits used to rationalize imposing austerity not only on the poor by cutting social programs but also on higher education, including reduced funding for research, which intensifies competition and makes universities more vulnerable to corporate influence.

Piecework in Unwaged Work

While Marx's analysis of piecework and piece-wages focuses on formally waged work, we can apply his analysis beyond that realm in various spheres of unwaged work. Not only is much unwaged work organized by task, rather than by the hour, but much de facto payment for that work is also organized by the piece. As a result, many of the characteristics of piecework in capitalist industry can also be found in various parts of the larger social factory.

Piecework in Schools

Once you recognize the piecework character of the work of professors in universities, it is easy to see how those professors, and the administrators for whom they work, impose the same kind of logic on their students. As students progress through elementary, middle and high schools (K-12), careful supervision is increasingly complemented by unsupervised homework. While parents are often admonished to make sure they do it, some do, many don't. At the university level, although there are a few professors who behave like schoolteachers and take attendance, for the most part students can come or not come to classes as they like. They are expected to impose the discipline of coming to class on themselves—and most do. For the most part, university students' work is unsupervised study whose accomplishment depends totally on the student's self-discipline.

At all levels, most schoolwork consists in the accomplishment of specific tasks, such as writing papers or preparing for and taking tests. Given the large number of courses most students are expected or required to take and the associated large number of tasks set by each teacher or professor, they rarely have either time or energy left over for any autonomous study or real appropriation of knowledge.[29] Indeed, students are notorious among their would-be teachers for doing *only* what is required to prepare for a test or to write a paper.

---

29. See my essay on "Learning, Understanding and Appropriating" (https://webspace. utexas.edu/hcleaver/www/Appropriation.htm).

Such shirking follows from the imposition of fully specified degree plans, with pre-established sets of tasks, at the expense of self-directed study, motivated by students' curiosity. In short, students suffer the imposition of externally imposed, alienated labor of the sort Marx analyzed in the *1844 Manuscripts* and I discussed in my commentary on Chapter 7. As a result, a great many students seek to minimize the amount of time and energy devoted to meeting those requirements. They want to know which pieces of knowledge they will have to know for tests and don't want to waste their time on other, useless, topics. Similarly, the first question about required papers is "How long does it have to be? How many pages? How many footnotes? How many sources?" So commonplace is such minimization of effort, that nowadays, in the age of computers, some professors go to the extent of specifying such things as font size, margins or word count to force students to crank out the specified amount of work.

Associated with such structuring of schoolwork by the piece are piece-rate-like payment systems. The most universal of these is grading in which students are "paid" by the piece, a grade for each task accomplished, each quiz, each test, each paper, each research report, etc. Grades, of course, are not money payments; but the promises that school administrators, professors and future employers attach to grades—that the better grades you get, the better jobs and higher wages you will eventually obtain—makes them "IOUs" on future income. Like piece-wages, grades are handed out according to the number of pieces accomplished and according to the "quality" of those pieces. Teachers and professors, of course, play the role of quality control inspectors; they do the grading, they decide which piece is worth an "A," which is only worth a "B" and so on. In the enlightening thermodynamic metaphor pointed out by George Caffentzis, they play the role of "Maxwell's Daemon," sorting students according to their degree of entropy, i.e., the degree to which they are willing to make their energy available for work.[30]

From this, we can see that whereas piece-wages in industry produces a hierarchy of better and worse paid workers, piecework in schools produces a grade hierarchy, promised to eventually translate into an income hierarchy. As with all such hierarchies, this kind of grading system encourages competition and many students strive to get higher grades than others—both for the immediate satisfaction of demonstrating their superiority and in the hope that later they may get better jobs.

Hence too, the common phenomenon of students banding together in various ways to overcome this alienation. One form of such banding are

---

30. George Caffentzis, "The Work/Energy Crisis and the Apocalypse", *Midnight Notes II*, vol. 1, 1980 (www.midnightnotes.org/workenergyapoc.html).

simple study groups or cheating networks whereby students help each other out in pre-test study or in the tests themselves to minimize the amount of alienated work and to maximize their grades. Fraternities, sororities and other kinds of clubs and associations provide other vehicles for students to collaborate to reduce their schoolwork and increase the time and fun they have outside their academic requirements. All these forms of collaboration try to improve working conditions and outsmart their professorial bosses.

Beyond such small group strategies, large-scale student movements mobilize in their collective self-defense not only to challenge working conditions, but also to demand the elimination or reduction of tasks (e.g., the elimination of redundant comprehensive exams, easier grading), changes in curriculum and the possibility of self-structured programs to allow their work to correspond more closely to their own intellectual interests instead of someone else's notion of what they *should* be doing. All these demands were common in the student movements of the 1960s and 1970s and have reappeared since. More recently, acting in collective self-defense has taken on new meaning in the wake of mass shootings in schools at all levels. The nationwide mobilization of students since the massacre at Stoneman Douglas High School demanding increased gun control constitutes both an angry protest of the failure of politicians to defy the National Rifle Association and the gun industry and a demand for improved working conditions.

Piecework in the Home

We can find similar structures of work and resistance in the larger community, especially in the home. While in Marx's time working-class men, women and children were all finding themselves herded into factories and mines, dramatically shrinking the sphere of domestic life, their eventual success in reducing the length of the working day and in banning of child labor, coupled with the exclusion of women from some jobs made the nuclear family—with only one wage-earner—dominant. One result was an expanding sphere of housework, undertaken by wives and sometimes by children (when not in school).

As discussed in Part Three, capitalists intervened directly and systematically to control the shape of housework: who did it, how it was structured, what technologies were used, what standards would apply, and so on. Any careful examination of housework reveals the piecework character of its organization. Although parents may supervise children's "chores," as a rule no one directly supervises housewives. But governments and private industry do set standards that housewives are expected to meet—and husbands, relatives, welfare agents and even neighbors, co-workers and bosses act as quality control inspectors who check to see that the standards are met.

Let's begin with governments. Generally responding to pressure from business, they formulate things like pro-natalist policies to encourage women to bear more children to expand the available labor force (or conversely, in other times and places, implement family planning programs to limit procreation). Pro-natalist programs are sometimes accompanied by "family allocation" payments to women according to the number of children they produce—a bump in pay for each new child. In China, on the other hand, for nearly 40 years those who violated its 1979 One-Child Policy faced fines and other legal sanctions. Aiming to increase the fertility rate, the Chinese government relaxed the policy in 2013 and a Two-Child policy was implemented in 2016. Governments also create welfare programs in which social workers monitor the housework of welfare recipients, checking up on such things as the degree of cleanliness, whether children's health is properly cared for, whether single mothers are engaged in illegal relationships with men, and so on.

Such intrusiveness has also been observed in the efforts by some employers to shape their workers' family lives. Robert Owen structured workers' homes and community to shape both work and non-work life. Years later, Henry Ford tried to monitor his employees' home life, and met with so much resistance that he had to abandon the effort. Today, it is common for some corporations to try to structure the off-the-job lives of their employees in various ways such as providing gyms and organizing sports teams, picnics, etc. The electronic giant Motorola calls its employees "Motorolans" and utilizes just such mechanisms to shape their employees' private lives.

Beyond such direct interventions, capitalists also set standards for housework. As corporations have developed more and more products for household work, their advertising constantly pesters housewives (indeed all the denizens of the home) with images and detailed specifications of what housework *should* consist of, and what standards *should* be met, e.g., for cleanliness ("next," we were long reminded, "to Godliness"). When housewives washed clothes by hand, and only occasionally because of the physical difficulty, no one expected—nor judged others ill—for appearing in less than sparkling clean attire. Today people have complex and effective washing machines that dramatically reduce the wear and tear on housewives' hands and arms. But given the heightened standards of what is "clean," they wind up spending as much or more time running washes, drying, ironing and folding as they used to with more primitive technology. Despite the introduction of this kind of "labor-saving" household technology, the amount of household piecework has been increased rather than decreased. By convincing people that every corner of every home must be spotless, corporations have developed, and advertisers have peddled, a wide variety of household cleaning agents for clothes, floors, dishes, furniture, windows, kitchen surfaces, toilets, tubs, and so on. Fomenting fears of illness, they have lately pushed "antibacterial" soaps and cleansers of all sorts.[31]

One prototypical advertisement produced for Wisk—the first liquid laundry detergent developed in 1956—claimed it would remove the "oil, dirt and grime that gathers around the neck" and rubs off on the inside of white business shirts. Dreamed up by Madison Avenue ad-man James Jordan, the advertisement offered a solution for frustrated housewives struggling to meet this new standard—the absence of "ring around the collar"—to avoid condemnation from bosses, fellow employers, friends and neighbors, all presumably exposed to, and convinced by, the same advertising. In effect, housewives were being taught to fear that everyday people would act as quality control managers for this kind of household piecework!

Later Wisk's slogan changed from "Wisk beats ring around the collar" to "America needs dirt" and its advertising campaign encouraged children to play hard and get dirty. In an age of growing child obesity and too much television, too many computer games and addictive social media, hard physical exercise out there in the dirt is good for everyone. Wisk could always get us clean again (and boost Wisk profits too).

Another example is the peddling of dishwasher detergents like "Cascade" to prevent "embarrassing" spots on glassware. In the ads, dinner guests are shown casting critical eyes on the crystal, raising eyebrows over water spots, or smiling approvingly at perfect, spotless, gleaming glass. The message is clear: meet the standard—artificially set by the capitalist corporation to get you to buy its product—or suffer the contempt of your friends.

Most of this advertising is done, of course, on television or in magazine ads against backdrops of beautifully clean, spotless homes of the sort portrayed in magazines like *Home Beautiful* and in virtually every soap opera and sit-com set in upper- and middle-class life. The results are explicit and implicit messages of acceptable standards by which anyone and everyone can judge the work of a given housewife, or more rarely, a househusband.

Such analysis can be extended to any number of tasks undertaken by the complex labor of housework: the clothing, cleaning, and feeding of children and spouses, the nursing of the sick and the psychological support given to the worn out and beaten down, and even the provision of sensual and sexual services to spouses. While some such tasks are inherent in any relationship, the number, frequency and character have all been quite consciously

---

31. Like the use of antibiotics in factory farming, the constant use of such "antibacterial" soaps has come under attack for gestating the evolution of antibiotic resistant bacteria, thus undermining, instead of contributing to health. Of course, from the point of view of industry, this just provides new opportunities for developing new antibiotics, more sales and more profits. See "FDA Taking Closer Look at 'Antibacterial' Soap" (www.fda.gov/ForConsumers/ConsumerUpdates/ucm378393.htm).

shaped by capitalist social planners, advertisers and policymakers with the aim of making sure that they contribute not to the happiness or well-being of family members but to corporate sales and the reproduction of lives as labor-power.

Piecework in the Countryside

A final example of extending Marx's analysis of piecework concerns farmers and peasants who produce at least in part for the market. Although economists and capitalist ideologues like to paint such people's work as that of small businesses—producing commodities to be sold on the market with the hope of a profit—the vast bulk of such producers earn barely enough to maintain themselves on their land and in their communities. Indeed, the history of both primitive and ongoing accumulation, of the ever-greater concentration of agricultural land in the hands of corporate agribusiness shows quite clearly that most small farmers and peasants in the United States and Europe have *not* made profits but have been driven off their lands. (Listen to John Mellencamp's song "Rain on the Scarecrow" on YouTube, also cited in my notes on Chapter 27.)

For such small farmers and peasants, the price of their output, e.g., the price of a bushel of wheat or corn, amounts to a piece-rate for their work, with the rates so low that the income they receive, on average, barely allows them to survive. As with other piecework, it is rarely supervised (unless they work under a putting-out arrangement with some corporation). Low prices/piece-rates impose long, intense hours of work—and often on all family members. Because farmers have varied abilities and varied circumstances, their varied success results, once again, in an income hierarchy (unless they band together in cooperatives) in which a very few may turn enough of a profit to invest, to expand their operations, to hire growing numbers of waged workers and actually *become* the capitalists they are portrayed as being.

CHAPTER 22: NATIONAL DIFFERENCES IN WAGES

Outline of Marx's Analysis

Comparing wages in different countries requires that we consider all the factors that determine changes in the value of labor-power. These include:

– the price and extent of the necessities of life in natural and historical development

▶

- the costs of training workers
- the part played by the labor of women and children
- the productivity of labor
- the extensive and intensive magnitude of labor
- the reduction of the average daily wage for the same trades to a uniform working day
- time-wages must be translated into piece-wages

Each country has a certain average intensity of labor
- but with a scale "whose unit of measure is the average unit of universal labor"
- where the average national labor is more intense, then there is more value and more money

Each country has a certain average productivity
- but with a scale (or hierarchy)
- more productive labor amounts to more intensity and more value
- as long as the absence of competition means no lowering of selling price

Because the development of capitalism brings increases in productivity and in the intensity of labor,
- above average development means above average levels of these characteristics

Suppose we have the same kind of commodity being produced during the same working time in different countries. Given the above we should expect:
- different unit values and different prices in different countries
- the relative value of money will be less in more developed countries
- *nominal* wages will be higher in more developed countries
- but *real* wages may be lower in more developed countries

Case study #1: spinning industry in England and Continental Europe
- productivity, wages and c/v are all lower on the continent
- data for the ratio spindles/worker (the technical composition of capital) in several countries
- hours of work are longer
- two main cases: Germany and Russia
- Russia: "over-work" (long hours) and "shameful under-payment of the workers" (low wages),
- yet, manufacturing "vegetates" due to protectionism

Case study #2: British railroad construction in Eastern Europe and Asia
  – firms use both British and foreign labor
  – British labor: more intense and gets paid higher wages
  – foreign labor: less intense and gets paid lower wages
  – price of labor in relation to the product is still high
Marx ends with critiques of economist Henry Carey

Commentary

Marx's analysis provides more of a cursory indication of what should be taken into account in studying "national differences in wages" than a systematic treatment. He begins with seven factors, but his ensuing discussion deals with only two: variations in intensity and in productivity across countries. The implications for workers everywhere of the international wage hierarchy was and continues to be an extremely important and contentious issue. In the nineteenth century, British capitalists were pitting cheap Irish labor against higher paid English workers, while exploiting labor in colonies abroad. Today, capitalists are still pitting immigrant workers against local ones and outsourcing production to areas of lower-cost and less powerful labor. The resulting fear of and antagonism toward multinational workers from low-wage countries has become widespread, while anger over corporate relocation of production facilities to countries where wages are low has also become common.

As recent work by historians Peter Linebaugh and Marcus Rediker has begun to document, the internationalization of the labor force developed as part and parcel of capitalist foreign investment and trade.[32] Capitalists did not merely employ workers at home, but shipped them abroad and put them to work in colonies, hired crews from all nations for their commercial and war fleets, entered the slave trade to redistribute African workers internationally and enslaved workers in every colonial area possible. In short, throughout virtually its entire history capitalism has imposed work on people over as much of the world as it could conquer, reorganizing both itself and its labor force to maximize profit and control.

With the extensive development of multinational corporations and rapid rebound of international trade in the post-World War II period such international organization and reorganization became evermore essential and rapid. The more capitalists have come to produce at a multinational

---

32. Linebaugh and Rediker, *The Many-Headed Hydra*.

level and the more international trade developed to redistribute the results globally, the more important this subject has become.

By the end of the twentieth century, capitalist attacks on higher paid workers by shifting production overseas to lower paid labor pools and their drive for so-called "free trade" to facilitate the re-import of outsourced production has made consideration of international wage differentials of growing importance. The current expanding use of outsourcing of business operations has become a hot political topic as the slow growth of jobs during the recovery from recent financial crises and recessions has made the displacement of American jobs—whether at home or abroad—anathema to American workers. Resentment has also flared in Europe in response to the recent influx of refugees from wars in the Middle East and immigrants from Eastern Europe and Africa.

In this light, we can see Marx's interest in "national differences in wages" lay not in simply making international comparisons or constructing some United Nations-like index of standards of living. It lay, instead, in drawing attention to how global capitalist development creates and tries to manipulate an international hierarchy of wages and living standards to pit workers against each other across the face of the earth, and in pointing out the necessity for workers to organize across national boundaries—precisely the objective of the First International with which he was deeply involved.

Price and Extent of the Necessities of Life

Some determinants of the costs of reproducing labor-power, as his original list makes clear, have to do with "natural" factors, e.g., the cost of reproducing labor in northern countries may be higher than that in the tropics because winters mean greater costs of housing, heating and clothing. But most factors are historically determined, and, as we have seen throughout *Capital*, at the core of that historical determination is class struggle.

For example, remember Marx's amusement—cited in my commentary on Section 5 of Chapter 10—at capitalist desires to reinstitute slavery in the British Caribbean in the nineteenth century because of the difficulty in getting freed slaves to work for them. The owners of the island plantations had enslaved Africans and put them to work producing sugar sold around the Atlantic—an international investment in labor force creation and trade. But with the end of legal slavery—won by slaves and abolitionists—the labor force suddenly became less available. So, the planters whined that without compulsion workers *would* only work enough to earn what little they needed for their own consumption, without regard for capitalist profits. The reason why they *could* work so little was because food was apparently plentiful and cheap.

At the same time, it should be clear that whether slavery could be reintroduced or whether large numbers of workers could be brought to Jamaica would be determined by class struggle, by the respective power of capitalists and workers, not just in Jamaica but in Britain (where both workers and economists such as John Stuart Mill opposed the reintroduction of slavery) and Africa (where without slavery very few Africans might be interested in moving to Jamaica, especially at near-slave wages).[33]

A serious survey of conditions throughout the colonial world of that period reveals again and again how colonizers sought to monopolize the production of food crops (and turn them into exports) and where that was infeasible to impose some alternative method for overcoming their availability to the indigenous population. Slavery was one such alternative. Another was the imposition of a "hut" tax, where colonized people were forced to pay taxes with the colonizer's money and the only means to obtain such money was to work for their new overlords. Where the latter method was used, wages were kept low, even below subsistence, to force those who entered the labor force to work long hours. They *could* be kept so low because much of the workers' subsistence was produced by either the workers or their families.

We find similar situations in the post-colonial world, a world where, in general, when they were forced out by independence movements, colonial powers left behind neo-colonial elites who continued the economic policies of their mentors. Throughout these periods, the changing hierarchical pattern of "national differences in wages" was determined by different historical paths of class struggle.

In industrial countries—or what Marx in this chapter calls the "more developed" countries—the cost of the necessities of life has been just as important in determining the value of labor-power, and thus the level of wages. Never was this more obvious than in the debate over the Corn Laws in Britain, analyzed by Marx in Chapter 17. Whereas tariffs kept up the price of grain, and hence bread, benefiting landlords and by necessitating higher wages hurt capitalist profits, their repeal resulted in lower prices, cheaper bread and reduced wages! In more recent times, capitalist policies have sometimes been aimed at keeping food prices low and sometimes at raising them depending on the desired impact on real wages. In the post-World War II period, cheap fertilizer and cheap imported labor (e.g., Braceros in the US, workers from the Mediterranean basin in Northern

---

33. A hundred years later, finding themselves low in the wage hierarchy of the British Commonwealth, many workers from the West Indies—as well as from other ex-colonies such as Pakistan, India and Nigeria—immigrated to Britain, now ready to accept them because the struggles of women in the UK had led to declining local birth rates.

Europe) kept food prices low, supporting higher real wages negotiated through productivity deals. In the 1970s, when rising money wages were outstripping productivity growth and undermining those deals, and when they didn't have the power to lower money wages directly—because of well-organized worker opposition—capitalist policymakers used *increases* in food prices to undermine the real value of wages.[34] In the 1980s and 1990s, during the international debt crisis engineered by US central bank policy, one common austerity strategy deployed by policymakers was currency devaluation that increased the cost of food imports, undermining real wages in so-called "debtor" countries.[35]

From the above discussion, we can see three things. First, "price and extent of the necessities of life" in each country depends only partly on "natural" circumstances and mainly on the "historical development"—especially of class struggle. Second, "national" differences depend not only upon local circumstances, both natural and historical, but also on international ones as well, i.e., the overall pattern of class struggle across countries. Third, that overall pattern involves both capitalist strategies for controlling labor and worker resistance to those strategies as well as their struggles to realize their own desires, e.g., good food, less work and more opportunity for self-directed activities.

The Costs of Training Workers

This topic was discussed by Marx in Chapter 6 on the labor market where he dealt with the value of labor-power and thus deserves attention in dealing with wage differentials at the international level. The costs of training are determined, for the most part, by the character of work for

---

34. In 1972, with the rationale of countering a declining American trade surplus, the US government used existing law to cut back grain production (reducing supply) while arranging, with the collaboration of a handful of international grain trading companies, huge new exports of grain to the Soviet Union (increasing demand) to jack up food prices. Two years later, when OPEC quadrupled the price of oil, a vital input in the production of nitrogen fertilizers and other agricultural inputs, US acceptance of that price increase also contributed to increasing the costs of grain production, the price of grain itself, and the price of food (and other consumer goods) more generally—once again undermining the real value of wages.

35. The FED engineered the international debt crisis by intentionally driving up interest rates in the US, which quickly drove up rates everywhere else. The result was such a dramatic increase in debt servicing obligations on existing international loans that country after country declared, or threatened to declare, default. To protect the income of the banks that had made the loans, the US and organizations such as the International Monetary Fund agreed to rollover those debts, but only in exchange for austerity programs that directly attacked the living standards of workers, reducing demand and freeing up export revenues for debt repayment.

which workers are trained. Clearly, it costs more to train an engineer than an assembly-line worker and if engineers tend to rear future engineers, and assembly-line workers to rear future assembly-line workers, then the former need higher wages than the latter. (Sociological studies show that despite the presence of some upward mobility, the wage hierarchy in capitalism tends to reproduce itself.)

From the time of colonialism to the mid-twentieth century, global capitalism was characterized by a division of labor in which, for the most part, the colonized and then decolonized, yet still "less-developed" world mainly produced raw materials (either means of subsistence or means of production). The so-called "developed world," on the other hand, mainly specialized in manufacturing and later service production. Therefore, in general, those put to work by capitalists in the "less-developed" world have been employed throughout most of modern history in such activities as agriculture and mining. Although both of those kinds of industry require a few workers trained in technical skills, most require little training. Moreover, given the colonial and neocolonial history of such industries, much of the required skilled labor has been drawn from the abroad. As a result, the level and cost of training of the labor force in such countries has been low. It doesn't take a university education to learn how to collect palm nuts, or dig peanuts, or shovel debris in copper, diamond or gold mines. Thus, insofar as the wages of such unskilled workers in those countries have been determined by the need to cover their education, they could be kept low.

In the "more developed" capitalist countries where industries such as manufacturing (from toolmaking to computers) and more sophisticated services (from health care and finance to software development) are more common, the costs of training for many workers has been greater. It does take a university education to train an electrical or software engineer as well as considerable on-the-job training. Obviously, there are a great many unskilled or low-skilled workers in those industries, workers who require little more training than their counterparts in the "less developed" world, but they are a smaller proportion of the labor force and therefore the *average* cost of training and level of wages tends to be higher in these countries.

In more recent times, the kind of outsourcing mentioned above has included the displacement first of manufacturing labor and most recently of some service labor from the "developed" to the "less-developed" world. Unfortunately for local average wages, most of the jobs in outsourced manufacturing and services have been low-skilled ones, e.g., assembly labor in the first case, routine call-center work in the second, requiring little education and thus requiring only low wages. This has been changing, to varying degrees in different places. Some capitalists have invested in the training of more skilled workers, e.g., software engineers in India and China, while others have invested less, e.g., clothing production in Bangladesh. As history has amply demonstrated, understanding how the capitalist global "division of labor" changes, requires understanding not just changes in capitalist strategies, but the struggles of workers causing and responding to those strategies.

Women and Children

Although he doesn't discuss this factor in this chapter, elsewhere in *Capital* it is clear enough that Marx's concern with the "part played by women and children" primarily involves the way they were being increasingly drafted into the labor force as cheap labor to undermine more highly paid male labor. In other words, the drafting of women and children was a capitalist strategy to hold down or lower wages. This has been true within countries and across different countries. There can be little doubt that in recent years one reason some capitalists have embraced feminist demands for the removal of traditional patriarchal obstacles to women obtaining waged jobs has been the desire for an expansion of the supply of labor and downward pressure on wages. The associated feminist demand for wage equality, of course, is designed to counter this aspect of capitalist strategy. (So too has been the feminist demand for "wages for housework"—which, in such forms as family allocations, pay for work already done and reduce the need for a second wage from an employer.)

The battle over child labor around the world has resulted in a much greater public awareness of such issues. The emphasis of those fighting to eliminate child labor has been on the low wages and execrable working conditions of children. As in Marx's time, those still opposed to its elimination have pointed to the low wages of their parents and their families' need for the extra money, however little the children bring in. In other words, the benefits to children achieved by the elimination of child labor, it is argued, would be offset by the increased poverty and suffering of their family. Clearly one issue in that debate should be the size of effects. The elimination of child labor would reduce family income from the children, but it would also reduce the labor supply which would, *ceteris paribus*, tend to raise wages. Would the rise in wages be enough to offset the fall in income? The answer to this question cannot be given *a priori* but depends upon labor market conditions that may vary from place to place. Nor, I hasten to add, is it necessarily a deciding issue; even if wages did not rise enough to offset the reduction of income caused by the elimination of child labor, some other offsetting mechanism, e.g., minimum wage laws or income transfers, are possible.

Beyond this kind of discussion, my comments on earlier chapters have hopefully made clear that there is another dimension to the "part played by women and children" in the determination of average national wages and in the determination of national differences in wages—namely, the unwaged labor of women and children in the home and community that contribute to the production and reproduction of labor-power. As I indicated in my discussion of the circuit of the reproduction of labor-power, the more work done by women and children in homes and gardens, the lower the wage required to obtain a given quality of reproduction. Two examples relevant to the international wage hierarchy follow.

First is housework. As I have indicated, the less control women have over their own bodies, the higher the birth rate, the greater the supply of labor and the downward pressure on wages. Not surprisingly, a loose correlation exists between the international hierarchy of wages and that of women's autonomous power. Also, the more wives and children in the typical patriarchal family do the work of growing and preparing food, the lower the value of labor-power and the less wages are required to support the family. The importance of this in rural areas helps explain the hierarchy of wages within all countries. In the Global South, agricultural production in extended families often makes possible still lower wages, even below what would be required for subsistence in the absence of such work.

Second is schoolwork. Where the generalized imposition of elementary and secondary education has replaced on-the-job training and apprentice-ships, children go to school (which is not everywhere). Whereas educational opportunities were severely limited in colonized countries, once liberated the new post-colonial elites dramatically expanded them, in part to provide employment as teachers for those already educated.[36] Today, although there are still many areas in the Global South with few or no schools, especially for girls and young women, most countries have created systems of primary, secondary and higher education. Those systems tend to be geared to local labor force requirements and thus to replicate a country's position in the international hierarchy of development and wages. As capitalist invest-ment has moved from manufacturing to large-scale industry to the service sector and diversified internationally, so too has education. For many years, students from better-off families in the Global South have been sent for higher education in the Global North, but over time investment in educa-tional systems in the former have contributed to the education of students capable of competing with those of the latter. That development has facil-itated the outsourcing from North to South of both industrial and service

---

36. For an analysis of this dynamic, see Carnoy, *Education as Cultural Imperialism*.

sector jobs, from automobile production in Mexico and Brazil to software development in India and China.

The Productivity of Labor

As mentioned at the outset, Marx deals more with the productivity than with those "factors" discussed above. The main reason why differences in the average level of national productivity is important in determining differences in the average level of national wages is revealed in Chapters 12–15's analysis of relative surplus-value. There we saw that increases in the productivity of the labor that produces the means of subsistence lowers their per unit value and when this is translated in the market into lower per unit prices, it lowers the nominal wage necessary to supply a given real wage.

Therefore, we should expect that to the degree that productivity is higher in one country than another, the lower the value per unit of subsistence goods in the higher-productivity country. All other things equal, we should therefore expect the prices of those subsistence goods to be lower, and therefore *lower wages* to reproduce labor-power.

However, all other things are not equal. To the degree that the higher productivity is itself the product of worker struggles that have induced capitalists to substitute machinery and other technology for labor, and to the degree that those same workers have been able to force capital to share the fruits of rising productivity, they receive *higher* real income. Depending on the size of the various forces, it is, paradoxically, possible that the higher nominal wages of workers in the higher-productivity countries actually buy a lower *value* package of consumer goods than the lower nominal wages of workers in less developed countries.[37]

The second factor on which Marx dwells in this chapter—the relative average intensity of labor—also can contribute to the existence of an international scale or hierarchy of wages. Given his discussion in Chapters 12–15 of the influence of capitalist organization and the use of machinery to set the rhythm of work, we might expect intensity to be higher in more

---

37. A fundamental problem with this sort of reasoning, however, is that capitalist production is global and levels of productivity in one country are therefore connected to levels of productivity in other countries. In Marx's day, for example, the high productivity of cotton textile manufacturing in England (and then in New England) was directly connected to the low productivity of cotton production by slaves (and then sharecroppers) in the American South. Cheap cotton kept input prices low and profits high enough to finance the investments in machinery that raised productivity and made it possible to meet demands by textile workers for wages above the income of slaves (and sharecroppers).

developed capitalist countries. This may or may not, however, be the case
because, as always, other things are not generally the same. For instance, it
may be that the relative weakness of workers in a less developed area—say,
forced to work for extremely low piece-wages—may drive them to the very
limits of the intensity possible to any human being. It may also be the
case that good self-organization of workers in the more developed areas
may shift work from piece to hourly wages and force up the level of those
wages while imposing work rules that limit work to a more leisurely pace.
About all that can be said *a priori* is that capital always seeks the highest
intensity that it can impose and that workers resist this. Given differences
in the balance of power between capital and workers across countries we
can expect that the degree of intensity will vary and that that variation will
play a part in shaping the global wage hierarchy.

Case Study #1: Spinning

Marx's example of differences in the spinning industry between Britain
and the European continent and among countries on that continent can
be generalized. As a rule, Britain led the development of textile production technology at every stage of production, from the growing of the
raw materials through the spinning of thread and weaving of cloth to the
sewing of clothing. Therefore, Marx's observation that British spinning
labor was more intense was likely applicable throughout the industry. The
basis for his argument that spinning labor was more intense in Britain was
data on the number of spindles per worker. The more spindles for which
each worker was responsible, the more intense would be the labor of taking
care of them. Although, it is worth noting, in the period in which spinning
and weaving were being gathered from homes into factories and then
automated with water and then steam-driven machines, it is quite possible
that the still-at-home handloom weavers, who were struggling to survive
in the face of factory competition and falling prices, might well have been
working not only longer hours but more intensely than factory operatives.
While it is relatively easy to observe changes in the pace of work (speed-up
or slowdown) it is not so easy to obtain any absolute value for intensity. One
can imagine the use of modern scientific apparatus to measure something
like BTUs burned per hour per worker, but I have never heard of such a
thing being done, much less done systematically in such a way as to permit
cross-industry or cross-country comparisons.

At any rate, Marx presumes the higher productivity and higher intensity
of labor in the English factories follows from more machinery per worker,
which allows higher wages in England than on the continent. As we have

seen above, this would be at least the *tendency* although other factors would have to be considered in a concrete historical analysis.

Case Study #2: Railroad Construction

This case is of interest for several reasons. First, it is a case of British foreign investment. Considerable British capital was invested in railroad construction not only in Eastern Europe and Asia but also in the United States. It was a major area of British overseas investment for quite a long time. One must suppose that such investment was undertaken based on familiarity with production conditions and costs in the various areas and the estimated conditions and costs (coupled with government subsidies such as grants of land and rights-of-way) were expected to yield competitive profits.

Second, when Marx notes that British labor was more "intensive" than local labor and got paid higher wages he doesn't specify any differences in either job categories or work behavior. We may assume, however, that he thought that the British firms were sending dedicated careerists to oversee such production and those overseers would be hiring mostly unskilled peasant labor to cut through forests and mountains and lay track. Such was certainly the case in the United States where large numbers of Chinese immigrant workers were hired by railroad robber barons such as Charles Crocker (1822–88) and Leland Stanford (1824–93) to lay the Central Pacific Railroad, east, west and through the Sierra Nevada mountains. In photographs from time, we can see both Chinese workers in traditional garb and well-dressed white men overseeing their work.[38] As research by historians such as Herbert Gutman (1928–85) has demonstrated, peasants drafted for industrial work often brought with them agrarian habits of time and work that were much more leisurely than those demanded by industrialists.[39] Extremely low wages and often brutal oversight were often required to inculcate habits of punctuality and work intensity desired by their employers. Under those circumstances, Marx's assertions seem likely to have been accurate.

Third, with the expansion of imperial investment during the colonial period and the post-colonial growth of multinational corporate investment, such differences in work habits (and consequent length and intensity of labor) have proved of decisive importance time and time again. There are a seemingly endless number of examples where multinational firms have displaced production facilities geographically to take advantage of lower

---

38. The pilot episode of the TV series *Kung Fu* (1972–75) vividly illustrated the use and exploitation of Chinese laborers in California.
39. See Gutman, *Work, Culture and Society*.

wages (and other lower costs). This was true—to choose an example in line with Marx's exposition—in the American textile industry that moved first from New England to the US Sun Belt, and then later into Mexico and Asia. But it is also true that not every country that has extremely low wages has been able to attract such foreign investment hell-bent on escaping rising labor costs at home. Among the reasons why many pools of labor have been bypassed by such movements are precisely the work habits (and habits of struggle) of the people there. In the post-World War II era, anti-colonial struggles and insurgency, e.g., Indochina, dissuaded such investment. Even later in the post-colonial era, in India, for example, workers have demonstrated the nasty habit of going on strike using *gheraos*, or sit-ins, that surround their employers and refuse to let them out until they capitulate. This may be hard to believe, inasmuch as American high-tech investment in India has become common. It becomes more believable, however, when we recognize that such investment involves the hiring not of feisty, blue-collar Indian workers but of relatively well-educated and well-conditioned middle-class workers.[40]

Marx's overall treatment, of course, draws our attention not only to the question of the intensity of effort of such workers hired abroad but also to that of their productivity. Lack of skill at even low-skilled jobs may result in lower productivity and even render such investment unprofitable. In recent years, there have been some cases where the productivity of outsourced workers turned out to be so low as to lead to the abandonment of such foreign investment. One example is that of technical assistance call centers relocated abroad. Despite newsworthy efforts by Indians to relearn English pronunciation so they can sound like Americans on the phone (and their adoption of false American names), the impatience of many parochial American callers with both their accents and their skill has been so great as to lead more than one company to abandon their investment and repatriate the jobs. The costs of repeated hang-ups by impatient customers, irritation with the company and the resulting bad satisfaction ratings have outweighed the reduced cost of low foreign wages.

Critical Comments on Carey

Henry Charles Carey (1793–1879) was an American economist and advisor to President Lincoln who supported protectionist measures by the United States against the "diabolical influence of England." Commenting

---

40. Similar methods have been used by workers in South Korea, but a repressive police-state apparatus—backed up by thousands of American troops and American-trained Korean troops—kept such tactics in check until recently, thus permitting a much higher level of direct foreign investment than in India.

on Carey's 1835 *Essay on the Rate of Wages*, Marx sees Carey's understanding of the determinants of wages, and relative wages across countries, as simplistic. For example, Carey tried to prove that differences in national wages are directly proportional to the degree of productivity. As one might suspect, on the basis of this chapter, Marx argues this is wrong, because so many other factors have to be taken into account. He also notes both the contradiction between Carey's stated belief in free trade and his advocacy of protectionism and how his support for the former "became the secret source of the harmonious wisdom of a Bastiat, and of all the other free-trade optimists of the present day."[41]

Foreign Direct Investment and "Free Trade"

Current debates about differences in wages among various countries have arisen amidst larger debates about so-called "free trade" agreements, such as NAFTA and the more recent, hotly contested, Trans Pacific Partnership. Negotiated in secret—in the first case by the governments and capitalists of the United States, Canada and Mexico, and in the second case by those of the United States and eleven other countries around the Pacific Ocean—these agreements have been met with widespread opposition.[42]

As explained earlier, literally hundreds of grassroots groups mobilized against NAFTA and created a network of organizing across national borders. Those efforts provoked dissent within the legislative branches of all three governments as the draft of the agreement was posted to the Internet and became available for anyone and everyone to read.

Among the arguments against the agreement was one based on existing "national differences in wages" between the United States and Canada (minor differences) and between those countries and Mexico (major differences). The fact that wages were so much lower in Mexico than in the United States or Canada led many to argue that successful passage of NAFTA would make it easier for Canadian and US corporations to move, or threaten to move, their production operations south into Mexico. Third-party candidate for president in the 1992 and 1996 election cycles, Texan billionaire Ross Perot (1930–) became famous for his evocation of a possible "great sucking sound" as jobs were drawn out of the United States into Mexico by low wages.

---

41. Frédéric Bastiat (1801–50) was a well-known French advocate of unrestricted free market and opponent of protectionism.

42. Despite Trump's pulling the US out of TPP in January 2017, the other eleven countries went on, a year later, to form a new treaty—the Comprehensive and Progressive Agreement for Trans-Pacific Partnership (CPTPP, or TPP-2)—that includes most of the provisions in the original TPP.

This issue, which focused on the same topic as Marx does in this chapter, was, however, only part of a larger debate. Those who were worried about US or Canadian corporations shifting jobs into Mexico also addressed many other dimensions that bore on the issue. For example, they pointed out how even though Mexico had reasonable environmental laws, the ease with which they could be bypassed through bribery (*la mordida*) added to the allure of low wages by further reducing the costs of production. Moreover, they also pointed to the organizational weakness of Mexican labor, how the only trade unions tolerated by the Mexico government were those that had sold out to the PRI, the then dominant party in that virtually one-party state. Yes, a growth of investment would mean more jobs and an expansion of the labor force, but political repression would prevent both new and existing workers from fighting for their rights, higher wages, better working conditions, and so on. As it turned out, the professional political classes of Canada, the United States and Mexico ratified NAFTA, narrowly, despite this opposition.

The defeat of the opposition to NAFTA was soon followed by the same debate on a much larger scale: namely about the newly created WTO, spearheaded by the United States and aimed at accelerating the freedom of movement for multinational capital. Because the WTO had dozens of members rather than just three, and because it amounted to the imposition of the same set of trading rules on all its members, opposition to it, to its rules and to the implementation of those rules was soon global in scope. As in the case of NAFTA, opposition forces created networks to share information and organize against it. The first sign of the seriousness of that opposition came when opponents besieged WTO meetings in Geneva, Switzerland in 1998. Organized by People's Global Action (PGA), some 20,000 from around the world protested. It was followed by the much more widely reported siege of the WTO meetings in Seattle, Washington in 1999. The "Battle of Seattle" saw some 30,000 protestors from dozens of countries converge on Seattle and successfully shut down the WTO meetings.[43] Among those protestors were a very large number of blue-collar workers from the US labor movement as well as environmentalists, left-wing party members, anarchists, university students and so on.

---

43. Watch *Showdown in Seattle: Five Days that Shook the WTO* (1999) (available on YouTube) and read Keven Danaher and Roger Burbach (eds.), *Globalize This! The Battle Against the World Trade Organization and Corporate Rule*, Monroe, MA: Common Courage Press, 2000; Eddie Yuen, Daniel B. Rose and George Katsiaficas (eds.), *The Battle of Seattle: The New Challenge to Capitalist Globalization*, New York: Soft Skull Press, 2001; and Notes from Nowhere (ed.), *we are everywhere: the irresistible rise of global anticapitalism*, London: Verso, 2003.

Once again, the issue of "national wage differences" was front and center for many protestors—most obviously for those in the labor movement—for the same reason it had been during the debate over NAFTA: the fear that more trade with countries with very low wage rates would make it easier for multinational corporations to undermine better paid workers elsewhere. Once again, that argument was buttressed by the consideration of many other issues.

The protests at Geneva and Seattle were the first of their kind. When Marx was writing in the mid-1800s, it was only with great difficulty that workers and activists were able to collaborate across national boundaries. Even throughout most of the twentieth century this was also true. There were cases of collaboration—such as opposition in the United States to counter-insurgency in Vietnam, or support around the world for the anti-apartheid struggle in South Africa—but creating and mobilizing networks was a slow process. Those earlier transborder collaborations lacked the capacity to organize collective demonstrations of tens of thousands such as those that exploded in Geneva and Seattle.

There were two key factors leading to these anti-WTO mobilizations. First, was the gathering of some 3,000 grassroots activists in Chiapas, Mexico in the summer of 1996 for an "Intercontinental Encounter Against Neoliberalism and For Humanity" called by the Zapatista movement that had challenged NAFTA, the Mexican government and sparked an indigenous renaissance around the world. Almost a week of discussions and networking among activists from over 40 countries led to the recognition of how neoliberal policies were being implemented everywhere and triggered a new surge of cross-border organizing to oppose them. When the encounter was over, and participants went home, they carried with them a vision of global networking and global, collaborative mobilization. Among the fruits of that vision were the PGA and the anti-WTO protests.

Beginning with the organizing that produced the Battle of Seattle, global grassroots networking accelerated and evolved new dimensions, especially the elaboration of Internet channels of communication of which the one key new form was Indymedia—websites that could post news from a grassroots perspective almost instantly, including audio, photographic imagery and streamed video. The possibilities were demonstrated during the confrontations in Seattle, when for the first-time dozens of independent reporters armed with camcorders circulated amidst the demonstrations and then streamed their filming directly onto the Web, bypassing the capitalist-controlled mass media. The difference between the images broadcast by media such as CNN (generally emphasizing the breaking of McDonald's windows by a few) and those broadcast by Indymedia (generally showing non-violent protestors and violent police actions) was dramatic. After that, Indymedia operations sprang up in country after country, city after city. As mass mobilizations were mounted against other capitalist organizations such as the International Monetary Fund, the World Bank, the World Economic Forum at Davos, Switzerland and the G-8 meetings, Indymedia would provide alternative coverage of events.

Alongside the issue of the uses to which capitalists try to put "national differences in wages"—pitting workers against workers—and the attempt to overcome that strategy by organizing across borders, the very success of such demonstrations made visible another way in which workers were divided by those wage differentials. In all these large-scale demonstrations, it soon became obvious that most of the demonstrators were from countries high on the international wage and income hierarchy. Traveling intercontinentally to participate in such demonstrations was something most of the world's workers could hardly afford. A cluster of villages or a city might pool its resources to send a representative, but the resources required is large and the numbers sent small.

One response to this problem has been the diffusion of protests. Instead of gathering very large numbers of people in one spot, à la Seattle, even larger numbers of people have mobilized for the same purpose with the same kind of target at a multiplicity of easier-to-reach sites around the world. The issues are the same, although often mixed with purely local ones, but one message is common: the unity of vast numbers of people in many different countries against capitalist policies. How to make such global mobilization more effective is an ongoing subject of discussion in these early years of the twenty-first century.

10

Part Seven
The Process of Accumulation
of Capital

These three chapters complete Marx's theoretical analysis of capitalism in this volume. After laying the groundwork by describing what the mere maintenance of capitalist system requires, he analyzes "accumulation" or the "expanded reproduction" of capitalist society.

Chapter 23: Simple Reproduction. For capitalism to reproduce itself at all, "simple" reproduction requires recreating all those elements whose roles we have seen analyzed in previous chapters: money, means of production, labor-power, production and final products. The most important, of course, is the reproduction of labor-power, the recreation of a labor force able and willing to be put to work with all the other elements.

Chapter 24: The Transformation of Surplus-Value into Capital. Turning surplus-value into capital requires investing it. In simple reproduction, elements that have been used up are simply replaced. In expanded reproduction or accumulation surplus-value is used to buy extra means of production and labor-power to increase production, output, sales and the total amount of surplus-value generated. Along the way, Marx critiques economists' understanding of these processes and some of their ideological justifications.

Chapter 25: The General Law of Capitalist Accumulation. Growth, or accumulation, is, above all, the accumulation of the classes and of class struggle. Here, for the first time in this book, Marx seriously analyzes how the reproduction of the working class involves not only waged labor, but also unwaged labor. The unwaged or "surplus" part of the working class—making up what he calls "the reserve army"—consists of at least three sectors: the floating, the latent and the stagnant. Drawing on previous commentary, I show how the terms "surplus" and "reserve" can be as misleading as "unemployed," given the diverse forms of work occupying people in these sectors, creating and reproducing labor-power.

CHAPTER 23: SIMPLE REPRODUCTION

Outline of Marx's Analysis

Reproduction
- continuous production
- continuous valorization of value advanced as capital

Reproduction = replacement of ALL elements of the circuit of capital
- reproduction of means of production, *MP* = replacement of used up raw materials and worn-out machinery, buildings, etc.
- reproduction of labor-power, *LP*, requires production of necessary means of subsistence, *MS*

Labor fund = the means of subsistence required for reproduction of labor-power
- variable capital
- product of peasants' own land/labor (under feudalism)

Simple reproduction
- the "mere continuity of the production process"
- "converts all capital into accumulated capital"

Alienation
- of workers' labor, sold by them to capitalist
- alienation of worker's product, owned by capitalist, an "alien power that dominates and exploits him"

Reproduction of the worker

Workers' consumption is of two kinds:
- productive consumption of *MP* during work—allows capital to live
- individual consumption of *MS* outside work—allows worker to live
- abusive consumption: where individual consumption is *merely* the means to "keep his [the worker's] labor-power in motion, just as coal and water are supplied to the steam-engine"

At the aggregate level of the classes:
- investment of variable capital = "reconversion of the means of subsistence... into fresh labor-power"
- as such, "individual consumption"... remains an aspect of the production and reproduction of capital"

▶

- but "the capitalist may safely leave this [individual consumption] to the worker's drive for self-preservation and propagation"
- exceptions, e.g., mine-owners who force their workers to eat beans to increase their strength and work
- for capital, workers' consumption above what is needed for reproduction of labor-power is *unproductive*
- reproduction of workers also involves "transmission and accumulation of skills from one generation to another"

Capitalist understanding
  Quotes from a spokesperson for English cotton textile industry against worker emigration during cotton famine
    - workers are machines that should be kept on hand and in order
    - if they left, it would take a generation to replace them with a new batch of skilled workers
    - therefore, the cotton industry and other, related industries would suffer
    - therefore, the workers should be kept via forced public works
  The Times newspaper editorial also worried that:
    - "human machinery *will* rust under inaction"
    - "human machinery will, as we have just seen, get the steam up of its own accord, and burst or run amuck in our great towns"
  Marx concludes his example by noting Parliament passed an Act "empowering the municipal corporations to keep the workers in a state of semi-starvation, i.e., to exploit them without paying the normal wages"

Commentary

Marx's two-page introduction to Part Seven of *Capital*, alerts us to its simplifying assumptions. The most important one in this chapter, and the one that differentiates this chapter and its analysis of *simple* reproduction from that of *expanded* reproduction in the subsequent chapters, is that capitalists consume all value generated over and above requirements for replacing used-up means of production and replacing workers. In other words, this chapter deals with how production must reproduce all elements of the capitalist organization of production abstracting from investment to generate growth.

  Most of what Marx writes should already be familiar from preceding chapters, especially Chapter 6 that deals explicitly with the reproduction of labor-power, and indeed he often refers to those discussions. There are, however, a couple of points, one minor and another major, that are worthy of examination.

Alienation

As discussed in my commentary on Chapter 7 on the labor process, there has been a debate as to whether there was a fundamental change in Marx's analysis of capitalism from his discussion of alienation in the *1844 Manuscripts* to the theory laid out in *Capital*. I argue that *Capital* includes concrete elaborations of his earlier theoretical discussion of four forms of alienation, i.e., of how capital: 1) controls workers on the job thus alienating them from their labor; 2) owns their product and uses it against them; 3) pits workers against each other, alienating them from each other; and 4) by imposing its will, alienates workers from their very species-being.

Substantiation of this argument requires showing how Marx's analysis in *Capital* elaborates these themes despite the absence of any explicit use of the term "alienation." In this chapter, however, he *does* use the term and his use deserves some attention:

> Since, before he enters the process, his own labour has already been alienated [*enfremdet*] from him, appropriated by the capitalist, and incorporated with capital, it now, in the course of the process, constantly objectifies itself so that it becomes a product alien to him [*fremder Produkt*].[1]

Marx here describes two forms of "alienation." The first refers simply to the sale of labor-power. This is a vernacular use of the term "alienation," just meaning to go away from or be taken away from; here the term does not seem to refer to any of the four forms that Marx discussed in the *1844 Manuscripts*. The second use, however, refers to what happens "in the course of the [labor] process," during production. The capitalist utilization of the use-value of the worker's labor-power results in a product owned by the capitalist. This is the second form mentioned above. When Marx goes on to point out how that product becomes "capital, i.e., into value that sucks up the worker's value-creating power" and thereby becomes "an alien power that dominates and exploits him,"[2] we have, explicitly, all the elements of the second form of alienation discussed in the *Manuscripts*.

---

1. *Capital, Vol. I*, p. 716.
2. Ibid.

The Reproduction of the Worker

The more important issue concerns the reproduction of workers and their labor-power as an integral part of capitalist reproduction. The key passage concerns the reproduction of capital as a social whole, of "the capitalist class and the working class."

> The capital given in return for labour-power is converted into means of subsistence which have to be consumed to reproduce the muscles, nerves, bones and brains of existing workers, and to bring new workers into existence. Within the limits of what is absolutely necessary, therefore, the individual consumption of the working class is the reconversion of the means of subsistence given by capital in return for labour-power into fresh labour-power which capital is then again able to exploit. It is the production and reproduction of the capitalist's most indispensable means of production: the worker. The individual consumption of the worker, whether it occurs inside or outside the workshop, inside or outside the labour process, remains as aspect of the production and reproduction of capital, just as the cleaning of machinery does, whether it is done during the labour process, or when intervals in that process permit. The fact that the worker performs acts of individual consumption in his own interest, and not to please the capitalist, is something entirely irrelevant to the matter.[3]

Let us examine this passage in some detail. First, "the capital given in return for labour-power" is the wage, the variable capital invested in the hiring of workers. As we have seen before, this can be represented, from the capitalist point of view, as $M - LP$, the exchange of money for labor-power. Or, from the worker's point of view as $LP - M$, the sale of labor-power for money. Second, the "conversion" of the wage into "the means of subsistence" refers to all those expenditures workers make on commodities necessary to reproduce their labor-power, e.g., food, clothing, music, transportation, housing, and so on, or $M - C(MS)$. Third, all such things "must be consumed" in order "to reproduce the muscles, nerves, bones and brains of existing workers, and to bring new workers into existence." In other words, individual consumption must reproduce the labor-power of existing workers and produce the next generation and its labor-power. The key point: from the capitalist point of view, their *consumption* must be *production*—the production of labor-power.

---

3. Ibid., pp. 717–718.

Leaving it to the Workers?

Now Marx's final comment in the above passage notes that "The fact that the worker performs acts of individual consumption in his own interest, and not to please the capitalist, is something entirely irrelevant to the matter." From the workers' point of view their entry into the labor market provides a means toward their "own interest," the elaboration of their own lives; for them, consumption is *not* production, it is simply living! On this Marx elaborates in Chapter 1, Volume II of *Capital*:

> [$M - L$] is the sale of labour-power on the part of the worker, the owner of labour-power (we can say "labour" here, as the wage form is presupposed). What is $M - C$ *($M - L$)* for the purchaser, is here, as in every other sale, $L - M$ *($C - M$)* for the seller (the worker), in this case the sale of his labour-power. The latter is for the seller of labour the first stage of circulation, or the first metamorphosis, of the commodity (Vol I, Chapter 3, 2a); it is the transformation of his commodity into its money form. The worker spends the money thus received bit by bit on a sum of commodities that satisfy his needs, on articles of consumption. The overall circulation of his commodity thus presents itself as $L - M - C$, i.e., firstly as $L - M$ *($C - M$)* and secondly $M - C$, i.e., the general form of the simple circulation of commodities, $C - M - C$, where money figures simply as an evanescent means of circulation, as merely mediating the conversion of one commodity for another.[4]

But this "little circuit," $L - M - C$, fails to capture the central point of this part of Chapter 23: from the capitalist point of view working-class *consumption* must involve the *production* of labor-power.

As we have seen, the industrial circuit of capital can be represented by the following sequence, what Marx calls the circuit of money capital:

$$M - C(LP, MP) ...P_I... \; C' - M'$$

where $...P_I...$ stands for the industrial production process. Nowhere in Marx's writings, not even in Part One of Volume II of *Capital* where he sketches a detailed analysis of that circuit, and analyses it from two other points of view, is there a parallel symbolic representation for consumption qua production of labor-power.[5] However, there is nothing to prevent us

---

4. *Capital, Vol. II*, pp. 112–113.
5. The two other points of view are those of the reproduction of the production process, i.e., the circuit of productive capital, and the reproduction of commodity capital, i.e., the circuit of commodity capital.

from using his same notation to represent just such a parallel process. Thus, as I suggested in my comments on Chapter 1, we can represent what Marx is saying in the above passage by:

$$LP - M - C(MS) ...P_C... LP^*$$

where $...P_C...$ represents consumption as production of labor-power and LP^* is the labor-power produced. The sense of this "circuit of the reproduction of labor-power" is the same as his circuits of industrial capital: it represents a sequence of processes through which a key element of capital is reproduced. Recall that I have given the final LP^* an asterisk instead of a prime (e.g., LP') because while in Marx's notation primes are used to designate unambiguous *increases* in value, the work of consumption has ambiguous effects. Procreation that generates new workers, or worker success in struggle may *increase* the value of labor-power; but more housework that substitutes for purchased goods or services may *reduce* the value of labor-power.

After the passage quoted above, Marx comments that "the capitalist may safely leave this [consumption qua production of labor-power] to the worker's drives for self-preservation and propagation."[6] Almost immediately, however, he gives a counter-example of South American mine-owners forcing their workers to eat beans as well as bread to increase their strength and productivity.[7] What are we to make of this contradiction?

Marx's comments reflect what he was seeing around him in England and what he was reading in the reports of the Factory Acts inspectors: a general tendency on the part of capital to minimize wages and neglect the needs of workers. He also drew repeatedly from Engels's book *The Condition of the English Working Class* (1845) that gives many vivid illustrations of such minimization and neglect and the resulting misery of British workers.[8]

Although Marx calls the South American mine-owners' oversight of their workers' diet "crude," in historical retrospect we can see them as harbingers of the capitalist future. As workers' struggles reduced the working day to 12 hours, then ten hours and then eight hours, they freed more and more time for living. More and more consumption could be freed from mere production of labor-power. Those working-class successes forced capitalists to rely more and more upon two strategies, one that Marx analyzed extensively and one that he did not. The first was relative surplus-value; the second was intervening in workers' off-the-job lives, in their "free time" to

6. *Capital, Vol. I*, p. 718.
7. Ibid., p. 718, fn 9.
8. *MECW, vol. 4*, pp. 295–596. Engels's book, it is worth noting, has held up well to critical scrutiny by subsequent generations of historians.

make sure that their consumption resulted in the production and reproduction of labor-power. Chapters 12–15 detail Marx's analysis of the former strategy. The sketchiness of this chapter shows how little attention he paid to the latter strategy. We must do better. As capitalists' active interventions in shaping workers' lives have multiplied, so has our need to understand what they have been doing—so that, as in production, we can discover how best to deal with their efforts.

Analyzing those interventions requires applying to capitalist strategies in the sphere of reproduction the same kind of close, detailed examination that Marx applied in the sphere of production. Where he examined the basic outlines of the labor process (Chapter 7), some forms of cooperation (Chapter 13), the division of labor in industry (Chapter 14) and the dynamics of technological change (in Chapter 15), we need to examine the concrete forms of such relationships in reproduction relevant to our contemporary struggles, not just as "examples" to illustrate the theory, but to help us decide what future directions we should take.

While a systematic investigation goes beyond the scope of these commentaries, I will briefly illustrate applying his analysis of the labor process to the sphere of reproduction. In Marx's analysis there are three elements: the workers, their tools and the raw materials upon which they work to fabricate commodities. When the commodity being fabricated is labor-power, how are we to understand these elements? The *workers* include all kinds of people beginning with housewives and children-in-school and continuing through waged workers on and off the job, prostitutes, teachers and so on. The *tools* would include everything used by those people to produce and reproduce labor-power: kitchen and dining equipment, washing machines, irons, beds, computers, school books, training manuals, self-help books, playgrounds, footballs, condoms and sex paraphernalia, music CDs, film DVDs and so on. And the *raw materials*? Those are the people themselves: from children to adults. Applying Marx's understanding of the labor process—as active workers using tools to transform passive, will-less, nature—to reproduction reveals how efforts to shape human beings according to capitalist needs involves destroying the autonomy of their own will and subordinating it to that of capital. The process is easy to recognize in the human subordination of other animals' wills, e.g., "breaking" horses to the saddle, or slaving oxen to the plow, and in the enslavement of some humans by others. Harder to recognize is the parallel relationship between capitalists and ostensibly "free" workers. Yet this is precisely what we discover in the analysis of primitive accumulation and in that of alienation. To the degree that capitalists are successful in such subordination, we must recognize how family life, procreation, childrearing, education and training are not shared activities of socially interactive, free human beings; they are poisoned by alienated relations of power.

Once we understand this, we can grasp the nastier aspects of the various hierarchies capital imposes on our relationships, e.g., the patriarchal dimension of capitalist reproduction. Men's power over women in their daily lives not only mediates the latter's relationship with capital, but requires their dehumanization, via the subordination of their will, directly to that of men, indirectly to that of capital. For years feminists have pointed out how patriarchy involves men demanding services from women. But where those services merely reproduce male labor-power, their own labor counts as work-for-capital as well as work-for-men—whether those services are provided on-the-job by waged women or off by the unwaged. Recently brought back into the spotlight by the #MeToo movement, one aspect of men's efforts to dominate women has been sexual, to satisfy male desires for control, sexual release and progeny with the desires of women either ignored or manipulated into compliance. That movement should remind us that one of the discoveries by feminists in the 1970s was how few of their mothers and grandmothers ever experienced any real pleasure in sex and mostly viewed it as an onerous obligation—sometimes tolerated and sometimes rejected (by deploying such weapons of the weak as fatigue, headaches or nervous breakdowns, feigned or real). In this domain, the labor process of reproduction involves the dehumanization of women to the degree that they are beaten—physically and/or psychologically—into will-enslaved objects to be used and abused. Parallel concrete forms of such dehumanization and alienation can be discovered within the many, many different labor processes in the sphere of reproduction. Recognizing and revealing such relationships has been key to organizing collective resistance and to beginning the search for more fulfilling alternatives. The personal narratives that triggered the #MeToo movement not only resulted in an outpouring of hitherto hidden stories of manipulation and domination but fueled a resistance already spurred by attacks on women in other domains, e.g., rights to good health care, including abortion. Such is the circulation of struggle in the sphere of reproduction out of shadows and into light.

Schemas of Reproduction

In Chapters 23 through 25 as Marx distinguishes between simple and expanded reproduction, his exposition is largely verbal. In Volume II of *Capital*, however, he reworks the *Tableau Économique* of Francois Quesnay (1694–1774) to model the requirements of reproduction and to distinguish between simple and expanded forms. Quesnay, the main theorist of the "Physiocrat" school of political economy in the eighteenth century, developed his *Tableau* to trace/demonstrate the interlinkages of the economy and to argue how, in his view, all expansion could be traced back to the work of farmers on the land—the only *truly* productive workers.

Like Adam Smith before him, Marx found Quesnay's approach to analyzing the "circular flows" of the economy useful, while disagreeing with his interpretation, especially his privileging of land/farming as the unique source of value. So, in Volume II of *Capital*, he suggests his own formulation of those flows, first for simple reproduction and then for expanded reproduction. In what follows I will only sketch his analysis of simple reproduction, holding a discussion of his parallel treatment of expanded reproduction over for Chapter 24 that deals with that subject.

Marx's analysis divides the economy into two sectors, or "departments." All those circuits of industrial capital that produce the means of production are regrouped, or aggregated, into Department I; all those circuits of industrial capital that produce the means of subsistence are aggregated into Department II. Using his value theory, the value of the output of each department can be represented in the same manner:

$$Department\ I = C_1 + V_1 + S_1$$
$$Department\ II = C_2 + V_2 + S_2$$

For capitalist society to reproduce itself, certain conditions must be met. First, Department I must produce enough of the means of production to replace those used up in its own activities, C_1, plus enough to replace those used up in the activities of Department II, C_2. Second, Department II must produce enough means of subsistence to sustain/reproduce the labor-power employed in its own activities, V_2, plus enough to sustain/reproduce the labor-power employed in Department I, V_1. Third, given the assumption that none of the surplus-value is reinvested, but is consumed by capitalists, Department II must also produce enough consumer goods for the capitalists of both departments to buy with their surplus-value. These conditions can be represented in the following manner:

$$Department\ I\ must\ produce\ C_1 + C_2$$
$$Department\ II\ must\ produce\ V_1 + V_2 + S_1 + S_2$$

If, and only if, these conditions are met can simple reproduction take place, i.e., can the system reproduce itself from period to period.

In the language of Chapter 23, not only must capital organize its productive activities to maintain the quantity of its raw materials and the effectiveness of its tools and machines at the current level, but it must also make sure that enough food, clothing, housing, etc. are produced to make possible the reproduction of the current number (and effectiveness) of the labor force. Meeting these requirements necessitates an appropriate balance between the activities of the two departments; failure to achieve that balance creates a crisis in the ability of the system to reproduce itself. Indeed, some Marxists have leaned heavily on these schemes in advancing the thesis that capitalist crises originate in such "disproportionalities."

There are limits to this schema. First, there is no discussion of the labor processes in either Department, only their outcomes in terms of value—neither the processes of replacing depreciated physical capital, nor the processes of maintaining labor-power. These processes, and the parallels between them, are touched on in Chapter 23, but not in these schemas. Second, as Marx will make clear in Chapter 25, the ability of capital to keep its currently employed workers working (at profitable wages) also requires that it produce and reproduce what he calls the "reserve army"—unwaged workers whose demands for jobs and wages keep pressure on those with jobs to accept wages and working conditions that they might refuse in the absence of such pressure. This is true whether we are talking about simple reproduction (Chapter 23) or expanded reproduction (Chapter 25). In both cases, capital must reproduce not only those who are waged, but also those who are unwaged. Therefore, the output of the means of subsistence in Department II destined for the working class, i.e., $V_1 + V_2$ must be sufficient to feed, clothe, etc. (to greatly varying degrees, of course) not only the waged but also the unwaged. But nowhere is this explicit in the schema. I will return to this in my analysis of Chapter 25.

Economists: "Productive" and "Unproductive" Consumption

Marx highlights how both capitalists and political economists have differentiated between working-class consumption necessary to capital and any consumption that goes beyond that and only benefits the workers themselves.[9] He cites James Mill, David Ricardo and Thomas Malthus as all considering any working-class consumption over and above what capital requires as "unproductive." Their concepts of what constitutes "productive" versus "unproductive" consumption clearly express the viewpoint of capital itself.

Adam Smith insisted on distinguishing between the unproductive use of money, e.g., rich landlords hiring large numbers of retainers, and the productive use of money as capital, i.e., hiring workers who produced products upon which a profit could be earned. Marx, in Volume III of *Capital*, retained a similar distinction between investments of money in

---

9. *Capital, Vol. I*, pp. 718–719.

mere mercantile buying and selling or financial dealings versus investments in industrial production.

In this chapter's discussion of working-class consumption Marx accepts the economists' usage, even embracing Thomas Malthus's assertion that workers' consumption is not even productive to themselves:

> The workman. . . is a productive consumer to the person who employs him, and to the state, but not, strictly speaking, to himself.[10]

Marx's formulation is: "In reality, the individual consumption of the worker is unproductive even from his own point of view, for it simply reproduces the needy individual. . ."[11]

But he follows this with: "Even its [the working-class's] individual consumption is, within limits, a mere aspect of the process of capital's reproduction." The caveat "within limits" refers, of course, to the degree to which workers achieve some degree of life autonomous from capital over and beyond the simple reproduction of their labor-power. This was the worry of the capitalists and of their economists; they knew that in periods of upturn and tight labor markets workers were sometimes able to achieve increases in wages from which they alone benefited. Marx was well aware of this phenomenon, not only because the economists that he read were aware, but because such increases in wages were occurring around him during upswings and because there was debate among working-class strategists about the importance of struggles to win such gains. Embracing such struggles, Marx argued against those who thought they were a waste of time because eventual downturns and rising unemployment would eventually hammer wages back down.[12]

The important point here, I think, has nothing to do with the periodic fluctuations in wages, and hence variations in the degree to which working-class consumption became "unproductive" for their employers, but rather the simple fact that such consumption could, and has, occurred and that therefore, there is something like a counter-concept of "productivity" from our point of view! To the degree that we consume in ways that escape or go beyond simply reproducing our labor-power, that consumption is autonomously "productive" of *our* lives, even if "unproductive" from the point of view of capital. Instead of being part of the self-valorization

---

10.   Ibid., p. 719, fn 12.

11.   Ibid., p. 719.

12.   See his arguments against Weston's opposition to wage struggles and trade unionism spelled out in his essay "Value, Price and Profit," an address to the First International in 1865. *MECW, vol. 20*, pp. 101–149.

of capital, it becomes an aspect of our own self-valorization autonomous of capital's desires and projects.

Vocabulary: Their and Ours

Terms such as "productive," "unproductive," "self-valorization," as well as their roots (production, valorization) and even "consumption" fit the vocabulary of capital, even if we use them in an inverse sense to express our own point of view. We do better, I think, to seek out, and use, a vocabulary untainted by such vile origins and associations. Capital may find it convenient—both theoretically and ideologically—to reduce our various life activities to the categories of "consumption" and "production," but we will find it more enlightening to break out of such reductionism and to contemplate our activities as irreducible and complex variety.

When we prepare, serve and eat food, especially in a social setting, we are not merely "consuming," something the fast-food industry seeks to make brief, for high turnover and increased sales and profit. On the contrary, in preparing food we can be engaged in a creative search for (as the Chinese say of their cooking) a harmonious combination of tastes, shapes, smells, colors and textures. We can also be engaged in the preparation of gifts for our friends and/or families—gifts of ourselves objectified in our dishes. In that preparation, we may well be engaged in cooperation and collaboration—mutual aid, in the language of Kropotkin. In eating together, we can be sharing the pleasures of food laced with love and the joys of cooperation; our mealtimes can be moments of the sharing of our lives through conversation, stories, body language and facial expressions. Eating together may have collective spiritual significance, and so forth. Let us not allow the reductionism of capital's economists to guide our language and our lives. Let us rather learn from poets and artists how to talk about and appreciate all the dimensions of human experience, both individual and social.[13]

Labor-Power and the "Transmission of Skills"

The chapter ends with a discussion of how the reproduction of workers and their labor-power requires "the transmission and accumulation of skills [especially] from one generation to another."[14] Marx already touched upon this in Chapter 6 but here he takes the opportunity to illustrate how acutely aware capitalists are of this necessity. He quotes at some length from

---

13.   My previous remarks on the need for new language to think about, and talk about, post-capitalist relationships mainly concerned "labor" and "work." Those remarks can be found in my essay titled "Work is Still the Central Issue!" (1999).

14.   *Capital, Vol. I*, p. 719.

Edmund Potter (1802–83) who argues against allowing cotton millworkers to emigrate away from British mills during the downturn in employment brought on by the disruption in cotton imports caused by the American Civil War. Potter emphasizes how such workers "are the mental and trained power which cannot be replaced for a generation." Better than allowing them to emigrate, he argues, the state should spend the money necessary to force them to accept "some [local] occupation or labour." While, in response, the *Times* of London mocks Mr. Potter's proposal to "sustain them by alms" and, most likely, "to keep down their discontent by force," it too worries about the loss of skill due to unemployment—"Human machinery *will* rust under inaction, oil and rub it as you may"—and the possibilities of such workers running "amuck in our great towns."[15]

Over time, these kinds of concerns did lead to increasing state intervention in "the transmission and accumulation of skills [especially] from one generation to another," often under the goad of private enterprise or their philanthropic spin-offs, such as Rockefeller's General Education Board. Today, part of the crisis of the school brought on by both student struggles and capitalist efforts to reorganize its labor force for better control has been a fierce debate over the relative role of private versus public schools. Capitalists have sought to frame that debate, not surprisingly, primarily in terms of which kind of school, private or public, can best prepare young people for the labor market. That framing obviously seeks to exclude other questions we might well consider more important: such as which kind of school provides a better terrain for fighting to liberate learning from its subordination to "skill transmission" and the capitalist world of work?

CHAPTER 24: THE TRANSFORMATION OF SURPLUS-VALUE INTO CAPITAL

Overview of Chapter

Section 1: Capitalist Production on a Progressively Increasing Scale. The Inversion which Converts the Property Laws of Commodity Production into Laws of Capitalist Appropriation

Section 2: The Political Economists' Erroneous Conception of Reproduction on an Increasing Scale

Section 3: Division of Surplus-value into Capital and Revenue. The Abstinence Theory ▶

---

15. Ibid., pp. 722–723.

Section 4: The Circumstances which, Independently of the Proportional Division of Surplus-Value into Capital and Revenue,
Determine the Extent of Accumulation, Namely, [1] the Degree
of Exploitation of Labor-Power, [2] the Productivity of Labor, [3]
the Growing Difference in Amount between Capital Employed
and Capital Consumed, and [4] the Magnitude of the Capital
Advanced
Section 5: The So-called Labor Fund

Preliminary Commentary

This chapter opens the discussion of expanded reproduction, or accumulation, by highlighting the utilization of surplus-value for investment.
Extremes of income and wealth inequality in capitalism have often
provoked critics to emphasize greed as the motivation for capitalist actions,
especially policies that have enriched some and impoverished others, such
as repeated tax cuts for the very rich and attacks on social programs that
benefit working families. One result has been a long history of capitalists being caricaturized as obese Mr. Moneybags, surrounded by bags of
money, sometimes sitting on the shoulders of gaunt, ill-clothed workers.
Such motivations on the part of individuals and such policies, while quite
real and recurrent within capitalism, are considered by Marx as secondary,
albeit functional, to the primary social use of surplus-value as investment,
as the expenditure of money on the resources and labor necessary to impose
ever more work, and thus the extension of the capitalist social order.

Section 1: Capitalist Production on a Progressively Increasing Scale.
The Inversion which Converts the Property Laws of Commodity
Production into Laws of Capitalist Appropriation

Outline of Marx's Analysis

Surplus-value can be employed
  – for capitalist consumption, as revenue
  – for investment, as capital
Net revenue (sales minus costs)
  – is the money form of surplus-value
  – it becomes capital when invested in more means of production
    and the hiring of more labor
  ▶

Expanded reproduction must include:
- new *MP*, beyond replacement of used-up *MP*
- new *LP* (workers)
- new *MS* to sustain them
- wages to purchase enough *MS* to support an expanding labor force
- not a circle, but an expanding spiral

The *laws of private property* that assume equal exchange
- hide the real relationship
- equal exchange (assuming wages = value of labor-power)
  - mystifies the real *content* of the relationship,
  - i.e., surplus-value = unpaid labor stolen from workers

Property rights were once grounded in labor
- e.g., John Locke's theory of property[16]
- but in capitalism, property = the right to appropriate the labor of others

"General law of commodity production" = "law of exchange" = exchange of equal values
- Marx assumes this to always hold
- yet exploitation exists

Generalization of commodity production only occurs when labor-power becomes a commodity

Commentary

There are two basic points in this section. First, for capitalism to expand beyond simple reproduction the surplus-value earned through the exploitation of workers and accruing to capitalists as money realized through the sale of the commodities produced by those workers, must be *invested* rather than consumed. Second, in his analysis of such investment, Marx assumes *equality in exchange*. But, because the extraction of surplus-value constitutes the very *unequal* exploitation of workers, the "laws of exchange" hide the reality of the situation.

Investment: by Corporations, by Philanthropies and by the State

In simple reproduction—where the existing situation is merely reproduced— all surplus-value is consumed, either by the capitalist class to whom it

---

16. See John Locke, *Second Treatise of Civil Government* (1690), Chapter V: Of Property.

belongs or, perhaps, by the beneficiaries of any charity the capitalists might distribute to the poor. Marx doesn't discuss charity, but others of his time were aware of this secondary "consumption" of surplus-value. Some, such as the Parson Thomas Malthus, upon whom Marx both draws and frequently mocks, argued against it.[17] Others, such as the French novelist Émile Zola (1840–1902), in *Germinal* (1885)—based on investigative research into the mining industry—sketched biting portraits of such condescension in the annual bestowal of charity on impoverished coal miners by the mine-owners' wives. Louisa May Alcott's *Little Women* (1868) portrays such charity during the American Civil War.[18]

In expanded reproduction, or accumulation, surplus-value is invested to buy more means of production and acquire additional labour.[19] This expands the imposition of work, the scale of production, the amount of output and the amount of surplus-value/money realized from enlarged sales. For this to occur, current production must supply not only replacement means of production but also *new* raw materials and equipment to *expand* production. At the same time, it must also supply sufficient means of *subsistence* to support an expanding working class. Thus, in accumulation "ordinary wages [must] suffice, not only to maintain [existing workers] but also to increase [their] numbers."[20]

In the language and symbolism of Marx's reproduction schemes, for the present organization of capitalist society to reproduce itself on an expanded scale, new conditions must be met. First, Department I must produce enough of the means of production to replace those used up in Department I and II and *enough to meet the needs of new investment in each department.* Second, Department II must produce enough of the means of subsistence to sustain/reproduce the labor-power employed in Departments I and II and *enough to sustain/reproduce whatever new labor is employed with the surplus-value realized and invested in each department.* These conditions can be represented in the following manner:

$$Department\ I\ must\ produce\ C_1 + C_2 + C_{1new} + C_{2new}$$
$$Department\ II\ must\ produce\ V_1 + V_2 + V_{1new} + V_{2new}$$

---

17.   See Thomas Malthus, *An Essay on the principle of Population* (1798).

18.   Film versions of both novels have been frequent. The most recent version of *Germinal* (1993) was directed by Claude Berri. A 2017 made-for-TV version of *Little Women* was produced by the BBC and directed by Vanessa Caswell.

19.   Marx notes that "additional labour" could be acquired by either hiring more workers *or* an increase in "the exploitation of workers already employed. . . either extensively [more hours] or intensively." *Capital, Vol. I*, p. 727.

20.   Ibid.

If, and only if, these conditions are met can investment be successful and expanded reproduction take place.

While in Marx's exposition the production of new means of production and the expansion of the labor force were financed by new investments, the nineteenth and early twentieth centuries saw a few, extremely wealthy capitalists discover a new way to achieve these same goals: "philanthropy"— which must be distinguished from charity. Most people understand *charity* to be made up of small gifts, sometimes drawn from capitalist profits but more often drawn from wages, offered to improve the lives of a few in dire need, these days often deductible from one's taxable income. But *philanthropy* is a much more extensive use, not of wages, but of surplus-value for purposes of social engineering. Any close examination of such well-known philanthropies as those associated with the Rockefellers, with Henry Ford or with Bill Gates reveals that their expenditures amount to sizeable *investments* in either the shaping of labor-power, or in the development of new technologies and strategies aimed at achieving socio-political goals. A few examples follow.

The early efforts by John D. Rockefeller's General Education Board to support the expansion of public schooling in the Southern states and to transform the Southern family through the development of home economics, were paralleled by those of the Rockefeller Sanitary Commission (1909–15) that financed an anti-hookworm campaign in the same region.[21] Both "philanthropic" expenditures were *investments*, designed quite consciously to transform and improve the quality of the Southern labor force.[22] Unlike, say the corporate financing of a gym to help *their own employees* stay in shape, be productive and reduce health care costs, these philanthropic investments were aimed at improving the quality of the labor force in the region, no matter who their future employers might be. These capitalist philanthropies finance social investments in the interests of the capitalist class as a whole.[23]

---

21. This effort was followed by a Rockefeller Foundation campaign against malaria in the South and in various other countries. More recently, the Gates Foundation launched a campaign against HIV in sub-Saharan Africa.

22. I write "quite consciously" because I read letters written by the field representatives of the GEB and archived by the Rockefeller Foundation as part of my dissertation research. See Harry Cleaver, "The Origins of the Green Revolution", Stanford University dissertation, 1974, Chapter III: The Southern Colony or the Attempt to Transform Southern Agriculture and Make It Safe for 'Democracy' and Profits."

23. To some degree, these investments also benefited those parts of the working class directly affected. This was certainly true for the eradication of hookworm. See Hoyt Bleakley, "Disease and Development: Evidence from Hookworm Eradication in the American South", *Quarterly Journal of Economics*, vol. 122, no. 1, 2007, pp. 73–117. The benefits of public schooling are less clear, for all the reasons discussed heretofore.

Similarly, philanthropies have often invested in the development of new technologies aimed at improving productivity throughout much of society, far beyond any personal profit motives of those supplying the funds underwriting such research. Motivated by the desire for a more stable labor force, the funding of agricultural research centers by the Rockefeller and Ford Foundations in the post-World War II period was aimed at the development of new, higher-yielding varieties of grain to boost food supplies in the Third World.[24] They believed this could reduce unrest and rebellion caused by hunger. The new high-yielding varieties of wheat and rice at the heart of the so-called "Green Revolution" were aimed at removing causes of "Red Revolutions."[25] In all these cases, surplus-value was expended not to improve the means of production or to expand the labor force of *particular* corporations, and thus not aimed, directly, at expanded reproduction, but rather at the expanded reproduction of an exploitable labor force (as opposed to a rebellious one) necessary for accumulation and/or improved productivity that would generate greater relative surplus-value and greater profits generally. Thus, philanthropy involves *social* investment and *social engineering*.

Not surprisingly, given the influence of powerful capitalists on public policy as well as the demonstration effect of successful private programs, these private philanthropic investments have often become the starting point for similar investments by the state. The General Education Board's lobbying in support of public education in the Southern states successfully led to the organization of public schooling by state governments. Similarly, the Rockefeller Sanitary Commission's campaigns led to broader government programs of public health.[26] And, of course, there have been extensive government expenditures on productivity-raising research of all kinds. For the most part, such government efforts have been financed with taxpayer money, mostly drawn from the wages of workers.

---

24. These included, most notably, International Center for the Improvement of Corn and Wheat in Mexico, founded in 1940 and the International Rice Research Institute in the Philippines, set up in 1960.

25. See Harry Cleaver, "The Contradictions of the Green Revolution", *American Economic Review*, vol. 62, issue 2, May 1972, pp. 177–185, and *Monthly Review*, vol. 24, no. 2, June 1972, pp. 80–111.

26. For more on such connections, see Harry Cleaver, "Malaria, the Politics of Public Health and the International Crisis", *Review of Radical Political Economics*, vol. 9, no. 1, Spring 1977, pp. 81–103.

Section 2: The Political Economists' Erroneous Conception of Reproduction on an Increasing Scale

---

Outline of Marx's Analysis

The classical political economists were *correct*
  - to emphasize how hired retainers, e.g., butlers, housemaids, are *unproductive* because they produced no new products on which a profit could be realized
  - whereas industrial workers, who produce such profitable products, are *productive*

They were also *correct* to distinguish
  - *hoarding* where money or things are just piled up, from:
  - *capital investment* where money is spent to buy new means of production and labor-power that are put to work,[27] so
  - consumption of surplus product by productive workers is, indeed, "a characteristic feature of the process of accumulation."

Adam Smith is *wrong*
  - to pretend that accumulation is "nothing more" than that consumption
  - because invested surplus-value takes the form of both constant and variable capital
  - because wages buy the means of subsistence "which are consumed, not by 'productive labor', but by the 'productive worker'"

Commentary

Marx dwells on this "error" of classical political economy because "it goes without saying that political economy has not failed to exploit, in the interests of the capitalist class, Adam Smith's doctrine that the whole of that part of the net product which is transformed into capital is consumed by the working class." How is this doctrine "exploited"? By providing an ideological cover for the real exploitation of workers. Evoking this doctrine, business can tout how workers gain from capitalist profits and their investment, because, ultimately, the workers consume it all.[28] In both this section

---

27. As discussed in Chapter 3, the temporary hoarding of *some* money as a reserve to deal with fluctuations in the need for money is a natural part of the circulation of capital.
28. The modern parallel to this doctrine can be found in the neoclassical pretense that ultimately what is produced is determined by consumer demand, thus the system meets people's needs.

and in the next, Marx critiques this ideological ploy and, along the way, further clarifies his own analysis of how the *normal* functioning of capitalism involves the exploitation of workers.

Marx's acceptance of the classical political economy distinction between productive and unproductive labor can be found not only in this chapter but in many places, especially Volume III where he uses it to distinguish between the *productive* labor of workers in industry and the *unproductive* labor of workers in commerce and finance. It turns out that Marx's retention of this distinction is much more problematic than its original use by Smith.

Working during the latter part of the eighteenth century—the *Wealth of Nations* was published in 1776—Smith was preoccupied with calling attention to how manufacturing industry was supplanting landed property as the major source of wealth. The traditional landed aristocracy in Britain maintained huge country estates, opulently furnished inside and surrounded by extensive and lavish formal gardens, tended inside and out by hordes of retainers paid out of *rents* obtained from tenants on the owners' vast land holdings.[29] The supplanting of rents by profits occurred both in the gradual transformation in the management of the great landed estates from mere rent-taking to capitalist methods (Chapter 29) and in the rise of capitalist manufacturing (Chapter 31).

Writing in the nineteenth century and primarily focused on a fully developed capitalist system, Marx sharply distinguishes between the spheres of exchange/circulation and of production. Indeed, we are not formally introduced to the sphere of production until Chapter 7 on the labor process. Here, Marx draws the same sharp line between equality in the sphere of exchange/circulation and inequality in the sphere of production as he did at the end of Chapter 6:

> The sphere of circulation or commodity exchange. . . is in fact a very Eden of the innate rights of man. It is the exclusive realm of Freedom, Equality, Property and Bentham. . . When we leave this sphere of simple circulation, or the exchange of commodities. . . a certain change takes place, or so it appears, in the physiognomy of our *dramatis personae*. He who was previously the money-owner now strides out in front as a capitalist; the possessor of labor-power follows as his worker. The one smirks

---

29. Those estates were portrayed in many an eighteenth- and nineteenth-century novel, such as Jane Austen's *Pride and Prejudice* (1813), where Mr. Darcy's estate Pemberley so awed Lizzy. Many of them, now owned by the National Trust, have been used as settings for film versions of those novels, e.g., Lyme Park in Cheshire for Pemberley (exterior), Sudbury Hall in Derbyshire for Pemberley (interior) in the 1995 BBC/A&E TV mini-series and Highclere Castle for Downton Abbey in the Carnival Films/WGBH-TV mini-series (2010–15).

self-importantly and is intent on business; the other is timid and holds back, like someone who has brought his own hide to market and now has nothing else to expect but—a tanning.[30]

Despite this sharp association of productive labor with factories and the industrial production of things, there are times when Marx recognizes how service labor, when organized by capitalists—as opposed to servants working for the wealthy—can also be productive of surplus-value. One example analyzed in Part One of Volume II of *Capital* is *transportation*. On the face of it, the transportation of commodities seems an obvious moment of circulation, a necessary moment of buying and selling because buyers are often far from the location of the producer. This is true whether the seller is the original industrial capitalist or wholesalers and retailers who have bought to resell. Actual sale, therefore, depends on transportation to deliver the use-value to purchasers.

However, Marx recognizes that transportation is *more* than just a moment of circulation. He notes that while physically a commodity at point A may be the same after being transported to point B—whether miles of roads or oceans away—there is a real difference. A shirt manufactured and warehoused in Manchester, England has zero use-value for a buyer located in the United States, Australia or India. For the seller to sell, the buyer must be able to realize the use-value of the item purchased and for that to happen the commodity must be transported to the buyer. When this happens, he writes, "What the transportation industry sells is change of location."[31] Therefore, he continues,

> The useful effect is inseparably connected with the process of transportation, i.e., the productive process of the transport industry. . . The exchange value of this useful effect is determined, like that of any other commodity, by the value of the elements of production (labor-power and means of production) consumed in it plus the surplus-value created by the surplus-labor of laborers employed in transportation.[32]

In Marx's time, this meant the labor of loading vehicles, lighters and ships, driving or sailing them and unloading them all counted as productive labor. As transportation methods improved rapidly in the nineteenth century—railroads were being built and steam ships were replacing sailing vessels—the new kinds of labor associated with these technologies counted,

---

30. *Capital, Vol. I*, p. 280.
31. *Capital, Vol. II*, p. 135.
32. Ibid.

in Marx's view, as productive labor. As in manufacturing, capitalists in the transportation sector were investing in new kinds of machines and new kinds of labor to put people to work and extract surplus-value.

The key questions for deciding whether any labor is *productive* are: 1) does that labor produce a new product (be it a thing, a service or a "useful effect"); and 2) does the sale of that new product realize a surplus-value? It is entirely secondary, according to Marx in Volume II, whether such labor takes place within "the sphere of production" or "the sphere of circulation." Accepting this reasoning means we must ask the same questions of labor employed everywhere. Let's examine this issue in the spheres of education and of finance.

Education and the Question of Productive versus Unproductive Labor

Investment in education can be productive of surplus-value in two ways. First, raising the productivity of labor-power results in a rise in the relative surplus-value. The investments of the Rockefellers' General Education Board successfully promoted state investment in public schooling and raised the productivity of the Southern labor force. Second, capital can also be invested in private schools with the aim of directly realizing surplus-value from the labor of teachers (and other school employees). Marx used just such an example "from outside the sphere of material production" in Chapter 16 and in "Results of the Immediate Process of Production." In the latter text Marx writes,

> A schoolmaster who instructs others is not a productive worker [e.g., the governesses and tutors of upper-class children, who would be counted among those unproductive retainers discussed above]. But a school-master who works for wages in an institution along with others, using his own labor to increase the money of the entrepreneur who owns the knowledge-mongering institution, is a productive worker. But for the most part, work of this sort has scarcely reached the stage of being subsumed even formally under capital and belongs essentially to a transitional stage.[33]

But, as workers forced down the length of the working day and freed their children from waged labor (something which has *not* yet been achieved by millions of families around the world), the number of "knowledge-mongering institutions" multiplied. Sometimes they have been by-products of capitalist efforts such as those of the Rockefeller General

---

33. *Capital, Vol. I,* p. 1044.

Education Board. Sometimes they have been direct investments, such as the recently proliferating for-profit technical schools. In retrospect, what he was observing was an early moment of a truly epochal transition from a capitalism based primarily on manufacturing to one based primarily on services.

Similarly, services provided by unproductive retainers on the great estates have come to be provided by waged workers employed by capitalists. Where the landed gentry employed extensive kitchen staffs, housemaids, launderers and gardeners, increasingly such work is done by caterers, restaurants, laundry, cleaning and landscaping services, all employing waged workers generating surplus-value. Where the masters of such estates hired nannies and tutors for their children, such work was taken over by for-profit day-care centers and schools. Over time, these capitalist-provided services became available to waged and salaried workers as well. Successful struggles to raise wages and reduce the working day led to increasing expenditures of wages and salaries on services. This has been especially true where women have fought to substitute purchased services for their own unwaged domestic labor (cooking, cleaning, childcare, etc.), intensified where women have entered the labor force and sought to avoid a "double working day" of waged work in one part of the day and unwaged work in the other.

But what of administrators, teachers and staff in *public schools*, whose costs, including fixed capital costs, salaries and wages, are paid for by tax revenues and are ostensibly non-profit. Because neither the service being produced—the conversion of life into labor-power—nor the product—labor-power—are sold for a profit, such workers clearly do not *directly* generate surplus-value/profits in the same manner as those employed in for-profit private schools. However, as with the activities of students, to the degree that their labor does successfully produce labor-power and the cost of that labor-power to the capitalists who buy it is lower than it would be otherwise, their profits will be higher. Therefore, the labor of those administrators, teachers and staff in public schools, like that of students, turns out to be productive-for-capital in the sense that the higher the productivity of the labor-power produced, the greater the surplus-value. Hence, the ceaseless efforts by private industry both to shape public schooling to produce the kinds of workers desired and to ensure public schooling is mostly financed out of workers' wages.[34]

---

34. Although state universities claim to be "non-profit," many realize surplus-value—from the investment of endowments, from taking cuts of research funding and from patents on creations stemming from that research—and reinvest it to expand their operations just like their overtly profit-making counterparts.

Finance and the Question of Productive versus Unproductive Labor

Turning to labor expended in the sphere of finance—which Marx quite pointedly considered unproductive in Volume III of *Capital*—we are obliged today to examine that sphere as carefully as he examined transportation and schooling in his day.

Workers in the financial industry produce services that their bosses sell. One service many workers find vital are mortgages, loans that allow them to buy homes today and pay for them over a long period of time. Another is banking services: insured deposits, where money can be safely stored, and credit cards that, like mortgages, allow workers to obtain goods today and pay for them later. Such loan services may be far costlier than the borrower initially realizes—even fraudulently marketed. But that is true with many products, from foods, supplements and drugs that don't supply the nutrition or health benefits advertised, to automobiles and other products that do not perform as marketed. Nevertheless, they are still new products produced by workers for their employers and sold by the latter to make a profit.

Once identified, the labor processes that produce services provided by the financial industry can be researched just as with industrial production or transportation or schooling. Traditionally, legions of "Bartleby's" scrivened away in the back rooms of financial houses creating and processing the paperwork used to provide such services.[35] More recently, investment in computers has spread dramatically in the financial industry, displacing some workers, but many still fill forms and shape the final products. That this labor has proved profitable has been glaringly obvious to those who have followed recent financial crises, brought on, in part, by how the financial industry has fashioned and handled the marketing of its products. That a few profited immensely, while many lost their jobs, wages and commissions characterizes most capitalist crises.

So why did Marx consider the financial industry, and the labor employed within it, to be unproductive? The answer he gave in Volume III of *Capital* argued that the profits of the financial industry (summarized as "interest") were but a share of the surplus-value that resulted from the labor of workers in "productive industrial spheres." This paralleled his reasoning about the "unproductive" nature of labor in commerce. In both cases, he thought, *to the degree that* such labor merely contributed to buying and selling and thus took place uniquely in the sphere of exchange—where he *assumed* equality—it was unproductive and constituted merely the *faux frais* of cir-

---

35. The reference, of course, is to Herman Melville's short story "Bartleby, the Scrivener: A Story of Wall Street" published in 1853. Now in *Great Short Works of Herman Melville*, New York: Perennial Classics, 1969 and available at www.gutenberg.org/ebooks/11231.

culation. The above examples show that a far closer examination of the financial industry is required than Marx provided. A cursory dismissal of all labor in that industry as unproductive just won't do.[36]

Section 3: Division of Surplus-Value into Capital and Revenue. The Abstinence Theory

---

Outline of Marx's Analysis

Surplus-value can be either
  – consumed by capitalists, S_c
  – or invested, S_i
Capitalists can do *both*: consume some surplus-value and invest some.
Total $S = S_i + S_c$
  In the short run, this is a zero-sum game: $\uparrow S_i \Rightarrow \downarrow S_c$
As capital "personified," the "motivating force" is S_i
  – diversion into S_c "counts as a robbery committed against the accumulation of his capital"
Historically, there is an evolution in the attitudes of capitalists
  – early on, "the capitalist of the classical type brands individual consumption as a sin against his function"
  – as capitalist development proceeds, as surplus-value grows and as the availability of luxury goods expands, capitalists' attitudes change. "There develops in the breast of the capitalist a Faustian conflict between the passion for accumulation and the desire for enjoyment."
  – Marx quotes Dr. Aikin at length on this historical evolution
  – an historical turning point came with the July Revolution in France
    – rebellion on both sides of the Channel
    – Owenism in England, Saint-Simonism and Fourierism in France
Senior's "abstinence theory" replaces "capital" with "abstinence"
  – but this is totally inappropriate in an epoch in which capitalists live in luxury, with the ratio S_c/S_i extremely low
Rather, it is the workers who are forced to *abstain from consumption* due to their endless exploitation by capitalists

---

36. I elaborate this argument in *Rupturing the Dialectic*.

Commentary

Following several pages sketching the history of capitalist attitudes toward consumption and investment, Marx critiques and mocks Nassau Senior's "abstinence theory"—a theory concocted by replacing the word "capital, considered as a means of production" with the word "abstinence" that refers to capitalists' choices. Senior's theory, he shows, amounts to the resurrection and glorification of the attitudes and practices of the capitalists of a much earlier era, when individual capitalists struggled to accumulate, a struggle often requiring personal sacrifice. But, he maintains, it is totally inappropriate for the more modern capitalism of the nineteenth century, when capitalist enterprise and development have grown to such a degree that the "conventional degree of prodigality" requires very little diversion of surplus-value and therefore has very little effect on the rate of accumulation. Senior would, Marx sneers, have us feel sorry for "the self-chastisement of this modern penitent of Vishnu, the capitalist" and revere "that peculiar saint, that knight of the woeful countenance, the 'abstaining' capitalist."[37]

In the "dawn" of the capitalist era, it was easy to find emphatic rants against self-indulgence on the part of those who extracted surplus-value. In a footnote, Marx provides a very long quote from Martin Luther (1483–1546) condemning usurers "that old-fashioned but ever-renewed specimen of the capitalist." Luther wrote:

> Whoever eats up, robs, and steals the nourishment of another, that man commits as great a murder (so far as in him lies) as he who starves a man or utterly undoes him. Such does a usurer, and sits the while safe on his stool, when he ought rather to be hanging on the gallows, and be eaten by as many ravens as he has stolen guilders, if only there were so much flesh on him, that so many ravens could stick their beaks in and share it.[38]

He might also have quoted almost any of the merchant capitalists whose sage advice to their monarch almost always included tirades against consumption and calls for abstinence and investment. One such was Thomas Mun who condemned:

---

37. *Capital, Vol. I*, pp. 745–746. "Penitent of Vishnu" refers to those worshipers of the Hindu god who have contributed over a certain amount to the support of his priests and temples. The "knight of the woeful countenance" refers to Don Quixote de la Mancha who gave up all his fortune in the pursuit of doing good as a knight errant.

38. *Capital, Vol. I*, p. 740.

the general leprosie of our Piping, Potting, Feasting, Fashions, and mis-spending of our time in Idleness and Pleasure (contrary to the Law of God, and the use of other Nations) hath made us effeminate in our bodies, weak in our knowledge, poor in our Treasure, declined in our Valour, unfortunate in our Enterprises, and condemned by our Enemies.[39]

Once "a conventional degree of prodigality, which is also an exhibition of wealth, and consequently a source of credit, becomes a business necessity, luxury enters into capital's expenses of representation." This "necessity" can be understood in two senses. First, with the expansion of capitalist operations, both at home and abroad through colonialism and foreign trade, the ability to obtain credit from the ever more important but also ever more unstable financial sector, required a solid reputation in the business world. Reputations depended on successful investments but also the perception of success created by one's "representation" of oneself and one's enterprise.

Second, the rising capitalist class challenged the old landed elite, not only in terms of providing the wealth of nations but politically and socially. New capitalist money vied with old landed money for recognition and social valorization. Although capitalists would eventually displace the landed aristocracy as the ruling elite, they fought to do so not only in the formal political sphere (e.g., pushing the supremacy of the House of Commons over the House of Lords in Britain) but also in the social sphere. For a good while, they did so by emulating many of the social practices and graces of the old aristocracy. Thus, another need for luxurious display as an essential element of self-representation.

This social tension was treated extensively in the novels and social commentaries of the time, my favorite being Jane Austen's portrayal of the vainglorious Bingley sisters in *Pride and Prejudice* (1813) who repeatedly make fun of those "in trade," i.e., capitalists. The role of self-representation was taken up and made famous by the American economist Thorstein Veblen in his analysis of "conspicuous consumption." While we can debate the degree to which Veblen's ideas were derived from Marx, both clearly perceived how capitalists divert at least some of their profits into "self-representation" for both business and social motives.

Whatever an individual capitalist's personal proclivities, Marx insists,

the development of capitalist production makes it necessary constantly to increase the amount of capital laid out in a given industrial under-

---

39. Mun, *Englands Treasure by Forraign Trade*.

taking, and competition subordinates every individual capitalist to the immanent laws of capitalist production, as external and coercive laws.[40]

In other words, the capitalists who ignore the pressures of competition and divert too much of their surplus-value into personal consumption may soon find themselves outcompeted and driven from the field by those who have devoted more attention and resources to accumulation.[41] This is one of the reasons why, for the most part, Marx is only concerned with individual capitalists to the extent that their behavior accurately embodies the values and dynamics of the system. Thus, there are "good" capitalists whose behavior strengthens the system—especially those who invest surplus-value to expand the means of production and the number of people put to work— and "bad" capitalists who behave as if they think the only purpose of being a capitalist is to get rich and flaunt one's wealth. The latter often pursue money and wealth along paths of speculation and get-rich-quick schemes instead of contributing through real investment to the expansion of the social relations of capitalism.

I first came across economists critiquing such "bad" capitalists while I was in graduate school in the 1960s. The topic was economic development in the Third World and the critique blasted the strategy, put forward by W. A. Lewis, to spur investment by transferring income from consumers to capitalists.[42] The problem with the theory, suggested my professor, Tibor Scitovsky (1910–2002), was that it assumed that the capitalists who received the increased income would invest it. History has amply demonstrated, he argued, that many so-called capitalists were more interested in buying expensive houses on the Italian Riviera or new racehorses or fast cars than they were in investing in the expansion of production and employment. Indeed, for many years a great many economists were convinced that in newly independent countries government policymakers—often trained and groomed by their once-colonial masters—were the primary repository of the skills required for managing capitalist investment and accumulation. This was one source of the plethora of state enterprises that would, many years later, come under attack by neoliberal ideologues as being inefficient and deserving of privatization.

In the 1980s as union-busting, attacks on wages, the deregulation of business, especially of finance, and the Reagan era celebration of getting rich spread, such critiques began to reappear in American culture. One

---

40. *Capital, Vol I*, p. 739.
41. Many sudden failures of new enterprises during the dot.com bubble of the late 1990s were attributed to such diversions.
42. On this early "supply-side" strategy, see my commentary on Chapter 29.

example was the movie *Wall Street* (1987) with Michael Douglas playing Gordon Gekko, an unscrupulous corporate raider who became famous for uttering a line already associated with the Reagan era: "Greed is good." Three years later came *Pretty Woman* (1990) in which Richard Gere played another corporate raider, only this time the raider was rescued and brought into the domain of "good capitalism" (putting people to work building "big ships") by the intervention of a hooker-with-a-heart-of-gold played by Julia Roberts.

With the latest financial crisis (2007–12) also brought on by financial fraud and rampant unregulated speculation, new movies were made in the same vein. These included the documentaries *Capitalism: A Love Story* (2009) directed by Michael Moore, *Inside Job* (2010) directed by Charles Ferguson, HBO's drama *Too Big to Fail* (2011), a new *Wall Street: Money Never Sleeps* (2010) with Michael Douglas still playing Gordon Gekko, *Margin Call* (2011) directed by J. C. Chandor and, most recently, *The Wolf of Wall Street* (2013) based on the memoirs of a Wall Street speculator enriched by securities fraud and corruption.

In short, understanding what makes for successful accumulation and what undermines it shapes one's grasp of both its successes and its failures, its periods of booms and its periods of crash and collapse.

Section 4: The Circumstances which, Independently of the Proportional Division of Surplus-Value into Capital and Revenue, Determine the Extent of Accumulation, Namely, [1] the Degree of Exploitation of Labor-power, [2] the Productivity of Labor, [3] the Growing Difference in Amount between Capital Employed and Capital Consumed, and [4] the Magnitude of the Capital Advanced

---

Outline of Marx's Analysis

Rate of surplus-value, s/v = the degree of the exploitation of labor-power
  ↑ in s/v *can* result from ↑ productivity of labor
  ↑ in s/v *can* result from ↑ hours of work
  ↑ in s/v *can* result from ↓ wages
We have assumed wages = value of labor-power, equal exchange of *LP* for *M*, but:
  – capitalist efforts to ↓ wages, even below the value of labor-power, have been common
  – capitalists in one country have often complained about local wages being higher than those in other countries   ▶

- capitalists have examined diets to see how close wages could be pushed to the bare minimum of biological subsistence
- adulteration of food and medicines have reduced their prices, and thus the minimum subsistence wage
- parish charity, the poor rate or the workhouse have helped keep wages below the value of labor-power

Longer hours, while keeping total wages constant,
  - raises the amount of surplus product, the amount of absolute surplus-value and the rate of surplus-value, s/v
  - reduces the cost of tools (per unit of output) and raises the rate of profit and rate of accumulation
  - especially in extractive industries (e.g., mining, quarrying) where tools are the only constant capital.

With ↑ productivity and s/v constant, the mass of S rises. If S_i/S_c constant, then consumption of capitalist can rise with no decrease in the fund for accumulation—no more zero-sum game

With an ↑ in productivity and a higher level of s/v, real wages can rise, even as the value of labor-power falls
  - but a ↓ in the value of labor-power ⇒ "the same value in variable capital therefore sets in motion more labor-power and consequently, more labor"

An ↑ in the productivity of labor also lowers the value of constant capital, c, as the application of science to industry improves technology, so old machines are replaced by newer and cheaper, but generally more productive ones

Therefore, a given amount of surplus-value can generate more and more accumulation as time goes on

as the # of workers and mass of capital increases, "the more does the sum of value increase that is divided into a fund for consumption $[S_c]$ and a fund for accumulation $[S_i]$"

With the total mass of $S_i + S_c$ growing, "The capitalist can therefore live a more pleasant life, and at the same time 'renounce' more," i.e., allow S_c/S_i to fall

Commentary

The first part of this section provides a rare moment in *Capital*—apart from Part Six—where Marx discusses the wage struggle, focusing on the desire and sometimes the efforts of capitalists to lower wages to increase surplus-value/profits and accumulation. With his frequent quoting of various authors lamenting "high" wages of English workers, as opposed to those in other countries, these paragraphs are reminiscent of Chapter 10 on the struggle over the length of the working day and his later discussion in Chapter 22 on "National Differences in Wages." Among those quoted are an unnamed eighteenth-century writer who reveals, Marx says, "the innermost secret of English capital," i.e., the effort to "force down English wages to the French and Dutch level." That writer, in turn, quotes a north Hampshire manufacturer who claims workers in France survive very well on a diet considerably more restricted than that of English workers. The American Benjamin Thompson (1773–1814) goes so far as to propose a specific recipe for the preparation of a cheap soup—based on barley, Indian corn and herring—sufficient, he says, to feed 64 men.

Such quotations demonstrate how carefully capitalists have calculated the minimum wage that could—imaginably—support workers at the level of bare subsistence. When the classical economists spoke of a "subsistence wage" they meant exactly that. However, it is worth remembering Marx's analysis in Chapter 6 on the buying and selling of labor-power that "subsistence" is socially and historically determined. Today economists and sociologists determine "basic needs" or the "poverty line," i.e., the income below which one is declared to be "poor" or "in poverty," varying their estimates according to local requirements. Thus, to avoid being poor in New York City requires more money than avoiding being poor in Podunk, Mississippi because of differences in the cost of things like food, clothing, housing, heating and transportation. What is true across regions is also true through time as requirements for producing and reproducing labor-power changes. Computer techs working for Dell in Austin, Texas today need to be able to buy computers to keep up their skills, unlike cowboys on the King Ranch when beef production dominated the Texas economy in the nineteenth century, or workers juggling pipes and chains on drilling rigs around Beaumont during the oil boom in early twentieth century.

One part of this discussion throws some light on the debates of the early nineteenth century over the Corn Laws, introduced in 1815 at the end of the Napoleonic Wars to artificially sustain the high price of wheat which had prevailed when imports from the continent were cut off. On one side, capitalists and their spokespersons, including David Ricardo, wanted to remove the laws and sought to mobilize workers to that end with promises of cheaper bread. On the other side, landlords, whose rents were high as a result of the laws, and their supporters, including Thomas Malthus, fought to keep the laws and high rents intact. What the capitalists kept from the workers to whom they appealed for support was how their calculations of the subsistence wage would drop with any fall in the price of bread. Their real objective was to reduce rents and wages while increasing profits.

As Marx goes on to show, wherever it was feasible capitalists would try to pay *less* than the bare minimum if they could get someone else to provide the difference between what they paid and that minimum. One source of such support was parish charity and the workhouse. If, for example, local charities would provide workers with clothes, wages could be reduced accordingly.

The contemporary relevance of this material should be obvious. In place of parish relief, a variety of federal, state and local programs provide the difference between existing wages and a subsistence income, making it possible for capitalists to hire workers for less than the value of their labor-power. The level of wages is still determined by struggle, but among the least powerful sectors of the working class we find millions who cannot even earn a subsistence wage and depend on taxpayer-financed public subsidies to survive, subsidies as diverse as food stamps, food banks, school lunches, general hospitals for the indigent, homeless shelters, and so on. Such underpaid workers can be found in places as diverse as Walmart and the University of Texas at Austin. To such obvious subsidies we must add all of those that reduce the costs of basic subsistence goods, such as food and clothing. I am referring here to the vast federal and state agricultural subsidies, paid for primarily by taxes on middle-class income, that keep down the price of food and raw materials. These last include cotton (used in clothing), not to mention subsidies to the energy sector that keeps down the costs of fertilizer, other agricultural chemicals, the raw materials of synthetic fibers and, most recently, the price of ethanol. Just as the capitalists fought to eliminate the Corn Laws in the early nineteenth century to reduce the price of bread, so have they in the twentieth and twenty-first centuries lobbied for and obtained vast subsidies to keep down the price of bread and many other consumption goods, so they can pay low wages.

Of course, it is also true that *reducing* such subsidies is a weapon for attacking the real wage and forcing it down, not only for workers living with a subsistence income but for all workers. Such reductions have been common elements of the structural adjustment policies imposed by the International Monetary Fund and capitalist banks during the decades of the "international debt crisis" of the 1980s and 1990s as well as the current efforts to impose "austerity"—read reduced real wages and standards of living—on the working classes in Europe and the United States.

All of these attacks are capitalist responses to earlier working-class successes in fighting to *increase* wages, benefits and programs that have subsidized their income and standards of living. The dominant rationale for current attacks is the existence of "debt crises" wherein various governments have borrowed heavily from the international banking system to finance their expenditures (including those that support working-class income and well-being). Naturally, when we examine the reductions demanded by these austerity policies, we discover that the main cuts in government expenditures are those that benefit workers.

Section 5: The So-called Labor Fund

Outline of Marx's Analysis

Marx: "capital . . . fluctuates with the division of surplus-value into revenue and additional capital"

Yet, "Classical political economy has always liked to conceive social capital as a fixed magnitude of a fixed degree of efficiency"
– this became dogma with Bentham

This dogma has been used:
- to argue that the amount of capital that can be converted into labor-power is fixed
- to justify telling workers that there is no point in fighting for higher wages
  - because fixed, it can only be redistributed over available workers
- to put the division of the total capital into constant and variable capital off-limits to discussion or negotiation

Classical political economists, such as H. Fawcett, equated the "wages-fund" with the "circulating capital of a country"
- the average possible wage will be determined by the size of the labor force over which it is distributed
- fixed and circulating capital ≠ constant and variable capital

Commentary

Eventually economists set aside the "Wages-Fund Doctrine," as it is mostly known today, in part because they came to recognize precisely the point that Marx made about the flexible and fluctuating character both of capital in general and of the part invested in hiring labor.

John Stuart Mill, for example, after having set out and embraced the doctrine in his *Principles of Political Economy* published in 1848, recanted his support in an 1869 book review article.[43] "The theory," he writes, "rests on what may be called the doctrine of the wages-fund." "But is there," he

---

43. John Stuart Mill, *Principles of Political Economy* (1848), vols. 2 and 3, *Collected Works of John Stuart Mill*, Indianapolis, IN: Liberty Fund, 2006.

then asks, "such a thing as a wages-fund, in the sense here implied? Exists there any fixed amount which, and neither more nor less than which, is destined to be expended on wages?" His answer? "There is not."

He made his case thusly:

If we choose to call the whole of what he possesses applicable to the payment of wages, the wages-fund, that fund is co-extensive with the whole proceeds of his business, after keeping up his machinery, buildings and materials, and feeding his family; and it is expended jointly upon himself and his labourers. The less he expends on the one, the more may be expended on the other, and vice versa. The price of labour, instead of being determined by the division of the proceeds between the employer and the labourers, determines it. If he gets his labour cheaper, he can afford to spend more upon himself. If he has to pay more for labour, the additional payment comes out of his own income; perhaps from the part which he would have saved and added to capital $[S_t]$, thus anticipating his voluntary economy by a compulsory one; perhaps from what he would have expended on his private wants or pleasures $[S_c]$. There is no law of nature making it inherently impossible for wages to rise to the point of absorbing not only the funds which he had intended to devote to carrying on his business, but the whole of what he allows for his private expenses, beyond the necessaries of life. The real limit to the rise is the practical consideration, how much would ruin him, or drive him to abandon the business: not the inexorable limits of the wages-fund.

This, of course, was one of Marx's points published two years earlier!

As with Marx, Mill very clearly sees how this doctrine has been used to undermine workers' wage struggles and how once we recognize the falsity of the doctrine, we must also see that it cannot be used to justify arguing against those struggles. Mill wrote:

The doctrine hitherto taught by all or most economists (including myself), which denied it to be possible that trade combinations can raise wages, or which limited their operation in that respect to the somewhat earlier attainment of a rise which the competition of the market would have produced without them, this doctrine is deprived of its scientific foundation, and must be thrown aside. The right and wrong of the proceedings of Trades Unions becomes a common question of prudence and social duty, not one which is peremptorily decided by unbending necessities of political economy.

Finally, Mill argues that this critique justifies the struggles of workers and their unions for a greater share of the wealth they produce:

> It has made it necessary for us to contemplate, not as an impossibility but as a possibility, that employers, by taking advantage of the inability of labourers to hold out, may keep wages lower than there is any natural necessity for; and *converso*, that if work-people can by combination be enabled to hold out so long as to cause an inconvenience to the employers greater than that of a rise of wages, a rise may be obtained which, but for the combination, not only would not have happened so soon, but possibly might not have happened at all. The power of Trades Unions may therefore be so exercised as to obtain for the labouring classes collectively, both a larger share and a larger positive amount of the produce of labour; increasing, therefore, one of the two factors on which the remuneration of the individual labourer depends.

Spreading rejection of the wages-fund doctrine in the latter part of the nineteenth century was facilitated by the rise of a new economic doctrine that provided new weapons against workers' wage struggles. That new doctrine was "marginalism"; its rise often called the "Marginal Revolution," and the name we know it by today is neoclassical microeconomics. The fruit of the work of several economists, of whom those most closely associated with its crafting were William Stanley Jevons (1835–82), Marie-Esprit-Léon Walras (1834–1910) and Carl Menger (1840–1921). Its spread to hegemony in the English-speaking world was primarily due to its embrace by Alfred Marshall (1842–1924) who elaborated these new ideas in *The Economics of Industry* (1879) written with his wife Mary Paley (1850–1944) and in his *Principles of Economics* (1890).[44]

The weapon provided by the new marginalist or neoclassical doctrine was the concept of the "marginal productivity of labor," or, put more generally, the neoclassical doctrine that each factor of production is due the value of its marginal product. Whereas the wages-fund supposedly defined an absolute upper limit to what workers could possibly receive, so, according to this new doctrine, labor should neither expect, nor struggle, to achieve any more than the value of its marginal product. Moreover, the doctrine argued that given free markets, labor *would* receive neither more nor less than the value of that product. (The only possibilities of "exploitation" in this theory were those few cases, due to imperfectly competitive markets, where labor received *less* than the value of its marginal product.)

---

44. Alfred Marshall and Mary Paley, *The Economics of Industry* (1879), vols. I and II, Lexington, KY: Ulan Press, 2012. Alfred Marshall, *Principles of Economics* (1890), 9th edn., London: Macmillan and Co., 1961.

The theory raised an obvious question: "what is meant by the *value* of a factor's marginal product?" The marginal revolutionists' answer was to replace labor as the *source* of value, by "utility." Jeremy Bentham—the same Bentham Marx mocks in this chapter—was one of those who popularized the concept of "utility" as a replacement for labor as a source of value.[45] That this new doctrine provided a weapon against the struggles by labor to raise wages (and other benefits) is not surprising, given the attitudes of its creators. Let us examine those of Jevons, who saw great dangers to both workers and society in union wage struggles. In a lecture given in 1866 to primary school-teachers about the importance of teaching economics to working-class children to avoid the evils of class struggle, we find the following:

> The best example I can give, however, of the evils and disasters which may accompany progress is to be found in trade unions and the strikes they originate and conduct. Of these I may say, in the words of a recent article of the *Times*, that "every year sees these organizations more powerful, more pitiless, and more unjust". Such atrocities as that reported from Sheffield are but the extreme cases of a tyranny which is at this very moment paralyzing the large part of the trades of the country. . . there is one great disaster almost the greatest that I can figure to myself. It is that our working classes, with their growing numbers and powers of combination, may be led by ignorance to arrest the true growth of our liberty, political and commercial.[46]

So strongly did Jevons fear such struggles that two years later in 1868 he undertook to lecture trades unionists directly. While he approved of the efforts by unionists to reduce working hours and improve working conditions, he deplored any effort by them to raise wages above the value of their marginal product and argued that not only would such efforts be doomed to failure, but any success would be "injurious to the welfare of the community." He told them that if *some* of them succeeded, it would be at

---

45. Utility theory ran into trouble when it was recognized that the *marginal utility* of any commodity (including money) declines as the quantity of its consumption rises. That led some to argue for the *redistribution* of money from the rich to the laboring poor to increase the total utility of society. In response, economists reworked neoclassical theory in the twentieth century to get rid of "utility," "marginal utility" and "declining marginal utility" such that the only concept of "value" that remained was market value, or price.

46. William Stanley Jevons, "The Importance of Diffusing a Knowledge of Political Economy", a lecture delivered on October 12, 1866, in R. D. Collison Black (ed.), *Papers and Correspondence of William Stanley Jevons, vol. VII: Papers on Political Economy*, London: Macmillan Press, 1981, and available at: http://la.utexas.edu/users/hcleaver/368/368JevonsDiffusingtable.pdf.

the expense of others. Higher wages, he said, would lead to higher prices and thus a lower standard of living for other workers who had to consume the higher priced goods. If workers as a class succeeded it would raise all prices thereby undermining the value of whatever increase had been gained. *Real* wages would still be limited.

In short, Jevons's interpretation of the new marginalist doctrine accepted—in a manner altogether parallel to the reasoning of those who had embraced the wages-fund doctrine—that wages had an upper limit. In the new theory this limit was set by the value of its marginal product and any effort to exceed that limit was doomed. The implication that Jevons draws from this, for the edification of workers, is that the best way to achieve increases in wages is to collaborate with their employers in improving the productivity of labor, which will, through market forces, be returned to them in the form of higher wages. Now it must be noted that Jevons not only saw, and argued, that this path was a better one for raising wages but that it was a path to the transcendence of the class struggle. He argued that as wages rose, workers could earn enough and save enough to become capitalists themselves and as they did, they would abandon their objections to capitalism:

> But all this is changed for the man who has even a moderate amount of savings. Not only does he disarm sickness or misfortune of half its terrors, but he may also, by cooperation, become his own employer; and then he will, I presume, cease to complain of the tyranny of capital.[47]

Marx's analysis, of course, has demonstrated why such a path *may* work for this or that worker but it is delusional to think that it would work for all, or even for most, given the nature and dynamics of capitalism.

Despite his opposition to wage struggles, there was a progressive insight at the core of Jevons's thinking, one that would be largely ignored by capitalists for many years to come. The insight was how *increases in labor productivity made it possible for real wages to rise without undermining profits (the marginal productivity of capital) or provoking inflation.* Over time a few economists, such as Alfred Marshall, and a few capitalists, like Henry Ford, would recognize and accept this principle, but it would not be until John Maynard Keynes demonstrated that the principle was applicable at the level of the whole economy that capitalists would begin to see wage

---

47.   Jevons, "Trades Societies: Their Objects and Policy", a lecture delivered at the request of the Trades Unionists' Political Association in Manchester, March 31, 1868. W. Stanley Jevons, *Methods of Social Reform*, London: Macmillan & Company, 1883 and available at: http://la.utexas.edu/users/hcleaver/368/368JevonsTradestable.pdf.

struggles and wage increases as not only compatible with the system but potentially a vital motor of its development.

All of this was implicit in Marx's analysis of relative surplus-value, but unlike these economists who were devoted to the promulgation of capitalism, he was not preoccupied with discovering how workers' struggles might be compatible with it but rather with how they might lead beyond it.

CHAPTER 25: THE GENERAL LAW OF CAPITALIST ACCUMULATION

Overview of Chapter

Section 1: A Growing Demand for Labor-Power Accompanies Accumulation if the Composition of Capital Remains the Same

Section 2: A Relative Diminution of the Variable Part of Capital Occurs in the Course of the Further Progress of Accumulation and of the Concentration Accompanying it

Section 3: The Progressive Production of a Relative Surplus Population or Industrial Reserve Army

Section 4: Different Forms of Existence of the Relative Surplus Population. The General Law of Capitalist Accumulation

Section 5: Illustrations of the General Law of Capitalist Accumulation
    (a) England from 1846 to 1866
    (b) The Badly Paid Strata of the British Industrial Working Class
    (c) The Nomadic Population
    (d) Effect of Crises on the Best Paid Section of the Working Class
    (e) The British Agricultural Proletariat
    (f) Ireland

Section 1: A Growing Demand for Labor-Power Accompanies Accumulation if the Composition of Capital Remains the Same

---

Outline of Marx's Analysis

Composition of capital
    – *value* composition: ratio of constant to variable capital, c/v
    – *technical* composition: arrangement of means of production and living labor-power, MP/LP

▶

- *organic* composition: value composition *in so far as* it is determined by the technical composition, c_o/v_o

Individual capitals and branches of production
  - compositions differ within a branch
  - average gives composition of branch

Total social capital of a country
  - average of branch compositions = average composition of total social capital
  - growth of total social capital means growth of the working class
  - reproduction on an expanded scale = *accumulation*
  - accumulation = expanded reproduction of the classes, multiplication of the proletariat
  - proletarian = wage laborer

Classical political economists
  - recognized essential role of labor in growth of capital
  - argued workers had to be kept poor to have incentive to work, but not too poor
  - Malthus's "principle of population" blamed workers for their poverty
    - rising wages, he said, meant more workers and lower wages
    - policy conclusion: keep wages low, no Poor Laws
    - Marx mocks him as a plagiarist and many of his fellow Protestant pastors as hypocrites

Business cycle?
  - against Malthus blaming cycle on changes in workers' wages
  - Marx argues wages fluctuate primarily as a function of the demand for labor
    - in periods of rapid growth, demand rises, wages rise
    - in downturns demand falls, wages fall

Commentary

Marx's opening remarks on the "composition of capital" harken back to the analysis in Chapter 15 on relative surplus-value. There we saw how efforts to offset reductions in the working day by raising productivity involved capitalists replacing troublesome workers with compliant machinery. He suggests that the introduction of more machinery per worker can be formulated as a rise in the *technical composition* of capital, something we can represent symbolically by *MP/LP*, the material configuration of means of production and labor-power.[48] Looked at from the point of view of value invested, increased expenditure on machinery raises the *value composition* of capital, or c/v, a ratio of the value invested in constant capital, c, to that invested in variable capital, v. However, because the value composition can change independently of any change in the technical composition,[49] Marx calls the value composition—when changes are *only* due to changes in the technical composition—the *organic composition* of capital. To differentiate, we can represent the organic composition of capital as c/v_o. So, c/v can change, even if c/v_o does not; but any change in c/v_o is also a change in c/v. Therefore, whenever he refers to changes in the organic composition he is talking about a change in the technical composition, but in value terms. Eventually—especially in Volume III of *Capital*—we find that Marx's analysis of some tendencies to crisis are formulated in terms of the *organic composition* of capital.[50]

Although we can analyze these various "compositions of capital" at every level of the economy, from individual enterprises through branches of industry to the total social capital, it is "with this [last] alone that we are concerned here."[51] In other words, the subject is the expansion of the total social capital. It is therefore vital to be clear about what Marx means by *accumulation*.

Had he defined accumulation merely as an expansion of the total social capital, it would be easy to confuse accumulation with economists' concepts of "growth," or, taking qualitative changes into account, with concepts of "economic development." But he doesn't leave it at that; he carefully defines accumulation in social terms as the reproduction "of the capital-relation on an expanded scale, with more capitalists, or bigger capitalists, at one pole, and more wage-laborers at the other pole."[52] In other words, what is being accumulated are the antagonistic class relationships of capitalism. Unlike economists who recognize neither classes nor class antagonism, and think of growth in terms of aggregate production functions such as $Q = f(K, L)$, where factors of production K (capital) and L (labor) produce output

---

48. Because *MP* and *LP* are heterogeneous, as a representation of the arrangement of means of production and labor-power *MP/LP* might better be thought of as an array rather than a ratio.

49. For example, take the cotton textile industry. Fluctuations in weather can affect the value of a bale of cotton, changing c and thus c/v. Or worker successes or failures in struggles over the value of their labor-power, v, can change v and thus c/v.

50. In the voluminous literature interpreting Marx's writings on crisis, differences in understanding the relationship between the value composition and the organic composition have led to different interpretations of his analysis, especially that of "the tendency of the rate of profit to fall." See Cleaver, "Karl Marx: Economist or Revolutionary?"

51. *Capital, Vol. I*, p. 763.

52. Ibid.

(Q) that grows as the economy expands, Marx re-emphasizes here that his interest is precisely those antagonistic relationships within which K (MP or c), L (LP in action or v) and Q (C' and M') are only elements or moments.

He then proceeds to discuss the dynamics of accumulation in terms of the relationships between the classes. In this first section he assumes that the composition of capital (by each definition) remains the same, so that when capitalists invest, their money buys more means of production, MP, and labor-power, LP, in the existing configuration. (He relaxes this assumption in the next section.) Under this assumption, capitalist investment increases the demand for labor-power and puts upward pressure on wages as capitalists compete for available workers.[53]

Marx then brings this association between investment and the demand for labor to bear on the analysis of the fluctuations in business activity. He recognizes how downturns and upturns were recurring periodically, but his real interest lay not in their periodicity but how major downturns constituted *crises* for capitalism. That is to say, large-scale layoffs, rising unemployment and increased poverty could lead to worker-led uprisings and a crisis for capitalist control. Although capitalists had repeatedly overcome such crises and restored accumulation, he never assumed that they would always succeed. Unlike economists who prefer the term *business cycle*, optimistically presuming that downturns will always be followed by upturns, for Marx each major crisis opened the possibility of the revolutionary overthrow of capitalism.

Assuming a constant composition of capital, as he does in this section, rapid accumulation was achieved by capitalists hiring more labor, sometimes buying new machines and processing more raw materials to produce more output, whether in agriculture, manufacturing or services. At some point, however, accumulation slows and then turns down; the boom becomes a bust, a crisis for capital, often a dramatic collapse with bank panics, firms going bankrupt or being taken over by others. Among a working-class population whose wages are already near subsistence, the associated rapidly rising unemployment and falling wages create another kind of crisis: sickness, evictions and starvation. Forced to bear the human

---

53.   He is well aware that capitalists have often sought to reduce such upward pressure on wages by importing cheap labor to expand the pool of available workers. In his day, Irish workers were brought over and pitted against British workers. In the years after decolonization, British capitalists imported workers from the West Indies and South Asia. Since the collapse of Soviet-style regimes, contemporary British capitalists have been hiring workers from Eastern Europe. Such pitting of foreign against domestic workers—widespread today—can escape capitalist control, through immigrant/migrant worker struggle, through local worker efforts to limit competition in labor markets or through local and foreign workers joining forces.

costs of downturns, workers sometimes agree that they have "nothing to lose but their chains" and explode in revolt.

Such explosions were not just a theoretical possibility for Marx but part of his own experience. The dramatic international economic crisis of 1847 was followed by the 1848 revolutions on the European mainland. Marx and Engels followed the crisis closely, analyzing it in their journalism.[54] When revolution erupted in Germany, both traveled there to participate in the uprising. Although the rising failed and both returned to England, Marx subsequently provided a detailed analysis of the parallel uprising in France in a series of articles later published under the title "The Class Struggles in France."[55]

Among theories of the business cycle put forward by economists, that of Malthus became popular with business. He argued that two related phenomena caused downturns: 1) the emergence of a "glut," more output being produced than the market could bear, resulting in falling sales, prices and profits; and 2) rising wages. Although rising wages might help absorb rising output, he warned, they would also result in workers having more children. The resulting expansion of the supply of labor, he argued, would soon reduce wages, reduce buying power and accentuate glut. His reasoning assumed workers breed like rabbits, that increased income would inevitably result in more children. In his theory, the only checks on population growth were hunger, disease or war. In short, his theory argued against wage increases and was wielded against both workers' efforts to utilize tight labor markets to raise wages and against the "poor laws" of the time—supported by middle-class humanitarians—that sought to support the income of the unemployed through various forms of welfare.

Against this theory that blamed workers for their poverty, Marx argued that the primary determinant of the rise or fall of wages was fluctuations in the demand for labor-power. Accumulation, he reasoned, often tightened labor markets as the demand for labor expanded and facilitated workers' battles for higher wages. But the fall in wages occurring during downturns were due to cutbacks in investment that reduced demand for labor-power, not an excessive growth of population. Eventually, demographers, studying the relationship between income and family size, would provide support for Marx's position on this issue. Identifying what they came to call the "demographic transition," they would observe how rising income would lead people to *reduce* the birth rate and the size of their families—the exact opposite of Malthus's assumption.[56]

---

54. See, for example, F. Engels, "The Commercial Crisis in England—The Chartist Movement—Ireland" (written October 23, 1847), *MECW*, vol. 6, pp. 307–309.

55. *MECW*, vol. 10, pp. 45–145.

56. By admitting—in the second edition of his book on population—that workers

The real source of downturns, Marx argued, was reduced investment in response to declines in profits. When, as a result of rising wages, "the surplus labor that nourishes capital is no longer supplied in normal quantity, a reaction sets in: a smaller part of revenue is capitalized [invested], accumulation slows down, and rising wages come up against an obstacle.[57] The rise of wages is therefore confined within limits that not only leave intact the foundations of the capitalist system, but also secure its reproduction on an expanding scale."[58] Despite such limits on increases in wages, Marx supported struggles to raise wages and those that sought to limit their reduction during downturns.[59] Although he doesn't discuss it at this point, Marx argues that one source of Malthus's "glut" lies in the tendency of capitalists to hold down wages, which in turn limits the ability of workers to purchase the goods they have produced.[60]

Marx ends this section by evoking how different things would be if "objective wealth" was "there to satisfy the worker's own need for development" instead of capitalists' need for profits and control.[61]

Section 2: A Relative Diminution of the Variable Part of Capital Occurs in the Course of the Further Progress of Accumulation and of the Concentration Accompanying it

---

Outline of Marx's Analysis

As capitalists invest in machinery,
- MP/LP rises, so too does c/v
- but c/v rises *less* than MP/LP because per unit value of MP declines   ▶

---

could exercise "moral restraint" and limit the size of their families, Malthus effectively undermined his theory. This admission has largely remained unnoticed, or ignored, by all those who have enjoyed using his theory to attack workers' wage demands and welfare support for those without wages.

57.   Here he recognizes how worker success in raising wages can undermine profits. Those who have emphasized this phenomenon often speak of "profit-squeeze" as a source of crisis.

58.   *Capital, Vol. I*, p. 771.

59.   See his arguments against Weston's opposition to wage struggles and trade unionism spelled out in his essay "Value, Price and Profit".

60.   Both Marxists and non-Marxists, e.g., John A. Hobson (1858–1940) and Albert F. Mummery (1855–95) in *Physiology of Industry* (1889), New York: Routledge/Thoemmes Press, 1992, who have emphasized this problem speak of "underconsumption" as a cause of crisis. Like Keynes who, years later, took Hobson to task, Marx recognized that consumption demand was only one element of aggregate demand.

61.   *Capital, Vol. I*, p. 772.

> Increase in social productivity of labor, via MP/LP, involves:
> - cooperation on a large scale
> - creation of systems of machinery
> - harnessing of gigantic natural forces
>
> Accumulation evolves increased scale of production via two processes:
> - the *concentration* of capital via investment that creates new capital
> - the *centralization* of existing capital via mergers and takeovers of existing capital

Commentary

In this section, Marx drops the assumption that the composition of capital remains the same and analyses some aspects of what is involved as the LP in MP/LP and the v in c/v experience a relative diminution as a result of the relative surplus-value strategy.

He notes how the *value composition* of capital, c/v, tends to rise less than the *technical composition*, MP/LP, because the introduction of productivity-raising machinery in the production of the means of production reduces their per unit value. So, while labor-power is employed using ever more machinery and transforming ever more raw materials, the decline in the value of the means of production means that the "increase of the difference between constant and variable capital is therefore much less than that of the difference between the mass of the means of production into which the constant capital, and the mass of labor-power into which the variable capital is converted. The former difference increases less with the latter, but in a smaller degree."[62] Clearly, as in Part Four, what motivated this analysis was Marx's observation of the spreading use of machinery in factories, mines and agriculture and the associated relative decline in the use of labor-power. Unexamined here, but previously evoked in his *Grundrisse* notebooks of 1857 and later implied in his comments in Volume III of *Capital* on the results of a rising organic composition of capital, is the dangerous consequence of this capitalist strategy: a declining need for labor to produce wealth, a decline that undercuts capital's ability to impose work and can inspire the rejection of any need for capitalists as managers of production.[63]

---

62. Ibid., p. 774. It is worth noting that in this analysis Marx ignores a key element of the argument he made in Part Four about capital's relative surplus-value strategy: namely, that increases in productivity in the production of the means of *subsistence* lowers the value of variable capital, thus raising the rate of exploitation s/v and the rate of profit $s/(c+v)$. Ignoring this parallel effect, as he does in this passage, only makes sense if you assume that the value per unit of c is declining faster than that of v.

63. The analysis in Volume III of *Capital* unfolds in Part Three, Chapters 13–15.

As capitalists strove to cope with workers' struggles for less work and to expand markets, the scale of production grew steadily. Marx examines two ways capitalists achieve greater scale. First, individual capitalists invest in expanding their operations. They build new factories, buy machinery for those factories, produce or contract for raw materials and hire more workers. This process, he calls the *concentration* of capital. Second, one capitalist buys out, or takes over, the operations of another, combining existing production facilities. Such combining he calls the *centralization* of capital. This choice of words can be confusing because it became common for economists to speak of increasing industrial concentration when referring to what Marx calls the centralization of capital. Indeed, governments compile statistics on the degree to which various industries are "concentrated" as part of their effort to monitor the degree of competition and the need for anti-trust regulation. That preoccupation arose as the result of public opposition to monopolistic practices and the demand for anti-trust regulation, thanks in large part to the revelations of investigative journalists into the practices of large-scale business operations.[64]

Drawing on some changes introduced by Marx in the French transla-tion of *Capital*, Engels rewrote some of Marx's analysis to highlight the role of credit in the form of limited liability or "joint stock" companies. Throughout the 1850s and 1860s, Marx followed the rapid expansion of the financial industry and published many articles on the growing role of credit in financing both concentration and centralization. The issuance of "stock," or the exchange of certificates of part-ownership in a firm for money, facilitated the "drawing together" of disposable money, whether the retained profits of firms or the savings of individuals. This process enabled centralization "in the twinkling of an eye," a vast speed-up in what had hitherto been a much slower process.[65] The preoccupation here, however, is not with the modes of centralization but only with their impact on the relationship between capital and labor.

Marx concludes his analysis by noting that whether achieved by concen-tration or centralization the increasing scale of production either "attracts fewer and fewer workers in proportion to its magnitude" or "repels more

---

64. Among the many highly critiqued "trusts," whose behavior led to public outcry and eventually anti-trust regulation, was the "oil trust" of John D. Rockefeller, whose "philanthropic" investments in social engineering are cited in several of these com-mentaries. Counterparts today can be found in controversies surrounding mergers in telecommunications, such as that between Comcast and AT&T or the continuing expansion of the right-wing Sinclair Broadcast Group and their consequences for con-sumer costs and access to information.

65. Both Marx's original passage and Engels's rewritten one can be found in *Capital*, *Vol. I*, pp. 777–780.

and more of the workers formerly employed."[66] Both observations prepare the next section on the genesis of a reserve army of the unemployed.

Section 3: The Progressive Production of a Relative Surplus Population or Industrial Reserve Army

---

Outline of Marx's Analysis

As total invested capital, $c + v$, rises, so does the demand for labor

But, the organic composition, c_0/v_0, of the total social capital rises quicker than social wealth

- because simple accumulation is accompanied by centralization
- so, the demand for labor, determined by v_0, "falls relatively to the magnitude of the total capital"
- as a result, while size of the working population grows, capital produces a "relatively redundant" or "surplus" population

The growth in surplus population involves:

- the "extrusion" of workers (laying off or firing)
- increased difficulty in "absorbing" a growing working class
- "violent fluctuations" in the economy

Law of population in capitalism: workers produce both:

- the accumulation of capital
- the means of their redundancy

Accumulation = growth in number of waged workers + growth in "industrial reserve army"

Industrial reserve army is a vital component of capital

- provides a mass of workers available when needed
- cycle of expansion and contraction produces and absorbs the surplus population
- duration of cycle is variable, will gradually shorten

Political economists and their popularizers recognized the need for an industrial reserve army

Increases in c_0/v_0

- reduce *MP*'s capacity to employ workers
- increase the number of unwaged and enforces idleness
- facilitate increased intensity of labor and overwork
  - partly by speed-up (machine driven work rhythms)

▶

---

66.   Ibid., p. 781.

>   – partly by the pressure of the unwaged reserve army on
>   employed waged workers
> Therefore, the movements of wages are:
>   – determined by fluctuations in demand for labor
>   – NOT determined by fluctuations in supply of labor as Malthus et
>   al. claimed
>   – fluctuations in the supply of labor are much too slow to meet
>   capital's fluctuating demands
>   – labor moves in response to variation in wage rates
>   – from low wage spheres of production to higher wage spheres
>   – a movement that eventually lowers higher wages
> Apologetics of political economists—sycophants of capital
>   – prate virtues of supply and demand when they meet the needs of
>   capital
>   – abandon supply and demand and resort to force when they do
>   not

Commentary

Marx's analysis in this section makes unambiguously clear that accumulation, i.e., the expanded reproduction of the antagonistic social relationships of capitalism, includes both the waged and the unwaged sectors of the working class. This implies rejecting the standard twentieth-century position of orthodox Marxism-Leninism that defined the working class purely in terms of its waged components and sought to subordinate the struggles of the unwaged to those of the waged. Working through this section, the need to complement analysis of the waged with that of the unwaged becomes obvious.

Marx's demonstration of why accumulation includes the unwaged consists of showing, first, how capital constantly regenerates an industrial reserve army, and second, how that regeneration is vital to the dynamics of its development.

The regeneration of the industrial reserve army takes place as capital's strategy of increasing the organic composition of capital results both in the *expulsion* of some waged workers and a *reduction in the ability to absorb* new unwaged additions to the growing labor force. Among both Marxists and economists, the emphasis has usually been on the expulsion—the laying off or firing—of workers and has derived from concerns about the loss of wages and reduced standard of living of such workers and the potential for revolt. Such concerns have been recurrent during periodic crises, especially during severe ones with high levels of unemployment.

Concern with the ability of capital to absorb new unwaged additions to the working class has been associated with several different phenomena. First, lengthy, slow "jobless" recoveries from crises eventually worry economists not only because of the anger of those expelled who lost wages, but because of growing youth unemployment as new entrants to the working class are unable to find waged work. Having been subjected to fewer years of the discipline of imposed labor, young workers are less patient and more likely to revolt against the conditions in which they find themselves. Second, new entrants to the labor market come not only from population growth but also from new enclosures of subsistence agriculture. Where real investment has been weak and involving a high organic composition, accumulation has been unable to generate enough jobs to absorb rural–urban migrants who have formed a huge "informal sector" of largely unwaged workers who survive by organizing themselves in communities rather than being organized by capital in factories and offices. Capital's control of such unwaged sectors has, therefore, required supplementary methods, e.g., police repression and urban planning (repeated physical destruction and dispersion of autonomous communities).[67] Where such methods have been severe, they have spurred both resistance and exodus, involving an often difficult-to-control level of working-class mobility, including cross-border migration.

Along with his own analysis of the genesis of the industrial reserve army, Marx also highlights the recognition by political economists and historians such as Malthus and Merivale (1806–74), whom he quotes at some length, of the need for readily available unwaged workers. He also quotes the well-known popularizer for such political economic views, Harriet Martineau (1802–76), who wrote stories embodying the apologetics of economists with the aim of convincing her readers that workers should accept their sorry lot as the inevitable consequence of the natural dynamics of social development. It was undoubtedly because of this role that Marx dismissively refers to her as "an old maid" (she remained unmarried until her death). His dismissal was unfortunate because despite her role as an apologist for capitalism, a great many of Martineau's writings called attention to and provided analyses of various aspects of the work of the unwaged. Indeed, in recent years she has been celebrated not only as the first woman sociologist but as an early analyst of the domestic labor of

---

67. In the United States, such destruction is often rationalized under the euphemism of "urban renewal." For one example of such struggles in Mexico, see Harry Cleaver, "The Uses of an Earthquake", *Visa Versa* (Quebec), December/January 1987, *Midnight Notes* (US), no. 9, May 1988, *Wildcat* (Germany), Winter 1988, and *Commonsense* (Scotland), no. 9, 1989 and available at: http://la.utexas.edu/users/hcleaver/earthquake.html.

reproduction.[68] Instead of dismissing her, and her work, Marx would have done better to draw on it to amplify his own analysis of the reserve army.

He then returns to the issue of the causes of fluctuations in wages and reiterates his argument that they are primarily the result of fluctuations in the capitalist demand for labor rather than the results of changes in labor supply. He makes this argument taking into account such phenomena as increases in the intensity of labor—associated as he showed in Chapter 15 with the subordination of work to the rhythm of machines—and the replacement of better organized workers by those more vulnerable.

Evoking his analysis of how machinery is used to impose more work—through speed-up and the intensification of labor—instead of freeing workers from labor, Marx points out the irony and injustice of the way capitalist development imposes overwork on some while denying others any chance to earn a wage. As he also made clear in Chapter 10, overwork is not just a theft of daily life time and energy, it also kills. In Japan, where it is all too common, death-by-overwork has a name: *karōshi*.[69] It should have a name everywhere.

His uncritical acceptance of the conventional vision of the jobless alternative to waged overwork as "enforced idleness" also limits his analysis. He readily uses the term "unemployed" to designate those without jobs. As I've indicated in my commentary on earlier chapters, the unwaged are rarely "idle," the "unemployed" generally must employ their skills to survive; both those who have lost their jobs and those who have yet to find one must work at trying to stretch what little money they have or finding ways to get more, whether from welfare or a new waged job or some creative, temporary gig in the "informal economy." When, in the next section, Marx offers an analysis of the composition of the industrial reserve army, the absence of this recognition becomes apparent. Fortunately, since he was writing, others have filled this gap in his work and often applied his ideas to the analysis of various domains of unwaged labor.

Marx ends this section by mocking the hypocrisy of economists and other priests of capitalism who preach the virtues of the markets capitalists impose on us, but quickly abandon their catechism when force and state intervention serves them better. His examples we have seen before—crackdowns on workers' self-organization at home and violent colonization abroad. Recognizing such hypocrisy is particularly important today, when once again, in this era of neoliberalism, market-worship forms the central

---

68.   See, for example, Michael Hill and Susan Hoecker-Drysdale (eds.), *Harriet Martineau: Theoretical and Methodological Perspectives*, New York: Routledge, 2002.

69.   National Defense Counsel for Victims of Karoshi, *Karoshi: When the "Corporate Warrior" Dies*, Tokyo: Mado-Sha, 1990.

ideological framework of contemporary economics and public policy, while the state wholeheartedly represses workers at home and abroad.

Markets and force have always gone hand in hand. The state has always been the enforcer and protector of capitalist markets, from their forcible imposition to the use of force to maintain them, against both efforts to escape them and any violation of their rules (property ownership). In so doing, the state has played as central a role in the shaping of markets as private capitalists. Perhaps not since overt colonialism has this been as clear as during this period of trade agreements among capitalist nation-states. Whether multilateral or bilateral they are ostensibly negotiated by governments, and then overseen by such supranational state institutions such as the World Trade Organization. In reality, such agreements are designed in secret and in collusion with capitalists, who desire arrangements that facilitate pitting weaker (generally lower waged) workers overseas against stronger ones at home. Only by being able to export back to the country from whose workers they have fled can companies take advantage of cheap labor abroad to produce for domestic markets.

Section 4: Different Forms of Existence of the Relative Surplus Population. The General Law of Capitalist Accumulation

---

Outline of Marx's Analysis

Relative surplus population possesses three forms:
  – floating, latent, stagnant
Floating includes:
  – dismissed male workers who have reached maturity
    – some emigrate, following emigrant capital
    – replaced by younger workers, often female, often children
      – work in large-scale industry burns up lives, shortens them
      – early marriages produce child replacements
Latent includes:
  – those working in agriculture, not yet repulsed from the land
  – as capitalist development in agriculture proceeds, it generates a
    constant flow of out-migration
Stagnant includes:
  – those with extremely irregular employment
  – typically, maximum of working time, minimum of wages
  – chief form: so-called "domestic industry"
  – constitutes a growing proportion of surplus population

▶

- workers' family size inversely related to income
- lowest sphere of stagnant exist in sphere of pauperism
  - lumpenproletariat, i.e., vagabonds, criminals, prostitutes
  - those able to work
  - orphans and pauper children
  - the demoralized, ragged and unable to work
    - older people
    - victims of industry: the mutilated, sickly, widows, etc.
  - "Pauperism is the hospital of the active labour-army and the dead weight of the industrial reserve army"
Absolute general law of capitalist accumulation:
  - the greater social wealth, the greater the industrial reserve army
  - the greater the reserve army, the greater the mass of surplus population
  - the greater the surplus population, the greater pauperism
Political economists have recognized some of this
  - Ortes, Townsend, Storch, Sismondi, Steuart

Commentary

This analysis of the composition of the unwaged industrial reserve army and surplus population not only details the conditions of life and situations facing various sectors but also argues their essential role in accumulation. Effectively, Marx shows, with few exceptions, how the surplus population is not really a surplus at all but necessary for capital to be able to meet its ever-changing demands for labor-power and keep in check those it hires.

The Floating Form

Today, the *floating form* corresponds to the US Bureau of Labor Statistics' category of currently unemployed members of the labor force who are looking for waged work. Just as governments estimate the number of new hires—additions to the active labor army—as one index of the state of accumulation and the economy, so too do they estimate the number of the unemployed and their percentage of the labor force, the rate of unemployment. Drops in the rate are interpreted as a sign of accelerating accumulation and economic "health"; increases in the rate are taken as measures of deceleration or recession. These government-generated figures are regularly and dutifully reported by the capitalist media. Only outspoken critics of current government policies make a habit of pointing out how the rate of unemployment underestimates the degree of actual joblessness by ignoring those who have stopped looking for work and dropped out of the labor force.

Underestimation serves the ideological needs of capital by hiding from frequent consideration all those sectors of the reserve army not included in the narrow definition of "looking for work." The situation is akin to what we saw in Chapters 19–21, how the wage—when defined as payment for labor (as opposed to payment for labor-power)—hides the existence of surplus labor. Marx reveals how, once you take into account the dynamics of their relationship to work, most members of the population—with the exception of the leisured few who live off the work of others, of the bedridden casualties of labor and of preschool infants and toddlers—make up a *working* class, whether they receive wages or salaries or not. Despite this, officialdom treats all of those sectors of the reserve army of labor who are not currently looking for paid employment as entirely separate phenomena.

Although his treatment here is brief, his comments on how overwork burns up the lives of workers, shortening their life expectancy is worth noting. So too is the correlation between short life spans and large families. When he speaks of the "premium" set on the production of children, he undoubtedly had in mind the growing tendency of capital to replace adult with child workers and the need of poverty-stricken working-class families to render up their children to exploitation. Today, thanks to considerable research, we know a great deal more about both of these phenomena.

As we saw in Section 3 of Chapter 10, work can not only kill quickly in industrial accidents, but also more slowly through continuous exposure to low levels of toxic chemicals and noxious substances, e.g., cotton dust in textile mills, rock and coal dust in mining that cause byssinosis, silicosis and pneumoconiosis, respectively. Then there's the poisoning of water, land and air by pollution from industrial factories, mining, factory-farming and energy generation. Added to such physical abuse, we also now know how stress, anxiety and depression weaken the body and lead to health-destroying behaviors outside, as well as within, working hours. Beyond such direct workplace-related dangers we are increasingly conscious of how the mining and burning of fossil fuels contribute not only to pollution and acid rain but to global warming, which affects not only those working but the larger environment and all of those living in it, human and non-human. Economists call such capitalist-spawned plagues by the euphemistic and depreciating term of "negative externalities."

The work of demographers revealing how the success of workers in raising their income generally results in smaller families—because fewer children are needed as income-earners—must be complemented by more gender-specific considerations. Feminists have pointed out how the size of families is also determined by the degree of control that women are able to exercise over their own bodies. Against the patriarchal relationships that capital inherited, adopted and promoted, women have long organized for greater freedom and self-determination. Part of that self-determination is the choice of whether or to what extent to have children. Everywhere women have won access to various methods of birth control and abortion, they have reduced the average number of children they have been willing to bear, and the size of families has dropped accordingly. To some degree, there has been a correlation between working-class income and the success of such struggles. Where income is higher, and women win access to that income, their battles for self-determination are more easily financed, including their access to methods of contraception. Therefore, in those countries with higher average income and standards of living, women have been more successful in gaining control over their own bodies, procreating and rearing fewer children.

The Latent Form

When we turn to the composition of the *latent* reserve army, it is evident that who can be considered a part of this sector varies historically. When Marx was writing, those still attached to the land, still being periodically driven off by the development of capitalist agriculture, constituted the larger part. Even today, a great many people are still subject to such repulsion. Enclosures, which once constituted *primitive* accumulation, have become a recurrent strategy of ongoing accumulation. But even in that earlier period, there were parallels between the situation of those still in agriculture and the situation of women and children in the families of waged workers in manufacturing. They were not immediately and automatically available as members of the floating reserve any more than those attached to the land were immediately available for employment in factories. Although some women and children sought independent income, many had to be driven into the labor market—mostly by poverty—as others had to be driven off the land. Later, years after Marx died, when workers were successful in imposing not only further restrictions on the length of the working day but labor laws that liberated children from waged labor, they were effectively shifted from part of the active army or floating reserve into a position of latency. Typically, child labor laws forbid employers from hiring children, from birth to some legally determined age, usually in the teens. There were often exceptions, both legal, such as family and farm labor, and illegal, such as human trafficking, but vast numbers of children are only a latent source of potential labor-power.

As I have discussed in earlier commentaries, capitalists' need those children, temporarily free from waged employment and exploitation, to be properly prepared to eventually enter the floating reserve. Thus, their incarceration in schools structured and designed to produce compliant and exploitable future participants in both the reserve and active armies of labor. Although school children are not engaged in producing commodities on which a profit can be earned, they are put to work producing labor-power. So, although workers' struggles have liberated most children from waged exploitation, their youth is still being poisoned by the forced labor of schooling through which they are disciplined into accepting authority— today of teachers, tomorrow of employers—and acquiring, to a greater or lesser degree, depending on their resistance, the skills and abilities required by those future employers. Although latent with respect to the active army of labor, capital still manages to impose unwaged work on children.

The position of women, vis-à-vis labor, has also varied over time, the result of both capital's demands and women's struggles. In Marx's time, along with children they were being driven from work in the latent to work in the active army. In the late nineteenth- and early twentieth-century United States, laws and rules were passed excluding women from certain jobs, pushing many back into the latent reserves, despite a wave of feminist-suffragette struggle when women marched out of workplaces and homes into the streets. In both the First and Second World Wars, women were drawn into waged labor to replace men mobilized as soldiers. Then, as soon as the wars were over, despite having demonstrated both their ability and willingness to work in industry, vast numbers of women had their wages snatched away and handed to demobilized soldiers as a "family wage." With the rise of "second-wave" feminism in the 1960s, autonomously organized women fought for universal access to, and equal treatment in, whatever form of work they choose.

The Stagnant Form

The closest modern equivalent of what Marx calls the *stagnant* form is made up of what economists call the "structurally unemployed." This section, however, shows that to be a poor parallel. The structurally unemployed are defined as those who, having lost a job, discover it impossible to find another of the same kind. But the "chief sort" of the stagnant surplus population for Marx were workers actually at work in so-called "domestic industry." As he explained in Section 8 of Chapter 15, the domesticity of this industry refers only to workers being employed in other workers' homes. There, he provided details of the exploitation of women and children; here, he largely evokes such conditions and points out how they favor large and pauperized families. *Stagnant* describes the social condition and immobility of persons caught in such circumstances. Whereas workers in the floating and latent forms may eventually, or periodically, find jobs in one industry or another, those in the stagnant form are largely stuck. If they can work, they work at the most miserable, low-paying jobs. If they cannot work for wages—too old, mutilated by capitalist machinery or sickly because poisoned by working conditions—they may still contribute to the reproduction of labor-power. Although Marx refers to pauperism as the "hospital of the active labor-army," it does not function like a real hospital where impediments to work may be repaired, but rather as a kind of obscene social-hospice to which some are condemned to slowly die.

The Lumpenproletariat

In this sub-sector of the surplus population, which Marx places within general category of pauperism, he includes vagabonds, criminals and prostitutes. We have already seen in Part Eight on primitive accumulation, how vagabondage and petty crime were, like begging, active alternatives to the meek acceptance of entering the labor market in search of waged labor. Since Marx touched only briefly on such alternatives, we have been fortunate enough to have several Marxist historians delve much more deeply into examples drawn from the same period to which he makes reference, including the authors of such books as *Albion's Fatal Tree*, *Between the Devil and the Deep Blue Sea* and *The London Hanged*.[70] From such studies we have learned much about the complicated relationships that have existed between wage-earning and alternative modes of survival. Such studies have revealed how individual lumpenproletarians, that in Marx's brief treatment appear to be stuck in a stagnant state of pauperism, have often been quite mobile, moving among the alternatives available to them, including waged labor. Studies of more recent periods, including the present, have revealed much the same.

Prostitution is one survival strategy, which Marx includes among those of the lumpenproletariat, that deserves closer treatment than he accords it. In the nineteenth century, the dominant image of the prostitute seems to have been "the fallen woman"—often a woman who had not "fallen" but been pitched into poverty and recourse to prostitution by being "gotten with child" and then abandoned by the man responsible. With the extended family rapidly disappearing under the pressure of expropriation and the need to seek wages wherever they could be found, such single-mothers often had few options for earning a living. These were

---

70.   Thompson et al., *Albion's Fatal Tree*; Marcus Rediker, *Between the Devil and the Deep Blue Sea: Merchant Seamen, Pirates and the Anglo-American Maritime World, 1700–1750*, Cambridge: Cambridge University Press, 1989; Linebaugh, *The London Hanged*.

the streetwalkers and brothel sex-workers often portrayed in literature. But we know that, as in so many other domains, there has always been a hierarchy of prostitutes, both female and male, from the paupers evoked in Marx's text to well-kept courtesans and mistresses living among the wealthiest in society. In Victorian England, such diversity was well-known but kept in the shadows, except in a more or less underground literature and salacious journalism. Elsewhere, say in mining towns and those with military barracks, brothels functioned with greater openness and often government sanction. In more recent times, feminist works, such as Simon de Beauvoir's *Le Deuxième Sexe* (1949), and success in overcoming obscenity laws have allowed a more open circulation of literary treatments of sexual relationships forcing a more general recognition of this diversity. Along the way, some authors, often feminists, have drawn parallels between formal prostitution—in which sex and other reproductive services are provided in what amount to short-term contracts—and marriage (formal or de facto) where those same services are provided in exchange for long-term contracts. Such observations harken back to Marx and Engels's critique of marriage in the *Communist Manifesto* that blasted its conventions within capitalism as exploitative of women.

Unfortunately, while describing these various strata of the reserve army or surplus population, Marx gives us little sense of the various forms of struggle undertaken by individuals and groups, nor of how movement from one strategy of survival to another might constitute such a struggle. Beyond the struggle for a wage, of movement from the reserve to active army, are many other struggles unfolding within the various sectors of the surplus population and contributing to the political recomposition of the working class. Knowledge of all of these can inform useful strategies for circulating our efforts from one sector to another.

Section 5: Illustrations of the General Law of Capitalist Accumulation

---

Overview of Section

(a) England from 1846 to 1866
(b) The Badly Paid Strata of the British Industrial Working Class
(c) The Nomadic Population
(d) Effect of Crises on the Best Paid Section of the Working Class
(e) The British Agricultural Proletariat
(f) Ireland

(a) England from 1846 to 1866

Outline of Marx's Analysis

- rapid growth, but slowing
- accelerating increase in income from profits and rents
- increasing concentration and centralization of land and production
- parallel increase in working-class poverty
- real wages undercut by rise in consumer prices, debt
- steady growth in pauperism, ill health and starvation
- must take into account situation of workers outside of production

---

Commentary

The bulk of this section presents statistics—mainly drawn from official government documents—illustrating the historical accuracy of Marx's previous analysis of accumulation. He shows how the rapid growth, concentration and centralization of wealth in the hands of the rich was paralleled by an equally rapid spread of poverty and pauperism. Against evidence of some increase in wages, among some sectors of the working class, he provides evidence of increases in the prices of the means of subsistence that has undercut real wages. These kinds of statistics have also been used to attack Marx's theory of the "pauperization" of the working class. Pro-capitalist economists and historians have used increases in real wages and various measures of standards of living in England (and in other industrialized countries) to argue that the pauperization that Marx illustrates here was soon reversed as capitalism continued to develop. Among Marxist responses to such attacks has been the argument that with the spread of colonialism and primitive accumulation abroad, the issue of pauperization has to be reframed in international terms. Following the early period of slavery for the production of industrial inputs, of colonial conquest, of the seizure of the best lands and their conversion from local food production to export agriculture and of mining operations, global capitalist accumulation displaced the locus of pauperism from industrial England, where concessions were granted to an increasingly well-organized and militant working class, to the colonies (and later neo-colonies). Even in this section, however, Marx is not arguing that all workers will be reduced to paupers, only that the dynamics of capitalist development, including downturns in business activity that cause many to lose their wages, continually produces paupers and on an expanding scale.

In one of the few passages in this volume where he brings up the issue of debt, he does so in a quotation from Henry Fawcett's book on *The*

Economic Condition of the British Labourer (1865). "They (the workers) become almost the slaves of the tradesman to whom they owe money."[71] The increasing dependence of workers upon credit from tradesmen, Marx notes in a footnote to that passage, "is the consequence of the frequent oscillations and interruptions in their employment." In other words, with wages at, or very near, subsistence, the loss of wages forces workers to pawn their few worldly possessions and to beg credit from local merchants who supply subsistence goods. Once in debt, the risk of near slavery—or what some economists and historians call "debt peonage"—lay in the way some tradesmen manipulated debt accounting to prevent workers' escape, even if, and when, wages could once again be obtained. In a period in which workers' income and wealth was so low as to make access to bank credit impossible, such were the limited legal possibilities open to them, short of being turned out into the street, starving or entering the prison-like workhouses.

To my mind, however, the most important point in this section is that:

> for a full elucidation of the law of accumulation, [workers'] condition *outside the workshop* must also be looked at, his condition as to food and accommodation.[72] [my emphasis]

Just as Sections 3 and 4 of this chapter have shown how the unwaged are an integral and necessary part of the working class, reproduced on an expanding scale, so too must an analysis of accumulation take into account the character of the lives of workers, both waged and unwaged, outside of places of waged employment. This is a shift from Chapter 23 where Marx thought it sufficient to point out 1) that the reproduction of the class was part of the reproduction of capital and 2) that the capitalists mostly leave it to workers to take care of that reproduction. Here he examines the conditions of that reproduction, especially workers' ability to eat, to clothe themselves and to find shelter. Largely missing from his analysis in the next few sections, however, is the kind of close examination of work outside the workshop that he undertook inside it.

(b) The Badly Paid Strata of the British Industrial Working Class

Outline of Marx's Analysis

– illustrations from public health reports
– food intake often near or below biological subsistence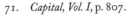

---

71. *Capital, Vol. I,* p. 807.
72. Ibid.

- working-class housing is execrable, conducive to disease
- made worse by city "improvements" that benefit capitalists
- made worse by public health measures
- made worse by speculation
- made worse by overcrowding
- made worse by sudden influxes of workers

Commentary

Drawing on a series of Public Health Reports, commissioned in response to the appalling conditions in both cities and countryside, Marx cites statistics and comments by the authors of those reports as to the malnourishment of the waged, active labor army of the English working class. For present-day readers from middle and upper levels of the global hierarchy of working-class income, where discussion of food intake has largely shifted from requirements to maintain biological subsistence to how to avoid overeating and obesity, the statistics Marx cites may seem quaint and passé. However, although advances in science have made such measurement more sophisticated today, estimates of nutritional requirements for the maintenance of life are not all that different from Marx's time. Instead of calculating the intake of grains of carbon and nitrogen, requirements are now calculated for things like general energy intake and nutrients, e.g., amino acids, carbohydrates, essential fatty acids and a variety of vitamins and minerals. Moreover, whereas in the Public Health Reports of the mid-1860s differentiation was only made between men and women, today nutritional requirements are calculated for males and females over their entire life cycle, from gestation and infancy to old age, taking into account things such as activity and body characteristics.

As in the days of the reports cited here, those preoccupied today with fighting hunger, whether working in governmental or non-governmental agencies, study the close relationship between malnutrition and susceptibility to illness and disease. Marx's analysis makes clear that the situation was so dire among so many workers as to risk the spread of disease to "respectable people," i.e., the bourgeoisie. As a result, public health measures were demanded, not out of any benevolent attitude towards workers but from self-defense. To this motivation must be added the demand by capitalists for healthy, productive workers. Often unwilling to implement costly changes within their own production facilities that would improve the health of their workers, or to pay wages sufficient to support a healthy life, capitalist support for public health measures always wanted the cost to be borne by other taxpayers. As capitalist investment moved into disease-ridden areas, either at home (the American South) or abroad (the colonies or otherwise subordinated nations), there too capitalists began to demand public health measures to reduce their own labor costs.[73]

When Marx turns from food to housing, the Public Health Reports upon which he draws are even more graphic in describing the terrible living conditions of waged workers, especially those in urban areas.[74] Poorly built, ill-maintained, often with little or no access to light, air, water or sanitation, the typical tiny apartments were often overcrowded, ill-furnished (especially when wages were lost and furniture was pawned); they were homes of the malnourished and breeding places of disease. Although it is still possible to find similar conditions in the ghettos and poor neighborhoods of the Global North, those conditions are more rampant in the sprawling shanty towns and slums of the Global South. Often created and then packed with rural–urban migrants escaping the enclosure of their lands in the countryside, only through great effort and collective struggle are workers who dwell in such favelas, barrios or bidonvilles able to gradually convert their hovels into decent housing and obtain utilities such as electricity and running water. To what degree there was collective self-organization in the nineteenth-century slums of England's great cities, such as London and Newcastle upon Tyne, we are not told; we are only offered an account of the dynamics of exploitation and impoverishment.[75]

Those dynamics include such familiar phenomena as urban renewal and real-estate speculation. Urban renewal projects, which in Marx's time were called "city improvements," replaced the old with the new, often at the expense of workers' housing. Ill-built and ill-kept housing (tenement or row houses)[76] were demolished to make way for wider roads (for

---

73. Thus, the efforts mentioned earlier of the GEB and Rockefeller Sanitary Commission in the Southern states. For an overview of capitalist responses to one disease— prevalent in the Global South—see Cleaver, "Malaria, the Politics of Public Health and the International Crisis" (1977). For a broader overview, see Peter Linebaugh, "Lizard Talk; Or, Ten Plagues and Another: An Historical Reprise in Celebration of Boston ACT UP", February 26, 1989, and available at: http://la.utexas.edu/users/hcleaver/LizardTalkOriginal.pdf.

74. Marx's analysis was preceded by Engels's vivid portrayals of workers' housing in his *Condition of the Working Class in England* and followed by his more polemical 1872 analysis of "The Housing Question", *MECW, vol. 23*, pp. 317–391.

75. A similar absence marked Upton Sinclair's novel of immigrant life in Chicago's meatpacking districts, *The Jungle* (1906). As James Barrett points out in his introduction to *The Jungle* (Urbana: University of Illinois Press, 1988), Sinclair completely missed the networks of mutual aid in those communities.

76. Keep in mind that in Marx's day, while some agricultural tenants lived in standalone single-family houses/farms, workers in urban areas had no access to bank credit or mortgages and the only housing they could afford was a room or two in a tenement.

commerce), bigger, better buildings (for businesses and for homes for the wealthy), tramways (to bring workers to work from increasingly marginalized distant neighborhoods), sanitation systems (to protect the bourgeoisie from disease) and so on. That projects to improve "public" health should have such adverse consequences for workers is especially bitter. Subjected to the worst living conditions, they were displaced by such "remedies" only to find themselves in even worse conditions! Such reorganization of cities to meet capitalist needs has been going on ever since. As workers have become better organized in their communities, however poor, they have learned to fight back against such attacks. In recent years, pitched battles have been fought against such projects as new airports or sports stadiums intended to benefit commercial airline and sports industries at the expense of local people. Such conflicts erupt every time whole working-class neighborhoods are demolished to make way for World Cup or Olympic stadiums and associated buildings.[77]

Anticipation (or insider knowledge) of such projects also feeds real-estate speculation—buying cheap today to be richly compensated tomorrow by the state for property subjected to imminent domain. Such speculation proceeds even in the absence of such large-scale projects because the growth of capitalist industry in cities and the associated growth of the working class increases the value that can be realized from rents and thus from land. As land rent rises, so too does the price of homes and the cost of rental housing, especially during periods of rapid growth. Today, when the middle- and upper-income strata of the working class have obtained access to bank credit and mortgages, the same phenomena—complete with speculation—puts upward pressure on the price of single-family dwellings. It was precisely such speculation—coupled with widespread fraud—that inflated the "bubble" in housing prices in the early 2000s, whose bursting triggered the great financial collapse of 2007–08.

(c) The Nomadic Population

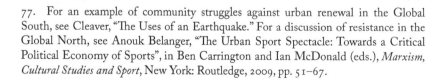

Outline of Marx's Analysis

– the "light infantry" of capital
– they march from workplace to workplace   ▶

---

77. For an example of community struggles against urban renewal in the Global South, see Cleaver, "The Uses of an Earthquake." For a discussion of resistance in the Global North, see Anouk Belanger, "The Urban Sport Spectacle: Towards a Critical Political Economy of Sports", in Ben Carrington and Ian McDonald (eds.), *Marxism, Cultural Studies and Sport*, New York: Routledge, 2009, pp. 51–67.

> – they are execrably housed
> – they spread disease
> – they are exploited as waged labor and as tenants

Commentary

Despite its title, this section does not deal with traditional nomads, neither subsistence pastoral tribes who move their herds according to season and available forage, nor geographically restless, itinerant groups such as the Romani or the Irish Travelers. Instead, Marx analyzes the living conditions of workers only able to obtain temporary employment who are forced to move more frequently than most. High unemployment and rapid changes in industrial demands for labor, coupled with capitalist efforts to minimize the cost of labor, combine to result in horrible housing for such workers, even worse than that in cities surrounding factories, often in more isolated, temporary work spaces, such as construction sites and mining camps. In this section, he illustrates such conditions by drawing on the reports of official government inspectors. Typical are flimsy, overcrowded shacks (or even caves) with no running water, no sanitation, no ventilation, no drainage, no health services and often built in proximity to toxic wastes.

Because of these conditions, suffering and death proliferate as contagious diseases spread easily from worker to worker, from parent to child. The Public Health Reports are particularly scathing in their condemnation of the living conditions of such workers. At best, special houses are provided to separate those with diseases such as smallpox, typhus, scarlet fever and cholera. But in the absence of medical care and sanitation, those diseases spread not only to other workers but to people in the surrounding areas. All of this unfolded in the absence of both modern understanding of the vectors of disease or of effective methods of treatment.

In these conditions, Marx notes, capitalists exploit their workers "in two directions at once—as soldiers of industry and as tenants." Even among relatively highly paid workers, such as miners, employers minimize their costs by treating such things as housing, fuel and water—"be it good or bad"— as payments in kind, deducting their costs from wages. These patterns of abuse in living conditions parallel those at the point of production. The minimization of expenditure on life outside mines or construction sites replicates the minimization of expenditures on "protective measures against dangerous machinery in the factory, from safety appliances and means of ventilation in the mines, and so on."[78] Such consistent efforts to minimize costs and maximize profits have condemned workers to injury and ill health.

Those familiar with the conditions of life available to today's "nomadic" segments of the working class will be struck by how uneven changes have been since the mid-1860s. In the Global North some workers have succeeded in escaping from such conditions. For example, through decades of arduous struggle, often against violent repression, miners, through collective resistance, have won recognition for their unions, collective bargaining, higher wages and escape from isolated mining camps into better living conditions. Another example has been the successful resistance of some migratory agricultural laborers. In the United States, in the 1960s, the United Farm Workers in California (UFW) evolved an innovative strategy that complemented strikes and protest marches with consumer boycotts of farm produce. Their success forced grower recognition of the UFW and negotiations that have brought better wages, less dangerous working conditions and improved temporary living conditions. More recently, the Coalition of Immokalee Workers' (CIW) anti-slavery campaign has "uncovered, investigated, and assisted in the prosecution of numerous multi-state farm slavery operations across the Southeastern U.S., helping liberate over 1,200 workers held against their will since the early 1990's."[79] On the other side of the country, in Washington state, Familias Unidas por la Justicia (FUJ), an organization of mostly indigenous migrant farmworkers has recently won a collective bargaining agreement with Sakuma Brothers Farms.[80]

On the other hand, vast numbers of the estimated 150 million migrant workers in the world today continue to suffer all the ills described in this section of *Capital*. In construction sites around the globe, it is easy to spot crude shacks, lacking all the same amenities described here, thrown up to house temporary migrant labor, often imported from far away. Most recently, such practices have been revealed in the construction of sports facilities, e.g., those for the World Cup in Brazil in 2014 and currently in Qatar in preparation for 2022.[81] Similarly, while some agricultural workers, such as those who organized the UFW and CIW, have made substantial

---

78. *Capital, Vol. I*, p. 821.
79. See their webpage for a description of all their programs to improve agricultural workers' rights, conditions of employment and conditions of life more generally.
80. See http://familiasunidasjusticia.org/en/2017/06/17/historic-union-contract-ratified-by-members-of-familias-unidas-por-la-justicia/
81. "Brazil World Cup Workers 'Face Slave-like Conditions'", *BBC News*, September 26, 2013; "Qatar 2022: World Cup Project Workers Living in Slum Conditions Behind Glitz of Oil-Rich Country", *ABC News*, July 14, 2015.

gains, millions of other workers, toil and continue to struggle against intolerable conditions of both work and life.

(d) Effect of Crises on the Best Paid Section of the Working Class

---

Outline of Marx's Analysis

Example # 1: Impact of crisis of 1866 on English workers
- overproduction and speculation in shipbuilding fed by diversion of capital in response to cotton famine
- result: financial crisis and mass unemployment of skilled mechanics and artisans
- thousands out of savings, out of things to pawn, in workhouses, on parish relief or starving

Example #2: Impact of crisis on Belgian workers
- "workers' paradise"? No unions, no factory acts!
- average worker income is less than that of soldiers, sailors or even prisoners!
- 1855 study shows most with minimum subsistence
- any downturn, any loss of income = disaster

Commentary

Newspaper reports on the crisis of 1866 in England illustrate the catastrophic effects of that downturn on even the highest paid workers, e.g., shipbuilders, who tended to be highly skilled mechanics or artisans. Those reports detail the miserable condition of workers, whether admitted to workhouses, where they break rocks or pick oakum for less than subsistence wages, or desperately besiege factory gates in hopes of obtaining some relief, however little.[82] Marx also gives us an interesting analysis of the causes of the 1866 crisis. First, the crisis came in the wake of an industrial crisis in the textile industry resulting from the "cotton famine" caused by the American Civil War that cut off cotton exports to the United Kingdom causing a dearth of raw materials and a spike in cotton prices. Second, the financial panic that set off the crisis was due to the collapse of a speculative wave of investments, in shipbuilding among other industries, fed by capitalists throwing "much capital from its accustomed sphere into the great centers of the money-market."[83] Thus, from a global perspective, the crisis

---

82. "Picking oakum" refers to the tedious labor of picking apart old tarry ropes and cordage to make new materials for caulking the seams in wooden ships.
83. *Capital, Vol. I,* p. 822.

was not merely due to financial speculation but also to workers' struggles—those of slaves and those of waged workers in the Union Army—to end the Confederate use of slavery to undercut the income of waged labor. In Volume III of *Capital*, in an expanded, year-by-year analysis of the cotton famine and its consequences for workers, Marx also reports on the effects on British workers of the substitution of weaker, shorter fiber Surat cotton from India for stronger, longer fiber American cotton, a substitution made possible by the British conquest of the subcontinent and its annexation of the labor of Gujarati cotton workers.[84] In these two cases, we can see not only the global reach of capital, but the interconnectedness of workers' struggles in different parts of the world. The victory of the Union against slavery and the militancy of British workers, evident in the so-called Hyde Park Riot where thousands faced down police and government troops, resulted in the passage of the Reform Act of 1867 enfranchising most English and Welsh male workers.

In the Belgium case, often admired by English capitalists, Marx quotes from an 1855 report by the inspector-general of prisons and charitable institutions whose data show that the average working-class family receives less real income than soldiers, sailors and even prisoners. Moreover, that data also revealed income so close to bare biological subsistence that even the slightest downturn in economic activity, any reduction of wages or employment, or any increase in the price of basic necessities throws the average family into destitution and pauperism.[85]

(e) The British Agricultural Proletariat

Outline of Marx's Analysis

- wage and living conditions have steadily worsened
- wages often below subsistence
- housing execrable, gross overcrowding, conducive to illness and spread of disease
- worsening conditions parallel rapid investment and growth of agricultural productivity
- enclosures, evictions associated with primitive accumulation continue, produces surplus population
  - reduces capitalist farmer and landlord contributions to poor rates

▶

---

84. *Capital, Vol. III*, Chapter 6, Section 3: "General Illustration: The Cotton Crisis 1961–65", pp. 228–229.
85. *Capital, Vol. I*, pp. 825–828.

> – subjects farm workers to housing at great distances
> – cheap hovels built in open villages, let at high rents to expelled farmers
> – many examples drawn from various official reports
> – both labor surpluses and dearth of labor during periods of peak need, e.g., harvests
> – gang system of subcontracted labor, employing men, women and children

Commentary

The living conditions of agricultural workers differ little from that of the "nomadic" working-class population analyzed in section (c) above. The former are less mobile; the latter more so, but both were subjected to extremely low and precarious wages and forced to live under horrible conditions of overcrowded, often deteriorating huts with no sanitation or running water, rampant disease, etc. What this section shows is why at the very beginning of his analysis of proletarian nomads, Marx states that their "origin is rural." Here he examines the forces that continue to drive agricultural laborers off the land, into open villages and sometimes further afield in search of the kinds of jobs discussed in section (c).

Those forces are twofold. First, a revolution in agricultural technology that dates from the mid-seventeenth century produced investments in new methods of land drainage and cultivation that often involved labor-displacing machinery. Second, far from sharing the resulting increased productivity of the land with those retained to work it, capitalist farmers transformed and reduced the cost of their labor force. Whereas in earlier times a great many agricultural workers were housed on the ever-growing estates, as this "revolution" progressed, the owners of those estates found it more profitable to evict their workers and force them to find worse housing many miles away in local "open" villages.

The various reports upon which Marx draws reveal a continuation of the processes analyzed in Part Eight on primitive accumulation: the expulsion from the land to distant villages or small towns and an ever-growing concentration of control over the means of production, both the land and the tools to work it. Yet, as with manufacturing, agriculture requires workers—who must now walk miles to and from their assigned fields. As in the towns surrounding factories, the Poor Laws and those laws and police practices aimed at curbing resistance force them to remain in the local "labor market" and subject to exploitation by their employers in the countryside and by landlords and merchants in the villages.

These processes—complemented over time by other exploitative methods, such as debt peonage and taxation—have been constant elements of ongoing accumulation ever since Marx wrote. The development of the American Midwest—the Corn and Wheat Belt—enabled by railroads to serve far markets, was marked by the invention and deployment of first reapers, then threshers then combines, all labor-displacing machinery.[86] A parallel process of mechanization in American cotton-growing—of planting, picking and baling—displaced millions of Black farmers and workers from the land. A more recent great "revolution" in agricultural technology was the advent of the Green Revolution in the 1950s and 1960s that involved the introduction of new high-yielding wheat and rice in the Global South. The nature of the new plants (short, with heavy heads of grain) and the switch to monoculture required increased investment—in controlled irrigation, heavy use of fertilizers, pesticides and herbicides—and the profits from the resulting increased productivity permitted many better-off farmers in places like Mexico, India and Pakistan to purchase and use, for the first time, labor-displacing technologies such as reapers and threshers, once more depriving rural laborers of jobs. Not surprisingly, the "Green" revolution turned "Red" in many places as unemployed and destitute rural workers fought back against their worsening poverty.[87]

In other words, this section reveals how capitalist development in agriculture paralleled its development in manufacturing; how the replacement of labor by machinery—investments that raised the organic composition of capital—contributed to the production of a "surplus population" that constituted parts of the "floating" reserve army of labor, and more broadly, elements of the "latent" reserve that, over time would gradually escape the poverty of fields and village to find employment elsewhere in construction sites, mines, factory towns or cities.

After giving abundant illustrations of these dynamics, Marx ends this section by focusing our attention on the way the increasingly precarious employment of agricultural workers came to be organized through processes of subcontracting, known at the time as the "gang system." Whether the gangs were of the "public, common or tramping" types, organized by an

---

86. While a graduate student at Stanford, I was employed as a research assistant to Paul David (1935–), who was researching the spread of the reaper in the Midwest. Although he framed his study using the neoclassical theory of factor substitution, the results replicated Marx's analysis that increases in wages spurred the adoption of labor-displacing machinery. See his "The Mechanization of Reaping in the Ante-Bellum Midwest," published in a 1966 volume edited by Henry Rosovsky, *Industrialization in Two Systems: Essays in Honor of Alexander Gerschenkron*, New York: John Wiley & Sons, 1966, pp. 3–39.

87. See Cleaver, "The Contradictions of the Green Revolution."

agricultural worker turned "gang-master," or of the "private" type, organized by "some old farm servant," the pattern is the same. The intermediary negotiates with the farmer on the one side and the workers on the other. They work for him, not the owners of the land and his income derives from his leverage on both sides. This organization of labor proved highly profitable for capitalist farmers, by reducing their labor costs and because workers could be mobilized and moved from farm to farm as needed. In such movement, of course, they resembled that "nomadic population" discussed earlier.

This method of labor organization, while growing in Marx's time, has exploded in recent years. An element of local "outsourcing," it is no longer confined to the countryside and the employment of farm labor but has infected cities and industry where a wide variety of workers, e.g., custodial workers, clerical labor, domestic labor and so on, are organized through such mediation. It has been an essential element of the increasing precariousness of labor in recent decades as members of what has been dubbed the "precariat" are hired part-time, with few or no benefits and find themselves dependent on intermediaries for repeated employment and income.

(f) Ireland

Outline of Marx's Analysis

Ireland = "merely an agricultural district of England"
- that provides "corn, wool, cattle and industrial and military recruits"
- run by a government "which is maintained only by bayonets and by a state of siege"
- dramatic decrease in population beginning with famine year of 1846, over 1 million died
   - fourteenth-century plague
- increased poverty provoked massive emigration, over a million persons fled the country, mostly to America
- deaths plus emigration meant big increase in concentration of agricultural land
- decrease in population, decrease in production, but increased proportion of "surplus product"
- despite fall in population, decline in real wages as price increases outstripped nominal gains
   - refutes Malthusian claims about decline in population raising wages

▶

- increased resistance to British rule both in Ireland and among
  emigrants
- increased surplus product + increase in prices = increased profits for
  capitalists and landlords
- forced from land, agricultural laborers formed a reserve army in
  towns for work on farms, similar to situation of British agricultural
  workers but with less possibility of escaping to cities and industry

Commentary

All commentary on conditions in Ireland in the mid-nineteenth century
must keep in mind that Ireland, along with Scotland and Wales, were the
first colonies of the British Empire. From the early Norman invasion of the
late twelfth century, through the invasion, conquest and rape of the country
by Oliver Cromwell in 1649–50, just three years after the great famine the
mostly impoverished Irish population was subjected to systematic expropriation and exploitation by the British, and by local Irish capitalists and
landlords who sided with them. The characterization by Marx of Ireland as
being "merely an agricultural district of England" was not only correct but
would be applicable to colony after colony as the British Empire expanded,
annexing lands and people's labor in the Americas, the Middle East, Africa,
Asia and Oceania. Place after place was colonized to provide raw materials
and the cheap labor to produce them for British industry, first the textile
industry and then others.[88]

Never completely assimilated or subdued, the history of Ireland was
one of repeated rebellion against British control and exploitation. The
consistency of that resistance, fueled partly by Gaelic nationalism, partly
by Catholic refusal to accept Henry VIII's imposition of Protestantism,
was the source of the government's dependence on "bayonets and a state
of siege." British rule in Ireland was what historian Peter Linebaugh has
called a thanatocracy, rule by death, whether the method was starvation,
local police and courts or military repression.[89]

Marx's primary interest here, however, within the context of illustrating
the character of accumulation and its impact on the working class, is how

---

88. Colonization, of course, also provided export markets for British industry and
investment options for its capitalists, both at home in the expansion of commercial and
naval fleets and armies and abroad in conquest, the expansion of export production and
infrastructure development. The raw materials acquisition that Marx treats here was
only one element of British imperialism.

89. Linebaugh, *The London Hanged*, Chapter 2: "Old Mr Glory and the Thanatocracy."

capitalists profited from the vast suffering caused not only by the potato blight that wiped out workers' basic food stuff, bringing on the Great Hunger (*an Gorta Mór*) of 1842 to 1852, but by the conditions of colonialism that had made them dependent on that one food and by the response of the colonialists to their plight. Instead of helping the Irish cope, the colonizers, from local landlords (such as Lord Dufferin) to English economists (such as Nassau Senior) welcomed the famine and the exodus of emigration because it undermined resistance and increased the rate of exploitation. Despite the dramatic reduction of both population and agricultural output, capitalists and landlords managed to appropriate an increased proportion of output as "surplus" earning profit and rent for them.

Having already debunked Malthus's analysis of the relationships among wages, changes in population and crises in the very first section of this chapter, Marx points to the way the evolution of events in Ireland illustrate the errors of the Malthusian argument, i.e., the dramatic decline in population instead of raising real wages was accompanied by their fall and by a rise in profits and rents.[90]

This redistribution of income, from workers to capitalists and landlords, took place not only within the context of the vast suffering of Irish workers, but also through a massive reorganization of agriculture. Here Marx highlights two phenomena: the concentration of land and farms as families died off or moved away and a change in the composition of agricultural production. The reduction in the number of small farms meant a reduction in the production of food crops to support the local population. The abolition of the Corn Laws, which had encouraged the production of wheat for export to Britain, brought on the conversion of cultivated land to grazing land to provide meat and wool to British markets, and with it a reduction in the demand for agricultural labor and greater poverty for Irish farmworkers.

---

90.   While he does cite evidence of a rise in some nominal wages, Marx doesn't address the consequences of the famine on birth rates that fell an estimated 14 percent over this period. See Phelim P. Boyle and Cormac Ó Gráda, "Fertility Trends, Excess Mortality, and the Great Irish Famine", *Demography*, vol. 23, no. 4, November 1986, pp. 543–562.

11
Conclusion

One of the hazards of reading *Capital* is the danger of becoming depressed—not in the clinical sense but depressed about the state of the world around us. I didn't realize this when I first read it because I had already been studying the evils of capitalism for some time and was only looking to see if Marx's analysis of the source of those evils and the struggles against it made sense to me. So mostly I just added his horror stories to those I already knew and focused on his theory. But once I began teaching the book, my students soon brought to my attention how depressing its study could be. Because of its emphasis on capitalism's bloody origins and of its ongoing methods of exploitation and alienation, some found reading chapter after chapter, hundreds of pages—and realizing that it's all still relevant—had the depressing effect of heightening their awareness of how virtually all aspects of our daily lives have been warped and tainted by those methods. Grasping the overall portrayal of the capitalist world, as laid out in *Capital*, does tend to replace the rose-tinted glasses that capitalists try to get us to wear—through which, like Dr. Pangloss in Voltaire's *Candide* (1759), we see ourselves in the best of all possible worlds—with a new, dismaying way of seeing reality. We are like the drifter in the film *They Live* (1988), who puts on a pair of accidentally found dark glasses and discovers not only aliens disguised as humans, but their subliminal messages plastered everywhere of work, work, buy, buy, and submit to authority. Or like Neo in *The Matrix* (1999), who, upon swallowing the red pill, discovers that he, along with all other humans, are having their life energy drained by an exploitative machine, a modern update of Marx's characterization of capitalism as being "vampire-like," sucking up our life energy. The more thorough the awareness, the more depressing.

There can be little doubt that after discovering in *Capital* how capitalists have imposed their kind of social organization—one that subordinates our lives to work—it is impossible, in our waged and salaried jobs, not to recognize how work time dominates our lives, day after day, week after week, year after year, monopolizing our time and energy, depriving us of opportunities to live, love and create alternatives. After reading Marx's analysis of how capitalists pit us against each other in our jobs—whether we like those jobs or not—we cannot avoid seeing hierarchies of income and power, and often of race, ethnicity, age and gender, all designed to undermine our ability to organize both against our bosses and for what we want. That perception also leads to seeing how our time is also stolen in preparations for, getting to and from our jobs and recuperating from them. We don't just "hate Mondays," we wake up at least five days a week with the depressing awareness that we are about to lose another day to the work imposed on us.

Extending the analysis in *Capital* to domains outside of jobs—ones Marx largely neglected—such as the home, family and schooling makes it even worse. All day, every day we are surrounded by things and services with price tags, and constant, intrusive advertisements—disrupting TV shows, cluttering magazines and newspapers, blocking the view on roadside billboards, blazing in neon distractions, filling first our mailboxes then our recycling bins—most appealing to our worst inclinations or fears and all urging us to buy more. But having read the analysis in *Capital* of commodities, we cannot avoid seeing them for what they are: alienated products being used against us, first to force us to work—because we require some of them to live—and then to convince us that we "need" them and thus to do the work required to earn the money to buy them. So, sitting at home we find ourselves a bit like Edward Norton in *Fight Club* (1999) in the scene where he's in his apartment looking around at all his stuff and sees, superimposed over each item, catalog information describing each and giving their price. Only, having read not just catalogs but also *Capital*, when *we* look, we now wonder about the working conditions of those who made each item, how much poison is contained in the materials used and how much of what we paid for them went to workers and how much was pocketed by the capitalist who sold them to us. The less we estimate went to the workers and the more to the capitalists, the more depressing.

Before hurrying off to our jobs, when we sit down for a quick breakfast, say of coffee, eggs, bacon and toast, Marx's discussion of colonialism in Chapter 31 makes us wonder where the coffee came from, who picked it, under what conditions, and how much was wasted by being burned up to keep supply down and prices up. While musing on this, Dolly Parton's "9 to 5" line about a "cup of ambition" may run through our heads as we know we're caffeinating in order to wake enough to get to work and do our job. As we take a bite of our toast, having read Chapter 10, Section 3, we wonder if the cellulose added to the bread is better or worse for us than the chalk added to flour in Marx's time. Thinking back up the "supply chain," we pray whatever grain was used to make the bread wasn't weeded and poisoned with glycophosphate or some other nasty substance, and that no farmworkers were poisoned along the way. Even if we've never read Sinclair's *The Jungle* or Schlosser's *Fast Food Nation* or watched the *Meatrix* films (2003,

2006) or one of those horrifying covert documentaries about the mistreatment of animals in factory farms, when we eat our eggs, we wonder under what conditions those who lay them were kept. We wonder the same about the pigs who lives were sacrificed so we could enjoy a hearty breakfast. In both cases, reading *Capital* makes it hard for us to imagine capitalists providing decent lives for either chickens or pigs, when they don't even do so for millions of human workers. And if we've complemented *Capital* with Hribal's writings, contemplation of the bacon is likely to provoke the thought "Poor bastards! Should I be eating my fellow workers?" Breakfast, they say, is the most important meal of the day, but when it's haunted by awareness of the source of everything on our plates, it can be depressing.

If, instead of heading off to a job, we stay home—as a housewife perhaps—and clean up after breakfast, such musings can only continue. Closing up the plastic bag containing the bread, having read *Capital* thoughts may wander both upstream—back to the oil, oil wars and refining that provided the plastic, the blood spilled and the natural environments polluted—and downstream to whether the bag can be recycled or must go into landfill, and how many other such bags are now part of the massive, floating islands of plastic trash polluting the oceans and killing sea life. With *Capital* enhancing our awareness, instead of being amused by the phrase "One word: plastics" offered to Ben in *The Graduate* (1967), we're more likely to remember the penguin in *Happy Feet* (2006) being slowly strangled by a plastic six-pack holder and then the threat of capitalist overfishing that threatens not only all penguins but our own food supply as well. While cleaning up, any houseworker who has read *Capital*, must wonder to what degree the just finished breakfast was anything more than a quick soaking up of stimulants and calories to fuel the day's work. Depressing.

Some of us, instead of leaving for waged work in factories, offices, fields or mines, or staying behind to do the unwaged work of cleaning up, head off to school as students or teachers. If we have read *Capital*, especially Chapters 6 and 23, we can't avoid thinking about all the depressingly alienating schoolwork that lies ahead in buildings and courses designed for teachers to mold students into obedient workers. We've been told that schools are for our enlightenment, that we study things like history and literature to get to know our cultural heritage and civics to become active citizens, but our experience as K-12 students has revealed that in our edu-factories those subjects have mostly been sterilized of any dangerous knowledge (by narrow-minded, interfering school boards) and as teachers we are forced to shovel those subjects too fast for students to have time for serious contemplation or to gear them to preparation for time-wasting standardized tests. And we also know STEM subjects like math, various sciences and computer programming, while intrinsically interesting, are shaped and aimed at preparing students for jobs, not to feed our curiosity or convey a sense of awe at the wonders of our environment or the universe. Every day, instead of finding rich opportunities for teaching and learning, we find instead a structure of one active lecturer and many passive listeners, with the latter mandated to sit quietly and compete against each other in tests, and the former condemned to do the work of quality control, while all are subject to the dynamics of piecework spelled out by Marx in Chapter 21. After reading *Capital*, both students and teachers are forced to recognize "education" as little more than the work of reshaping human being into labor-power. Depressing.

But...

Does the "heightened sense of awareness" that comes from reading *Capital* only breed depression? Not necessarily. For one thing, that awareness must provoke anger over the damage to humans and nature wrought by capitalism. And anger is an important source of energy. Unfortunately, these days we see capitalists diverting anger (along with fear and frustration) from their real causes to made-up ones, such as immigrants and others said to be threats to our income and security. From *Capital*, we can learn to focus our anger against the real source of our problems, the capitalist system of endless work, of thoughtless pollution, of pitting us against each other. As I have sought to show, a careful reading of *Capital* can produce an increased awareness not only of capitalist exploitation and the resulting alienations and distortions of our lives and environment but also how those evils have always been resisted and how angry people have repeatedly succeeded in not only resisting but maintaining or creating spheres of autonomy for self-determined activities. One can begin to offset the depression caused by reading Marx's lengthy analysis of how capitalism poisons our lives by absorbing his briefer but ultimately more important emphasis on workers' resistance and creativity. Yes, we learn from *Capital* how carefully crafted institutions drain our time and energy by turning so many of our activities into the work of producing commodities. But *Capital* can also help us discover sources of energy available to us to replenish what capitalists steal.

From the Past...

One source of energy are his histories of struggle. From Part Eight on peasant resistance to being expropriated and most people's resistance to colonialism, through Part Three on resistance to extensions in the working day and then on successful struggles to reduce it, to Part Four on resistance to the subordination of workers and their organizations to machine discipline, *Capital* offers us energy from inspiring past struggles. In the Americas, we are taught to be inspired by the courage of our "founding fathers" who fought for independence from colonial exploitation, but *Capital* and the bottom-up and subaltern histories it has spawned, provide us with a much broader array of sources of inspiration and energy. Beyond resistance to European rule, we can draw energy from slave revolts, from the revolution in Haiti and from the successful conclusion to the Civil War that ended most out-and-out slavery in the US. We have been taught to be inspired by the bravery of pioneers and frontier homesteaders, but—thanks to the work of indigenous historians—we have become more and more aware of the bravery of those who defended their way of life from encroaching Europeans; we can be inspired by them too. That homesteaders and the indigenous were mostly pitted against each other, instead of finding ways to coexist, was tragic—especially for the latter—but both struggles clearly provide sources of energy to those who study and appreciate them.

Both Chapter 10 on industrial struggles over the length of the working day and *Our Own Time* about similar struggles in the US illustrate how generations of workers have drawn energy from the struggles of those who came before to continue the fight to free more and more time and energy from capitalist-imposed work. Similarly, from the Luddite resistance to machines that threatened their livelihoods—discussed by Marx in Chapter 15—to the subsequent formation of industrial unions and cooperatives, we can recognize and be inspired by the long history of stalwart resistance to how capitalists have turned worker inventiveness and the technological change it has produced against us.

In the Present...

But all these historical examples, inspiring though they may be, provide something more. They also show us where to look for present sources of energy. The historical examples of yeoman farmers in England or clans in Scotland or indigenous resistance to enclosure in the Western hemisphere should awaken us to the contemporary struggles of the MST landless in Brazil, to the Zapatistas in Chiapas, to Native Americans in the US and First Peoples in Canada struggling to take back land or fiercely resisting new efforts at enclosure, at mining and pipeline desecrations. The historical example of Africans resisting slavery and slaves fighting to be free must wake us up to the demands of their great-grandchildren fighting to make Black Lives Matter and to contemporary mobilizations against attacks on voting rights and the promulgation of racial and ethnic hatred by the current administration in Washington, DC. The historical example of the Irish flight from the British colonization of Ireland should inspire us every bit as much as that of the Pilgrims from religious persecution. But it should also give us empathy with the struggles of contemporary refugees and immigrants from the Middle East and Central America fleeing war, criminal and political persecution—the contemporary legacies of past imperialisms. Their bravery in crossing waters, deserts and borders in search of more promising shores should give us energy to help them resist capitalist repression, in both their countries of origin and in the lands to which they are trying to escape. All these righteous struggles constitute wellsprings of energy, some fueled by anger, but some fueled by hope and excitement that people are on the march, challenging virtually every aspect of this vile system.

Indeed, everywhere we look we can find mobilizations of resistance to the contemporary crimes of capitalism—both at home and abroad—and the excitement of discovering them should provide new sources of energy upon which we can draw to replenish what we lose to the capitalist vampires we confront daily. On the job, joining with others by organizing collectively instead of competing, is a source of energy, one we can try to channel into fighting for less work and freeing up energy for figuring out better ways to live. Knowing you have comrades at work with whom you can conspire against the boss makes going to work easier. Keeping watch beyond the shop floor and office reveals the existence of networks of resistance to efforts to roll back regulations protecting us, from those of OSHA to those of the EPA. Yes, Trump and his minions are trying to gut those agencies, but there are many fighting to stop them, or replace them with others who will reverse the damage being done. Yet others are mobilizing against all sorts of poisoning caused by capitalists in workplaces or in the wider environment—of land, of water and of air—as well as their contribution to global warming and species extinction driven by greed for short-term profits and neglect of long-term effects.

Although plagued by an unceasing onslaught of commodities and advertisements, a little investigation will reveal the decades-old existence of a diverse "consumer movement" dedicated to discovering and protecting us from capitalist lies (or silence) about the true nature of their products. This includes financial services. Vigilance and protest once forced the creation of regulations to protect us from speculation, real estate and stock market booms and busts and now resist deregulation and financial squeezes on personal and student debt. There are also groups investigating all those sites of production along the "supply chain" where others are put to work in near or actual slave labor, in manufacturing sweatshops, mines, agricultural fields, brick kilns, brothels, fishing vessels and fish-processing camps—labor that keeps the prices we pay down and profits up. Numerous groups seek to at least mitigate these horrors by fighting such labor conditions and by developing "fair trade" networks in which the share of value retained by workers is greatly improved.

So, if we pay attention and investigate, we can know where our coffee comes from, whether glycophosphate has been banned from grain cultivation, whether the chickens who lay the eggs we eat are confined in crippling cages or allowed to roam free, whether the pigs whose flesh we eat are similarly confined in ag-factories or had a decent life on family farms while they lived. With a little more effort, we can also discover the progress being made in moving toward a more vegetarian diet and sparing animals from slavery and murder. Recognizing all these efforts should provide energy to cope with our awareness when we sit down to eat.

The same goes for the homemaker contemplating the plastic bag containing the bread from which we made toast. Attention downstream reveals both the possibilities of recycling already won and the increasingly widespread campaigns against plastic this and plastic that, from throwaway grocery store bags to unrecyclable Styrofoam boxes (winding up in landfills), to tossed aside six-pack holders (that strangle not only penguins but many other animals), straws (that torture sea birds and turtles), beach and ocean clean-up efforts and even a campaign to live entirely "plastic free." Attention upstream reveals groups in both producer and consumer countries fighting the pollution of the oil industry and others fighting to end both reliance on hydrocarbons and wars over their availability. All that human energy generated in those hopeful campaigns helps in figuring out not only what to do with the bread bag when it's emptied but where one can join one or another of these battles.

For those of us who go from breakfast to school, we have many potential allies among our schoolmates or among our colleagues. Yes, administrators—at the behest of business—impose rigidities that cripple our learning and teaching. But the possibilities of resistance among students has been amply demonstrated by both local and widespread student movements, among teachers at the K-12 level by recent successful mobilizations and strikes in a growing number of states and at the university level by TAs and adjuncts forming unions. In courses, students can minimize doing what they are told to do and divert their energy into following their own individual and collective intellectual and political noses, while teachers can undermine rigid curricula by introducing more interesting materials and giving students as much time as possible to contemplate and think about them. They can subvert the whole edu-factory system by bringing its character to students' attention, by suggesting that they find ways to use available resources for their own purposes and by opening discussions about alternatives to incarcerated learning.

In the Future...

Perhaps all these examples, past and present, suggest a final, thirty-fourth lesson from reading *Capital*. Even as things change in ways we can barely foresee, as we invent new technologies and face new efforts by capitalists to turn them against us, because Marx's analysis grasps essential aspects of capitalism it will continue to be relevant and useful for understanding and struggle. In the middle of the twentieth century, Jean-Paul Sartre argued that as long as capitalism survives, Marx will remain relevant.[1] Already by that time, much had changed, but his point was already clear. While Marx did not, could not, imagine the technologies involved in the rise of the commercial airline, radio, television or social media industries, his analysis of the roles of the transportation and communication methods of his time have made the subordination of the new technologies to capitalism perfectly intelligible. Although Marx spent few words in *Capital*, or elsewhere, on the capitalist use of culture and education, what he did write provided solid points of departure for the work of the Frankfurt School, critical theorists, the Situationists and those who have followed them on how capitalists turned radio, television and now the Internet into modern means of diversion, proliferating moments of a very capitalist "society of the spectacle" and reduced education to ideology and the production of labor-power. Although there is no discussion of robots in Chapter 15— other than the evocation of the dreams of ancient Greeks—the analysis of machine systems and of machines building machines provide excellent insights into how first industrial and now consumer robots are functioning to shape life on the shop floor and in homes. While nowhere in *Capital* is there any premonition of the kinds of potentially catastrophic crises of climate change and mass extinction that we now face, his analysis in Chapter 7 of non-human nature as mere resources and in Chapter 15 of how capitalist manipulation of the non-human world disrupts all natural "metabolisms," once again provide points of departure for confronting both the present and the future. Today, two decades into the twenty-first century, Sartre's claim continues to be validated.

But beyond providing us with keys to unlocking changes within this system and alerting us to sources of energy to fuel resistance to it, by providing a guide to so many noxious aspects of capitalism, *Capital* also provides criteria for judging our efforts to invent alternatives. Because we

---

1. "[Marxism] reste donc la philosophie de notre temps; it est indépassable parce que les circonstances qui l'ont engendré ne sont pas encore dépassés." "*Questions de méthode*" (1957), Jean Paul Sartre, *Critique de la raison dialectique, Tome I*, Paris: Éditions Gallimard, 1960, p. 29.

invent in and against capitalism our inventions are inevitably scarred by the circumstances of their creation. The clearer we are about what we do not want, the easier it is to design alternatives that minimize such taint. So, it matters how you understand what you find in the book. When readers of *Capital* have seen capitalism in terms of property ownership—the owners of capital having the power to exploit others through the imposition of alienating labor—they invented a socialism based on redistributing ownership and power from individual capitalists to the state in order to liberate workers. Unfortunately, that conception resulted in continuing the very capitalist subordination of life to work. When readers have read Marx's analysis of money and markets as merely critiquing their use by capitalists, they have tried to imagine alternative monetary systems and forms of "market socialism," despite Marx's detailed critique of earlier Proudhonist schemes for "People's Banks." Seeing work itself as the means of social control, and money as the embodiment of the value of labor to capital, as I have argued here, implies that escaping capitalism must involve the reduction of work to one voluntary activity among others in such a manner as to free everyone to explore alternative means of self-fulfillment, both individually and collectively and the liberation of social relationships from being measured by any singular value.

We bring our reading, whatever its nature, to the evaluation of all the resistance we see around us and to every effort to create alternatives. Are the moments of resistance well aimed, or could they better target more essential aspects of the system? Are proposed alternatives truly different and better, or still carrying so many characteristics of the system that they are susceptible to co-optation? If we set aside, as Marx did, any all-encompassing utopian proposals and focus instead on shaping current struggles to achieve as much change as we can manage, we can minimize their susceptibility to co-optation and maximize the chances of them being stepping stones toward even better alternatives.

To truly conclude, while *Capital* reveals how the history of capitalism has been all too long and all too dark, it also shows how struggles have been ever renewed and how the victories won account for most of what we appreciate about life today. Moreover, the book's demonstration of the dependence of capitalists on imposing exploitative and alienating work shows why struggles will never cease and thus the possibility of getting beyond it never dies. Moreover, his analysis of the imagination and creativity at the heart of living labor shows that we have what we need to invent new worlds. Thus, the new glasses that *Capital* offers reveal not only the depressing darkness shadowing the world but also the optimism of a kaleidoscope of light generated by ongoing struggles.

Index

abortion, attacks on, 215; fight for, 367, 459

absenteeism, in the 1960s, 3, 371; bypassing bureaucrats, 371; inclination to, 269; workers' "nibbling", 235–7

abstinence, Malthus on, 432–4; Mun on, 432–3; vs prodigality and self-representation, 433; *see* Veblen

absolute surplus value, 186–271; defeat and relative surplus value, 325–6; formal subsumption of labor, 199; framing history, 2; intensity constant, 202; return of, 373–4; as strategy, 2, 202–3, 248; *see* surplus value

abstract labor, 112–3; semantic meaning of, 109–10, 119, 122; in simple value form, 116–21; substance of value, 100, 109, 113, 119; and useful labor, 112, 114

accumulation, 406–76; of antagonistic classes, 65, 96, 446–7; primitive, 16–97; and simple reproduction, 407–19; as expanded reproduction, 419–76; schemes of, 414–16, 422–3; of waged and unwaged, 453–6; ruptured by struggle, 280; in post-capitalist world, 358; includes reproduction of labor power, 215, 411, 418–9, 422; rate of, 432; role of state, 75, 76–7, 90, 434; historical tendency, 85–91; crises of, 250, 447–8; wages and, 274, 436–8, 448–9; business cycles, 447–8; government statistics, 457–8; and pauperization, 463; and life outside the workshop, 464; socialist, 90, 95; *see* reserve army of labor

adjuncts, 383fn; unions, 483; as piece-workers, 383fn; *see* precariat

advertising, and consumerism, 106, 201; Tom Wait's mockery 146; to increase demand, 183; cultivation of modes of housework, 211, 387–8; complementing women's struggles, 315; washing machines, 316–7; by the hollow corporation 342

adulteration, 241–2; of bread, 183; in meatpacking industry, 242; reduces value, 183–4

Africa, 30, 229, 393 475; apartheid, 261, 404; Abeokuta women's revolt, 77; Rhodesian Bush War, 239fn; cooperatives for women, 294fn; enslavement of Africans, 9, 41, 54, 84, 392, 481; Gates Foundation in, 423fn; workers in Western Europe, 134, 374, 392; *see* slave trade

African-Americans, *see* racism; Black Lives Matter Movement

agrarian capital, origins, 58–65; displacement of food by raw material production, 70, 463

agribusiness, cowboy strikes, 61; government aid, 59; range wars, 61; foreclosures, 42–3, 61; immigrant labor, 62; monoculture, 71; short-handled hoe, 309; child slavery, 329; poisoning the earth with chemicals, 239; disruption of human/earth metabolism, 346; *see* Bracero Program

agriculture, 345–6; commercialization of, 29; cooperatives, 61; Downton Abbey, 34; Native American, 40; traditional small farm, 71–2; proletarianization, 61; colonial, 63; organic, 241; Kropotkin and,

346; import problems, 356; *see* Corn Laws; productivity in, 70–2; machinery in, 450, 473; new enclosures, 454; export agriculture, 463; labor, 62, 472; Green Revolution; self-sustaining, 40; payment-in-kind, 363; use of chemicals in, 239; in California, 381; latent reserve army, 459; land concentration, 476; in Southern US, 423; *see* agribusiness

alienation, 203–17; of commodities, 142; of work, 204, 206–7; of individuals, 20; from one's product, 204, 207–8; of life, 203; resentment, 204–6, 209; estrangement, 205; in songs, 146; in reproduction, 209–15; resistance, 215–6; of capitalists, 216–7; of students, 213; vernacular use, 409; four kinds, 207; psychological, 205; songs about, 217; of housewives, 214–6; cultural manifestations, 205; from collective creativity, 215

Alger, Horatio, 20, 76

alter-globalization movement, 11, 81, 261; *see* Zapatistas

alternatives, 1–2, 7, 10, 12, 24–7, 59, 100, 184, 198, 212, 327, 350, 477, 483–5; to the labor market, 461–2; money can finance, 147

Althusser, Louis, on reading *Capital*, 15; structural model, 22; on the young vs the mature Marx, 208fn

Amazon rainforest, 45–6

American Civil War, charity during, 422; cotton famine, 340, 419, 470; and eight hours agitation, 57; English capitalist support for South, 57; fate of ex-slaves, 7, 53–5, 60, 178fn

American Federation of Labor, 300

anger, of capitalists, 245; over damage to humans and nature, 480; diversion of, 480; energy for struggle, 480, 482; function of changes in income,

182; of "les gilets jaunes", 213; against immigrants and outsourcing, 391; against teachers, 129; transferred, 326; of unemployed, 454; of workers and reformists, 52

animals, circulation of damage to, 39; differences with humans, 188–9, 191; enslavement by humans, 191fn, 413; in family farms, 60; Hegel on, 189, 193; humans' spiritual relation with, 46; hurt by plastic, 483; Kropotkin on cooperation among, 290–1; questions of will, tool making and puzzle solving, 190, 192fn; mistreatment of, 479; murder of, 483; play of, 192fn; poisoning of, 72; vivisection, 1; as part of working class, 191, 479

anti-colonial struggles, 9, 77; post-World War II, 401

appearance, hides essence, 363–4; in metamorphosis, 103; money wage and value of labor power, 363; of value, 126

appropriate technology, 228

Arab Spring, circulation of, 262; use of social media during, 290

Argentina, debt crisis in 1980s, 164, 167; financial crisis of 2001–2002, 83; Gauchos, 61fn, 308fn; hides from, 61; La Plata, 307–8

Ariosto, Ludovico, on wrongs to women, 44fn

Aristotle, dreams of, 192fn, 323, 357

Asia, 30, 38; American textile industry moved to, 401; crisis of 1997, 83; pre-capitalist communities, 303; railroad construction, 400; *see* South-East Asia; use of silver as money, 165fn; wet-paddy rice culture, 72; workers from, 400, 447fn; *see* Asia Minor

Asia Minor, vs Roman tribute, 175

associated producers, self-management of, 287; *see* communism austerity, use of currency devaluation, 394; response to financial crisis, 164; imposition on workers, 83, 107–8, 438; in New York City, 107fn; versus raising taxes, 107; resistance to, 290; role of IMF, 394fn; tax cuts to rationalize, 384

Australia, slaughter of aboriginal population, 93; source of raw materials and export markets, 339; transportation of workers, 280; *see* Wakefield

authority, and cooperation in industry, 283–7; Engels on, 284–5; revolt against, 213, 216; of managers, 302

auto industry, failure of management, 302fn; sabotage, 236; *see* General Motors; mass worker, Taylorism, Fordism

autonomists, anarchists in Marx's day, 285; contemporary Italian, 68fn, 299

autonomy, and authority, 285; from capital, 24; of cooperation, 290; destruction in reproduction, 413–4; indigenous culture, 25–7, 46, 290; Spartacus and Nat Turner, 103; spheres of, 480; *see* Zapatistas

Baltimore, Maryland, refusal of water prices, 135

Balzac, Honoré de, 146

Bangladesh, clothing production in, 396

barter, 66, 108, 115, 143; Adam Smith and Marx on, 106–7; *see* exchange value

begging, 48, 461; alternative to factory, 49–50

Bengal, famine, 77

Bentham, Jeremy, egotism, 185; utility, 442; panopticon, 301; *see* Foucault, Michel

biopiracy, 351–2

boycott, of grapes, 62, 240; of Nestlé, 69; UFW's, 469

Black Lives Matter, 129fn; and slavery, 481; and social media, 290

Black Studies, result of protests, 130, 214, 259

Bolsheviks, debate over peasants, 94fn; overthrow of soviets and factory committees, 285; policy of accelerating capitalist development, 22; *see* Lenin

Bonaparte, Napoleon, *see* Napoleonic Wars

Bonfil Batalla, Guillermo, *Mexico Profundo*, 27fn

boyars, *see* corvée labor

Bracero Program, 62

Brazil, Black slavery, 56; burning coffee beans, 154; debt crisis in 1980s, 164, 167; indigenous and rubber tappers, 46; indexed wages, 64; inflation politics, 64; landless laborers, 38, 481; slave-like labor for 2014 World Cup, 469; sugar industry, 71

Britain, attitudes toward American Civil War, 57; colonialism, 124; cotton industry, 340; defeat in 1812, 356; factory inspectors, 242; immigrant labor, 393, 447fn; Keynes's observations, 355–6; landed aristocracy, 426; Opium Wars, 138–9; opposition to slavery, 393; pre-capitalist forms, 26; spinning industry, 399–400; struggles over working day, 254–62, witch hunts, 43; *see* Corn Laws; Napoleonic Wars

Brontë, Charlotte, *The Professor*, vs self-made man, 20; on competition, 279–80

bullionists, fetishism of, 162

Bush, George W., tax breaks for rich, 146

business cycles, vs crises, 447; Malthus on, 448

Caffentzis, George, on Marx after demonetization of gold, 159fn; on

Maxwell's Daemon, 385; on money debasement, 151fn

Cambridge controversy, 359fn

Cantillon, Richard, versus bullionists, 162; on money supply and investment, 157fn; on velocity of money, 156–7

capitalists, fetishistic, 228; as functionaries, 76, 121, 172–3, 200fn, 216, 268–9; "good" vs "bad", 434–5; qua individuals, 74, 172; "properly speaking", 268

Carey, Henry, on wages, 401–2

Carlyle, Thomas, on slavery, 245–6

Central America, CIA overthrow of Guatemalan government, 71; workers from, 374, 482

centralization, of capital, 86, 451; of land, 61; of wealth, 463

Chaplin, Charlie, on harassment, 235; on speed-up, 331; time clocks, 372; workers as part of machinery, 48

children, abuse in the home, 326fn, 327, 366fn; allowances, 366; blunting of creativity, 321; Common on, 148; competition in schools, 288, 332; exploitation of, 197fn; home economics, 211; in hospital asylums, 49; housework, 212–3, 216, 306, 315, 386, 397; Jevons on, 442; labor of, 9-10, 84, 133, 257, 324, 326, 328–9, 396; Marx on post-capitalist education of children, 344; Malthus on, 448; mediation between parents and children, 128, 133, 212, 215; natalist policies, 387; night work, 243; problem of controlling, 233, 327; procreation and rearing of, 179, 182, 197, 212, 219, 236, 243, 269, 288, 299, 306, 344, 365, 413–14, 459; resentment, 197–8; as part of reserve army, 459–60; resistance, 128–9, 243–4, 279, 367; scalping of Native American, 77; shootings, 332; skill loss, 68, 304; work-

houses, 179, 305; see GEB; Owen; schoolwork; students

China, Child Policy, 387; forced labor, 55fn; Lobby, 74fn; Opium Wars, 78fn, 138–9; peasant resistance, 95; revolution, 38, 94; role of Marxism, 94–5; software engineers, 396 398; walls, 78

circuit, of capital, 98, 169–76, 187, 411; of commodities, 153–5; little circuit, 180, 181, 183, 411; material circuits, 80fn, 239–40; of money, 155–8; of the reproduction of labor power, 181–2, 412; of struggle, 240; see resistance

circulation of struggle, 26fn, 80fn, 129–30, 240; electronic, 4, 25, 26fn, 262, 290; international, 58, 261, 482–3; in sphere of reproduction, 213, 261, 414, 462

civil rights, 213; attacks on, 290; movement, 129, 258; see Black Lives Matter

Clare, John, "The Mores", 31–2

class, analysis, 50; antagonism, 32, 79, 91, 123, 130, 164, 173, 284, 285, 293, 335–6, 344, 367, 375, 391, 446; capitalist, 58–5; composition, 37, 67fn, 299, 304, 306, 334; decomposition, 35, 332, initiative in struggle, 128, 230, 244, 250, 257, 258–9, 285, 371; in-itself and for-itself, 121, 189; landed gentry, 33, 36, 339, 429; lived dichotomy, 269; middle class, 269; personification of, 172, 256; recomposition, 128, 129, 462; reconciliation, 32; rule, 51; see working class

coalition, opposition to NAFTA, 81; of Immokalee Workers, 469

coffee, restriction of supply, 154, 183, 478; stimulant for work, 219, 251, 253, 478

coin, 131, 150, 158–9; debasement, 151

collective worker, 297, 300, 349; composition of, 341; productivity of, 307;

waged and unwaged, 304; *see* mass worker
colonialism, 9, 76–8, 303fn; in antiquity, 175; British, 38; creation of labor reserves, 134; division of labor, 395; imposition of language, 30; as infinite expansion, 124; in Ireland, 475–6; local cultures, 24–5, 26–7; pauperism reframed, 463; trade, 77–9; violence of, 30, 75, 77; *see* slavery; Wakefield
combinations, of labor, 51, 297, 344, 440–1, 442; Acts, 52; of species characteristics, 190
commercial crises, *see* crises
commodity, aborted production of, 154; circulation of, 153–5; commodification of life, 145–7; commodity-form, 99–100fn, 116–7, 140, 193; disvalorization, 68–9, 296; as exchange value, 106–8; form of wealth, 99; labor-power as, 176–8; land as, 152; life-cycle and planned obsolescence, 184–5fn; money, 150, 157, 160; owners of, 142–4; songs against, 146–7; things and services, 105–6; things-for-us, 193; transportation of, 314–5; as use-value, 104–6; *see* adulteration; alienation; circuits; consumerism; consumption; exchange value; fetishism; labor-power; trade; use-value; value
commons, 9, 18, 65, 75, 317, 335; Bills for the Enclosure of, 28; drawn and quartered, 45; enclosure of, 9, 28–46, 67, 75; House of, 51, 433; knowledge, 317; public lands, 75; struggle to expand, 65; *see* Diggers
communication, 262; adaptation to industrial development, 314; difficulties of, 36; evolving technology, 484; factories facilitate, 262; Internet, 404; as service, 105; social media, 4, 25fn, 262, 290, 302fn, 331, 388, 484; in working-class organization, 4, 26fn, 262, 366, 283

communism, 87–90; associated producers, 202, 287; debates in Russia, 22; multiple paths to, 88; possibilities of less work, 201–2; social property, 87, 89; *see* Marx, Karl, "Manifesto of the Communist Party"
Communist Party, of China, 95; of France, 15
compensation theory, 337–9
competition, among capitalists, 216, 279–81; animal spirits, 287; austerity increases, 384; between boys, 288; versus collaboration, 287–9; collective action vs, 214; laws of, 280; in contests, 288; cooperatives as alternative, 290–4; within families, 288; between girls, 288; ideology of, 216; "imperfect", 200; inner nature, 280; inter-firm, 289; invention fairs, 321; Lenin on, 285–7; between locals and immigrants, 261, 289; in microeconomics, 200fn; and nativism, 129, 261, 289; in piece-wages, 378; among professors, 130, 383; and racism, 9, 129, 261; rejection of, 216; in schools, 288–9; among scientists, 383; for status, 20, 216, 270, 288; in sports, 288; and war, 289; among workers, 207, 289–90; *see* hierarchy
composition of capital, organic, 446 450, 453, 454, 473; technical, 445–6, 450; value, 446, 450
composition of class, *see* class, composition
computers, games, 328; in finance, 430; to impose work, 3; metrics; in reproduction, 4, 312, 413, 437; in schools, 4, 385; ubiquitous, 3
concentration of capital, 451, 463; vs centralization, 451
constant capital, 217–9, 223, 225–6, 267; depreciation of, 217, 224, 226; investment in, 267, 338, 339, 446;

means of production; value of, 202, 224; *see* composition of capital

consumerism, advertising, 211, 315–6, 342fn, 387–8; consumer movement, 106, 482; critical theory's critique of, 250; ideology of, 106, 201; relation to work, 250

contradiction, between availability of land and labor market, 93–5, 246; between classes, 91 103, 154; of commodity and money, 154; of Carey's positions on trade, 402; in dialectics, 91; definition of, 103; between differing organic compositions and general rate of profit, 267–8; in general formula for capital, 173–6; between humans and nature, 188; between Marxists, 6; of misers, 162; between rising organic composition and imposition of work, 277–9; between use and exchange value, 143, 153; in USSR, 76; in value forms, 121, 122, 126

consumption, autonomous appropriation of, 245, 250; by capitalists, 172, 338–9; capitalist shaping of, 181, 195, 196, 211, 249, 250; charity, 421–2; in expanded reproduction, 422–4; individual, 195, 410–1, 417; for Keynes, 96; of labor-power, 184; leaving it to workers, 412; of life, 54; as living, 105; luxury, 357; means of subsistence, 43, 100, 105, 133, 142, 169–70, 180, 182, 200, 202, 206, 219, 275, 330, 338, 355, 364, 395, 398, 410, 415–6, 422, 450fn, 463; machines as elements of, 314; Malthus on, 417; material circuit of, 80, 239; money mediates, 155; necessary product, 228; ostentatious, 172; productive and real, 330, 335; in simple reproduction, 411–6; tirades against, 432–3; transportation as, 315; unproductive, 416–8; of use-values, 171; Veblen on conspicuous, 172fn; by workers as production

of labor-power, 181–2, 411–2; *see* abstinence; underconsumption

cooperation, 281–94; in agriculture, 70; among animals, 290; and "animal spirits", 287, 288; capitalism reorganizes, 283; in communism, 89, 91, 287, 290; coordination of, 283–5; diffused factory, 342; Lenin on, 285–6; liberation of, 290; of machines, 314; in manufacturing, 319–20, 341–2; and productivity, 283, 297; in productivity deals, 356; in science, 319–21; second negation preserves, 91; as social process, 282–3; among students, 214; among workers vs capital, 289–90, 297; *see* authority; cooperative movement; Fourier; Kropotkin; Owen; Taylorism

cooperative movement, 290–4; Marx on, 293–4; *see* Owen

Corn Laws, 357, 437; contemporary counterparts, 394, 438; results of abolition, 393, 476; Malthus-Ricardo debate, 357, 437

corvée labor, reveals surplus labor, 234–5, 364

cotton, exports and overworking of slaves, 54; famine and crisis in industry, 339–40; fluff and byssinosis, 238; foundation of British textile mills, 55–6, 84, 105; Guajarati workers, 471; Seven Cent Cotton, 60; yarn, 223–5; *see* American Civil War; mechanization

Cournot, Antoine, developed demand functions, 152fn

credit, and business cycle, 42, 62; and commercial crises, 163; creditors vs debtors, 106; crisis of 2007–8, 164, 435, 467; debt peonage, 60, 178fn, 464, 473; fiscal crises, 130, 164fn; fraud, 106, 163, 164, 201, 430, 435, 467; housing bubble, 467; joint stock companies, 451; from local merchants, 464; loan sharks,

164; means of payment, 163–5; mortgages, 42, 106; 430, 466fn, 467; pawning, 340, 464; potential crisis, 163; prodigality as source of, 433; Third World debt crisis, 166–7; wages and workers' uses, 106, 430
Crédit Mobilier, 82, 83
crisis, of 1847, 228, 448; of 1866, 470; of 1930s, 80; of 1980–82, 278; of 2007–12, 83, 164, 467; in Argentina in 2001–2, 83; Asian in 1997, 83; as business cycle, 447; for capital, 447; of capitalist control, 447; collapse of savings and loan industry in 1987, 108; commercial crisis, 154, 448fn; credit/debt crises, 63, 64fn, 290; cyclical character, 42, 62; debate between Ricardo and Malthus, 154fn; of democracy, 146fn; of disproportionality, 416; of ecological balance, 39; of the family, 213–5; Fed and, 166–7, 394; financial panic, 470; fiscal crises, 107, 119, 130, 163; international debt in 1980s-90s, 83, 108, 163, 438; international monetary of 1960s-70s, 150; Keynes on, 154fn; of Keynesianism, 74; of Marx's analysis, 159fn; in New York City 1974–75, 164; of peso in 1994, 83; potentials for, 154; of production, 158; profit-squeeze, 449; in Puerto Rico, 163; relation to wages, 275; and reproduction, 327, 340; and revolution, 228, 447–8; Russian in 1998, 83; of the school, 419; tendency of the rate of profit to fall, 446fn; Turkish in 2000, 83; underconsumption, 449fn; and unemployment, 24, 228, 271, 274m 275fn, 278, 279, 417, 447, 453, 457; work/energy, 385fn; for workers, 106, 447–8, 471; and workers' struggles, 135, 228, 250, 470; *see* American Civil War, *see* Diggers
critical theory, 484; critique of consumerism, 250

Cromwell, Oliver, revolt in army, 36; rape of Ireland, 475

Dalla Costa, Giovanna Franca, 249fn
Dalla Costa, Mariarosa, *Our Mother Ocean,* 40fn; seminal essay on unwaged labor, 134fn
debasement of money, 151; *see* Caffentzis, George
debt, *see* credit
debt crises, *see* crisis
demand, 153fn, 267; aggregate, 449fn; analysis of, 152fn; capitalist manipulation of, 65fn, 183, 201, 387–8, 394fn; changes in business cycle, 448; consumer, 96, 201, 211, 249, 315, 319fn, 338, 355fn, 425fn; effect of changes on prices, 151; frequency of changes, 152, 339, 342; for gold, 150fn; for labor-power, 41, 178, 444–9, 455, 457, 468, 476; for labor-saving devices, 315–7, 387–8; life-cycle, 184–5fn; mathematical function, 152fn; Say's Law, 154fn; sensitivity to changes in price, 242fn; transactions and precautionary, 161; *see* advertising; consumption
demand for less work, by waged workers, 2, 211, 246–8, 257, 259, 278, 279, 326, 394, 451, 482; by students, 4, 214, 236, 243–4, 248, 258–9, 279; as fruit of increases in productivity, 277–9, 309–10; by women, 4, 198, 214, 216, 236, 243–4, 250; shortening of working day, 254–9; *see* wages for housework
demographic transition, 448
deregulation, of finance, 3, 82, 108, 434; neoliberal, 75, 278, 343; resistance to, 482; of safety rules, 75, 241, 278
deskilling, disvalorization, 68–9, 296; in factories, 296, 334; in the home, 304–5; machines and, 69
determinism, technological, 336

Detroit, Michigan, austerity, 164; fight over price of water, 135fn

devalorization, loss of skill and meaning, 68–9, 296; vs valorization, 68–70, 80fn, 240; *see* disvalorisation

dialectical materialism, 21–2

Dickens, Charles, *Hard Times*, 19–20, 172

Diggers, struggle to reverse enclosure, 36–7; *see* Winstanley, Gerard

dialectics, 90–1; *see* Engels, Frederick

direct appropriation, 50; during blackouts, 134fn; of means of production by workers, 67, 134, 236; property laws against, 67; refusal of price, 134; response to enclosure, 17; of wood by peasants, 67fn

disease, 309; black lung, 239fn, 240, 241fn; byssinosis, 238–9, 241fn; cloaking idleness, 50; Gates Foundation and HIV, 423fn; hookworm, 423; limit to population growth, 448; malaria, 466fn; of potters, 239fn; and housing, 466–8, 472; stress and heart disease, 232, 331; *see* Linebaugh, Peter, *Lizard Talk*; malnutrition; public health; Rockefeller Sanitary Commission

disposable time, 309–10

Disraeli, Benjamin, and Owen, 292–3

disvalorization, via capitalist appropriation, 68–9

division of labor, capitalist despotism, 301–2; crippling effect on workers, 308; differentials in power, 299–300; expansion of planning, 303; Fordism, 300; in education, 305; in the family, 214, 304–6; in manufacturing, 294–311; multinational, 23, 340, 395–6; in reproduction, 304–6, 397–8; in science, 322; simplification of tasks, 109; in society, 111; and syllogism, 302; and wage hierarchy, 298; *see* class composition; collective worker; colonialism; hierarchy; Taylorism

dollar, "Day the Dollar Die", 167; devaluation of, 166; diplomacy, 83fn, 159fn; dollar reserves, 161; exchange value of, 150fn; as international money, 159fn, 161; petrodollars, 65, 83

domestic industry, 341; and stagnant reserve army, 460–1

domestic labor; *see* housework

Downton Abbey, tenant rents, 180–1; resistance to change, 34

Dunayevskaya, Raya, diverse paths to revolution, 350

education, *see* labor; professors; schools; schoolwork; students; teachers

Ejército Zapatista de Liberación Nacional, 25; *see* Zapatistas

ejidos, 25, 94

Elliot, George, *Silas Marner*, 33, 162; *Felix Holt*, 33

emigration, due to Irish famine, 476; response to displacement by machinery, 340; threat to capital, 419

enclosures, 28–46; continuing, 65, 75, 164fn, 454, 459; debate about, 23fn; resistance to, 26, 29, 30, 34–9, 43, 65, 480–1; of subsistence agriculture, 454; unevenness, 36; in the US, 7, 30fn, 40–3, 59; of water, 38–40; of women's bodies, 43–4; *see* Clare, John; Diggers; Sutherland, Duchess of

energy, and alienation, 207; for alternatives, 384; from *Capital*, 480–3; capital qua vampire, 477; to consume, 183; diversion of, 249; entropy, 385; extraction of, 297; factor of production, 109; fracking, 201; Dr. Frankenstein, 193; in housework, 326; human, 106, 315; hydrocarbon, 106; libidinal, 44fn; non-human, 106, 272, 314; in nutrition, 465–6; overtime, 276fn; racist diversion, 375; reproducing lost, 276fn; Rick Perry, 241; for struggle, 62, 258, student, 216, 384–5; subsidies, 438; theory of value, 109; use-values of, 62; withholding, 315, 385; work drains, 62, 326, 477; and work intensity, 355; *see* anger

Engels, Friedrich, *Anti-Dühring*, 21; *Communist Manifesto*, 1, 21, 32, 78, 88, 89fn, 306, 325, 462; *Condition of the Working Class in England*, 346, 466fn; *The Dialectics of Nature*, 21

entrepreneurship, myth of, 74–6

essence, controversy over, 363–4; in Hegel, 120fn; in metamorphosis, 103; metaphysical, 218; of surplus value, 352; value as, 218

Europe, 1848 Revolutions, 1, 88, 228, 260, 448; austerity, 438; oil importer cartel, 65fn; capitalist development in, 351; European Union, 80; Exchange Rate Mechanism, 83; genesis of capitalism in, 22–3, 59; overfishing in, 39; indentured, 41; invasion of Western Hemisphere, 40, 41, 77, 481; leather exports to, 308; Marshall Plan, 80; monetary union, 83; protectionism, 78; reductions in work, 278–9, 371; sixteenth century inflation, 157–8; use of immigrant labor, 374, 447; refugees, 392; relative intensity of labor, 399; Right-wing groups in, 289; rigidities of guilds, 69; vacation time, 375; witch hunts, 43–4; *see* Corn Laws; Napoleonic Wars

Evans, Mary Ann, *see* Elliot, George

exchange, barter, 106, 108, 115; of commodities, 103; equal and unequal, 42, 118fn; Exchange Rate Mechanism, 83; fixed exchange rates, 150, 166; foreign exchange reserves, 161–2; form of value, 114–35; history of, 144–5; of labor-power, 118, 121, 123, 132–3; marriage and prostitution, 462;

as mediation, 153–6; money in, 143–4; money for bonds, 161; between owners, 142–3; process of, 103, 141–7; non-equivalent reciprocity, 108; resolves contradiction, 103; reveals value, 112; role of hoard, 160–2; is worth, 107fn; *see* exchange-value; value

exchange-value, contradiction with use-value, 103; different class meanings, 107; of dollar, 166; as final goal, 171; form of value, 107–8, 114–35; of gold, 150fn; "is worth", 117–18; metamorphosis, 103–4; and nature, 109fn, 141; money as quintessential form, 131; martyr to, 162; price as monetary expression of, 112; unequal, 175; universal equivalent, 127, 144; *see* value

expanded reproduction, *see* accumulation

exploitation, as benevolence, 172–3; of children, 76, 84–5, 328–9, 460, 458; of Chinese laborers in California, 400; collaboration to limit, 58, 130, 216, 261, 289, 386, 404; clocks as tools for, 105; colonies for, 75, 77; debt peonage, 60; of the earth, 45, 345; emigration as escape from, 476; the frontier as escape from, 41–2; home as refuge from, 210; ideological cover for, 86, 425–6; of immigrant workers, 62, 93, 128, 211, 239, 242fn, 375, 391, 400, 447fn, 466fn, 482; of the Irish, 475–6; land as basis for resistance, 43, 95, 351; role of land in, 45, 75; by landlords and merchants, 472; mortgage men and bankers, 42; money against, 147; necessary and surplus labor, 200; in neoclassical economics, 200, 359, 441; Populist Revolt against, 59; rate of, 220–7, 264–8, 360; relative surplus value strategy of, 276–7, 450fn; resistance to, 36, 75, 287, 378–80; role of unwaged, 365; songs about, 42–3, 62, 253; unevenness of, 36; valorization, 198–203; how wages hide, 361, 364, 372–3, 378; *see* labor

extinction, of handloom weavers, 335; of old ruling class, 33; of species, 45, 482, 484

factory, assembly line, 3, 48, 129, 170, 216, 235, 238fn, 300, 332, 378fn; behavior indicators, 291; committees, 285; cripples, 307–9; diffused, 342; edu-factories, 13, 128, 479, 483; farming, 388fn, 478–9; as incarceration, 252, 334–5; inspectors, 2, 227, 235fn, 238fn, 242, 259, 305, 326, 329, 339, 380, 412, 468; as means of control, 301; mitigated jails, 334; Motorola, 248, 387; Red Star Tractor, 380; refusal of, 48; reorganization as decomposition, 332; seizures of, 134; social, 4, 128, 132fn, 236, 304, 309, 327, 331, 384; songs about, 20, 197, 252, 379; street as alternative, 49–50; towns, 382, 462, 473; *see* Disraeli; Gaskell, Elizabeth, *Mary Barton*; London, Jack, "The Apostate"; Owen; sabotage

Factory Acts, and child labor, 254–7; contradictory effects, 241; health clauses, 343–4; requirements for education, 344; Senior's opposition to, 225–7; working conditions, 344; and working hours, 2, 225, 234–5

fair trade, 483

family, nuclear, alienations of, 209–16; allocations, 276, 367, 387, 396; capitalist intervention, 210–12; celebrated in TV shows, 258; to control women, 10; crisis of, 213–5, 327; division of labor in, 10, 214, 216, 243, 306, 386; efforts to restore, 215, 327; escaping, 214, 243; income, 214, 315, 396; laws to regulate, 43–4, 181, 211–12; parents as truant officers and drill sergeants, 215;

patriarchal character and hierarchy, 10, 216; as "private sphere", 212; piece-work in home, 386–9; as refuge, 210; single-family dwellings, 335, 466fn, 467; new structures, 327; as vehicle of control, 10; wage, 275, 365, 374, 460; women vs patriarchal power, 213; youth revolt, 213; *see* Fourier; General Education Board; housework; Owen; wages for housework

farm workers, Bracero Program, 62, 393; consumer boycotts in assistance to, 62, 240, 469; Familias Unidas por la Justicia, 469; housing of, 467–70; poisoning of, 72, 239, 240; short-handled hoe, 309, 331; songs about, 62; Texas Farm Workers, 239; United Farm Workers, 62, 239, 469; yeoman, 28, 59, 481

farmers, American Farm Federation, 61; capitalist, 58–65; contracts, 60, 473; cooperatives, 61, 294; debt peonage, 60; effects of inflation, 64; efforts to reclaim land, 36–8, 94; enclosure of, 28–36, 40–3; family, 41–3, 59–61, 71, 268, 294, 483; Green Revolution, 11, 424, 472, 473; labor-saving machines, 473; and latent reserve army, 459; orthodox Marxism on, 94; output prices as piece-wages, 389; physiocrats on, 415; resistance to market, 59–61; songs about, 60, 389; subsidies, 42, 63, 438; "scissors" against, 60fn; terms of trade, 56, 59, 60fn; Wakefield on American, 95; *see* agribusiness; agriculture; Diggers, gang system; Populist Revolt

Federici, Silvia, 134fn

Federal Reserve, 107, 163, 167, 394fn

fetishism, of bullionists, 162; commodity, 135–41, 193; of mainstream economics, 139–41; misers, 162; money, 139, 144, 162; of narrow pursuit of profit, 237; and overcoming, 166; religion, 137–8, 193–4; sexual, 137

feudalism, no nostalgia for, 31; surplus labor in, 234; *see* corvée labor

Feuerbach, Ludwig Andreas, Eleventh Thesis on, 7; on religion, 138

finance, capitalist uses, 82, 107, 167, 202, 268, 398fn, 423; colonialism, 75, 76–9; deregulation of, 3, 434; financial intermediation, 82; government loans, 83; international banks, 438; loans to state, 81–2, 83; Marshall Plan, 80; monetary policy, 83; mortgages, 42; of penal system, 53; productive labor in, 105, 426, 430–1; sources of, 74; vouchers, 75; of resistance, 366, 459; workers' uses, 106, 430; *see Crédit Mobilier*; crisis; debt; Hilferding, Rudolf, *Finance Capital*; philanthropy; speculation

First International, *see* International Working Men's Association

fiscal crisis, *see* credit

floating reserve, those looking for work, 457–9; schools as preparation for, 459–60

food, banks, 438; Bengal famine, 77; boycotts, 69fn; canning clubs, 210; colonialism, 77, 393, 463; commercialization, 146; beyond consumption, 418; consumption as production, 410, 464; direct appropriation, 67; disruption of metabolism, 346; diversity of, 69; domestic production and value of labor-power, 181, 397; effect of devaluation of currency, 394; in family farming, 71; *Fast Food Nation*, 242, 478; from food to raw material production, 70; IMF vs subsidies, 438–9; Irish famine, 476; Meat Inspection Act, 242; minimal requirements, 182–3, 465; OPEC and prices, 394fn; overfishing, 479; Pure Food and Drug Act, 242; price policies, 63, 393–4; reduction

in variety 69; requirements for reproduction, 392, 415; riots, 35; school lunches, 438; stamps, 49fn, 438; tickets, 49; toxic, 240, 242; use-values of, 105; work of preparation, 180, 306; *see* adulteration; agriculture; Corn Laws; farmers; Gaskell, Elizabeth, *Mary Barton*; Green Revolution

Ford, Henry, Taylorism on assembly lines, 3; monitoring employees' lives, 387; recognition of wage as demand, 443; *see* Fordism, philanthropy

Ford Foundation, agricultural research, 424, *see* philanthropy

Fordism, 300

Foucault, Michel, 302fn, 335

Fourier, Charles, plans, 291, 293; Marx beyond, 309; mitigated jails, 334

foreign exchange reserves, role as hoard, 162; *see* International Monetary Fund

Fowkes, Ben, 7, 120fn, 171

Fox, Michael J., myth in *The Secret of My Success*, 20

France, Bastiat, 402; *Capital* published in, 1, 7, 14, 451; *la chaine*, 300; colonialism, 77, 124; crowd support for beggers, 50; employer subsidized job search, 213fn; Great Riot in Lyons, 49; National Front Party, 375; Paris Commune, 88; peasants, 94; reduction in working hours, 279; Revolution of 1848, 260, 448; *sage femmes*, 43; vacations, 375; *see* Althusser, Louis; Bonaparte, Napoleon; Cournot, Antoine; *Crédit Mobilier*; Fourier; Marx, Karl, *Civil War in France* and *Class Struggles in France*; Napoleonic Wars; Sartre, Jean-Paul; Zola, Émile, *Germinal*

fracking, 201

Frankfurt School, 484

Franklin, Benjamin, on humans as tool-makers, 191

free trade, Carey on, 402; comparative advantage, 78, 80; direct investment and, 57, 402–5; ideology of, 74fn; List on, 78–9; Marx on, 78, 79; and outsourcing, 80–1, 392; vs protectionism, 78–9; resistance to, 289; *see* General Agreement on Tariffs and Trade; Marshall Plan; NAFTA; neoliberalism; Ricardo, David
full employment, 228

gang system, 473–4
Gaskell, Elizabeth, *Mary Barton*, 32, 306, 329; *North and South*, 32
GATT, *see* General Agreement on Tariffs and Trade
Gaughan, Dick, on Winstanley's song, 37
GEB, *see* General Education Board
gender, capital mediates, 128; discrimination, 124fn; for division, 4, 10, 128, 260; struggle against, 213–14, 216, 258, 458–9 315; *see* hierarchy, women
General Agreement on Tariffs and Trade, 80
General Education Board, shaping labor-power, 210, 423, 428; promoting public schooling, 423, 424, 428; reshaping the home, 210–11; *see* philanthropy
General Motors, 81fn
Germany, absolutist state, 88; education in, 244; immigrant labor, 375; peasant revolt in, 94; Revolution of 1848, 88, 448; vacation days, 375; workers' councils, 290; working hours, 279; post-World War I looting of, 165; *see* Treaty of Versailles
globalization, 260, 289, 374; neoliberal, 9; alter-, 261
glut; *see* Malthus
Global South, 24, 63–4, 167, 182fn; appropriate technology, 228; clothes washing, 315fn; colonialism pillaged, 76, 134; deregulation, 83; distinct ways of life, 27; lower wages, 57, 260, 397; favelas and barrios, 466; malaria, 466fn; payment in kind, 363; schools, 397; subsistence agriculture, 327; state-generated inflation, 64; struggles against urban renewal, 467fn; Third International in, 22; *see* Green Revolution
global warming, 46, 458; struggle against hydrocarbon energy, 106, 482
gold, bullionists, 162; coins 151, 165; colonial plundering, 77fn, 157; demonetization, 135, 159, 165–6; goldsmiths, 268; gold supply and trade, 166; as hoard, 160–2; imports and exports, 162; mining, 395; as money, 131, 150, 165; price of,150fn, 166; quantity required, 157–8; standard, 96, 165; *see* Caffentzis; debasement; hoard, *see* Populist Revolt
gothic metaphors, necromancy, 193; vampire-like, 208, 232, 477, 482; werewolf-like, 208
Gramsci, Antonio, organic intellectuals, 13
grades, 331, 370, 386; competition, 214, 288; computer tracking, 4; hierarchy, 385; inflation, 4; as piece-wages, 243, 385; resistance, 385–6
"Great Eel Robbery, The", 38–40
Great Depression, destruction of farm animals, 154fn; protectionism, 80; working uprisings, 228
greed, 37, 79–80fn, 482; beyond, 172; exploitation of children, 329; "is good", 146, 435; misers, 162; as secondary issue, 167, 420
Green Revolution, early, 70; vs Red Revolutions, 11, 424, 473; *see* Philanthropy
growth, 83, 446; after capitalism, 234, 358; aggregate production functions, 446–7; of alternatives, 23,

90; investment for, 419–24; of labor
force, 229, 403, 467; limited by low
wages, 319; of markets, 30, 65–70,
163, 475fn; in mass of misery, 463;
of multinational investment, 400;
of population, 448, 454; of productivity, 278, 394; requirements for,
408; savings and, 154fn; in scale of
production, 283; slow, 392; spurred
by high wages, 319fn; technological change for, 326; theory, 200fn;
of working-class power, 51, 88; *see*
accumulation, relative surplus value
Griffith, Melanie, myth in *Working
Girl*, 20
Guatemala, CIA overthrow of
government, 71
Guthrie, Woody, 25fn

Hegel, G. W. E., on appearance and
essence, 363; commodities and
owners, 142; dialectics as cosmology,
90–1; good and bad infinity, 125;
on humans and other animals,
188–90, 193; masters and slaves
103fn; negation, 90–1; on reflection,
120; *Science of Logic* as model for
organization of *Capital*, 98; syllogistic mediation, 127, 128, 155, 302;
taking possession, 192fn; valorization, 173
hierarchy, competition and, 207, 288,
378; in division of labor, 24, 298;
in the family, 214; of farmers and
peasants, 389, of gender, 214, 315,
397; of grades, 385; of health, 181;
and immigration, 128; income, 24,
74, 385; international, 261, 362,
391, 392, 397, 398, 405, 465; of
labor powers, 298–9; of power, 299;
of prostitutes, 462; in schools, 128,
397; students against, 214, 385–6; of
waged and unwaged, 20, 128, 182,
214, 216, 221fn, 269–70, 299, 393fn,
395; women against, 214, 216;
upward mobility, 24; *see* piece wages

highland clearances, 29, 172
Hilferding, Rudolf, power of banks,
106, 107
Hill, Christopher, *The World Turned
Upside Down*, 36–7, *see* Diggers
Hill, Joe, 25fn
historical materialism, 20–4; journal,
22; Marx's refusal of, 22–3
hoard, 160–2; *see* foreign exchange
reserves; *see* International Monetary
Fund
home, affective skills, 305; alienation
within, 49, 209, 212–13, 288, 326,
367; capitalist intervention in,
210–12, 316, 386–9; children's
rebellion, 213, 216; competition in,
288; division of labor, 306; *doble
jornada*, 215, 243, 374; domestic
industry, 341–2, 460–1; economics,
211, 423; "feeling at", 205, 209, 246;
homework, 133, 235, 243, 244, 248,
269, 384; loss through enclosure,
9, 29, 43, 50; loss through foreclo-
sure, 107, 108, 164; machines in,
4, 315–17, 328, 342, 484; market,
65–72, 79, 100, 304; proper modes
of labor, 211; piece-work in, 386–9;
price of, 467; as refuge, 210, 212;
standards of cleanliness, 4, 278,
387–8; time in, 211, 326, 327, 373;
women escape from, 214, 460; as
workplace, 133, 197–8, 215, 230,
235, 243, 248, 249, 305, 370; *see*
Dalla Costa, Mariarosa; Dalla
Costa, Giovanna; family; General
Education Board; housework;
Owen; patriarchy
Homes & Gardens magazine, 4
housing, booms and bubbles, 163, 164,
467; cooperative, 294; communal,
335; costs of, 392, 437; distance from
work places, 472; as means of subsistence, 410, 415; of migrant workers,
469; of nomadic[migrant] workers,
468; Owen upgrades, 291; self-pro-
vision by peasants, 43; self-reduction

of rent, 134–5; speculation, 467; tenant rent, 340, 468; urban renewal, 466–7; of workers, 466

housework, alienation, 209–15; child-rearing, 243; and collective worker, 304–5; de-skilling, 304–5; division of labor, 304, 306; imputed monetary value, 365; lack of special-ization, 304; machines in, 315–17; Marx and, 304; night-work, 243; piece-work character, 386–9; pro-creation, 43–4, 179, 182, 197, 209, 365, 387, 397, 412, 413–14; in reproduction of labor-power, 180–2, 184, 212–13, 219, 479; sharing of, 216, 311; and standards, 4, 386, 387; as substitute for purchased commodities, 182; supervision, 210; as unwaged labor, 10, 214; and the value of labor power, 181, 397, 412; wage hides, 365; women's resistance to, 4, 214, 216, 275, 279, 311, 315; see family, nuclear; Gaskell, Elizabeth, *Mary Barton*; piece-work; wages for housework

human nature, Bentham on, 185fn; Franklin on, 191; Hegel on, 189, 190; Marx on, 188–94, 207–8; Sartre on, 189

humans, crimes against, 8; trafficking, 9; human nature, 185fn; and nature, 21, 45–6, 71–2, 75, 111–2, 141, 187–98; see human nature; labor

Hume, David, 138, 156fn

Hyde Park Riot, 471

hypocrisy, of market worship, 75, 455–6; about private property, 86–7, 93; see entrepreneurship

ILO, see International Labor Organization

IMF, see International Monetary Fund

immigrants, and competition, 375; diversion of anger, 289, 375, 480; in Britain, 391; in Europe, 375, 392; labor, 62; vs locals, 50, 93, 128, 130;

peasant, 211; and unenclosed land, 93; songs about, 62; struggles, 129, 239, 242fn, 447, 466fn, 482; in the US, 62, 400; see refugees; Sinclair, Upton, *The Jungle*

incarceration, in factories, 333–5; in jails, 335; as paradigm of social control, 335; in schools, 248, 252, 335, 460

indentured, 41, 56–7

India, burying of silver, 160fn; call centers, 401; colonial usurpation of lobal markets, 77; commune, 144; cotton, 63, 339–40, 471; emigration to Britain, 393fn; gheraos, 401; independent development of capitalism, 351; software engineers, 396, 398; struggles for land, 94; Marx's writings on, 303fn; hand washing, 315; waterworks, 351; see Green Revolution

indigenous, cultural diversity, 46; vs cultural genocide, 9, 25, 94; defense of land, 25–6, 45, 351; farm workers, 469; historians, 481; imposition of colonialists' languages, 30; knowledge, 351; maroon communi-ties, 57fn; refusal of assimilation, 40, 41; rebellion, 9, 25, 64; renaissance, 9, 350, 404; resistance to Europeans, 63, 481; spiritual relation to nature, 45; social media, 290; studies, 41; see ejidos; NAFTA; Zapatistas

Indonesia, palm oil production, 46

industrial capital, genesis of; circuit of, 71–85; home market for, 65–72; role of finance, 81–3; quintessential form, 171; and transportation, 314–15; see Gaskell, Elizabeth, *Mary Barton*

Indymedia, 404–5

infinity, beyond capital, 125; Hegel's bad and good, 125, 128, 154; tendency of capitalism to expand, 124, 233; of value, 125, 127–8, 171

inflation, capitalist uses of, 64–5, 96, 183; and wages, 107, 167, 443; of

grades, 4, 130, 212; Keynes on,
    64fn; differential indexation, 64;
    Volcker against, 107; in sixteenth
    century, 157–8; W. A. Lewis on state
    generated, 96
informal sector, 9, 454, 455
infrastructure development, in colo-
    nialism, 475; railroads, 312, 400–1,
    427, 473
innovation, in agriculture, 70; best
    practices, 381; indigenous, 351;
    forced, 341; by Owen, 291; role of
    social individuals, 75–6, 366; living
    labor as source, 124–5, 337; tradi-
    tional barriers, 325
intellectuals, discontented, 228;
    organic, 13; reformist, 52; in USSR,
    22, 286
intensity of labor, 70, 113, 119, 129,
    202, 263, 266, 329–31, 349, 355,
    357, 380, 381; historical tendency,
    325, 332–3; machines increase,
    329, 332, 455; relative and wage
    hierarchy, 398–400; and relative
    surplus value, 267, 330–1; in schools,
    331; *see* speed-up
Intercontinental Encounter Against
    Neoliberalism and for Humanity,
    261, 404
international debt crisis, currency
    devaluation, 394; resistance, 290;
    result of action by Fed, 83, 107–8,
    163, 164fn, 394fn; *see* austerity
International Labor Organization, on
    forced labor, 84; for international
    labor standards, 261, need for jobs,
    229
International Monetary Fund, debt
    rollover, 63, 394fn; oil facility,
    162; and planning, 303; pooling
    of foreign exchange reserves, 161;
    protests against, 405; role, 80, 161;
    structural adjustment, 438; *see*
    austerity; crisis
International Working Men's Asso-
    ciation, address on wage struggles,

417fn; objective of, 260, 392; Marx's
    letter to Lincoln, 57
Internet, capitalist use, 4, 484; our use,
    4, 366, 404; and schoolwork, 311,
    317; NAFTA leaked to, 402; *see*
    Indymedia
investment, in advertising, 106, 183,
    201, 211, 315–16, 387; in computers,
    430; vs consumption, 172, 432–3;
    demand for labor-power, 447–8;
    deregulation to encourage, 64,
    75, 80fn; in disease ridden areas,
    465–6; in education, 397, 428–9;
    one element of imperialism, 30, 303;
    extension agents, 61; vs hoard, 162;
    in human capital, 320; imposition
    of work, 147, 170, 172–3, 203, 228,
    271; via inflation, 64; Keynes on,
    222fn, 355; by managers, 268; in
    Mexico, 25, 64, 401, 403; multi-
    national, 260, 303, 392, 400, 402,
    475fn; and NAFTA, 25–6, 64, 80–1,
    402–4; out of personal savings, 74;
    by philanthropists, 423–4, 451fn;
    pressures driving, 275; policies of
    the state, 424; productive vs unpro-
    ductive, 416–17; real investment
    vs speculation, 82–3, 106, 434;
    resistance to, 30, 401; in science
    research and development, 322, 326;
    by the state, 326, 434; stocks and
    bonds to finance, 161; and surplus
    value, 184, 201, 202, 222, 224–6,
    232, 268, 329, 360, 420; tax cuts
    and, 75; wages and, 96, 154fn, 167,
    318–19, 326, 398fn, 449; *see* agri-
    business; agriculture; appropriate
    technology; Cantillon on; composi-
    tion of capital; *Crédit Mobilier*; crisis;
    machinery; Preobrazhensky, Yevgeni;
    slavery; WTO
Ireland, 474–6; as agricultural district
    of England, 475; bakers in, 238;
    colonization of, 25, 475, 481;
    emigration, 481; example contra-
    dicts Malthus, 476; famine, 475–6;

immigrants, 481; Northern, 38; resistance and rebellion in, 38–9, 475

Italy, beggers, 49–50; Dalla Costa, Mariarosa, 134fn; diffused factory, 342; Marxist innovations, 299–300; mass worker, 300; Negri, 68fn, 275fn; self-reduction of prices, 135fn; water works, 351

Japan, management, 302fn; post-World War II recovery, 166; vacation days, 375; *see karōshi*

Jevons, William Stanley, marginalist, 441; progressive insight, 443; on unions and wage struggles, 442–3

joint stock companies, and centralization, 451; diffusion of ownership, 268

karōshi, 232, 455; *see* overwork

Keynes, John Maynard, and capitalist planning, 303; consumption and savings, 96; crisis of Keynesianism, 74; on demand for money, 161; harnessing working-class struggle, 96, 374, 443–4; vs Hobson, 449fm; and inflation, 64; macroeconomics, 96, 139; marginal efficiency of capital, 222; political insight, 96, 355–6; and productivity deals, 250, 325–6, 278, 371; return to gold standard, 96; vs Treaty of Versailles, 165; on wages and profits, 355

Kropotkin, Peter, future in the present, 96, 291; mutual aid, 290–1, 418; studying workers' struggles, 34

labor, abstract, 100, 104, 108–10, 112–14, 119, 120, 122; agricultural, 95; revolt, 35–8; alienated, 203–4, 206–7; alternatives to, 49–50; American Federation of, 300; as basis of property, 86; byproductive, 197fn; camps, 53, 55fn; cheap, 25, 53, 54; child, 10, 84; cognitive, 373; colonial, 63; corvée, 234–5, 364; creating value, 218, 409; dead, 76; demand for, 41; deskilled, 334; division of, 23, 24, 109; endlessness in capitalism, 10, 16, 46, 168, 172, 187, 228, 234–5, 270, 325, 480; family, 41–2, 59–62; force, 9, 10, 31, 70; formal subsumption, 199; fund, 439–44; gang system, 473–4; generic concept, 112, 187, 195, 349; immigrant, 62, 128, 211, 239, 242fn, 315, 375, 391, 400, 447fn, 466fn; imposition of, 77, 109, 113; indentured, 56; as one input, 109; indigenous refusal, 40; intensity of, 70, 113; kills, 208; liberation from waged, 10; living, 76; marginal productivity of, 355fn, 441, 443; market, 9, 23, 43, 46, 52, 56, 93; mass of, 267, 450; mental and manual, 309, 337, 373; migrant or nomadic, 248, 467–70, 454, 466, 469; mobility, 56; and nature, 31, 109fn, 111, 141, 187–95, 203, 314, 350–2, 413, 484; necessary and surplus, 200–2; one of three elements, 191, 196, 413; paid and unpaid, 84, 180fn, 249fn, 348, 360; prison/convict, 53–5; private, 139; process, 67; products of, 99, 117; productive vs unproductive, 426–31; productivity of, 71, 114, 119; prostitution, 44, 84, 461–2; one kind of purposeful activity, 191; real subsumption, 199, 357; of reproduction, 196–8, 209–15, 221, 232, 236, 275, 278, 304, 305; rights, 31, 51fn; in schools, 4, 130, 197, 210–11, 216, 235, 288, 301fn, 305, 309, 317, 367, 384–6, 460, 479; simple and complex, 112; skilled, 383, 395; slave, 7, 9, 22, 40, 53, 55–7, 84, 103fn; as social control, 110, 113, 114; socially necessary, 100, 113–14, 122; songs about, 48, 62, 197, 251–4, 326fn, 379, 389; as source of innovation, 75–6, 125, 337; struggles against, 10, 24; supply, 28–58, 54, 64fn; time of,

3, 113–14; two-fold character, 104, 110–14; unalienated, 207–8; un- or low-skilled, 395, 401; unwaged, 9, 55–8; useful, 104, 108, 110, 111–12, 119; use-value of, 110; waged, 9, 10, 42, 53, 93; white-collar, 13; of women, 10, 43; and work, 195fn; *see* Clare, John; cooperation; housework; Lenin; Petty, William; schoolwork; surplus labor; Taylorism

labor-power; capitalists purchase, 86; definition, 86–7, 121; use-values of, 184–5; repair of, 219; what workers sell, 86, 118; *see* labor

labor theory of value, classical, 139–40, 159, 352, 359, 360; core of Marx's theory, 6; critique of, 109; reason for, 15, 16; as theory of the value of labor to capital, 110, 113; *see* value

land reform, 37, 53, 94

Lenin, Vladimir, on encouraging competition, 285–7; overthrow of soviets, 285; on peasants, 94fn; and Taylorism, 336–7

Leontiev, A., 115fn

Levellers, *see* Diggers

Lewis, Sinclair, *Babbitt*, 22

Lewis, W. A., on use of inflation, 64, 96; critique of, 434

liberalism, nineteenth century, 63, 74fn; *see* neoliberalism

Linebaugh, Peter, *Lizard Talk*, 466fn; *London Hanged, The*, 50fn, 67fn, 363fn; *Many-headed Hydra*, 41, 391; thanatocracy, 67, 475

liquidity, 165; *see* money

List, Friedrich, 78–9

little circuit, 180, 181, 183, 411–12; *see* circuit of the reproduction of labor-power

Liverpool, England, dockers, 261

loan sharks, 164

Locke, John, Caffentzis on, 151fn; on education for the poor, 179; on money and prices, 156, 157; on property, 86, 421

London, England, adulteration of bread, 241; building worker strike, 371; fishmongers, 38; *London Labour and the London Poor*, 50; Linebaugh Peter, *London Hanged*, 50fn, 67, 283fn, 363fn, 461, 475; merchant bank, 163fn; slums, 466

London, Jack, Johnny in "The Apostate", 247, 308, 330, 377–8; piece-rates in "South of the Slot", 379

Luddites, machine breaking, 336, 481; in *Shirley*, 279–80; *see* relative surplus value

lumpenrproletariat, 461–2

machinery, in agriculture, 345, 450, 473; assembly line, 300; breaking, 48, 69, 279–80, 336; and capitalist flexibility, 339–40; computers, 327–8; cooperation of, 314; and deskilling, 334; and emigration, 340; female and child labor; repair of, 218, 328–9; and handicrafts, 340–3; in homes, 106, 211, 315–17; to impose work, 104, 110, 203; incentives to introduce, 275–6, 318–19; to increase productivity, 114, 265fn, 277fn; as input, 86, 109; intensification of work, 329–31; labor-displacing, 265fn, 276, 277fn, 279, 314, 337–8, 340, 473; machi-no-facture, 295; paradox of, 313–14, 324–5; and recreation, 327; repair of, 218, 219; resistance to, 331–3, 335–7; robots, 192, 312; in schools, 317; in the social factory, 312, 314; song about, 327; tending, 69, 209, 295, 314; and tools, 312–14; and toxics, 239fn; transferring value from, 218, 318; workers as, 48, 185; vs skilled workers' control, 311; *see* Chaplin, Charlie, *Modern Times*; class decomposition; collective worker; Ford, Henry; Luddites; relative surplus value; Taylorism

malnutrition, and disease, 465; hunger, 448

Malthus, Thomas, on charity, 422; on Corn Laws, 357, 437; on crisis, 154fn, 448–9; Irish famine refutes, 476; on need for unwaged, 454; on piece-work, 378; on population, 422fn, 448–9; on unproductive consumption, 416–17; on wages, 152fn; *see* demographic transition

Manchester, England, textile mills, 55; *see* Gaskell, Elizabeth, *Mary Barton*

manufacturing, definition of, 295; division of labor in, 294–311; origins, 296; handicraft workers' control, 295, 297; payment in kind in early, 363; Smith, Adam, on, 308; two forms of, 296; *see* collective worker

Mao, Zedong, 38

Marcuse, Herbert, on consumption, 250; and Freud, 44fn; on "repressive tolerance", 130fn

Marginalism, *see* neoclassical economics

Marjory Stoneman Douglas High School, 129

market, coercion of, 56; Downton Abbey and, 34; exploitation via, 59–60; financial, 81–3; and force, 455; free-, 63; gold, 150fn; home, 65–72; imposition of, 23fn, 66–7; vs planning, 303; prices, 139; property laws, 46–53, 67; requires owners, 142; resistance to, 59–61, 63–4; socialism, 90; songs about, 60, 146; stock, 82, 83, 87, 161, 451, 482; terms of trade, 60; women, 77; worship, 74fn, 455–6; *see* colonialism; exchange; glut; Keynes, John Maynard; labor; realization problem

marriage, 44, 196, 211, 215, 250fn, 258, 316fn, 366, 462

Marshall, Alfred and Mary, marginalism, 441; on wages and profits, 355, 443

Marshall Plan, 80, 83

Marshall, Sahlins, 350

Martineau, Harriet, 454–5

Marx, Karl, *Capital Vol. II*, 100, 132, 411, 427; *Capital Vol. III*, 360, 471; *"Comments on James Mill*, 204; *Communist Manifesto*, 1, 21, 32, 78, 88, 89fn, 306, 325, 340, 462; *Contribution to the Critique of Political Economy*, 21, 103, 104, 140, 143, 145, 151fn, 154, 155, 156fn; *Contribution to the Critique of Hegel's Philosophy of Right*, 138, 142, 189, 192fn, 193; *Economic and Philosophical Manuscripts of 1844*, 188, 204; *Eighteenth Brumaire of Louis Napoleon*, 31fn, 94fn; *Eleventh Thesis on Feuerbach*, 7; *Grundrisse*, 48, 115, 125fn, 145, 206–7, 245, 309–10, 357, 450; *Theories of Surplus Value*, 95fn, 140, 181

Marxism-Leninism, 453

mass worker, 300; *see* Taylorism; Fordism; United Auto Workers, 300

material circuits, of commodities, 80fn, 239; of valorization, 240

means of production, consume workers, 209, 271; as dead labor, 76; directly appropriated, 67; element of accumulation, 65; expropriation of, 28–46; heterogeneous, 446fn; means of command, 206, 271, 355; means to profit, 170; objectified as monster, 206; ownership of, 87, 142, 268; as passive element, 193; possession in common, 87, 89; private property in, 86, 95; replacement of used-up, 408, 422; requirements for simple and expanded reproduction, 415–6; workers as indispensable element, 410, 422–3; *see* adulteration; composition of capital; class composition; technology; value; Wakefield

means of subsistence, control to impose work, 206; expropriation of, 28–46; loss of, 43; material, 105; money buys, 169–70; necessary labor, 200; need for, 100, 133; physically indispensable, 182; prices of, 463; *see* compensation theory; little circuit; relative surplus value; value; witch hunts

meatpacking, *see The Jungle*

mediation, breaking, 129; reflective, 119–21, 127; refusing and bypassing, 128–30, 134–5; syllogistic, 127–8; universal, 127

Meek, Ronald, 109fn; on the form of value, 115

Men of No Property, *see* "Great Eel Robbery, The"

metamorphosis, of exchange value, 103, 153; of labor-power, 411; metaphor, 103, 176; of capital, 173

metrics, bio-, 372; in industry, 3; in education, 4

Mexican-American, studies, 4; workers, 128

Mexico, debt crisis of 1982, 63, 164, 167; direct investment in, 80–1, 401, 402; environmental laws, 81, 403; The Other Campaign, 26; outsourcing to, 81, 398; peonage, 178fn; people of the corn, 194; peso crisis of 1994, 83; profundo, 27; Revolution of 1910, 25, 93–4; trade unions in, 403; urban renewal, 454fn; workers, 260, 374; wages, 81, 402; *see* Green Revolution; NAFTA; Rage Against the Machine; urban renewal; Zapatistas

Middle East, refugees from, 229, 392, 482; source of resources, 475; *see* OPEC

Mikhailovski, Nicolai K, 22

Mill, James, 204, 416

Mill, John Stuart, on effects of machines, 313; on the wages-fund, 439–41; vs slavery, 246, 393

mir, peasant, 22; possibilities of, 23, 89

misers, 162

money, bullion, 162, 165; -capital and industrial investment, 82; commodity, 150, 157, 160; to control research, 240, 322, 424; credit, 159, 163; crises, 158; debasement of, 151, 158; disposable, 327, 451; endogenous vs exogenous, 158; in exchange, 143–4; expressions domain of capital, 131; fetish, 144, 162, 166, 172; forced levies, 35; illusion, 64; loaned, 82; as magic wand, 132; as means of circulation, 153–9; means of payment, 149, 163–5; as measure of value, 99, 149–51; monetary policy, 83, 96–7, 303; names, 150–1; need for money, 143–4, 161, 425fn; origin of, 144–5; -owner vs capitalist, 426–7; paper, 158–9; as power, 147–8; quantity theory, 156–8; redistribution of, 170, 442fn, 476; refusal of, 135; right-wing, 74fn; songs about, 147–8, 167; spent vs advanced, 170; as standard of price, 99, 149–52; supply of, 59, 151, 156, 158fn, 164–5, 166, 222fn; tribute, 175; as universal equivalent and mediator, 131–5, 143–5; value of, 145, 151, 158, 363; velocity of, 156–9, 161; wages, 354, 355fn, 361–405; as weapon, 148, 167, 366–7, 438; weight-names, 150; world, 165–7; *see* coin; *Crédit Mobilier;* hoard; inflation; petrodollars; price, value, money form of

money form, secret of, 116–7; *see* value

Moore, Thomas, on beggers, 50

Motorola, commuter work, 248; and reproduction of labor-power, 387

Mun, Thomas, vs bullionists, 162; against non-work, 227fn, 432–3

music, Celtic, 25fn; as commodity, 25fn, 146, 410; competition, 288; as critique, 20; escaping commercialization, 250; hip-hop, 148; of memory, 29; about money, 147–8, 167; preservation of indigenous, 25;

of protest, 25, 146; of resistance, 26, 42; role in circulating struggles, 25, 62; and school spirit, 288; as tool, 413; against work, 251–4

NAFTA, *see* North American Free Trade Agreement
National School Walkout, 129
Native American, cultural preservation, 24; extermination, 40, 59, 77; historians, 41; ignorance about, 40; vs pipelines, 351 481; resistance, 24, 40, 45, 481; studies, 41; traditional relations to nature, 45
nativism, to create divisions, 261; anti-immigrant, 129, 289
nature, appropriation of, 190; capitalist destruction of, 273, 480; confronting, 187–8, 351; and exchange value, 141; family farming and, 60–1, 71–2; forces of, 190, 285; human, 188–90, 207–8; in humanity, 189; as one input, 141; in the labor process, 187–98; metabolism between man and, 111, 346, 484; Native American relation to, 45; neoliberalism vs, 30; non-work relations with, 191; passive, 188–9, 192, 193, 413; plenitude of, 350; as resources, 190, 484; and species-being, 194; transformation into use-values, 193; *see* Clare, John; Engels, Frederick, *The Dialectics of Nature*; humans
necessary labor, *see* labor
neoclassical economics, 114fn, 139, 152fn, 184fn, 200fn, 232fn, 319, 355fn, 441
neo-conservatives, and neo-liberalism, 74
neoliberalism, alter-globalization movement against, 11, 74fn, 81, 261, 403–4; and deregulation, 3, 75, 82, 108, 278, 343, 434, 482; as ideology, 63, 74; and privatization, 26, 124, 434; as strategy, 75; Trump and

Putin, 76; Zapatista critique of, 26; *see* NAFTA; Zapatistas
Napoleonic wars, effect on trade, 70fn, 279, 356, 437; *see* Corn Laws
New York City, fiscal crisis, 107fn, 163, 164; cost of living, 437; blackout in, 134
nibbling and cribbling, by capitalists, 235, 373; by workers, 235–7
Nietzsche, Friedrich, on history, 6; on projection, 138
noblesse oblige, sense of by some capitalists, 172
North American Free Trade Agreement, constitutional amendment in Mexico, 25, 94; corporate purposes for, 80–1, 402; to facilitate outsourcing, 404; grassroots opposition to, 81, 402–3; threat to indigenous, 25–6, 94; *see* WTO; Zapatistas

Occupational Safety and Health Administration, efforts to roll back protections of, 241, 482
Occupy movement, 262; role of social media, 290
oil, conflicts in producing countries, 167; crisis for importers, 83, 162, 163, 166; palm, 46; pollution, 479, 483; quadrupling of prices, 64, 162, 394; supply restriction, 183; Texas boom, 437; trust, 451fn; wars, 479; *see* OPEC
OPEC, *see* Organization of Petroleum Exporting Countries
opium, British control in India, 77; eaters, 138; as painkiller, 139; wars, 78fn, 138–9
organic composition of capital, problem of job generation, 454; and technical composition, 446; tendency to rise, 450, 453; and reserve army, 473, *see* relative surplus value

Organization of Petroleum Exporting
  Countries, quadrupling of oil prices,
  64, 162, 394; petrodollars, 65, 83;
  and debt crisis, 167; internal crises,
  167; US acceptance of increased
  prices, 65fn, 394fn; impact on food
  prices, 394fn
OSHA, *see* Occupational Safety and
  Health Administration
Other Campaign, The, *see* Zapatistas
out-sourcing, international, 81, 124,
  391, 395–6, 398; local, 341, 342, 474;
  debate on, 58fn, 392, *see* free trade,
  NAFTA
overfishing, 39, 479; vs careful
  management at Lough Neagh, 40
overwork, connection to stress and
  disease, 232, 331; Juliet Schor
  on, 258fn, 373–4; kills, 455, 458;
  and life-expectancy, 232, 458; *see*
  Walkley, Mary Anne; Japan
Owen, Robert, cooperative movement,
  292; fictional counterpart, 292–3;
  innovations, 180, 291–2; utopian
  socialist, 291

Palestinians, solidarity with, 261
panopticon, 301fn
Paris Commune, 88, 290; Marx on,
  88–9
Parliament, acts of enclosure, 29; laws
  against combinations 52; workers
  used, 259, 325; *see* Factory Acts
pathologies, industrial, 308; in the
  social factory, 269, 309, 331
patriarchy, in capitalist reproduction,
  215, 315, 397, 414; in "primitive"
  community, 144; in religion, 138;
  revolt against, 213–4, 216, 258, 459;
  in slavery, 54; in waged and salaried
  labor, 396; *see* family, nuclear
pauperism, 463; and wages, 355, 471; as
  social-hospice, 461; displacement of
  locus, 463; *see* lumpenproletariat
peasants, 35, 268; cooperatives, 294;
  as unwaged, 9, 389; at heart of

twentieth century revolutions, 9;
  Russian populists, 22; expropriation of in ancient Rome, 22; *see*
  ejidos; Kropotkin on, 34fn; Marx on
  French, 31; in Mexican Revolution,
  25, 37, 93–4; *mir*, 27, 31, 89; Salinas
  attack on, 94; in Vietnam, 38, 62;
  expropriation of, 29, 30, 43, 82;
  de- and disvalorization, 68–70, 296;
  landless, 71; and markets, 63–4;
  Marxist attacks on, 94; exploitation
  in USSR, 60, 90, 95; subsistence,
  268, 327; piece-work, 389; agrarian
  habits, 211, 400; weapons of the
  weak, 367; world of, 31; resistance,
  35–6, 67, 71, 93, 95, 480–1; *see*
  farmers
People's Global Action, 81, 403, 404
petrodollars; *see* Organization of
  Petroleum Exporting Countries
Petty, William, on labor, 112; on
  velocity of money, 157
Peuchet, Jacques, on suicide, 8fn
philanthropy, vs charity, 423; as
  investment in social engineering,
  423–4; investment in new technologies, 423; *see* Green Revolution;
  General Education Board; Rockefeller Foundation; Rockefeller Sanitary
  Commission; Ford Foundation
physiocrats, *see* Quesnay, Francois
piecework, benchmarks, 381; in
  California, 380–1; in coal mining,
  382; commissions, 383; competition,
  378, 385; of farmers and peasants,
  389; in the "gig" economy, 383;
  hides exploitation, 378; in the home,
  386–9; in Hungary, 380; Malthus
  on, 378; of professors, 383; quality
  control, 381–2, 383; reduced supervision, 377; resistance to, 378–9,
  385–6; song about, 379; strategy;
  of students, 384; *see* London, Jack,
  "South of the Slot" and "The
  Apostate"; wages

planning, counter-, 236; ever broader, 303; despotic, 301–2; in education, 130, 385; family, 215, 387–9; in industry, 70fn, 185fn, 281–2, 342fn; international, 80, 303; of labor power, 387; vs markets, 302; national, 303; in production, 282–4; regulation, 343; on the shop floor, 301–2; in state capitalism, 90, 95; urban, 454; worker subversion, 52, 130, 236, 271, 332, 454; see GEB; IMF; Owen; panopticon; WTO

plastic, campaign against, 483; see pollution

political economy, classical, 93fn, 100, 359, 426; critique of, 14–15, 140–1, 425; myth of, 19–20; Physiocrat school of, 414–5; quantity theory of, 157; texts of, 100, 439–41

pollution, 240, 458, 480; plastics, 45, 479; pesticides, 72, 239, 240; herbicides, 239, 473; struggle against, 483; films about, 240fn

poor laws, 247, 472; Malthus against, 448

population, aboriginal, 93; agricultural, 28–46; decline in Ireland, 475–6; disposable working, 344; reduction in eel and fish, 39, 479; expropriation of, 28–46; indigenous, 30fn, 393; institutions to reproduce, 10; jobs to control, 228; Malthus on, 422, 448, 476; Native American, 40; nomadic, 467–70, 474; surplus, 452–62; see reserve army

Populist Revolt, 42, 59, 61, 62, 165fn; song from, 42; see farmers

precariat, 383, 474

precautionary demand, 161fn

preference theory, 352

Preobrazhensky, Yevgeni, 90fn

price, 132; acceptable, 154; of basic necessities, 338, 392–4, 438, 471; of bread, 49, 184, 356–7, 393, 437–8; of capital, 359fn; in catalogs, 478; of coffee, 154fn, 478; of cotton, 60, 223, 398fn, 470; of credit, 163; crop prices, 389; differ from value, 151–2, 159, 166, 174–5, 354; of eels, 39; farm, 42, 59–63; -form, 132,157; and glut, 448; of gold, 166; in Great Depression, 154fn; of homes, 467; inflation, 64, 107; of labor, 364, 440; of labor-power, 182–3, 245–6, 352–8, 361–405; Locke on, 156–7; maxims, 35; in merchant capitalism, 169, 171; money expression of value, 131–2; money as standard of, 149–50; of oil, 64, 162, 167; price policies, 393–4; and productivity, 183, 279, 355, 398; protectionism, 78–80, 393; quantity of money and, 156–8; and real wages, 79, 183, 354, 355fn, 443, 463; reduction and transformation problem, 112–3; refusal of, 134; "scissors" in USSR, 60; self-reduction of, 135fn; sensitivity of demand to changes in, 241–2fn; and slave labor, 482; and structural adjustment, 438; of sugar, 71, 79; supports, 63–4, 438; tags, 175, 478; theory, 139, 152; of things without value, 132, 152; as value of marginal product, 319; of water, 135fn; see adulteration; Cambridge Controversy; coin; consumerism; Corn Laws; Cournot, Antoine; inflation

price-form, see money form; price

price theory, see neoclassical economics

privatization, of space exploration, 124; of state enterprises, 434

procreation, see children; housework; women, and reproduction of labor-power

production functions, 109, 141, 359; aggregate and growth, 320, 446–7; and technological change, 319

productive labor, see labor

productivity, and amount of work, 2–3, 277–9, 309–10, 330, 257–8; and competition, 279–81, 336; and cooperation, 287, 296; counter-concept, 417; deals, 3, 250, 326, 356, 371, 394; distribution of fruits of rising, 2–3, 183fn, 201, 276–8, 291, 354–6, 472; food and, 412, 424; impact on value, 114, 119, 183; international connections of, 398fn; and land tenure, 71–2; marginal, 441–2; in neoclassical economics, 114fn, 355; and piece rates, 378–80, 381fn; role of science, 320–1, 322; of the soil, 190; specialization and, 297; and standards of living, 201; in unwaged work, 426–9; of useful labor, 210, 275; impact on wages, 273–81; 398–9, 401; *see* composition of capital; Green Revolution; Owen; relative surplus value, value

professors, adjuncts, 249, 383fn, 483; beyond "unite and fight", 130; competition among, 383–4; as mediators, 128, 130, 133, 134; as piece-work, 383–4; night-work, 249; quality control of, 383; second jobs, 249; work of, 4, 235, 238fn, 317, 385; and working class, 13; *see* Brontë, Charlotte, *The Professor*; grades; hierarchy

profit, and antibiotics, 388fn; challenges to, 352; classical failure to explain source, 352; and crises, 250, 449; deaths for, 53–4, 475–6; farmers' lack of, 389; fetishistic pursuit of, 39, 62, 228, 237, 482; from finance, 430; and gang system, 473–4; and gluts, 448–9; and imposition of work, 147, 171–2, 195–6, 391; and inflation, 64–5, 183, 443; from interest, 106, 107; and jobs, 228; lack of skill can undermine, 401; maximization of, 319, 339, 469; minimization of costs, 241, 398fn, 469; in neoclassical theory, 319, 359; neoliberal support for, 75; non-, 429fn; "our", 253; Owen's innovations and, 291; as part of savings, 96, 200fn;

personal, 20, 424; and piece-wages, 380–4; potential rates of, 222; and productive workers, 181, 210; and productivity, 276–8, 473; protectionism and, 78–81; rate of, 220–2, 232, 264fn, 267–8, 360, 446fn; regulations and, 241–2; retained, 451; from schools, 180, 322, 429; for self-representation, 433; Senior on, 225–7; and "shut-down", 184fn; through social investment/engineering, 424; songs about, 62, 253; squeeze, 449fn; and turnover, 243fn; in valorization, 68; and wages, 64–5, 355–6, 370, 443; *see* compensation theory; Corn Laws; philanthropy; surplus value

proletarianization, 61

property, private; capitalist vs personal, 86, 91, 95; vs communal, 94; control through stock, 200; crimes against, 50, 53; established by force in colonies, 30; ideology of, 86, 93; justification for, 86; laws of, 357; limited liability, 87; Locke on, 86; vs Owen's experiments, 291; and relations of production, 21; vs social, 87, 89; *see* commodity; Diggers; ejidos; Men of No Property

prostitution, 44, 84, 461–2

Proudhon, Pierre-Joseph, People's Banks, 485

public debt, in accumulation, 81–3; *see* credit; fiscal crisis

public health, Public Health Reports (UK), 465–6, 468; to reduce costs of labor-power, 466; as working-class income, 370; *see* disease; Rockefeller Sanitary Commission

public schools, capitalist intervention in, 429; vs private, 419; and production of labor-power, 180; profits from, 180fn; science curriculum, 320; teachers in, 429; *see* GEB; schools

quantity theory, 157; Marx vs, 157–8

Quashees, 245, 350
Quesnay, Francois, Tableau Économique, 414–5

racism, 9–10, 40, 124fn, 128, 129, 245–6, 260, 261, 270, 289, 351, 375, 481; see Black Lives Matter Movement, competition; hierarchy; refugees; slavery
Rage Against the Machine, "People of the Sun", 26; *The Battle of Mexico City*, 26fn
rate of surplus value, see surplus value
Reagan era, attacks on workers, 373; non-enforcement of laws, 51fn, 343; greed is good, 146, 434, 435; tax breaks for rich, 146; depression, 278; films about, 434–5; songs of, 147–8; see neoliberalism
real estate speculation, 82, 466–7, 482
realization problem, 152
reciprocity, between commodities, 66, 127fn; non-capitalist systems of, 118fn; non-equivalent, 108fn
reduction/transformation problem, 112–3
reflection, in class relationship, 121; in expanded form, 122; gives expression of value; in Hegel, 103fn, 120; form of mediation; in general form, 127; in money form, 132; in simple form, 119–20
Reform Act of 1832, 292
Reform Act of 1867, 471
refugees, 229, 289, 375, 392, 482
relative surplus value, benefits to both classes, 354–5; and competition, 280–1; displacement of workers, 2, 276, 316, 337–9, 340, 345, 449–52, 452–6; historical character, 275, 325; via increased productivity, 275; institutionalization, 325–6; and less work, 277–9, 313, 316–17, 324–5; as an object, 276; and intensity of labor, 329–33; investment in research and development, 322; response to

increases in cost of labor, 318–19; as strategy, 272, 276–7; undermines social control through work, 450; undermine workers' self-organization, 2, 276, 296; real subsumption of labor, 199, 357; see Luddites; productivity, deals
religion, as opiate, 138–9; and relation with nature, 189–90; see fetishism
reproduction, circuits of, 173, 181–2, 411–12; circulation of struggle in, 240, 414; expropriation of means of, 43; expanded, 419–76; individual consumption within, 417; of labor power, 124, 179–83, 196–8, 410–14, 418–19; post-capitalism, 344, 346, 357; schemas of, 414–16, 422–3; simple, 407–19; of slaves, 54; sphere of, 197–8, 209–15, 413–14; subversion of, 198, 213–16; unwaged work of, 180–1, 209–15; see accumulation; alienation; crisis; education; hierarchy; home; housework; schools; students; women
reserve army of labor, 276, 452–6; composition of, 455–62; floating, 457–9; latent, 30, 459–60, 473; lumpenproletariat, 461–2; recognition by economists, 454; regeneration of, 453–4; stagnant, 460–2; underestimation of, 457–8; of unwaged, 133, 365, 416; world-wide, 134; see labor; machinery; Martineau, Harriet; relative surplus value
resistance, to absolute surplus value, 278–9, 325, 235–7, 240–1, 244–59, 325–6, 371, 480; to alienation, 209, 212, 213–15; Arab Spring, 290; armed, 40, 54–5, 77, 88, 290, 366; to austerity, 290; creating alternatives, 198, 214–16, 350; analyzing, 34, 198, 239–40; of animals, 191fn; *Capital* as aid to, 2–4, 9, 14, 240–1, 259, 480–1, 484–5; circulation of, 239–40, 414; collective, 130, 198, 283, 290, 332, 414, 469; to colo-

nialism, 480; competition diverts, 378; via computer games, 328; to consumerism, 482, 483; continent-wide, 289; during crises, 182fn, 228, 447–8, 453; to deregulation, 482; of discontented intellectuals, 228fn; to enclosures, 36–46; exodus, 454, 476, 482; of farm labor, 469; in films, 37, 46, 250; financed by wages, 366–7; of First Peoples, 351, 481; of fishermen, 38–40; forces change, 198; in the future, 484–5; *Grande Rebeine*, 49; of handicraft workers, 310–11; caused by hunger, 424; to imposed labor, 46–58, 109–10, 114; indigenous, 40, 45–6, 63, 350, 481; Irish, 475; isolated, 36; Laborer's Revolt, 36; of landed elite to change, 34; of London building workers, 371; long-buried stories of, 11, 34–6; to machines, 279–80, 331–2, 336, 480–1; to markets, 59–60, 63; measured by repression, 19, 46; Mexican Revolution, 37; music has circulated, 62, 250–4; against parental authority, 213; of peasants and small farmers, 29, 37, 42–3, 62, 93–4, 480; Native American, 40–1, 351, 481; new social movements, 124fn; on-the-job, 231, 235–7, 240–1, 254–7, 283, 332, 371–2, 382, 481, 482; Paris Commune, 290; to piece-work, 378–80, 382, 384–6; to reduction in real wages, 356; of refugees, 482; revolutions of 1848, 1, 88–9, 228, 448; in schools, 4, 129, 130, 198, 213, 252–3, 258–9, 306, 317, 366, 460, 483; vs slavery, 57, 103fn, 367fn, 481, 482; in social factory, 4; via social media, 26, 290; songs of, 37, 42–3; to subsumption, 5, 25, 240, 269; on TV, 124, 258; to Trump, 290, 482; to urban renewal, 467fn; urban uprisings in the US, 49fn, 134–5; in USSR, 71, 286–7, 336; Whiskey Rebellion, 42; of

women, 43, 77, 181, 213–14, 219, 236, 243, 250, 258, 315, 357, 367, 414; of youth, 213, 250; *see* Black Lives Matter; Clare, John; farmers; Kropotkin; Luddites; peasants; Populist Revolt; sabotage; students; women; Zapatistas
revolution, *see* resistance
Ricardo, David, on Corn Laws, 357, 437; on crises, 154; Marx on, 140; on profits, 352; on trade, 78, 80, 174; on value, 140; on workers' consumption, 416
Ricardo, Salvatore, on New England farmers, 61; on gauchos, 61fn
rights, attacks on, 31, 51fn, 290, 375, 403; of capitalists, 231; civil, 129, 213, 258; to exploitation of public lands, 30fn, 45; fishing, 38–9; indigenous, 26; immigrant, 129; LGBTQ, 215; property, 86–7; student, 214; Hegel's things without, 189; voting, 292, 471, 481; of women, 43, 77, 261, 367, 414; of workers, 80, 231, 382, 469fn
Robin Hood, 67
Robinson, Edward Arlngton, "Richard Cory", 20, 217
Robinson, Joan, 24
robots, industrial and consumer, 321fn, 484; in science fiction, 192; *see* Aristotle
Rockefeller Foundation, agricultural research, 424; campaign against malaria, 423fn; *see* philanthropy
Rockefeller Sanitary Commission, 423, 466fn; *see* philanthropy
Rossellson, Leon, songs, 37
Rubin, Isaak Illich, on value, 115fn
runaway shops, *see* outsourcing
Russia, capitalism in, 22; financial crisis of 1998, 83; grain exports, 70fn; Mikhailovski, 22; peasant *mir*, 22–3, 25, 27, 31, 70, 89, 350; subsistence peasant plots, 95; Revolution of 1917, 9, 22, 37, 94, 356; post-USSR,

95; Zasulich, 23; *see* Kropotkin; Lenin

sabotage, in production, 3, 35, 134, 215–16, 218, 236, 310, 332, 371, 379; the revolution, 286; by slaves, 367fn
Sahlins, Marshall, 350
Sartre, Jean-Paul, on being, 189; on relevance of Marx, 484; on reflexive mediation, 120fn
savings and loan industry, crisis of, 83, 108
Say's law, 154fn
schools, access to, 367; benchmarks, 381; boards, 479; books, 413; capitalist shaping of, 189fn, 209, 210–11, 269, 429; in colonies, 397; use of computers, 4; for control of children, 10; edu-factories, 128, 258, 479; fiscal crisis, 128; in Global South, 397; as incarceration, 248, 252, 271, 335, 460; Jevons' lectures, 442; and latent reserve army, 459–60; Locke on, 179fn; lunches, 438; private vs public, 75, 419; profits from, 180fn, 428–9; Senior on, 344; shootings, 129, 252–3, 332, 386; skipping, 367; songs, 60, 252; strikes, 198fn, 271; right-wing attacks, 130; terrains of struggle, 230, 419; waged/unwaged divisions, 367; walkouts, 129; and work ethic, 204; *see* competition; GEB; hierarchy; Owen; panopticon; schoolwork
schoolwork, and alienation, 20, 209, 214–16, 479; to avoid chores, 367; competition, 288–9, 332fn; coping with, 197, 252; division of labor, 304–6; forced labor, 84fn, 460; home economics, 210, 211, 423; homework, 373, 384; impact of computers, 4, 317; Marx on, 344; mind-deadening, 197; night work, 235, 243–4, 249; piecework, 384–6,

480; produces labor-power, 180, 184, 198, 365, 413, 423, 460, 480; labor process, 197–8; productive labor in, 349; speedup, 4, 331; struggle against, 4, 128, 129–30, 244, 248, 258–9, 275, 279, 311, 317, 367, 385–6, 483; STEM, 320–1, 479–80; struggle over curricula, 4, 130, 213, 261, 386; unwaged, 10, 133, 273, 460; and value of labor-power, 181–2; wages for, 367; *see* competition; resistance
science, in agriculture, 12, 345–6; collective activity, 319, 320–2; competition in, 20, 321, 383; division of labor, 337; dynamics of investment in, 322, 326; fiction, 46, 124, 320; invention and science fairs, 288, 321; as labor, 319, 337; of nutrition, 465; public perception, 320; "no royal road to", 14fn; Sputnik and curriculum, 320; technology, 319; STEM, 320–1, 322, 479–80; *see* cooperation; Kropotkin
Scitovsky, Tibor, on "bad" capitalists, 434
Scotland, anti-vagrant laws, 7; clans in, 29, 481; as colony, 25fn, 475; Duchess of Sutherland, 29; enclosures, 29; New Lanark, 291; oats, 105fn; *see* Ariosto, Ludovico
Second International, hope for peaceful transition, 88; failure with World War I, 260–1
Second Wave feminism, 258, 279
Seeger, Pete, 25fn, 60fn
self-valorization, of capital, 68, 173; workers' autonomous, 68fn, 247, 315, 417–8
Senior, Nassau W., on abstinence, 432; on famine, 476; on labor hours, 220, 223, 225–7; on the school day, 344
serfs, *see* corvée labor
services, as commodity, 68, 123, 178, 181, 183, 184fn, 429; credit as, 430; demand for 429; domestic, 49;

financial, 106; housework and, 412; industries, 3, 105, 344, 395, 429; job-search as, 213; largely ignored by Marx, 105; marriage, 462; for men, 414; out-sourced, 395, 397–8; personal, 180; product of useful labor, 111; public health, 370; by retainers, 427, 429; of "schoolmasters", 349; sexual, 219, 388, 414; transportation as, 314–14; in USSR, 181fn; workers, 371, 430

sharecroppers, 59, 60, 178fn, 398fn

silver, as bullion, 165; Dorothy's shoes, 60; trade restrictions, 162; as hoard, 160; imports in sixteenth century, 157–8; monetization, 59, 165fn; preference for in Asia, 165fn

Sinclair Broadcast Group, 451; *see* centralization

Sinclair, Upton, *The Jungle*, 239, 242, 247–8, 466fn; *King Coal*, 382

Situationists, 249, 484

skilled labor, drawn from abroad, 395; educational requirements, 182, 305; hierarchy of, 299; in housework, 211, 304–5, 326; power of, 296, 300, 310; indigenous, 27; multi-skilled, 296; requirements, 437; in schoolwork, 383; vs simple, 112; unwaged, 118, 211, 455; *see* American Federation of Labor

slavery, of Africans, 9, 41, 84; ancient, 22–3, 56, 163–4, 234, 364; Anti-Slavery Society, 84; campaigns against, 469; Carlyle-Mill debate, 245–6, 393; of children, 84, 328–9; colonial, 76, 124, 158, 393; debate among Marxists, 55; debt, 464; defacto, 9, 60; farm slavery operations, 469; hides work for self, 364; illegal, 9; impact on wage labor, 57, 260; interspecies, 191, 194, 483; Marx's letter to Lincoln, 57; near-slave labor, 7, 53–4, 482; plantation, 84, 287, 392; resistance to, 57, 260, 471, 481; Spartacus and

Nat Turner, 103fn; sugar, 79–80fn; as unwaged labor, 9, 60, 234, 364; in the US, 54, 55, 56, 178fn, 234, 364, 398fn; wage-slavery, 55, 84, 234fn; of the will, 103fn, 413–4; Eric Williams on, 56–7; *see* labor; Quashees

slave trade, 84fn; forced migration, 84; Atlantic working class, 41, 391; consequences of abolition, 392, 471

Smith, Adam, on barter, 106–7; capital as command over labor, 360; on export of gold and silver, 162–3; on form of value, 140; Marx's commentaries on, 140, 181fn; on negative consequences of division of labor, 308; on net product and workers' consumption, 425; on productive and unproductive labor, 180–1, 416, 426; on Quesnay, 415; on trade, 78, 162–3; *Wealth of Nations*, 2, 14fn, 100, 426

SNLT, *see* socially necessary labor time

social capital, 446

social Darwinism, 280, 290

social factory, 4, 128, 132fn, 236, 304, 309, 327, 331, 384

socialism, 284; Bolshevik-style, 287; vs communism, 89; state capitalism, 90; state ownership, 485; market, 485; *see* Lenin

social workers, 387

socially necessary labor time, *see* value

society of the spectacle, *see* Situationists

South America, colonial empires, 30; mine owners, 412

Southeast Asia, peasant resistance, 62; outsourcing to, 374

South Korea, strike methods, 401fn

Soviet Union, appropriation of Marx, 90; collectivization, 71, 95; despotism of, 287; Gorbachev, 76; grain deal of 1972, 394fn; gulag, 53; industrialization, 201; Marxism as ideology of exploitation, 94–5; Material Product System, 181fn;

official ideology, 22; overthrow of soviets, 285; peasant resistance, 71, 95; the "scissors", 60fn; Taylorism in, 336; Third International, 261fn; *see* Lenin

specialized worker, *see* collective worker

speculation, 3, 82–3, 106, 201, 434, 435, 466–7, 470–1, 482; Casino economy, 82–3; motive for holding money, 161fn; in shipbuilding, 470; *see Crédit Mobilier*; investment; savings and loan Industry

speed-up, and breakdown, 331; in centralization, 451; in schools, 4, 129; in industry, 237, 330, 455; and piece-wages, 380; resistance to, 332–3; *see* Chaplin, Charlie, *Modern Times*; intensity; machines; relative surplus value; sabotage

species-being, *see* humans

sports facilities, construction of, 469; displacement of worker housing, 467

stagnant, real wages, 279, reserve army, 460–2; *see* lumpenproletariat

state, absolutist, 88; in capitalist development, 76–81, 90; charters, 75; debt, 81–3; farms, 71, 75; fiscal policy, 130, 153, 164, 303, 384; as government, 25, 26, 43, 49, 51, 53–5, 61, 62, 74fn, 451, 467, 475, 485; Keynesian, 74, 303, 325–6; Marxist theories of, 51fn; monetary policy, 64, 108; paternalism, 75; in primitive accumulation, 51, 75; regulation and deregulation, 3, 30, 51, 63, 75, 82–3, 108, 212, 241, 257, 278, 302, 303, 309, 343, 344, 434, 482; of siege, 475; subsidies, 63; as terrain of class conflict, 51, 52; welfare, 75; *see* colonialism

Stewart, Andy, "The Highland Clearances," 29

students, alienation of, 213, 216, 385, 386; bullying, 332fn; bypassing mediators, 128–9, 134; breaking mediations, 129; homework, 248–9; internal tension, 269; minimizing effort, 384–5; need for jobs, 249; resentment, 197–8; struggles, 128–30, 198, 213–4, 216, 236, 258–9, 279, 311, 317, 342–3, 367, 386, 403, 483; unwaged, 133, 134, 365; wages for, 236fn, 244, 248, 367; *see* competition; schools, schoolwork

subsumption of labor, formal and real, 199, 357

sugar, in film, 63; history of, 79–80fn, 84, 392; price, 71; tariffs, 78; *see* Quashees

supply and demand, law of, 338; manipulation of, 183; Marx's analysis of, 152; neoclassical theory, 152; price of gold, 150; *see* Cournot, Antoine

surplus labor, before capitalism, 233–4; beyond capitalism, 201–2; endless quest, 203; measures of, 220–2; vs necessary labor, 200; as unpaid labor, 84fn, 348, 359–60; were-wolf hunger for, 208, 233–7; within capitalism, 199–200

surplus population, *see* labor, reserve army of labor

surplus product, 227–9; in class societies, 349; ratio to necessary product, 228

surplus value, abstinence, 431–5; consumption of, 339, 415, 420, 434; contribution of education to, 428–9; as exploitation, 221; historical evolution, 275–6, 325–6, 348–9, 357; hours that produce, 225–7, 230–2; investment of, 184, 202, 360, 419–24; mass of, 264–6; none in communism, 358; to perpetuate social control, 184, 203; rate of vs rate of profit, 220–2; rent as portion of, 59; source of, 174, 176–7, 352; subverting, 3; and surplus labor, 200; *Theories of*, 7, 95fn, 140, 181; three laws of, 262–8; as use-value of labor-power, 104, 177, 184; valorization,

198–203; voracious appetite for, 233–7; *see* absolute surplus value; exploitation; intensity; machinery; profit; relative surplus value; surplus product

Sutherland, Duchess of, enclosure of land, 29, 172; enclosure of seashore, 38

Sweezy, Paul M., 109fn; on the form of value, 115

syllogistic mediation, between commodities, 127; in the capitalist organization of control, 128, 211; role of money, 155

Taylor, Frederick, and scientific management, 3

Taylorism, vs handicraft and skilled labor, 300, 311; *see* Ford, Henry; Lenin

taxes, austerity instead of raising, 107; in colonies, 393, 466; cuts for wealthy to produce deficits, 146, 384, 420; deductible charity, 423; to finance production of labor-power, 180fn, 429, 438; to finance repression, 75; to finance subsidies to industry, 75, 164, 322, 326, 424, 438, 465–6; to finance wages for housework, 367; to repay public debt, 81–3; "supply-side" cuts, 75; as tribute, 175

teachers, anger against, 129; authority of, 460; Brontë, Charlotte, *The Professor*, 20; bypassing, 129; distracting, 311; as employment for the educated, 228–9fn, 397; imposed curricula, 197; Jevons lecture to, 422; mediation of relationship to students, 128, 130; night-work, 235, 249; as producer of labor-power, 413, 479–80; as producers of surplus-value, 428–9; quality controllers, 385; reading *Capital*, 480; resentment, 198; schoolwork versus, 181; second jobs, 249; strikes, 130,

271, 483; subversion, 483; unions, 129, 198; work of, 212, 235, 317, 321, 384–6, 479–80

technology, against workers, 277, 336; agricultural extension, 61; appropriate, 228; and authority, 283–5; biometrics, 372; in Brontë, Charlotte, *Shirley*, 279–80; collective worker as source of innovation, 321–2, 337; development as response to worker struggles, 110, 398; household, 315–17, 387–8; investment in, 322, 326; manipulation to impose more work, 271; in mining, 277fn; never politically neutral, 336; and over-fishing, 39; priority of command over labor, 270; and productivity, 202fn; revolutions in agricultural, 472, 473; role of competition, 336; and science, 319–20; in science fiction, 320; and spread of popular culture, 251; STEM, 322; and wages, 356, 398; and working day, 350, 372; *see* class composition; Green Revolution; machinery; relative surplus value

technical composition of capital, 445–6, 450

Texas Farm Workers, 239

thanatocracy, 67, 475

time clocks and biometrics, 372

trade, blockades, 280, 340, 356, 470; bullionists on, 162; Carey on, 401–2; with China, 78, 80; class content of, 81; colonial, 56, 63, 77, 78; comparative advantage, 78, 80, 174; cotton famine, 340, 470–1; declining American surplus, 394fn; deficits, 161; fair, 483; and foreign investment, 64, 260, 391–2, 402–3; and famine, 77; "free", 57, 74fn, 78–80, 362; fur, 40; gains from, 78; GATT, 80; List on, 79; market women, 77; Marshall Plan, 80; Marx on, 79, 303fn; money reserves, 165–6; Mun on, 227fn; owners, 142;

policies, 63fn; protests, 81, 402–5; Ricardo on, 78, 80; sex, 84; Roman, 175; shipping labor, 391; slave, 41, 54, 84, 328–9, 391; terms of, 56, 59–60; world, 56; WTO, 81, 303; zones, 80; *see* colonialism; credit; crisis; exchange-value; globalization; IMF; Napoleonic Wars; outsourcing; protectionism; NAFTA

trade unions, of adjuncts, 483; -busting, 278, 434; collective bargaining, 356; and Combination Acts, 52; contracts, 143, 278, 303, 326, 356; craft, 300; dues, 366; of farm workers, 62, 239; of eel fishermen, 39; gender discrimination in, 258; of graduate students, 367, 483; industrial, 216, 289, 300, 303, 326, 356, 481; international, 303; Jevons on, 442–3; Los Obreros Unidos, 382; Marx vs Weston, 417; in Mexico, 403; Mill on, 440–1; vs NAFTA; rank-and-file vs officials, 128, 198fn, 229, 278, 371; recognition won, 356, 469; of skilled workers, 300; strikes, 36, 48, 52, 54, 62, 88, 130, 134, 271 332, 336, 356, 367fn, 401, 442, 469, 483; strike funds, 366; of teachers, 129, 198; and wages, 417fn; wildcat strikes, 3, 128, 198, 277fn, 297, 332, 371–2; vs WTO, 81; *see* Coalition of Immokalee Workers; Familias Unidas por la Justicia; Texas Farm Workers; United Farm Workers

transportation, of convicts, 280; as consumer good, 315, 437; demand for as byproduct of industrialization, 338; industry sells change in location, 427; productive labor in, 427–8; as moment of circulation, 427; in reproduction, 315, 410; as service, 105, 430

transactions demand, 161fn

Treaty of Versailles, 165fn

tropics, abundance 350; diversity of life, 351; value of labor power in, 392; *see* biopiracy; Sahlins, Marshall

Trump, Donald, appointment of industry shills, 241; attacks on civil rights, 290; authoritarianism, 76; despoiling of public lands, 30fn; incarnation of Dickens' Bounderby, 19fn, 20fn; nativism and anti-immigrant policies, 289, 375; non-enforcement and deregulation, 51, 343, 482; projection, 138; tax breaks for rich, 146; threat to Dreamers, 129; on trade, 402fn

two-fold character of labor, *see* labor

underconsumption, 449fn

unemployed, alienation of, 213; day-labor, 229; number of, 457–8; payments to, 276, 354, 370, 448; rarely idle, 406–7, 455; released retainers, 31; rural workers, 473; street-dwellers, 134; structurally, 460; struggles of, 36, 49–50; 271, 316, 419, 447, 453–4, 473; work of, 212–13, 370; *see* labor, migrant or nomadic; reserve army

unemployment, debt crises and, 108; female and family health, 327; and loss of skill, 419; during Napoleonic Wars, 279; rate of, 457; resulting from technological change, 276, 280; and sickness, 447; stick of, 24; youth, 454; and wages, 274, 276fn, 278, 417, 447; *see* crisis; Luddites; machines; relative surplus value; reserve army

unions, *see* trade unions

United Farm Workers, 62, 239, 469

United States, austerity in, 373–4, 438; debt peonage, 178fn; Department of Agriculture, 61, 210, 242; enclosures in, 40–3, 77; family farming, 59–62, 389; farm worker struggles, 469; Federal Reserve, 107, 163, 167, 394fn; financial deregulation, 82–3;

foreign loans, 83; immigrant labor, 211; laws excluding women, 460; Marx on, 57; National Science Foundation, 322; neoliberalism in, 74; peasant immigration to, 211; piece-work, 379; pipelines, 351; prison labor, 53, 54–5; privatization of space exploration, 124; productivity deals, 3, 250, 326, 356, 371, 394; railroads, 400; Roosevelt administration, 356; small farmers as workers 389; struggle over work time, 2, 257–8, 278, 373–4; trade, 80, 401–2; teacher strikes, 130; textile industry, 401; unique communities, 24; vagrancy laws, 53–5; War against Vietnamese independence, 12, 404; the western frontier, 7, 41, 481; women's struggles, 258, 460; *see* child labor; deregulation; farm workers; NAFTA; Native Americans; OPEC; Populist Revolt; privatization; savings and loan crisis; slavery; trade; trade unions; Trump; unemployment; United Farm Workers; urban renewal; WTO

universal equivalent, *see* value

universities, anti-war struggles, 146, 214, 404; as edu-factories, 13, 128, 483; research, 20, 204fn, 235, 240, 321–2; state, 429; *see* division of labor; piecework; students

unwaged, 9–10, 24, 55–8, 123fn, 132fn, 133–4, 180–2, 452–62; accumulation includes, 452–62; alienation of, 209–16; exploitation of, 36, 60; labor processes, 413–14; mediation of, 133; struggles of, 134, 228, 243–4, 252, 258, 275–6, 311, 316, 385–6, 462; working day, 232, 235, 236, 429; *see* children; collective worker; farmers; indentured; housework; Martineau, Harriet; peasants; piecework; reserve army of labor; schoolwork; slavery; students;

unemployed; value, of labor power; women, as unwaged workers

upward mobility, 395; ideology of, 74; promise of, 24

urban "marginals", 9

Ure, Andrew, idleness and immorality, 227; power of skilled workers, 310

useful labor, *see* labor

use-value, for buyer, 143; as commodity, 111; contradiction with exchange-value, 103; determinate forms, 104; different class meaning, 105–6; of energy, 105; expresses value, 104; as final goal, 171; of food, 105; of labor, 110; of loaned money, 106; qualities of, 104, 106; quantities of, 104; for seller, 143; *see* labor-power; value

USSR, *see* Soviet Union

utility, replacing labor in value theory, 139fn, 352, 442, 459; political dangers of, 442fn; *see* Bentham, Jeremy

utopianism, Marx's rejection of, 31, 89; *see* Fourier; Owen

vagrancy laws, in England, 46–50; in the US, 53–5

valorization, of capital, 68, 171–4, 198–203, 240; social, 433; *see* disvalorization

value, capital, 64; composition, 446; creating, 68, 218; destruction of, 68; dis-, 68; equivalent form of, 117, 119–21; exchange-value, 78, 100, 103–8, 106; expanded form, 122–5; form of, 5, 98, 101, 114–35; general form of, 125–30; of gold, 157–9; of labor-power, 179–84; of labor to capital, 110, 113, 114, 137, 485; labor theory of, 6, 14, 15, 16, 109, 110, 113, 138fn; -less, 45; liberation from any singular, 485; measure, of, 5, 98, 100, 113–14, 149–52; money value, 32; of money, 145, 151; money form, 98, 131–5, 148; money represents, 159fn; money as store of, 160–2; opportunity for imposing work, 113 119, 131, 132, 173, 174; preserving, 218; price form, 132, 150; prices rarely equal, 152; and productivity, 114, 119; realization of, 152, 168; redistribution of, 175; relative form of, 117–19, 120, 122–3, 126; replacement by disposable time, 309–10; revealed in exchange, 112; simple form, 116–22; substance, of, 5, 68, 100, 108–10, 113, 119; symbol of, 158–9, 166; transfer, 64; use-value, 100, 103, 104–6; see abstract labor, exchange-value; fetishism; labor-power; metamorphosis; reflection; surplus value; syllogistic mediation; use-value, wage

vampire, capital as, 208, 232, 477

Veblen, Thorstein, on conspicuous consumption, 172fn, 433; on sabotage, 236

vegetarianism, vs murder of animals, 483

velocity, see money; Cantillion; Petty

Vietnam, colonial exploitation of, 63; racism against, 289; struggles for independence, 9, 38, 77, 94, 404; US war against, 12

vivisection, 1

vocabulary, capital's and ours, 118fn, 418; of workers, 235fn

Volcker, Paul, 107, 167, 278

wage, 361–405; Carey on, 401–2; comparable worth, 299; children's, 328–9, 396; and consumption, 66–70, 96, 100, 154, 155, 170, 183, 246, 319fn, 410, 416–18, 429; as defining class, 13, 268–70; as equivalent form, 118; escape from, 24, 49–50, 93–5, 134, 170, 245–8; 288; family wage, 322, 374, 422, 460; Fund, 2, 439–41; and education and training, 182, 298–9, 394–6, 418–19, 428–9 459–60; hide exploitation,

372–3, 378; hides unwaged, 458; for housework, 134, 219; imposition of, 46–58; indexation of, 64; Keynes and, 64, 96–7, 319fn, 355–6, 374; in kind, 67; little access to, 9; living wage, 24; Malthus on, 448, 476; manipulation of, 288, 369–71, 392; in microeconomics, 200, 355fn, 359, 441–3; money, 133, 254; national differences, 389–405; nominal and real, 64–5, 79, 107, 183, 354, 355fn, 394, 443; normalization of, 178; overtime, 276 373–4; and personal ownership, 86; piece-wages, 375–84; and power, 299; precarious, 106; as price of labor-power, 354; and productivity, 2, 3, 64, 201, 275, 326, 398–9, 473fn; and profits, 2, 64, 319, 355, 443–4, 437; savings, 200fn; songs about, 147–8, 253–4; struggles over, 3, 35, 57–8, 61, 62, 64–5, 81, 106, 107–8, 128, 134, 147, 164, 167, 180, 182fn, 183–4, 211, 229–30, 241, 246, 249–50, 260–1, 266, 274–9, 289, 304, 340, 356–7, 269–74, 378–9, 402–5, 417, 434, 436–9, 447fn, 449, 456; for students, 236fn; subsistence, 274; time-wages, 368–75; working day for, 229–62; see austerity; Corn Laws; credit; crisis; direct appropriation; GEB; inflation; hierarchy; labor; market; labor-power; little circuit; machinery; means of subsistence; Owen; piecework; Quashees; relative surplus value; taxes; unwaged

wages for housework, Campaign, 134, 219, logic of, 134fn; see Dalla Costa, Mariarosa, Federici, Silvia

wages-fund doctrine, 439–44

Wakefield, Edward Gibbon, 93–7

Walkley, Mary Anne, 238

Wall Street, Bartleby, 430; films about, 435

war, 289; American Civil, 7, 42, 54, 56–7, 59, 60, 178fn, 180, 340,

364fn, 419, 422, 470, 481; between
  classes, 260; in France, 88–9; over
  oil, 479; counterinsurgency, 62; *see*
  Napoleonic Wars
weight-names, *see* money
welfare, agents, 386; corporate, 75;
  general social, 172, 442; payments,
  247, 276, 367, 370, 448; programs,
  387, 455, 449fn; recipients, 107, 387;
  state, 75
West Indies, 246, workers from, 393fn,
  447fn; *see* Quashees
wildcat strikes, *see* trade unions, wildcat
  strikes
Wilson, Alice, 32
Winstanley, Gerard, 36–7; *see* Diggers
women, vs alienation, 214; authors,
  306; autonomous organization of,
  214, 306; commercialization of,
  146; contraception and abortion,
  261, 367, 459; cooperatives, 294fn;
  dehumanization of, 215, 414; *doble
  jornada*, 243, 429; in domestic
  industries, 341–2; in factories, 9–10,
  257, 304, 324, 326, 382, 396; in
  families, 214, 215, 216, 243, 315,
  316, 327, 386–9; foot binding,
  137; and latent reserve army, 460;
  LGBTQ rights, 215; magazines,
  316; marches, 129, 262; market
  women, 77; mediation and, 128,
  129, 130, 134, 211, 414; Native
  American, 77; night work, 243; vs
  patriarchal authority, 213, 216, 258,
  414; and reproduction of labor-
  power, 43–4, 179, 182, 197, 209,
  211, 212, 215, 219, 236, 243, 249,
  257, 261, 269, 288, 299, 306, 311,
  326–7, 344, 365, 387, 397, 412,
  413–4, 454–5, 459; restrictions on
  waged jobs, 10, 211, 258, 326, 386;
  right to vote, 88, 258; in science,
  320–1; Second Wave feminism, 258,
  279; sexuality repressed, 44, 414;
  struggles of, 4, 43, 77, 130, 133, 198,
  213–4, 216, 236, 243–4, 250, 258,

299, 306, 315, 327, 367, 414, 429,
  458–9; studies, 4, 130, 214, 259,
  261, 279, 289, 393fn; on television,
  258; "unproductive", 338; unwaged,
  128, 133–4, 306, 365; witch hunts
  and enclosure of bodies, 43–4, 215;
  work of reproducing labor-power,
  215; *see* Dalla Costa; Dalla Costa,
  Giovanna; family, nuclear; Federici,
  Silvia; Gaskell, Elizabeth; GEB;
  housework; marriage; Martineau,
  Harriet; patriarchy; piecework; prostitution; wages for housework
Woodward, C. Vann, *Origins of the
  New South*, 53, 54–5
work, *see* labor; over-work
Workers' Inquiry, 242fn, 243fn, 304
working class, accumulation of,
  406–76; alienation in production,
  203–9; alienation in reproduction,
  209–15; exploitation of, 198–203,
  220–9, 229–71; 272–360; fate
  of, 85–91; genesis of, 9, 16, 18,
  28–58; in-itself, and for-itself, 121;
  wages of, 361–405; *see* adjuncts;
  African-Americans; alter-globalization movement; animals, as
  part of working class; autonomists;
  children; circulation of struggle;
  collective worker; class, composition,
  recomposition, decomposition; combinations, of labor; farm workers;
  farmers; immigrants; indentured;
  indigenous; intellectuals; Luddites;
  lumpenproletariat; mass worker;
  Native American; peasants;
  precariat; professors; Quashees;
  refugees; reserve army of labor;
  sharecroppers; slavery; students;
  teachers; women; Zapatistas
working class struggle, *see* resistance
working day, beyond capitalism, 357–8;
  definition of, 229–30; determination of, 260; *doble jornada*, 429;
  escape from, 246–8; of housework,
  243, 249; hypnopedia, 249; and

life expectancy, 232, 458; limits of, 230–3, 242–4; machinery and, 323–5, 329–31, 350; morality of, 227fn; songs about, 197, 251–4; nibbling and cribbling, 235–6, 248–9; overtime, 276 373–4; piece-wages and, 380; and productivity, 277–8; representation of, 230–1; of teachers and professors, 249; of salaried, 230fn, 248–9; Senior vs shortening, 225–7; struggles over, 2, 3, 10, 229–30, 232, 234, 237–8, 240, 243–59, 250–1, 270, 274, 275–6, 278–9, 288, 304, 309–11, 331–3, 350, 371–2, 412, 480; of students, 235–6, 243, 248–9, 258–9, 261–2; *see* absolute surplus value; housework; *karōshi*, relative surplus value; sabotage, schoolwork, students

World Bank, protests, 405
World Trade Organization, international capitalist planning, 303, 456; opposition to, 81, 403–4; *see* People's Global Action
World War I, 88, 260; after, 96, 165fn, 356
World War II, 260, 289; after, 70fn, 77, 80, 83, 159fn, 161, 166, 228, 258, 299, 309, 370, 371, 374, 391, 393, 401, 424
WTO, *see* World Trade Organization

Zapatistas, encounters, 404; film, 46; uprising, 9, 11, 25–6, 38, 64, 74fn, 261, 350
Zasulich, Vera, 23
zerowork, 3
Zola, Emile, *Germinal*, 422

Printed and bound by CPI Group (UK) Ltd, Croydon, CR0 4YY

16/04/2025

14658481-0005